Lecture Notes in Computer Science   951

Edited by G. Goos, J. Hartmanis and J. van Leeuwen

Advisory Board: W. Brauer   D. Gries   J. Stoer

Springer

Berlin
Heidelberg
New York
Barcelona
Budapest
Hong Kong
London
Milan
Paris
Tokyo

Max J. Egenhofer John R. Herring (Eds.)

Advances in Spatial Databases

4th International Symposium, SSD '95
Portland, ME, USA, August 6-9, 1995
Proceedings

 Springer

Series Editors

Gerhard Goos, Universität Karlsruhe, Germany
Juris Hartmanis, Cornell University, NY, USA
Jan van Leeuwen, Utrecht University, The Netherlands

Volume Editors

Max J. Egenhofer
National Center for Geographic Information andAnalysis
Department of Spatial Information Science and Engineering
and Department of Computer Science, University of Maine
5711 Boardman Hall, Orono, ME 04469-5711, USA

John R. Herring
Oracle Corporation
3 Bethesda Metro Center, Suite 1400, Bethesda, MD 20814, USA

Cataloging-in-Publication Data applied for

Die Deutsche Bibliothek - CIP-Einheitsaufnahme

Advances in spatial databases : 4th international symposium ;
proceedings / SSD '95, Portland, ME, USA, August 6 - 9, 1995.
Max J. Egenhofer ; John R. Herring (ed.). - Berlin ; Heidelberg
; New York : Springer, 1995
  (Lecture notes in computer science ; Vol. 951)
  ISBN 3-540-60159-7
NE: Egenhofer, Max J. [Hrsg.]; SSD <4, 1995, Portland, Me.>; GT

CR Subject Classification (1991): H.2-3, H.5, I.4, I.5, J.2

ISBN 3-540-60159-7 Springer-Verlag Berlin Heidelberg New York

© Springer-Verlag Berlin Heidelberg 1995
Printed in Germany

Typesetting: Camera-ready by author
SPIN 10486460   06/3142 – 5 4 3 2 1 0   Printed on acid-free paper

Message from the Chairs

These proceedings contain the technical papers selected for presentation at the Fourth International Symposium on Large Spatial Databases (SSD '95) held in Portland, Maine, August 6-9, 1995. With the conferences in Santa Barbara (1989), Zurich (1991), and Singapore (1993), the International Symposium on Large Spatial Databases has become the premier meeting for researchers, developers, and practitioners focusing on the integration between database management systems and geographic information systems. SSD '95 brought together computer scientists and GIS experts to explore advances in modeling, storage, and retrieval of massive spatial data sets, and to discuss the requirements from new, demanding application domains.

From among sixty submissions of full papers by authors from sixteen countries, the program committee selected twenty-three outstanding papers for inclusion in this volume. The acceptance rate at SSD continues to be highly competitive, which we believe is a sign of an active research community.

The papers included in this volume show that we are on the verge of a new generation of spatial database management systems motivated by the needs of digital spatial libraries, interoperable systems and Open GIS, and the World-Wide Web. Discussions have moved away from the design of new spatial access methods, more SQL extensions, or yet another object-oriented spatial data model. This is not to say that the problems of spatial query languages and conceptual modeling for spatial data have been solved, but rather the attention for innovative advancements has shifted. New, exciting topics have come up, such as data mining in large spatial databases. Other areas have been established as topics with great potential for advanced use such as spatial joins and spatial reasoning for intelligent access to spatial data.

The conference included two tutorials on spatial databases (by Hanan Samet) and spatio-temporal information systems (by Mike Worboys). Also two panels on Open GIS and New Applications of Spatial Databases were included to stimulate discussion of emerging issues. For the first time at SSD, we offered a software demonstration session.

We are in debt to the many people who made this event happen. The program committee and the external referees provided invaluable assistance with their reviews. Hanan Samet deserves special thanks for hosting the program committee meeting at the University of Maryland. The conference would have been impossible without the local organization of Kathleen Hornsby. We also very much appreciated the assistance of Eileen Herring and Blane Shaw.

We are very grateful for the support given by our corporate sponsors: Environmental Systems Research Institute, Inc., Lockheed Martin, Management & Data Systems, and Oracle Corporation. Cooperation with ACM SIGMOD and the National Center for Geographic Information and Analysis is also gratefully acknowledged.

Max J. Egenhofer
General Chair

John R. Herring
Program Chair

Portland, Maine, USA, August 1995

Acknowledgments

In Cooperation with ACM SIGMOD

Sponsors:

Environmental Systems Research Institute, Inc.

Lockheed Martin, Management & Data Systems

National Center for Geographic Information and Analysis

Oracle Corporation

Conference Organization

General Chair:
Max J. Egenhofer, University of Maine

Program Committee Chair:
John R. Herring, Oracle Corporation

Local Arrangements:
Kathleen Hornsby, University of Maine

Program Committee:
David Abel, CSIRO, Australia
Walid Aref, Matsushita Information Technology Laboratory, Panasonic
    Technologies, Inc.
Mark Ashworth, Unisys Corporation
Renato Barrera, Intergraph Corporation
Gilberto Camara, Instituto Nacional de Pesquisas Espaciais (INPE), Brazil
Marco Casanova, IBM Brazil
Eliseo Clementini, Università de l'Aquila, Italy
Umesh Dayal, Hewlett-Packard Laboratories
Jim Farley, University of Arkansas
Robin Feagus, US Geological Survey
Leila de Floriani, Università de Genoa, Italy
Andrew Frank, Technical University Vienna, Austria
Randolph Franklin, Rensselaer Polytechnic Institute
Kenn Gardels, University of California - Berkeley
Mike Goodchild, University of California - Santa Barbara
Oliver Günther, Humboldt Universität, Germany
Ralf Hartmut Güting, Fernuniversität Hagen, Germany
Klaus Hinrichs, Universität Münster, Germany
Erland Jungert, Swedish Defense Establishment, Sweden
Curt Kolovson, Hewlett-Packard
Hans-Peter Kriegel, Universität München, Germany
Gail Langran Kucera, Intergraph Corporation
Ron Lake, MDA, Canada
Scott Morehouse, ESRI, Inc.
John O'Callaghan, CSIRO, Australia
Beng Chin Ooi, University of Singapore
Peter van Oosterom, TNO Physics and Electronics Laboratory,
    The Netherlands
Dimitris Papadias, University of California - San Diego
Niki Pissinou, Univeristy of SW Louisiana
Hanan Samet, University of Maryland

Hans Schek, ETH Zürich, Switzerland
Michel Scholl, INRIA, France
Timos Sellis, National Technical University Athens, Greece
Cliff Shaffer, Virginia Polytechnic Institute and State University
Terry Smith, University of California - Santa Barbara
Mark Sondheim, Ministry of Environment, Lands and Parks, Canada
Agnès Voisard, Freie Universität Berlin, Germany
Gio Wiederhold, Stanford University
Mike Worboys, University of Keele, UK

Additional Reviewers:
Chuan Heng Ang
Stefan Berchtold
Thomas Brinkhoff
Michael Dillencourt
Claudio Esperanca
Martin Ester
Gabriel Kuper
Kia Makki
Enrico Puppo
Alan Saalfeld
Michael Schiwietz
Thomas Seidl
Jayant Sharma
Emmanuel Stefanakis
Yannis Theodoridis
Tom Vijlbrief

Contents

Spatial Data Models

Lossless Representation of Topological Spatial Data
Bart Kuijpers, Jan Paredaens, Jan Van den Bussche 1

On the Desirability and Limitations of Linear Spatial
Database Models
Luc Vandeurzen, Marc Gyssens, Dirk Van Gucht 14

The Quad View Data Structure — A Representation for
Planar Subdivisions
Ulrich Finke, Klaus H. Hinrichs 29

Spatial Data Mining

Discovery of Spatial Association Rules in
Geographic Information Databases
Krzysztof Koperski, Jiawei Han 47

Knowledge Discovery in Large Spatial Databases:
Focusing Techniques for Efficient Class Identification
Martin Ester, Hans-Peter Kriegel, Xiaowei Xu 67

Spatial Query Processing

Ranking in Spatial Databases
Gísli R. Hjaltason, Hanan Samet 83

Optimal Redundancy in Spatial Database Systems
Volker Gaede 96

Accessing Geographical Metafiles through a
Database Storage System
Stephen Blott, Andrej Vckovski 117

Extending a Spatial Access Structure to Support
Additional Standard Attributes
Andreas Henrich, Jens Möller 132

Multiple Representations

Towards a Formal Model for Multiresolution Spatial Maps
Enrico Puppo, Giuliana Dettori 152

Multi-Scale Partitions: Application to Spatial and
Statistical Databases
Philippe Rigaux, Michel Scholl 170

Open GIS

Specifying Open GIS with Functional Languages
Andrew U. Frank, Werner Kuhn 184

Geo-algorithms

Load-Balancing in High Performance GIS: Declustering
Polygonal Maps
Shashi Shekhar, Sivakumar Ravada, Vipin Kumar,
Douglas Chubb, Greg Turner 196

Implementation of the ROSE Algebra: Efficient
Algorithms for Realm-Based Spatial Data Types
Ralf Hartmut Güting, Thomas de Ridder, Markus Schneider 216

A 3D Molecular Surface Representation Supporting
Neighborhood Queries
Thomas Seidl, Hans-Peter Kriegel 240

Reasoning about Spatial Relations

An Inferencing Language for Automated Spatial Reasoning
about Graphic Entities
Paul Scarponcini, Daniel C. St. Clair, George W. Zobrist 259

Inferences from Combined Knowledge about Topology and
Directions
Jayant Sharma, Douglas M. Flewelling 279

2D Projection Interval Relationships: A Symbolic
Representation of Spatial Relationships
Mohammad Nabil, John Shepherd, Anne H.H. Ngu 292

Topological Relations between Discrete Regions
Stephan Winter 310

Spatial Joins

Generating Seeded Trees from Data Sets
Ming-Ling Lo, Chinya V. Ravishankar 328

Spatial Join Strategies in Distributed Spatial DBMS
David J. Abel, Beng Chin Ooi, Kian-Lee Tan, Robert Power,
Jeffrey X. Yu 348

Benchmarks

Comparison and Benchmarks for Import of VPF Geographic Data from
Object-Oriented and Relational Database Files
David Arctur, Eman Anwar, John Alexander, Sharma Chakravarthy,
Miyi Chung, Maria Cobb, Kevin Shaw 368

Compressing Elevation Data
Wm. Randolph Franklin 385

Author Index 405

Lossless Representation of Topological Spatial Data

Bart Kuijpers[1], Jan Paredaens[1] and Jan Van den Bussche[2]*

[1] University of Antwerp (UIA), Dept. Math. & Computer Sci.,
Universiteitsplein 1, B-2610 Antwerp, Belgium
Email: {kuijpers, pareda}@uia.ua.ac.be
[2] INRIA Rocquencourt, BP 105, F-78153 Le Chesnay Cedex, France
Email: jan.van_den_bussche@inria.fr

Abstract. We present a data structure used to represent planar spatial databases in the topological data model. Conceptually, such databases consist of points, lines between these points, and areas formed by these lines. The data structure has the distinctive feature that it is geared toward supporting queries involving topological properties of the database only: two databases that are topologically equivalent have the same representation. Moreover, no information is lost in this way: two databases that are not topologically equivalent never have the same representation.

1 Introduction

Spatial database applications [7] can be classified according to the particular geometrical concepts that are involved in the interpretation of the spatial information. This interpretation is apparent from the type of queries that are important for the application. For example, in queries involving directions such as "Give all cities on the west bank of the St. Lawrence river north of Québec," only differences in longitude and latitude are important. Other, metric, queries deal only with distances, such as "Is there a highway within ten miles of my house?"

A major class of queries is formed by those involving only properties of the database that are topological in nature. In this class, concepts such as adjacency, connectivity, and containment are in the focus. Queries like "Is there a highway connecting Boston to Portland?" or "Give all states of the US adjacent to the Atlantic" are typical in this respect. Characteristic of topological properties is that they do not distinguish between two databases that can be obtained from each other by a topological deformation. We will call such databases *topologically equivalent* (this notion will be made precise later).

In the present paper, we elaborate on the idea of topological property in the context of databases consisting of points, lines between these points, and areas formed by these lines [13]. A survey of application domains that can be

---

* On leave from the University of Antwerp. Research assistant of the Belgian National Fund for Scientific Research.

modeled in this manner was given by Laurini and Thompson [10]. In particular, applications that are topological in nature are common in this context. As an illustration of topologically equivalent databases, we refer to subway or railroad maps such as the one depicted in Fig. 1. Such maps are topological deformations of reality: the length of the lines has no correspondence to the actual length of the trajectory, and the physical track is not as straight as its drawing in the map. We say that such a map is topologically equivalent with a classical map that obeys the reality more closely.

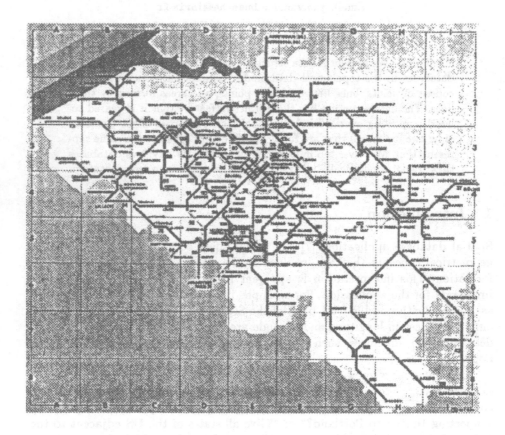

Fig. 1. A railroad map

A common representation of point-line-area spatial databases is by a data structure listing for each point its incident lines and its adjacent areas, arranged in the order in which they appear as one proceeds clockwise around the point. We call this data structure an observation-structure. Essentially this structure underlies the TIGRIS system [8], as well as the topological layer of the ARC/INFO system [12], and the original design of the cartography system of the Census Bureau of the United States [1]. It is also a common data structure for planar graph embeddings [15].

Of course, not just any structure consisting of a number of point names together with arbitrary circular listings of line and area names is the description of a database. We will show that those structures that are "sound", in this sense, can be effectively recognized by an efficient algorithm. This can be viewed as a necessary and sufficient integrity test for the topological data model (also known as "error identification" [10, Chapter 5.3]).

If only topological properties are under consideration, it may be desirable to be able to work with a representation of the database which is *topologically invariant*, meaning that two topologically equivalent databases will be represented identically. Ideally, a representation should also be *lossless*, in the sense that two databases that are *not* topologically equivalent will be represented differently. It is clear that the representation of a database by means of observation-structures, as mentioned above, is topologically invariant. The issue of its losslessness has been somewhat neglected, however. In fact, we will show that it is not lossless.

Although, as we will see, the same observation-structure can represent spatial databases of quite drastically different appearances, we will also show that this phenomenon has one single cause. Indeed, we will show that by explicitly marking one of the areas to be the unbounded one (i.e., the infinitude of space on the "outside" of the database), losslessness is achieved. The formal proof of this claim proceeds by reasoning on the nesting structure of the connected components of the database, and involves the careful composition of local isotopies.

It might seem probable to the reader that the issue of losslessness has already been addressed in the mathematical theory of planar graph embeddings or in the field of planar graph drawing. Indeed, this was also the sentiment of the authors at the initial stages of this investigation. However, this is not the case. In mathematics, the primary interest lies in embeddings on the sphere rather than in the plane. Topological equivalence on the sphere is not equal to topological equivalence in the plane. In graph drawing, one is interested in drawing *one particular* planar embedding of a given planar graph, according to certain criteria, rather than characterizing a unique such embedding in terms of a certain data structure. Moreover, both approaches do not consider the areas as first-class objects.

Our work is driven by the same motivations as those concerning the large body of work done on "spatial relationships" in spatial databases. In particular the various topological relationships that can exist between two specified spatial objects have been extensively investigated by Egenhofer and his collaborators [2, 3, 4, 5]. One way to think of our results is that we generalize these ideas to global topological properties of the entire spatial database [14]. The issues are also relevant from a user interface point of view: a topologically invariant, lossless representation of the database corresponds to an interface which allows the user to concentrate only on the topological aspects of the spatial data, and on all of them, if he so desires.

2 Spatial Databases and Observations

In this section, we define what a spatial database is in the present discussion. We will also introduce the notion of an observation.

In the following, we work in the real Euclidean plane.

Definition. A *spatial database* consists of a finite set of named points, a finite set of named lines and a finite set of named areas. Each point name is assigned to a distinct point in the plane. Each line name is assigned to a distinct non-selfintersecting continuous curve[1] in the plane that starts and ends in a named point and does not contain any other named points except these. Each area name is assigned to a distinct area formed by the named lines.

We remark that this definition allows lines to start and end in the same point, i.e., the database may contain loops. It also may contain more than one line between the same two points. Fig. 2 gives an example of a spatial database. This database has eight points, ten lines and five areas.

We apply the following notational convention throughout the remainder of the paper: Roman characters $p, q, \ldots$ denote point names, Roman capitals $A, B, \ldots$ denote line names and Greek characters $\alpha, \beta, \ldots$ are used for area names.

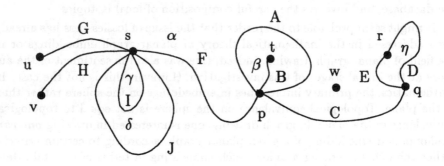

Fig. 2. An example of a spatial database

As a first step in achieving an effective, finite representation of a spatial database, we introduce the notion of *an observation of a spatial database from one of its points*.

For each named point in a spatial database, we make a circular alternating list of area names and line names corresponding respectively to the areas and lines

---

[1] Formally speaking, a simple Jordan Curve [11].

that an observer, placed in the named point, sees when he makes one clockwise full turn and scans the environment of the point. This is illustrated in Fig. 3. There, the alternating list for the point with name p is $(\alpha\ B\ \alpha\ A\ \beta\ C\ \beta\ A)$.

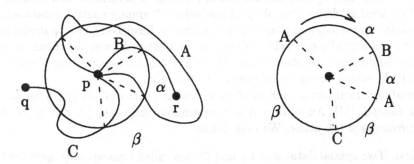

Fig. 3. An observation of a figure from one of its points

We make this more formal. A point p is the endpoint of a finite number of lines (and loops) of the spatial database. We choose a circle with center the point p and a radius such that the circle has at least two intersection points with each loop in p and at least one intersection point in each line ending in p. Such a circle always exists. In Fig. 3, two lines start from the point p and there is one loop. The circle in Fig. 3 has an appropriate radius for it cuts the loop in at least two points and the lines in at least one.

We next mark on the chosen circle the intersection points where the lines and loops "first" intersect with the circle as we follow the lines and loops starting from the point. For a line there is one such point, for a loop there are two such points (one on the right and one on the left). Knowing these markings, we make a circular alternating list of line names and area names, as is illustrated in Fig. 3.

A point which is isolated from the remainder of the database gives rise to an observation consisting of one single area name. For example, the observation of the spatial database of Fig. 2 from the point w is (α). The concept of observation is well-defined. Indeed:

The definition of observation is independent of the chosen radius. Any radius that is sufficiently small produces the same circular list. We can therefore, independently of a radius, write $O_\mathcal{D}(p)$ for an *observation of the spatial database $\mathcal{D}$ from one of its points named p*.

We refer to the list of observations of a spatial database from each of its named points as *the observation of the spatial database*.

3   A Lossless Representation

In this section, we use the notion of observation, as a building block of a data structure that is a topologically invariant and lossless representation of a spatial database.

In order to formally specify the notions of topological invariance and losslessness we first need to define "topological equivalence" among spatial databases. Fig. 4 depicts two topologically equivalent databases. Intuitively, two spatial databases are topologically equivalent if one can be obtained from the other by a continuous deformation. In other words, there is a "continuous motion picture" in the plane by which one is transformed into the other.

The mathematical formalization of such "motion pictures" is given by the notion of *isotopy* [11]. An isotopy h is a continuous series $(h_t \mid 0 \le t \le 1)$ of homeomorphisms of the plane. We thus define:

Definition. Two spatial databases $\mathcal{D}_1$ and $\mathcal{D}_2$ are called *topologically equivalent* if there exists an isotopy h such that $h_0(\mathcal{D}_1) = \mathcal{D}_1$ and $h_1(\mathcal{D}_1) = \mathcal{D}_2$, with the understanding that h respects the names of points, lines and areas.

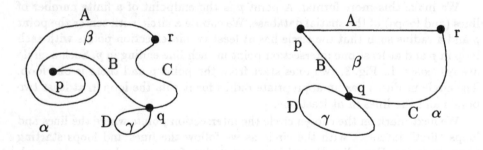

Fig. 4. Two topologically equivalent databases

Definition. A representation of a spatial database is called *topologically invariant* if any two topologically equivalent spatial databases are represented in the same way. A representation of a spatial database is called *lossless* if any two spatial databases that are not topologically equivalent are distinguished by the representation.

As motivated in the Introduction, it may be desirable to represent spatial databases by means of data structures that are topologically invariant and lossless. The data structures of Sect. 2 are topologically invariant representation of a spatial database. More precisely:

Property. Two topologically equivalent databases have the same observation.

The proof of this fact is quite straightforward. A circle with center the point p, that is located inside a topological deformation of a (possibly other) circle that was used to obtain an observation from p, gives rise to an identical observation as the original circle.

Is this representation, on the other hand, lossless? The answer is *no*. Fig. 5 contains two spatial databases that are represented by identical lists of observations. These databases are however clearly not continuously deformable into each other.

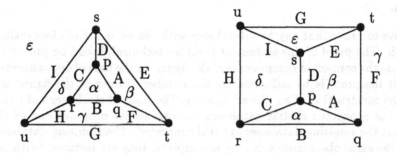

Fig. 5. Two spatial databases that are not topologically equivalent but that have the same observation list

A key observation that can be made in Fig. 5 is that ε is the unbounded region in the first database, but not in the second. Indeed, a necessary condition for two spatial databases to be topologically equivalent is that for both the unbounded area has the same label. We note that a spatial database has only one unbounded area. It is therefore justified to reserve a special label for the unbounded area: α^∞.

In Fig. 6, we have a simpler example that captures the essence of the problem. These two databases have the same list of observations. If embedded in the sphere, these two databases could be deformed into each other (by pulling the loop over the sphere). In the plane, however, this is not possible. Here however it is obvious that giving the unbounded area a special status is also sufficient to distinguish between the two databases.

Is giving, in addition to the list of the observations of a spatial database from all its named points, the information that the unbounded area has the name α^∞ not only necessary but also sufficient to obtain losslessness? We answer this question affirmative in the following theorem.

Theorem. Suppose we have two databases that give the unbounded area the

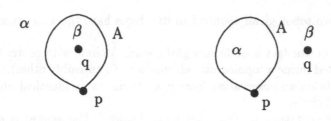

Fig. 6. Is α^∞ enough?

same name α^∞. If they are not topologically equivalent they have different observations.

We have to prove that any two databases with the same list of observations are isotopic. The proof of this statement is rather technical. It can be proved by induction on the connected components of the figure. In the case of one connected component the proof is by induction on the number of lines of the figure and involves the construction of an "local" isotopy. The basis of the latter induction is trivial. For connected spatial databases, we can always drop out one of the lines so that the resulting databases are still connected. The resulting databases also have the same observations. So, by assumption, they are isotopic. With the information of the observations, there is isotopically only one way to put the line back. What remains is gluing the local isotopies together in the proper way into one global isotopy.

We now have a data structure that is invariant and lossless. We therefore give it a name.

Definition. For a given spatial database $\mathcal{D}$, we call the data structure $(\mathcal{P}, \mathcal{L}, \mathcal{A}, \alpha^\infty, \text{Obs}())$ the *PLA-structure of $\mathcal{D}$* if $\mathcal{P}$ is the set of point names of $\mathcal{D}$, $\mathcal{L}$ is the set of line names of $\mathcal{D}$, $\mathcal{A}$ is the set of area names of $\mathcal{D}$, α^∞ is the name of the unbounded area of $\mathcal{D}$, and $\text{Obs}()$ is a function that associates with each element p of $\mathcal{P}$, $O_{\mathcal{D}}(p)$, the observation of $\mathcal{D}$ from p.

4 An Efficient Algorithm to Recognize PLA-structures

In this section, we deal with error identification problems in PLA-structures. We will give an algorithm that can be used as an integrity test for representations of spatial databases. More precisely, not every structure consisting of a number of point names, line names, area names together with arbitrary circular listings of line and area names for each point name describes a spatial database.

For example, it is easily verified that the structure $\mathcal{S} = (\{p\}, \{A\}, \{\alpha^\infty, \beta\}, \alpha^\infty, \text{Obs}())$, with $\text{Obs}(p) = (\alpha^\infty A)$ is not the PLA-structure of any spatial database. On the other hand for $\text{Obs}(p) = (\alpha^\infty A\beta A)$, Fig. 7 depicts a database for which it is the PLA-structure. So, there are structures that "look" like PLA-structures, but make no real sense. This broader class of structures can be characterized as follows.

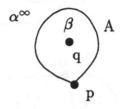

Fig. 7. A loop

Definition. We call any tuple

$$(\mathcal{P}, \mathcal{L}, \mathcal{A}, \alpha^\infty, \mathrm{Obs}())$$

a structure if $\mathcal{P}$, $\mathcal{L}$, respectively $\mathcal{A}$ are finite sets, α^∞ is an element of $\mathcal{A}$, and Obs() is a function that associates to each element of $\mathcal{P}$ or a circular list of alternatingly elements of $\mathcal{L}$ and $\mathcal{A}$ or just one element of $\mathcal{A}$.

Clearly, PLA-structures are exactly those structures that represent a spatial database.

In this section we give a positive answer to the following question.

Is it syntactically decidable whether a given structure is a PLA-structure?

We will describe an efficient decision procedure to solve this problem. Suppose we are given an arbitrary structure $\mathcal{S} = (\mathcal{P}, \mathcal{L}, \mathcal{A}, \alpha^\infty, \mathrm{Obs}())$. To decide whether or not it is a PLA-structure of a spatial database, we start by constructing what we will refer to as the *dual graph* $\mathcal{G}_{\mathcal{S}}$ of $\mathcal{S}$. Fig. 8 illustrates this construction for a loop and a line. $\mathcal{G}_{\mathcal{S}}$ is an undirected graph and consists of a set of vertices V and a set of edges E.

V contains a vertex for each point name, for each line name and each area name in $\mathcal{S}$. In addition to these, V contains a different vertex for each occurrence of a line name in an observation (called an observation vertex of the line) and a different vertex for each occurrence of an area in an observation (called an observation vertex of the area). E contains an edge between the vertex of a line name A and and each observation vertex of A, an edge between the vertex of an area name α and and each observation vertex of α. If $\mathrm{Obs}(p) = (\alpha)$, E contains an edge between the vertex of p and the corresponding observation vertex of α, and an edge from the corresponding observation vertex of α to itself. If, on the

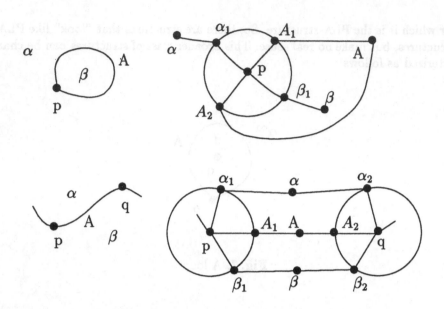

Fig. 8. The dual graph of a loop and a line

other hand, $\text{Obs}(p) = (A_1\alpha_1 \ldots A_n\alpha_n)$, E contains an edge between the vertex of p and the $2n$ corresponding observation vertices, and an edge between two successive observation vertices and between the observation vertices of α_n and of A_1. We refer to the latter series of $2n$ edges as the *cycle of p*.

We now give our decision procedure in terms of decidable properties of the dual graph and of the structure $\mathcal{S}$.

Decision procedure. The following are necessary and sufficient conditions for a structure $\mathcal{S}$ to be a PLA-structure:
• If $\alpha A\beta$ occurs in the observation from p, then there is a point q (possibly equal to p) such that $\beta A\alpha$ occurs in the observation from q. Both occurrences of A are different and are the only occurrences of A in an observation.
• $\mathcal{G}_\mathcal{S}$ is a connected graph.
• $\mathcal{G}_\mathcal{S}$ is a planar graph.

We will briefly outline the (rather technical) proof of the correctness of this procedure. The conditions are clearly necessary. Indeed, if $\mathcal{S}$ is a PLA-structure then there is a spatial database $\mathcal{D}$ of which $\mathcal{S}$ is the PLA-structure. We can very easily transform the database in the dual graph $\mathcal{G}_\mathcal{S}$. $\mathcal{G}_\mathcal{S}$ is planar and connected. Furthermore, each line A has to endpoints, say p and q. This results in two occurrences of A in the way as specified the first condition.

To prove sufficiency, we start with a planar embedding of $\mathcal{G}_S$ in the plane. This embedding exists because of the third condition. For each point that is located outside the interior of its cycle, we switch the interior and the exterior of the cycle with the result that it is inside. With a similar inversion, we can make sure that the vertex of α^∞ is in the unbounded area of the embedding. For some of the points the cycles may have the wrong, i.e., counterclockwise orientation. It can be proved that the points with a wrong orientation are "clustered" together and can all be turned without affecting the points with a clockwise cycle. It is easy to derive the wanted spatial database from an embedding of the dual graph in which α^∞ is located in the unbounded area and each point is located inside its correctly oriented cycle.

We end this section with the comment that this decision algorithm is efficient. The construction of the dual graph is linear in the size of the structure. Also the first condition can be checked in linear time. For both the second and the third condition efficient algorithms are known [6].

5   Further Remarks

In Sect. 3 we have defined two spatial databases to be topologically equivalent if they are isotopic. Intuitively this means that one database can be continuously deformed into the other. In classical topology, however, two figures are usually called topologically equivalent if they are *homeomorphic*. Homeomorphisms form a broader class of continuous transformations than the one that we have considered. The reflection ρ of the plane along the y-axis is a homeomorphism of the the plane but not an isotopy. ρ transforms a left hand continuously a right hand, as is illustrated in Fig. 9. This continuous transformation can not be achieved by a continuous deformation in the plane. To deform a left hand continuously into a right hand it is necessary to leave the plane and to use a third dimension.

The following well-known result classifies homeomorphisms of the real plane as either being continuous deformations or composed of a reflection followed by a continuous deformation (see e.g. [16]).

Property. A homeomorphism of the plane is either isotopic to the identity or to ρ.

This property allows us to define an invariant and lossless representation for spatial databases if toplogically equivalent corresponds to homeomorphic. The reflection ρ reverses the orientation and as a consequence also each observation of a spatial database from one of its points. For the databases in Fig. 9 this is best visible for the point p. Two isotopic spatial databases have the same clockwise, respectively counterclockwise observations. For two homeomorphic but non-isotopic spatial databases the clockwise observations of the first correspond to the counterclockwise observations of the other and vice versa.

12

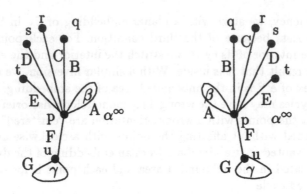

Fig. 9. Two spatial databases: a left and a right hand

Acknowledgements

The authors would like to thank Rudi Penne and Johan Van Biesen for many helpful discussions. Furthermore, we would like to thank Jan Hidders [9] and Xiao-Song Lin for useful suggestions concerning the proof of losslessness.

References

1. J.P. Corbett. *Topological Principles of Cartography.* Technical Paper No. 48, US Bureau of the Census, Washington, DC, USA: US Government Printing Office, 1979.
2. M. Egenhofer. Reasoning about Binary Topological Relations. *Advances in Spatial Databases, Lecture Notes in Computer Science, 525,* (eds. O. Günther and H.-J. Schek), 143–160, Springer-Verlag, 1991.
3. M. Egenhofer. Topological Relations between Regions of $\mathbf{R}^2$ and $\mathbf{Z}^2$. *Advances in Spatial Databases, Lecture Notes in Computer Science, 692,* (eds. D. Abel and B.C. Ooi), 316–336, Springer-Verlag, 1993.
4. M. Egenhofer and R. Franzosa. On the equivalence of topological relations. *International Journal of Geographical Information Systems,* 523–542, 1994.
5. M. Egenhofer and J. Herring A mathematical framework for the definition of topological relationships. *Proceedings of the Fourth International Symposium on Spatial Data Handling,* Zurich, Switzerland (eds. K. Brassel and H. Kishimoto), 803–813, 1990.
6. S. Even. *Graph Algorithms.* Computer Science Press, 1979.
7. R.H. Güting. An Introduction to Spatial Database Systems. *The VLDB Journal,* 3(4), 1994.
8. J. Herring. TIGRIS: Topologically Integrated Geographic Information Systems. *Proceedings of Auto Carto 8 Conference,* Baltimore, MD, (ed. N.R. Chrisman), 1987.

9. J. Hidders. An Isotopic Invariant for Planar Drawings of Connected Planar Graphs. Computing Science Note, 95/04, Eindhoven University of Technology, 1995.
10. R. Laurini and D. Thompson. *Fundamentals of Spatial Information Systems.* The A.P.I.C. Series, 37, Academic Press, 1992.
11. E.E. Moise. *Geometric Topology in Dimensions 2 and 3.* Graduate Texts in Mathematics, 47, Springer-Verlag, 1977.
12. S. Morehouse. The architecture of ARC/INFO. *Proceedings of the Auto Carto 9 Conference*, Baltimore, MD, American Society for Photogrammetry and Remote Sensing/American Congress for Surveying and Mapping, 266–277, 1989.
13. J. Paredaens. Spatial Databases. The Final Frontier. *Database Theory - ICDT '95, Lecture Notes in Computer Science, 893*, 14–32, Springer-Verlag, 1995.
14. J. Paredaens, J. Van den Bussche and D. Van Gucht. Towards a Theory of Spatial Database Queries. *Proceedings of the 13th ACM SIGACT-SIGMOD-SIGART Symposium on the Principles of Database Systems*, 279–288, ACM Press, 1994.
15. P. Preparata and M.I. Shamos. *Computational geometry.* Springer-Verlag, 1985.
16. J. Stillwell. *Classical Topology and Combinatorial Group Theory.* Graduate Texts in Mathematics, 72, Springer-Verlag, 1980.

On the Desirability and Limitations of Linear Spatial Database Models

Luc Vandeurzen[1], Marc Gyssens[1], Dirk Van Gucht[2]

[1] Dept. WNI, University of Limburg, B-3590 Diepenbeek, Belgium,
lvdeurze@alpha.luc.ac.be, gyssens@charlie.luc.ac.be.
[2] Computer Science Dept., Indiana Univ., Bloomington, IN 47405-4101, USA,
vgucht@cs.indiana.edu.

Abstract. A general linear spatial database model is presented in which both the representation and the manipulation of non-spatial data is based on first-order logic over the real numbers with addition. We first argue the naturalness of our model and propose it as a general framework to study and compare linear spatial database models. However, we also establish that no reasonable safe extension of our data manipulation language can be complete for the linear spatial queries in that even very simple queries such as deciding colinearity or computing convex hull of a finite set of points cannot be expressed. We show that this fundamental result has serious ramifications for the way in which query languages for linear spatial database models have to be designed.

1 Introduction

There are many database applications that need the ability to store and manipulate geometric data, such as geographic information systems (GIS), geometric modeling systems (CAD), and temporal databases. We refer the reader to the following papers for more background on the work done about spatial and temporal databases[3]. [12, 29]

In a recent paper [18], Güting specified requirements for spatial database systems: a spatial database system must first and foremost be a database system, meaning that it should offer the tools needed to represent, store, and manipulate both conventional and geometric data objects; in addition it should offer spatial data types in its data model and query language; and finally it should support spatial data types in its implementation, e.g., by making available spatial indexing and algorithms for spatial joins.

Spatial database models designed in accordance with the above requirements can roughly be categorized in models based on fixed and variable spatial dimensions. In models based on fixed spatial dimensions (e.g., [2, 16, 17, 35, 33]), the spatial data types are subclasses of all possible point sets of a Euclidean space of some fixed dimension (usually 1, 2, or 3), such as, e.g., points, lines, and polygons.

---

[3] Since temporal databases can be interpreted as 1-dimensional spatial databases, we shall not give them separate consideration.

Unfortunately, the particular choices of spatial data types and corresponding operators in these models are somewhat "ad hoc" as no singular set of spatial data types and corresponding operators is known to serve well all spatial purposes. Models based on variable spatial dimensions (e.g., [10, 22, 24, 28]) avoid this lack of generality by adopting a more declarative approach. However, some of the latter models may be too general from an implementational perspective.

It is the purpose of this paper to bridge the gap between the two main approaches by presenting a general, variable-dimensional, *linear* spatial database model as a formal framework to study the representation and manipulation of linear spatial data. In Section 2, we introduce our model as a restriction of the very general (non-linear) spatial database model considered by Paredaens et al. [28]. The point sets in the model thus obtained are called semi-linear sets and are characterized as definable in the first-order theory over the real numbers with addition. By providing some alternative characterizations and establishing desirable closure properties semi-linear sets on the one hand, and by proposing a simple and natural declarative, calculus-like query language, called FO + linear, for which an equivalent procedural algebra can be defined, on the other hand, we argue the appropriateness of our model for the purpose it is intended. In Section 3, we study the expressiveness of FO + linear. Although certain complex geometric decision problems and computations can be expressed in an elegant way, we were able to prove that no reasonable safe extension of FO + linear can be complete for the linear spatial queries in that even very simple queries such as deciding colinearity or computing convex hull of a finite set of points cannot be expressed. The viability of alternative strategies to obtain a richer language that circumvent the deep inherent problem identified in this paper are examined. In Section 4, finally, we discuss the ramifications of our main result and compare our approach with other work.

2 A General Linear Spatial Database Model

2.1 Semi-linear Sets

Linear spatial database models and prototypes proposed in the literature typically focus on a finite number of specific spatial data types one might designate as "linear," the particular choice of these primitives usually being driven by the applications that are intended. The choice of these "linear" data types is further motivated by the observation that many geometrical operations on typical linear data, such as lines, and polygons, and their counterparts in three dimensional space, have efficient algorithms. Thus, linear data types are also attractive from an implementational perspective. Variable-dimension models avoid the "ad-hoc" approach of choosing a set of data types and operators satisfying all application needs by offering a general, declarative framework. It goes without saying that such a general framework offers a tool to study spatial databases and their properties in a formal way, as is the case for conventional databases. In our model we try to combine the benefits of these two approaches. It is our purpose to study linear, spatial databases from a general perspective by offering a constraint-based data model and a calculus-like query language with an equivalent algebra. To do this, we took the most liberal restriction possible of an existing very general and non-linear spatial database model, considered by Paredaens et al. [28].

Paredaens, Van den Bussche, and Van Gucht considered as spatial data all geometrical figures definable in elementary geometry, i.e., first-order logic over the real numbers with addition and multiplication. These figures are called *semi-algebraic sets* in real algebraic geometry. [4] The rationale behind this approach was that the first-order theory of the reals is decidable by means of a very strong form of effective quantifier elimination [11, 3], and that, consequently, many properties of semi-algebraic sets are decidable, too. [20]

A formula in the first-order logic of the reals, a *real formula* for short, is built from *atomic real formulae* using boolean operators and quantification over real variables; *atomic real formulae* are conditions built from *real terms* using one of the six binary comparison relations $=, <, >, \leq, \geq$, and $\neq$; and *real terms* are polynomials in real variables with integer coefficients.

A very general and appealing way to obtain linear figures is to consider only those real formulae that are exclusively built from real terms that are *linear* polynomials; these real formulae will be called *linear formulae* and the real terms from which they are built will be called *linear terms*. Clearly, linear formulae can be characterized as first-order formulae over the real numbers with addition only. Without loss of generality, we may assume that *atomic linear formulae* are of the form $\sum_{i=1}^{m} a_i x_i \, \theta \, a$, where $x_1, \ldots, x_m$ are real variables, $a_1, \ldots, a_m$ are integer coefficients, a is an integer, and θ is one of $=, >, \geq, <, \leq$, and $\neq$.

Every linear formula $\varphi(x_1, \ldots, x_m)$ with free real variables $x_1, \ldots, x_m$ defines a geometrical figure $\{(x_1, \ldots, x_m) \mid \varphi(x_1, \ldots, x_m)\}$ in m-dimensional Euclidean space $\mathbf{R}^m$ by letting real variables range over the real numbers. Semi-algebraic sets defined in this way are called *semi-linear sets*. Examples of semi-linear sets are given in Example 1.

It is of course important that these semi-linear sets satisfy several desirable closure properties:

Proposition 1. *Semi-linear sets are closed under the set operations union, difference, intersection, and Cartesian product, and under projection.*

The proof of the above proposition is straightforward and is therefore omitted. Notice that the above closure properties can also be regarded as providing interpretations for the various Boolean operators occurring in linear formulae. In particular, existential quantification can be interpreted as a projection. Finally, notice that negation can easily be computed, as the negation of an atomic linear formula is obtained by appropriately changing the comparison relation.

Next, the above closure properties allow us to establish two alternative characterizations of semi-linear sets.

Günther [15] defines *polyhedral chains* as a representation scheme for geometric data. A *polyhedral chain* in a Euclidean space (of arbitrary dimension) is defined as a finite sum of *cells* each of which is a finite intersection of half-spaces.

A polyhedral chain is called *semi-linear* if its cells can be described by equations with rational coefficients.

Proposition 2. *Semi-linear sets and semi-linear polyhedral chains represent the same class of figures.*

Proof. Since semi-linear polyhedral chains can be defined in terms of half-spaces that can clearly be described by atomic linear formulae, Proposition 1 yields that they are semi-linear sets.

Conversely, an atomic linear formula represents either a hyperplane or an open or closed half-space or the complement of a hyperplane, which is the union of two open half-spaces. It is therefore easy to see that any semi-linear set defined by a linear formula *without* quantifiers can alternatively be defined as a semi-linear polyhedral chain. This result extends to semi-linear sets defined by *general* linear formulae, as the quantifiers can be eliminated [21, 19] (details omitted).

Another practical tool to deal with semi-linear sets is *polytopes*. A *polytope* in a Euclidean space (of arbitrary dimension) is defined as the convex hull of a non-empty finite set of points in that space. [7, 27, 23]. A polytope is called *semi-linear* if it can be defined in terms of points with rational coefficients. An *open polytope* is the topological interior of a polytope with respect to the smallest sub-space containing the polytope.

Proposition 3. *Bounded semi-linear sets and finite unions of open semi-linear polytopes are equivalent.*

Proof. Every open semi-linear polytope can be written as a finite intersection of open half-spaces of which the bounding hyperplanes can be described by equations with rational coefficients. Therefore, it is possible to write the union of open semi-linear polytopes as a semi-linear polyhedral chain. Conversely, a bounded semi-linear set can be written as a semi-linear polyhedral chain. Because of the boundedness of the semi-linear set, all cells of the polyhedral chain are bounded and can therefore be shown to be the union of open semi-linear polytopes (details omitted).

The above characterizations allow us to conclude that most spatial data types found in the literature are sub-types of the semi-linear sets. Güting [16, 17] in his geo-relational algebra proposes the spatial data types *point*, *line*, and *polygon*, which can be seen as 0-, 1-, and 2-dimensional polytopes, respectively.[4] Egenhofer [13] in his spatial data representation model proposes as basic objects *simplices*, which are special kinds of polytopes.

In summary, semi-linear sets constitute a very general and elegant paradigm to represent linear spatial data, which are the kind of spatial data that are most often considered. As opposed to general semi-algebraic sets which are *too*

---

[4] The polygons considered by Güting are not necessarily convex, but can always be decomposed into convex polygons.

complex, we believe semi-linear sets have the potential for efficient implementation. The alternative characterizations we presented offer the opportunity to use polyhedral chains or polytopes as internal representation for semi-linear sets. Günther [15] has described efficient algorithms to perform set-operations on polyhedral chains. Algorithms to compute efficiently the union or intersection of n-dimensional polytopes are provided by Putnam et al. [31]. Several operations and techniques in computational geometry, such as plane sweep and divide-and-conquer, can be used for this purpose. [26, 36, 8, 30] Brodsky et al. [6] introduced canonical forms for semi-linear sets to make efficient implementation of operations on semi-linear sets possible. Lassez et al. [25, 19] have proposed variable elimination algorithms for sets of linear constraints. Finally, the notion of semi-linear set is not bound to any particular dimension. Even though practical applications are rarely situated in a dimension higher than 4, this generality of semi-linear sets is of relevance, since—as pointed out earlier— semi-linear sets defined by existentially quantified linear formulae can straightforwardly be interpreted as projections of higher-dimensional semi-linear sets defined by unquantified linear formulae.

2.2 The Data Representation Model

A linear spatial database *scheme*, S, is a finite set of *relation names*. Each relation name, R, has a type which is a pair of natural numbers, $[n, m]$. Here, n denotes the number of non-spatial columns and m the dimension of the single spatial column of R. Consider a relation type $[n, m]$. A *syntactic tuple* of type $[n, m]$ has the form $(a_1, \ldots, a_n; \varphi(x_1, \ldots, x_m))$, with $a_1, \ldots, a_n$ non-spatial values of some domain, U, and $\varphi(x_1, \ldots, x_m)$ a linear formula with m free variables. As already observed, we may assume without loss of generality that this formula is quantifier-free. A *syntactic relation* of type $[n, m]$ is a finite set of syntactic tuples of type $[n, m]$. A *syntactic instance*, finally, is a mapping assigning to each relation name of a scheme S a syntactic relation of the same type.

The semantics of a syntactic tuple $t = (a_1, \ldots, a_n; \varphi(x_1, \ldots, x_m))$ of type $[n, m]$ is the possibly infinite subset of $U^n \times \mathbf{R}^m$ denoted as $I(t)$ and defined as the Cartesian product $\{(a_1, \ldots, a_n)\} \times S$, in which $S \subseteq \mathbf{R}^m$ is the semi-linear set $\{(x_1, \ldots, x_m) \mid \varphi(x_1, \ldots, x_m)\}$. This subset of $U^n \times \mathbf{R}^m$ can be interpreted as a possibly infinite $(n + m)$-ary relation, called *semantic relations*, the tuples of which are called *semantic tuples*. The semantics of a syntactic relation, r, is the semantic relation denoted as $I(r)$ and defined as $\bigcup_{t \in r} I(t)$. Finally, the semantics of a syntactic instance, $\mathcal{I}$, over a database scheme S is the mapping assigning to each relation name R in S the semantic relation $I(\mathcal{I}(R))$.

Example 1. The example in Figure 1 shows a spatial database representing geographical information about Belgium.

Notice that a syntactic relation has exactly one spatial attribute. Since applications which would require more spatial attributes can be simulated with one spatial attribute using Cartesian product, we chose not to complicate the formalism by relaxing the restriction we imposed.

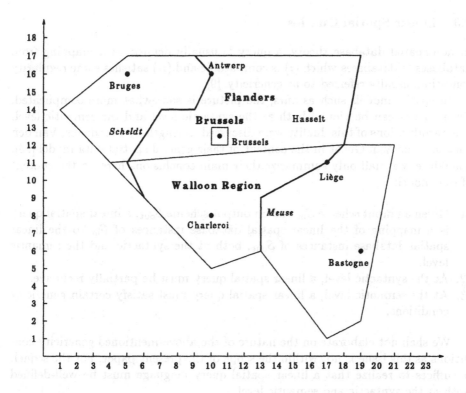

Regions

Name	Geometry
Brussels	$(y \leq 13) \wedge (x \leq 11) \wedge (y \geq 12) \wedge (x \geq 10)$
Flanders	$(y \leq 17) \wedge (3x - 4y \geq -53) \wedge (x - 14y \leq -150) \wedge (x + y \geq 45) \wedge$ $(4x - y \leq 78) \wedge (\neg((y \leq 13) \wedge (x \leq 11) \wedge (y \geq 12) \wedge (x \geq 10)))$
Walloon Region	$((x - 14y \leq -150) \wedge (y \leq 12) \wedge (19x + 7y \leq 375) \wedge$ $(x - 2y \leq 15) \wedge (5x + 4y \geq 89) \wedge (x \geq 13)) \vee ((-x + 3y \geq 5) \wedge$ $(x + y \geq 45) \wedge (x - 14y \geq -150) \wedge (x \geq 13))$

Cities

Name	Geometry
Antwerp	$(x = 10) \wedge (y = 16)$
Bastogne	$(x = 19) \wedge (y = 6)$
Bruges	$(x = 5) \wedge (y = 16)$
Brussels	$(x = 10.5) \wedge$ $(y = 12.5)$
Charleroi	$(x = 10) \wedge (y = 8)$
Hasselt	$(x = 16) \wedge (y = 14)$
Liège	$(x = 17) \wedge (y = 11)$

Rivers

Name	Geometry
Meuse	$((y \leq 17) \wedge (5x - y \leq 78) \wedge (y \geq 12)) \vee$ $((y \leq 12) \wedge (x - y = 6) \wedge (y \geq 11)) \vee$ $((y \leq 11) \wedge (x - 2y = -5) \wedge (y \geq 9)) \vee$ $((y \leq 9) \wedge (x = 13) \wedge (y \geq 6))$
Scheldt	$((y \leq 17) \wedge (x + y = 26) \wedge (y \geq 16)) \vee$ $((y \leq 16) \wedge (2x - y = 4) \wedge (y \geq 14)) \vee$ $((x \leq 9) \wedge (x \geq 7) \wedge (y = 14)) \vee$ $((y \leq 14) \wedge (-3x + 2y = 7) \wedge (y \geq 11)) \vee$ $((y \leq 11) \wedge (2x + y = 21) \wedge (y \geq 9))$

Fig. 1. Example of a spatial database.

2.3   Linear Spatial Queries

In non-spatial database theory, a query is usually defined as a mapping from databases to databases which (i) is computable and (ii) satisfies some regularity condition, usually referred to as genericity. [9]

In spatial models such as ours, the picture is somewhat more complicated, since queries can be viewed both at the syntactic level and the semantic level. The ramifications of this duality were discussed at length by Paredaens, Van den Bussche, and Van Gucht in the context of their general spatial data model [28]. Therefore, we shall only summarize their main conclusions here, in the context of our model:

1. Given an input scheme S_{in} and an output scheme S_{out}, a linear spatial query is a mapping of the linear spatial database instances of S_{in} to the linear spatial database instances of S_{out}, both at the syntactic and the semantic level.
2. At the syntactic level, a linear spatial query must be partially recursive.
3. At the semantic level, a linear spatial query must satisfy certain genericity conditions.

We shall not elaborate on the nature of the above-mentioned genericity conditions as this issue is not within the scope of the present paper. For the sequel, it suffices to realize that a linear spatial query language must be well-defined both at the syntactic and semantic level.

Example 2. An example of a (very simple) linear spatial query on the database in Example 1 is *"Find all cities that lie on a river and give their names and the names of the rivers they lie on."* More complicated linear spatial queries are given in Section 3.1.

2.4   The Linear Spatial Calculus and Algebra

In this section, we present two query languages, a calculus and an algebra, and establish their equivalence. As both languages in our opinion were kept as simple as can reasonably expected, we feel that our equivalence result emphasizes the naturalness of both languages.

We first define the *linear calculus*. The *linear calculus* is obtained by adding to the language of linear formulae defined in Section 2.1 the following:

- a totally ordered infinite set of variables called *non-spatial variables*, disjoint from the set of real variables;
- atomic formulae of the form $v_1 = v_2$, with v_1 and v_2 non-spatial variables;
- atomic formulae of the form $R(v_1, \ldots, v_n; p_1, \ldots, p_m)$, with R a relation name of type $[n, m]$, $v_1, \ldots, v_n$ non-spatial variables, and $p_1, \ldots, p_m$ linear terms; and
- universal and existential quantification of non-spatial variables.

Linear calculus formulae can be interpreted as mappings from linear spatial database instances to linear spatial database instances *at the semantic level* in the standard way.[5]

In a straightforward manner, the spatial algebra of Paredaens, Van den Bussche, and Van Gucht [28] can be restricted to a *linear algebra* of which the expressions can be interpreted as computable mappings from linear spatial database instances to linear spatial database instances *at the syntactic level*.

Using the same techniques as Paredaens et al., it is possible to establish the following result:

Proposition 4. *Every linear calculus formula can be effectively converted into a linear algebra expression and vice-versa, in such a way that both express the same mapping from linear spatial database instances to linear spatial database instances, respectively at the semantic and syntactic level.*

The equivalence result in Proposition 4 also establishes that the linear calculus (or algebra) is indeed a spatial query language in the sense of Section 2.3.

Example 3. The query in Example 2 can be expressed by the following linear calculus expression:

$$\{(c, r) \mid (\exists x)(\exists y)(\text{Cities}(c, x, y) \wedge \text{Rivers}(r, x, y))\} \ .$$

3 Expressiveness of Linear Spatial Query Languages

In this section, we shall give results concerning both the expressiveness and limitations of the linear spatial calculus of Section 2.4, which will be referred to as FO + linear for brevity. The spatial calculus of Paredaens, Van den Bussche, and Van Gucht [28] designed to manipulate geometric objects definable by general real formulae shall be referred to as FO + poly.

3.1 Expressiveness of FO + linear

Up to now, a precise characterization of the expressive power of FO + linear is still wide open. In this section, we try to give a feeling for the kind of queries that can be solved in FO + linear by presenting some typical examples of topological or geometrical properties computable in FO + linear.

In order to state the solutions to our example queries concisely, we shall use some abbreviations. We shall use vector notion to denote points. In this notation, equations such as $\mathbf{x} - \mathbf{y} < \mathbf{z}$ should be interpreted coordinate-wise. In particular, $\neg(\mathbf{x} = 0)$ denotes that $\mathbf{x}$ is not the origin of the coordinate system, whereas $\mathbf{x} \neq 0$ denotes that *none* of the coordinates of $\mathbf{x}$ equals 0! In all the queries below, the input database consists of one relation name S of an arbitrary purely spatial

---

[5] The linear calculus can also be shown to satisfy a genericity condition, but we shall not digress on this issue here.

type. The restriction on S is justified since in FO + linear manipulation of both conventional and geometric data can be done in a straightforward manner as is shown earlier (Example 3).

Example 4. The following FO + linear expression decides whether S is *discrete*:

$$(\forall x)(\exists d)((d \neq 0) \wedge S(x) \Rightarrow \neg(\exists y)(\neg(y = x) \wedge (x - d < y < x + d))) .$$

Since discrete semi-algebraic sets are necessarily finite [4], the same property holds a fortiori also for semi-linear sets. Conversely, a finite semi-linear is necessarily discrete. Hence the above expression can also be used to decide whether S is *finite*. It is however possible to decide finiteness of semi-linear sets without having to rely on the above property of semi-algebraic sets as for an arbitrary set in a Euclidean space finiteness is always equivalent to discreteness *and boundedness*. The following FO + linear expression decides whether S is *bounded*:

$$(\exists d)(\forall x)(\forall y)(S(x) \wedge S(y) \Rightarrow -d < y - x < d) .$$

Example 5. In this example, we show that several topological properties of a semi-linear set can be computed in FO + linear. For instance, the topological interior of S is computed by the following FO + linear expression:

$$(\exists d)((d \neq 0) \wedge (\forall y)(x - d < y < x + d) \Rightarrow S(y)) .$$

Similarly, the topological closure of S is computed by the following FO + linear expression:

$$(\forall d)((d \neq 0) \Rightarrow (\exists y)(S(y) \wedge x - d < y < x + d)) .$$

Hence, also the topological boundary of S can be computed as the difference of the topological closure and the topological interior. We note that Egenhofer in his paper [13] showed that with these topological operations, a whole class of topological properties can be expressed in $\mathbf{R}^2$.

Due to space limitations, we conclude this section with some useful queries that can be expressed in FO + linear, without giving the formulae.

– Is a semi-linear set of $\mathbf{R}^n$ n-dimensional (i.e., not embeddable in a space of lower dimension)?
– Compute the regularization[6] of a semi-linear set. Because of this query, the regularization of the set operations union, intersection and difference can be computed. This is an important result since in practice it turns out that the regularized set operations are more important than the standard set operations.
– Translate or scale a semi-linear set. Reflection according to some axis or the origin is also computable.

---

[6] Intuitively, a regular set has no dangling or isolated boundary points.

3.2 Limitations of FO + linear

In this section, we demonstrate that there are fundamental, *inherent* limitations to safe calculus-like languages for linear spatial databases, which in particular apply to FO+linear. By *safe*, we mean that the language can *only* express linear queries.

Definition 5. Let $\mathbf{x}$, $\mathbf{y}$ and $\mathbf{z}$ be m-dimensional vectors of real variables. The $3m$-ary *colinearity* predicate $\text{line}_m(\mathbf{x}, \mathbf{y}, \mathbf{z})$ evaluates to *true* if in m-dimensional Euclidean space the points with coordinates $\mathbf{x}$, $\mathbf{y}$, and $\mathbf{z}$ are colinear.

Theorem 6. *The language* FO+linear+colinearity *is equivalent to the language* FO + poly.

Proof. Obviously, the colinearity predicate $\text{line}_m(\mathbf{x}, \mathbf{y}, \mathbf{z})$ can be expressed in FO + poly by the following formula:

$$(\mathbf{x} = \mathbf{y}) \vee (\exists \lambda)(\mathbf{z} = \lambda \mathbf{x} + (1 - \lambda)\mathbf{y}) \ .$$

Conversely, consider the ternary multiplication predicate $\text{product}(x, y, z)$ which is true if $z = xy$. Let $\mathbf{x}$ and $\mathbf{z}$ be m-ary vectors of real variables of which the first components are x and z, respectively, and let $\mathbf{e_2}$ and $\mathbf{y}$ be m-ary vectors of real variables of which the second components are 1 and y, respectively. All other components of $\mathbf{e_2}$, $\mathbf{x}$, $\mathbf{y}$, and $\mathbf{z}$ are 0. In m-dimensional Euclidean space, this predicate can be expressed by the following formula in FO + linear + colinearity:

$$(\forall \mathbf{u})\neg(\text{line}_m(\mathbf{x}, \mathbf{e_2}, \mathbf{u}) \wedge \text{line}_m(\mathbf{z}, \mathbf{y}, \mathbf{u})) \ .$$

The above formula expresses the geometric construction of the product of two real numbers (see, e.g., [34], p. 144), whence its correctness. (The expression is not correct in case of $y = 1$, $y = 0$ or $x = 0$. However, these individual cases can be treated separately.) Clearly, any atomic real formula can be expressed in FO + linear extended with the above multiplication predicate. Therefore, FO + linear + colinearity and FO + poly are equivalent.

Corollary 7. *The convex hull of a set of n points in m-dimensional Euclidean space cannot be expressed as a $m(n + 1)$-ary predicate in any safe extension of* FO + linear *if $m \geq 2$ and $n \geq 2$.*

Proof. The proof follows immediately from the above theorem and the observation that three points in m-dimensional Euclidean space are colinear if and only if one of them is on the line segment defined by the other two, which is the convex hull of that pair of points.

Notice that the convex hull of any m-dimensional (semi-algebraic) set S can be expressed in FO + poly as

$$\{(\mathbf{z}) \mid (\exists \mathbf{x_i})(\exists \lambda_i)(\bigwedge_{i=0}^{m} S(\mathbf{x_i}) \wedge \bigwedge_{i=0}^{m}(\lambda_i \geq 0) \wedge (\sum_{i=0}^{m} \lambda_i = 1) \wedge (\mathbf{z} = \sum_{i=0}^{m} \lambda_i \mathbf{x_i}))\} \ .$$

It is interesting to note that in FO + linear convexity is decidable:

Proposition 8. [32] *It is decidable in* FO + linear *whether a semi-linear set is convex.*

Proof. The following FO + linear expression decides whether S is *convex*:

$$(\forall \mathbf{x})(\forall \mathbf{y})((S(\mathbf{x}) \wedge S(\mathbf{y})) \Rightarrow (\exists \mathbf{z})(S(\mathbf{z}) \wedge (2\mathbf{z} = \mathbf{x} + \mathbf{y}))) .$$

Similarly, one may ask if in FO + linear it is decidable whether a semi-linear set is a line, even though colinearity is not computable.

3.3 Extensions of FO + linear

The question arises whether "reasonable," "non-trivial" safe proper extensions of FO + linear exist at all. In this section, we review some mechanisms for extension proposed by other authors and discuss to which extent they might be useful for our purposes.

In recent papers, Afrati, Cosmadakis, Grumbach, and Kuper [10, 1] proposed a calculus in which they extended a language similar to FO+linear with variables that range over lines. Unfortunately, they were able to show that their language is also equivalent to FO + poly. Thus, extending FO + linear with line variables does not lead to a safe proper extension of FO + linear.

In a series of papers, J.-L. Lassez et al. (e.g., [25]) proposed so-called *parameterized queries*. A *parameterized query* is of the form

$$\{(\alpha_1, \ldots, \alpha_n, \beta) \mid (\forall y_1) \ldots, (\forall y_n)(S(y_1, \ldots, y_n) \Rightarrow$$
$$((\alpha_1 y_1 + \cdots + \alpha_n y_n \leq \beta) \wedge \varphi(\alpha_1, \ldots, \alpha_n, \beta)))\}$$

where S is a set of linear constraints on $y_1, \ldots, y_n$ and φ is a set of linear constraints on the parameters $\alpha_1, \ldots, \alpha_n$ and β. Observe that because of the term $\alpha_1 y_1 + \cdots + \alpha_n y_n$ this formula violates the syntax of FO + linear. However, it follows from a result by T. Huynh, C. Lassez, and J.-L. Lassez [19] that parameterized queries are safe linear spatial queries.

The precise relationship between FO+linear and the language of parametrized queries is as of yet still unclear. On the one hand, some FO + linear queries may not be expressible by parametrized queries, but on the other hand, not all parameterized may be expressible by FO + linear queries because they violate FO + linear syntax. A mechanism such as used in parametrized queries remains a viable candidate for extending FO + linear, provided sufficient syntactic restrictions are built in to prevent that, e.g., colinearity can be expressed.

We want to point out that languages such as FO + linear rely heavily on the use of subqueries as a tool to solve more complicated queries. A possible approach towards extending FO + linear might therefore be adding some non-expressible linear queries which may not be applied arbitrarily to the results of subqueries. This is currently under investigation.

4 Discussion

In this paper, we have proposed a general linear spatial database model that tries to combine the benefits of both fixed dimensional linear spatial database models and general variable dimensional databases. We used this model as a framework to study the manipulation and representation properties of formal and still implementable linear spatial database models in general.

The proposed model uses semi-linear sets as spatial data type. We showed by establishing the equivalence of semi-linear sets with the data types used in fixed dimensional linear spatial database models that semi-linear sets have the right properties to be used as a practical spatial data type. Otherwise, semi-linear sets form a specialization of semi-algebraic sets, which are the data type used in the variable-dimension database model considered by Paredaens et al. [28]. Also the query language, FO + linear, is a specialization of the query language defined in [28] and is equivalent with a procedural algebra language. Both our spatial data and query language (FO + linear) have linear constraints as their fundamentals, and can therefore serve as a formal framework to study the intended properties.

Although a lot of interesting practical queries can be expressed in FO+linear, we found that FO + linear nevertheless has serious shortcomings with respect to expressive power, and can therefore not be considered fully adequate as a *querying tool* for linear spatial databases. The central issue in this regard is that certain natural linear queries (such as deciding colinearity or computing convex hull of a finite set of points) cannot be expressed. However, the problem encountered is not merely a deficiency of our particular model, but is of a deep fundamental nature, since we have shown that extending FO + linear to accommodate these queries leads to languages which are no longer safe in the sense that also non-linear data can be derived.

We have shown by considering some other proposals for linear spatial database query languages that there is no obvious way to circumvent this problem. In this connection, we want to mention two more approaches to linear spatial databases.

Brodsky and Kornatzky [6] propose a complex-object object-oriented spatial database models in which the data in the objects are represented as linear constraints and are therefore equivalent to semi-linear sets. Therefore, they face the same expressibility problems as we do. The issue of complex-object types is orthogonal to the more fundamental issue of reasoning about data types specific to spatial and temporal data.

Kanellakis and Goldin [22] describe a general framework for pure spatial relations with as query language the union of some existing query language and a decidable logical theory. Unfortunately, they only work out the dense order constraint case by giving an appropriate algebra. They only suggest the practical importance of linear constraints, but do not say anything about their expressiveness.

Our paper has therefore elicited a fundamental problem in the design of logic-based query languages for linear spatial databases.

In order to overcome this problem it may perhaps be necessary to first restrict FO + linear before extending it. As hinted at towards the end of the previous section, the main culprit of the problem we identified seems to be the absence of any limits to the use of (existential) quantification—geometrically corresponding to projection—in FO+linear. In retrospect, an algebraic approach similar to that of Güting [16] may be most promising and therefore deserves further study in this new light.

References

1. F. Afrati, S. Cosmadakis, S. Grumbach, and G. Kuper, "Linear Versus Polynomial Constraints in Database Query Languages," in Proceedings *2nd Int'l Workshop on Principles and Practice of Constraint Programming* (Rosario, WA), A. Borning, ed., *Lecture Notes in Computer Science*, vol. 874, Springer-Verlag, Berlin, 1994, pp. 181–192.

2. W.G. Aref and H. Samet, "Extending a Database with Spatial Operations," in Proceedings *2nd Symposium on Advances in Spatial Databases*, O. Günther, H.-J. Schek, eds., *Lecture Notes in Computer Science*, vol. 525, Springer-Verlag, Berlin, 1991, pp. 299–319.

3. D.S. Arnon, "Geometric Reasoning with Logic and Algebra," *Artificial Intelligence*, 37, 1988, pp. 37–60.

4. J. Bochnak, M. Coste, and M.F. Roy, *Géométrie algébrique réelle*, in *Ergebnisse der Mathematik und ihrer Grenzgebiete*, 3. Folge, Band 12, Springer-Verlag, Berlin, 1987.

5. A. Brodsky, J. Jaffar, and M.J. Maher, "Toward Practical Constraint Databases," in Proceedings *19th Int'l Conf. on Very Large Databases* (Dublin, Ireland), 1993, pp. 567–580.

6. A. Brodsky and Y. Kornatzky, "The LyriC Language: Querying Constraint Objects," in Proceedings *Post-ILPS'94 Workshop on Constraints and Databases* (Ithaca, NY), 1994.

7. A. Brøndsted, *An Introduction to Convex Polytopes*, in *Graduate Texts in Mathematics*, vol. 90, Springer-Verlag, New York, 1983.

8. I. Carlbom, "An Algorithm for Geometric Set Operations Using Cellular Subdivision Techniques," *IEEE Computer Graphics and Applications*, 7:5, 1987, pp. 44–55.

9. A. Chandra and D. Harel, "Computable Queries for Relational Database Systems," *Journal of Computer and System Sciences*, 21:2, 1980, pp. 156–178.

10. S.S. Cosmadakis and G.M. Kuper, "Expressiveness of First-Order Constraint Languages," *Technical Report*, ECRC-94-13, European Computer-Industry Research Centre, Munich, 1994.

11. G.E. Collins, "Quantifier Elimination for Real Closed Fields by Cylindrical Algebraic Decomposition," in Proceedings *2nd GI Conf. on Automata Theory and Formal Languages* (Kaiserslautern, Germany), H. Brakhage, ed., *Lecture Notes in Computer Science*, vol. 33, 1975, pp. 134–183.

12. J. Nievergelt and M. Freeston, eds., Special issue on spatial data, *Computer Journal*, 37:1, 1994.

13. M.J. Egenhofer, "A Formal Definition of Binary Topological Relationships," in Proceedings *Foundations of Data Organization and Algorithms*, W. Litwin and H.-J. Schek, eds., *Lecture Notes in Computer Science*, vol. 367, Springer-Verlag, Berlin, 1989, pp. 457–472.

14. M.J. Egenhofer, "Why not SQL!", *Int'l J. on Geographical Information Systems*, 6:2, 1992, pp. 71–85.

15. O. Günther, ed., *Efficient Structures for Geometric Data Management*, in *Lecture Notes in Computer Science*, vol. 337, Springer-Verlag, Berlin, 1988.

16. R.H. Güting, "Geo-Relational Algebra: A Model and Query Language for Geometric Database Systems," in *Advances in Database Technology—EDBT '88*, Proceedings *Int'l Conf. on Extending Database Technology* (Venice, Italy), J.W. Schmidt, S. Ceri, and M. Missikoff, eds., *Lecture Notes in Computer Science*, vol. 303, Soringer-Verlag, Berlin, 1988, pp. 506–527.

17. R.H. Güting, "Gral: An Extensible Relational Database System for Geometric Applications," in Proceedings *15th Int'l Conf. on Very Large Databases* (Amsterdam, the Netherlands), 1989, pp. 33–34.

18. R.H. Güting, "An Introduction to Spatial Database Systems," *VLDB-Journal*, 3:4, 1994, pp. 357–399.

19. T. Huynh, C. Lassez, and J.-L. Lassez. Fourier Algorithm Revisited. In Proceedings *2nd Int'l Conf. on Algebraic an Logic Programming*, H. Kirchner and W. Wechler, eds. *Lecture Notes in Computer Science*, volume 463. Springer Verlag, Berlin, 1990, pp. 117–131.

20. J. Heintz, T. Recio, and M.F. Roy. "Algorithms in Real Algebraic Geometry and Applications to Computational Geometry," in *Discrete and Computational Geometry*, W. Steiger, J. Goodman, and R. Pollack, eds., *DIMACS Series in Discrete Mathematics and Theoretical Computer Science*, vol. 6, AMS-ACM, 1991, pp. 137–163.

21. J.E. Hopcroft and J.D. Ullman, *Introduction to Automata Theory, Languages, and Computation*, Addison-Wesley Publ. Co.,, Reading, MA, 1979, pp. 355–357.

22. P.C. Kanellakis and D.Q. Goldin, "Constraint Programming and Database Query Languages," in Proceedings *2nd Conf. on Theoretical Aspects of Computer Software*, M. Hagiya and J.C. Mitchell, eds., *Lecture Notes in Computer Science*, vol. 789, Springer-Verlag, Berlin, 1994.

23. P.J. Kelly and M.L. Weiss. *Geometry and Convexity: a Study in Mathematical Methods*, J. Wiley and Sons, New York, 1979.

24. P.C. Kanellakis, G.M. Kuper and P.Z. Revesz, "Constraint Query Languages," *Journal of Computer and System Sciences*, to appear, also in Proceedings *9th ACM SIGACT-SIGMOD-SIGART Symposium on Principles of Database Systems* (Nashville, TN), 1990, pp. 299–313.

25. J.-L. Lassez, "Querying Constraints," in Proceedings *9th ACM SIGACT-SIGMOD-SIGART Symposium on Principles of Database Systems* (Nashville, TN), 1990, pp. 288–298.

26. M. Liebling and A. Prodon, "Algorithmic Geometry," in *Scientific Visualization and Graphics Simulation*, D. Thalmann, ed., J. Wiley and Sons. pp. 14–25.

27. P. McMullen and G.C. Shephard, *Convex Polytopes and the Upper Bound Conjecture*, University Press, Cambridge, 1971.

28. J. Paredaens, J. Van den Bussche, and D. Van Gucht, "Towards a Theory of Spatial Database Queries," in Proceedings *13th ACM SIGACT-SIGMOD-SIGART Symposium on Principles of Database Systems* (Minneapolis, MN), 1994. pp. 279–288.

29. N. Pissinou, R. Snodgrass, R. Elmasri, I. Mumick, T. Özsu, B. Pernici, A. Segef. B. Theodoulidis, and U. Dayal, "Towards an Infrastructure for Temporal Databases," *SIGMOD Records*, 23:1, 1994, pp. 35–51.

30. F.P. Preparata and D.E. Muller. "Finding the Intersection of n Half-Spaces in Time O(nlogn)," *Theoretical Computer Science*, 8, 1979, pp. 45–55.
31. L.K. Putnam and P.A. Subrahmanyan, "Boolean Operations on n-Dimensional Objects," *IEEE Computer Graphics and Applications*, 6:6, 1986, pp. 43–51.
32. E. Robertson, *personal communications*, 1994.
33. N. Roussopoulos, C. Faloutsos, and T. Sellis, "An Efficient Pictorial Database System for PSQL," *IEEE Transactions on Software Engineering*, 14:5, 1988, pp. 639–650.
34. W. Schwabhauser, W. Szmielew, and A. Tarski. *Metamathematische Methoden in der Geometrie*, Springer-Verlag, Berlin, 1983.
35. P. Svensson and Z. Huang, "Geo-Sal: A Query Language for Spatial Data Analysis," in Proceedings *2nd Symposium on Advances in Spatial Databases*, O. Günther and H.-J. Schek, eds. *Lecture Notes in Computer Science*, vol. 525. Springer-Verlag, Berlin, 1991, pp. 119–140.
36. B. Tilove, "Set Membership Classification: a Unified Approach to Geometric Intersection Problems," *IEEE Transactions on Computers*, C-29:10, 1980, pp. 874–883.

The Quad View Data Structure - a Representation for Planar Subdivisions

Ulrich Finke   Klaus H. Hinrichs

FB 15, Informatik, Westfälische Wilhelms-Universität
Einsteinstr. 62, D - 48149 Münster, Germany
E-Mail: finke, khh @ math.uni-muenster.de

Abstract. Applications in cartography, computer graphics and computer aided engineering require the representation and manipulation of planar subdivisions. Topology-oriented approaches represent the relations existing between the vertices, edges and faces of a planar subdivision. We extend this standard approach by decomposing the faces into trapezoidal views. By defining a neighborhood relation among the views we obtain the view graph which forms the basis of the quad view data structure - a new data structure for representing planar subdivisions. We present some basic operations on this data structure, and we show how it can be used to traverse a planar subdivision. Furthermore we sketch an algorithm for overlaying planar subdivisions represented by the quad view data structure. This algorithm is optimal for simply connected planar subdivisions: its time and storage requirements are linear in the size of the output subdivision. Finally we apply this overlay algorithm to implement locational vector-based map overlay operations.

1   Introduction

A *planar subdivision* is a partition Π of the 2-dimensional plane $\mathbb{R}^2$ into three finite collections of disjoint parts: the set of *vertices* V (each vertex $v \in V$ is a singleton {p} where $p \in \mathbb{R}^2$), the set of *edges* E and the set of *faces* F, i.e. $\Pi = V \cup E \cup F$. Each edge $e \in E$ connects two vertices in V, and each vertex in V is an end point of at least one edge in E. The boundary of each face $f \in F$ is formed by vertices from V and edges from E.

Planar subdivisions can be further classified by imposing additional restrictions:

Each closed path lying completely in one region of a *simply connected subdivision* can be topologically contracted to a point. Therefore a region in a simply-connected subdivision cannot contain any other region.

For any pair of points lying in a region of a *path connected subdivision* there exists a path which connects the two points and lies completely in this region. Therefore regions of a path connected subdivision can contain other regions.

Some topology-oriented approaches represent the relations existing between the vertices, edges and faces of a planar subdivision (Fig. 1). The arrows in Fig. 1 indicate the direction in which direct access is possible. The number specifies how many topological objects are referenced. [Woo85] analyzes different representations with respect to efficiency of certain operations and storage requirements.

The data structures mentioned in Fig. 1 allow to represent simply connected subdivisions. Path connected subdivisions can be transformed into simply connected subdivisions by inserting "invisible" edges.

Other representations, e.g. the loop approach by [Weil86], avoid "invisible" edges by extending the vertex-edge-face scheme by a further element. We will follow a similar track.

A face of a planar subdivision can be a complex geometric object, especially if it is bounded by a large number of edges (and vertices). Therefore algorithms operating on faces tend to be complicated and inefficient. We try to circumvent this problem by decomposing each face into smaller simpler geometric objects. As will be shown in section 4 our approach allows to perform the overlay of two simply connected planar subdivisions more efficiently than other known algorithms: its time and storage requirements are linear in the size of the output subdivision.

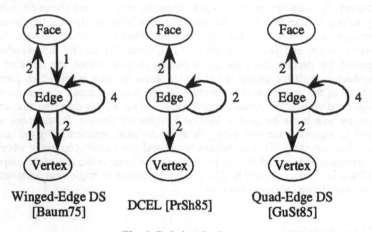

Fig. 1. Relational schemes

2 The Quad View Data Structure

In order to simplify the subsequent discussion we make the following assumptions:

- The plane $\mathbb{R}^2$ is topologically equivalent to a cylinder by identifying the points at "infinity", i.e. $(-\infty, y)$ and (∞, y), $y \in \mathbb{R}$, are identical. The plane $\mathbb{R}^2$ is bounded "above" and "below" by two horizontal edges $e_{-\infty}$ and e_{∞}, i.e. each point of $\mathbb{R}^2$ lies above (resp. below) the edge $e_{-\infty}$ (resp. e_{∞}). The plane is bounded "left" resp. "right" by a vertex $v_{\infty} = \{(\infty, 0)\}$.
- All edges of a planar subdivision are line segments.
- No edge is vertical.

[Fink 94] shows how to overcome the last two restrictions. Line segments can be generalized to curves which are defined by a finite number of points, e.g. Bezier or Spline curves. A set of non-vertical edges intersecting a given vertical line can be ordered in a natural way. This ordering can be extended to allow vertical edges. The algorithms presented in this paper can handle vertical edges by using this modified total ordering.

Each face of a planar subdivision Π can be decomposed into trapezoids: Through each vertex v of the partition we draw a vertical which ends at the edges lying directly above and below v (Fig. 2).

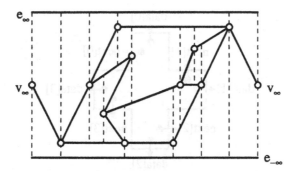

Fig. 2. Trapezoidal decomposition

The trapezoids and triangles obtained by this partitioning are called *views*. The left (resp. right) boundary of a view t is formed by a vertical which passes through the vertex $v_0(t)$ (resp. $v_1(t)$) which we call the *left* (resp. *right*) *bounding vertex* of t. The lower (resp. upper) boundary of t is formed by the *lower* (resp. *upper*) *bounding edge* $e_0(t)$ (resp. $e_1(t)$). In the following we denote by $T(\Pi)$ the set of views of a planar partition Π (Fig. 3).

If v denotes the number of vertices and e the number of edges of Π, then the number of views $|T(\Pi)|$ can be determined by building Π incrementally: $|T(\Pi)| = v + e - 2$. We define a neighborhood relation $\ddagger$ on $T(\Pi)$:

Definition: Two views $t_1 \neq t_2$ are neighbors, denoted by $t_1 \ddagger t_2$, if they have a common bounding vertex and a common bounding edge.

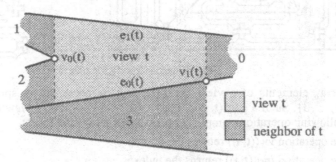

Fig. 3. A view t and its four neighbors

It is easy to show that a view can have at most four neighbors. Since $\ddagger$ is a symmetric relation on the set of views the *view graph* with vertex set $T(\Pi)$ and edge set $\ddagger(T(\Pi))$ is an undirected graph. View graphs are represented by the *quad view data structure*: A view t is represented by arrays data and next each consisting of four elements (Fig. 4):

- data[i] points for $i \in \{0, 2\}$ to $e_{1-i/2}(t)$ and for $i \in \{1, 3\}$ to $v_{(i-1)/2}(t)$.
- next[i] points to that neighbor of t which has $v_{\lfloor ((i+3) \bmod 4)/2 \rfloor}(t)$ as bounding vertex and $e_{\lfloor ((i+2) \bmod 4)/2 \rfloor}(t)$ as bounding edge.

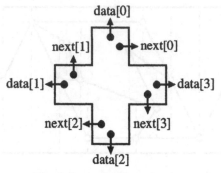

Fig. 4. Representation of a view

The next-pointers ensure that the views form doubly-linked rings around the vertices and edges of a partition. The ring of views around a vertex is called a *vertex ring*, the ring of views around an edge is called an *edge ring* (Fig. 5).

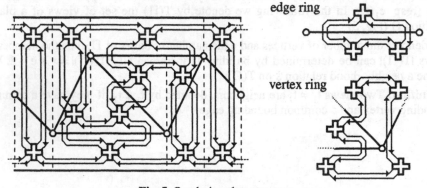

Fig. 5. Quad-view data structure

The array elements of a view $t \in T(\Pi)$ can be accessed by specifying an index $i \in \{0, ..., 3\}$. Such a pair $(t, i) \in T(\Pi) \times \{0, ..., 3\}$ is called a *view reference* (Fig. 6). The following operations simplify processing of view references:

* The operation $vw((t, i))$ returns the view t.
* The operation $ind((t, i))$ returns the index i.
* The operation $inc((t, i), j)$ returns the view reference $(t, (i+j) \bmod 4)$.

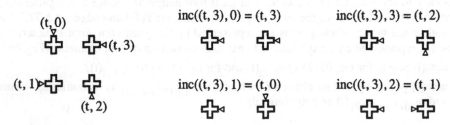

Fig. 6. View references

For each view reference $(t, i) \in T(\Pi) \times \{0, ..., 3\}$ the pointer t.next[i] references the next view in counterclockwise direction in the ring around t.data[i]. The successor view reference (Fig. 7) of (t, i) in this ring is

- (t.next[i], i), if t.next[i].data[i] = t.data[i],
- (t.next[i], (i+2) mod 4) otherwise.

In the first case we call (t, i) a *continuous*, in the second case a *discontinuous* view reference.

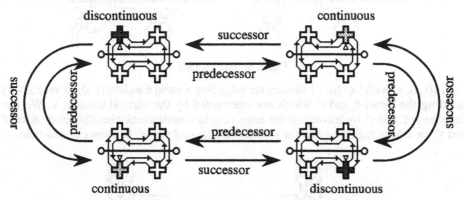

Fig. 7. Successors and predecessors of view references

Determining the successor (t', i') of a view reference (t, i) can be accelerated by storing in t.next[i] the view reference (t', i'). For ease of notation we write

- $next((t, i))$ instead of t.next[i].
- $data((t, i))$ instead of t.data[i].

Since the vertex and edge rings are doubly-linked we can determine for each view reference (t, i) also its predecessor view reference $prev((t, i))$ (see Fig. 8) which is given by $inc(next(inc((t, i), 1)), 1)$.

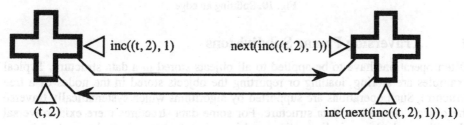

Fig. 8. Computing the predecessor

The following operations are used to generate and manipulate the quad view data structure:

$split((t, i), g)$ separates from t a view t' and generates a ring consisting of t and t' around the geometric object g. Fig. 9 shows how a new vertex can be inserted by splitting a view.

$merge((t, i))$ is the reverse of $split((t, i), g)$, i.e. performing a split followed by a merge does not change the data structure. If t and $vw(next((t, i)))$ form a ring around g this operation removes the geometric object $g = data((t, i))$ from the data structure.

34

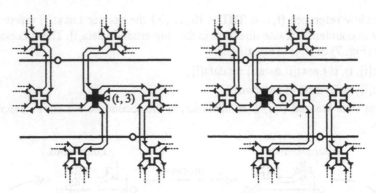

Fig. 9. Splitting a view

esplit((t, i), v) with i ∈ {0, 2} divides the edge ring around e = *data*((t, i)) at vertex v by splitting the views t' and t" which are intersected by the vertical through v. We can determine t' and t" by traversing the edge ring in counterclockwise direction. After t' and t" have been split we generate a vertex ring around v. Fig. 10 shows an example.

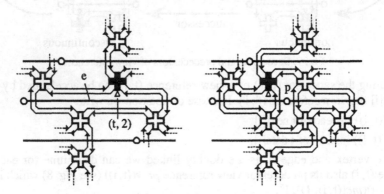

Fig. 10. Splitting an edge

3   Traversing Planar Subdivisions

Often operations have to be applied to all objects stored in a data structure. Typical examples are storing, loading or reporting the objects stored in the nodes of a tree structure. Such operations are supported by algorithms which systematically traverse the objects stored in a data structure. For some data structures there exist traversal algorithms which run in linear time and have constant space requirements, e.g. the triple tree traversal algorithm for binary trees [NiHi 93]. In the following we describe an algorithm which systematically traverses the edge rings of a quad view data structure.

The traversal starts with a view reference b ∈ T(Π) × {0, 2}. In the following the view reference c determines the status of the traversal, i.e. the current position in the quad view data structure. In the beginning c is initialized with b. The traversal of the ring around *data*(c) is performed in two phases (Fig. 11).

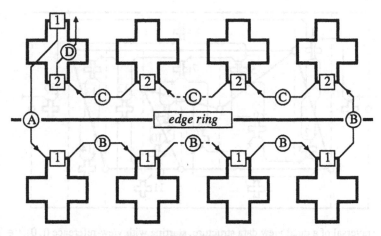

Fig. 11. Traversal of a edge ring

The traversal is in phase [1] if $ind(c) = ind(b)$. If the view reference $c' := inc(c, 2)$ is continuous the succeeding view reference (case (B) in Fig. 11) is obtained by $c := next(c)$. Otherwise the traversal around $data(c)$ is interrupted, and the traversal around $data(c')$ is started by $c := next(c')$ (case (A) in Fig. 11).

The traversal is in phase [2] if $ind(c) = ind(inc(b, 2))$. If the view reference c is continuous the succeeding view reference (case (C) in Fig. 11) is obtained by $c := next(c)$. Otherwise the traversal around $data(c)$ is finished, and by $c := next(inc(c, 2))$ (cases (D) and (B) in Fig. 11) the traversal continues in the ring whose traversal has been interrupted previously.

The traversal is finished as soon as c becomes equal to b. Fig. 12 shows the traversal of a quad view data structure.

The traversal algorithm is implemented by the following procedure:

```
procedure Traverse (b: ViewReference)
var c: ViewReference;
begin
    c := b;
    repeat
            op(vw(c));
            if (ind(b) = ind(next(inc(c, 2)))) then
(*A*)       c := next(inc(c, 2));
            else begin
                while (ind(c) ≠ ind(next(c))) do begin
(*B*)               c := next(c);
(*C*)               while (ind(c) = ind(next(c))) do c := next(c);
(*D*)               c := inc(c, 2);
                end;
(*B*)           c := next(c);
            end;
    until c = b;
end (* Traverse *);
```

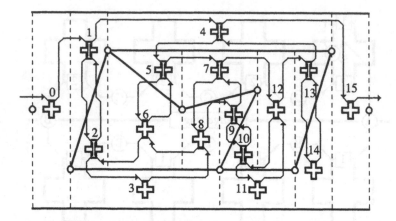

Fig. 12. Traversal of a quad view data structure, starting with view-reference $(t, 0), t \in T(\Pi)$

For each view t of the quad view data structure an operation *op* is performed once during phase [1]. The sequence in which the operation is applied to the views is determined by the traversal path. The numbering of the views in Fig. 12 gives an example. Different sequences are obtained by placing the operation calls in different positions in the procedure 'Traverse'. Furthermore this algorithm can be adapted for the traversal of vertex rings.

4   Overlay Algorithm

Algorithms to compute the overlay of planar subdivisions are of theoretical and practical significance. They can be applied to solve the map overlay problem in spatial information systems, the hidden surface problem in computer graphics or design rule checking in VLSI layout design. In this section we present an algorithm which computes the overlay $\Pi_b \cap^{\Pi} \Pi_g$ of two simply connected planar subdivisions Π_b and Π_g; we assume that Π_b and all its components are colored in blue, and Π_g and all its components are colored in green. Π_b (resp. Π_g) is called the blue (resp. green) partition. The overlay $\Pi_b \cap^{\Pi} \Pi_g$ consists of all non-empty sets $b \cap g$ with $b \in \Pi_b$ and $g \in \Pi_g$. The input and output subdivisions are represented by the quad view data structure. The algorithm is based on a graph exploration technique and computes from the trapezoidations of Π_b and Π_g the trapezoidation of the overlay $\Pi_b \cap^{\Pi} \Pi_g$. However, the algorithm does not compute the overlay of the trapezoidations, i.e. it does not compute the intersections between the verticals obtained by the trapezoidations and the edges of Π_b and Π_g. The algorithm operates destructively on its input subdivisions, i.e. the algorithm interweaves Π_b and Π_g into the overlay $\Pi_b \cap^{\Pi} \Pi_g$. Those components of Π_b and Π_g which are also contained in $\Pi_b \cap^{\Pi} \Pi_g$ are taken over implicitly and are not touched by the algorithm. The algorithm runs in $O(n + k)$ time and space, where n denotes the total number of edges of Π_b and Π_g and k the number of intersections between blue and green edges. The algorithm presented in this section is explained in more detail in [FiHi 95].

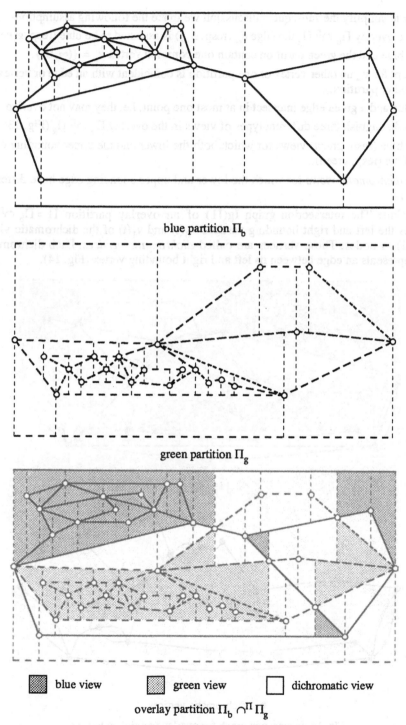

blue partition Π_b

green partition Π_g

blue view   green view   dichromatic view

overlay partition $\Pi_b \cap^{\Pi} \Pi_g$

Fig. 13. Three different types of views

In order to simplify the subsequent discussion we make the following assumptions:

- In the overlay $\Pi_b \cap^\Pi \Pi_g$ the edge e_∞ (resp. $e_{-\infty}$) is assumed to be blue (resp. green).
- The blue and the green partition contain one common vertex $v_\infty = \{(\infty, 0)\}$.
- Except for v_∞ no other vertex of one partition is coincident with an edge or vertex of the other partition.
- A blue and a green edge intersect in at most one point, i.e. they may not overlap.

We can distinguish three different types of views in the overlay $\Pi_b \cap^\Pi \Pi_g$ (Fig. 13):

- The blue (resp. green) views for which both the lower and the upper bounding edge are blue (resp. green).
- The *dichromatic views* for which the lower and upper bounding edge have different colors.

Definition: The intersection graph $Ig(\Pi)$ of an overlay partition $\Pi = \Pi_b \cap^\Pi \Pi_g$ contains the left and right bounding vertices $v_0(t)$ and $v_1(t)$ of the dichromatic views $t \in T(\Pi)$ as nodes. These vertices are called *dichromatic vertices*. Each dichromatic view represents an edge between its left and right bounding vertex (Fig. 14).

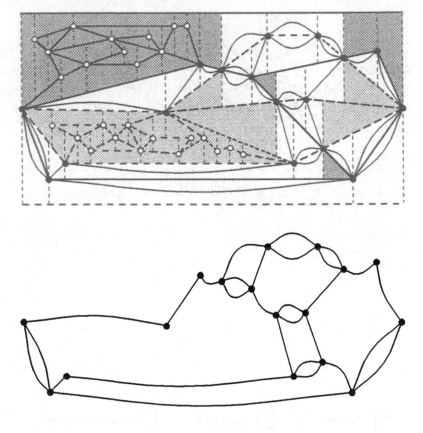

● dichromatic vertices

Fig. 14. Intersection graph for overlay partition in Fig. 13

The intersection graph $Ig(\Pi_b \cap^\Pi \Pi_g)$ has two important properties: It contains all the intersection points between edges of Π_b and edges of Π_g as nodes. Furthermore it can be shown that the intersection graph consists of a single connected component if Π_b and Π_g are simply connected.

A blue (resp. green) view t in the overlay is identical to or contained in a view of the blue (resp. green) input subdivision (Fig. 15). In the first case t is called an *original view*, in the latter case at least one of the bounding vertices of t is a dichromatic vertex and t is called a *clipped view*. Since the clipped and dichromatic views are bounded by dichromatic vertices the overlay is obtained by computing for each dichromatic vertex v all views which have v as a bounding vertex, and taking over the original views from the input subdivisions which are not bounded by at least one dichromatic vertex.

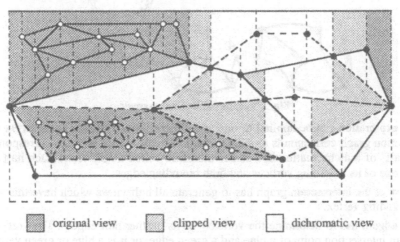

original view   clipped view   dichromatic view

Fig. 15. Original and clipped views

Our overlay algorithm takes advantage of the connectivity of the intersection graph to determine the overlay partition. It uses the graph exploration technique to build the intersection graph.

4.1   Graph Exploration

A connected graph can be constructed successively from its already known components by graph exploration. Each edge of a graph can be considered to consist of two *half edges* (Fig. 16).

Fig. 16. Each edge consists of two half edges

During the graph exploration vertices and half edges have to perform different tasks. When a vertex v is created it has to generate all half edges emanating from v. A half edge only knows the vertex by which it was created. Each half edge h has to perform three tasks:

1. First, h has to determine the vertex of its partner half edge p with which it forms an edge of the graph.

2.   If p's vertex does not yet exist then h generates this vertex.

3.   Finally, h and p merge to form an edge of the graph.

If the graph to be constructed is connected and all vertices and half edges perform their tasks the complete graph can be constructed by starting at any known vertex (Fig. 17).

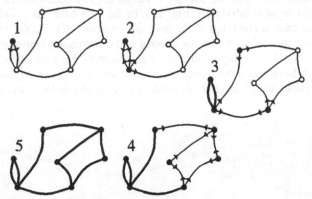

Fig. 17. Graph exploration example

Graph exploration can be applied to intersection graphs as follows: Each vertex of an intersection graph corresponds to a dichromatic vertex. Each half edge corresponds to one "half" of a dichromatic view and is therefore called a *half view*. Each half view knows one of its bounding vertices and both bounding edges.

A vertex of the intersection graph has to generate all half views which have this vertex as a bounding vertex.

A half edge h has to determine the vertex v of its partner half edge p. The vertex v is either an intersection point of a blue and a green edge, or it is a blue or green vertex. If v has not yet been generated, i.e. if the partner p does not yet exist, then h generates the vertex v. Then the new vertex v generates all half views emanating from v, and therefore also the partner p. The half view h can now merge with its partner p to form an edge of the intersection graph, i.e. a dichromatic view of the overlay partition. The implementation of this graph exploration for intersection graphs requires

- a representation of half views in the quad view data structure,

- an algorithm to perform the task of a vertex (vertex algorithm),

- an algorithm to perform the tasks of a half edge (half edge algorithm), and

- the implementation of a control mechanism which initializes and controls the process of graph exploration.

4.2   Representation of Half Views

A half view h is determined by a bounding vertex v and its two bounding edges e_0 and e_1 which have different colors (Fig. 18). Therefore the elements of the array data of h point to v, e_0 and e_1. The element of data which corresponds to the unknown bounding vertex is initialized with NULL. In the following we assume that the index of this array element is $i \in \{1, 3\}$. This index determines the direction in which one has to search for the vertex of the partner half view p.

Topologically a half view h is part of a blue and a green edge ring around the bounding edges e_0 and e_1 (Fig. 18). Therefore $next((h, i))$ and $next(inc((h, i), 1))$ point to a blue and a green view which are not part of the overlay partition and which determine the position of h in the blue and green partition. $next(inc((h, i), 2))$ and $next(inc((h, i), 3))$ determine other half views or green, blue or dichromatic views which are part of the overlay.

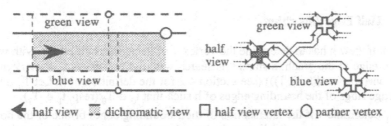

Fig. 18. Representation of a half view

4.3 Vertex Algorithm

During the graph exploration a vertex v has to generate all half views emanating from v. We assume that the vertex v for which the vertex algorithm has to be executed is contained in the blue and green partition, i.e. there exists a blue vertex ring T_b and a green vertex ring T_g around v. To ensure this a half edge h eventually has to split views and edges in the second step.

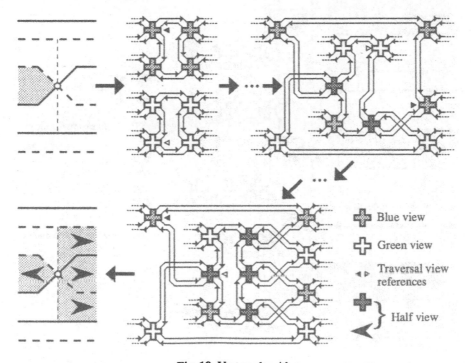

Fig. 19. Vertex algorithm

The vertex algorithm traverses the vertex rings T_b and T_g around v synchronously in counterclockwise direction. During the traversal a new vertex ring is constructed which contains all half views emanating from v. Since blue and green views can be transferred from the original blue and green vertex rings we do not only construct the intersection graph but also the overlay partition. Fig. 19 shows the effect of the vertex algorithm on the quad view data structure.

4.4 Half Edge Algorithm

First, a half view h has to determine the vertex v of its partner half edge p with which it forms an edge of the graph. h starts this search with the two views $t_0 = vw(next((h, i)))$ and $t_1 = vw(next(inc((h, i), 1)))$ (see section 4.2 for the definition of i). Let T_0 (resp. T_1) be the edge rings of the bounding edges of h such that $t_0 \in T_0$ (resp. $t_1 \in T_1$).

t_0 and t_1 determine v if the intersection of their bounding edges or one of the bounding vertices $v_{(i-1)/2}(t_0)$ or $v_{(i-1)/2}(t_1)$ lies on the boundary $\partial(t_0 \cap t_1)$ of their intersection.

If t_0 and t_1 do not determine v we exchange that view $t \in \{t_0, t_1\}$ for which the bounding vertex data[i] is closer in horizontal direction to the bounding vertex $data(inc((h, i), 2))$. The view t is replaced by that neighbor in its edge ring T_j which has not yet been considered, i.e. which lies in the direction determined by i (Fig. 20).

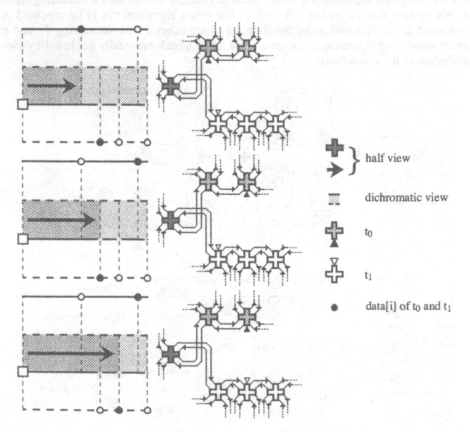

Fig. 20. Determining the vertex of the partner half view

If t_0 and t_1 determine v the half edge algorithm has to check in its second step whether v has already been generated by the vertex algorithm before. This is the case if t_0 and t_1 are linked to the partner half view p, and therefore the vertex algorithm must not be executed. If this is not the case the half view calls the vertex algorithm for v. As mentioned in section 4.3, eventually the half edge algorithm has to split views and edges before calling the vertex algorithm to ensure that v is contained as a vertex in both Π_b and Π_g. The vertex algorithm starts its traversal with the views t_0 and t_1.

The last step guarantees the existence of the partner half view p of h. In the third step h and p are merged to form a new dichromatic view of $\Pi_b \cap^{\Pi} \Pi_g$ (Fig. 21).

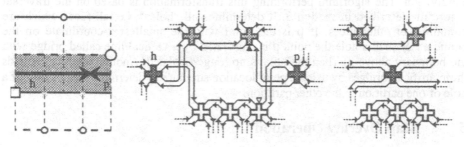

Fig. 21. Merging a half view and its partner to form a new dichromatic view

4.5   Control of Graph Exploration

The control mechanism which initializes and controls the process of graph exploration is implemented by a waiting system W which stores references to the currently existing half views. Since there is no distinguished sequence in which the half views should be processed it does not matter in what order the half views are fetched from W, i.e. W can be implemented by a stack or a first-in first-out queue.

For starting the graph exploration it is necessary to know at least one half view. The initial half views are obtained by executing the vertex algorithm for the vertex v_∞ which is common to both Π_b and Π_g. The references to these initial half views are passed to the waiting system W. Then we iterate a loop until W becomes empty. In each iteration we fetch a reference to a half view h from W. If h has not yet merged with another half view to form a dichromatic view in the overlay partition we execute the half edge algorithm for h. References to the half views generated by the half edge algorithm are passed to W. If h has already been merged with its partner half view before, the storage occupied by h can be released.

After the loop has terminated the complete overlay partition $\Pi_b \cap^{\Pi} \Pi_g$ is stored in the quad view data structure.

4.6   Analysis and Extensions

In the following we denote by n the total number of edges in the blue partition Π_b and the green partition Π_g, and by k the number of intersections between blue and green edges. The number of views in Π_b and Π_g is bounded linearly by n, since in an incremental construction of a partition the number of views increases by at most three with each additional edge. For the same reason the number of views in the overlay partition $\Pi_b \cap^{\Pi} \Pi_g$ is bounded linearly by $n + k$. Therefore the storage requirement of this algorithm is $O(n + k)$. The time needed for all executions of the vertex algorithm is $O(n + k)$, since the time to process a view is constant and the total number of views in $\Pi_b \cap^\Pi \Pi_g$ is bounded linearly by $n + k$. The same is true for the control mechanism. [FiHi 95], [Fink 94] show that the time needed for all executions of the half edge algorithm is $O(n + k)$. Hence the overlay of two simply connected planar subdivisions Π_b and Π_g is computed in $O(n + k)$ time and storage space.

In most applications the input subdivisions are not simply connected but path connected. Our algorithm can also be applied in this situation: By inserting additional edges a path connected subdivision can be transformed into a simply connected subdivision. The algorithm performing this transformation is based on the traversal algorithm described in section 3. It determines all "holes", i.e. all faces which are contained in other faces. If p is the point with the smallest x-coordinate on the boundary of such a hole the point p is connected by a vertical line called bridge with the boundary above p. Then the hole is no longer isolated. Another approach avoids these artificial bridges by using a point location structure to determine the position of a hole of one partition in the other partition.

5   Map Overlay Operation

The computation of new maps from existing information is a kernel operation in every spatial information system. The most general operation for this task is the map overlay [Toml 90]: Given one or more thematic map layers the overlay operation computes a new map in which the thematic attribute value of each location is a function of the thematic attribute values of the corresponding locations in the input maps. This overlay function enables manifold applications of the map overlay operation. Besides composing, overlaying or superimposing thematic maps it is also possible to update maps by inserting, deleting or merging given regions [Fran 87] or to perform simple queries like window- and region-queries.

The computation of a map overlay can be performed in three phases:

- *overlay phase*:
  In this phase the spatial relationship between the two maps is obtained by overlaying the underlying subdivisions.

- *function phase*:
  In this phase the thematic values of the faces in the result map are determined by applying the overlay function. We only consider *locational* overlay functions, i.e. the thematic value of a point in the result map does only depend on the thematic values of this point in the input maps. One could also imagine overlay functions where the thematic value of a point p in the result map depends on the thematic values of the points in a vicinity of p in the input maps.

- *merging phase*:
  In the function phase adjacent faces in the result map may be assigned the same thematic value. Furthermore inaccuracies in the input maps may lead to sliver polygons. In order to increase storage occupancy and to avoid unnecessary computations sliver polygons and thematically not necessary edges should be removed, i.e. the corresponding faces should be merged.

Fig. 22 shows the phases for the map overlay operation *LocalMin*. This operation determines point by point the minimum of the thematic values of two maps.

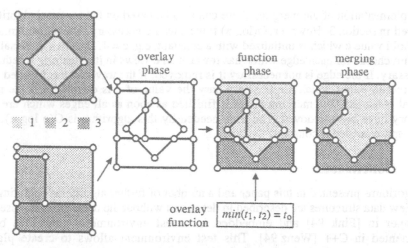

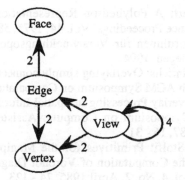

Fig. 22. Phases of map overlay operation

The algorithms and data structures presented in sections 2 to 4 allow the efficient implementation of locational map overlay operations.

The quad view data structure has to be extended to represent thematic maps (Fig. 23): For each edge two pointers reference two faces which are separated by this edge, each face stores its thematic attribute value.

Fig. 23. Extended quad view data structure

In the overlay phase we use the overlay algorithm described in section 4.

In the map Π_{bg} which is obtained by overlaying the maps Π_b and Π_g the edges still reference the faces of Π_b and Π_g. The implementation of the function phase is based on the traversal algorithm described in section 3: If we encounter during the traversal a face f_{bg} of Π_{bg} which has not been considered before a new face record is created. This record contains the thematic value obtained by applying the overlay function to the thematic values of the faces $f_b \in \Pi_b$ and $f_g \in \Pi_g$ which contain f_{bg}. The algorithm memorizes in each Π_b and Π_g the last edge crossed during the traversal and therefore knows f_b and f_g. The time needed for performing the function phase is $O(n)$ where n denotes the number of edges of Π_{bg}, the storage space needed is constant; this does not include the time needed to apply the overlay function and the space needed for storing the thematic values of Π_{bg}.

The implementation of the merging phase can also be based on the traversal algorithm described in section 3. However, O(log n) traversals are necessary. The algorithm uses a threshold value c which is initialized with a constant, e.g. c = 4. During a traversal the algorithm checks for each edge which has fewer than c views in its edge ring whether it is necessary. If the edge is not necessary it is removed. If the traversal has finished and there are still edges which are not necessary the value of c is doubled and the next traversal is started. The merging phase is finished as soon as all edges which are not necessary have been removed. The time needed by this algorithm is O(n log n), the storage space needed is constant.

6   Conclusions

The algorithms presented in this paper and a number of further algorithms operating on quad view data structures are described in detail and without the restrictions imposed in this paper in [Fink 94] and embedded in a test environment which has been implemented in C++ [Wenz 94]. This test environment allows to create planar subdivisions interactively; an interface allows to import maps from a commercial geographic information system (GIS). All implemented algorithms operating on quad view data structures can be animated. It is possible to observe the half views and the waiting system during execution of the overlay algorithm. Furthermore the actual time and storage requirements of the overlay algorithm can be measured.

References

[Baum 75]   B. G. Baumgart: A Polyhedron Representation for Computer Vision, AFIPS Conference Proceedings, Vol. 44, 1975, 580 - 596.

[Fink 94]   U. Finke: Algorithmen für Verschneidungsoperationen, Ph. D. Thesis, University of Siegen, 1994.

[FiHi 95]   U. Finke, K. Hinrichs: Overlaying simply connected planar subdivisions in linear time, 11th ACM Symposium on Computational Geometry (1995).

[Fran 87]   A. U. Frank: Overlay Processing in Spatial Information Systems, Proc. 8th International Symposium on Computer-Assisted Cartography (AUTO-CARTO 8), 1987, 16 - 31.

[GuSt 85]   L. Guibas, J. Stolfi: Primitives for the Manipulation of General Sub-divisions and the Computation of Voronoi Diagrams, ACM Transactions on Graphics, Vol. 4, No. 2, April 1985, 74 - 123.

[NiHi 93]   J. Nievergelt, K. H. Hinrichs: Algorithms & Data Structures - with applications to graphics and geometry, Prentice-Hall, 1993.

[PrSh 85]   F. P. Preparata, M. I. Shamos: Computational Geometry - An Introduction, Texts and Monographs in Computer Science, Springer-Verlag, 1985.

[Toml 90]   C. D. Tomlin: Geographic Information Systems and Cartographic Modeling, Prentice Hall, Englewood Cliffs, NJ, 1990.

[Weil 86]   K. Weiler: Topological structures for geometric modeling, Ph. D. dissertation, Depart. of Comp. and Syst. Eng., Renselaer Polytechnic Inst., Troy, New York, August 1986.

[Wenz 94]   M. Wenzel: Verschneidungsoperationen für Geo-Informationsysteme, Diploma Thesis, University of Münster, 1994.

[Woo 85]   T. Woo: A Combinatorial Analysis of Boundary Data Structure Schemata, IEEE Comp. Graphics and Applications, Vol. 5 (1985), No. 3, 19 - 27.

Discovery of Spatial Association Rules in Geographic Information Databases *

Krzysztof Koperski and Jiawei Han

School of Computing Science
Simon Fraser University
Burnaby, B.C., Canada V5A 1S6
e-mail: {koperski, han}@cs.sfu.ca

Abstract. Spatial data mining, i.e., discovery of interesting, implicit knowledge in spatial databases, is an important task for understanding and use of spatial data- and knowledge-bases. In this paper, an efficient method for mining strong spatial association rules in geographic information databases is proposed and studied. A spatial association rule is a rule indicating certain association relationship among a set of spatial and possibly some nonspatial predicates. A strong rule indicates that the patterns in the rule have relatively frequent occurrences in the database and strong implication relationships. Several optimization techniques are explored, including a two-step spatial computation technique (approximate computation on large sets, and refined computations on small promising patterns), shared processing in the derivation of large predicates at multiple concept levels, etc. Our analysis shows that interesting association rules can be discovered efficiently in large spatial databases.

1 Introduction

With wide applications of remote sensing technology and automatic data collection tools, tremendous amounts of spatial and nonspatial data have been collected and stored in large spatial databases. Traditional data organization and retrieval tools can only handle the storage and retrieval of explicitly stored data. The extraction and comprehension of the knowledge implied by the huge amount of spatial data, though highly desirable, pose great challenges to currently available spatial database technologies.

This situation demands new technologies for knowledge discovery in large spatial databases, or spatial data mining, that is, *extraction of implicit knowledge, spatial relations, or other patterns not explicitly stored in spatial databases.*

Recently, there have been a lot of research activities on knowledge discovery in large databases (data mining) [9, 16]. These studies led to a set of interesting techniques developed, including mining strong association and dependency

---

* This research was supported in part by the research grant NSERC-OGP003723 from the Natural Sciences and Engineering Research Council of Canada and an NCE/IRIS research grant from the Networks of Centres of Excellence of Canada.

rules [1, 2], attribute-oriented induction for mining characteristic and discriminant rules [12], etc. Such studies set a foundation and provide some interesting methods for the exploration of highly promising spatial data mining techniques.

Spatial data mining can be categorized based on the kinds of rules to be discovered in spatial databases. A spatial characteristic rule is a *general description of a set of spatial-related data*. For example, the description of the general weather patterns in a set of geographic regions is a spatial characteristic rule. A spatial discriminant rule is the *general description of the contrasting or discriminating features of a class of spatial-related data from other class(es)*. For example, the comparison of the weather patterns in two geographic regions is a spatial discriminant rule. A spatial association rule is a *rule which describes the implication of one or a set of features by another set of features in spatial databases*. For example, a rule like *"most big cities in Canada are close to the Canada-U.S. border"* is a spatial association rule.

There have been some interesting studies related to the mining of spatial characteristic rules and spatial discriminant rules [14, 15]. However, there is lack of studies on mining spatial association rules. In this paper, we study the extension of the techniques for mining association rules in transaction-based databases to mining spatial association rules.

A spatial association rule is a rule of the form $"X \rightarrow Y"$, where X and Y are sets of predicates and some of which are spatial ones. In a large database many association relationships may exist but some may occur rarely or may not hold in most cases. To focus our study to the patterns which are relatively strong, i.e., which occur frequently and hold in most cases, the concepts of *minimum support* and *minimum confidence* are introduced [1, 2]. Informally, the support of a pattern A in a set of spatial objects S is the probability that a member of S satisfies pattern A; and the confidence of $A \rightarrow B$ is the probability that pattern B occurs if pattern A occurs. A user or an expert may specify thresholds to confine the rules to be discovered to be *strong* ones.

For example, one may find that 92% of cities within British Columbia (bc) and adjacent to water are close to U.S.A., as shown in (1), which associates predicates *is_a*, *within*, and *adjacent_to* with spatial predicate *close_to*.

$$is\_a(X, city) \wedge within(X, bc) \wedge adjacent\_to(X, water) \rightarrow close\_to(X, us). \ (92\%)(1)$$

Although such rules are usually not 100% true, they carry some nontrivial knowledge about spatial associations, and thus it is interesting to "mine" (i.e., "discover") them from large spatial databases. The discovered rules will be useful in geography, environmental studies, biology, engineering and other fields.

In this paper, efficient methods for mining spatial association rules are studied, with a top-down, progressive deepening search technique proposed. The technique firstly searches at a high concept level for large (i.e., frequently occurring) patterns and strong implication relationships among the large patterns at a coarse resolution scale. Then only for those large patterns, it deepens the search to lower concept levels (i.e., their lower level descendants). Such a deepening search process continues until no large patterns can be found. An important optimization technique is that the search for large patterns at high concept levels may apply efficient spatial computation algorithms at a coarse resolution scale (such as generalized close_to (g_close_to), using approximate spatial computation algorithms, such as R-trees or plane-sweep techniques operating on minimum bounding rectangles (MBRs). Only the candidate spatial predicates, which are worth detailed examination, will be computed by refined spatial techniques(giving detailed predicates such as intersect, contain, etc.). Such multiple-level approach saves much computations because it is very expensive to perform detailed spatial computation for all the possible spatial association relationships.

In Sect. 2 of our paper, existing spatial data mining methods are surveyed. In Sect. 3, the concept of spatial association rules and its data mining methods are outlined. In Sect. 4, an algorithm for the discovery of spatial association rules is presented. In Sect. 5 we discuss the advantages of the algorithm and its possible extensions. The study is summarized in Sect. 6.

2 Previous Work Related to Spatial Data Mining

In this section, previous studies related to spatial data mining are overviewed, which provides a short survey of the topic and associates the previous work with our study.

2.1 Statistical Analysis

Until now statistical spatial analysis has been one of the most common techniques for analyzing spatial data [10]. Statistical methods handle well numerical data, contain a large number of algorithms, have a strong possibility of getting models of spatial phenomena, and allow optimizations. However, statistical analysis usually requires the assumptions regarding to statistical independence of spatially distributed data. Such assumptions are often unrealistic due to the influence of neighboring regions. To deal with such problems, spatial models can include trend surface or dummy variables. If data in one region are influenced by features of neighboring regions, the analyst may fit a regression model with a spatial lagged forms of the dependent variables. Statistical analysis also deals poorly with symbolic data like names.

$$expensive(condo) \leftrightarrow inside(condo, downtown) \wedge area(condo, large). \qquad (2)$$

Nonlinear rules in the form of (2) cannot be described using standard methods in statistical spatial analysis. Statistical approach requires a lot of domain and statistical knowledge. Thus, it should be performed by domain experts with the experience in statistics. Another problem related to statistical spatial analysis is expensive computation of the results.

2.2 Generalization-based Spatial Data Mining

One major approach in spatial data mining is to apply generalization techniques to spatial and nonspatial data to generalize detailed spatial data to certain high level and study the general characteristics and data distributions at this level.

An attribute-oriented induction method has been proposed in [14]. It generalizes data to high level concepts and describes general relationships between spatial and nonspatial data. Two algorithms were proposed in the study: (1) *nonspatial-dominant generalization*, and (2) *spatial-dominant generalization*.

The nonspatial-dominant generalization algorithm first performs attribute-oriented generalization on task-relevant nonspatial data describing the properties of spatial objects. In this step, numerical data can be generalized to ranges or descriptive high level concepts (e.g., $-9°C$ to a range value "$-10\_to\_0°C$" or *cold*), and symbolic values to higher level concepts (e.g., *potatoes* and *beets* to *vegetables*). By doing so, low level distinctive values may be generalized to identical high level values, and such high-level identical values among different tuples can be merged together with their spatial pointers clustered into one slot in the spatial attribute. Finally, the map consists of a small number of regions with high level descriptions.

The spatial-dominant generalization first performs generalization on query-related spatial data. Data are generalized using spatial data hierarchies (such as geographic or administrative regions) provided by users/experts or hierarchical data structures (such as quad-trees [19] or R-trees [11]). The generalized spatial entities (such as the merged regions) cluster the related nonspatial data together. After generalization of non-spatial data, every region can be described at a high concept level by one or a set of predicates.

Spatial hierarchies are not always given *a priori*. It is often necessary to describe spatial behavior of similar objects or to determine characteristic features of distinct clusters. In [15], the attribute-oriented induction method was combined with some efficient spatial clustering algorithms, which can still be classified into *spatial-dominant* vs. *nonspatial-dominant* methods. The *spatial-dominant* method classifies task-relevant spatial objects (such as points) into clusters using an efficient clustering algorithm and then perform an attribute-oriented induction for each cluster to extract rules describing general properties of a cluster. The *nonspatial-dominant* method first generalizes nonspatial attributes of query-related objects to high concept levels and then cluster the spatial objects with the same nonspatial descriptions. Then one may find that *"expensive single houses in Vancouver area are clustered along the beach and around two city parks"*.

2.3   Other Relevant Studies

Also knowledge mining in image databases, which can be treated as a special type of spatial databases, has been studied recently. Method for the classification of sky objects and another method for recogntion of volcanos on the surface of Venus are described in [8], where classification trees were used to make final decisions.

Sky objects were classified as stars or galaxies. In the first step of the algorithm, basic attributes describing each object were extracted. Attributes like area, sky brightness, positions of peak brightness, and intensity image moments, etc. were produced. The training set was classified by astronomers, and attributes mentioned above were used to construct the decision tree.

In the study of volcanos attributes recognized by humans like diameters and central peaks are not sufficient for the classification. Thus, eigenvalues of matrices representing images of possible volcanos were used as attributes for the classification algorithm.

The studies on data mining in relational databases [1, 2, 12, 13, 16] are closely related to spatial data mining. In particular, the previous studies on mining association rules [1, 2, 13] are closely related to this study.

An *association rule* is a general form of dependency rule and is defined on transaction-based databases [1]. It is in the form of "$W \rightarrow B$ $(c\%)$", explained as, "*if a pattern W appears in a transaction, there is c% possibility (confidence) that the pattern B holds in the same transaction*", where W and B are a set of attribute values. Moreover, to ensure that such rules are interesting enough to cover frequently encountered patterns in a database, the concept of the *support* of a rule "$W \rightarrow B$" is introduced, which is defined as the ratio that the patterns of W and B occurring together in the transactions vs. the total number of transactions in the database. For example, in a shopping transaction database one may find a rule like "*butter $\rightarrow$ bread (90%)*", which means that *90% of customers who buy butter also purchase bread*. Efficient algorithms for the discovery of such kind of rules in transaction-based databases have been studied [1, 2].

3 Spatial Association Rules

Generalization-based spatial data mining methods [14, 15] discover spatial and nonspatial relationships at a general concept level, where spatial objects are expressed as merged spatial regions [14] or clustered spatial points [15]. However, these methods cannot discover rules reflecting structure of spatial objects and spatial/spatial or spatial/nonspatial relationships which contain spatial predicates, such as *adjacent_to, near_by, inside, close_to, intersecting*, etc.

As a complementary, spatial association rules represents object/predicate relationships containing spatial predicates. For example, the following rules are spatial association rules.

– Nonspatial consequent with spatial antecedent(s).

$$is\_a(x, house) \land close\_to(x, beach) \rightarrow is\_expensive(x). \quad (90\%)$$

– Spatial consequent with non-spatial/spatial antecedent(s).

$$is\_a(x, gas\_station) \rightarrow close\_to(x, highway). \quad (75\%)$$

Various kinds of spatial predicates can be involved in spatial association rules. They may represent topological relationships [6] between spatial objects, such as *disjoint, intersects, inside/outside, adjacent_to, covers/covered_by, equal*, etc. They may also represent spatial orientation or ordering, such as *left, right, north, east*, etc., or contain some distance information, such as *close_to, far_away*, etc.

For systematic study the mining of spatial association rules, we first introduce some preliminary concepts.

Definition 1. A **spatial association rule** is a rule in the form of

$$P_1 \wedge \ldots \wedge P_m \rightarrow Q_1 \wedge \ldots \wedge Q_n. \quad (c\%) \qquad (3)$$

where at least one of the predicates $P_1, \ldots, P_m, Q_1, \ldots, Q_n$ is a spatial predicate, and c% is the *confidence* of the rule which indicates that c% of objects satisfying the antecedent of the rule will also satisfy the consequent of the rule. $\square$

Following this definition, a large number of spatial association rules can be derived from a large spatial database. However, most people will be only interested in the patterns which occur relatively frequently (i.e., with *large supports*) and the rules which have strong implications (i.e., with *high confidence*). The rules with large supports and high confidence are *strong rules*.

Definition 2. The **support** of a conjunction of predicates, $P = P_1 \wedge \ldots \wedge P_k$, in a set S, denoted as $\sigma(P/S)$, is the number of objects in S which satisfy P versus the cardinality (i.e., the total number of objects) of S. The **confidence** of a rule $P \rightarrow Q$ in S, $\varphi(P \rightarrow Q/S)$, is the ratio of $\sigma(P \wedge Q/S)$ versus $\sigma(P/S)$, i.e., the possibility that Q is satisfied by a member of S when P is satisfied by the same member of S. A single predicate is called **1-predicate**. A conjunction of k single predicates is called a **k-predicate**. $\square$

Since most people are interested in rules with large supports and high confidence, two kinds of thresholds: *minimum support* and *minimum confidence*, can be introduced. Moreover, since many predicates and concepts may have strong association relationships at a relatively high concept level, the thresholds should be defined at different concept levels. For example, it is difficult to find regular association patterns between a *particular house* and a *particular beach*, however, there may be strong associations between many *expensive houses* and *luxurious beaches*. Therefore, it is expected that many spatial association rules are expressed at a relatively high concept level.

Definition 3. A set of predicates P is **large** in set S at level k if the support of P is no less than its minimum support threshold σ'_k for level k, and all ancestors of P from the concept hierarchy are large at their corresponding levels. The confidence of a rule "$P \rightarrow Q/S$" is **high** at level k if its confidence is no less than its corresponding minimum confidence threshold φ'_k. $\square$

Definition 4. A rule "$P \rightarrow Q/S$" is **strong** if predicate "$P \wedge Q$" is *large* in set S and the *confidence* of "$P \rightarrow Q/S$" is high. $\square$

Based on these definitions, an example is presented for the explanation of the process of mining strong spatial association rules in large databases. To facilitate the specification of the primitives for spatial data mining, an SQL-like spatial data mining query interface, which is designed based on a spatial SQL proposed in [7], has been specified for an experimental spatial data mining system prototype, GeoMiner, which is currently under implementation and experimentation.

Example 1. Let the spatial database to be studied adopt an extended-relational data model and a SAND (spatial-and-nonspatial database) architecture [3]. That is, it consists of a set of spatial objects and a relational database describing nonspatial properties of these objects.

Our study of spatial association relationships is confined to British Columbia, a province in Canada, whose map is presented in Fig. 1, with the following database relations for organizing and representing spatial objects.

1. *town(name, type, population, geo, ...)*.
2. *road(name, type, geo, ...)*.
3. *water(name, type, geo, ...)*.
4. *mine(name, type, geo, ...)*.
5. *boundary(name, type, admin_region_1, admin_region_2, geo, ...)*.

Notice that in the above relational schemata, the attribute *"geo"* represents a spatial object (a point, line, area, etc.) whose spatial pointer is stored in a tuple of the relation and points to a geographic map. The attribute *"type"* of a relation is used to categorize the types of spatial objects in the relation. For example, the types for *road* could be {*national highway, local highway, street, back_lane*}, and the types for *water* could be {*ocean, sea, inlets, lakes, rivers, bay, creeks*}. The *boundary* relation specifies the boundary between two administrative regions, such as B.C. and U.S.A. (or Alberta). The omitted fields may contain other pieces of information, such as the area of a lake and the flow of a river.

Suppose a user is interested in finding within the map of British Columbia the strong spatial association relationships between large towns and other "near_by" objects including mines, country boundary, water (sea, lake, or river) and major highways. The GeoMiner query is presented below.

> **discover spatial association rules**
> **inside British_Columbia**
> **from road R, water W, mines M, boundary B**
> **in relevance to town T**
> **where g_close_to(T.geo, X.geo) and X in {R, W, M, B}**
>   **and T.type = ''large'' and R.type in {divided_highway}**
>   **and W.type in {sea, ocean, large_lake, large_river}**
>   **and B.admin_region_1 in ''B.C.''**
>   **and B.admin_region_2 in ''U.S.A.''**

Notice that in the query, a relational variable X is used to represent one of a set of four variables {R, W, M, B}, a predicate close_to(A, B) says that a spatial objects A and B are close one to another, and g_close_to is a predefined generalized predicate which covers a set of spatial predicates: *intersect, adjacent_to, contains, close_to*.

Moreover, "close_to" is a condition-dependent predicate and is defined by a set of knowledge rules. For example, a rule in (4) states if X is a town and Y is a country, then X is close to Y if their distance is within 80 kms.

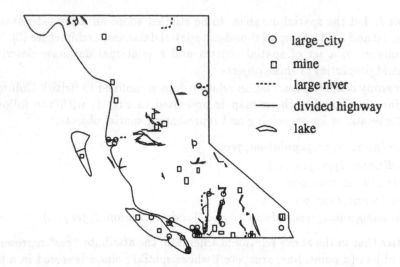

large_city ○
mine ▫
large river ·····
divided highway ——
lake �

Fig. 1. The map of BC.

$$close\_to(X, Y) \leftarrow is\_a(X, town) \wedge is\_a(Y, country) \wedge dist(X, Y, d) \wedge d < 80 \ km. \quad (4)$$
$$close\_to(X, Y) \leftarrow is\_a(X, town) \wedge is\_a(Y, road) \wedge dist(X, Y, d) \wedge d < 5 \ km. \quad (5)$$

However, "close_to" between a town and a road will be defined by a smaller distance such as (5).

Furthermore, we assume in the B.C. map, admin_region_1 always contains a region in B.C., and thus "U.S.A." or its states must be in "B.admin_region_2". Since there is no constraint on the relation "mine", it essentially means, "M.type in ANY", which is thus omitted in the query.

To facilitate mining multiple-level association rules and efficient processing, concept hierarchies are provided for both data and spatial predicates.

A set of hierarchies for data relations are defined as follows.

– A concept hierarchy for *towns*:
  (town (large_town (big_city, medium_sized_city), small_town (...) ...) ...).
– A concept hierarchy for *water*:

>   (water (sea (strait (Georgia_Strait, ...), Inlet (...), ...),
>   river (large_river (Fraser_River, ...), ...),
>   lake (large_lake (Okanagan_Lake, ...), ...), ...), ...)

– A concept hierarchy for *road*:

>   (road (national_highway (route1, ...),
>   provincial_highway (highway_7, ...),
>   city_drive (Hasting St., Kingsway, ...),
>   city_street (E_1st Ave., ...), ...), ...)

Spatial predicates (topological relations) should also be arranged into a hierarchy for computation of approximate spatial relations (like "*g_close_to*" in Fig.

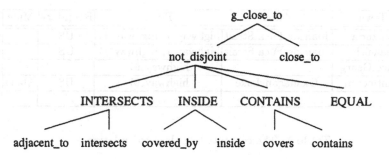

Fig. 2. The hierarchy of topological relations.

2) using efficient algorithms with coarse resolution at a high concept level and refine the computation when it is confined to a set of more focused candidate objects. □

4 A Method for Mining Spatial Association Rules

4.1 An Example of Mining Spatial Association Rules

Example 2. We examine how the data mining query posed in Example 1 is processed, which illustrates the method for mining spatial association rules.

Firstly, the set of relevant data is retrieved by execution of the data retrieval methods [3] of the data mining query, which extracts the following data sets whose spatial portion is inside B.C.: (1) towns: only large towns; (2) roads: only divided highways[2]; (3) water: only seas, oceans, large lakes and large rivers; (4) mines: any mines; and (5) boundary: only the boundary of B.C., and U.S.A.

Secondly, the "generalized close_to" (g_close_to) relationship between (large) towns and the other four classes of entities is computed at a relatively coarse resolution level using a less expensive spatial algorithm such as the MBR data structure and a plane sweeping algorithm [18], or R*-trees and other approximations [5]. The derived spatial predicates are collected in a "g_close_to" table (Table 1), which follows an extended relational model: each slot of the table may contain a set of entries. The support of each entry is then computed and those whose support is below the minimum support threshold, such as the column "mine", are removed from the table.

Notice that from the computed g_close_to relation, interesting large item sets can be discovered at different concept levels and the spatial association rules can be presented accordingly. For example, the following two spatial association rules can be discovered from this relation.

$$is\_a(X, large\_town) \rightarrow g\_close\_to(X, water). \quad (80\%)$$

$$is\_a(X, large\_town) \wedge g\_close\_to(X, sea) \rightarrow g\_close\_to(X, us\_boundary). (92\%)$$

---

[2] Not all the segments of national and provincial highways in Canada are divided ones, our computation only counts the divided ones. Also, "provincial divided highway" is abbreviated to "provincial highway" in later presentations.

Town	Water	Road	Boundary	Mine
Victoria	Juan_de_Fuca_Strait	highway_1, highway_17	US	
Saanich	Juan_de_Fuca_Strait	highway_1, highway_17	US	
Prince_George		highway_97		
Pentincton	Okanagan_Lake	highway_97	US	Alalla
...	...	...	...	...

Table 1. The computed "g_close_to" relation.

The detailed computation process is not presented here since it is similar to mining association rules for exact spatial relationships to be presented below.

Since many people may not be satisfied with approximate spatial relationships, such as *g_close_to*, more detailed spatial computation often needs to be performed to find the refined (or precise) spatial relationships in the spatial predicate hierarchy. Thus we have the following steps.

Refined computation is performed on the large predicate sets, i.e., those retained in the *g_close_to* table. Each *g_close_to* predicate is replaced by one or a set of concrete predicate(s) such as *intersect, adjacent_to, close_to, inside*, etc. Such a process results in Table 2.

Town	Water	Road	Boundary
Victoria	⟨adjacent_to, J.Fuca_Strait⟩	⟨intersects, highway_1⟩, ⟨intersects, highway_17⟩	⟨close_to, US⟩
Saanich	⟨adjacent_to, J.Fuca_Strait⟩	⟨intersects, highway_1⟩, ⟨close_to, highway_17⟩	⟨close_to, US⟩
Prince_George		⟨intersects, highway_97⟩	
Pentincton	⟨adjacent_to, Okanagan_Lake⟩	⟨intersects, highway_97⟩	⟨close_to, US⟩
...	...	...	...

Table 2. Detailed spatial relationships for large sets.

Table 2 forms a base for the computation of detailed spatial relationships at multiple concept levels. The level-by-level detailed computation of large predicates and the corresponding association rules is presented as follows.

The computation starts at the top-most concept level and computes large predicates at this level. For example, for each row of Table 2 (i.e., each large town), if the *water* attribute is nonempty, the count of water is incremented by one. Such a count accumulation forms 1-predicate rows (with $k = 1$) of Table 3 where the support count registered. If the (support) count of a row is smaller than the minimum support threshold, the row is removed from the table. For example, the minimum support is set to 50% at level 1, a row whose count is less than 20, if any, is removed from the table. The 2-predicate rows (i.e.,

$k = 2$) are formed by the pair-wise combination of the large 1-predicates, with their count accumulated (by checking against Table 2). The rows with the count smaller than the minimum support will be removed. Similarly, the 3-predicates are computed. Thus, the computation of large k-predicates results in Table 3.

k	large k-predicate set	count
1	⟨adjacent_to, water⟩	32
1	⟨intersects, highway⟩	29
1	⟨close_to, highway⟩	29
1	⟨close_to, us_boundary⟩	28
2	⟨adjacent_to, water⟩, ⟨intersects, highway⟩	25
2	⟨adjacent_to, water⟩, ⟨close_to, us_boundary⟩	23
2	⟨close_to, us_boundary⟩, ⟨intersects, highway⟩	26
3	⟨adjacent_to, water⟩, ⟨close_to, us_boundary⟩, ⟨intersects, highway⟩	22

Table 3. Large k-predicate sets at the top concept level (for 40 large towns in B.C.).

Spatial association rules can be extracted directly from Table 3. For example, since ⟨intersects, highway⟩ has a support count of 29, and ⟨adjacent_to, water⟩, ⟨intersects, highway⟩ has a support count of 25, and $25/29 \doteq 86\%$, we have the association rule (6).

$$is\_a(X, large\_town) \wedge intersects(X, highway) \rightarrow adjacent\_to(X, water). \ (86\%)(6)$$

Notice that a predicate "$is\_a(X, large\_town)$" is added in the antecedent of the rule since the rule is related only to large_town.

Similarly, one may derive another rule (7). However, if the minimum confidence threshold were set to 75%, this rule (with only 72% confidence) would have been removed from the list of the association rules to be generated.

$$is\_a(X, large\_town) \wedge adjacent\_to(X, water) \rightarrow close\_to(X, us\_boundary).(72\%)(7)$$

After mining rules at the highest level of the concept hierarchy, large k-predicates can be computed in the same way at the lower concept levels, which results in Tables 4 and 5. Notice that at the lower levels, usually the minimum support and possibly the minimum confidence may need to be reduced in order to derive enough interesting rules. For example, the minimum support of level 2 is set to 25% and thus the row with support count of 10 is included in Table 4; whereas the minimum support of level 3 is set to 15% and thus the row with support count of 7 is included in Table 5.

Similarly, spatial association rules can be derived directly from the large k-predicate set tables at levels 2 and 3. For example, rule (8) is found at level 2, and rule (9) is found at level 3.

$$is\_a(X, large\_town) \rightarrow adjacent\_to(X, sea) \ (52.5\%) \ (8)$$
$$is\_a(X, large\_town) \wedge adjacent\_to(X, georgia\_strait) \rightarrow close\_to(X, us).(78\%) \ (9)$$

k	large k-predicate set	count
1	⟨adjacent_to, sea⟩	21
1	⟨adjacent_to, large_river⟩	11
1	⟨close_to, us_boundary⟩	28
1	⟨intersects, provincial highway⟩	21
1	⟨close_to, provincial highway⟩	24
2	⟨adjacent_to, sea⟩, ⟨close_to, us_boundary⟩	15
2	⟨close_to, us_boundary⟩, ⟨intersects, provincial highway⟩	19
2	⟨adjacent_to, sea⟩, ⟨close_to, provincial highway⟩	11
2	⟨close_to, us_boundary⟩, ⟨close_to, provincial highway⟩	22
3	⟨adjacent_to, sea⟩, ⟨close_to, us_boundary⟩, ⟨close_to, provincial highway⟩	10

Table 4. Large k-predicate sets at the second level (for 40 large towns in B.C.).

k	large k-predicate set	count
1	⟨adjacent_to, georgia strait⟩	9
1	⟨adjacent_to, fraser_river⟩	10
1	⟨close_to, us_boundary⟩	28
2	⟨adjacent_to, georgia_strait⟩, ⟨close_to, us_boundary⟩	7

Table 5. Large k-predicate sets at the third level (for 40 large towns in B.C.).

Notice that only the descendants of the large 1-predicates will be examined at a lower concept level. For example, the number of large towns adjacent to a lake is small and thus ⟨adjacent_to, lake⟩ is not represented in Table 4. Then the predicates like ⟨adjacent_to, okanagan_lake⟩ will not be even considered at the third level. The mining process stops at the lowest level of the hierarchies or when an empty large 1-predicate set is derived.

As an alternative of the problem, large_towns may also be further partitioned into *big_cities* (such as towns with a population larger than 50,000 people), *other_large_towns*, etc. and rules like rule (10) can be derived by a similar mining process.

$$is\_a(X, big\_city) \wedge adjacent\_to(X, sea) \rightarrow close\_to(X, us\_boundary). (100\%) \ (10)$$

4.2 An Algorithm for Mining Spatial Association Rules

The above rule mining process can be summarized in the following algorithm.

Algorithm 4.1 Mining the spatial association rules defined by Definition 1 in a large spatial database.

Input: The input consists of a spatial database, a mining query, and a set of thresholds as follows.

1. A database, which consists of three parts: (1) a spatial database, *SDB*, containing a set of spatial objects, (2) a relational database, *RDB*, describing nonspatial properties of spatial objects, and (3) a set of concept hierarchies,
2. a query, which consist of: (1) a reference class S, (2) a set of task-relevant classes for spatial objects $C_1, ..., C_n$, and (3) a set of task-relevant spatial relations, and
3. two thresholds: minimum support ($minsup[l]$) and minimum confidence ($minconf[l]$) for each level l of description.

Output: Strong multiple-level spatial association rules for the relevant sets of objects and relations.

Method: Mining spatial association rules proceeds as follows.

Step 1: $Task\_relevant\_DB :=$ extract_task_relevant_objects(SDB, RDB);

Step 2: $Coarse\_predicate\_DB :=$
   coarse_spatial_computation($Task\_relevant\_DB$);

Step 3: $Large\_Coarse\_predicate\_DB :=$
   filtering_with_minimum_support($Coarse\_predicate\_DB$);

Step 4: $Fine\_predicate\_DB :=$
   refined_spatial_computation($Large\_Coarse\_predicate\_DB$);

Step 5: Find_large_predicates_and_mine_rules($Fine\_predicate\_DB$);

Explanation of the detailed steps of the algorithm.

Step 1 is accomplished by the execution of a spatial query. All the task-relevant objects are collected into one database: $Task\_relevant\_DB$.

Step 2 is accomplished by execution of some efficient spatial algorithms at a coarse resolution level. For example, R-trees [4] or fast MBR technique and plane-sweep algorithm [18] can be applied to extract the objects which are approximately close to each other, corresponding to computing g_close_to for the $Task\_relevant\_DB$. The efficiency of the method is reasoned in the next subsection. Predicates describing spatial relations between objects are stored in an extended relational database, called $Coarse\_predicate\_DB$, which allows an attribute value to be either a single value or a set of values (i.e., in non-first-normal form).

Step 3 computes the support for each predicate in $Coarse\_predicate\_DB$, (and registers them in a predicate-support table), and filters out those entries whose support is below the minimum support threshold at the top level, i.e., $minsup[1]$. This filtering process results in a database which contains all large 1-predicates, which is called $Large\_Coarse\_predicate\_DB$. Notice that spatial association rules can also be generated at this resolution level, if desired. Since this process is similar to the process of Step 5, the detailed processing of Step 3 is not presented here.

Step 4 is accomplished by execution of some efficient spatial computation algorithms [5] at a fine resolution level on $Large\_Coarse\_predicate\_DB$ obtained in Step 3. Notice that although such computation is performed for the interesting portion of the spatial database, the computation is only on those pairs which have passed the corresponding spatial testing at a coarse resolution level. Thus, the number of object pairs which need to be computed at this level is substantially smaller that the number of pairs computed at a coarse level. Moreover, as an optimization technique, one can use the support count of an approximate predicate in *Large_Coarse_predicate_DB* to predict whether there is still hope for a predicate at a fine level to pass the minimum support threshold. For example, if the current support for predicate P plus the remaining number of support for its corresponding predicate *P_coarse* is less than the minimum support threshold, no further test of P is necessary in the remaining processing.

Step 5 computes the large k-predicates for all the k's and generates the strong association rules at multiple concept levels. This step is essential for mining multiple-level association rules and is thus examined in detail.

This step is outlined as follows. First, obtain large k-predicates (for all the k's) at a top concept level. Second, for the large 1-predicates at level 1, get their corresponding large 1-predicates at level 2, and then get all large k-predicates at this level. This process repeats until an empty large 1-predicate set is returned or bottom level in the hierarchy was explored. A detailed study of such a progressive deepening process for mining multiple-level association rules in a transaction-based (but not spatial) database is presented in [13].

At each level, the computation of large k-predicates for all k's proceeds from computing large-1 predicates, then large-2 predicates (using the pair-wise combination of large 1-predicates as the candidate set), large-3 predicates (using the combinations of large 2-predicates as the candidate set), and so on, until an empty candidate set or an empty computed k-predicate set is obtained. Such a process of computing large k-predicate sets (called large k-itemsets in [1]) using previously computed $(k-1)$-predicate sets in a transaction-based database is studied in [1], and is called *Algorithm Apriori*.

Notice that this k-predicate sets computation algorithm is fairly efficient one since it generates candidate k-predicate sets by full exploration of the combination of $(k-1)$-predicate sets before testing the k-predicate pairs against the predicate database. For example, Table 4 contains large 2-predicates "(adjacent_to, sea), (close_to, us_boundary)" and "(close_to, us_boundary), (intersects, provincial highway)" but does not contain "(adjacent_to, sea), (intersects, provincial highway)". It cannot form a candidate 3-predicate "(adjacent_to, sea), (close_to, us_boundary), (intersects, provincial highway)". Thus the effort of testing such a 3-predicate against the predicate database can be saved.

After finding large k-predicates, the set of association rules for each level l can be derived based on the minimum confidence at this level, *minconf[l]*. This is performed as follows [1]. For every large n-predicate A, if m-predicate B is not a subset of A, the rule "$A \rightarrow B$" is added into the result of the query if $support(A \wedge B)/support(A) \geq minconf[l]$.

The process is summarized in the following procedure, where $\mathcal{LL}[l]$ is the large predicate set table at level l, and $\mathcal{L}[l, k]$ is the large k-predicate set table at level l. The syntax of the procedure is similar to C and Pascal.

(1)   procedure find_large_predicates_and_mine_rules(DB);
(2)   for ($l := 1$; $\mathcal{L}[l, 1] \neq \emptyset$ and $l < max\_level$; $l++$) do begin

```
(3)          L[l, 1] := get_large_1_predicate_sets(DB, l);
(4)          for (k := 2; L[l, k − 1] ≠ ∅; k++) do begin
(5)             Pₖ := get_candidate_set(L[l, k − 1]);
(6)             foreach object s in S do begin
(7)                Pₛ := get_subsets(Pₖ, s); {Candidates satisfied by s}
(8)                foreach candidate p ∈ Pₛ do p.support++;
(9)             end;
(10)            L[l, k] := {p ∈ Pₖ|p.support ≥ minsup[l]};
(11)         end;
(12)         LL[l] := ⋃ₖ L[l, k];
(13)         output := generate_association_rules(LL[l]);
(14)      end
(15)   end  □
```

In this procedure, line (2) shows that the mining of the association rules is performed level-by-level, starting from the top-most level, until either the large 1-predicate set table is empty or it reaches the maximum concept level. For each level l, line (3) computes the large 1-predicate sets and put into table $L[l, 1]$. Lines (4)-(11) computes the large k-predicate sets $L[l, k]$ for all $k > 1$ at the level l progressively, essentially using the Apriori algorithm [1], as we discuss above. Line (12) collects all the large k predicate at each level l into one table $LL[l]$, and finally line (13) generates the spatial association rules at each concept level from the large predicate table $LL[l]$. □

The generated rules may need to be examined by human experts or pass through some automatic rule quality testing program [17] in order to filter out some obvious or redundant rules and output only those fairly new and interesting ones to the users.

4.3 A Discussion of the Algorithm

Algorithm 4.1 is an interesting and efficient algorithm for mining multiple-level strong spatial association rules in large spatial databases. Here we reason on the two essential properties of this algorithm: its correctness and its efficiency.

Correctness of the algorithm.

First, we show that Algorithm 4.1 discovers the correct and complete set of association rules given by the Definition 1.

Step 1 is a query processing process which extracts all data which are relevant to the spatial data mining process based on the completeness and correctness of query processing. Step 2 applies a coarse spatial computation method which computes the whole set of relevant data and thus still ensures its completeness and correctness. Step 3 filters out those 1-predicates whose support is smaller than the minimum support threshold. Obviously, predicates filtered out are those which has no hope to generate rules with support reaching the minimum support. Step 4 applies a fine spatial computation method which computes predicates from the set of derived coarse predicates and thus still ensures the completeness and correctness based on the nature of the spatial computation methods. Finally, Step 5 ensures to find the complete set of association rules at multiple concept levels based on the previous studies at mining multiple-level association rules in transaction-based databases [1, 13]. Therefore, the algorithm discovers the correct and complete set of association rules.

Efficiency of the algorithm.

We have the following theorem for the efficiency of the algorithm.

Theorem 5. *Let the average costs for computing each spatial predicate at a coarse and fine resolution level be C_c and C_f respectively. The worst-case time complexity of Steps 2-5 of Algorithm 4.1 is $O(C_c \times n_c + C_f \times n_f + C_{nonspatial})$, where n_c is the number of predicates to be coarsely computed in the relevant spatial data sets, n_f is the number of predicates to be finely computed from the coarse predicate database, and $C_{nonspatial}$ is the total cost of rule mining in a predicate database.*

Proof sketch.

Step 1 applies a spatial database query processing method whose computational complexity has been excluded from the total cost of the computation according to the statement of the theorem.

Step 2 involves the computation of the largest set of spatial predicates since each pair of objects needs to be checked to see whether it potentially and approximately satisfies the predicate to be coarsely computed. Since there are totally n_c predicates with distinct object sets as variables to be coarsely computed in the relevant spatial data sets, and the cost of computing each spatial predicate at a coarse resolution level is C_c, the total processing cost at this step should be $O(C_c \times n_c)$.

To avoid checking the predicates which will not be used later in the fine computation, approximate computation can be performed at a coarse resolution level. To accelerate this process, every object can be described using its MBR and coarse predicates can be derived using R-tree technique for spatial join [4] or plane sweep technique [18].

Furthermore, to computations faster one may use the data generalized and approximated data. For example, sinusoity of lines can be reduced, and small regions can be converted to points, etc.

With a similar reasoning, Step 4 involves the computation of the spatial predicates at a refined level. More detailed spatial computation algorithms will be applied at this stage. Since there are totally n_f predicates with distinct object sets as variables to be finely computed in the relevant data sets, and the cost of computing each spatial predicate at a fine resolution level is C_f, the total processing cost at this step should be $O(C_f \times n_f)$. Notice in most cases, $C_f > C_c$, but $n_f \ll n_c$, which ensures that the total cost of computation is reasonable.

According to the algorithm, the computation of support counts, threshold testing, and rule generation will not involve further spatial computation. Thus the total computation cost for Steps 3 and 5 will be $O(C_{nonspatial})$, where $C_{nonspatial}$ is the total cost of rule mining in a nonspatial predicate database.

Adding all costs together, we have the formula presented in the theorem. □

Execution time of the above mining algorithm can be estimated using the results of spatial join computations based on real data [4, 5] and on our experience on mining multilevel association rules [13]. Time of finding multiple level association rules by algorithm 4.1 is presented by (11). Component $C_c' \times N$ of this equation presents time of the execution of step 2 of the algorithm, $C_{filter} \times N_{nsp}$ is the time of filtering small coarse predicates, $C_f \times F_{ratio} \times N_c$ presents execution time of finding fine predicates and $C_{nsp} \times F_{ratio} \times N_{nsp}$ presents mining association rules from the set of fine predicates. Curve "coarse+filter+fine" on Fig. 3 shows the execution time of algorithm 4.1. In case when filtering in Step 2 of the algorithm is not used t_2 time is needed as it is shown by curve "coarse+fine". Execution time of naive algorithm when no tree structure is used for finding coarse predicates can be computed by (13). This time is presented by curve "naive+filter+fine". Table 6 lists some parameters used in the cost analysis. Estimated time shown in Fig. 3 indicates a substantial improvement of performance when tree structure is used to compute coarse predicates. It also shows large acceleration of computation process by filtering out coarse predicates not leading to large predicates, which avoids fine computations on such predicates.

$$t_1 = C_c' \times N + C_{filter} \times N_{nsp} + C_f \times F_{ratio} \times N_c + C_{nsp} \times F_{ratio} \times N_{nsp} \quad (11)$$

$$t_2 = C_c' \times N + C_f \times N_c + C_{nsp} \times N_{nsp} \quad (12)$$

$$t_3 = C_c'' \times N^2 + C_{filter} \times N_{nsp} + C_f \times F_{ratio} \times N_c + C_{nsp} \times F_{ratio} \times N_{nsp} \quad (13)$$

Name	Value	Meaning
C_c'	0.5 ms	constant for finding coarse predicates using R-trees [4]
C_c''	0.2 ms	constant for finding coarse predicates using naive algorithm
C_f	10 ms	cost of computing one fine predicate using TR*-trees [5]
C_{nsp}	1.5 ms	constant for finding association rules in a predicates database
C_{filter}	0.5 ms	constant for filtering out predicates in step 3 of the algorithm 4.1
N_{nsp}	$0.2 \times N$	number of tuples in a predicates database
N_c	$0.8 \times N$	number of coarse predicates from step 2 of the algorithm 4.1
F_{ratio}	0.1	ratio of coarse predicate possibly leading to large predicates

Table 6. Database parameters.

5 Discussion

5.1 Major Strengths of the Method

The spatial data mining method developed in the previous section has the following major strengths for mining spatial association rules.

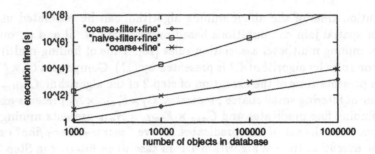

Fig. 3. Execution time.

- Focused data mining guided by user's query.
  The data mining process is directed by a user's query which specifies the relevant objects and spatial association relationships to be explored. This not only confines the mining process to a relatively small set of data and rules for efficient processing but also leads to desirable results.
- User-controlled interactive mining.
  Users may control, usually via a graphical user interface (GUI), minimum support and confidence thresholds at each abstraction level interactively based on the currently returned mining results.
- Approximate spatial computation: Substantial reduction of the candidate set.
  Less costly but approximate spatial computation is performed at an abstraction level first on a large set of data which substantially reduces the set of candidate data to be examined in the future.
- Detailed spatial computation: Performed once and used for knowledge mining at multiple levels.
  The computation of support counts at each level can be performed by scanning through the same computed spatial predicate table.
- Optimizations on computation of k-predicate sets and on multiple-level mining.
  These two optimization techniques are shared with the techniques for mining other (i.e., nonspatial) multiple-level association rules [13]. First, it uses the $(k-1)$-predicate sets to derive the candidate k-predicate sets at each level, which is similar to the *apriori* algorithm developed in [1]. Second, it starts at the top-most concept level and applies a progressive deepening technique to examine at a lower level only the descendants of the large 1-predicates, which is similar to the technique developed in [13].

5.2 Alternatives of the Method

Many variations and extensions of the method can be explored to enhance the power and performance of spatial association rule mining. Some of these are listed as follows.

- Integration with nonspatial attributes and predicates.
  The relevant set of predicates examined in our examples are mainly spatial ones, such as *close_to, inside*, etc. Such a process can be integrated with

the generalization and association of nonspatial data, which may lead to the rules, such as *"if a house is big and expensive, it is located in West Vancouver or Vancouver West-End (with 75% of confidence)"*, etc.

- Mining spatial association rules in multiple thematic maps.

  In principle, the method developed here can be applied to handle the spatial databases with multiple thematic maps. The rule mining process will be similar to the one presented above since the judgement of $g\_close\_to(X, Y)$ or $intersect(X, Y)$ can be performed by an approximate or detailed map overlay. The mining algorithm itself will remain intact.

- Multiple and dynamic concept hierarchies.

  Our method can also handle the cases when there exist multiple concept hierarchies or when the concept hierarchies need to be adjusted dynamically based on data distributions. For example, *towns* can be classified into *large* or *small* according to an existing hierarchy, *coast* or *in-land* according to their distance to the ocean, or *southwest, southeast*, etc. according to their geographic areas. Different characteristics will be discovered based on different hierarchies or their adjustments, which is similar to execute the same algorithm based on different knowledge-bases.

6 Conclusion

Based on the previous studies on spatial data mining and mining association rules in transaction-based databases, we proposed and studied an interesting method in this paper for mining strong spatial association rules in large spatial databases. Discovery of spatial association rules may disclose interesting relationships among spatial and/or nonspatial data in large spatial databases and thus it represents a new and promising direction in spatial data mining.

The method developed in this paper explores efficient mining of spatial association rules at multiple approximation and abstraction levels. It proposes first to perform less costly, approximate spatial computation to obtain approximate spatial relationships at a high abstraction level and then refine the spatial computation only for those data or predicates, according to the approximate computation, whose refined computation may contribute to the discovery of strong association rules. Such a two-step spatial mining method facilitates mining strong spatial association rules at multiple concept levels by a top-down, progressive deepening technique.

Our study is based on the assumption that a user has reasonably good knowledge on what s/he wants to find, and that there exists good knowledge (such as concept or operation hierarchies) for nonspatial or spatial generalization. Such assumptions, though valid in many cases, may enforce some strong restrictions to naive users or to some complex spatial databases with poorly understood structures or knowledge. More studies are needed to overcome these restrictions.

The method investigated in this study is currently under implementation and experimentation as one of several spatial data mining methods being developed in the spatial data mining system prototype, GeoMiner. We plan to integrate this technique with the generalization-based spatial data mining technique developed before [14, 15] and will report the prototype implementation and the experiments with reasonably large spatial databases in the future.

References

1. R. Agrawal and R. Srikant. Fast algorithms for mining association rules. In *Proc. 1994 Int. Conf. VLDB*, pp. 487–499, Santiago, Chile, Sept. 1994.
2. R. Agrawal, T. Imielinski, and A. Swami. Mining association rules between sets of items in large databases. In *Proc. 1993 ACM-SIGMOD Int. Conf. Management of Data*, pp. 207–216, Washington, D.C., May 1993.
3. W. G. Aref, and H. Samet. Optimization Strategies for Spatial Query Processing. In *Proc. 17th Int. Conf. VLDB*, Barcelona, Spain, pp. 81–90, Sept. 1991.
4. T. Brinkhoff, H. P. Kriegel, B. Seege. Efficient Processing of Spatial Joins Using R-trees. In *Proc. 1993 ACM-SIGMOD Conf. Management of Data*, Washington, D.C. pp. 237–246, May 1993.
5. T. Brinkhoff, H. P. Kriegel, R. Schneider, B. Seege. Multistep Processing of Spatial Joins. In *Proc. 1994 ACM-SIGMOD Conf. Management of Data*, Minneapolis, Minnesota, pp. 197–208, May 1994.
6. M. Egenhofer. Reasoning about Binary Topological Relations. In *Proc. 2nd Sympp. SSD'91*, Zurich, Switzerland, pp. 143–160, Aug. 1991.
7. M. Egenhofer. Spatial SQL: A Query and Presentation Language. In *IEEE Trans. Knowledge and Data Engineering*, 6:86-95, 1994.
8. U. Fayyad, and P. Smyth. Image Database Exploration: Progress and Challenges. In *Proc. 1993 Knowledge Discovery in Databases Workshop*, pp. 14-27, Washington, D.C..
9. U. Fayyad, G. Piatetsky-Shapiro, P. Smyth, and R. Uthurusamy. *Advances in Knowledge Discovery and Data Mining*, AAAI/MIT Press, 1995.
10. S. Fotheringham, and P. Rogerson. *Spatial Analysis and GIS*, Taylor and Francis, 1994.
11. A. Guttman. R-trees: A Dynamic Index Structure for Spatial Searching. In *Proc. ACM SIGMOD Int. Conf. on Management of Data*, Boston, MA, 1984, pp. 47-57.
12. J. Han, Y. Cai, and N. Cercone. Data-driven Discovery of Quantitative Rules in Relational Databases. *IEEE Trans. Knowledge and Data Eng.*, 5:29-40, 1993.
13. J. Han, and Y. Fu. Discovery of Multiple-Level Association Rules from Large Databases in *Proc. 1995 VLDB*, Zurich, Switzerland, Sept. 1995.
14. W. Lu, J. Han, and B. C. Ooi. Discovery of General Knowledge in Large Spatial Databases. In *Proc. Far East Workshop on Geographic Information Systems* pp. 275-289, Singapore, June 1993.
15. R. Ng, and J. Han. Efficient and effective clustering method for spatial data mining. In *Proc. 1994 Int. Conf. VLDB*, pp. 144–155, Santiago, Chile, Sept. 1994
16. G. Piatetsky-Shapiro, and W. J. Frawley. Knowledge Discovery in Databases, AAAI/MIT Press, 1991.
17. G. Piatesky-Shapiro, C. J. Matheus. The Interestingness of Deviations. In *Proc. 1994 Workshop on Knowledge Discovery in Databases*, Seattle, WA, pp. 25-36.
18. F. P. Preparata, and M. I. Shamos. *Computational Geometry: An Introduction.* Springer-Verlag, 1985.
19. H. Samet. *The Design and Analysis of Spatial Data Structures*, Addison-Wesley, 1990.

Knowledge Discovery in Large Spatial Databases: Focusing Techniques for Efficient Class Identification[1]

Martin Ester, Hans-Peter Kriegel, Xiaowei Xu

Institute for Computer Science, University of Munich
Leopoldstr. 11 B, D-80802 München, Germany
{ester | kriegel | xu} @informatik.uni-muenchen.de

Abstract. Both, the number and the size of spatial databases are rapidly growing because of the large amount of data obtained from satellite images, X-ray crystallography or other scientific equipment. Therefore, automated knowledge discovery becomes more and more important in spatial databases. So far, most of the methods for knowledge discovery in databases (KDD) have been based on relational database systems. In this paper, we address the task of class identification in spatial databases using clustering techniques. We put special emphasis on the integration of the discovery methods with the DB interface, which is crucial for the efficiency of KDD on large databases. The key to this integration is the use of a well-known spatial access method, the R*-tree. The focusing component of a KDD system determines which parts of the database are relevant for the knowledge discovery task. We present several strategies for focusing: selecting representatives from a spatial database, focusing on the relevant clusters and retrieving all objects of a given cluster. We have applied the proposed techniques to real data from a large protein database used for predicting protein-protein docking. A performance evaluation on this database indicates that clustering on large spatial databases can be performed, both, efficiently and effectively.

1 Introduction

Numerous applications require the management of geometric, geographic or *spatial data*, i.e. data related to space. The specific space may be, e. g. a two-dimensional projection of the surface of the earth, in a geographic information system, or a 3D space containing a protein molecule in an application in molecular biology. *Spatial Database Systems (SDBS)* [Gue 94] are database systems for the management of spatial data.

Both, the number and the size of spatial databases are rapidly growing because of the large amount of data obtained from satellite images, X-ray crystallography or other scientific equipment. This growth by far exceeds human capacities to analyze the databases in order to find implicit regularities, rules or clusters hidden in the data. Therefore, automated knowledge discovery becomes more and more important in spatial databases. *Knowledge discovery in databases (KDD)* is the non-trivial extraction of implicit, previously unknown, and potentially useful information from databases [FPM 91]. So far, most of the KDD methods have been based on relational database systems which are appropriate to handle non-spatial data, but not spatial data.

---

1. This research was funded by the German Minister for Research and Technology (BMFT) under grant no. 01 IB 307 B. The authors are responsible for the contents of this paper.

One of the well-known techniques for KDD is induction. [HCC 93] assumes the existence of concept hierarchies in the application domain and uses them to generalize the tuples of a relation into characteristic rules and classification rules. [LHO 93] extends this method for SDBS by adding spatial concept hierarchies and performing spatial induction. However, these hierarchies may not be available in many applications and, if available, they will not be appropriate for all KDD tasks. Therefore, [NH 94] does not rely on any domain knowledge and explores the applicability of cluster analysis techniques for KDD in SDBS. An algorithm called CLARANS (Clustering Large Applications based on RANdomized Search) is presented, which is both, efficient and effective for databases of some thousand objects.

[NH 94] assumes that all objects to be clustered can reside in main memory at the same time. However, this does not hold for large databases. Furthermore, the runtime of CLARANS is prohibitive on large databases. In general, the issue of interfacing KDD systems with a database management system (DBMS) has received little attention in the KDD literature and many systems are not yet integrated with a DBMS (c.f. [MCP 93]). [MCP 93] proposes an architecture of a KDD system including a DBMS interface and a focusing component. Well-known techniques are, e.g. focusing on a small subset of all tuples or focusing on a subset of all attributes. [AIS 93] presents a set of basic operations for solving different KDD tasks and shows how to apply them for efficient *classification*, i.e. finding rules that partition the database into a given set of groups. Good performance even on a large database is obtained by splitting the search space into independent parts, which is possible because different branches of a decision tree may be expanded independently from each other. [HK 94] addresses the issue of classification on large databases for relational database systems. Splitting the given relation into a lot of relatively small binary relations, i.e. focusing on one attribute at a time, [HK 94] always keeps the relevant part of the database in main memory. Additional histograms for each of the binary relations efficiently support the expensive computation of rule quality.

The task considered in this paper is *class identification*, i.e. the grouping of the objects of the database into meaningful subclasses (c.f. [MCP 93]).We show how to integrate CLARANS with a SDBS in order to perform class identification on large spatial databases, which can only partially be loaded into main memory. The key to this integration is the use of a well-known spatial access method, the R*-tree [BKSS 90]. The R*-tree, designed for supporting spatial queries, provides an efficient interface to a SDBS. This DB interface supports several focusing techniques allowing efficient class identification even on large spatial databases. The rest of the paper is organized as follows. Chapter 2 gives a brief introduction into CLARANS and discusses its application to large databases. An architecture for KDD in SDBS is outlined in chapter 3, giving special attention to the SDB interface. The focusing component of our KDD system, a main contribution of this paper, is presented in chapter 4. We perform an evaluation of both, efficiency and effectiveness on a protein database (chapter 5) and finish with the conclusion in chapter 6.

2 CLARANS on Large Databases

Cluster analysis techniques are attractive for KDD, because they can find hidden structures in data without using any additional domain knowledge. Different kinds of clustering algorithms have been developed (see [KR 90] for a survey), *k-mean* being one of the most prominent ones. The methods of type k-mean (e.g. ISODATA), however, suffer from some important drawbacks when applied to databases. First, these algorithm are quite sensitive to outliers, i.e. objects which are far away from the rest of the objects. Second, the cluster centers are no objects of the database, i.e. they may have no meaning in the domain of the application. Third, k-mean can only be applied when the mean of a cluster of objects is defined, which may not be the case in some applications, e.g. when the attributes are non-numeric. *k-medoid* algorithms avoid these drawbacks. Their goal is to find representative objects, called *medoids*. To achieve this goal, only the definition of a distance for any two objects is needed. Note that a distance function is also required by k-mean algorithms. Each object is assigned to the closest medoid so that the database of objects is partitioned into a set of clusters. Because of the above advantages, we have chosen the type k-medoid as the basis for our approach.

In the following, we introduce some basic notions for this paper. Let O be a *set of n objects*. $M \subseteq O$ denotes the set of *k* medoids, $NM = O - M$ denotes the *set of non-medoids*. We assume the objects to be polyhedrons, a common assumption for SDBS. Thus, each object is given by a list of its edges, and an edge is given by a list of two vertices, being points. Let $P \subseteq R^3$ be the set of all *points*. In general, the objects are spatial, and we define the *center of an object* to be the arithmetic mean of its vertices.

$$center: O \rightarrow P$$

Let *dist* be a *distance function*:

$$dist: P \times P \rightarrow R_0^+$$

In the following, we assume *dist* to be the euclidean distance, which is a natural choice for spatial clustering. Distance function *dist* can naturally be extended from points to polyhedron objects via the center function:

$$dist: O \times O \rightarrow R_0^+$$

$$dist\ (o_i,\ o_j) = dist\ (center(o_i),\ center(o_j))$$

Now each object is assigned to one of the medoids, such that the distance of its center to its medoid is minimal. Therefore, we define a function medoid:

$$medoid: O \rightarrow M$$

$$medoid\ (o) = m_i,\ m_i \in M,\ \forall\ m_j \in M: dist\ (o, m_i) \leq dist\ (o, m_j)$$

Finally, we define the *cluster* of medoid m_i to be the subset of all objects from O with medoid(o) = m_i and a *clustering* to be a set of clusters partitioning O. Let C_O be the set of all possible clusterings of O. The *total distance* of a clustering is used to measure its quality:

$$total\_distance: C_O \rightarrow R_0^+$$

$$total\_distance(c) = \sum_{m_i \in M}\ \sum_{o \in cluster(m_i)} dist\ (o, m_i)$$

PAM (Partitioning Around Medoids, see [KR 90]) is an algorithm of type k-medoid. It starts from an initial set of medoids and iteratively replaces one of the medoids by one of the non-medoids as long as the total distance of the resulting clustering is improved. PAM works efficiently for small data sets, but its runtime is prohibitive for large databases. [NH 94] proposes a clustering method called CLARANS (Clustering Large Applications based on RANdomized Search) based on PAM with a new heuristic search strategy. The key idea is not to consider all possible replacements of one medoid by one non-medoid and to select the optimal one, but to perform the first replacement improving the quality of the clustering. The clustering obtained after performing a single replacement is called a *neighbor* of the current clustering. The number of neighbors tried is restricted by a parameter provided by the user (*maxneighbor*) and the selection of these neighbors is random. Each iteration of CLARANS yields a local optimum, i.e. a clustering for which no neighbor with a better quality was found. Note that not all neighbors are considered for a local optimum but only *maxneighbor* of them. The parameter *numlocal* allows the user to define the number of these local optima to be searched. In the following, we present the algorithm CLARANS in a C++-like notation. *O*, *k*, *dist*, *numlocal*, and *maxneighbor* are given as input. The output consists of a set of *k* clusters.

Algorithm CLARANS (int k, function dist, int numlocal, int maxneighbor)

```
for (i = 1; i++; i <= numlocal) {
    current.create_randomly(k);
    j = 1;
    while (j < maxneighbor) {
        current.select_randomly(old, new);
        diff = current.calculate_distance_difference(old, new);
        if (diff < 0) {
            current.exchange(old, new);
            j = 1;
        } // end if
    } // end while (inner loop)
    dist = current.calculate_total_distance();
    if (dist < smallest_dist) {
        best = current;
        smallest_dist = dist;
    } // end if
} // end for (outer loop)
```

The algorithm assumes the existence of a class `clustering` with methods of the following meaning:
- `create_randomly(k)`
  Creates a random clustering with k clusters, i.e. it selects randomly *k* of the *n* objects as medoids. This selection is random, because it is performed inside the outer loop of the algorithm so that a different selection is required for each iteration.
- `select_randomly(old, new)`
  Selects randomly one of the medoids as `old` and one of the non-medoids as new.

- `calculate_distance_difference(old, new)`
  Calculates the difference in total distance between the current clustering and the hypothetical clustering obtained when replacing medoid `old` by `new`. A naive implementation sums up the distance differences for each object implied by the replacement.
- `exchange(old, new)`
  Exchange `old` (a selected medoid) and `new` (a selected non-medoid), i.e. old becomes a non-medoid and new becomes a medoid. Consequently, the assignment of objects to medoids has to be updated.
- `calculate_total_distance()`
  Calculates the total distance for the current clustering.

Note that the algorithm is mainly based on relative distances. No total distance is calculated for the initial clustering of each iteration, and only differences of distances implied by changing medoids are calculated until a local minimum is found. Only then, the total distance is calculated for the current clustering.

Now, we want to analyse the cost of CLARANS, when applied to a database. Our analysis is based on the following assumptions. Let c be the average number of objects stored on one page. The small set of medoids is resident in main memory, while the large set of non-medoids has to reside on disk. The I/O-cost heavily dominates the CPU cost. Therefore, we take the number of disk pages to be read as the cost measure, which is a common approach for database systems. We obtain the following cost for one call of the different methods:

- `create_randomly`
  has to choose k medoids, i.e. it has to read k pages in the worst case.
- `select_randomly`
  has to read just one of the non-medoids, i.e. one page.
- `calculate_distance_difference`
  accesses all objects, i.e. it reads n/c pages.
- `exchange`
  only updates the set of medoids and thus does not access to the disk.
- `calculate_total_distance`
  has to access all objects, i.e. has cost n/c.

The calculation of the number of calls, i.e. the number of iterations in the inner loop, cannot be done in an analytic way because of the heuristic nature of the algorithm. Therefore, we only distinguish whether a method is called within the inner loop (a lot of iterations) or within the outer loop (*numlocal* iterations) of the algorithm.

Thus, the cost of CLARANS is dominated by the cost of the method `calculate_distance_difference`, because its cost is $O(n)$ and it is called inside the inner loop of the algorithm. All other methods are either not as expensive per single call or are not called in the inner loop of the algorithm. A similar observation can be found in [HK 94] stating that in their case the main problem is the efficient computation of the quality of all possible rules. As a consequence of our analysis, in chapter 4 we propose several techniques to improve the efficiency of CLARANS on large databases.

3 An Architecture for Knowledge Discovery in SDBS

[MCP 93] proposes an architecture for a KDD system (cf. figure 1) consisting of the following components: controller, DB interface, focus, pattern extraction, evaluation and knowledge base.

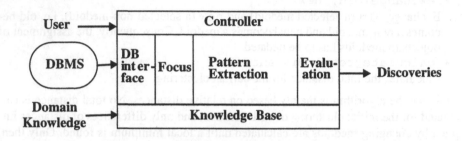

Fig. 1. architecture of a KDD system

So far, we have only considered the task of class identification, a kind of *unsupervised learning*, i.e. learning only from the data without using additional domain knowledge. Thus, we do not require the controller and the knowledge base. In the following, we sketch the components of our KDD system in terms of the above architecture.

The *DB interface* allows the KDD system to select a set of objects from the database fulfilling a given condition on their attributes. Typical queries for SDBS are *region queries* (return all objects from the database intersecting a query polygon) and *nearest neighbor queries* (return the object closest to a query object) [Gue 94]. *Spatial access methods* (SAM) have been developed to support efficient processing of such queries (cf. [BHKS 93] [BKSS 94]). An *approximation* is a simple object with limited complexity preserving the main properties of a complex spatial object. The most common approximation is the *bounding box* (BB), i.e. the minimal rectilinear rectangle containing a given spatial object. Therefore, most SAMs are designed to manage rectangles.

The *R*-tree* [BKSS 90] is a SAM which is very efficient for points and rectangles. Each node of the tree represents a *page*, the unit of transfer from secondary storage to main memory. Therefore, the number of rectangles per node is constrained by a lower and an upper limit, such that a high storage utilization is obtained and consequently the number of disk pages to be read for query processing is as small as possible. The nodes storing the data objects are called *data pages*, the nodes organizing the directory are called *directory pages*. As soon as overlapping data rectangles do not fit into the same page, an overlap of directory pages will occur. This overlap of directory pages has to be minimized for efficient query processing. Therefore, the R*-tree uses a heuristic splitting strategy when the capacity of a page is exceeded after the insertion of a new object.

The *focusing component* determines which parts of the database are relevant for pattern extraction. In relational DBS, e.g. one could focus on some attributes of the tuples yielding most information or focus on a randomly drawn sample of all tuples. Finally, the focusing component asks queries to the DB interface obtaining the input for pattern extraction. The focusing component is outlined in chapter 4.

Pattern Extraction is based on the data returned by the focusing component. In general, pattern extraction is a multi-step process, i.e. a cluster might be input for another step of cluster analysis. For example, a first step might cluster the data according to a non-spatial attribute like landuse, and a second step would cluster all data within one of the resulting clusters according to the spatial attributes.

The *evaluation component* should determine the statistical significance of the extracted patterns and support an application-specific evaluation of their usefulness by the user. So far, we do not compute the significance. The clusters extracted are visualized to the user in a graphical way, either all clusters at the same time or one cluster at a time together with its neighboring clusters.

4 The Focusing Component

In chapter 2, we have concluded that the most expensive operation of CLARANS is calculating the difference of the total distances of two clusterings. There are two approaches to improve the efficiency of this operation. First, a reduction of the number n of all objects will result in a significant speed-up, because the calculation of the distance difference is $O(n)$. Second, a careful analysis shows that actually not all n objects contribute to the result of the operation, so that efficiency can be improved by restricting the access to the relevant objects. In this chapter, we present three different focusing techniques exploiting both approaches.

4.1 Focus on Representative Objects

The number of all possible clusterings of a database depends on n and k. In order to reduce the time complexity, we propose to apply CLARANS not to the whole database, but to select a relatively small number of representatives from the database and to apply CLARANS only to these representatives. This is a kind of *sampling*, a technique common in KDD systems, e.g. [KR 90]. The quality of the sampling is crucial for the quality of the resulting clustering. Our DB interface supports a new way of selecting representatives from a SDBS. From each data page of the R*-tree, we select the most central object as a representative. Thus, the clustering strategy of the R*-tree, which minimizes the overlap between directory rectangles, yields a well-distributed set of representatives.

Let the *center of the data page* be the center of the bounding box of its objects. The *most central object* in a data page is the object with the minimal distance of its center from the center of the data page. Figure 2 illustrates the selection of representatives according to this definition for some data pages.

An obvious question is, whether it is reasonable to let the R*-tree perform the whole clustering in one step without using CLARANS in a second step. The answer is "no" because of the following reasons:

- The R*-tree does not allow the users to specify the number k of clusters, it derives k indirectly from n and from the capacity of a page. This k may be inappropriate for a given application and may yield clusterings with a high total distance.

- All clusters (i.e. the directory rectangles) have a rectangular shape and, furthermore, these rectangles have to be parallel to the axes of the coordinate system.

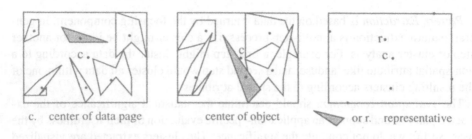

c. center of data page   center of object   or r. representative

Fig. 2. example data pages of an R*-tree with representatives selected

We propose to combine the good properties of the R*-tree and of CLARANS in the following two-step approach:

1.) Extract one representative for each data page of the R*-tree.
2.) Cluster the representatives using CLARANS and return k medoids.

For the purpose of extracting the representatives, we need a new query, called *centroid query*, returning the most central object for each data page. This query requires a scan over all data pages of an R*-tree, i.e. n/c pages have to be read. On the other hand, when focusing on representatives, CLARANS only has to cluster n/c objects instead of n objects.

4.2 Focus on Relevant Clusters

In this section, we take a closer look at the calculation of the difference of total distance between two neighbor clusterings, i.e. clusterings differing in exactly one medoid. This method gives the main contribution to the cost of CLARANS. The algorithm presented by [NH 94] performs a loop over all non-medoid objects for calculating the difference of distance. This is prohibitive when working on a database, because all these objects would have to be loaded into main memory. Therefore, our goal is to restrict the calculation to the relevant parts of the database.

There are four different cases of non-medoid objects o to be distinguished when calculating the distance difference between a current clustering and the resulting clustering after exchanging a medoid *old* with a non-medoid *new*. They are illustrated in the following figures by examples of 2D-points.

1.) The current medoid of o is *old,* and o is closer to its second closest medoid than to *new*. Then o will be inserted into the cluster whose medoid is its second closest medoid (see figure 3).

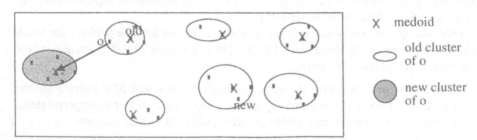

Fig. 3. Example of Case 1

2.) The current medoid of *o* is *old*, and o is closer to *new* than to its second closest medoid. Then *o* will be inserted into the cluster whose medoid is *new* (see figure 4).

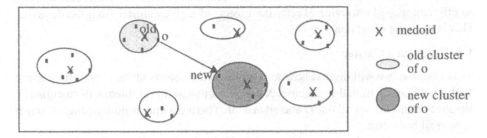

Fig. 4. Example of Case 2

3.) The current medoid of *o* is different from *old* and o is closer to its medoid than to *new*. Then *o* will stay in its cluster (see figure 5).

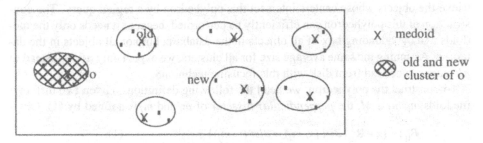

Fig. 5. Example of Case 3

4.) The current medoid of *o* is different from *old*, and o is closer to *new* than to its current medoid. Then *o* will be inserted into the cluster whose medoid is *new* (see figure 6).

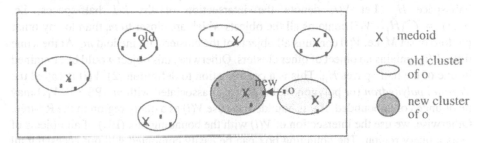

Fig. 6. Example of Case 4

Only in cases 1.), 2.) and 4.) *o* will be moved to another cluster, i.e. only in these cases the total distance for *o* will change. The objects of case 1.) form a subset of the objects with medoid *old*, cases 2.) and 4.) cover the objects with medoid *new*. Thus, only the objects belonging to the clusters of *old* and *new* contribute to the distance difference. Instead of reading all non-medoid objects from disk (i.e. the objects of all k clusters), we just have to read the objects of two clusters. Assuming the same average size for all clusters, we expect a performance gain of $k/2$ compared to [NH 94]. However, we need an efficient way of retrieving exactly the objects of a given cluster from the database. This is the issue of section 4.3.

4.3 Focus on a Cluster

In this section, we will discuss how to retrieve all the objects of the cluster for a given medoid efficiently from the database. A naive solution of this problem will calculate all distances $dist(o,m)$, for all $o \in O$ and all $m \in M$. This technique would require n/c pages to be read from disk.

Now, we want to solve this problem more efficiently. According to chapter 2, the distance of polyhedron objects is defined by using the distance of points. Thus, in the following, we only consider point objects without loss of generality. We construct a polyhedron for a medoid m_i such that all objects within this polyhedron belong to the cluster with medoid m_i while no objects from other clusters are contained in it. Then, we retrieve the objects whose centers intersect this polyhedron by a region query. The construction of this polyhedron can efficiently be performed, because it needs only the medoids and the bounding box of all objects in the database, but not all objects in the database. Assuming the same average size for all clusters, we expect only $n/k*c$ instead of n/c pages to be read from disk with this focusing technique.

To construct the polyhedron, we need the following definitions. Given two different medoids $m_i, m_j \in M$, the *perpendicular bisector* of m_i and m_j is defined by (1). Obvi-

$$B_{ij} := \{x \in \mathbb{R}^3 \mid dist\,(x,\, m_i) = dist\,(x,\, m_j)\} \qquad (1)$$

ously, the bisector is a plane bounding the *half-space* H_{ij}, which is defined by (2).

$$H_{ij} := \{x \in \mathbb{R}^3 \mid dist\,(x,\, m_i) \leq dist\,(x,\, m_j)\} \qquad (2)$$

For any medoids m_i and m_j, all objects closer to m_i than to m_j are located in the half-space H_{ij}. Let $V(i)$ denote the intersection of the $k\text{-}1$ half-spaces, i.e. $V(i) = \bigcap H_{ij}$. $V(i)$ contains all the objects which are closer to m_i than to any other medoid of set M, i.e. $V(i)$ contains all objects of the cluster with medoid m_i. At the same time, $V(i)$ contains no object of other clusters. Otherwise, this object would be contained in one of the half-spaces H_{ij}. This is a contradiction to definition (2). $V(i)$ is called the *Voronoi polyhedron* (or polygon in the 2D case) associated with m_i [PS 85]. $V(i)$ may be bounded or unbounded. If it is bounded, we use $V(i)$ as a query region to the R*-tree. Otherwise, we use the intersection of $V(i)$ with the bounding box (BB) of all objects of O as a query region. The bounding box can be easily computed without accessing all the objects of the database only by using the root of the R*-tree. Figure 7 illustrates the constructed query region for a small database of 2D-polygons.

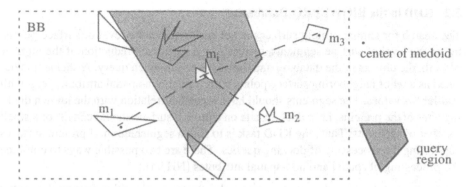

Fig. 7. The query region for all objects of the cluster with medoid m_i

5 Application and Performance Evaluation

We apply the proposed clustering techniques to a large protein database and evaluate their performance in this context. We introduce the protein database (section 5.1), illustrate the KDD task in this application (section 5.2) and evaluate focusing on representatives with respect to effectiveness and efficiency (section 5.3).

5.1 BIOWEPRO - a SDBS for Protein-Protein Docking

Proteins are biomolecules consisting of some hundreds to some thousands of atoms. Their mode of operation lies in the interaction with other biomolecules, for example proteins, DNA or smaller partner molecules. These interactions are performed by connecting the partner molecules, and are therefore called *docking*.

Molecular biologists point out that the geometry of the molecular surfaces at the interaction site plays an important role, along with the physicochemical properties of the molecules. A necessary condition for protein-protein docking is the complementarity of the interaction site with respect to surface shape, electrostatic potential, hydrophobicity etc. Therefore, a database system for protein-protein docking has to process queries for proteins with similar or complementary surfaces.

In the BIOWEPRO (Biomolecular Interactions of Proteins) project (cf. [EKSX 95], [SK 95]) we are developing a SDBS to support protein-protein docking. We use the crystallographically determined atom coordinates of proteins and protein complexes from the Brookhaven Protein Data Bank ([Ber 77], [PDB 94]), presently containing some 3,000 proteins. Each protein has a triangulated surface with some 10,000 3D points. For each point on the protein surface, several geometric and physicochemical features are computed. The *solid angle (SA)*, e.g., [Con 86] is a geometric feature describing the degree of convexity or concavity of the surface in the neighborhood of the considered point.

5.2 KDD in the BIOWEPRO Database

The search for similar protein surfaces is not performed at the level of surface points, but at the level of surface segments, resulting in a significant reduction of the number of both, the objects in the database and the answers to a given query. A *segment* is defined as a set of neighboring surface points with similar non-spatial attributes, e.g. with similar SA values. The segments should have a good correlation with the known docking sites of the proteins, i.e. a docking site on a protein surface should consist of a small number of segments. Thus, the KDD task is to find a segmentation of protein surfaces supporting the processing of docking queries. There are two possible ways to combine the processing of spatial and non-spatial attributes [NH 94]:

1.) *Spatial dominated approach.* Apply the clustering algorithm first on the spatial attribute to obtain segments. The number of clusters is determined heuristically by using the number of local extrema of SA. Then generalize the non-spatial attributes for all 3D points of a given segment to classify the shape of the segment.

2.) *Non-spatial dominated approach.* Apply the clustering algorithm first on the non-spatial attributes with the number of clusters, e.g., set to 5. In the second step, we cluster each of the 5 non-spatial clusters using the spatial attributes such that these clusters are split into segments of neighboring points.

For an illustration, we sketch the application of the spatial dominated approach in the BIOWEPRO database. Figure 8 depicts some of the segments found on the surface of protein 2ptc by spatial clustering.

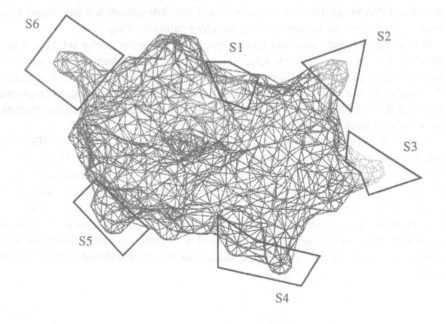

Fig. 8. Example segments on the surface of protein 2ptc

Based on the values of SA, three classes of shapes (convex, neutral and concave) can be distinguished. Since no crisp definitions of these classes are available, we perform fuzzy classification. Figure 9 presents our fuzzy membership functions for the three classes.

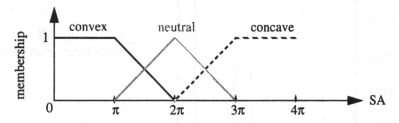

Fig. 9. Fuzzy membership functions for the three classes of shape

According to the membership functions, segment S1 is neutral (with grade 0.826) and convex (with grade 0.174), whereas S2 is convex (with grade 0.981) and neutral (with grade 0.019).

5.3 Evaluation of Focusing on Representatives

In this section, we present experimental results from the BIOWEPRO database evaluating the technique of focusing on representatives with respect to efficiency and effectiveness. Our measure of effectiveness is the average distance of the resulting clusterings, i.e. the average distance of an object from its medoid. Efficiency is measured by the CPU runtime of the whole processing. All experiments have been run on an HP 9000/735 workstation.

We use the protein hemoglobin (4hhb) for our experiments, because it is one of the largest objects in the database. The surface of 4hhb consists of 50,559 points, and for each of these points we store the 3D-coordinates along with the value of SA. The number of clusters is set to 10 and *numlocal* set to 2. In the first set of experiments, we directly apply CLARANS on 4hhb with *maxneighbor* varying from 250 over 500 to 1,000. In the second set of experiments, we use "focusing on representatives". We obtain 1,027 representatives out of the 50,559 points for 4hhb, and CLARANS is then applied to this set of representatives.

The results on effectiveness in terms of the average distance are presented in figure 10. Using the focusing technique, we observe a decrease of effectiveness ranging

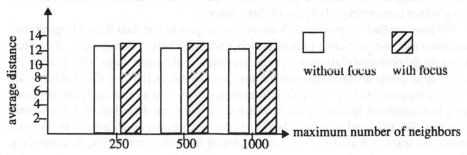

Fig. 10. Comparison of Effectiveness

from 1.5% to 3.2% compared to clustering without focus. Figure 11 depicts the results of the comparison of efficiency. Focusing improves the efficiency by a factor ranging from 48 to 158 in comparison to clustering without focus.

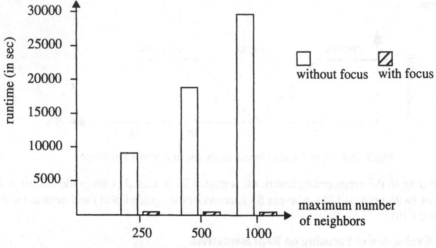

Fig. 11. Comparison of Efficiency

To conclude, focusing improves efficiency by a factor of 48 to 158, whereas the loss of effectiveness is only 1.5% to 3.2%.

6 Conclusion

We use the clustering algorithm CLARANS [NH 94] for class identification in SDBS. Our analysis points out that the most expensive operation of CLARANS, when applied to a large SDB, is calculating the difference of the total distances of two clusterings.

The DB interface of our KDD system is based on the R*-tree, a well-known spatial access method. For the purpose of focusing, we need a new query, called centroid query, returning the most central object for each data page.

The focusing component supports three types of focusing. Focusing on representative objects significantly reduces the number of objects to be clustered. Focusing on relevant clusters restricts the calculation of the difference of distance between two clusterings to the relevant clusters, i.e. to the cluster of the medoid and the cluster of the non-medoid to be exchanged. Focusing on a given cluster is performed by determining the minimum polyhedron intersecting all objects of this cluster.

We have applied the proposed clustering techniques to real data from a large protein database used for predicting protein-protein docking. There are other types of applications for the proposed clustering method, because its only requirement is the availability of an appropriate distance function for any two objects. In [NH 94] CLARANS is applied in the context of a geographic information system. We want to apply our approach to a k-dimensional feature space, in which CAD parts are described by k non-spatial features. The first goal is to find classes of CAD parts based on their features. Furthermore, we want to discover associations between the different features, indicating e.g. the redundancy of a given feature.

We have performed an evaluation of focusing on representatives on the protein database. In terms of efficiency, CLARANS with focusing outperforms CLARANS by a factor of 48 to 158. The decrease of effectiveness, using the focus on representatives, is only 1.5% to 3.2% compared to CLARANS. Thus, focusing on representatives offers a very good trade off between efficiency and effectivity.

Future research will have to consider the following issues. CLARANS randomly selects two objects to be exchanged and does not consider any alternatives if the exchange results in a reduction of the total distance of the clustering. Heuristic strategies for selection should reduce the huge size of the search space and thus improve the efficiency of pattern extraction. So far, we have created crisp clusterings, i.e. each object has been assigned to a unique cluster. However, due to the spatial nature of the objects, it is possible that an object intersects the area of two clusters at the same time. A similar situation occurs when two objects have the same distance from two different medoids. In both cases, fuzzy clustering techniques, assigning an object to several clusters with varying degrees of membership, seem to be more appropriate than crisp clustering methods. We intend to explore them in our future work.

Acknowledgment

We thank Thomas Seidl for engaging and fruitful discussions on the subject of this paper and for his support in the performance evaluation on the BIOWEPRO data.

References

[AIS 93] Agrawal R., Imielinski T., Swami A.: *"Database Mining: A Performance Perspective"*, IEEE Transactions on Knowledge and Data Engineering, Vol.5, No.6, 1993, pp. 914-925.

[Ber 77] Bernstein F. C., Koetzle T. F., Williams G. J., Meyer E. F., Brice M. D., Rodgers J. R., Kennard O., Shimanovichi T., Tasumi M.: *'The Protein Data Bank: a Computer-based Archival File for Macromolecular Structures'*, Journal of Molecular Biology, Vol. 112, 1977, pp. 535-542.

[BHKS 93] Brinkhoff T., Horn H., Kriegel H.-P., Schneider R.: *'A Storage and Access Architecture for Efficient Query Processing in Spatial Database Systems'*, Proc. 3rd Int. Symp. on Large Spatial Databases, Singapore, 1993, Lecture Notes in Computer Science, Vol. 692, Springer, pp. 357-376.

[BKSS 90] Beckmann N., Kriegel H.-P., Schneider R., Seeger B.: *'The R*-tree: An Efficient and Robust Access Method for Points and Rectangles'*, Proc. ACM SIGMOD Int. Conf. on Management of Data, Atlantic City, NJ, 1990, pp. 322-331.

[BKSS 94] Brinkhoff T., Kriegel H.-P., Schneider R., Seeger B.: *'Efficient Multi-Step Processing of Spatial Joins'*, Proc. ACM SIGMOD Int. Conf. on Management of Data, Minneapolis, MN, 1994, pp. 197-208.

[Con 86] Connolly M. L.: *'Measurement of protein surface shape by solid angles'*, Journal of Molecular Graphics, Vol. 4, No. 1, 1986, pp. 3-6.

[EKSX 95] Ester M., Kriegel H.-P., Seidl T., Xu X.: "Shape-based Retrieval of Complementary 3D Surfaces in Protein Databases", (in German), Proc. GI Conf. on Database Systems for Office Automation, Engineering, and Scientific Applications.1995, Berlin: Springer 1995.

[FPM 91] Frawley W.J., Piatetsky-Shapiro G., Matheus J.: *"Knowledge Discovery in Databases: An Overview"*, in: Knowledge Discovery in Databases, AAAI Press, Menlo Park, 1991, pp. 1-27.

[Gue 94] Gueting R.H.: *"An Introduction to Spatial Database Systems"*, Special Issue on Spatial Database Systems of the VLDB Journal, Vol.3, No.4, October 1994.

[HCC 93] Han J., Cai Y., Cercone N.: *"Data-driven Discovery of Quantitative Rules in Relational Databases"*, IEEE Transactions on Knowledge and Data Engineering, Vol.5, No.1, 1993, pp. 29-40.

[HK 94] Holsheimer M., Kersten M.L.: *"Architectural Support for Data Mining"*, Proc. AAAI Workshop on Knowledge Discovery in Databases, Seattle, Washington, 1994, pp. 217-228

[KR 90] Kaufman L., Rousseeuw P.J.: *"Finding Groups in Data: an Introduction to Cluster Analysis"*, John Wiley & Sons, 1990.

[LHO 93] Lu W., Han J., Ooi B.C.: *"Discovery of General Knowledge in Large Spatial Databases"*, Proc. Far East Workshop on Geographic Information Systems, Singapore, 1993, pp. 275-289.

[MCP 93] Matheus C.J., Chan P.K., Piatetsky-Shapiro G.: *"Systems for Knowledge Discovery in Databases"*, IEEE Transactions on Knowledge and Data Engineering, Vol.5, No.6, 1993, pp. 903-913.

[NH 94] Ng R.T., Han J.: *"Efficient and Effective Clustering Methods for Spatial Data Mining"*, Proc. 20th Int. Conf. on Very Large Data Bases, Santiago, Chile, 1994, pp. 144-155.

[PDB 94] Protein Data Bank: *'Quarterly Newsletter No. 70 (Oct. 1994)'*, Brookhaven National Laboratory, Upton, NY, 1994.

[PS 85] Preparata F. P., Shamos M. I.: *"Computational Geometry"*, Springer 1985.

[SK 95] Seidl T., Kriegel H.-P.: *'Solvent Accessible Surface Representation in a Database System for Protein Docking'*, Proc. 3rd Int. Conference on Intelligent Systems for Molecular Biology (ISMB–95), Cambridge, UK, AAAI Press, 1995.

Ranking in Spatial Databases*

Gísli R. Hjaltason and Hanan Samet

Computer Science Department, Center for Automation Research, and Institute for
Advanced Computer Studies, University of Maryland, College Park, MD 20742, USA

Abstract. An algorithm for ranking spatial objects according to increasing distance from a query object is introduced and analyzed. The
algorithm makes use of a hierarchical spatial data structure. The intended application area is a database environment, where the spatial
data structure serves as an index. The algorithm is incremental in the
sense that objects are reported one by one, so that a query processor can
use the algorithm in a pipelined fashion for complex queries involving
proximity. It is well suited for k nearest neighbor queries, and has the
property that k needs not be fixed in advance.

1 Introduction

Indexes are used in databases to facilitate retrieval of records with similar values.
For a particular attribute, an index yields an ordering of all records in increasing
(or decreasing) order of the attribute value. Extending this idea to more than one
attribute is a bit complex. One approach is to make the first attribute a primary
attribute and the additional attribute a secondary attribute. Thus we first sort
the records according to the value of the first attribute and we break ties by use
of the second attribute. This is fine as long as we only want the records sorted
by the value of the first attribute. If we want the records ordered by the value of
the second attribute, then our index is useless as consecutive records obtained by
the index are not necessarily ordered by the value of the second attribute. One
solution is to build an additional index on the second attribute. This is feasible
but does take up more space.

The solution of adding a second index is acceptable as long as queries do
not make use of a combination of the attribute values. Such a combination is
generally meaningless if the dimensional units of the attribute values differ. For
example, if one attribute is age and the other is weight, then the corresponding
dimensional units could be years and pounds. In this case, we are not likely to
try to determine the nearest record to the one with name John Jones in terms
of age and weight as we don't have a commonly accepted notion of the meaning
of the year-pound unit.

Spatial databases are distinguished from conventional databases, in part, by
the fact that some of the attributes are locational and in which case they have

---

* This work was supported in part by the National Science Foundation under grants
IRI-92-16970 and ASC-93-18183.

the same dimensional unit. More importantly, this common dimensional unit is distance in space. The distance unit is the same regardless of the dimensionality of the space spanned by the locational (i.e., spatial) attributes of the records as long as they cover the same space. What this means is that if we combine the attributes, and seek to determine the nearest record of type t to the one with name Chicago, then the corresponding unit would be distance regardless of whether there are two or three (or even more) locational attributes associated with t. Note that just because an attribute has a dimensional unit of distance does not make it a locational attribute. For example, size attributes are also measured in terms of distance yet they are not locational. Thus attributes corresponding to a person's height and waist are not locational attributes and cannot be combined.

In addition, different spatial databases can be distinguished according to the types of records that they store. There are two types: points and objects. We define the former to have a zero volumetric measure, while the latter have a nonzero volumetric measure. In other words, the latter have an extent while the former do not (i.e., they are discrete). Note that the records in a conventional database are always discrete, and can be viewed as points in a higher dimensional space. The difference is that in the case of spatial data, the dimensional unit of the attribute is distance in space.

Regardless of the distinction between the types of data stored in a spatial database, we are often interested in ordering the records on the basis of some combination of the values of the locational attributes. This ordering is used to facilitate storage of the records as the storage methods are inherently one-dimensional. It is desirable for this ordering to also preserve proximity in the sense that records that are close to each other in the multidimensional space formed by ranges of the values of the locational attributes are also close to each other in the ordering. Of course, if there is just one locational attribute, then the ordering is the same as that used for a non-locational attribute.

An example of such an ordering technique is hashing. There are two variants of hashing, depending on whether the resulting ordering is explicit or implicit. An explicit ordering results from the use of a particular mapping from the higher dimensional space to a one-dimensional space. An example mapping is one that interleaves the individual bits in the binary representation of the locational attribute values. Such mappings result in what are known as space-filling curves [5] (e.g., Peano, Hilbert, Sierpinsky, etc.) although no curve has the property that all records that are close to each other in the multidimensional space formed by the ranges of the locational attribute values are also close to each other in the range of the mapping.

Bucketing methods are examples of an implicit ordering. In this case, the records are sorted on the basis of the space that they occupy (i.e., the space formed by the values of their locational attribute) and are grouped into cells (i.e., buckets) of a finite capacity. Of course, if there is just one locational attribute, then the implicit and explicit orderings are equivalent. When the records are such that they also have an extent (e.g., non-point spatial objects), then the notion of a bucket is more meaningful. In particular, there are two possible approaches [14].

The first approach finds a minimum bounding box for the object. These boxes may be subsequently aggregated by use of hierarchies. In such a case, the minimum bounding boxes may not necessarily be disjoint. The drawback is that an object is associated with just one bounding box. Thus if we are given a particular point p, and we search for an object that contains p, then just because we don't find an object that contains p in a bounding box b containing p does not mean that objects in other bounding boxes do not contain p.

An alternative approach decomposes the objects so that the bounding boxes that contain them are disjoint. Once again, these boxes may be subsequently aggregated into hierarchies. Now, for each point p there is just one bounding box b that contains p and if none of the objects in b contain p, then none of the objects in the database will contain p and the query fails. The drawback is that an object can be decomposed into several pieces and hence associated with many boxes. Thus if we want to determine which objects are associated with a region that spans several bounding boxes, then we may report a particular object more than once. For such queries we must have a post-processing step that removes duplicate answers. The process of removing duplicate may require a process as complex as sorting although, depending on the nature of the object, other methods may be applicable (e.g., [2]).

The ordering provided by an index is useful for ranking the data based on its closeness to a particular value v of the attribute a. The ability to perform the ranking does not depend on whether a record r exists in the database such that attribute a of r has value v. Value v serves as a reference point for the ranking.

In this paper, we focus on the issue of ranking in spatial databases. For the moment, assume that we have just one attribute and that it can be locational or non-locational. In this case the explicit and implicit indexes are equivalent, and we can derive the ranking directly from the index for the attribute. In particular, the index is obtained by sorting the data with respect to a particular reference point (usually the smallest possible value — e.g., zero for an attribute whose value is of type ratio). For example, consider the non-locational attribute weight and its corresponding index. Suppose that the database records correspond to individuals, and we want to find all individuals in the order of the closeness of their weight to that of John Smith whose weight is 150 pounds. The answer is computed by looking up the value 150 in the index and then proceeding in two directions along the index to get the nearest individuals by weight in constant time. We do not have to rebuild the index if we want to be able to answer the next query which deals with Sam Jones whose weight is 200 pounds.

In the case of more than one locational attribute all of whose values are of type distance, we wish to obtain a ranking of the records in terms of their distance from a particular value v of the locational attributes. If the index is explicit, then we cannot derive this ranking directly from the index for the locational attributes. As an example, we could have built an index on the basis of the distance of the records from a particular reference point P_1 using a given distance metric. However, if we want to obtain the records in order with respect to a new reference point P_2, we must resort them. In other words, we cannot simply say that their distance from P_2 is equal to the addition or subtraction of some constant equal to the distance from P_1 to P_2 depending on the relative position of the record with respect to P_1 and P_2, which is what is done when there is just one attribute (regardless of whether or not it is locational). Thus we have to rebuild the index, which is a costly process if we need to do it for each query. Thus, what is usually done is to use an implicit index such as the one discussed earlier that is based on sorting the objects with respect to the space that they occupy rather than with respect to each other or some fixed reference point.

Ranking queries are frequently used in spatial databases (e.g., in browsing applications). For example, we may wish to find all the houses in the database in the order of their distance from a point at location P. Often the desired ranking is partial. For example, we may wish to find the nearest city of population greater than 100,000 to Las Vegas. In this case, if we make use of the index on the locational attributes corresponding to the location of the cities, then we want to obtain the cities in the order of the cities' distance from Las Vegas. The population of the cities is examined in increasing order of their distance from Las Vegas. The process ceases once the condition on the value of the non-locational population attribute is satisfied. It should be clear that the query to find the closest city to Las Vegas is also a partial ranking query. Observe that the key to the utility of the ranking process is that if the closest record does not satisfy the query condition, then we can continue the search from where we computed the current answer. We do not restart the search again from reference point of the index.

In this paper we show how to respond to ranking queries in a spatial database when the spatial data is organized using an implicit index. There are a number of possible solutions depending on the nature of the implicit index. We present a general solution which is designed to minimize the number of blocks of the underlying decomposition that are examined. In order to be able to analyze its execution cost, we must have a concrete representation. We choose a representation that decomposes the objects so that the bounding boxes that contain them are disjoint. Moreover, we assume a regular decomposition such as that provided by the PMR quadtree [9]. Of course, other representations (e.g., the R^+-tree [15]) could also have been used as well as an implementation where the bounding boxes are not disjoint (e.g., an R-tree [6]). Our methods are equally applicable to these representations.

2 Data Structure

As we mentioned earlier, our algorithm was developed for the PMR quadtree but can be adapted to many other hierarchical spatial data structures that make use of what we term *container block*. This term is used here to denote an area in space which may itself be decomposed further on basis of the number or particular nature of the spatial objects that it contains. Examples of such structures include

R-trees [6], R$^+$-trees [15], and k-d-b-trees [10].

The PMR quadtree uses a regular decomposition of space to index spatial objects. Each quadtree block is a square, or a hypercube in higher dimensions. Leaf blocks contain the spatial objects (or pointers to them), whereas non-leaf blocks are decomposed into 2^d sub-blocks, where d is the number of dimensions. Fig. 1 presents an example two-dimensional PMR quadtree with a splitting threshold of one where the objects are points representing cities. The cities are inserted in the order Chicago, Mobile, Toronto, Buffalo, Denver, Omaha, Atlanta, Miami. The inherent definition of a quadtree is a representation that recursively decomposes space into congruent blocks until some condition is satisfied. The retrieval of the blocks that comprise the quadtree is facilitated using a number of different access structures [13]. The most common access structures are a tree having four sons at each level (see Fig. 1b) or a tree such as a B$^+$-tree [4] that is based on finding an ordering on the blocks. An example of such an ordering is that achieved by interleaving the bits comprising the binary representations of the x and y coordinates of the upper-left corners of each block. These numbers are then used as keys in the B$^+$-tree. We use the former implementation in the discussion of our algorithm, although it also works for the latter implementation.

PMR quadtrees differ from other quadtree variants in the way in which object insertions trigger decomposition of quadtree blocks. In particular, if, upon insertion of an object, the number of objects in a leaf block l intersected by the object exceeds a threshold value s (similar to a bucket capacity but not quite the same concept), then l is split once and the objects in l are reinserted into the new sub-blocks of l that they intersect. Note that the number of objects in a leaf block may exceed the threshold value. However, the number of objects in a leaf block at depth i is bounded by $s + i$, assuming there is no limit on the depth of the tree.

3   Overview of the Algorithm

We present a top-down solution. An alternative is to use a bottom-up solution. In this case, the algorithm locates the block b containing the query object q and then finds the nearest object o by examining the adjacent neighboring blocks of b in a clockwise order. Depending on the nature of the distance metric that is employed, we may have to examine blocks that are not immediately adjacent to b. This technique is termed *bottom-up* because we are obtaining the neighbors using neighbor-finding techniques [12] that do not restart the search at the root of the tree. In the case of a pointer-based (i.e., a tree) quadtree representation, they have been shown to visit a constant number of blocks for each neighbor-finding operation. This method could be very fast especially if o is in block b or one of the brothers of b. However, it may have to visit all of the blocks around the node [7]. Worse of all, if we need the next closest object, then we have to restart the search from the beginning rather than from where we last left off, making it unsuitable for ranking. In contrast, our algorithm can simply continue the search from the object it last found.

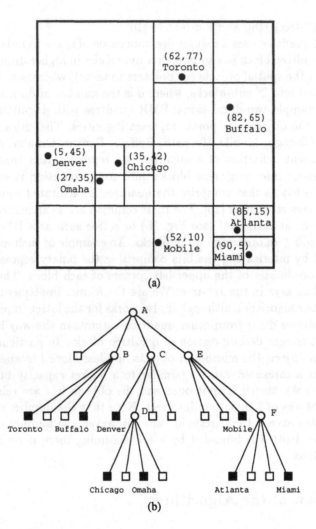

Fig. 1. A PMR quadtree representing points corresponding to cities. (a) The block decomposition induced by the quadtree, and (b) a tree access structure for the blocks in (a)

The key to the efficiency of the bottom-up method is that it works on the principle that if block b is empty, then the three siblings of b must contain at least $s+1$ objects or we would not have decomposed the space. This acts as a pruning device on the search. However, as we are interested in obtaining a ranking, we make use of the top-down method. First, we find leaf nodes containing q. We then use the recursion to keep track of what blocks have already been seen. Once we visit a leaf node, we also want to remember the objects that we have already encountered in the block which may still not yet be the closest ones. We achieve this by modifying the top-down algorithm to maintain a priority queue to record the blocks whose descendants have not been visited yet as well as the objects which have not yet been visited.

Using the top-down method, it is easy to find a leaf node containing q. Nevertheless, we need to be able to extend this technique to find the nearest object as the leaf may be empty or the other object in the leaf may be quite far from the query object. The problem here is that we have to unwind the recursion to find the nearest object. However, if we want to find the second nearest object, then the solution becomes even tougher. To resolve this problem, we replace the recursion stack where the next block to be examined is the block nearest to q with a priority queue. The key to our solution is that the objects are also stored in the priority queue. Once a leaf block b is encountered, we attempt to insert the objects stored in b into the priority queue. We can only insert an object o if it has not already been reported. This can be determined by checking if o's distance from the query object q is less than the distance of b from q. In this case, o was contained in a block c which was closer to q than b, and hence already processed earlier.

Observe that the data objects as well as the query objects can be of arbitrary type (e.g., points, rectangles, polygons, etc.). The only requirement is that there be a distance function between the query object type and the object type stored in the index (feature metric), and the query object type and the container block type (block metric). The two distance functions must be consistent with each other. Consistency means that for a feature f with a distance d from the query object q, there must exist a block b containing f such that the distance from b to q is less than or equal to d. This will hold if both distance functions are based on the same distance metric, of which some common examples are the Euclidean, Manhattan and Chessboard metrics. The consistency assumption also means that the distance from a query object to a block that contains it is zero.

The algorithm works for any dimension, although the examples we give are restricted to two dimensions. Also the query object need not be in the space of the dataset.

4 Algorithm

We first consider a regular recursive top-down traversal of the index to locate a leaf block containing a query object. Note that there could be more than one such block. The traversal is initiated with the root block as the second argument.

FINDLEAF($QueryObject$, $Block$)
1 **if** $QueryObject$ is in container block $Block$ **then**
2   **if** $Block$ is a leaf block **then**
3   Report leaf block $Block$
4   **else**
5   **for** each $Child$ block of container block $Block$ **do**
6   FINDLEAF($QueryObject$, $Child$)
7   **enddo**
8   **endif**
9 **endif**

The first task is to extend the algorithm to find the nearest object to the query object. In particular, once the leaf block containing the *QueryObject* has been found in line 3, we could start by examining the objects contained in that block. The object closest to the query object might reside in another quadtree block. Finding that block may in fact require unwinding the recursion to the top and descending again deeper into the tree. Furthermore, once that block has been found, it doesn't aid in finding the next nearest object.

To resolve this dilemma, we replace the recursion stack of the regular top-down traversal with a priority queue. In addition to using the priority queue for container blocks, objects are also put on the queue as leaf blocks are processed. The key used to order the elements on the queue is their distance from a query object. In order to distinguish between two elements at an equal distance from the query object, we adopt the convention that blocks are ordered before objects, while different objects are ordered according to some arbitrary (but unique) rule. This makes it possible to avoid reporting a particular object more than once, which is necessary when using a disjoint decomposition where an object may be associated with more than one block (e.g., PMR quadtree, R$^+$-tree).

A container block is not examined until it reaches the head of the queue. At this time, all blocks and objects closer to the query object have been looked at. Initially, the container block spanning the whole index space is the sole element in the priority queue. In subsequent steps, the element at the head of the queue (i.e., the closest element not yet examined) is retrieved until the queue has been emptied.

INCNEAREST(*QueryObject, SpatialIndex*)

```
1   Queue ← NEWPRIORITYQUEUE()
2   Block ← ROOTBLOCK(SpatialIndex)
3   ENQUEUE(Queue, DIST(Block, QueryObject), Block)
4   while not ISEMPTY(Queue) do
5     Element ← DEQUEUE(Queue)
6     if Element is a spatial object then
7       while Element = FIRST(Queue) do
8         DELETEFIRST(Queue)
9       enddo
10      Report Element
11    elsif Element is a leaf block then
12      for each Object in leaf block Element do
13        if DIST(Object, QueryObject) ≥ DIST(Element, QueryObject) then
14          ENQUEUE(Queue, DIST(Object, QueryObject), Object)
15        endif
16      enddo
17    else /* Element is a non-leaf container block */
18      for each Child block of container block Element in SpatialIndex do
19        ENQUEUE(Queue, DIST(Child, QueryObject), Child)
20      enddo
```

21   **endif**
22 **enddo**

Lines 1–3 initialize the quadtree. In line 10, the next closest object is reported. At that point, some other routine (such as a query processor) could take control, possibly resuming the algorithm at a later time to get the next closest object, or alternately terminate it if no more objects are desired.

Recall that for some representations, a spatial object may span several container blocks. The algorithm must thus guard against objects being reported more than once [2]. The test (i.e., the **if** statement) in line 13 ensures that objects that have already been reported are not put on the queue again. For this to work properly, blocks must be retrieved from the queue before spatial objects at the same distance. Otherwise, a feature may be retrieved from the queue before a block b containing it that is at the same or less distance from the query object. When the feature then is encountered again in block b, there is no way of knowing that it has already been reported. The loop in lines 7–9 eliminate duplicate instances of an object from the queue. By inducing an ordering on features that are at the same distance from the query object, all of the instances of an object will be clustered at the front of the queue when the first instance reaches the front. The reason we check for duplicates in this manner is that for many representations of a priority queue it is not efficient to test for membership. Thus, the removal of duplicates is largely a byproduct of the algorithm.

We now give an example to illustrate how the algorithm works. Consider the simple database given in Fig. 2a containing two-dimensional point data. Assuming a Euclidean distance metric, we want to "find the city closest to the point (65,62) which has a population of at least 1 million". In our scenario, a query processor interacts with our algorithm to retrieve cities in the order of their distance from the point. Note that the algorithm inserts a city c into the queue even if its population is not high enough to satisfy our query condition. The reason is that checking for the satisfaction of this condition would require a database access. Such an access might be unnecessary as c's distance from the query point may result in c not coming to the front of the queue by the time the algorithm terminates (i.e., by the time enough answers have been output).

Figure 2b shows a PMR quadtree with a splitting threshold value of 1 containing the points corresponding to the cities. Cities with a population of more than 1 million are denoted with solid dots and the query point is denoted with with an 'x'. Several concentric circles are drawn around the query point to make relative distances more obvious. Most of the leaf blocks are labelled with a number. In the description below, a PMR quadtree block is denoted by its depth and the label in its North-Westernmost descendant leaf block. The root block is thus denoted by 0/1 and its NE son by 1/2. The elements in the priority queue are listed within brackets in the order of their distance from the query point.

Initially, the queue contains only the root block, i.e., [0/1]. In the first step, the root block is retrieved from the queue, and as it is a non-leaf block, its sub-blocks are put on the queue: [1/2, 1/13, 1/1, 1/6]. Next, the block 1/2 is dequeued, and its sub-blocks enqueued: [2/4, 2/5, 1/13, 2/2, 1/1, 2/3, 1/6]. In

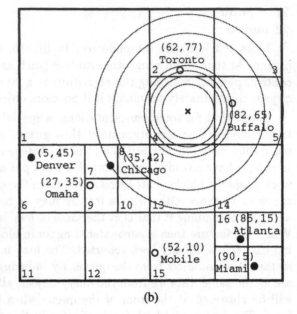

City	Pop.	Pos.
Atlanta	4,129	(85,15)
Buffalo	764	(82,65)
Chicago	6,532	(35,42)
Denver	1,381	(5,45)
Mobile	504	(52,10)
Omaha	416	(27,35)
Toronto	904	(62,77)
Miami	5,250	(90,5)

(a)　　　　　　　　　　(b)

Fig. 2. Example data set and nearest neighbor query

the next step, the leaf block 2/4 is dequeued, but it contains no objects. The leaf block 2/5, however, contains Buffalo, so Buffalo is inserted in the queue: [1/13, 2/2, 1/1, 2/3, Buffalo, 1/6]. In the next three steps, the sub-blocks of 1/13 are put on the queue, the leaf 2/13 is retrieved from the queue but contains no objects, and the city Toronto is enqueued as the leaf block 2/2 is processed: [1/1, Toronto, 2/14, 2/3, Buffalo, 1/6, 2/15, 2/16]. No action is taken as 1/1 is dequeued since it is empty, but Toronto is the first city to be reported to the query processor. The query processor discards it as it has a population less than 1 million and requests the next closest city. The top two elements on the queue, 2/14 and 2/3, are empty leaf blocks, so no action is taken. Next, Buffalo is reported to the query processor but its population is too low. At this point, the queue contains [1/6, 2/15, 2/16]. Now, 1/6 is taken off the queue and its sub-blocks enqueued, resulting in [2/7, 2/15, 2/16, 2/12, 2/6, 2/11]. The sub-blocks of 2/7 are then put on the queue, resulting in [3/8, 3/10, 3/7, 3/9, 2/15, 2/16, 2/12, 2/6, 2/11]. The blocks 3/8 and 3/10 are empty, but 3/7 contains Chicago, so it is put on the queue: [Chicago, 3/9, 2/15, 2/16, 2/12, 2/6, 2/11]. Finally, Chicago is reported to the query processor, which terminates the search and returns Chicago as the result of the query.

5　Analysis

Our solution to the problem of finding the nearest object is not more efficient than other known methods [3, 7]. However, it is more general in several respects.

The algorithm presented in [3] only works with point data and relies on a specialized data structure to achieve optimality in execution time for approximate nearest neighbor queries. This structure is static and must be rebuilt if more points are introduced. In addition, it is not amenable to practical implementation. Thus the authors implemented a greatly simplified data structure (thereby sacrificing the optimality guarantee of their algorithm while still yielding an approximate answer) that resembles k-d trees, and also use a priority queue in the query process. In contrast, our algorithm can be used for arbitrary data objects as well as a large class of spatial indices. Of course, its level of efficiency may depend on the type of spatial index used. The main advantage of our method compared to the one proposed in [7] is that the latter can not be efficiently used to find several of the nearest objects, only the nearest. Also, that method relies on a quadtree-like decomposition. The algorithm presented in [11] is limited to points as query objects and the R-tree as spatial index, although it may possibly be extended to work for a wider class of query objects and spatial indices.

The algorithm that we presented can be used to find the k nearest neighbors to a query object. However, in our case, the k is not fixed a-priory. This is in contrast with the algorithm in [11] for finding k nearest neighbors. In particular, once it has computed the k nearest neighbors, if the $k+1^{st}$ nearest neighbor is desired, then the algorithm must be restarted anew.

The analysis below, although incomplete, gives an indication of the worst-case behavior of the algorithm. Various simplifications are made to ease the task. First, we assume that calculating the distance metric takes a constant amount of time. This is true for simple objects such as points and lines, but may not be true for more complex ones (e.g., polygons).

Second, the spatial index is assumed to have some of the properties of the PMR quadtree. Suppose that there are N objects. For some object types (e.g., points, lines) it can be shown that under certain assumptions on the data distribution and the tree depth, the number of blocks in a PMR quadtree is proportional to N [8]. We also assume that the objects in question are already stored in a spatial index and ignore the cost of the preprocessing needed to build the index.

In order to complete our analysis of the space requirements of the algorithm, we need to know the maximum size of the priority queue. Let us consider the queue at an arbitrary time during the execution of the algorithm, and let d be the distance from the object at the head of the queue to the query object. All of the objects in the queue are at a distance of at least d from the query object and are contained in blocks at a distance of at most d from the query object (these are blocks that have been retrieved from the queue and processed). A worst-case scenario is such that all leaf blocks containing objects are closer to the query object than is the nearest object. In this case, all objects will be inserted into the queue before the nearest one is found. This gives a worst-case bound of $O(N)$ on the size of the queue. However, this is a pathological case, which is unlikely to arise. In practice, the maximum size of the queue is much smaller.

If all the objects need to be ranked by their distance from the query object, then the execution time of the algorithm is at worst $O(N \log M)$ where N is the number of leaf blocks in the spatial index and M is the maximum number of items in the priority queue. This assumes a priority queue implementation where update operations take $O(\log M)$ time. As discussed above, M is $O(N)$ in the worst case, which gives a bound of $O(N \log N)$. This compares favorably with one-dimensional sorting algorithms.

An alternative solution for ranking all the objects is to compute the distance for all of them from the query object and then to sort them using a conventional sorting technique. The cost of this is $O(N \log N)$ where N is the number of objects. In contrast, our ranking algorithm has the advantage that it doesn't have to retrieve all of the objects at once. It is dynamic. Also, we can achieve a better result than $O(N \log N)$ in practice as often we don't sort on the objects; instead, we sort on the container blocks. This is quite important when executing in a disk-based environment as the inspection of a container blocks often does not require us to examine their contents which may require a disk access.

In our ranking algorithm, container blocks are inserted in the priority queue even though they may be empty leaf blocks. We could examine blocks before putting them on the queue and just insert the non-empty ones. The problem here is that if we were executing in a disk-based system, then we would require a disk access every time we check if a container is empty. In contrast, when we insert all the blocks into the priority queue without regard to their contents, we may not have to look at many of them as they may get pruned from the search by virtue of their distance from the query object (i.e., if the search is terminated after finding an object closer to the query object). However, if we want a ranking of all of the objects, then it may be advantageous to inspect blocks before putting them on the queue, since then fewer priority queue operations are needed in addition to the queue being smaller.

For a partial ranking of the objects, our algorithm visits a minimal number of container blocks in the sense that given that the kth nearest neighbor is at a distance of d_k from the query object q, only the container blocks that lie completely or in part within d_k of q have had their contents examined by the time the k nearest neighbors have been found. However, note that all of the container blocks could be within d_k of q, regardless of the value of k. Thus the worst-case execution time is the same as for finding a total ranking, $O(N \log N)$.

6 Conclusion

The algorithm presented in this paper was designed to work in the SAND [1] spatial database environment, where a PMR quadtree is used as the underlying spatial index. However, the algorithm is not limited to a PMR quadtree. It should work (with minor modifications) for a wide class of spatial indices, that includes R-tree variants and k-d-b-trees. We have already successfully adapted the algorithm to work with an R*-tree index. The basic requirement that a spatial index must satisfy for the algorithm to be useful is that the spatial index decomposes space into blocks that are organized hierarchically in a tree-like fashion. Of course, much of our analysis of the execution time of the algorithm depends on characteristics of the PMR quadtree, and may change for other spatial data structures.

References

1. W. G. Aref and H. Samet. Extending a DBMS with spatial operations. In O. Günther and H. J. Schek, editors, *Advances in Spatial Databases - 2nd Symposium, SSD'91*, pages 299–318, Berlin, 1991. Springer-Verlag. (also Lecture Notes in Computer Science 525).

2. W. G. Aref and H. Samet. Uniquely reporting spatial objects: yet another operation for comparing spatial data structures. In *Proceedings of the Fifth International Symposium on Spatial Data Handling*, pages 178–189, Charleston, South Carolina, August 1992.

3. S. Arya, D. M. Mount, N. S. Netanyahu, R. Silverman, and A. Wu. An optimal algorithm for approximate nearest neighbor searching. In *Proceedings of the Fifth Annual ACM-SIAM Symposium on Discrete Algorithms*, pages 573–582, Arlington, VA., January 1994.

4. D. Comer. The ubiquitous B–tree. *ACM Computing Surveys*, 11(2):121–137, June 1979.

5. L. M. Goldschlager. Short algorithms for space-filling curves. *Software - Practice and Experience*, 11(1):99, January 1981.

6. A. Guttman. R–trees: a dynamic index structure for spatial searching. In *Proceedings of the SIGMOD Conference*, pages 47–57, Boston, June 1984.

7. E. G. Hoel and H. Samet. Efficient processing of spatial queries in line segment databases. In O. Günther and H. J. Schek, editors, *Advances in Spatial Databases - 2nd Symposium, SSD'91*, pages 237–256. Springer-Verlag, Berlin, 1991. (also Lecture Notes in Computer Science 525).

8. M. Lindenbaum and H. Samet. A probabilistic analysis of trie-based sorting of large collections of line segments. Department of Computer Science CS-TR-3455, University of Maryland, College Park, MD, April 1995.

9. R. C. Nelson and H. Samet. A population analysis for hierarchical data structures. In *Proceedings of the SIGMOD Conference*, pages 270–277, San Francisco, May 1987.

10. J. T. Robinson. The *k-d-b*-tree: a search structure for large multidimensional dynamic indexes. In *Proceedings of the SIGMOD Conference*, pages 10–18, Ann Arbor, MI, April 1981.

11. N. Roussopoulos, S. Kelley, and F. Vincent. Nearest neighbor queries. In *Proceedings of the 1995 ACM SIGMOD International Conference on Management of Data*, pages 71–79, San Jose, CA, May 1995.

12. H. Samet. Neighbor finding techniques for images represented by quadtrees. *Computer Graphics and Image Processing*, 18(1):37–57, January 1982.

13. H. Samet. *Applications of Spatial Data Structures: Computer Graphics, Image Processing, and GIS*. Addison-Wesley, Reading, MA, 1990.

14. H. Samet. *The Design and Analysis of Spatial Data Structures*. Addison-Wesley, Reading, MA, 1990.

15. M. Stonebraker, T. Sellis, and E. Hanson. An analysis of rule indexing implementations in data base systems. In *Proceedings of the First International Conference on Expert Database Systems*, pages 353–364, Charleston, SC, April 1986.

Optimal Redundancy in Spatial Database Systems

Volker Gaede

Institut für Wirtschaftsinformatik

Humboldt-Universität zu Berlin

Spandauer Str. 1

10178 Berlin, Germany

gaede@wiwi.hu-berlin.de

Abstract

In spatial database systems rectangles are commonly used to approximate real spatial data. A technique that approximates extended objects with a *collection* of rectangles is the *z-ordering* method. Since each of these rectangles eventually corresponds to an entry in a spatial index, the object may be referenced several times. This *redundancy* effect is controllable. In this paper, we present an empirically derived formula to assess the expected redundancy for the z-ordering approximation technique given some simple parameters. After showing the applicability of this formula to a large class of different object geometries, we make use of this result to determine the optimal redundancy for real spatial data by means of theoretical considerations. In order to verify our theoretical results, we conducted several experiments using real spatial data and found a good correspondence.

1 Introduction

Spatial indexing or spatial access methods have found great attention in recent years, culminating in numerous different approaches. Among those approaches one can roughly distinguish between two different classes of techniques. First, those techniques based on the approximation (parameterization) of the original object and second, those dealing with the original geometry. Well-known examples for the first class include the R-tree (Guttman 1984), the grid file (Nievergelt, Hinterberger, and Sevcik 1984), the R^+-tree (Sellis, Roussopoulos, and Faloutsos 1987), and the R^*-tree (Beckmann, Kriegel, Schneider, and Seeger 1990). An example of the second class is the cell tree (Günther 1988). The techniques in the second class have primarily been invented to overcome the major drawback of the former, which is the introduction of additional space (*dead space*), i.e., the artificial augmentation of the geometry.

For approximation schemes one obtains a two-step strategy for query processing:

1. **Filter step:** By using a spatial access method based on approximated geometries, one obtains a set of candidate objects. With this step one eliminates most objects that do not satisfy the query, but usually includes some false hits.

2. **Refinement step:** To identify false hits in the candidate set, it is necessary to fetch the qualifying objects into main memory and perform a (computationally expensive) test on the actual geometry.

The larger the dead space, the less selective is the filter step. Techniques, such as *z-ordering* (cf. for example (Orenstein and Merrett 1984)), which use multiple rectangles (*z-regions*) for the approximation, can achieve a better approximation than a single rectangle. For z-ordering a global underlying grid determines the shape and position of these rectangles. As a consequence of the fixed grid, each z-region can be labelled with a a unique identifier (*z-value*), which eventually corresponds to an index entry. These z-values are organized in a point (single key) index structure such as a B^+-tree (Comer 1979). In the remainder of this text, we will use the terms z-region and z-value interchangeable.

The fact that one object usually corresponds to multiple rectangles (index entries) is called *redundancy*. As Orenstein (1989a) pointed out, there are two possibly conflicting objectives: On the one hand, a detailed approximation induces a substantial amount of redundacy and leads to a large index, but less false hits in the filter step. On the other hand, using too few z-regions causes poor approximation of the object, i.e., a less selective filtering step. Thus numerous false hits are fetched into main memory and tested against the (possibly expensive) predicate.

As Orenstein shows, there is an optimum between those opposite aims. Unfortunately, he fails to report an analytical and generalizable guideline for the choice of the optimal parameters, to be used for more general settings.

Since z-ordering allows to control redundancy, it is important to have a limit when to stop approximating. Orenstein (1989b) identifies the following limits:

1. **error-bound:** If a certain fixed accuracy (e.g., distance between object boundary and approximating geometry) is reached, stop.

2. **size-bound:** Use a given maximum number of z-regions to approximate it.

3. **granularity-bound** (precise): Approximate each object until a certain finest granularity (maximum number of decompositions or maximal resolution) is achieved.

Note that the granularity-bound strategy is the limiting case of the others. For the second item the number of index entries (z-values) is predetermined, whereas for the first and the third item the answer is not obvious. In the following, we will provide a formula to assess the redundancy associated with the granularity-bound approach. However, the presented results generalize to the error-bound technique as long as the data is homogeneous (that is, about the same size and shape). The paper is organized as follows. In Section 2 we give a more detailed introduction to z-ordering. After discussing several aspects of this technique, we will provide a formula to predict the number of expected index entries given some parameters. This formula is shown to be applicable to a broad range of different scenarios. These results are used in Section 3 to determine theoretically the optimal granularity for intersection queries. Likewise in this section practical results are reported. Section 4 summarizes our results.

2 Z-Ordering

The z-ordering technique is based on a simple but efficient technique for approximating a given object. Starting from a fixed world size, the world is decomposed by dividing it recursively into two halves along a certain axis (more generally, hyperplane). Every time this is done, a test for intersection with the given object is conducted. If there is an intersection, the object is split by this hyperplane and one proceeds with the two pieces and the next axis. This implies that the axes have to be visited in fixed order. If there is no intersection, one tests where the object is located relative to the hyperplane and proceeds with the subspace where the object is to be found and the next axis. This process is recursively repeated until a termination criterion (granularity, error, ...) is met. The procedure how to decompose a given object into a number of z-regions is shown in Figure 1.

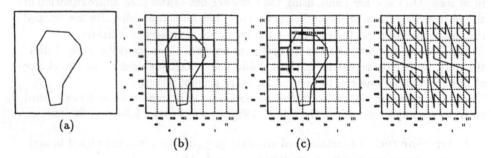

Figure 1: Figure (a) shows the polygon to be approximated. The frame represents the "world size". After the decomposition starting with the x-axis we obtain Figure (b). The object is approximated by 9 rectangles of different sizes. Finally, in Figure (c) each z-region is labelled with the corresponding z-value.

Figure 2: Peano-enumeration of the cells for the finest granularity.

The maximum number of decomposition steps is called *granularity*. For each granularity i one obtains a tiled decomposition of the plane (in the 2-dimensional case). Depending on the granularity i these tiles have different sizes and shapes.

The enumeration of the tiles is done according to the Peano curve as shown in Figure 2. The tags for the rectangles can also be obtained by bit-interleaving the corresponding bit-sequences z_x, z_y of the respective axes. As an example, consider $(z_x, z_y) = (01, 0) = 001_z$.

Definition 1 (01-representation, granularity) *A z-value z is in* 01-**represen-tation** *iff it is composed of a sequence of 0's and 1's. We further call the total number of 0's and 1's the* z-**value length***, denoted by zlen or $|z|$. The maximum length $|z|_{\max}$ is called* **granularity***.*

Definition 2 (Hull) *Given a z-value z in* 01-*representation, we call all z-values z' prefixed by z the* **lower hull***. Similarly, all z-values z' prefixing z are called the* **upper hull***. The union of the lower and the upper hull is termed* **hull** *for z. The procedure of computing all z-values is called a* **closure***. The lower hull is denoted by $\underline{z}$, the upper hull $\overline{z}$, and the hull closure z^+.*

This definition generalizes easily to sets of z-values by applying the definition to each element of this set.

As an example, 001 is in the lower hull of 00. Vice versa 00 is in the upper hull of 001. The upper hull for $z = 001$ is $\overline{z} = \{0, 00\}$. Z-ordering is *conservative*; this means that the object is guaranteed to be enclosed in the confining z-regions. If the z-value of a given region prefixes another z-value, then the former region encloses the latter; for instance, the region with the z-value 00 encloses 001 and 000. From this discussion it becomes clear that zeros are significant.

Incentives for the use of z-ordering in spatial database systems technique include: (i) it can be integrated easily into today's commercial database systems (relational or object-oriented) since z-values can be represented as integers; (ii) it is possible to control redundancy; (iii) it is easy to implement and to maintain; (iiii) it can be extended easily to higher dimensions. In (Gaede and Riekert 1994) a formal model of query processing using z-ordering along with its implementation on top of an object-oriented database system is presented.

2.1 Fractal Z-Ordering Dimension

In order to determine the optimal granularity (redundancy), it is important to pre-dict the expected number of z-regions resulting from the approximation. To find a good estimate for the expected number of z-values generated during the approxi-mation, it is necessary to understand some peculiarities of the z-ordering approxi-mation. In case of the granularity-bound technique, the approximation stops under two conditions: Either further decomposition does not improve the approximation (e.g., the borderlines of the object are aligned with the underlying grid) or the final granularity is reached.

An example of the first case, where the boundaries are aligned with the z-ordering grid, is depicted in Figure 3 a. In this case the approximation returns two z-regions which are exactly congruent with the given object and independent of the granularity. In Figure 3 b the rectangle has been slightly tilted. Albeit its is not perceptible, this approximation (using the same granularity $g = 16$) resulted in 122 z-values instead of 2.

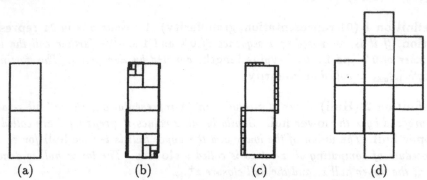

(a)　　　　　　(b)　　　　　　(c)　　　　　　(d)

Figure 3: Figure (a) shows a rectangle that is exactly aligned with the underlying grid, (number of z-values $|Z| = 2$). Figure (b) shows the same rectangle turned by 4 degrees ($g = 122$)). Figures (c) and (d) depict the approximation for a granularity of $g = 12$ ($|Z| = 30$) and $g = 6$ ($|Z| = 8$).

This large difference seems surprising and one might think that a reasonably good prediction of the expected number of z-values is not possible. However, according to our experience, it is a rare case, that the given object is congruent with the underlying grid structure and was actually never observed while working with real cartographic data. Nevertheless, this case cannot be ruled out, since especially maps containing human made objects (build-up areas, roads, ...) tend to have rectangular shapes. Another source of such rectangular objects could be for example a convex decomposition of a map.

Figures 3 c and 3 d illustrate the approximation for varying granularities for the slightly turned rectangle. Figure 3 c shows the approximation for the granularity $g = 12$ which seems to be a reasonable compromise between the number of z-values and the achieved approximation. On the other hand, the approximation depicted in Figure 3 d for $g = 6$ is poor. In fact, the area covered by the z-regions is 3 times the area of the object at hand. Thus, the dead space is greater than the object area, which would in turn lead to a poor selectivity of the filter step. Note that a bounding box approximation does a better job. Note also that the size of the z-regions in the interior of the object are independent of the granularity; only z-regions touching the boundaries are split for finer granularities

Besides the number of generated z-regions, the quality of the approximation is also of interest. As a measure, we use the ratio of polygon area to z-region area and refer to it as *load factor* Q. Figures 4 and 5 exemplify clearly the dichotomy of our objectives, where the Q and Z are shown for different granularities. On the one hand, to achieve a load factor of 0.9 (about 10 % dead space), a granularity of

13 is necessary. On the other hand, this granularity implies that we obtain more than 50 z-values (index entries). This is at least five times the number of z-values we obtain for $g = 7$, which corresponds to $Q = 0.4$ (60 % dead space). For the sake of discussion, we introduce the abbreviations listed in Table 1.

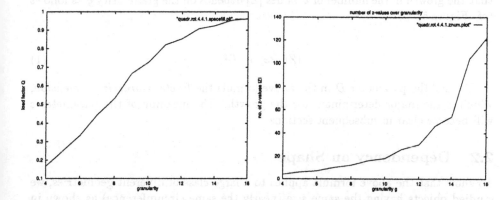

Figure 4: Load factor over granularity for the tilted rectangle.

Figure 5: The exponential growth of $|Z|$ over g for the tilted rectangle.

N	number of objects in the database
D	fractal z-ordering dimension
g	granularity (maximal z-value length)
$\zeta(g)$	number of index entries
μ_X	average number of objects per page (later introduced)
μ_ζ	average number of index entries per page (later introduced)
h	height of the B^+- tree (later introduced)
$|z|$	length of the z-value z
$|Z|$	cardinality of the z-value set Z
$\hbar_i$	minimal extension in direction i (later introduced)
$\eta \geq 1$	clustering factor (later introduced)
P	page size

Table 1: List of abbreviations used in the remainder of this text.

While looking at the number of z-values generated during the approximation process, we notice that the growth of z-values is exponential. This is a well-known phenomenon in the area of fractals (Mandelbrot 1983). A common example in this area is the computation of the length of a shoreline. The better the resolution of the map, the longer will be the shoreline, since one has to account for every new visible creek for higher resolutions. Eventually, for infinite resolution one obtains the paradoxon that the shoreline is infinitely long. The growth is determined by an object-specific fractal dimension D. This dimension D needs not to be unique to the object but offers a chance to classify objects. Mandelbrot (1983) provides a good survey on this topic and the results.

But how does this relate to our problem? In the following, we will demonstrate that the growth in the number of z-values $|Z|$ depends on the granularity g as follows (cf. Figure 5)

$$|Z| \approx c \cdot D^g \tag{1}$$

We call the parameter D in the above formula the *fractal z-ordering dimension*, which is the major determinant for the growth. The meaning of the parameter c will become clear in subsequent sections.

2.2 Dependency on Shape

To show that the above formula applies to a large class of different geometries, we studied objects having the same size (nearly the same circumference) as shown in Figure 6. Although the graphs in Figure 7 display some variation depending on the object geometry, they are all nearly linear on a logarithmic scale. To determine the fractal z-ordering dimension D for the objects, they have to be approximated for varying granularities g. Next, for the logarithm of $|Z|$ a linear regression analysis is conducted to determine D. Based on our experiments, the regression analysis for various extended geometries yields slopes between 0.25 and 0.44 which corresponds to a fractal z-ordering dimension D of 1.28 to 1.56.

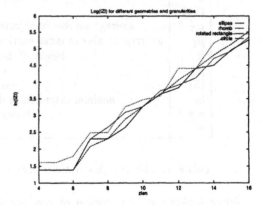

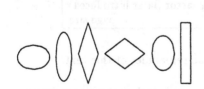

D=1.43   D=1.41   D=1.34   D=1.39   D=1.42   D=1.36

Figure 6: Different geometries and their fractal z-ordering dimension D.

Figure 7: Logarithm of the number of z-values for different geometries and different approximations.

The above geometries are quite compact, in the sense that the breadth is about the order of the height. Since long, narrow (line like) geometries (Figure 8), which are not parallel to the axes, are expected to yield more z-values, we further investigated these geometries. Although the long narrow rectangle (R_l) has the same area as the short, compact one (R_s), the approximation of R_l resulted in more than 20 z-values, whereas for R_s only 8 z-values were generated. Nevertheless, even for R_s and R_l we found our assumption confirmed.

To establish these results further, we investigated cartographic objects as the one depicted in Figure 9. The regression analysis of this object (Figure 10) yields a fractal z-ordering dimension $D = 1.47$. A repetition of the above test suite for this and other regions validated the fractal z-ordering observation.

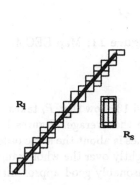

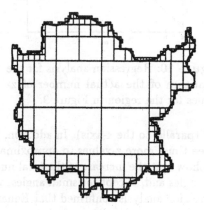

Figure 8: The investigated rectangles R_l $(D = 1.41)$ and R_s $(D = 1.36)$ of the same size and their approximation for different degrees of rotation.

Figure 9: Middle Franconia $(D = 1.47)$.

2.3 Dependency on Orientation

The next question to be answered is the dependency on the orientation relative to the conceptual grid. For this purpose, we rotated various geometries while approximating them for varying granularities. With the rotation of the rectangles R_s and R_l, the number of z-values generated increases as shown in Figure 12 and 13. It should be pointed out that the dependency on the rotation is different for different granularities. Consider, for example, Figure 12 where $|Z|$ increases for the granularity $g = 16$ depending on the rotation, but for $g = 15$ there is nearly no dependency. Besides this, the plot of the long narrow rectangle (Figure 12) is smoother than the one for R_s depicted in Figure 13. This illustrates the stronger dependency of $|Z|$ for objects spanning only a small number of z-regions on the orientation. However, due to the nature of the decomposition applied by z-ordering, geometries extending along the y-axis need less z-regions than geometries along the x-axis. This increase is reflected by the slight increase starting at $0°$ degrees (i.e., parallel to the y-axis) to

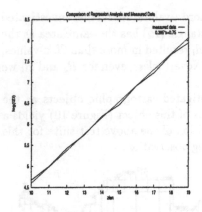

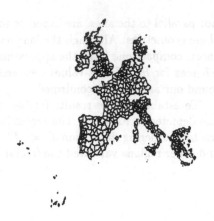

Figure 10: Regression analysis for the logarithm of the actual number of z-values for the region in Figure 9.

Figure 11: Map EEC 4.

90° (parallel to the x-axis). In addition, Figures 12 and 13 show that R_l takes about three times more z-values to approximate than R_s on the average. Figures 12 and 13 show that the increase of the total number of z-values is about the same order for all angles and, except for small angles, varies only slightly over the whole range. A regression analysis confirmed that Equation 1 is a reasonably good approximation.

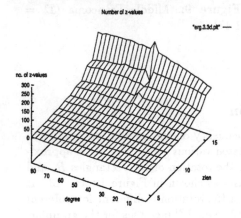

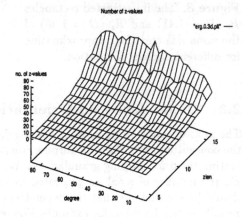

Figure 12: Number of generated z-values for the long narrow rectangle R_l for different rotations and granularities.

Figure 13: Number of generated z-values for the short compact rectangle R_s for different rotations and granularities.

Real geographic objects show almost *no dependency on the orientation*, since different orientations of the borderline segments level each other off during the rotation.

Without providing experimental evidence, we note that $|Z|$ is generally *independent of the location* of the object. So far, the investigated objects had about the same size relative to the world they are embedded in. In the next section, we will investigate the dependency on the size (more strictly, the perimeter) of the object.

2.4 Dependency on Perimeter

Apart from the shape of the object, the perimeter or, more general, the surface of the object is also a determinant. Equation 1 does not allow for this factor. To determine the dependency on the perimeter, we increased the perimeter of the object with constant world size (thus constant world perimeter) and vice versa. Figure 14 shows rhombuses with doubling perimeters. Notice that the interior of the rhombuses is covered with large z-regions, whereas the smaller ones are at the borderlines. Consequently, there are two diametrical effects: large objects having a long boundary need numerous rectangles to approximate it. On the other hand, large objects can accommodate large z-regions in the interior, thus result in less z-values.

Figure 15 suggest a linear dependency between the number of z-values and perimeter for the rhombuses shown in Figure 14. The x-axis is rescaled by the constant world perimeter to guarantee an invariant representation for different ratios of perimeter and world size.

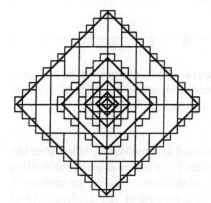

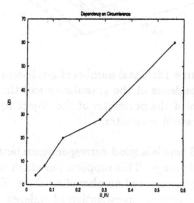

Figure 14: Different rhombuses and their z-value approximation. The perimeter doubles from one rhombus to the next.

Figure 15: The total number of z-values for the rhombuses of Figure 14 over the corresponding perimeters with constant world size.

Since this observation is not restricted to the reported results, but also applies to a broader range of geometries, we conclude that the *perimeter* is yet another determinant for the number of z-values. To take account of this fact, we modify Equation 1 by setting the constant c to $c_i \cdot \frac{U_i}{U}$ with U_i being the perimeter of the object, U the perimeter of the world, and c_i an object constant. Finally, we get

$$|Z| \approx c_i \cdot \frac{U_i}{U} \cdot D^g = \tilde{U} \cdot D^g \qquad (2)$$

To show that Equation 2 enables us to predict the expected number of z-values, we applied this formula to the region shown in Figure 9. Figure 16 shows the three-dimensional plot of the resulting z-values in dependence of the ratio of the perimeters $\frac{U_i}{U}$ and the granularity (zlen) for Equation 2. For reasons of presentation we did not plot the measured data graph. This, however, is done for varying $\frac{U_i}{U}$ and three granularities in Figure 17. In this figure, Equation 2 has been used to predict the expected number of z-values for the region depicted in Figure 9 given the ratio $\frac{U_i}{U}$ and the maximal granularity. As mentioned before, the fractal dimension of this object is $D = 1.47$.

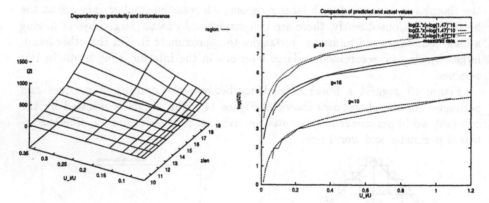

Figure 16: Total number of z-values in dependence of the granularity and the ratio of the perimeter of the object to the world perimeter.

Figure 17: Comparison of the predicted and actual number of z-values for the region of Figure 9.

There is a good correspondence between predicted and measured values over the whole range. This supports our claim that Equation 2 is a reasonable approximation for the expected number of z-values. To further establish our results, we undertook an extensive investigation of different objects and confirmed the applicability of Equation 2 for a large number of different geometries.

2.5 Generalization to Multiple Objects

The discussion so far is restricted to one object. For real geographic applications, where we have to deal with a multitude of heterogeneous objects, one might ask whether Equation 2 is still valid. In the remainder of this section, we shall show that Formula 3 is a good approximation for sets of objects:

$$|Z(g)| \approx \tilde{U} \cdot D^g \cdot N \qquad (3)$$

Here, $\tilde{U}$ can be interpreted as the characteristic perimeter ratio (it is no more a single perimeter we have to allow for) and N is the number of objects in the set. To confirm this formula, we undertook experiments with maps from the European Union (EEC 1990) (Figure 11) and from Africa (Gorny and Carter 1987). A detailed investigation of the used data along with several data parameters can be found in (Schiwietz 1993) (to a lesser extent (Schiwietz and Kriegel 1993)). As the reported parameters of map EEC 4 in Table 3 on page 17 show, the investigated objects *are inhomogeneous* and differ widely in shape.

Due to lack of space, we can not report other results. To make a long story short, we confirmed in our experiments Formula 3, i.e., sets of objects scale like single objects. For the map EEC 4, we obtained for example:

$$|Z(g)| = 0.0114 \cdot 1.499^g \cdot N$$

Figure 19 compares the measured and predicted number of index entries for the map EEC 4 and clearly reflects the exponential growth. Note for $g = 22$ we get 80,000 index entries for slightly more than 800 objects!

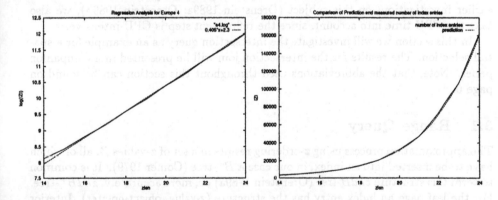

Figure 18: Regression analysis for the map EEC 4.

Figure 19: Comparison of the prediction and the measured data for the map EEC 4.

In summary, we found in the preceding sections that it is possible to provide a fractal z-ordering dimension D which applies for a wide variety of different geometries. By using D we can predict the expected number of z-regions generated during the z-ordering decomposition for a bound granularity g. It further generalizes to sets of objects by multiplying with the number of objects.

Albeit this an interesting observation on its own, the question is justified what this is all good for. In the following, we will show how the results presented so far can be utilized to determine the optimal redundancy. Before doing so, we have to make several comments on how to obtain the correct parameters for Equation 3. As long as there is no classification of the objects at hand, i.e., D and $\tilde{U}$ are unknown, there is no way around approximating the objects for different granularities. By fitting the obtained values $Z(g)$ to Equation 3, one can determine $\tilde{U}$ and D. This is the preferred method in any case. If D is known, one has to find a good choice for $\tilde{U}$. A good initial choice for $\tilde{U}$ is hard to find, although $\frac{\overline{U}}{2 \cdot U}$ represents a reasonable choice (with $\overline{U}$ denoting the arithmetic average of the perimeters). On the average, the maps contain a smaller number of big objects than small ones, thus $\tilde{U}$ is composed of the weighted average perimeter of the objects. Moreover, we found that $D = 1.5$ is a fairly good choice to determine an upper bound for our data.

3   Analysis of the Redundancy Problem

With the ideas presented so far, it is possible to address our initial problem, the determination of the optimal granularity. This will be done in two ways: First, we provide a model based on theoretical considerations and second, we will show that this model is suitable to predict a close to optimal granularity. In contrast to several earlier investigations on this subject (Orenstein 1989a; Orenstein 1989b), we also take the CPU time into account, since the refinement step is CPU-intensive.

In this section we will investigate the intersection query as an example for a spatial selection. The results for the intersection join will be presented in a companion paper. Note, that the abbreviations used throughout this section can be found on page 6.

3.1   Range Query

The approximation process using z-ordering results in a set of z-values Z, all of which have to be inserted into an index, in our case a B^+-tree (Comer 1979). It is common to term this structure $zkdB$-tree (Orenstein 1989a) or, more accurately, $zkdB^+$-tree. For the leaf page an index entry has the structure (z-value, object-pointer). Interior nodes are organized in the usual way (z-value, page-pointer). Before we proceed, we want to restate our problem. In short, for fine granularities we expect a large number of z-values, all of which representing an index entry, hence a large index is expected. A large index causes a lot of page faults during traversal, but only a few number of false hits have to be loaded for postprocessing on the actual geometry. On the other hand, if the objects are poorly approximated, the filter step (i.e., index traversal) is cheap, but the postprocessing step is expensive.

For our considerations, we assume that one object (more generally search region) is given and we want to retrieve all intersecting objects in the database. This kind of query is called an *intersection query* or *range query*. We further assume a fixed granularity g for the complete database. A given object is decomposed on the average into $\tilde{U} \cdot D^g$ z-values.

In case of an intersection query, the procedure to find matching objects is as follows: First, the given geometry is decomposed into a number of z-values and all relevant z-values are generated (i.e., compute a hull closure). Next, for each resulting z-value an index look-up is performed to find the matching object references (C_{ind}). In order to eliminate duplicates, the object references are hashed into a table (C_{hash}). To guarantee optimal page scheduling while loading the actual geometries (C_{geo}), the object identifiers have to be sorted by their corresponding page numbers. Finally, each loaded object is tested against the search region for intersection (C_{int}).

In our consideration, we assume that the object is already decomposed into a set of z-regions and all relevant (i.e., all possible z-regions which can contribute to the result) z-values are generated. Thus, the performance of the above algorithm is mostly dominated by I/O-costs and the intersection test. Consequently, the cost formula consists of the following four terms

$$C = C_{ind} + C_{hash} + C_{geo} + C_{int}$$

The number of index entries $\zeta(g)$ depends on the granularity as follows:

$$\zeta(g) = \tilde{U} \cdot D^g \cdot N$$

In the above formula $\tilde{U}$ denotes the perimeter obtained from the regression analysis. As an index we assume B^+-tree with height h of

$$h = \log_{\mu_\zeta}(\zeta(g)) = \log_{\mu_\zeta}(\tilde{U} D^g \cdot N)$$

with an average number of index entries per interior node of μ_ζ.

The finest resolution $\hbar_i$ along axis i with a maximal extension Δ_i (e.g., $\Delta_x = \max(x) - \min(x)$) for two dimensions is given by

$$\hbar_i = \frac{\Delta i}{2^{g/2}}$$

The approximation of the search region by various z-regions expands the search space. This expansion is again determined by the granularity g. For instance, the area of a given rectangle (not congruous with the grid) with width a and height b is increased at worst to

$$\Sigma(g) = (a + 2.25 \cdot \hbar_x) \cdot (b + 2.25 \cdot \hbar_y) = a \cdot b + 2.25(\hbar_y a + \hbar_x b) + (2.25^2 \cdot \hbar_x \hbar_y) = a \cdot b + \Gamma(g)$$

The factor 2.25 results from the consideration that we have to take account for this enlargement effect twice for each axis and that z-regions not having the minimal resolution $\hbar_i$ along dimension i also contribute (0.25). Thus, $\Gamma(y)$ is a guideline for the expected dead space. The slope of the above function is steeper than the one shown in Figure 4. So we assume a better adaption behaviour in the beginning. Assuming the same granularity for the searched region and the objects in the database, we have to allow for Γ twice (factor two in the equation below). We find for the percentage T^* of the search space covered by the z-regions:

$$T^* = \frac{a \cdot b}{\Delta X \cdot \Delta Y} + 2 \cdot \frac{\Gamma(g)}{\Delta X \cdot \Delta Y}$$

T is the percentage of the world covered by the region. We assume in our calculation that T^* is proportional to the number of loaded objects. Depending on the ratio between searched region and dead space the second part of the above formula can incur substantial costs as a result of dead space.

Assuming that for the search region, Equation 2 is also valid and that the ratio of perimeters is denoted by $\tilde{U}'$, we have to search for $\tilde{U}'D^g$ z-values. This is already a simplification, since during the hull closure more z-values are generated than the above equation reflects. We can avoid computing some of these superfluous z-values by keeping track of the z-value with the shortest length $|z|_{min}$. This prevents the generation of z-values for non-existing lengths. The effect of the remaining z-values can be compensated by sorting them. This simple means enables one to process several keys during a single look-up, since it is possible to exploit the locality principle by acting upon several entries placed on a single loaded page, what in turn decreases the expected number of index look-ups. In practice, it is quite common to achieve substantial savings by doing so.

The number of page accesses to find k records on m pages with n records using a B$^+$-tree with height h is given by (Yao 1977)

$$I_b(h, k, m, n) = \sum_{i=0}^{h-1} Y_i$$

with

$$Y_{-1} \stackrel{def}{=} k$$

$$Y_0 \stackrel{def}{=} Y(k, m, n) = m \cdot \left\{ 1 - \prod_{i=1}^{k} \frac{n - (n/m) - i + 1}{n - i + 1} \right\}$$

$$Y_i \stackrel{def}{=} Y(Y_{i-1}, \lceil \frac{m}{\mu_{\zeta X}^i} \rceil, \frac{m}{\mu_{\zeta X}^{i-1}})$$

The above formula assumes that the average number of index records on each page is equal to the fan-out and that the root page of the index tree resides in main memory. Note also that the Yao formula assumes that the k records are selected at random, which is not met completely by the z-values. However, since we omit the extra z-values resulting from the hull closure and due to the zigzag course of the Peano-enumeration, we regard this simplification as admissible. Yao further assumes that no buffering is performed, which is true for our application, but cannot be guaranteed for the operating system.

In summary, the cost induced by traversing the index is

$$C_{ind} = \lceil I(h, \tilde{U}'D^g, \lceil \frac{\zeta(g)}{\mu_\zeta} \rceil, \zeta(g)) \rceil C_{IO}$$

For all found index entries the object pointers have to be hashed into a table to eliminate duplicates.

$$C_{hash} = T^*\zeta(g) \cdot C_{lkup}$$

Provided that the number of found index entries is proportional to the number of qualifying objects, we have to load $F(g) = T^*N$ objects. The number of page faults is

$$C_{geo} = \lceil \eta \cdot \frac{F(g)}{\mu_X} \rceil C_{IO}$$

In the above formula η is the clustering factor. This clustering factor determines the skew, i.e., which indicates the quality of clustering. For optimal clustering η is equal to 1. With this factor one can also take account for huge objects, i.e., objects which cover more than one page.

Finally, all objects are tested for intersection with the given object. If the granularity is not sufficiently fine, a lot of objects have to be tested for intersection.

$$C_{int} = F(g)C_{inter}$$

The final formula is therefore given as

$$
\begin{aligned}
C(g) &= C_{ind} + C_{hash} + C_{geo} + C_{int} = \\
&= \lceil I(h, \tilde{U}'D^g, \lceil \frac{\zeta(g)}{\mu_\zeta} \rceil, \zeta(g)) \rceil C_{IO} + T^*\zeta(g) \cdot C_{lkup} + \lceil \eta \cdot \frac{F(g)}{\mu_X} \rceil C_{IO} + F(g)C_{inter}
\end{aligned}
\tag{4}
$$

There are several factors which determine the behaviour of the above equation:

1. $\tilde{U}'$: reflects the relative perimeter of our search region

2. fractal z-ordering dimension D: determines the complexity with regard to the z-ordering approximation. For simplicity, we assumed the same value for search region and stored objects.

3. μ_X: average number of objects per page. This is a measure for the size (complexity) of the objects (number of vertices).

It should be noted, that for simpler $\Gamma(g)$-functions it is possible to provide an algebraic approximation of the optimal granularity. For our analytical investigations, we used the parameters reported in Table 2 and 3.

C_{IO}	12 ms
C_{inter}	4 ms
C_{lkup}	0.0001 ms
D	1.499
$\tilde{U}$	0.0114
$\tilde{U}'$	0.023
T	0.053
η	1.3
P	1024 Bytes
μ_X	$P/\bar{v} \cdot 8$
μ_ζ	$P \cdot 0.7/8$

Table 2: The parameters used for the analytical investigation.

v_{min}	4
v_{max}	869
$\bar{v}$	82.9721
$\min(\frac{U_i}{U})$	0.0002
$\max(\frac{U_i}{U})$	0.1408
$\frac{U}{U}$	0.0142

Table 3: The different parameters found in the map EEC 4 with $N = 824$ objects.

In our experiments, we confirmed that the test for intersection, enclosure or containment can be very expensive for complex polygons. Note that in real applications the time to test for intersection of two polygons is not constant. In particular if not even the bounding boxes overlap one can dismiss the tuple on the spot. We further assume that each index entry and each vertex is 8 Byte in size and that the space utilization factor of the B^+-tree is 0.7.

It is not obvious in the above equation, how the different parameters interact, in particular, the influence of each of them. To study this interaction, we first varied the granularity to determine an optimal value. Next, we studied the dependency of the optimal granularity on the size of the stored objects and eventually on the number of objects in the database. The results of these theoretical investigations are depicted in Figures 20 through 22.

In Figure 20, the course of the expected execution time of Equation 4 is plotted. As expected, after a decrease of the execution time to a minimum around the granularity of 15, before the time increases again. The left side of this performance graph is dominated by fetching and testing of candidate objects. The execution time decreases as the selectivity increases. This continues until the time to scan the index becomes the dominating factor; this can be noticed on the right side of the graph: the exponential rise of $\zeta(g)$ is clearly reflected. This graph further supports our claim that the optimal granularity is critical for the overall performance. For a granularity of 22 the expected execution time is already about three times greater than the optimal.

In Figure 21 the effect on the optimum for different $\tilde{U}$ is plotted, which is roughly correlated to the area of the stored objects. As expected, the higher the perimeter of the objects the lower will be the minimal optimal granularity. It is worthwhile to notice that for larger values of $\tilde{U}$ the choice of the granularity is very important for the performance of the selection. We can summarize our results as follows: the smaller the objects (i.e., the smaller $\tilde{U}$), the greater one should choose the granularity g.

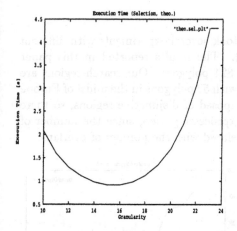

Figure 20: Expected execution time for different granularities.

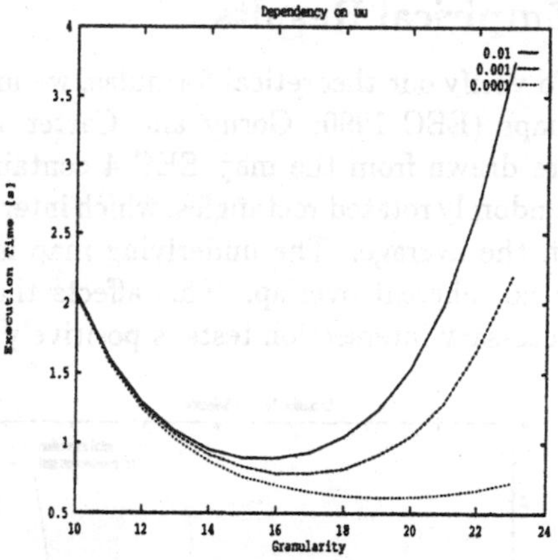

Figure 21: Dependency of the execution time on varying ratios $\tilde{U}$.

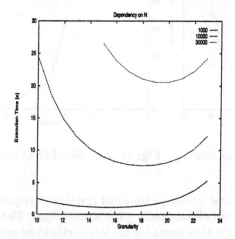

Figure 22: Dependency on the number of objects N in the database.

Besides the granularity the total number of objects in the database influences the optimum as depicted in Figure 22. The cost curve becomes steeper and the minimum more visible. This means that the more objects are in the database the more important it is to determine the optimal value for the granularity and the more advantageous it is to use a finer granularity. Obviously, the total execution time depends upon N.

114

Empirical Results

To verify our theoretical formulas, we undertook several experiments with different maps (EEC 1990; Gorny and Carter 1987). The results reported in this paper are drawn from the map EEC 4 containing 824 polygons. Our search regions are randomly rotated rectangles, which intersect with 52 polygons in the midst of Europe on the average. The underlying map is composed of disjunctive regions, so there is no inherent overlap. This affects the postprocessing step, since the number of necessary intersection tests is positively correlated with the number of overlaps.

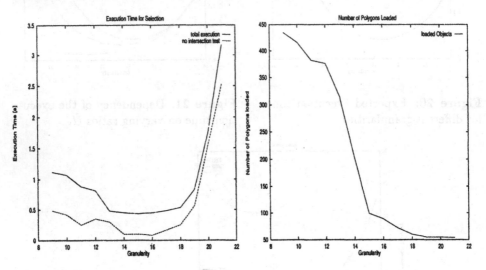

Figure 23: The total execution time measured for the selection.

Figure 24: Number of loaded polygons.

In Figure 23, we depict the total execution time and the time it required to scan the index and to load the objects (without testing for intersection). The difference between the two curves is the CPU time spent for the intersection test on the actual geometry. The left part of the figure shows clearly that the CPU time spent for the intersection test is more than the I/O time. Although the difference decreases as granularity increases, the reduction is not as strong as one might expect. The reason for this is that the majority of tests can be decided at an early stage. So the major portion of loaded objects can be rejected easily. There is a broad minimum around the granularity of 15 before the execution time increases again steeply. One might notice that the difference between the two curves has become smaller; hence the relative amount of I/O-time compared to the CPU time has increased. As expected, the left part of the diagram is dominated by the CPU intensive intersection test, whereas the right part by the I/O intensive index scan. The minimum found empirically comes close to the theoretically predicted minimum of 15, although the theoretical prediction for the execution time slightly overestimates the costs.

Figure 24 shows the number of loaded objects for the intersection test. For a granularity of 10, more than 400 polygons had to be fetched into memory. This means that the set of candidates is about 10 times greater than the number of hits. Thus more than 80 % of the loaded objects are false hits. Although a great deal of them can be rejected at an early stage, they still contribute to the total execution time. After a steep decrease around granularities between 12 and 15, the number of objects decreases only slightly with finer granularity.

4 Conclusions

In this paper, we have shown that controlled redundancy can be an important means for efficiently processing spatial queries. We provided an empirically derived formula to compute the expected number of index entries using z-ordering for a wide variety of different geometries. This formula contains two major determinants, the fractal z-ordering dimension D and the relative perimeter of the object to the embedding world. Several guidelines are provided on how to choose this parameters in case of unavailability, so that at least a worst case assessment can be ensured. We demonstrated the applicability of this formula to sets of objects. By using these results, we provided a theoretical model to determine the optimal redundancy for the spatial access method z-ordering. We verified the accuracy of our model by means of empirical experiments using real data for the intersection query.

The presented model covers only the spatial selection. We are currently working on a companion model for the intersection join. Similar to this work, we want to establish the theoretical formulae by experiments.

Acknowledgement

Thanks to Prof. J.C. Freytag and Prof. O. Günther (both of Humboldt-Universität zu Berlin), Dr. W.F. Riekert (FAW Ulm) and the unknown referees for improving the presentation of this paper. Furthermore, thanks to Dr. Mikhail Rachnikov (Humboldt-Universität zu Berlin) for his readiness to support this work.

References

Beckmann, N., H.-P. Kriegel, R. Schneider, and B. Seeger (1990). The R*-tree: An efficient and robust access method for points and rectangles. In *Proc. ACM SIGMOD Conference on Management of Data*, pp. 322–331.

Comer, D. (1979). The ubiquitous B–tree. *ACM Computing Surveys 11*(2), 121–138.

EEC (1990). Statistical bureau of the european union. Regions.

Gaede, V. and W.-F. Riekert (1994). Spatial access methods and query processing in the object-oriented GIS GODOT. In *Proc. of the AGDM'94 Workshop*, Delft, The Netherlands, pp. 40–52. Netherlands Geodetic Commission.

Gorny, A. and R. Carter (1987). World Data Bank II: General Users Guide. Technical report, U.S. Central Intelligence Agency, Washington.

Günther, O. (1988). *Efficient structures for geometric data management*. Number 337 in LNCS. Berlin: Springer–Verlag.

Guttman, A. (1984). R-trees: A dynamic index structure for spatial searching. In *Proc. ACM SIGMOD Conference on Management of Data*, pp. 47–54.

Mandelbrot, B. (1983). *Fractal geometry of nature*. San Francisco: W. H. Freeman.

Nievergelt, J., H. Hinterberger, and K. C. Sevcik (1984, March). The grid file: An adaptable, symmetric multikey file structure. *ACM Trans. on Database Systems 9*(1), 38–71.

Orenstein, J. (1989a). Redundancy in spatial databases. In *Proc. ACM SIGMOD Conference on Management of Data*, pp. 294–305.

Orenstein, J. (1989b). Strategies for optimizing the use of redundancy in spatial databases. In B. et al (Ed.), *Design and Implementation of Large Spatial Database Systems*, pp. 115–134. Springer–Verlag. LNCS No. 409.

Orenstein, J. and T. H. Merrett (1984). A class of data structures for associative searching. In *Proc. 3rd ACM SIGACT–SIGMOD Symposium on Principles of Database Systems*, pp. 181–190.

Schiwietz, M. (1993). *Speicherung und Anfragebearbeitung komplexer Geo-Objekte*. Ph. D. thesis, Ludwig-Maximilians Universität München. (in german).

Schiwietz, M. and H.-P. Kriegel (1993). Query proceeing of spatial objects: Complexity versus redundancy. In D. Abel and B. C. Ooi (Eds.), *Advances in Spatial Databases*, pp. 377–396. Springer Verlag. LNCS No. 692.

Sellis, T., N. Roussopoulos, and C. Faloutsos (1987). The R⁺-tree: A dynamic index for multi-dimensional objects. In *Proc. 13th Int. Conference on Very Large Data Bases*, pp. 507–518.

Yao, S. (1977). Approximating block accesses in database organizations. *Communications of the ACM 20*(4), 260–261.

Accessing Geographical Metafiles through a Database Storage System

Stephen Blott*   Andrej Vckovski[†]

Abstract

We describe a database storage extension for geographical metadata, discuss the retrieval requirements of such an extension, and describe the extension process itself.[1] Our aims in undertaking the work reported were twofold: on the one hand we wanted to better understand the basic requirements of a geographical metadata manager, and on the other we wanted to "stress-test" the storage model of our prototype storage system [19]. We discuss the following issues: What are the retrieval requirements of a geographical metadata manager? In what architectural contexts must such a manager operate? How can a database system be extended to meet both these classes of requirements? Characteristic of our approach is that such metadata remains primarily stored in files external to the database system, while indexing and query processing is carried out within the database system. We also report on our experiences in building such a prototype geographical metadata manager.

1 Geographical Metadata and Database Systems

The handling of metadata has gained importance in recent years, particularly within scientific and engineering disciplines. This importance is mostly related to the rapidly increasing amount of primary data being produced and exchanged within these various domains. In the field of geographical systems, the cost of data acquisition and datasets' sheer volumes heightens this importance further, making data discovery a key challenge in the computerisation of the discipline.

1.1 Geographical Metadata and Standards

A widely-used definition describes metadata as *data about data*; this is sometimes generalised to *information which makes data useful* [13]. From the data

---

*Institute for Information Systems, ETH Zentrum, CII-8092 Zürich, Switzerland; blott@inf.ethz.ch.

†Institute for Geographical Information Processing, University of Zürich, CH-8057 Zürich, Switzerland; vckovski@gis.geogr.unizh.ch.

[1]The term *metadata* has technical meanings in both the fields of geographical and database systems. To avoid confusion, we use the term *geographical metadata* in discussion from a geographical point of view, and *metafiles* when discussing geographical metadata from a database point of view. Database schema information is not discussed.

producer's point of view, metadata documents a dataset. The US Federal Geographic Data Committee (FGDC) and other organisations have created standards to support the uniform assessment of geographical metadata [8, 7, 12]. These standards cover content and semantics of metadata, that is what information is documented, and also define its digital representation. We will use the FGDC's *Metadata Content Standard* as our primary reference for geographical metadata [8]. A pseudo extract from such a geographical metadata file is illustrated in Figure 1. Such metadata is used with varying levels of detail in the following tasks:

Quality control: Detailed metadata is essential for quality control within organisations which produce and maintain large spatial datasets. It documents the entire life-cycle of data including its collection, pre-processing and maintenance [14]. This kind of metadata is usually very detailed.

Data exchange: Due to the high cost of acquisition, data exchange plays a major role in spatial information processing. The geographical metadata accompanying a dataset is the key to successful exploitation of that data. To be of value to a large community, metadata's contents must adhere to some standard, and therefore be accurately interpretable by its final users. Missing or misinterpreted metadata is one of the major sources of avoidable errors and uncertainties when using external datasets. Less detail is required of such metadata; however large datasets are usually accompanied by correspondingly detailed metadata.

Data directories: The need to reuse expensive datasets motivates the establishment of data directories. These allow users to browse content descriptions of datasets without requiring access to the primary data itself. For example, they may be interested in locating data sources covering a specific geographic region. Directories might be in-house within large organisations, or describe the contents of digital libraries available from other sources. Such geographical metadata typically requires the lowest level of detail.

Details of the production process are not required, and in contrast to the cases above the dataset itself need not be present. That is, metadata has storage and querying requirements independently to the primary data itself.

The first two of the examples above do not require geographical metadata to be available as a separate entity, it can rather be seen as a part of the primary data. Geographical Information Systems (GIS) usually offer some means of storing short descriptions of a dataset, its list of themes or its geographic region. The whole range of metadata content, however, is not supported by current systems. While it is an important requirement for a GIS to offer comprehensive handling of the metadata, this alone will not address the problem of metadata management within data directories. In those systems, the primary data being described is usually not available, and the information system applied need not be a GIS. The metadata may stem from datasets managed by a variety of different systems, each having its own mechanism for metadata management. Due to their ubiquity, such data is often managed directly within operating-system files. Common tools for its management include simple paper forms, scripts and custom database systems.

1.2 Database Systems and Geographical Metadata

As part of our on-going research activities, we have developed a storage-management kernel named CONCERT [19, 3]. This kernel is designed to support object managers such as RDBMSs, OODBBMSs, engineering systems and geographical systems. Such object managers extend the CONCERT kernel by embedding new types and their corresponding operations in the kernel; in a sense they *program* the kernel. The kernel's storage model is novel, and is based on the management of abstractly-defined objects. New types are added to the system as new implementations of a fixed set of abstract data types. To be sure that that model is sufficiently rich, we decided to "stress-test" it by *programming* it for the task of geographical metadata management. The variety of classes of information encompassed by such metadata, including spatial attributes, provides a very broad test of the flexibility of the storage model.

Databases supporting geographical applications must support the storage, querying and analysis of structured data, spatial data and its metadata. Current application of database technology, particularly with respect to metadata, is limited. There are a number of reasons for this. Firstly, the modelling and query-language concepts for metadata access remain poorly identified and supported; and secondly, the storage and query-processing strategies necessary are more complex than those supported by existing commercial systems. Though addressing the former is important (see, for example, [18]), only the latter is considered here.

One specific problem is the commitment associated with *one-giant-leap* solutions. Database systems typically require that objects are represented in the storage model of the system at hand, and operated upon only under the control of that system. This gives rise to a number of major problems in practice. Firstly, it implies that data must be translated from a data-exchange to a database-storage format. This implies the development of translation code, translation costs, and that pre-existing scripts and applications can no longer be used. The second problem is that mapping geographical metadata files to the relations or classes of a database system typically de-clusters the attributes of the file [22]. Different attributes will appear in different relations or classes, and the complexity of standards such as [8] is beyond that for which current commercial systems could provide the necessary (re-)clustering functionality. We conceive of our approach as being evolutionary rather than revolutionary: initially files are the primary storage representation, while over time we would like to support smooth migration to a database-system solution.

For both these reasons we decided to retain the file representations of geographical metadata files. In our approach, the primary representation is the file; however, secondary indexes are constructed within the database system, and query-processing across these indexes and the files themselves is managed from within the database system. For these purposes, it is necessary that the database system interpret the contents of those files, that is not treat them simply as BLOBS, and achieving this is one of the contribution of this paper. In some senses our problem is similar to those addressed by [1, 10, 5, 11], in which techniques for accessing (object-oriented) database objects through file-system interfaces (or *vice versa*) are described. Our contribution here differs from these, however, in a number of respects: firstly in that it elaborates a specific application-area problem, secondly in the complexity of the objects

```
Data_set_scale          1:250,000
Identification_code     23
Data_set_description    This dataset was derived from the
                        1:250,000-scale source by the U.S.
                        Geological Survey for the
                        Land-Use/Land-Cover program ...
Theme_keyword           hydrologic unit, river basin
Data_set_G-polygon      inside(49.10,-123.27    49.15,-116.27
                        49.16,-104.06 49.40,-95.12
                        48.12,-88.40 ...)
...
```

Figure 1: Pseudo Extract from a Geographical Metadata File

described, and thirdly in its special treatment of spatial data.

Document Structure. The remainder of this paper is structured as follows. In the following section we discuss the retrieval (and hence storage-management) requirements of geographical metadata. We then, in Sections 3 and 4, map those requirements to a database storage model and show how a metadata manager based on such a model can be built in practice. Finally, Section 5 concludes.

2   Metadata Retrieval Requirements

Structure of Geographical Metadata. The FGDC standard [8] supports data producers by defining the information to include within a dataset's metadata. It defines a set of attributes and their meaning. Due to the scope of different datasets to be documented, a very large set of attributes was needed. These were grouped and structured hierarchically in a similar manner to other geographical metadata standards [16]. The FGDC standard exposes a nested, tree-like structure of metadata entries, where each leaf is a particular *data element* and the nodes are *compound elements*. The wide scope of the standard's application leads to many optional attributes. Further, non-standard, instance-specific attributes may extend the standard where necessary.

Each *data element* is of one of the basic data types `integer`, `real`, `text`, `date` and `time`. The *domain* of a data element describes valid data values that can be assigned to that element. For example, the domain may constrain a real-element describing latitude/longitude coordinates to the ranges $[-90, 90]$ and $[-180, 180)$. An important data-element type is `textual`, for which certain instances are constrained to contain only certain strings. An example of this is the `Metadata Security Classification` which is constrained to contain the values such as `Top secret` and `Secret`, etc.

Compound elements are defined through production rules, describing the relationship between the compound element and its components. These are

```
1. SELECT (summary-or-entry) WHERE attribute operator value
   SELECT (summary-or-entry) WHERE PROGRESS = "Complete"
   SELECT (summary-or-entry) WHERE BNDGCOORDS OVERLAPS
   (12.2,45.5,13.1,48.2)

2. SELECT (summary-or-entry) WHERE any OVERLAPS
   (12.2,45.5,13.1,48.2)
   SELECT (summary-or-entry) WHERE any LIKE "%soil-type%"

3. SELECT (summary-or-entry) WHERE exists attribute
   SELECT (summary-or-entry) WHERE exists THEME
```

Figure 2: Example SQL-like queries over Geographical Metadata

formed through record, list and union constructions over sub-components, which are themselves either data elements or nested compound elements. Production rules specify which of components are *mandatory, mandatory-if-applicable* or *optional.* A number of the compound elements can rather be regarded as indivisible data elements of compound structure. Examples of this include Data_set_G-polygon, which is implemented as a list of point-pairs, but logically represents a spatial polygon. For effective storage management and query processing, this spatial interpretation is the one required, and the representation is typically of no concern.

Retrieval Requirements of Geographical Metadata. The retrieval modes fall into two basic classes. If a query yields several applicable metadata entries, then a list of *summary information*[2] is returned. This provides an overview of each matching metadata entry. If the result is a uniquely identified metadata entry, then the whole entry is retrieved. A typical user interface would allow the user to select items from the list of summary information and then retrieve the detailed metadata.

The query types are similar to queries within library systems. One can consider queries over arbitrary specific parts of the hierarchical structures; such would be similar to queries over nested relations [21]. However, other views are also important for query processing. *Universal type queries* retrieve entries where *any* data element or compound element of a given particular type matches the query predicate. For example, a query may apply to *any* textual or *any* spatial attribute. The third category of queries retrieves entries for which a specific attribute exists. Queries for existence also include entries where the specified attributed is a *null-value* as defined in [8]. This accommodates missing information: if the attribute with missing information is *applicable* to the meta-data entry, then the attribute is encoded using a data-type specific null-value. Missing information that is *not applicable* is not encoded and can be detected via queries for existence. This corresponds to the different types of null values discussed in [6] and [4]. Some examples of SQL-like metadata queries are given in Figure 2.

---

[2]The summary information is basically the content of the compound element Identification Information (ASTM tag IDENTINFO).

All queries allow both individual data elements and compound elements to be specified. Queries for contents of compound elements must accommodate the semantics of the compound element's components. For example, compound elements defining a spatial object (e.g., Data_set_G-polygon) might be queried using spatial operations such as enclosed-in or overlaps. Type information is required, therefore, over specific compound elements in addition to simple data elements.

3 Developing a Storage Model for Geographical Metadata

Our starting point is FGDC [8], and our assumption is that we have some set of metafiles conforming to that geographical metadata standard. The first issue to address is that of how the contents of such files can be made known to a general-purpose database system such that they may be indexed, perhaps replicated and queried from within the database system.

3.1 An Abstract-Object Storage Model

Our solution is based on our prototype storage kernel CONCERT [19]. CONCERT provides exactly two base types (SCALAR and UNKNOWN), and exactly five constructed types. These are RECORD and LIST, UNION, REFERENCE, and CONTINUUM. Two novel aspects of CONCERT are the treatment of externally-defined types in terms of their *likeness* to built-in types, and the treatment of the CONTINUUM type as a basic, common model of arbitrary-dimensional extended objects. As both details are important in the current context, we sketch them below.

Likeness. CONCERT provides a number of built-in types, and built-in implementations of these. However, these may in certain contexts prove inadequate, for example to meet performance particular requirements or accommodate existing externally-defined representations. Metafiles are an example of the latter. In these cases, new implementations of the known types may be embedded in the system, and their semantics made known through their *likeness* to the known types. For example, the basic structure of a metafile is that of a sequence of attribute-value pairs; hence their structure is *like* that of the built-in RECORD type, though their implementation is externally-defined. With respect to Figure 1, example attribute names would be Data_set_scale and Identification_code, with types scaleT and text-intT, respectively. Based on such a *likeness*, any physical-design or query-processing strategy which is applicable to records, is applicable also to these externally-defined records.

The types scaleT and text-intT are then themselves also externally-defined types, defined to be *like* the built-in SCALAR type. They both have (different) textual representations, but they behave something *like* scalars. Any physical-design or query-processing strategy which applicable to scalars, is applicable also to these externally-defined scalars. Types declared through such *likenesses* are referred to as *abstract-object types*.

The CONCERT kernel performs storage management and query processing to the level of selection and projection.[3] To achieve this, the kernel must be able to manipulate objects in accordance with the *likenesses* declared. Hence, operations must be provided over abstract-object types which prove—in a sense—those *likenesses*. For example, over the metafiles with their *likeness* to RECORD types, an operation would be required to project the component attributes of the record. Over the attributes themselves, which in the examples above were *like* the built-in type SCALAR, comparison (<, =) operations are required. These then suffice, for example, for access structures and the query evaluator to interpret the contents of metafiles. For example, one of the basic access structures in the kernel is a B-tree, and this could be used to index metafiles over any attribute which is *like* the SCALAR type. The record operations allow the individual attribute to be extracted, and the comparison operations determine how they are managed within the B-tree.

Spatial Objects as Continua. The second novel aspect of CONCERT is its treatment of spatial data as a special basic type named CONTINUUM. Continua enable the special semantics of spatially-extended objects to be embedded within the kernel. As with the other types, new CONTINUUM types must provide implementations of particular operations. In this case, they are partition, compose, is-empty, interval and overlaps.[4] When a *likeness* to a CONTINUUM type is declared, scalar types must be provided for each of its dimensions, as must implementations of the operations above over the new type. Take, for example, the Data_set_G-polygonT of the FGDC standard. Assume that the necessary SCALAR type textual-float is already declared. Attribute values of this new polygon type are declared to be *like* the CONTINUUM type in two dimensions of scalar textual-float. With the correspondingly-required operations, such externally-defined polygons can be indexed within access structures such as spatial grid-files and R-trees. This approach is a generalisation of that of our earlier prototype DASDBS [9, 20], and also has similarities with that of point-sets pursued in [17].

3.2 Describing Metafiles as Abstract-Object Types

Given metafiles' formats [8], and the storage model sketched above, we now describe those files' contents in terms of that model. This turned out to be relatively straight-forward.

Treatment of Errors. There are a number of reasons for which metafiles may be treated as erroneous: for example, they may be syntactically incorrect, or may include attribute values outwith the admitted ranges of those values. To function correctly, the storage system must be able to establish whether a given object is well-formed or not. One possibility is to treat this as a higher-level problem; however, we felt that it was possible to address it at a lower level and therefore we should. We considered two approaches, both based on UNION

---

[3]In this respect, the CONCERT kernel is at approximately the same architectural level as the RSS of System R [2], the Core of Starburst [15], or the DASDBS Kernel [20].

[4]The necessary operations are presented here from a logical point of view. In practice, particular care has been taken in defining the necessary operations such that: 1) trivial implementations are always possible and always logically correct; and 2) highly-specialised resource management is possible. Such details are particularly important, for example, if one considers the management of large raster-image data sets where excessive copying would present an unacceptable overhead.

```
           Lineage  =   0{ Source_Information }n +
                        0{ Process_Step }n

                        ⇓

    Source_InformationT' is-like '[ Source_InformationT ]'
    Process_StepT' is-like '[ Process_StepT ]'
    LineageT is-like '( Source_Information : Source_InformationT'
                       Process_Step : Process_StepT'   )'
```

Figure 3: Mapping FGDC Types to CONCERT Type *Likenesses*

types. The first solution would be to encode in each base type an abstract
UNION which is of one alternative if that attribute is well-formed, or of the
other if it is not. We discarded this option as being of an unnecessarily fine
granularity, with costs associated with almost every operation applied to leaf
attributes. The second solution was to describe an entire file as being *like* a
UNION between correct-dataT and incorrect-dataT. We chose this solution
as it is simple and allows a dataset to be partitioned horizontally into well-
formed and ill-formed partitions as new objects are inserted.

   Metafile Base Types as Abstract-Object Types. A number of standard representations are used within FGDC. These are described easily in terms
of their likenesses to the built-in base types. For example, calendar-dates,
times-of-day, and degrees-of-latitude and -longitude are all described as being
like the SCALAR type. Other values such as network addresses are described as
being *like* the built-in UNKNOWN type, and hence are managed as unstructured
objects. Since errors are managed at the top level, all constrained textual attributes are also described simply as being like the built-in type SCALAR. Spatial
attributes are described in terms of their *likeness* to CONTINUUM types.

   Constructed Abstract-Object Types. The basic constructions of
metafiles are records, lists and unions, and these map straight-forwardly to the
RECORD and LIST and UNION types of the storage model. For example, at the top
level metafiles consist of a sequence of named attributes. These are described
as abstract RECORD types. For attributes themselves, some additional types
had to be inserted. An example of such a description is given in Figure 3. The
top part is an extract from [8], and the bottom is the corresponding CONCERT
types. The first step is to un-nest the set constructions of Source_Information
and Process_Step, thereby generating two new types. The second is to map
the metafile specification concepts of set and record to the storage-management
concepts of LIST and RECORD, respectively.

3.3 Supporting Metafile Queries through Multiple Representations

Section 2 identified a number of special requirements of geographical metadata retrieval; these included *uniform type querying*, and the ability to retrieve objects on the basis of the existence of particular attributes. Both these aspects can be considered to be multiple-representation problems. These can be described in the CONCERT kernel through the use of RECORD-likenesses with computed attributes. Assume that an entire metafile's structure is described by the abstract-object type MD-structureT. Additional metafile representations (or views) are described by additional (computed) attributes.

```
MD-viewT is-like '(   MD-structure  : MD-structureT,
                      MD-strings    : [ stringT ],
                      MD-temporal   : [ timeT ],
                      MD-spatial    : [ Data_set_G-polygonT ∪ CoordinateT ],
                      MD-attributes : [ SCALAR ] )
```

The representation to query is selected by project-ing the appropriate attribute. Were one interested in *any* metafile containing the string "soil-type", one would query the MD-strings attribute. Were one interested in any object defining the attribute THEME, one would query the MD-attributes attribute.

4 Extending the Database System

Operations must be provided over abstract-object types in order that the kernel be able to manipulate abstract objects in terms of their *likenesses*. Exactly which operations are required is dependent on the type. In the current context, two issues arise in this respect:

Number of Operations. Firstly, while only a few examples were given in the previous sections, several hundreds of attributes are present in practice. This then implies the need for a very large number of operations to implement the necessary abstractions. We concluded that generating all those operations by hand would be problematic and error-prone. Instead, we developed a tool to generate these automatically. This is in keeping with our context of programming the kernel on behalf of a higher-level data manager.

Operational Model. The operations concerned must extract information from the metafiles themselves; this must be done as efficiently as possible. We chose a general implementation strategy for those operations based on their being interfaced directly to the buffer manager.

4.1 Automatic Generation of Extraction Operations

Standard tools such as lex and yacc provide some help in parsing the contents of structured files. However, using these alone the specification of the operations remains complex; further, adding new operations to interpret instance-specific attributes would require further detailed lex and yacc programming. However, large parts of geographical metafiles are regularly structured; sufficiently so, we concluded, that it should be possible to generate a large percentage of the

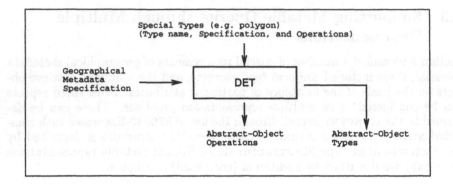

Figure 4: The Inputs/Outputs of the Database Extension Tool

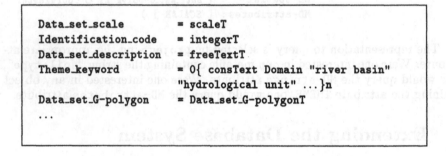

Figure 5: Extract from a DET Metafile Specification

necessary operations automatically. We therefore decided to develop a tool which would take a specification of a metafile-format as input, and generate both the CONCERT types and operations as output. We refer to this tool as the *Database Extension Tool* (DET). However, not all metafile attributes are regularly structured. Some compound elements, such as Data_set_G-polygonT, have semantics beyond that of their structure alone. Therefore, the DET must also accept the specification of some special types as inputs. The functionality of the DET is illustrated in Figure 4. Its inputs are a specification of the metafile format and the special types for which automatic generation is inappropriate, and its outputs are the CONCERT types and their corresponding operations.

The notation of the metafile specification language is broadly similar to that used in the specification document [8]. It allows various attributes to be specified: that is, their name and their type. Attribute types include a number of base types, a textual type, constrained textual types, unions, nestings, and the special types. An example extract from such a specification is given in Figure 5, this corresponds to that metafile extract given earlier in Figure 1. The types Data_set_G-polygonT and scaleT are examples of the special types which are not built into the DET. The DET generates types as described in the previous section; for example, it accommodates potential syntactic errors

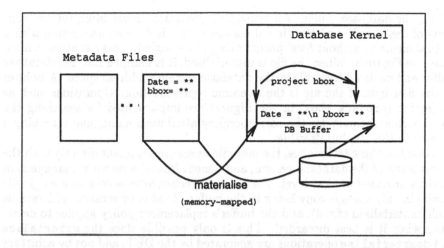

Figure 6: Materialising and Extracting Information from Metafiles

through the use of a UNION type, and replicates and aggregates all textual, temporal and spatial attributes and attribute names to the top level to support universal querying. The corresponding operations are generated automatically by the DET.

4.2 Operational Model

We had to decide on an operational model of what would actually happen when an operation over an externally-stored metafile was called. Clearly the cost of executing such operations should be minimised; however, other issues also arise. For example, multiple operations may be executed against the same metafile at the same time. This may result from a single query requiring multiple pieces of information from a file, from concurrent queries, or from parallelisation of a single query. In any of these cases, we would like that at most a single copy of the file be managed dynamically within the database, that copies of parts of that file only be made when necessary, and when access is no longer required, that the file be discarded and the resources it occupied be freed. These requirements are similar to those expected of a traditional database buffer.

The persistent representation of metafiles within the database system consists simply of the filename of the corresponding metafile. These are modelled within our storage manager as being *like* the built-in reference type. For any such reference, the operations materialise and dematerialise must be provided. In CONCERT, buffer management is based on direct (and uniform) access to database segments and files through the use of memory mapping [3]. Metafiles can therefore be accessed directly within the database buffer by *fixing* the appropriate file as if it were a database segment. By doing this, the materialise operation establishes addressability of metafiles within the virtual address space of the database system. Correspondingly, the dematerialise operation is implemented by *unfixing* the relevant buffer pages. Dynamic references, therefore, are simply virtual-memory pointers to metafiles' contents within the database buffer. All remaining operations must interpret the contents of the metafiles within virtual memory. This is done by navigation within virtual memory, without files' parts having to be copied. This situation is illustrated in Figure 6. When the file is materialised, it is mapped into the database buffer and made addressable in the database system's address space. A pointer to the first byte of the file is the dynamic representation. Operations such as projection (`project bbox`, in the Figure) are implemented by searching the file in virtual memory for the corresponding attribute's name, and returning a pointer to the attribute's value.

Based on these techniques, the metafile operations interact directly with the lowest levels of the database system, and benefit from the resource-management services provided at that level. For example, concurrent access to a single file results in only a single copy being in the buffer. That copy remains addressable while materialised (fixed), and the buffer's replacement policy applies to determine when it is best discarded. This is only possible since the `materialise` and `dematerialise` operations are generated by the DET, and not by arbitrary application programmers. That the buffer manager provides uniform addressability over multi-page objects [3] implies that neither the operations generated by the DET nor those associated with the special types need be concerned with page boundaries within the buffer.

4.3 Prototype

We have developed a prototype of the geographical metadata manager described here. It supports all the basic functionality discussed above except that its operations are not yet interfaced directly to the database buffer in the way described (though their implementations are as described). A detailed description of this implementation is given in [24].

5 Summary and Prospects

We have described the extension of a database storage-management system to the management of geographical metadata. This extension is based on the assumption that data resides in externally-stored files conforming to existing standard representations [8], while indexing, replication and query processing are performed from within the database system. We described the requirements of such a metadata manager, showed how externally-defined metafiles can be described in the storage model of our CONCERT prototype, and described how the very-large number of operations demanded by such a database extension may be supported by automatic generation. Our choice of FGDC as our standard was based on our particular application-area specific experience. An obvious alternative would be SGML, and we believe that our prototype could be easily adapted to that representation. An important aspect of our approach is that the data remains stored in the externally-defined files of the operating system, while it is indexed and queried from within the database system. This is somewhat similar to the approach to document management taken in the Rufus project [23].

Our aims in undertaking this work were two-fold: firstly to better understand the requirements of a geographical metadata manager, and secondly to stress-test the storage model of our CONCERT prototype. Despite the richness of the classes of metafile discussed, we always were able to describe the structures we required in our abstract-object storage model. Hence, we were able to support the functionality required of a metadata manager. One potential problem was that at several stages we were faced with a number of possibilities for the storage types to choose. This then implies that some form of data modelling is taking place at the storage-management layer, while such should really take place at a higher level. The other side of the same coin, however, is that we were able to describe multiple representations (or views) of the data directly within the storage system, thereby supporting the development of physical designs such as replication and indexing over those views. For example, we conceive of coupling our system to a textual indexing engine to provide improved support for textual querying.

A further consideration is how our approach extends to distributed environments. Clearly, some of the basic techniques applied (such those of memory management) are single-site in nature. However, one of the potential advantages of managing metadata within a database system is that the technology of distributed and federated database systems can be applied at a higher level. Coupling the access to externally-stored metafiles within a database system to technology for distributed access offers the potential for smooth migration to widely-available meta-databases.

In addition to *proof-of-concept*, the purpose of our prototype is to support improved querying of metafiles through the use of physical-design and query-processing support within a database system. We do not currently have sufficient data with which we can perform experimentation with such designs, nor do we have representative query classes and frequencies with which we could evaluate both those designs and our prototype as a whole. Were it to become available, such a benchmark suite would prove invaluable in the next phases of our project.

Acknowledgements

The authors would like to thank Thomas Etter who undertook the majority of the implementation work described, and also Gisbert Dröge, Lukas Relly, Hans-Jörg Schek and Andreas Wolf for their many helpful discussions and important contributions with respect to this and earlier related work.

References

[1] S. Abitoboul, S. Cluet, and T. Milo. Querying and Updating the File. In *Proceedings of the 19th Conference on Very Large Database Systems*, volume 19, Dublin, Ireland, 1993.

[2] M. M. Astrahan, M. W. Blasgen, D. D. Chamberlain, K. P. Eswaran, J. N. Gray, P. P. Griffiths, W. F. King, R. A. Lorrie, P. R. McJones, J. W. Mehl, G. R. Potzolu, I. L. Traiger, B. W. Wade, and V. Watson. System R: Relational Approach to Database Management. *ACM Transactions on Database Systems*, 1(2):97–141, 1976.

[3] Stephen Blott, Helmut Kaufmann, Lukas Relly, and Hans-Jörg Schek. Buffering Long Externally-Defined Objects. In *Proceedings of the Sixth International Workshop on Persistent Object Systems (POS6)*, pages 40–53, Tarascon, France, September 1994.

[4] K. Brassel, F. Bucher, E.-M. Stephan, and A. Vckovski. Completeness. In *Spatial Data Quality*. Elsevier Applied Science, London, 1995. in preparation.

[5] Michael J. Carey, David J. DeWitt, Michael J. Fanklin, Nancy E. Hall, Mark L. McAuliffe, Jeffre F. Naughton, Daniel T. Schuh, Marvin H. Solomon, C. K. Tan, Odysseas G. Tsatalos, Seth J. White, and Michael J. Zwilling. Shoring Up Persistent Applications. In *Proceedings of the ACM SIGMOD International Conference on Management of Data*, Minneapolis, Minnesota, USA, 1994.

[6] E. F. Codd. Missing information (applicable and inapplicable) in relational databases. *SIGMOD RECORD*, 15:53–78, 1986.

[7] (US) Federal Geographic Committee. *ASTM Draft Specification*. U.S. Geological Survey, 590 National Centre, Reston, Virginia 22092, USA, 1994.

[8] (US) Federal Geographic Committee. *Content Standard for Digital Geospatial Metadata*. U.S. Geological Survey, 590 National Centre, Reston, Virginia 22092, USA, (anonymous ftp: fgdc.er.usgs.gov), 1994.

[9] Gisbert Dröge, Hans-Jörg Schek, and Andreas Wolf. Erweiterbarkeit in DASDBS. *Informatik Forschung und Entwicklung*, 5:162–176, 1990 (in German).

[10] N. H. Gehani, H. V. Ragadish, and W. D. Roome. OdeFS: A File-System Interface to an Object-Oriented Database. In *Proceedings of the 20th International Conference on Very-Large Database Systems*, pages 249–260, Santiago, Chile, September 1994.

[11] Illustra Information Technologies (Inc). *Illustra Users Guide*. 1111 Broadway, Suite 2000, Oakland, CA 94607, Illustra Server Release 2.4.1 edition, March 1995.

[12] Arbeitsgruppe Geographische Informationssysteme. SIK-GIS Empfehlungen 1992. Technical report, Schweizerische Informatikkonferenz, Bern, September 1992.

[13] Francis P. Lenz, H. J.Bretherton and Paul T. Singley. Metadata: a user's view. In James C. French and Hans Hinterberger, editors, *Seventh International Working Conference on Scientific and Statistical Database Management*, pages 166–173. IEEE Computer Society Press, September 28–30 1994.

[14] H. J. Lenz. The conceptual schema and external schemata of metadata-bases. In James C. French and Hans Hinterberger, editors, *Seventh International Working Conference on Scientific and Statistical Database Management*, pages 160–165. IEEE Computer Society Press, September 28–30 1994.

[15] B. Lindsay, J. McPherson, and H. Pirahesh. A Data Management Extension Architecture. In *Proceedings of the 1987 ACM SIGMOD Conference on Management of Data*, pages 220–226, San Francisco, CA, USA, May 1987. ACM SIGMOD.

[16] National Aeronautics and Space Administration (NASA). *Directory Interchange Format Manual*, April 1993. Version 4.1.

[17] Jack A. Orenstein and Frank A. Manola. PROBE Spatial Data Modelling and Query Processing in an Image Database Application. *IEEE Transactions on Software Engineering*, 14(5):611–629, 1988.

[18] Ramesh Jain and Arun Hampapur. Metadata in Video Databases. *ACM SIGMOD Record*, 23(4):27–33, December 1994.

[19] Lukas Relly and Stephen Blott. Ein Speichersystem für Abstrakte Objekte. In *Proceedings of the 1995 Conference Datenbanksysteme in Büro, Technik, und Wissenshaft (BTW95); (in German)*, pages 338–347, March 1995.

[20] Hans-Jörg Schek, Heinz-Bernhard Paul, Marc H. Scholl, and Gerhard Weikum. The DASDBS Project: Objectives, Experiences, and Future Prospects. *IEEE Transactions on Knowledge and Data Engineering*, 2(1):25–43, March 1990.

[21] Hans-Jörg Schek and Marc Scholl. The relational model with relation-valued attributes. *Inormation Systems*, 11(2), 1986.

[22] SEQUOIA 2000 Metadata Schema for Satellite Images. Metadata in Video Databases. *ACM SIGMOD Record*, 23(4):42–48, December 1994.

[23] K. Shoens, A. Luniewski, P. Schwarz, J. Stamos, and J. Thomas. The Rufus System: Information Organisation for Semi-Structured Data. In *Proceedings of the 19th International Conference on Very-Large Database Systems*, pages 97–107, Dublin, Ireland, August 1993.

[24] Thomas Etter. Geospatial Metadata: Standards and Storage-Management Considerations. (Diplomarbeit thesis, Institute for Information Systems, ETH Zürich, Switzerland; in German), February 1995.

Extending a Spatial Access Structure to Support Additional Standard Attributes

Andreas Henrich[1] and Jens Möller[2]

[1] Universität Siegen, Fachbereich Elektrotechnik und Informatik, Praktische Informatik, D-57068 Siegen, henrich@informatik.uni-siegen.de
[2] FernUniversität Hagen, Fachbereich Informatik, Praktische Informatik IV, D-58084 Hagen, jens.moeller@fernuni-hagen.de

Abstract. In recent years, many access structures have been proposed supporting access to objects via their spatial location. However, additional non-geometric properties are always associated with geometric objects, and in practice it is often necessary to use select conditions based on spatial *and* standard attributes. An obvious idea to improve the performance of queries with mixed select conditions is to extend spatial access structures with additional dimensions for standard attributes. Whereas this idea seems to be simple and promising at first glance, a closer look brings up serious problems, especially with select conditions containing arithmetic expressions or select conditions for non-point objects and with Boolean operators like **or** and **not**.

In this paper we present a solution to overcome the problems sketched above which is based on three pillars: (1) We present powerful basic techniques to deal with arithmetic conditions containing mathematical operations (like '+', '−', '∗', and '/') and range queries for non-point objects. (2) We introduce a technique which allows to decompose select conditions containing Boolean operators and to reduce the processing of such a select condition to the processing of its elementary parts. (3) We show how other operations like joins and distance-scans can be integrated into this query processing architecture.

1 Introduction

In recent years, various efficient access structures for large sets of geometric objects have been developed. Most of these structures have been designed for multidimensional points [Rob81, NHS84, OMSD87, Fre87, LS89, SK90, KO91]. Some structures can also be used to maintain multidimensional intervals using the so-called transformation technique [Hin85, SK88]. Other structures have directly been designed to maintain non-point objects [Gut84, SRF87, BKSS90, HSW90, GB91].

The focus of most of the listed approaches has been on the performance of range queries (e.g. searching all objects lying in a given query region which may be a rectangle, a circle or a polygon in the 2-dimensional case). But also nearest-neighbour-, closest- and distance-scan-queries (sorting all objects with respect to their distance to a given point) can be performed well using such access

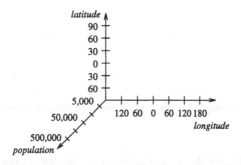

Fig. 1. Data space for an access structure for a spatial and a standard attribute

structures (see e.g. [Hen94]) and even joins based on spatial join conditions can be supported (see e.g. [BHF93]).

However, additional non-geometric properties are always associated with geometric objects, and in practice it is often necessary to use select conditions based on spatial *and* standard attributes.

A typical situation is the following: Suppose our database contains a relation (or class) *Cities* containing all cities on the earth. Besides others, the cities have the two attributes *CLocation* representing the geographical location of the centre of the city and *CPopulation*. If we want to retrieve all big cities in Germany and a polygon which describes the territory of Germany is known as constant *Germany*, the query may be written as:[3]

Cities σ [(CLocation **inside** Germany) **and** (CPopulation ≥ 100000)]

If our database has a spatial index for the attribute *CLocation* and a standard index, say, a B-tree, for *CPopulation*, we can use one of both in correspondence to the used optimisation strategy and select a preliminary result which has to be checked against the remaining part of the condition in a second step.

On the other hand, only every 100th city may be located in Germany and also approximately every 100th city may have a population of 100,000 or more inhabitants. Hence, if there are 1,000,000 cities in our database, the use of an index for one of the attributes *CLocation* or *CPopulation* would yield 10,000 cities, which have to be checked against the remaining condition in order to find the 100 cities in Germany with 100,000 or more inhabitants.

An obvious idea to improve the performance of queries with mixed select conditions is to extend spatial access structures with additional dimensions for standard attributes. Figure 1 shows the resulting data space for our example.

Whereas the idea of using a spatial access structure for additional standard attributes seems to be simple and promising, a closer look brings up serious

---

[3] The syntax used to state queries in this paper is that of the geo-relational algebra [Güt88], the query language of the Gral-system [Güt89]. The name of the relation is followed by the selection operator σ and the select condition in brackets.

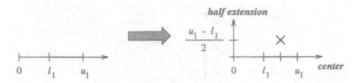

Fig. 2. 1-dimensional example for the transformation technique (centre representation)

problems. Let us consider the example above searching all big cities in Germany once again. This query would now introduce a complex polyhedron as our new 3-dimensional query region, and hence the comparisons of geometric objects needed in the access structure to perform our query are much harder than in the 2-dimensional world we have been concerned with before, when we were looking only at the attribute *CLocation*. Nevertheless, this is a relatively simple example.

To get a deeper understanding of the problems which arise from the *multi-attribute* approach, let us consider three further examples:

1. If the geometric attribute taken into concern is a non-point attribute, many spatial access structures use the so called transformation technique. In this case k-dimensional intervals (serving as bounding boxes for arbitrary complex non-point objects) are stored as $2k$-dimensional points. Two types of representations exist, the centre and the corner representation. The centre representation considers for each of the k dimensions the centre and the half extension of the interval to be distinct dimensions. Figure 2 shows this transformation for $k = 1$. The 1-dimensional interval $[l_1, u_1]$ is represented by the 2-dimensional point $\left(\frac{u_1+l_1}{2}, \frac{u_1-l_1}{2}\right)$.

   Assume, in our example above the attribute *CLocation* would be replaced by an attribute *Area* containing the area of each city as a polygon. Then an access structure taking into consideration the attributes *Area* and *CPopulation* would have five dimensions (the first, resp. third, dimension would relate to the centre of the interval of the bounding box of *Area* in longitude, resp. latitude, the second, resp. forth, dimension would relate to the half extension of the bounding box in longitude, resp. latitude, and the fifth dimension would relate to the population).

   In section 3.3 we will show that the problems which arise from the additional dimensions introduced by the transformation technique can be overcome using a reverse transformation for the data regions in the access structure. But this enforces a special treatment of the dimensions used to store non-point objects. As a consequence, we can not compute a homogeneous 5-dimensional query region, rather we have to separate the processing of the dimensions with respect to the corresponding attribute[4].

---

[4] It has to be mentioned, that the situation is by no means better for spatial access structures directly designed to maintain non-point objects, like e.g. the R-tree [Gut84, SRF87, BKSS90]. With the R-tree, point attributes (like *CPopulation*) have

2. As mentioned above, we are not only interested in range queries on spatial attributes. Another typical operation is e.g. a distance-scan. Assume we are looking for a 3 star hotel with a price of at most 70 US$ in the south west of the venue of our conference. Then we would like to have a list with all hotels fulfilling the conditions on the standard attributes (*Category* and *Price*) lying in the south west of the venue of our conference (a condition representing a range query on the spatial attribute *HLocation*) sorted in ascending order according to their distance to the venue of our conference. Hence, we have to combine three select conditions and a distance-scan.

3. Our third example arises if we consider arithmetic expressions in conditions. Suppose we have a relation *StatesStatistics*, which provides statistical data about states over a period of time. One may wish to find all states with a real gross national product per capita of at least 2500 US$ in 1994:

$$\text{StatesStatistics } \sigma \; [(\text{Year} = 1994) \textbf{ and}$$
$$((\text{GrossNationalProduct / SPopulation}) \geq 2500)]$$

As with this example, if arithmetic operations are used in a condition a transformation into a query region is often difficult, or may even be impossible. Hence, we need new techniques to deal with arithmetic expressions in multi-attribute access structures.

Our solution to overcome the problems sketched above is based on three pillars: First of all, we present powerful basic techniques to deal with arithmetic conditions and range queries for non-point objects. Second, we introduce a technique which allows to decompose complex select conditions and to reduce the processing of a complex select condition to the processing of its elementary parts. And third, we show how other operations like joins and distance-scans can be integrated into this query processing architecture.

The basic techniques are presented in section 3. Subsection 3.1 describes the processing of simple conditions like range queries on point objects. Subsection 3.2 presents a technique to deal with select conditions involving arithmetic expressions like e.g. $c_1 \cdot Attr_1 + c_2 \cdot Attr_2 \leq c_3$, or $(Attr_1 + c_1) \cdot (Attr_2 + c_2) \geq c_3$. In subsection 3.3 we describe an efficient way to process range queries on non-point objects stored in an access structure using the transformation technique.

Thereafter we present a technique to deal with select conditions combined from simpler conditions using Boolean operators like **and, or,** or **not**. This technique described in section 4 builds a superordinate technique with respect to the techniques described in section 3, i.e. it represents a strategy to decompose composite queries in a way that they can be performed easily combining the results of the basic techniques used for their components.

Finally in section 5 we give an idea of how the methods presented to support complex select conditions may be exploited to support other important types of queries. We will first outline an algorithm that processes joins with arbitrarily

---

to be treated like degenerated intervals and in contrast e.g. to the LSD-tree the fanout of the directory of an R-tree becomes worse for higher dimensions.

complex join conditions, and secondly give the idea of an efficient method to perform a large variety of closest- and distance-scan-queries.

Another important aspect, which we are not able to discuss here due to space limitations, arises from the observation that some attributes are normally accessed more frequently than others. An access structure should favour these attributes, providing a higher selectivity with respect to them. A discussion of this issue is presented in [HM95].

All proposed methods can be directly applied to multi-dimensional access structures which use a variant of the k-d-tree [Ben75] as directory [Rob81, OMSD87, LS89, HSW89b, KO91]. Furthermore an adaptation to other structures which are based on a hierarchical directory is possible. In this paper we use the LSD-tree as an example for a structure based on a generalised k-d-tree.

2   The LSD-tree as Geometric Access Structure

In this section, we restrict our discussion to the two-dimensional case and describe only those aspects which are essential for this paper. A detailed description is given in [HSW89b].

For geometric access structures it is important to distinguish points and extended, i.e. non-point, objects. Conceptually the LSD-Tree is an access structure for multi-dimensional points, but it was designed to maintain extended objects as well by applying the transformation technique.

Spatial access structures for points usually divide the data space into pairwise disjoint data cells, each of which is associated with a bucket of fixed size, storing all objects located in the cell. The data cell is normally called *bucket region*.

To introduce the basic idea of the LSD-tree we outline the construction of an LSD-tree, when new points are sequentially inserted.

Initially, the whole data space corresponds to one bucket. After a certain number of insertions the initial bucket has been filled, and an attempt to insert an additional object causes the need for a bucket split. For that purpose, a *split line* is determined, and the objects situated on one side of the split line are kept in the old bucket, while those lying on the other side are moved into a new one. After some further insertions, the capacity of some other bucket will be exceeded, which then is split in the same way. For example, consider the two-dimensional data space in figure 3. The first split has been made in the first dimension at co-ordinate 50, yielding buckets 1 and 2. Later, bucket 2 has been split in the second dimension at position 60, giving buckets 2 and 3, ...

The split lines of an LSD-tree are maintained in a directory, which is a generalised k-d-tree [Ben75]. Each inner node contains the dimension and position of a split line; the leaves of the tree point to the buckets. For example, the partitioning depicted in figure 3 results in the directory tree shown in figure 4.

Normally, the directory grows up to a point where it cannot be kept in main memory any longer. In this case, subtrees are paged out onto secondary storage, while the part near the root remains in main memory. The details of the paging algorithm are given in [HSW89a].

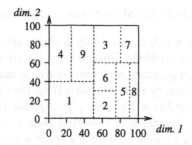

Fig. 3. Possible partition of the data space for an LSD-Tree

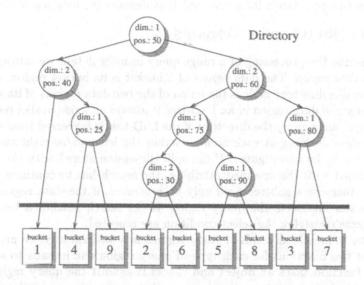

Fig. 4. The LSD-tree associated with the data space partition of figure 3

3 Techniques for Elementary Select Conditions

The LSD-tree, like all other spatial access structures, can be used as a multi-attribute access structure adding dimensions for the standard attributes under concern[5]. This has been illustrated in figure 1.

In this section we will describe some basic techniques to process what we call elementary select conditions in this paper. Roughly spoken an elementary select condition is a condition that does not include Boolean operators like **and**, **or**, or **not**.

---

[5] Obviously using this approach, we can use a spatial access structure as a multi-attribute access structure even if no spatial attribute is concerned.

3.1 Simple Conditions Involving one Attribute

Elementary conditions which involve only a single attribute may specify a geometric or non-geometric attribute. Such conditions are either explicitly based on a query region (e.g. a range query with respect to a geometric attribute) or can be easily translated into a query region (interval) on the dimension associated with the attribute. E.g. a condition like $Attr_1 \geq c$ yields the query interval $[c, \infty)$ for the corresponding dimension. Processing such a query in a multi-attribute access structure, all dimensions of the data space except those corresponding to the attribute under concern can be ignored.

If e.g. all cities near Cologne are to be retrieved, an elementary condition on a geometric attribute, which corresponds to a circular query region, would be used (here *Cologne* stands for a constant that denotes the location of Cologne):

Cities σ [**dist** (CLocation, Cologne) ≤ 75]

To describe the processing of a range query in more detail, we introduce the term of a *data region*. The *data region* of a bucket is its bucket region, and the *data region* of a directory node is the union of the two data regions of its sons. As a consequence, a data region in an LSD-tree is always an axis-parallel rectangle.

During a range query the directory of the LSD-tree is traversed from the root to the buckets deciding at each node, whether the left and/or right subtree of the node has to be investigated. If the split dimension stored with the node is not associated with the specified attribute, the search has to continue in both subtrees; otherwise a subtree need only be processed, if the data region of the respective son intersects the query region. If the search reaches a bucket, all found objects satisfying the select condition are reported.

In order to handle all kinds of query regions in a uniform way, we propose to implement two functions for each type of query region one intends to support. The first function takes an object and checks it against the query region. The second one tests for an intersection between the query region and a data region.

Actually, the second function does a little bit more: it determines the relationship between a data region and the query region to be either *Outside*, *Intersects*, or *Inside*. The meaning of these values is:

Outside The data region and the query region are disjoint. Hence, the respective subtree need not be traversed, because the select condition is false for all objects stored in this subtree.

Intersects The data region lies partly inside the query region, but is not entirely contained. Here a further detailed investigation of the subtree is required.

Inside The data region is part of the query region. In this case, all objects stored in the respective subtree can be reported without further examinations because the select condition is true for all objects in this subtree. In particular, the final test of the objects against the query region can be omitted.

Implementing the two proposed functions for each type of query region allows to leave the core of the range query algorithm unaltered for all types of selections.

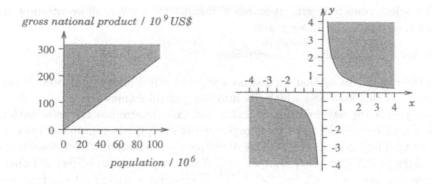

Fig. 5. Query Regions which can be handled with the *Vertices Approach*

There are mainly three types of select conditions which can not be treated in this simple way: (1) Conditions involving arithmetic expressions, (2) conditions on geometric non-point attributes, and (3) conditions including Boolean operators like **and**, **or**, or **not**. These types of conditions will be considered in the sections 3.2, 3.3, and 4.

3.2 Conditions Including Arithmetic Expressions

In section 1, we stated the following query to find all states with a real gross national product per capita of at least 2500 US\$ in 1994:

StatesStatistics σ [(Year $=$ 1994) **and**
$\qquad\qquad$ ((GrossNationalProduct / SPopulation) $\geq$ 2500)]

The second sub-expression of this query is an example for a select condition including an arithmetic expression; its graphical interpretation is given on the left side of figure 5.

The automatic translation of this condition into a geometric query region would still be possible; the reason is that the condition is only a linear condition. Multiplying both sides of the inequality by *SPopulation* leaves only a linear expression to be handled. However, non-linear expressions may also occur. Suppose e.g. the relation *StatesStatistics* would be replaced by a relation *States* which contains attributes for the current number of residents (*SPopulation*) and the growth rate of the population (*GrowthRate*) of the last year. One may be interested in those states for which the population is expected to exceed a number of 100 million people in the next year:

States σ [(SPopulation * GrowthRate) $\geq$ 100000000]

In this example, the corresponding query region is bounded by a hyperbola, which can be seen on the right side of figure 5, where the query region for the quite similar condition $x \cdot y \geq 1$ is depicted.

The select condition gets even more difficult to analyse, if we attempt to predict the situation in three years:

States σ [(SPopulation * (GrowthRate ^ 3)) $\geq$ 100000000]

In the rest of this section we discuss a method which allows to process many conditions of this kind and which fits into our general framework.

Our goal is the development of a function that determines the relationship between a data region and the query region without explicitly computing the corresponding query region. For reasons of simplicity, we assume select conditions to be given in the form $f(x_1, \ldots, x_m)$ *cop* 0 with *cop* being a comparison operator from the set $\{`<`, `\leq`, `=`, `\geq`, `>`\}$[6]. Furthermore, we expect the function f to be well-defined over the entire data space.

Our approach, which we call *Vertices Approach*, is as follows:

A data region is an orthogonal subspace of the whole data space, and, thus, its set of vertices may be considered. If all vertices are contained in (resp. situated outside of) the query region, we may – under certain assumptions – infer that the same even holds for the whole data region.

Which condition must hold to apply the proposed strategy? In the following analysis, $D = [\underline{w}_1, \overline{w}_1] \times \cdots \times [\underline{w}_m, \overline{w}_m]$ stands for a data region[7], and $\mathcal{D}$ denotes the whole data space. The vertices of a data region D are given by $Vertices(D) = \{\underline{w}_1, \overline{w}_1\} \times \cdots \times \{\underline{w}_m, \overline{w}_m\}$. Since in a condition of the form $f(x_1, \ldots, x_m)$ *cop* 0 only the sign of the result of the function f is relevant, we rewrite it as $(\text{sgn} \circ f)(x_1, \ldots, x_m) \in SignSet_{cop}$ with

$$SignSet_{cop} = \begin{cases} \{-1\}, & \text{if } cop = `<` \\ \{-1, 0\}, & \text{if } cop = `\leq` \\ \{0\}, & \text{if } cop = `=` \\ \{0, +1\}, & \text{if } cop = `\geq` \\ \{+1\}, & \text{if } cop = `>` \end{cases}$$

Requirement The *Vertices Approach* may be applied to a select condition of the form $f(x_1, \ldots, x_m)$ *cop* 0, $cop \in \{`<`, `\leq`, `=`, `\geq`, `>`\}$, f totally defined in the data space $\mathcal{D}$, if

$$\forall D \subseteq \mathcal{D} \; \forall cop \in \{`<`, `\leq`, `=`, `\geq`, `>`\} :$$
$$(\text{sgn} \circ f)(Vertices(D)) \subseteq SignSet_{cop} \Rightarrow (\text{sgn} \circ f)(D) \subseteq SignSet_{cop}$$

---

[6] The operator '$\neq$' is not considered here because of lacking selectivity. Moreover, it can be handled using the technique described in section 4 for **not** $(\ldots = \ldots)$.

[7] Irrespective of the fact that a data region for a bucket or a directory node w is a product of semi-open intervals, i.e. $D(w) = (\underline{w}_1, \overline{w}_1] \times \cdots \times (\underline{w}_m, \overline{w}_m]$, we will argue for a data region $D = [\underline{w}_1, \overline{w}_1] \times \cdots \times [\underline{w}_m, \overline{w}_m]$, because there is no other way to proceed for real values, and objects stored in a subtree of the LSD-tree corresponding to w are certainly contained in D. For attributes with a discrete domain, obviously $D = [succ(\underline{w}_1), \overline{w}_1] \times \cdots \times [succ(\underline{w}_m), \overline{w}_m]$ may be considered, which denotes the same region as $D(w) = (\underline{w}_1, \overline{w}_1] \times \cdots \times (\underline{w}_m, \overline{w}_m]$.

Obviously, this requirement guarantees that, if every vertex fulfils the select condition, the same is true for all points belonging to the data region, and, thus, the relationship is established to be *Inside*. For the other cases let us first consider the comparison operators '$<$', '$\leq$', '$\geq$', and '$>$': for these operators, the relationship is known to be *Outside*, if the select condition evaluates to false for all vertices. This property can easily be proofed as follows ($\overline{cop}$ denotes the complementary comparison operator, i.e. '$\geq$' for '$<$' etc.):

$$(\text{sgn} \circ f)(Vertices(D)) \cap SignSet_{cop} = \emptyset$$
$$\Rightarrow (\text{sgn} \circ f)(Vertices(D)) \subseteq SignSet_{\overline{cop}}$$
$$\Rightarrow (\text{sgn} \circ f)(D) \subseteq SignSet_{\overline{cop}}$$
$$\Rightarrow (\text{sgn} \circ f)(D) \cap SignSet_{cop} = \emptyset$$

In the remaining case, some vertices lie inside and others outside of the query region, and the relationship is *Intersects*.

For the operator '$=$', the relationship must be *Outside*, if all points of the data region fulfil either the condition $f(x_1, \ldots, x_m) < 0$ or $f(x_1, \ldots, x_m) > 0$. According to the discussion above this can be checked by $(Vertices(D)) \subseteq SignSet_{'<'}$ and $(Vertices(D)) \subseteq SignSet_{'>'}$. In the other cases, we compel further detailed investigations by assuming the relationship to be *Intersects*.

Since it is not apparent, whether a function fulfils the given requirement, we are now going to give a more convenient criterion.

Theorem A select condition of the form $f(x_1, \ldots, x_m) \, cop \, 0$, $cop \in \{$'$<$', '$\leq$', '$=$', '$\geq$', '$>$'$\}$, f totally defined in the data space $\mathcal{D}$, can be processed by the *Vertices Approach*, iff the function $(\text{sgn} \circ f)$ is monotonic, i.e.

$$\forall 1 \leq i \leq m \; \forall (x_1, \ldots, x_i, \ldots, x_m) \in \mathcal{D}:$$
$$[\forall x_i', (x_1, \ldots, x_{i-1}, x_i', x_{x+1}, \ldots, x_m) \in \mathcal{D} : x_i < x_i' \Rightarrow$$
$$(\text{sgn} \circ f)(x_1, \ldots, x_{i-1}, x_i, x_{x+1}, \ldots, x_m) \leq \quad \text{(increasing}$$
$$(\text{sgn} \circ f)(x_1, \ldots, x_{i-1}, x_i', x_{x+1}, \ldots, x_m)] \; \vee \quad \text{monotonicity)}$$
$$[\forall x_i', (x_1, \ldots, x_{i-1}, x_i', x_{x+1}, \ldots, x_m) \in \mathcal{D} : x_i < x_i' \Rightarrow$$
$$(\text{sgn} \circ f)(x_1, \ldots, x_{i-1}, x_i, x_{x+1}, \ldots, x_m) \geq \quad \text{(decreasing}$$
$$(\text{sgn} \circ f)(x_1, \ldots, x_{i-1}, x_i', x_{x+1}, \ldots, x_m)] \quad \text{monotonicity)}$$

Proof "$\Rightarrow$": Let $f(x_1, \ldots, x_m) \, cop \, 0$ be a select condition for which the *Vertices Approach* is applicable, i.e. which meets the requirement given above. Suppose that this condition does not satisfy the monotonicity criterion stated in the theorem. In this case, $(\text{sgn} \circ f)$ is not monotonic. Without any restrictions, we assume that $(\text{sgn} \circ f)$ is not monotonic in the first argument. Then, there exist vectors $\mathbf{x} = (x_1, x_2, \ldots, x_m)$, $\mathbf{x}' = (x_1', x_2, \ldots, x_m)$, and $\mathbf{x}'' = (x_1'', x_2, \ldots, x_m)$ in $\mathcal{D}$, $x_1' < x_1 < x_1''$, such that

$$[(\text{sgn} \circ f)(\mathbf{x}') < (\text{sgn} \circ f)(\mathbf{x}) \wedge (\text{sgn} \circ f)(\mathbf{x}'') < (\text{sgn} \circ f)(\mathbf{x})] \vee$$
$$[(\text{sgn} \circ f)(\mathbf{x}') > (\text{sgn} \circ f)(\mathbf{x}) \wedge (\text{sgn} \circ f)(\mathbf{x}'') > (\text{sgn} \circ f)(\mathbf{x})] \quad (i)$$

Now consider the data region $D = [x_1', x_1''] \times [x_2, x_2] \times \cdots \times [x_m, x_m]$ with its associated set of vertices given as $Vertices(D) = \{\mathbf{x}', \mathbf{x}''\}$. We uniquely choose the comparison operator *cop* so that $SignSet_{cop} = \{(\text{sgn} \circ f)(\mathbf{x}'), (\text{sgn} \circ f)(\mathbf{x}'')\}$, and thus $SignSet_{cop} = (\text{sgn} \circ f)(Vertices(D))$; this is always possible, since the case $\{(\text{sgn} \circ f)(\mathbf{x}'), (\text{sgn} \circ f)(\mathbf{x}'')\} = \{+1, -1\}$ can easily be excluded by (i). By the assumed requirement for f we obtain $(\text{sgn} \circ f)(D) \subseteq SignSet_{cop}$, and this leads for $\mathbf{x} \in D$ to $(\text{sgn} \circ f)(\mathbf{x}) \in SignSet_{cop}$ and finally to $(\text{sgn} \circ f)(\mathbf{x}) = (\text{sgn} \circ f)(\mathbf{x}') \vee (\text{sgn} \circ f)(\mathbf{x}) = (\text{sgn} \circ f)(\mathbf{x}'')$, which is a direct contradiction to (i).

"$\Leftarrow$": Suppose that $f(x_1, \ldots, x_m)$ *cop* 0 is a select condition that meets the monotonicity criterion given in the above theorem. Let $D = [\underline{w}_1, \overline{w}_1] \times \cdots \times [\underline{w}_m, \overline{w}_m]$ denote any data region and *cop* any comparison operator of the set $\{'<', '\leq', '=', '\geq', '>'\}$. We assume that f violates the requirement for some vector $\mathbf{x} \in D$, $\mathbf{x} = (x_1, \ldots, x_m)$, i.e.

$$(\text{sgn} \circ f)(Vertices(D)) \subseteq SignSet_{cop} \wedge (\text{sgn} \circ f)(\mathbf{x}) \notin SignSet_{cop}$$

Then we have $\mathbf{x} \notin Vertices(D)$, because $(\text{sgn} \circ f)(Vertices(D)) \subseteq SignSet_{cop}$. Hence, there is an index i, $1 \leq i \leq m$, such that $\underline{w}_i < x_i < \overline{w}_i$. Let $\mathbf{x}'$ and $\mathbf{x}''$ stand for the two vectors $(x_1, \ldots, x_{i-1}, \underline{w}_i, x_{i+1}, \ldots, x_m)$ and $(x_1, \ldots, x_{i-1}, \overline{w}_i, x_{i+1}, \ldots, x_m)$, respectively. If one of them also violates the requirement, consider it as new $\mathbf{x}$. Such a situation may occur at most m times, because then we have certainly reached a vertex of the data region.

Because of $(\text{sgn} \circ f)(Vertices(D)) \subseteq SignSet_{cop}$ we may now suppose $(\text{sgn} \circ f)(\mathbf{x}') \in SignSet_{cop}$ and $(\text{sgn} \circ f)(\mathbf{x}'') \in SignSet_{cop}$, i.e. $\{(\text{sgn} \circ f)(\mathbf{x}'), (\text{sgn} \circ f)(\mathbf{x}'')\} \subseteq SignSet_{cop}$. The monotonicity criterion, in connection with $\underline{w}_i < x_i < \overline{w}_i$ and $(\text{sgn} \circ f)(\mathbf{x}) \notin SignSet_{cop}$, implies

$$[(\text{sgn} \circ f)(\mathbf{x}') < (\text{sgn} \circ f)(\mathbf{x}) < (\text{sgn} \circ f)(\mathbf{x}'')] \vee$$
$$[(\text{sgn} \circ f)(\mathbf{x}') > (\text{sgn} \circ f)(\mathbf{x}) > (\text{sgn} \circ f)(\mathbf{x}'')]$$

As the function sgn only yields values of the set $\{-1, 0, +1\}$, this leads to $\{(\text{sgn} \circ f)(\mathbf{x}'), (\text{sgn} \circ f)(\mathbf{x}'')\} = \{-1, +1\}$, and by our last assumption to $\{-1, +1\} \subseteq SignSet_{cop}$, which is a contradiction, since no comparison operator is suited for satisfying this condition. $\qquad\square$

In particular, the criterion for applicability of the *Vertices Approach* is satisfied, if the function f is monotonic. This is e.g. the case for linear expressions like the one given in our first example and for all expressions of the form $c_1 \cdot Attr_1 + c_2 \cdot Attr_2 \leq c_3$, as well as for every non-linear expressions of the form $(Attr_1 + c_1) \cdot (Attr_2 + c_2) \geq c_3$ like the one of the second example. As a counterexample, the left side of figure 6 shows the query region corresponding to the select condition $x^2 - y \leq 0$; this condition does not meet the criterion in general, and, thus, the *Vertices Approach* may fail. However, for $x \geq 0$ the associated function f is monotonic; consequently, within a data space of, say, $\mathcal{D} = [0, 100] \times [0, 100]$ the *Vertices Approach* may still be applied.

A further disadvantage of the *Vertices Approach* is that the number of vertices is exponential in the number of attributes involved in the query. Also, the *Vertices Approach* is not suited for handling combined select conditions built by Boolean operators, even, if each sub-condition fulfils the criterion. Suppose one

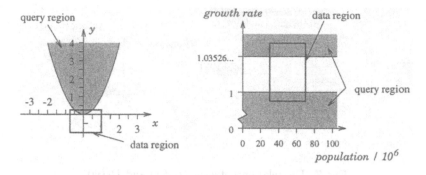

Fig. 6. Query Regions for which the *Vertices Approach* may fail

is interested in states with an unusual growth rate, i.e. in states with either a non-growing population or a population that is expected to double in number in the next twenty years:

States σ [(GrowthRate $\leq$ 1) or (GrowthRate $\geq$ (2 ^ (1 / 20)))]

The right side of figure 6 illustrates the select condition. Although the *Vertices Approach* can be applied to both sub-conditions, it fails on the whole expression.

To overcome the latter difficulty an integrated strategy, in which a condition is split into elementary sub-conditions, which may be processed with methods like the *Vertices Approach*, will be presented in section 4. But beforehand we will close our description of techniques for elementary select conditions with a look at the situation for geometric non-point attributes.

3.3 Range Queries on Geometric Non-Point Attributes

We explain the non-point situation for k-dimensional intervals which serve as bounding boxes for arbitrary geometric objects in many applications. To store a set of intervals in an LSD-tree we use the transformation technique as centre representation (see figure 2).

The transformation technique has two pitfalls: (1) Using the transformation technique the corresponding $2k$ dimensions of each data region build a $2k$-dimensional rectangle which can not be compared with a k-dimensional query region. (2) The transformation leads to a skew distribution of the image points.

With respect to the processing of range queries especially the first aspect is of importance, because the processing of range queries is based on the existence of k-dimensional data regions for buckets and directory nodes geometrically including all k-dimensional objects stored in the corresponding part of the access structure which can be compared with a query region.

Fortunately both pitfalls can be overcome.

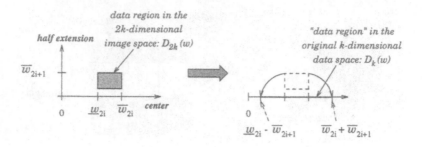

Fig. 7. The relation between $D_{2k}(w)$ and $D_k(w)$

The $2k$-dimensional data regions can be transformed into k-dimensional data regions[8]. If the $2k$-dimensional data region of a directory node or bucket w is given by $D_{2k}(w) = (\underline{w}_1 , \overline{w}_1] \times \ldots \times (\underline{w}_{2k} , \overline{w}_{2k}]$ a k-dimensional data region containing all rectangles for which the image point is in $D_{2k}(w)$ can be computed as follows:

$$D_k(w) = (\underline{w}_1 - \overline{w}_2 , \overline{w}_1 + \overline{w}_2] \times \ldots \ldots \times (\underline{w}_{2k-1} - \overline{w}_{2k} , \overline{w}_{2k-1} + \overline{w}_{2k}]$$

Here the region for the centres is extended with the upper bound for the half extension. Figure 7 illustrates the relation between $D_{2k}(w)$ and $D_k(w)$. The data region $D_k(w)$ can be used for comparisons in the processing of range queries and distance-scans.

Experience shows that $D_k(w)$ tends to be much greater than the region covered by the intervals actually stored in the structure. Hence, we store the actual data region $D_k^a(w)$, i.e. the minimal k-dimensional interval including all intervals stored in the corresponding part of the LSD-tree, with each reference to a bucket or an external directory page to avoid unnecessary page accesses[9].

The second pitfall of the transformation technique, the skew distribution of the image points, can be handled by the flexible directory of an LSD-tree using a special split strategy, which has been presented in [Hen94].

4   A Method for Complex Conditions

A complex select condition combined from elementary conditions using Boolean operators like **and, or,** and **not,** may be translated into a *query tree* as follows:

---

[8] If we talk about $2k$-dimensional data regions in the following, we mean the $2k$-dimensional axis-parallel rectangle built by the corresponding dimensions of the data region.

[9] Actually we do not store $D_k^a(w)$ itself but a coding of $D_k^a(w)$ relative to $D_k(w)$ in order to save space in the directory.

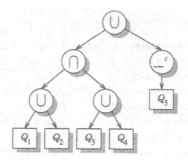

Fig. 8. Example of a Query Tree

1. In the case of a non-negated elementary condition, the query tree is given by a single leaf, which contains a representation of the corresponding query region; this representation may be implicit, as with the *Vertices Approach*.
2. For a negated condition, the query tree consists of a root, which denotes a complementation, and the query tree representing the negated condition.
3. Conditions that are built of an **and**- or **or**-connection of two sub-expressions are translated into a query tree which denotes an intersection or union of query regions in its root, respectively, and contains a query tree for each of the two sub-expressions as subtrees of the root.

Figure 8 shows a query tree for $((Cond_1$ **or** $Cond_2)$ **and**$(Cond_3$ **or** $Cond_4))$ **or** (**not** $Cond_5)$. Q_i denotes the corresponding query region for $Cond_i$, which may be stored implicitly or explicitly. Every single condition $Cond_1$ to $Cond_5$ may involve a geometric attribute or several standard attributes. Possible examples are $Attr_1 \leq Attr_2$, $Attr_1$ **intersects** $Const_1$, or **dist**$(Attr_1, Const_1) \leq Const_2$.

Basically, range queries with complex select conditions are processed in the same way as described in subsection 3.1: the traversal starts at the root of the LSD-tree; at each node the associated data region is compared with the query region to decide, which parts of the LSD-tree may contain objects that satisfy the select condition.

However, a comparison between a data region and the query region is now a little bit different, since the query region is represented as a query tree. At first, for each elementary query region given in a leaf of the query tree, the appropriate function that determines the relationship to the data region is called. If this reveals that the data region is totally contained in (resp. is disjoint with) the elementary query region, the respective leaf is substituted by the constant *Inside* (resp. *Outside*). After that, the query tree is simplified as far as possible according to the rules given in table 1.

For example, let us assume that the evaluation of the elementary query regions of the query tree depicted in figure 8 has resulted in *Inside* for Q_1 and Q_5, *Intersects* for Q_2 and Q_4, and *Outside* for Q_3. Then, a new query tree is computed as shown in figure 9.

Q_1	Q_2	Q_1^c	$Q_1 \cap Q_2$	$Q_1 \cup Q_2$
Inside	Inside		Inside	Inside
Inside	Intersects	Outside	Q_2	Inside
Inside	Outside		Outside	Inside
Intersects	Inside		Q_1	Inside
Intersects	Intersects	Q_1^c	$Q_1 \cap Q_2$	$Q_1 \cup Q_2$
Intersects	Outside		Outside	Q_1
Outside	Inside		Outside	Inside
Outside	Intersects	Inside	Outside	Q_2
Outside	Outside		Outside	Outside

Table 1. Rules for Simplification of the Query Tree

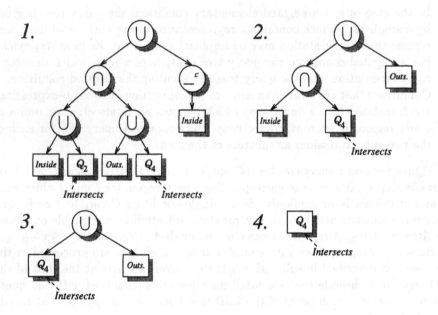

Fig. 9. Example for the Simplification of a Query Tree

Unless simplification yields *Outside* as the new root of the query tree, the traversal resumes afterwards as follows: if the data region for which the query tree has been evaluated belongs to a directory node, the new query tree replaces the old one for subsequent searches on the subtrees. In the other case a bucket has been reached, and the situations given below are distinguished:

1. The query tree has been simplified to *Inside*: all objects stored in the bucket belong to the query result and are reported without further investigation.

2. The query tree has not yet been simplified to a constant: each object found in the bucket has to be tested against the remaining query tree. This is done by checking the object against each elementary query region and combining the results: if a node denotes an intersection or union of query regions, the results from the sons are **and**- and **or**-connected, respectively; if the node stands for a complementation, the result of the son is negated.

Next, we are going to give an impression how the discussed strategy may be practically realised. At first, the select condition must be translated into a query tree. Each leaf stores a representation of the corresponding elementary query region and is marked with the kind of query (e.g. polygonal range query, mathematical query on numeric attributes). The latter information makes it possible to decide which function for checking a data region, respectively an object, against the query region should be called. Sub-conditions corresponding to query regions which cannot be supported – either because the required functions have not been implemented, or attributes are specified which are not considered in the LSD-tree – are stored literally and marked with a specific flag.

The range query is afterwards performed as presented resulting in a simplification of the query tree in each step. Leaves that contain non-supportable sub-conditions are ignored during the traversal of the directory and remain in the query tree if they can not be eliminated within the simplification process of the query tree. When a bucket is accessed, the remaining query tree is applied to each found object as outlined; non-supportable sub-conditions are then evaluated in the obvious way.

For the implementation one should note that whenever the query tree has to be checked against a data region of a directory node or bucket w only those leaves of the query tree must be considered which are associated with the split dimension stored in the directory node which is the father of w. The reason is that the data region of the son of a directory node coincides in all other dimensions with the one of its father, which has already been checked[10].

At the end of this section we briefly summarise the advantages of our approach:

1. Both geometric attributes and standard attributes are handled in a unified way and may be specified together in a single condition.
2. Select conditions which cannot be automatically converted into one or more geometric query regions can be processed.
3. For every sub-condition only those dimensions of the data space must be considered which correspond to attributes specified in it.
4. At each node of the directory only query regions affected by the split dimension associated with the father of the current node need to be examined.
5. Since sub-conditions which cannot be processed with the aid of an LSD-tree can be integrated into the proposed methods in a homogeneous way, we are not concerned with undesirable special cases.

---

[10] Obviously this is not true for comparisons against $D^a(w)$

5 Outline of the Methods for Join- and Nearest-Neighbour-Queries

After we have shown how selections are processed, we are now going to give an idea of how the proposed methods may be exploited to support other important types of queries.

In the introduction we have presented a query which retrieves all big cities of Germany. If we want to find all big cities of the neighbouring countries of, say, Switzerland, associated with the state they belong to, we require a join (here *Switzerland* denotes a polygon that describes the boundaries of Switzerland):

Cities States ⋈ [((CLocation **inside** Territory) **and**
(Territory **is_neighbour_of** Switzerland)) **and**
(CPopulation ≥ 100000)]

In this query, we assume the availability of an LSD-tree for the attributes *CLocation* and *CPopulation* of the relation *Cities*.

As for select conditions, join conditions may involve both geometric and standard attributes and may be composed of several elementary sub-conditions. Elementary sub-conditions possibly refer to both affected relations.

How could such a query be processed with the aid of an LSD-tree? The basic idea is that of repeated search: the non-indexed relation is scanned, and for each loaded object a search on the index is performed. The search is done with a select condition derived from the join condition as follows: the attribute names of attributes of the scanned relation are substituted by the attribute values of the current object; then, constant sub-expressions are evaluated, and the remaining condition is simplified as far as possible, leading to one of the following situations:

The condition has been simplified to *false*: the join condition cannot be satisfied regardless of with which object of the second relation the current object is joined; the object should be skipped.

The condition has been simplified to *true*: the current object being joined with any object of the second relation fulfils the required condition; a scan of the second relation has to be performed.

None of the previous cases apply: the simplified condition refers only to attributes of the second relation and can be used as select condition for a search on the LSD-tree; the current object is joined with each reported object.

In our example, while scanning the relation *States*, we may find the object for Spain. The attribute name *Territory* is then replaced by the polygon which represents the boundaries of this country. Since Spain is not a neighbouring country of Switzerland, the second sub-condition, which now is constant, evaluates to *false*. After simplification we realise that the object can be skipped. Later we may find the object for Germany. In this situation, the second sub-condition evaluates to *true*, and we end up with the selection discussed in the introduction.

In a closest-query, the geometric object(s) with a minimal distance from a given point are searched. As for range queries, the set of geometric objects to be considered may be restricted to objects with desired properties. A typical example would be to find the nearest city with an international airport relative to a certain location.

In practice, one is often interested in more information, e.g., if more than one airport may be in reachable distance – within a radius of 200 km, say – and one wants to compare the prices for a flight to a given destination. In this case, a sorted list of cities in ascending order according to their distance would suit best. This is exactly what a distance-scan yields. In [Hen94] an efficient algorithm for distance-scans is proposed. Roughly spoken, this algorithm works as follows:

We start at the root of the directory and search for the bucket for which the bucket region contains the starting point of the distance scan, say p. Every time during this search when we follow the left son, we insert the right son into an auxiliary data structure NPQ (= node priority queue), where the element with the smallest distance between p and its data region has highest priority, and every time we follow the right son, we insert the left son into NPQ.

Then the objects in the found bucket are inserted into another auxiliary data structure OPQ (= object priority queue), where the object with the smallest distance to p has highest priority. Thereafter the objects with a distance to p less than or equal to the minimal distance between p and data region of the first element in NPQ are taken from OPQ.

Now the directory node or bucket with highest priority is taken from NPQ. If it happens to be a directory node, a new search is started choosing always the son on the side of the split line facing p. The other son is inserted into NPQ. The bucket determined in this way is processed inserting the objects stored in this bucket into OPQ and removing the objects with a distance to p less than or equal to the minimal distance between p and the first element in NPQ from OPQ. Thereafter the process is continued in the same way.

If a distance scan is combined with a select condition, we can combine this distance scan algorithm with the proposed technique for select conditions in the following way.

Every time a directory node has to be considered, the data regions of both sons are checked against the query tree corresponding to the select condition. Then three cases have to be distinguished: (1) The computed relationship is *Outside* for both sons; in this case the investigation of the path under concern can be finished and the first element of NPQ has to be used to continue. (2) The computed relationship is *Outside* for exactly one son; then the other son is used to continue. (3) Otherwise; the son with the smaller minimal distance between p and its data region is used to continue, and the other son is inserted into NPQ together with the corresponding simplified query tree.

If an object has to be inserted into OPQ, it is checked against the query tree corresponding to the actual bucket. If this check is successful, the object is inserted into OPQ. Otherwise it is skipped.

The described integration of the join as well as the distance-scan algorithm and the proposed techniques for selections shows the broad applicability of our approach.

6 Summary and Further Developments

In this paper we have proposed methods which overcome the main problems which occur when spatial access structures are employed to maintain standard attributes in addition to geometric objects. Furthermore, we have shown how these methods help to perform join- as well as a large variety of nearest-neighbour-queries. For the LSD-tree the methods have been implemented into the Gral-system [Güt89]. The experiences made within this geometric database system have proven the practical usefulness of the methods.

Although a large number of elementary conditions on geometric as well as non-geometric attributes are supported, special methods for further query types, which e.g. involve both geometric attributes and non-geometric ones in a single elementary expression, may still be developed. The integration of the *Vertices Approach* provides a model for adding new methods to the existing framework.

Another area that deserves further investigation is the processing of joins in the case that more than one relation is maintained by an LSD-tree. For other multi-dimensional structures methods for executing equi-joins have been proposed, e.g. in [OB88, CFMT86, TRN86]; [KHT89] even considers *k-d*-trees. For more complex joins, we only know of one approach for grid files [NHS84], which is presented in [BHF93].

References

[Ben75]   J.L. Bentley. Multidimensional binary search trees used for associative searching. *Communications of the ACM*, 18(9):509–517, 1975.

[BHF93]   L. Becker, K. Hinrichs, and U. Finke. A New Algorithm for Computing Joins with Grid Files. In *Proc. IEEE Int'l. Conf. on Data Eng.*, pages 190–197, Vienna, Austria, April 1993.

[BKSS90]   N. Beckmann, H.-P. Kriegel, R. Schneider, and B. Seeger. The R*-tree: an efficient and robust access method for points and rectangles. In *Proceedings of the ACM SIGMOD Int. Conf. on Management of Data*, pages 322–331, Atlantic City, 1990.

[CFMT86]   J.P. Cheiney, P. Faudemay, R. Michel, and J.M. Thevenin. A Reliable Parallel Backend Using Multiattribute Clustering and Select-Join Operator. In *Procs. VLDB*, pages 220–227, 1986.

[Fre87]   M. Freeston. The BANG file: a new kind of grid file. In *Proc. of the ACM SIGMOD Intl. Conf. on Management of Data*, pages 260–269, San Francisco, 1987.

[GB91]   O. Günther and J. Bilmes. Tree-based access methods for spatial databases: implementation and performance evaluation. *IEEE Trans. on Knowledge and Data Engineering*, pages 342–356, 1991.

[Gut84]   A. Guttman. R-trees: A dynamic index structure for spatial searching. In *Proc. of the ACM SIGMOD Intl. Conf. on Management of Data*, pages 47–57, Boston, 1984.

[Güt88]   R.H. Güting. Geo-Relational-Algebra: A Model and Query Language for Geometric Database Systems. In J.W. Schmidt, S. Ceri, and M. Missikoff, editors, *'Advances in Database Technology – EDBT'*. Proc. of the Intl. Conf. on Extending Database Technology, pages 506–527, 1988.

[Güt89]   R.H. Güting. Gral: An Extensible Relational Database System for Geometric Applications. In *Proc. of the 15th Intl. Conf. on Very Large Databases*, 1989.

[Hen94]   A. Henrich. A distance-scan algorithm for spatial access structures. In *Proc. of the 2nd ACM Workshop on Advances in Geographic Information Systems*, 1994. to appear.

[Hin85]   K. Hinrichs. *The grid file system: implementation and case studies of applications*. Dissertation Nr. 7734, ETH Zürich, 1985.

[HM95]   A. Henrich and J. Möller. Die Nutzung mehrdimensionaler Zugriffsstrukturen für Standardattribute. In *Proc. GI-Fachtagung Datenbanksysteme in Büro, Technik und Wissenschaft*, Dresden, 1995. to appear.

[HSW89a] A. Henrich, H.-W. Six, and P. Widmayer. Paging binary trees with external balancing. In *Proc. 15th Intl. Conf. on Graph-Theoretic Concepts in Computer Science*, pages 260–276, Aachen, 1989.

[HSW89b] A. Henrich, H.-W. Six, and P. Widmayer. The LSD-tree: spatial access to multidimensional point and non point objects. In *Proc. 16th Intl. Conf. on Very Large Data Bases*, pages 45–53, Amsterdam, 1989.

[HSW90]   A. Hutflesz, H.-W. Six, and P. Widmayer. The R-File: An Efficient Access Structure for Proximity Queries. In *Proc. IEEE 6th Int. Conf. on Data Engineering*, pages 372–379, 1990.

[KHT89]   M. Kitsuregawa, L. Harada, and M. Takagi. Join Strategies on KD-Tree Indexed Relations. In *Proc. IEEE Conference on Data Engineering*, pages 85–93, 1989.

[KO91]   M.J. van Kreveld and M.H. Overmars. Divided k-d Trees. *Algorithmica*, 6:840–858, 1991.

[LS89]   D.B. Lomet and B. Salzberg. A Robust Multi-Attribute Search Structure. In *Proc. IEEE 5th Intl. Conf. on Data Engineering*, pages 296–304, 1989.

[NHS84]   J. Nievergelt, H. Hinterberger, and K.C. Sevcik. The Grid File: an adaptable, symmetric multikey file structure. *ACM Transactions on Database Systems*, 9(1):38–71, 1984.

[OB88]   E.A. Ozkarahan and C.H. Bozsahin. Join Strategies Using Data Space Partitioning. *New Generation Computing*, 6:19–39, 1988.

[OMSD87] B.C. Ooi, K.J. McDonell, and R. Sacks-Davis. Spatial kd-Tree: An Indexing Mechanism for Spatial Databases. In *IEEE COMPSAC*, pages 433–438, 1987.

[Rob81]   J.T. Robinson. The K-D-B-Tree: A Search Structure for Large Multdimensional Dynamic Indexes. In *Proc. of the ACM SIGMOD Intl. Conf. on Management of Data*, pages 10–18, 1981.

[SK88]   B. Seeger and H.-P. Kriegel. Techniques for design and implementation of efficient spatial access methods. In *Proc. 14th Intl. Conf. on Very Large Databases*, pages 360–371, 1988.

[SK90]   B. Seeger and H.-P. Kriegel. The buddy-tree: an efficient and robust access method for spatial data base systems. In *Proc. of the 16th Intl. Conf. on Very Large Data Bases*, pages 590–601, Brisbane, 1990.

[SRF87]   T. Sellis, N. Roussopoulos, and C. Faloutsos. The R+-tree: a dynamic index for multi-dimensional objects. In *Proc. 13th International Conference on Very Large Data Bases*, pages 507–518, 1987.

[TRN86]   J.A. Thom, K. Ramamohanarao, and L. Naish. A Superjoin Algorithm for Deductive Databases. In *Procs. VLDB*, pages 189–196, 1986.

Towards a Formal Model for Multiresolution Spatial Maps

Enrico Puppo and Giuliana Dettori

Istituto per la Matematica Applicata
Consiglio Nazionale delle Ricerche
Via De Marini, 6 - 16149 Genova - ITALY
Email: {PUPPO,DETTORI}@IMA.GE.CNR.IT

Abstract. Topological and metric aspects of the multiresolution representation of geographic maps are considered. The combinatorial structure of maps is mathematically modelled through *abstract cell complexes*, and maps at different detail are related through continuous functions over such complexes. Metric aspects of multiresolution are controlled through the concept of homotopy. Two alternative multiresolution models are proposed, which are implicitly defined by a sequence of map simplifications that fulfil both topological and metric consistency rules.

1 Introduction

The representation of spatial data at different resolution in the context of a unified model is a topic of relevant interest in spatial information theory. Indeed, multiresolution modelling offers interesting capabilities for spatial representation and reasoning: from support to map generalisation and automated cartography [15], to efficient browsing over large GISs, to structured solutions in wayfinding and planning [25].

Current GISs do not offer much in multiresolution data handling: apart from some hierarchical capabilities in raster modelling, which are essentially based on structures and tools inherited from image processing, there is an almost total lack of features for handling and relating spatial data at different resolutions. In order to support GISs of future generations, it seems worthwhile to pursue the definition of a formal framework for multiresolution representation of spatial entities based on a topological model that offers explicit description of spatial objects, and efficient encoding/retrieval of spatial relations.

A fair amount of work has been done in the last few years in the direction of a formal approach to the description and manipulation of spatial entities and their relationships [8, 17, 9, 27, 16, 5, 28, 12], and a number of models have been proposed in the literature for giving a comprehensive representation of the geometric structure of plane geographic maps (see, e.g., [14, 7, 21, 27, 22, 5]). Different models are characterised mostly by their expressive power, defined by the degree of generality of objects and configurations that they are able to represent, and by the different data structures that they require to support the representation of such objects and configurations.

Some research has also been undertaken that address multiple representations of spatial data in the context of GIS, concerning either the development of data models [2, 3, 15], or the assessment of consistency among different representations [10, 11, 13]. The possibility of developing models that can support the multiresolution representation of maps through hierarchical structures based on trees of cells has been outlined in [15]. A first hierarchical model that is formally defined on a mathematical basis has been proposed in [1]: such model is described by a tree of maps at different resolutions, where each map is the refined description of a simple region of its parent node in the tree.

In this paper, we exploit mathematical principles from the theory of cell complexes to establish a formal basis for the definition of multiresolution maps. The scope of this work is limited to generic geographic objects represented in the context of two-dimensional maps. For the sake of clarity, we list assumptions and guidelines on which we rely, before introducing the technical content of the paper.

1. A plane map is composed of spatial entities of three classes, namely *points*, *lines*, and *regions* embedded in the Euclidean plane: we will make distinction between such *entities* and spatial (semantic) *objects* that they represent.

2. A broad classification of relationships intercurring among spatial entities is into *topological* relations, *metric* relations, and *order* relations. The three classes of relationships involve different geometric properties, and can be studied independently: here, we do not consider issues concerning order relations.

3. Spatial entities forming a thematic map have disjoint relative interiors, i.e., they form a partition of the domain of the map, therefore they are allowed to take only the subset of topological relations, which exclude intersection of interiors.

4. Two maps of the same area at different resolutions can differ in two basic aspects:

   a) *detail*: some objects can be represented only in the map at higher resolution; objects that appear in both maps can be represented by entities of lower complexity and/or dimension in the context of the map at lower resolution; any object represented by an entity in the map at lower resolution must be also represented by either an entity or a group of entities in the map at higher resolution (monotonicity of simplification);

   b) *precision*: the spatial extent and location of any object in a map is approximated by the extent and location of the entity representing the object itself: the higher the resolution, the lower the approximation error.

   Changes in detail involve topological aspects, while changes in precision involve metric aspects: hence, they can be studied separately.

5. Two maps of the same area at different resolution must be consistent, i.e., objects that appear in both maps must maintain compatible spatial relationships.

The main results stated in this paper are the following. The topological structure of a geographic map is completely captured by a purely combinatorial structure called an *abstract cell complex*, which is, by all means, the only possible topological space apt to represent the map topology. *Map simplification*, i.e., an operation that relates two consistent maps at different detail, can be expressed through a continuous mapping between the abstract cell complexes representing the two maps. Moreover, suitable rules permit to control such functions in order to guarantee that simplification occurs through gradual changes. The metric aspects concerning changes in precision can be controlled separately through the concept of line homotopy: this part extends preliminary results stated in [1]. Through the iterative application of simplification mappings that satisfy both topological and metric constraints it is possible to define a sequence of gradually simplified maps of the same region. This sequence implicitly provides means to organise the maps, together with the mappings relating them in the sequence, either in a multi-layer model, or in a hierarchical model described by a tree, which extends the model proposed in [1].

The rest of the paper is organised as follows. In Section 2 we give a mathematical characterisation of spatial entities, we review their topological relationships, and we give a formal definition of map. In Section 3 we introduce abstract cell complexes, we state the main results about their properties as topological spaces, and we show that they represent the whole combinatorial structure of maps. In Section 4 we show simplification rules and functions that can be used to relate maps at different detail. In Section 5 we focus on metric aspects by using ε-homotopies to relate spatial entities at different precision. In Section 6 we propose two possible multiresolution models that can be obtained through simplification functions. Finally, in Section 7 we address possible extensions and future work on this subject.

2 Spatial Entities, Relations, and Maps

As we stated in the Introduction (item 1), a plane map is composed of *points*, *lines*, and *regions* embedded in the Euclidean plane $\mathbf{R}^2$.

- A point is uniquely defined by its coordinates in a coordinate system on $\mathbf{R}^2$.
- A line is defined by a continuous function $l : I \to \mathbf{R}^2$, where $I = [0, 1]$ is the unit interval on the real line[1]; if $l(0) = l(1)$, line l is said *closed*, otherwise it is said *open*; points $l(0)$ and $l(1)$ of an open line l are called the *endpoints* of l; the set formed by an open line l without its endpoints is called the *relative interior* of l, while the relative interior of a closed line is the line itself; a line is called *simple* if either l is injective on I, or l is closed and injective on $[0, 1)$.

---

[1] With abuse of notation, we will often use l interchangeably to denote the parametric function of a line, and its image $l(I)$, which corresponds to the realisation of the line on the plane.

By Jordan theorem, a simple closed line separates $\mathbf{R}^2$ into two open sets: one set is bounded, called the *internal set*, and denoted int(l); the other set is unbounded, called the *external set*, and denoted ext(l). A *chain* is a sequence of lines $c = (l_0, \ldots, l_{k-1})$ such that $\forall i = 1, \ldots, k - 1$, $l_{i-1}(1) = l_i(0)$. With abuse of notation, points $l_0(0)$ and $l_{k-1}(1)$ are called *endpoints* of c, only in case $l_0(0) \neq l_{k-1}(1)$; all other endpoints of lines forming c are called *joints* of c. A chain c admits itself a line parametrization:

$$c(x) = l_i(kx - i) \quad \text{for } x \in [\frac{i}{k}, \frac{i+1}{k}], \quad i = 0, \ldots, k - 1$$

A chain is said *simple, open,* or *closed* if it is simple, open, or closed as a line, respectively.

– A region is characterised by a simple closed line (or chain) l_0, called the *outer boundary*, plus possibly a set of simple closed lines (or chains) $\{l_1, \ldots, l_k\}$, called the *inner boundaries*, such that: (i) no two such lines intersect; (ii) for $i = 1, \ldots, k$ line l_i is contained in int(l_0) and in ext(l_j), $\forall \, 0 \neq j \neq i$. The region defined by $\{l_0, \ldots, l_k\}$ is the subset of $\mathbf{R}^2$ defined as

$$\cap_{i=1}^{k} \text{ext}(l_i) \cap \text{int}(l_0),$$

i.e., it is the region interior to the outer boundary, and exterior to all inner boundaries. Inner boundaries define *holes* in the region. The number $\chi(r) = k + 1$ of closed lines defining a region r is called the *characteristic* of r. A region r without holes has $\chi(r) = 1$, and it is said *simply connected*, while a region with holes has $\chi(r) > 1$, and it is said *multiply connected*. The *interior* and *closure* of a region r correspond to the standard interior and closure of r regarded as a set of $\mathbf{R}^2$ with the Euclidean topology. The *boundary* of r is the subset of $\mathbf{R}^2$ covered by the lines defining r, corresponding to the difference between its closure and its interior. We will usually refer to a region r by assuming it closed, otherwise we will call it explicitly *open region r*.

Topological relations between a pair of simply connected regions are usually classified according to the so-called 4-intersection relations [9], which are obtained combinatorially from a simple scheme involving the mutual intersections between interiors and boundaries. The following eight relations are possible: *disjoint, meet, contains, covers, equal, overlap, inside,* and *coveredBy*. For regions with holes the classification is obtained by combining the 4-intersections among the simply connected regions interior to the outer boundaries (i.e., those obtained by eliminating the holes), and the simply connected regions corresponding to the holes [12]. Topological relations can be extended easily to pairs of atomic entities, including also lines and points: in this case, also relations *bounds* and *boundedBy* are possible, between entities of different dimensions, and such that one is contained in the boundary of the other [5].

A map is often regarded as a disjoint covering of a portion D of the plane $\mathbf{R}^2$, called the *domain* of the map, with a collection of atomic entities. A disjoint covering is a set of entities such that the relative interiors of any two such entities never intersect. We make a weaker assumption stated by the following constraints: no pair of open regions can intersect; no line can intersect the relative interior of a different line; no point can coincide with a different point, or intersect the relative interior of a line. Nevertheless, isolated open lines and points can be completely *inside* or *coveredBy* a region: such lines and points are called *features* of the region, and are different from the remaining lines and points of the map in being not part of the boundary of any region, and being not endpoints of any line, respectively[2] (see also [5]). We call such a covering a *weakly disjoint covering* (see Fig. 1 for an example of map satisfying a weakly disjoint covering).

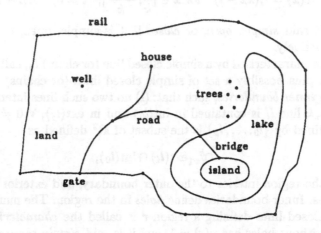

Fig. 1. An example of map: land, lake, and island are its regions; roads, trees, house, and well are features of land; bridge is a feature of lake; rail and gate form the boundary of land.

Given a generic set of atomic entities (which are the relevant entities to form a specific map, according to some semantics), a weakly disjoint covering of the portion of plane covered by such entities can be obtained by an overlay operation:

- whenever two open regions r, r' intersect, then they are fragmented into three sets of regions: the connected components of $r \setminus r'$; the connected components of $r' \setminus r$; the connected components of $r \cap r'$;
- whenever the relative interior of a line l intersects a point or another line l', then l is subdivided in two portions, joined at the intersection point.

Hence, a map can be represented as a triple $M = (P, L, R)$, where sets P, L, and R contain the points, lines, and regions of M, respectively. Note that M is completely characterised by P and L, since each region of R is understood as

---

[2] Some models of map require disjoint covering and do not accept features. We think that such a constraint is too strong to model real maps. On the other hand, it is possible to accept features while requiring disjoint covering if isolated lines (or chains) and points are considered as degenerated regions. This fact makes the definition of maps unwieldy, especially because any line *coveredBy* a region becomes part of the region boundary.

a maximal portion r of the plane such that any two points interior to r can be connected by a line that does not touch any line of L^3. This definition of map either conforms to, or extends models proposed previously in the literature (e.g., [21, 22, 5]).

The possible relations between pairs of entities in a map are highly simplified, with respect to the generic case. In the context of a single map, we can only have the following situations:

- two distinct regions either are *disjoint*, or they *meet* at a common boundary (possibly a single point);
- given a line l and a region r we can have one of the following: l and r are *disjoint*; l and r *meet* at a single point p, where p is an endpoint of l and p *bounds* r; l *bounds* r; l is *inside* r; l is *coveredBy* r (i.e., the relative interior of l is inside r, and one endpoint of l *bounds* r);
- given a point p and a region r we can have one of the following: p and r are *disjoint*; p *bounds* r (i.e., it is endpoint of two consecutive lines on the boundary of r); p is *inside* r;
- given two distinct lines they either are *disjoint*, or they *meet* at a common endpoint;
- given a point p and a line l they are either *disjoint*, or p *bounds* (i.e., it is an endpoint of) l;
- two distinct points are *disjoint*.

Note that for each non-symmetric relation listed above, the *converse* relation is verified too (e.g., l is *coveredBy* r if and only if r *covers* l).

We give the concepts of *combinatorial boundary* and *combinatorial coboundary*, or *star*, of entities in a map M, where each entity is regarded as an atom. The combinatorial boundary differs from the topological boundary defined before in being composed of a collection of cells, rather than being a subset of $\mathbf{R}^2$: the relation between the combinatorial and topological boundary is readily seen from the definition. In the sequel of the paper we will always omit the adjective combinatorial, whenever no ambiguity arises [20].

- The combinatorial boundary of any point $p \in P$ is empty; the combinatorial boundary of a line $l \in L$, denoted ∂l, is formed by its two endpoints if l is an open line, otherwise it is empty; the combinatorial boundary of a region $r \in R$, denoted ∂r, is formed by all lines and points of M contained either in r or in the Euclidean boundary of r.
- The star of a point $p \in P$, denoted $*p$, is either formed by all lines of L, and regions of R having p on their boundary, or is the region containing p in its interior, in case p is an isolated point or lies on a lineal feature; the star of a line $l \in L$, denoted $*l$, is either formed by the (at most two) regions having l as part of their boundary, or is the region containing l in its interior, in case l is a line feature; the star of a region $r \in R$ is r itself.

---

[3] This definition includes as a region of M also the infinite portion of plane surrounding the domain covered by the entities of M.

Given a map M, a chain c of lines in M is said a *free chain* if for any joint p of c, the only lines in $*p$ belonging to c. In other words, c meets no other lines of the map, except possibly at its endpoints.

On the basis of the concept of star, in the following section we make an abstraction over a map M, by considering only its combinatorial structure, while completely disregarding its metric structure. This fact will allow us to formally define and study separately all aspects of maps that are either purely combinatorial, or purely metric.

3   The Combinatorial Structure of Geographic Maps

The idea that geographic maps should be represented and studied as geometric cell complexes has been already stressed in the literature. Here, we handle the combinatorial aspects of maps through a structure that is more abstract than others proposed in the literature, such as simplicial complexes [7, 27], Plane Euclidean Graphs [5], or CW-complexes [22, 23]. Abstract cell complexes can capture the whole topological nature of maps, independently of their geometry [19, 20].

Let C be a finite set, called the *set of cells*. An *abstract cell complex* $\Gamma = (C, \prec, \dim)$ with cells in C is defined as follows:

- $\prec$ is a strict partial ordering on the elements of C (i.e., $\prec$ is an irreflexive, antisymmetric, and transitive binary relation) called the *bounding relation*;
- $\dim : C \to \mathbb{N}$, called the *dimension function*, is such that

$$\gamma' \prec \gamma'' \Rightarrow \dim(\gamma') < \dim(\gamma'').$$

A cell γ for which $\dim(\gamma) = k$ is called a *k-cell*. It is not restrictive to have $\dim$ such that there always exist some cells of dimension zero. A complex is called *d-dimensional* or a *d-complex* if $\max_{\gamma \in C}(\dim(\gamma)) = d$.

The *boundary*[4] of a cell γ of Γ is defined as $\partial \gamma = \{\xi \in C \mid \xi \prec \gamma\}$.

The *star* of a cell γ of Γ is defined as $*\gamma = \{\xi \in C \mid \gamma \prec \xi\} \cup \{\gamma\}$.

A *subcomplex* $\Gamma' = (C', \prec', \dim')$ of a given complex $\Gamma = (C, \prec, \dim)$ is a complex whose set C' is a subset of C, and relation $\prec'$ and function $\dim'$ are restrictions of $\prec$ and $\dim$ to C', respectively. A subcomplex Γ' of Γ is *open* if for every cell γ of Γ' all cells of the star of γ in Γ are also cells of Γ'. A subcomplex Γ' of Γ is *closed* if for every cell γ of Γ' all cells of the boundary of γ in Γ are also cells of Γ'. A subcomplex Γ' of Γ is *regular* if each cell γ of Γ' belongs to the star of some cell γ' of Γ' that has maximal dimension (possibly with $\gamma' = \gamma$). The *boundary* of a regular subcomplex Γ' is the set of cells of Γ' that belong to the boundary of some cell of $C \setminus C'$ in Γ; all other cells of Γ' are called *internal* cells.

It follows from the definitions above that in order to define a subcomplex Γ' of Γ it suffices to define the corresponding subset C' of the elements. All

---

[4] The overloading of terms *boundary* and *star* - that were already defined in the context of maps - is intentional here.

subcomplexes of Γ may be regarded as subsets of C, therefore, it is possible to use the common formulae of the set theory to define intersections, unions, and complements of subcomplexes of one and the same complex Γ. The following proposition was proven in [19]:

Proposition 3.1 *Let $\Gamma = (C, \prec, \dim)$ a cell complex. Let T_Γ be the (finite) set of all open subcomplexes of Γ. Then (C, T_Γ) is a separable topological space, and $B_\Gamma = \{*\gamma \mid \gamma \in C\}$ is a basis for (C, T_Γ).*

It is easy also to see that for any cell $\gamma \in \Gamma$, its star $*\gamma$ is indeed the smallest neighbourhood of γ; hence, all cells with maximum dimension are open sets.

The fact that Γ is a topological space is very important because allows us to exploit all results of topology - in particular, all results concerning mappings between topological spaces and homeomorphisms - to study the combinatorial structure of abstract cell complexes. Actually, an even stronger result states that each finite separable topological space is indeed an abstract cell complex [19]. For this reason the topology of cell complexes is called the *finite topology*: it is the only possible (non trivial) topology that one can consider on finite sets.

With this facts in mind, we observe that the family of all entities composing a map is indeed a finite set, and, thus, it should be possible to regard a map as an abstract cell complex. It is indeed straightforward to define an abstract cell complex on a map, which retains the whole combinatorial structure of M, while disregarding all its metric aspects. The proof of the following proposition is almost trivial, hence omitted.

Proposition 3.2 *Let $M = (P, L, R)$ be a map. Let us define $C = P \cup L \cup R$. Let $\prec$ be a relation on C defined as follows:*

$$x \prec y \Leftrightarrow x \subset y,$$

where the symbol $\subset$ denotes containment between sets of $\mathbf{R}^2$. Let $\dim$ be a function defined as follows:

$$\dim(x) = \begin{cases} 0 & \text{if } x \in P \\ 1 & \text{if } x \in L \\ 2 & \text{if } x \in R \end{cases}$$

Then, $\Gamma = (C, \prec, \dim)$ is an abstract cell complex.

From now on, when dealing with purely combinatorial aspects of maps, we will use interchangeably a map M, and its associated cell complex Γ, whenever no ambiguity arises. Also, we will speak of a *submap* of M by meaning its associated subcomplex $\Gamma' \subset \Gamma$. Therefore, we will speak of points, lines, and regions of a complex, by meaning its cells of dimension zero, one, and two, respectively. Note that purely geometric concepts defined on spatial entities, such as simple line, relative interior, portion, internal and external set, outer and inner boundary, hole, interior, and closure, have no meaning in the context of an abstract complex. Nevertheless, some concepts like endpoints, open and closed line, chain, characteristic of a region, and, thus, simply and multiply connected region, have a straightforward translation in the context of an abstract complex. It is interesting to notice that in abstract cell complexes we are still able to say whether a region has holes or not, although we cannot decide which adjacent regions lie inside the holes, and which in the outer space: there is indeed no concept of outer space! The concept of characteristic is extended to a regular subcomplex (and its relative submap) by counting the number of closed chains forming the boundary of the subcomplex, as defined before.

By means of mappings and homeomorphisms between cell complexes we are able to characterise the similarity and equivalence of spatial maps. Let $\Gamma = (C, \prec$, dim) and $\Gamma' = (C', \prec', \dim')$ be two cell complexes. We call *mapping*[5] between Γ and Γ' an application $F : C \to C'$. With abuse of notation, we will indicate $F : \Gamma \to \Gamma'$.

A mapping F defined as above is said *continuous* if for each U open set of Γ' (endowed with the finite topology) the inverse image $F^{-1}(U)$ is open in Γ (also in the finite topology). In particular, F is continuous in $\gamma \in \Gamma$ if $F^{-1}(*F(\gamma))$ is an open neighborhood of γ. Continuous mappings have nice properties such as preserving connectedness. Thus, if γ, ξ *meet* in Γ, and F is continuous, then $F(\gamma)$ and $F(\xi)$ cannot be *disjoint* in Γ'.

A one-to-one correspondence $F : \Gamma \to \Gamma'$ for which both F and the inverse function F^{-1} are continuous is a homeomorphism in the finite topology: in this case Γ and Γ' are said to be *isomorphic* [20]. The isomorphism between two complexes guarantees that their associated maps are combinatorially equivalent, i.e., that both the entities composing the maps, and their spatial relationships are in one-to-one correspondance[6].

4 Map Simplification

Different maps that correspond to non homeomorphic cell complexes are not topologically equivalent. However, we are interested in studying maps that can be converted into each other by means of reciprocal processes of simplification/refinement, in which details are either discarded or introduced while maintaining consistent the overall structure. In this section we will see that such maps can be related through continuous mappings.

First of all, we must informally understand what changes can involve simplifying a map M into a less detailed map M'. The monotonicity assumption (item 4a in the Introduction) guarantees that for each entity in map M' there must exist a corresponding entity in M; moreover, since each entity of M must correspond to something either simpler or equivalent in M', then a single entity

---

[5] In algebraic topology, an application between cell complexes is called a *map*. Here, we use the term *mapping* to avoid confusion with geographic maps, which are semantic objects whose structure is represented by cell complexes.

[6] In [13], *object homoemorphisms* and *relation homeomorphisms* between sets of spatial entities were defined. The isomorphism between cell complexes incorporates both the object homeomorphism, and the relation homeomorphism when spatial entities are considered in the context of a map.

of M can correspond to at most one entity in M'. These simple observations guarantee that the map-to-map correspondance describing a simplification from M to M' can be described by a surjective mapping $F : \Gamma \to \Gamma'$, that will be called a *simplification mapping*, where Γ and Γ' are the cell complexes describing M and M', respectively.

Let us consider now a generic entity e of a map M. We outline three possible basic simplifications of e into M':

- *preservation*: the object represented by e appears also in M' with the same dimension, and possibly with a simplified structure (e.g., if e is a region, its corresponding entity in M' will be also a region, possibly with a simplified boundary, or a smaller set of features, or a smaller characteristic).
- *reduction*: the object represented by e appears also in M', but with a lower dimension (e.g., if e is a region, its corresponding entity in M' could be a single point).
- *immersion*: the object represented by e disappears in M', i.e., it is immersed into some larger object.

If we translate the previous cases in terms of the simplification mapping we obtain:

- *preservation*: $\dim(F(\gamma)) = \dim(\gamma) \quad \wedge \quad \forall \tau \in \partial\gamma, \dim(F(\tau)) < \dim(\gamma)$;
- *reduction*: $\dim(F(\gamma)) < \dim(\gamma)$;
- *immersion*: $\dim(F(\gamma)) > \dim(\gamma) \quad \vee \quad (\dim(F(\gamma)) = \dim(\gamma) \quad \wedge$
$$\exists \tau \in \partial\gamma : \dim(F(\tau)) = \dim(\gamma)).$$

Note that when the image of a cell γ maintains the same dimension as γ itself, it may be either that γ is maintained in the simplification, or that it is immersed into a "larger" cell. Indeed, when a whole submap of M is simplified into a unique region r' of M', any cell γ corresponding to a region of such submap must have as image γ' corresponding to region r'. The discrimination between preservation and immersion is obtained through the condition on the boundary: indeed, if region r is immersed into region r', also one portion of the boundary of r must be immersed inside m'.

Further constraints on simplification are concerning the consistency of topological relationships in the domain and codomain. For instance, objects that *meet* before simplification, cannot possibly be *disjoint* in the simplified map; also, a point that is *disjoint* from a region cannot jump *inside* the region in the simplified map (unless both the point and the region are immersed into something bigger); on the other hand, it is possible that two *disjoint* regions r and s will *meet* after simplification, if, for instance, a third region t separating r from s is reduced to a line. A complete analysis of all possible cases arising from the simplification of pairs of entities is possible, on the basis of the admissible relationships between pairs of entities in a map (listed in Sect. 2). As one can easily guess, a result of such analysis is that a consistent simplification mapping must be continuous. Indeed, we need continuity if we want to guarantee that two objects that *meet* in the domain will not be *disjoint* in the codomain.

Although a complete analysis of possible cases is perhaps the most general approach to the formalization of consistency, it is quite involved and technical, hence not treated in this paper [6]. Here, we will rather give rules to define a continuous mapping, which reflect gradual changes, and can be used as constraints on the possible simplification mappings. So far, we have not given any constraint to guarantee the graduality of changes during simplification. The continuity of mappings guarantees consistency, but it is not sufficient to guarantee graduality: for instance, mapping of an arbitrarily complex structure into a map made of a single point is indeed continuous, but it is not much interesting! On the contrary, we wish to have simplification mappings that do not modify maps too abruptly, skipping meaningful intermediate representations.

We give rules only for the reductions of a single element that can happen without involving reductions of elements of higher dimension in its star, while reductions or immersions of elements of lower dimension are implied by the rules, and thus are defined inductively. The rules we list are not the only possible ones. Other consistent rules can be considered, depending on the application needs, still in the context of the same abstract framework. In the following, we use usual notations for regions, lines, and points, meaning their associated 2-, 1-, and 0-cells, respectively.

1. A line l can reduce to a point p' (Fig. 2a): in this case, also the endpoints of l are mapped to p'; the region(s) of $*l$ simplify to elements of $*p'$. In synthesis:

$$F(l) = p' \Leftrightarrow (\forall p \in \partial l,\ F(p) = p').$$

2. A free open chain c can reduce to an open line l' (Fig. 2b): in this case, all lines and joints of c are immersed into the same line l', while the endpoints of c are preserved into the endpoints of l'. In synthesis:

$$F(c) = l \Leftrightarrow (\forall l \text{ line of } c,\ F(l) = l')$$

$$\land$$

$$(\forall p \text{ joint of } c,\ F(p) = l')\ \land\ (\forall p \text{ endpoint of } c,\ F(p) \in \partial l').$$

The case of a closed chain that can reduce to a closed line is completely analogous: the condition on endpoints is just ignored.

3. A free open chain c can reduce to a point p': this case is easily derived from the composition of the previous two, hence not detailed.

4. A simply connected region r can reduce to a point p' (Fig. 2c): in this case, features and elements of the boundary of r are also reduced to p'. In synthesis:

$$F(r) = p' \Leftrightarrow \forall p, l \in \partial r,\ F(p) = F(l) = p'.$$

5. A simply connected region r can reduce to an open line l' (Fig. 2d-e): in this case, it must be possible to subdivide the boundary of r into four consecutive free chains $c_{p_0}, c_{l_0}, c_{p_1}, c_{l_1}$, where c_{p_0} and c_{p_1} can possibly be degenerate to single points (Fig. 2e), such that c_{l_0} and c_{l_1} reduce to l', and c_{p_0} and c_{p_1} reduce to the two endpoints of l', respectively. Endpoints and joints of chains

reduce consistently to such chains, according to rules 2 and 3. Let p'_0 and p'_2 denote the endpoints of l', and let symbol $\searrow$ denote a consistent reduction according to rule 2 or 3. In synthesis we have:

$$F(r) = l \Leftrightarrow (c_{l_0} \searrow l) \wedge (c_{l_1} \searrow l) \wedge (c_{p_0} \searrow p'_0) \wedge (c_{p_1} \searrow p'_1).$$

6. A regular submap $\bar{M}$ with characteristic k, containing more than one entity, can reduce to a single region r with characteristic k (Fig. 2f): in this case, all regions of $\bar{M}$ are immersed into r; all lines and point s internal to $\bar{M}$ are either immersed into r or mapped to features of r (through consistent mappings, according to rules 1, 2, 3); all lines and points forming the boundary of $\bar{M}$ are mapped to the boundary of r (through consistent mappings, according to rules 1, 2, 3). The synthetic description of this transformation is involved and omitted here for brevity [6].

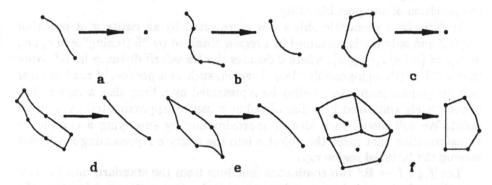

Fig. 2. Simplifications of entities and submaps: (a) from line to point; (b) from chain to line; (c) from region to point; (d,e) two different simplifications from region to line; (f) from submap to region.

It is easy to verify that a mapping $F : \Gamma \rightarrow \Gamma'$ satisfying the rules listed above will verify the following conditions on the inverse images of elements of Γ'.

- $\forall p'$ point of Γ', $F^{-1}(p')$ is formed either by a single point, or by an edge plus its endpoints, or by a free chain plus its joints and endpoints, or by a simply connected region plus the elements of its boundary.
- $\forall l'$ line of Γ', $F^{-1}(l')$ is formed either by a single line, or by the lines forming a free chain plus all joints of the chain, or by a simply connected region plus a portion of its boundary formed by two free chains without their endpoints, and such that the rest of the boundary is formed by two connected components, each of which is either a free chain or a point.
- $\forall r'$ region of Γ', $F^{-1}(r')$ is either a region, or an open regular submap of Γ having the same characteristic as r'.

By using such conditions it is easy (though tedious) to test that the inverse image of $*\gamma'$, for every $\gamma' \in \Gamma'$ is open in Γ, and hence, that a simplification F satisfying rules 1-6 is continuous [6].

5 Metric Aspects of Multiresolution

The previous discussion on map similarity takes into consideration only the combinatorial structure of maps. However, the fact that two maps have consistent structures does not imply that they are also metrically consistent. While variations in the combinatorial structure are related to the concept of detail in a map, variations of its metric aspects are related to the concept of precision (see item 4 in the Introduction).

In [1], the precision of a map was measured through the horizontal error in representing the lines in the map, formalised through the mathematical concept of ε-homotopy. Here, we extend and formalise further such concept to measure the precision of any possible entity.

Intuitively, a geometric object o is represented by an entity e at precision $\varepsilon \geq 0$ if and only if o is contained in a region obtained by "fattening" e of ε, i.e., in $r_{e,\varepsilon} = \{x \mid d(x,e) \leq \varepsilon\}$, where d denotes the Hausdorff distance in $\mathbb{R}^2$. Note that a "thin"(though possibly "long") region, such as a portion of road or river in a geographic map, can possibly be represented by a line; also, a region that is completely contained in a disc of radius ε can be approximated by a single point. We will model such idea of approximation by specifying a continuous transformation that maps the object o into the entity e representing it without leaving the fattened region $r_{e,\varepsilon}$.

Let $f, g : I \to \mathbb{R}^2$ two continuous functions from the standard unit interval into the real plane. A *homotopy* between f and g is a continuous function $H : I \times I \to \mathbb{R}^2$ such that $H(x,0) = f(x)$ and $H(x,1) = g(x)$ [24]. Such homotopy H defines a continuous deformation from f to g through all functions $H(\cdot,y)$, $y \in (0,1)$. For $\varepsilon \geq 0$, a homotopy H is called an ε-homotopy if

$$\forall x \in I, \ \forall y \in I, \ \ d(H(x,y), H(x,0)) < \varepsilon.$$

If H is an ε-homotopy between functions f and g, then f and g are said ε-homotopic. In particular, if f and g are two lines, this means that we can approximate f by g (or viceversa) with precision ε. Note that the ε-homotopy implies a condition much stronger than simply assuming g inside the region fattening f: indeed, ε-homotopy requires that any portion of g remains inside the fattened region of the corresponding portion of f; or, in other words, that two walkers synchronised to start together from $f(0)$ and $g(0)$, and to arrive together at $g(1)$ and $f(1)$ respectively, will always remain at a distance smaller or equal than ε. This fact excludes that g could possibly be a line going back and for an arbitrary number of times inside the "tube" surrounding f (see Fig. 3a), while it is admitted a fractal representation g that has a length much higher than f, but remains locally near f (see Fig. 3b).

Fig. 3. Approximations of lines (f is the thick line, g is the thin line): (left) g is not ε-homotopic to f; (right) g is ε-homotopic to f.

If f is a line and g is a constant function, then the fact that H is a ε-homotopy means that f can be approximated by a single point at precision ε.

Approximations of regions can be defined by considering ε-homotopies of the lines (chains) defining their boundaries. A region r can be approximated by a point p at precision ε if and only if the outer boundary of r is ε-homotopic to p (seen as a constant function). A region r can be approximated by a line l at precision ε if and only if the outer boundary of r can be subdivided into two chains such that each of them is ε-homotopic to l . A region r can be approximated by another region s if and only if (i) the outer boundary of r is ε-homotopic to the outer boundary of s, (ii) each inner boundary of s is ε-homotopic to an inner boundary of r, and (iii) any inner boundary of r that is not ε-homotopic to an inner boundary of s is ε-homotopic to a point. A regular submap $\bar{M}$ can be approximated by a region r at precision ε if and only if the region covered by $\bar{M}$ is ε-homotopic to r.

Based on the above definitions, we can introduce the concept of ε-simplification of a map. Given two maps M and M', a simplification $F : M \to M'$ is an *ε-simplification* if and only if

$$\forall e' \in M' \ e' \text{ approximates } F^{-1}(e') \text{ at precision } \varepsilon.$$

Hence, combinatorial and metric map simplifications, based respectively on variations of detail and of precision, are combined to obtain a simplified map that is consistent both in maintaining compatible topological and metric relations.

Note that the level of precision does not give by itself any condition on map elements that survive, and elements that are immersed, when simplifying M into M'. This is due to the fact that the degree of detail and the level of precision of a map are not necessarily related with each other, since there is no quantifiable dependence between the scale of a map and the fact that a given entity appears in it or not. Indeed, the relation between the relevance of an entity and the scale of a map can depend both on the size of the entity and on the semantics associated to the map. In actual implementations of systems for map generalisation, combinatorial and metric criteria must be strictly interrelated, together with semantic criteria, and all such information must be integrated to guide map simplification. The detail reduction, whose consistence we have analysed by formal methods, must be actually driven by metric checks on the actual map features, while reductions based on metric evaluations can be applied only as long as they do not violate structural consistency. However, we think that it is very important to separate the two components when working on theoretic aspects of multirepresentation, because the two levels involve different problems, and can be better studied in different mathematical environments.

6 Multiresolution Models

Let M_0 be a map at the maximum available resolution, and let M_1 be a simplification of M_0 through a simplification mapping F_1. If we apply a simplification mapping $F_2 : M_1 \rightarrow M_2$, and so on iteratively, we obtain a whole sequences of upward compatible maps,

$$M_0 \overset{F_1}{\rightarrow} M_1 \overset{F_2}{\rightarrow} \ldots \overset{F_3}{\rightarrow} M_n,$$

corresponding to less and less detailed descriptions of the same area. Note that the composed mapping

$$F^i = F_1 \circ F_2 \circ \cdots \circ F_i : M_0 \rightarrow M_i,$$

$\forall i = 1, \ldots, n$, is itself continuous, and it describes a *macro-simplification* of M_0, which transforms it abruptly from the full resolution to the i-th degree of detail. If we are further given an increasing sequence of tolerances $\varepsilon_1 < \varepsilon_2 < \ldots < \varepsilon_n$, such that the composed mapping F^i, $\forall i = 1, \ldots, n$, is a ε_i-simplification of M_0, then our sequence is consistent both with detail and precision simplification, and it is called a *multiresolution sequence*.

Let $\mathcal{M} = \{M_i \mid i = 0 \ldots, n\}$ be the whole family of maps of a multiresolution sequence, and let $\mathcal{F} = \{F_i \mid i = 1 \ldots, n\}$ be the corresponding family of simplifications, as defined above. The pair $(\mathcal{M}, \mathcal{F})$ is called a *layered multiresolution model*. A layered multiresolution model represents the map of a domain at different levels of resolution through different independent models that cover the whole domain. Models that are adjacent in the sequence are related through simplification mappings, which can be implemented as "vertical" links that allow browsing the model through the different levels of resolution, while "horizontal" browsing happens in the context of a single map.

In order to make more manageable the whole structure, it is possible to define an alternative model, in which every map $\mathcal{M}$ can be subdivided into independent submaps covering disjoint portions of the domain. In such a model a portion of a map can be handled without needing to consider the map of the whole domain. This approach gives rise to a hierarchy of maps similar to that proposed in [1], which is described by a tree structure. The hierarchy can be inductively defined on the basis of the multiresolution sequence. Since maps represented with more detail and precision contain a higher number of elements, the tree results reversed with respect to the layered model, i.e., it has as root the map at coarsest resolution.

Let M_n be the root node. The tree is defined inductively on the basis of the inverse image of elements inside each node. Given a generic node $M_{i,j}$, which is a submap of M_i (initially, we have $M_{n,1} = M_n$), we consider each element e_k

of $M_{i,j}$ whose inverse image through F_i^{-1} contains more than one cell. For each such element e_k we build a node[7]

$$M_{i-1,k} = \overline{F_i^{-1}(e_k)},$$

where $\overline{F_i^{-1}(e_k)}$ denotes the closure of $F_i^{-1}(e_k)$ (i.e., the inverse image is completed with its boundary). According to the usual terminology, $M_{i-1,k}$ is a *child* of $M_{i,j}$, labeled through e_k. Let $\mathcal{N} = \{M_n, M_{n-1,1}, \ldots, M_{0,h}\}$ be the whole family of submaps generated inductively as above, and let us define

$$\mathcal{E} = \{(M_{i,j}, M_{i-1,k}) \mid M_{i-1,k} \text{ is child of } M_{i,j}\}.$$

The pair $(\mathcal{N}, \mathcal{E})$ is called a *hierarchical multiresolution model*.

The child relationship expresses the *refinement* of (a portion of) a map, while the inverse *parent* relationship expresses a simplification. The root M_n represents the map over the whole domain, at precision ε_n; all nodes at level i represent portions of the map at the same resolution ε_i.

The model is richer than the hierarchical model described in [1], since the nodes of the tree are not simply refinements of regions, but they can also be non-regular submaps refining points and lines through chains, lines, and regions, as described in Section 4.

7 Concluding Remarks

We have given a formal framework that permits to study the representation of maps at multiple resolution by mathematical tools that keep combinatorial and geometric aspects separated. Abstract cell complexes and mappings appear promising means for handling the relations between maps at different detail, while ε-homotopies help handling multiple precision.

On the basis of such framework we have defined compatibility rules for mappings that define gradual simplifications of maps into less detailed ones. We have combined such mappings with metric aspects in order to obtain map transformations that take into account both combinatorial and metric aspects of multiresolution. We have derived multiresolution models that admit a natural and elegant definition on the basis of a sequence of successive simplification mappings. Such models are more general than other multiresolution models previously proposed.

We believe that this study can be widely developed towards a more synthetic and precise interpretation of integrated combinatorial and metric aspects of multiresolution, in order to obtain a sound theory for multiresolution representations.

Although the scope of this paper is limited to two-dimensional geographic maps, the same concepts and tools can be applied in the context of multidimensional representations based on decompositions of domains into cells. We plan to extend our study in the future to structures in arbitrary dimension.

---

[7] We assume here that k is an index that uniquely identifies an element of M_i.

We have intentionally left out of the scope of this paper all issues concerning data structures and computational aspects of multiresolution. Based on former experience on multiresolution models for terrains [4], we believe that a clear formalization and a sound theory are essential for an efficient implementation of models. The literature offers several schemes of data structures for multidimensional cell complexes, that seem suitable as a starting point to elaborate the necessary data structures to implement our representation framework. From the computational point of view, constructing a multiresolution representation implies classical problems of map simplification, hence requiring a variety of topological, metric and semantic bindings. We believe that our formalization helps providing topological and metric constraints to support logical deduction in the framework of hybrid systems for map simplification. We plan to tackle data structures and computational aspects in future work.

References

1. Bertolotto, M., De Floriani,L., Puppo, E.: Multiresolution topological maps. In Advanced Geographic Data Modelling - Spatial Data Modelling and Query Languages for 2D and 3D Applications, M. Molenaar, S. De Hoop (eds.), Netherland Geodetic Commission, Publications on Geodesy - New Series, 40, pp.179-190
2. Bruegger,B. , Frank, A. : Hierarchies over topological data structures. Proceedings ASPRS-ACSM Annual Convention, Baltimore, MD, 1989, pp.137-145
3. Bruegger, B., Kuhn, W.: Multiple topological representations. Technical Report 91-17, National Center for Geographic Information and Analysis, Santa Barbara, Ca, 1991
4. De Floriani, L., Puppo E.: A hierarchical triangle-based model for terrain description. In Theories and Methods of Spatio-Temporal Reasoning in Geographic Space, eds. A.U. Frank, I. Campari, U. Formentini, Lecture Notes in Computer Science 639, Springer-Verlag, 1992, pp.236-251
5. De Floriani, L., Marzano, P. Puppo, E.: Spatial queries and data models. In Spatial Information Theory - A theoretical basis for GIS, A.U. Frank, I. Campari (Eds.), Lecture Notes in Computer Science 716, Springer-Verlag, 1993, pp.113-138
6. Dettori, G., Puppo, E.: Simplification of combinatorial maps through continuous mappings. Technical Report, 3-95, Istituto per la Matematica Applicata, C.N.R., 1995, Genova, Italy
7. Egenhofer, M., Frank, A.U., Jackson, J.P.: A topological model for spatial databases. In Design and Implementation of Large Spatial Databases, (SSD'89), Lecture Notes in Computer Science, 409, 1989, pp.271-286
8. Egenhofer, M., Herring, J.: A mathematical framework for the definition of topological relationships. Proceedings 4th International Symposium on Spatial Data Handling, Zurich, Switzerland, 1990, pp.803-813
9. Egenhofer, M., Franzosa, R.: Point-set topological spatial relations. International Journal of Geographical Information Systems, 5 (2), 1991, pp.161-174
10. Egenhofer, M., Sharma, J.: Topological consistency. Proceedings 5th International Symposium on Spatial Data Handling, Charleston, SC, 1992, pp.335-343
11. Egenhofer, M., Al-Taha, K.: Reasoning about gradual changes of topological relationships. In Theories and Methods of Spatio-Temporal Reasoning in Geographic

Space, A.U. Frank, I. Campari, U. Formentini (Eds.), Lecture Notes in Computer Science **638**, Springer-Verlag, 1992, pp.196-219

12. Egenhofer, M., Clementini, E., Di Felice, P.: Topological relations between regions with holes. International Journal of Geographical Information Systems, **8** (2), 1994, pp.129-142

13. Egenhofer, M., Clementini, E., Di Felice, P.: Evaluating inconsistencies among multiple representations. Proceedings 6th International Symposium on Spatial Data Handling, Edinburgh, Scotland, 1994, pp.901-920

14. Frank, A., Kuhn, W.: Cell graph: a provable correct method for the storage of geometry. Proceedings 2nd International Symposium on Spatial data Handling, Seattle, WA, 1986

15. Frank, A., Timpf, S.: Multiple representations for cartographic objects in a multiscale tree – An intelligent graphical zoom. Computers & Graphics, **18**, 6 (1994) pp.823-829

16. Hadzilacos, T., Tryfona, N.: A model for expressing topological integrity constraints in geographic databases. Lecture Notes in Compute Science, **639**, Springer-Verlag, 1992, pp.252-268

17. Kainz, W.: Spatial relationships - Topology versus order. Proceedings 4th International Symposium on Spatial Data Handling, pp.814-819, Zurich, Switzerland, July 1990

18. Kelly, J.L.: General Topology. D. Van Nostrand Co., 1955

19. Kovalevsky, V.A.: Finite topology as applied to image analysis. Computer Vision, Graphics, and Image Processing, **46**, 1989, pp.141-161

20. Lundell, A.T., Weingram, S.: The Topology of CW Complexes. Van Nostrand Reinhold Comp., 1969

21. Molenaar, M.: Single valued vector maps - a concept in GIS. Geo-Informationssysteme, **2** (1), 1989

22. Pigot, S.: A topological model for a 3D spatial information system. Proceedings 5th International Symposium on Spatial Data Handling, Charleston, SC, August 3-7, 1992

23. Pigot, S.: Generalized singular 3-cell complexes'. Proceedings 6th International Symposium on Spatial Data Handling, Edinburgh, Scotland, 1994, pp.89-111

24. Rourke, C.P., Sanderson, B.J.: Introduction to Piecewise-linear Topology. Springer-Verlag, 1972

25. Timpf, S., Volta, G.S., Pollock, D.W., Egenhofer, M.: A conceptual model of wayfinding using multiple levels of abstraction. In Theories and Methods of Spatio-Temporal Reasoning in Geographic Space, eds. A.U. Frank, I. Campari, U. Formentini, Lecture Notes in Computer Science **639**, Springer-Verlag, pp.348-367

26. Worboys, M.F., Hearnshaw, H.M., Maguire, D.J.: Object-oriented data modelling for spatial databases. International Journal of Geographical Information Systems, **4** (4), 1990, pp.369-383

27. Worboys, M.F.: A generic model for planar geographic objects. International Journal of Geographical Information Systems, **6** (5), 1992, pp.353-372

28. Worboys, M.F., Bokafos, P: A canonical model for a class of areal spatial objects. Advances in Spatial Database (SSD93), D. Abel, B.C. Ooi (Ed.s), Lecture Notes in Computer Science, Springer-Verlag, 1993, pp.36-52

Multi-Scale Partitions: Application to Spatial and Statistical Databases*

Philippe Rigaux[1,2] and Michel Scholl[1,2]

[1] Cedric/CNAM, 292 rue St Martin, F-75141 Paris Cedex 03, France
[2] INRIA, BP 105, F-78153 Le Chesnay Cedex, France.
{rigaux,scholl}@asimov.cnam.fr

Abstract. We study the impact of scale on data representation from both the modelling and querying points of view. While our starting point was geographical applications, statistical databases also address this problem of data representation at various levels of abstraction. From these requirements, we propose a model which allows: (i) database querying without exact knowledge of the data abstraction level, (ii) the computation of multiple representations of data, one per abstraction level, and (iii) its application to the computation of statistical summaries. The model has been partially implemented with the DBMS O_2 by means of tree-structured domains: we give some examples which illustrate the above features.

1   Introduction

Multi-scale representation of data has raised attention for a long time in Geographic Information Systems (GIS), because of its major importance for cartographic representation [SM89, BM91, LR94, MLW95]. However, the *cartographic generalisation* process intended to convert spatial data from one scale-dependent representation to another may also be considered from an *abstract* point of view [BW88] in relation with non-cartographic requirements such as those of spatial analysis.

Abstract generalization is closely linked to *multiple representation* [BD89, Gup89, Jon91, vO91] within Database Management Systems (DBMS): object representation changes according to the level of abstraction at which data is represented (see [RS94] for a general overview of the multi-scale issues within GIS databases). In this paper we propose a model for multi-scale representation. We show that this model not only applies to spatial databases but also to statistical databases [Sho82, Gho86, RS90]. We restrict our attention to a simple but very common situation where data is defined as an *hierarchy of partitions* of a single space. The model we define allows to represent and query databases containing such hierarchies.

---

* Work partially supported by the French *CNRS GDR Cassini*.

We discuss different ways of implementing such hierarchies which use hierarchical atomic values domains. We show a few examples of queries using O_2SQL [BCD89], the query language of the object-oriented DBMS (ODBMS) O_2 [BDK91], and give some guidelines for query optimization in the presence of such hierarchies. In particular we show that by rewriting some queries one might avoid the expensive use of spatial indices, using instead some "logical" indexing mechanism as provided by the hierarchy of partitions.

Although motivated by applications where there is a strict decomposition of the space, this work is useful for a variety of situations beyond GIS and statistical data analysis. In particular hierarchical domains can solve problems related to cooperative query answering [Mot86, Mot88, CCL91]. We give an example where the user can query a database with incomplete knowledge of the domain of the attributes present in the query: the user does not know at which abstraction level data is represented.

Section 2 introduces the problem through examples. A model for multi-scale representation is proposed in Section 3. Section 4 shows how the model can be applied to solve the examples of Section 2 and simple cooperative query answering situations. In Section 5, an implementation with O_2SQL is illustrated.

2 Examples of Multi-Scale Databases

Spatial generalization: Figure 1.A shows three simple objects (land parcels). At a lower scale (Figure 1.B) we have a different view of land use: we can only tell apart cereals from flowers. As a consequence, space partitioning based on land use classification results in three or two objects depending on the scale[3].

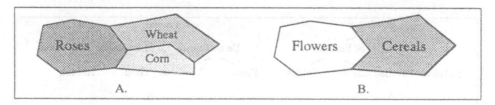

Fig. 1. : Impact of scale on spatial data

Statistical summaries: Table 1 displays a table of wine sales: for each wine (column) the sale in a given state (row) is given. Note that wines as well as states[4] are organized as *classification hierarchies* [RS90] with respective roots Bordeaux's wines and France. France is divided into administrative regions further split into states. Similarly, Bordeaux's wines are split into several production regions further split into single wines.

---

[3] The word *scale* will often be used in place of *level of abstraction* in the sequel.
[4] Such attributes are often denoted *category attributes* in the literature.

Wine sales		Bordeaux			
		Haut Médoc		St Emilion	
		St Julien	Pauillac	Lussac	Sables
Ile de France	Paris	1 500	870	550	700
	Yvelines	2 150	760	300	660
France Languedoc	Gard	1 900	800	500	460
Roussillon	Herault	1 100	670	330	230

Table 1: wine sales/states

Basically from Table 1, one would like to compute Table 2. In this table, sales are computed per administrative region and per production region. As a matter of fact, such a table is called a *summary* [Mal88, CMM88, dd94] of Table 1. Note that another *summary* of Table 2 would give the sale of Bordeaux per administrative region.

Wine sales		Bordeaux	
		Haut Médoc	St Emilion
	Ile de France	5 280	2 210
France	Languedoc Roussillon	5 140	1 750

Table 2: wine sales/region

Clearly from Tables 1 and 2, each *summary* is built on *tree-domain valued* category attributes represented in Figure 2 (A and B). More specifically, each *summary* includes for each category attribute only values from a given *abstract level* of the tree. {*St Julien, Pauillac, Lussac, Sables*} is an abstract level. {*Ht Medoc, St Emilion*}, is another abstract level (Figure 2.A).

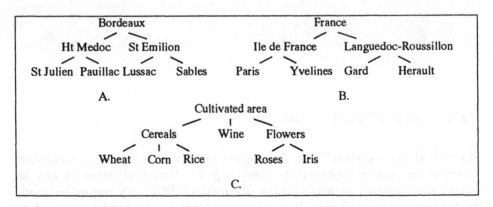

Fig. 2. : Tree-domain values

Land use (example 1) is also structured as a tree given in Figure 2.C: land use in Figure 1.A is taken among the leaves of the hierarchy in Figure 2.C, and simplified in a more abstract level including {*Flowers, Cereals*} in Figure 1.B.

A common feature to the above spatial and statistical multi-scale examples is the *partition* of objects according to some *descriptive* attribute (land use, sale state, wine). In both cases, a *simplification* of these attributes values relative to a change of scale implies an *aggregation* of some other attribute (in our examples: *geometric union* or *integer addition*).

We end this section with examples of queries on multi-scale databases. Consider the relation schema Parcel (land-owner, countyId, Luse, Geo): France Counties are split into smaller areas called parcels according to land use. The land owner of the parcel is recorded as well as the county to which it belongs and the geometry of the parcel. We assume that there is no other parcel in the same county with same land owner and same land use (a parcel might include several geometric zones). Here are two simple queries on such a relation.

1. Display the map of land use.

2. Classify counties in more abstract areas with schema (Luse, Geo) where the land use is chosen among $\{Wine, Cereals, Flowers, ...\}$ and the countyId and land-owner attributes have been projected out.

To answer query 1, one has to project first on (Luse, Geo) then nest [AB86] on Luse and finally compute for each tuple the parcel geometric union of the geometries (deleting inter parcel borders). Similarly, to answer query 2, one has first to project out attributes land-owner and countyId, then to replace attribute Luse by its ancestor in the hierarchy belonging to a more abstract level of the tree (e.g. Corn is replaced by Cereals), and then nest and perform the (geometric) union.

We started with a database including the single relation Parcel. One might as well have started with a set of administrative partitions of the French territory (e. g. one abstraction level for regions and one for counties) and a representation for the land use hierarchy. A typical query on such a database would be to obtain for example a (thematic) map of the Aquitaine counties where only the wine production areas (St Emilion, Pauillac, etc...) are represented. Such a query requires some overlay between the map of counties and the map of land use.

The following section presents a data model for such multiple scale databases. *Tree-domains, abstract levels, objects partitions* and *summaries* are more formally defined as well as a few operations for allowing queries such as those above.

3 A Model for Multiple Scale Partitions

3.1 Preliminaries

Let E be a subset of the plane: $E \subset R^2$ and $P \in 2^E$ be a partition of E, i.e. $\bigcup_P = E$ and $\forall p, p' \in P, p \cap p' = \emptyset$. Let $\wp(E)$ be the set of partitions of E and $\preceq$

be the following partial order on $\wp(E)$: $P \preceq P'$ iff $\forall p \in P, p' \in P', p \cap p' \in \{p', \emptyset\}$. Let $U = \{A_1, ..., A_n\}$ be the universe of *descriptive* attributes defined on domains $D(A_1), ..., D(A_n)$ and let O be any relation with schema $\{A_i^1, A_i^2, ..., A_i^q, Geo\}$, with $q \in [1, n]$ attributes in U and one geometric attribute Geo with domain $D(Geo) = 2^E$. O is called *geographic* relation.

Definition 1: A *cover* on E is a geographic relation O such that:

1. the relational projection $\pi_{Geo}(O)$ is a partition of E: $\pi_{Geo}(O) \in \wp(E)$

2. $A_1, ..., A_n \rightarrow Geo$ and $Geo \rightarrow A_1, ...A_n$[5].

An *elementary* cover is a cover with a single attribute $A \in U$. Let $\Omega(E)$ be the set of covers on E (for short Ω).

3.2 Geometric Operations on Ω

Let *intersect* be the intersection predicate $Geo \times Geo \rightarrow Bool$ and *intersection* $Geo \times Geo \rightarrow Geo$ be the set intersection on the plane. The *overlay* or *geometric join*[6] between two geographic relations O, O' denoted $O \bowtie_{Geo} O'$ is defined as:

$$O \bowtie_{Geo} O' = \{[a_1, ...a_m, a_1', ...a_p', g] | a_1, ...a_m, geo \in O, a_1', ...a_p', geo' \in O', geo \text{ intersect } geo', g = intersection (geo, geo')\}$$

Let O be a cover with schema $S' = \{A_1', ..., A_m', Geo\}$ and $S = \{A_1, ..., A_q\}$ be any subset of the descriptive attributes of S'. The *geometric projection* of O on S denoted $\prod_{S,Geo}(O)$ or $\prod_S(O)$ when there is no ambiguity, is defined as:

$$\prod_S(O) = apply_{\sum_{Geo}} (nest_S(\pi_{S,Geo}(O)))$$

where $apply_f(O)$ applies f to some attribute of each tuple of O, $nest_S$ is the N1NF grouping operation [BRS82, AB86, SS86] on S and $\sum_{Geo}: \{Geo\} \rightarrow Geo$ is the (geometric) sum agregate function where $+$ is (overloaded with) the set union over E[7].

Theorem 1: Ω is closed under geometric projection and geometric join.

Proof (sketch): one easily shows [Rig95] that $\pi_{Geo}(\prod_S(O))$ is a partition of E and that there is a bijection between $O' = \prod_S(O)$ and $\pi_{Geo}(O')$. The same argument holds for geometric join.

Corollary: $\pi_{Geo} : \Omega \rightarrow \wp(E)$ defines an homomorphism. $\bigcap$ is homomorphic to geometric join where $\bigcap$ is the intersection operation in $\wp(E)$ defined as follows: let $P1$ and $P2$ be two partitions; then $P1 \bigcap P2 = \{p_1 \text{ intersection } p2 | p_1 \in$

---

[5] where $\rightarrow$ denotes functional dependency.
[6] Also called in the literature *Spatial Join*.
[7] $nest_S(\pi_{S,Geo}(O))$ has for a schema $\{A_1, ..., A_q, B\}$ where B is of type $set(Geo)$. $\sum_{Geo}$ is applied to the B-value of each tuple of $nest_S(\pi_{S,Geo}(O))$.

$P1, p_2 \in P2, p_1 \text{ intersect } p_2\}$. We have: $\pi_{Geo}(O \bowtie_{Geo} O') = \pi_{Geo}(O) \cap \pi_{Geo}(O')$, and $\pi_{Geo}(\prod_{S,Geo}(O)) = h(\pi_{Geo}(O))$ where h is homomorphic to geometric projection.

Let $\leq$ be the partial order in Ω induced by $\preceq$: $O \leq O'$ iff $\pi_{Geo}(O) \preceq \pi_{Geo}(O')$. The following properties hold from the above:

Property 1: $\prod_S(O) \leq O, O \leq O \bowtie_{Geo} O', O' \leq O \bowtie_{Geo} O'$.

Property 2: $\prod_{A_1,\cdots,A_q,Geo}(O) = \prod_{A_1,Geo}(O) \bowtie_{Geo} \cdots \bowtie_{Geo} \prod_{A_q,Geo}(O)$.

Two remarks are noteworthy:

1. The above model is based on geographic objects, i.e. on the partition of a geometric space. We could have chosen any other set to be partitioned as well. As an example, instead of E, we might have chosen a set of people.

2. For the sake of generality we shall call such a set (e.g. geometry or people) a *population*. Then assume a set of populations $E_1, \cdots, E_p$, and let $\wp(E_i), i \in [1,p]$ denote the set of partitions on E_i. Now let G_i be an attribute with domain $\wp(E_i), i \in [1,p]$. A *generalized* cover is a geographic relation O with schema $\{A_1, \cdots, A_q, G_1, \cdots, G_p\}$ such that $\forall i \in [1,p]$, $\pi_{G_i}(O)$ is a partition in $\wp(E_i)$ and there is a bijection between O and $\pi_{G_i}(O)$. Because of space limitations, we refer to [Rig95] for the definition of the operations of (population) join and projection in that case[8]. As an example, we might consider for O a set of counties with descriptive attributes (the county name and the state name) and with population attributes (the set of people living in this county[9]) and the geometry of the county. A state's population and geometry is obtained by *geometric projection* on the state name, the people and the geometry. We might as well have only kept for each state either the set of people or the geometry (projecting out the other population attribute). In the sequel, we shall assume for the sake of simplicity there is a single "population" attribute *Geo* defined on E.

3.3 Tree Structured Domains and Statistical Summaries

We assume that a descriptive attribute A takes its values on a finite Poset $(D(A), \trianglelefteq)$. Graph G_A associated with poset $(D(A), \trianglelefteq)$ is defined as: elements of $D(A)$ are nodes of G_A and there is an edge from a to b iff $a \trianglelefteq b$ and there is no c such that $a \triangleleft c \triangleleft b$. We restrict G_A to be a tree denoted T_A. A *cut* in T_A is defined as:

1. Let R be the root of T_A. Then $\{R\}$ is a cut;

---

[8] The (population) projection is slightly more intricate than above: it involves the N1NF union [AB86].

[9] We assume that a single person cannot be reported in several counties.

2. $sons(R)$ is a cut, where $sons(a)$ is the set of sons of node a in the tree;

3. let C be a cut and $v \in C$ such that $sons(v) \neq \emptyset$. Then $C' = (C - v) \cup sons(v)$ is a cut.

The following holds: (a) $\forall c, c' \in C$, c and c' are not comparable, and (b) $\forall c \in T_A$ but $\notin C$, there exists $c' \in C$ such that either $c \lhd c'$ or $c' \lhd c$. We define the following partial order on cuts of a given tree. $C \ll C'$ iff $\forall y \in C', \exists x \in C$ such that $x \trianglelefteq y$. C is said to be more *abstract* than C'[10]. Figure 3 displays the set of cuts for the land-use tree domain of Figure 2.C, ordered by $\ll$. The most abstract cut is the root. $leaves(T_A)$, the set of leaves of T_A, is the least abstract cut (see Figure 3). A cut in the tree partitions the elements of $D(A)$ into two subsets $T_{A,<C} = \{e|e \in D(A), \exists c \in C, e \lhd c\}$ the set of elements "above" the cut and $T_{A,\geq C}$ the remaining elements. Let $v \in T_{A,\geq C}$. Then $Ancestor_C(v) \stackrel{def}{=} v' \in C|v' \trianglelefteq v$. Let $v \in T_{A,<C}$, then $Descendants_C(v) \stackrel{def}{=} \{v'|v' \in C, v \lhd v'\}$.

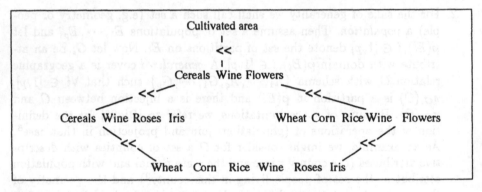

Fig. 3. : The cuts of the land-use tree domain of Figure 2.C

Interpretation of a set of cuts (on E): the interpretation of a set C of cuts on T_A is the mapping $I : C \to 2^{\Omega_A}$ from C to the powerset of elementary covers defined on A (O has for a schema $[A, Geo]$) such that: $I(R)$ is the singleton set of covers $\{o\}$, where o is the relation with single tuple $[A = R, Geo = E]$ and for each cut $C \in C$, $I(C) = O \in \Omega_A$ such that $\pi_A(O) = C$.

(Statistical) summaries: let O be a cover on E and A defined on an hierarchical domain $D(A)$ with tree T_A. We restrict Ω to the set of objects O such that $\pi_{A,Geo}(O) \in I(C)$. We call such objects *summaries*[11]. Let O be defined on cut C' and C be a more abstract cut than C': $C \ll C'$. Then we call *generalization of O up to C* denoted $gen_{A:C}(O)$ or $gen_C(O)$ when there is no ambiguity,

---

[10] A cut is a slice in a tree. It implements a *level of abstraction* as introduced in Section 2. Note that the values of a cut might not be at the same depth in T_A.

[11] Summaries may of course have other descriptive attributes: they are not necessarily elementary covers. These other attributes might be regular attributes or attributes also defined on a tree domain.

the expression: $gen_C(O) = apply_{A:Ancestor_C}(O)$, where in each tuple attribute A value a is replaced by its ancestor belonging to cut C. $gen_C(O)$ is no longer a cover in the general case, since there are several tuples with the same value for A and therefore $A_1, \cdots, A_q$ is not anymore a key for $gen_C(O)$. But the following expression:

$$apply_{\sum_{Geo}} (nest_{A_1 \cdots A \cdots A_q}(gen_{A:C}(O)))$$

denoted $summary_{A:C}(O)$ is a summary called *summary* of O on C.

Theorem 2: Ω (restricted to cuts) is closed under operation *summary*.

Proof: similar to that of Theorem 1 (see [Rig95]).

As an example look at the tree associated with the administrative splitting of the USA into states, counties, etc. Then a counties view of USA is a summary r with two attributes, ADM (whose value is a county name) and Geo (which describes the geometry of the county). ADM is defined on the "County" cut of the USA. Then let C be a more abstract cut on states. $summary_{ADM:C}(r)$ is a relation in which each tuple represents a state and has two attributes: the state name (ADM) and the state geometry (Geo). I induces an order on $I(C)$: $r1 \leq r2$ iff $C_1 \ll C_2$ where $r1$ ($r2$) is a summary of O on C_1 (C_2). We have also: $r1 \leq r2$ iff $\pi_{Geo}(r1) \preceq \pi_{Geo}(r2)$. Here are some properties on operations *gen* and *summary*:

Property 3: $gen_{A:C}(O \bowtie_{Geo} O') = gen_{A:C}(O) \bowtie_{Geo} O'$ where we assume that A is an attribute of cover O.

Property 4: $summary_{A:C}(O) = summary_{A:C}(\prod_{A,Geo}(O)) \bowtie_{Geo} \prod_{S-A}(O)$, where O has for schema S.

Property 5:
$summary_{A_1:C_1}(summary_{A_2:C_2}(O)) = summary_{A_2:C_2}(summary_{A_1:C_1}(O)) \overset{def}{=}$
$summary_{A_1:C_1,A_2:C_2}(O) \overset{def}{=} apply_{\sum_{Geo}} (nest_{A_1 A_2}(gen_{A_1:C_1,A_2:C_2}(O)))$ where
$gen_{A_1:C_1,A_2:C_2}(O) \overset{def}{=} gen_{A_1:C_1}(gen_{A_2:C_2}(O)) = gen_{A_2:C_2}(gen_{A_1:C_1}(O))$

This property states that (i) generalization on separate attributes is commutative, so is summary, and (ii) that one can save one (expensive) *nest* operation and one *apply* operation by doing at once all generalizations.

4 Applications of the Model

We shall first solve the queries of Section 2 by using the operations defined in Section 3. Consider first tables 1 and 2. Table 1 can be implemented by a relation with schema: WINESALE1(wine,area,amount), where wine is defined on the cut containing the leaves of the tree domain for wines, area is a state (belonging to the leaves cut of the administrative areas tree domain) and amount is the sale amount. Let CW be the more abstract cut {Haut Medoc, St Emilion} and CR be the cut of administrative regions. Then the *summary* in Table 2 is a relation WINESALE2 with same schema as WINESALE1 and equal to:

$$WINESALE2 = summary_{Wine:CW,Area:CR}(WINESALE1)$$

The second example we considered in Section 2 was that of Parcels (land-owner, countyId, Luse, Geo), where for each tuple land use is taken in the leaves cut of the hierarchy in Figure 2.C. The land use cover LUSE (Luse, Geo) is obtained by (geometric) projection $\Pi_{Luse,Geo}(Parcels)$.

$$summary_{Luse:CL}(\pi_{countyId,Luse,Geo}(Parcels))$$

computes a more abstract representation of Parcels on the T_{Luse} cut CL: {Cereals, Wine, Flowers,...}(see Figure 2.C).

Let ADMIN(admId, Geo) be a cover recording France (administrative) regions. The following expression computes the cover representing wine production areas in the Aquitaine region:

$$\sigma_{admId='Aquitaine'}(ADMIN) \bowtie_{Geo} \sigma_{Luse='Wine'}(LUSE).$$

We assume now that ADMIN is not anymore the administrative region cover but the counties cover (adminId is defined on the counties cut CC), and that LUSE is a cover defined on the cut CW {Ht Medoc, St Emilion}. Assume that we look for the administrative region where "St Emilion" is produced.

$$\sigma_{Luse='StEmilion'}(gen_{admId:CR}(ADMIN \bowtie_{Geo} LUSE))$$

computes such an answer. Indeed, we first overlay the covers LUSE and ADMIN, we then generalize the result to administrative regions (admId will take its values on the cut of regions) and finally make a selection on Luse. This expression is of course equivalent to: $gen_{admId:CR}(ADMIN) \bowtie_{Geo} \sigma_{Luse='StEmilion'}(LUSE)$, by pushing selection inside and using property 3.

The following expressions give the counties where 'St Emilion' is produced. The first expression assumes that ADMIN is the counties cover (defined on cut CC). The second one assumes ADMIN is the (administrative) regions cover and $Desc_{C'}(R)$ is defined as $\{c \in C'|gen_{A:C}(c)\ in\ R\}$ where attribute A of cover R is defined on cut C (more abstract than cut C').

$$ADMIN \bowtie_{Geo} \sigma_{Luse='StEmilion'}(LUSE)$$
$$DESC_{CC}(ADMIN \bowtie_{Geo} \sigma_{Luse='StEmilion'}(LUSE)) \bowtie_{Geo}$$
$$\sigma_{Luse='StEmilion'}(LUSE)$$

The second expression introduces a redundancy. It suggests to first select the regions which intersect the areas where St Emilion is produced (geometric join), then take all counties inside such regions ($DESC_{CC}$), and finally only for those counties perform the (geometric) join. The latter expression might provide a better performance depending on the implementation. Indeed instead of using for filtering a (physical) spatial index on counties expensive in terms of design and maintenance, it is suggested that the query optimizer chooses faster access paths provided by the semantics of the hierarchies application. Finally assume again ADMIN(admId, geo) is defined on the cut CC of counties and that in LUSE, Luse is defined on a cut {Pauillac, St Julien,...}. Then the query "Counties where 'Ht Medoc' is produced" is answered by the following expression:

$$ADMIN \bowtie_{Geo} \sigma_{Luse='HtMedoc'}(gen_{Luse:CW}(LUSE))$$

Such a query would provide a null answer with regular database query languages which require a complete knowledge of the attribute domain. In a companion paper [RS94] we suggested the use of attributes defined on tree structured domains to answer such queries, but without requiring a semantics as strong as that of Section 3 (without requiring the relations to be covers). Several authors have addressed this issue in a more general context known as "Cooperative Query Answering" which deals with syntactically correct queries which provide a NULL answer. For example, the *Type Abstraction Hierarchy* of [CCL91] combines an hierarchy similar to ours with object-oriented class hierarchies. [Mot86, Mot88] also allow some query generalization.

5 Implementation with O₂SQL

This model has already been partially implemented with the DBMS O_2 [Rig95, PR95]. We illustrate such an implementation by means of a few examples from Section 4. There are several ways of implementing a set of ordered covers. One simple way is to explicitly represent the usual covers by O_2 roots of persistence [BDK91], each object of a cover being explicitly linked to its "sons" in a less abstract cover and to its "father" in a more abstract cover. This is the case for the representation of administrative partitions of a country. Basically there would be the following roots of persistance:

Regions: set (Region), Counties: set(County)

defined on the classes Region and County with structure:

```
Class Region tuple (regionId:String,        Class County tuple(countyId: String,
              counties:set (County),                      region:Region,
              geo : Geo)                                  geo:Geo)
```

It is not clear whether the representation of several land use covers with explicit links would be useful or realistic since the choice of a cut in the land use tree domain is highly dynamic and dependent on the application or the query. Instead it is more realistic to represent a useful cover for land use (e.g. that including values such that "St Emilion", "Haut Medoc", etc.), and to implement the tree structured domain of landuse as follows[12]:

Class Landuse tuple (luse: String,
                 geo : Geo)

name Luses: set (Landuse)

Class Luse tuple (luse: String,
                 sons: set(Luse),
                 father: Luse)

name Treeluse: Luse

In the above, Luses is the database entry for the cover of land use, while TreeLuse is the root of the land use tree. Because of space limitations we shall only present the implementation of three among the queries of Section 4.

query 1: administrative region where "St Emilion" is produced. There are two ways of answering this query (one associated with each equivalent expression, see Section 4).

(i) **select** r
    from   r in Regions, c in r.counties, l in Luses
    where c.geo **intersect** l.geo
    and   l. luse = 'St Emilion'

We keep the counties whose geometry intersects St Emilion's area geometry and we follow an explicit path in the composition hierarchy. Obviously one will prefer the following expression. But the above expression would be the only way to answer the query if the geometry were only stored at the county level (and not at the region level).

(ii) **select** r
    from   r in Regions, l in Luses
    where r.geo **intersect** l.geo
    and   l. luse = 'St Emilion'

Checking only whether a region intersects the St Emilion's area is of course much faster than checking all counties since the number of regions is by several orders of magnitude smaller than the number of counties and since a single intersection test costs the same price whether it is a region or a county (in both cases the geometry is represented with a polygon of same complexity: the number of points of the polygon is of the same order). The optimizer should take into account property 3 (see Section 3.3) to rewrite query (i) into its equivalent form (ii).

query 2: Counties producing 'St Emilion'. For the same reasons the following redundant query takes advantage of the semantics of partitions to accelerate access to the relevant counties. It saves the use of a spatial index on counties.

---

[12] in [RS94] it is suggested to extend the O_2 data model by a poset constructor Poset($\preceq$, τ) which allows to represent a finite set of elements of type τ partially ordered by $\preceq$. This constructor is supposed to be equipped with several functions. This extension would allow a performant implementation of functions on posets.

```
select  c
from    r in Regions, c in r.counties, l in Luses
where   r.geo intersect l.geo
and     c.geo intersect l.geo
and     l.luse = 'St Emilion'
```

query 3: Counties where 'Ht Medoc' is produced. This query is similar to the previous one except for the last clause that selects all wines whose ancestor is 'Ht Medoc' in the tree with (named) root TreeLuse:

```
select  c
from    r in Regions, c in r.counties, l in Luses
where   r.geo intersect l.geo
and     c.geo intersect l.geo
and     TreeLuse→IsAncestor(l.luse,'Ht Medoc')
```

Assuming as in [RS94] an extension of O_2 with a Poset constructor, a root of persistance TreeLuse: Poset (Luse) for implementing the landuse hierarchy and a binary predicate $\preceq$ testing whether a node is an ancestor of another one in a given poset, the above query would be rewritten as:

```
select  c
from    r in Regions, c in r.counties, l in Luses, l' in Treeluse
where   r.geo intersect l.geo
and     c.geo intersect l.geo
and     l'.luse='Ht Medoc'
and     l'.luse $\preceq$ l.luse
```

Acknowlegments. We thank Gérard d'Aubigny for helpful discussions within the multi-scale representation group of the GDR Cassini. We are also indebted to Claudia Medeiros, Jean-Marc Saglio and the anonymous referees for their careful readings which significantly improved the quality of the paper.

References

[AB86]   S. Abiteboul and N. Bidoit. Non First Normal Form Relations: an Algebra Allowing Data Restructuring. *Journal of Computer and System Sciences*, 1986.

[BCD89] F. Bancilhon, S. Cluet, and C. Delobel. A Query Language for an Object-Oriented Database System. In *2nd Int. Worshop on Database Programming Languages (DBPL)*, pages 301–322, 1989.

[BD89]   B. P. Buttenfield and J. Delotto. Multiple Representation: Report on the Specialist Meeting. Technical Report 89-3, National Center for Geographic Information and Analysis, Santa Barbara, 1989.

[BDK91] F. Bancilhon, C. Delobel, and P. Kannelakis, editors. *The O_2 Book*. Morgan Kaufmann, 1991.

[BM91]   B.P. Buttenfield and R. P. McMaster. *Map Generalization: Making Rules for Knowledge Representation*. Longman Scientific&Technical, New-York, 1991.

[BRS82] F. Bancilhon, P. Richard, and M. Scholl. On Line Processing of Compacted Relations. In *8th Int. Conference on Very Large Data Bases (VLDB)*, Mexico, 1982.

[BW88]   K. E. Brassel and R. Weibel. A Review and Conceptual Framework of Automated Map Generalization. *Int. Journal of GIS*, 2(3):229–244, 1988.

[CCL91] W. W. Chu, Q. Chen, and R. Lee. Cooperative Query Answering via Type Abstraction Hierarchy. In S. M. Deen, editor, *Cooperating Knowledge Based Systems*, pages 271–292. Elsevier Science Publishing Co. Inc, 1991.

[CMM88] M. C. Chen, L. McNamee, and M. Melkanoff. A Model of Summary Data and its Application in Statistical Databases. In *Int. Conference on Statistical and Scientific Database Management (SSDBM)*, pages 356–387, Rome (Italy), 1988. LNCS No. 339, Springer-Verlag.

[dd94]   C. d'Aubigny and G. d'Aubigny. Agrégation Spatiale et Résumés Statistiques. *Revue de géomatique*, 4(3-4):307–336, 1994.

[Gho86] S. Ghosh. Statistical Relational Tables for Statistical Database Management. *IEEE Transactions on Software Engineering*, 12(12):1106–1116, 1986.

[Gup89] S. G. Guptill. Speculations on Seamless, Scaleless Cartographic Data Bases. In *Auto-Carto 9*, pages 436–443, 1989.

[Jon91] C. B. Jones. Database Architecture for Multi-scale GIS. In *ASPRS/ACSM*, pages 1–14, Baltimore, 1991.

[LR94]   J. P. Lagrange and A. Ruas. Data & Knowledge Modelling for Generalization. In *Int. Conference on Spatial Data Handling (SDH)*, pages 1099–1117, Edinburgh, 1994.

[Mal88] F. M. Malvestuto. The Derivation Problem for Summary Data. In *Int. Conference on Management of Data (ACM-SIGMOD)*, pages 82–89, Chicago, 1988.

[MLW95] J. C. Muller, J. P. Lagrange, and R. Weibel, editors. *GISs and Generalization*. Taylor & Francis, London, 1995.

[Mot86] A. Motro. Query Generalization: A Method for Interpreting Null Answers. In *Int. Workshop on Expert Database Systems*, pages 597–616, 1986.

[Mot88] A. Motro. VAGUE: a User Interface to Relational Databases that Permits Vague Queries. *ACM Transactions on Office Information Systems*, 6(3):187–214, 1988.

[PR95]   J. P. Peloux and P. Rigaux. A Loosely Coupled Interface to an Object-Oriented Geographic Database. In *Spatial Information Theory (COSIT)*, 1995. To appear.

[Rig95] P. Rigaux. Interfaces Visuelles et Représentation Multiple dans les Bases de Données Spatiales. Thèse de doctorat CNAM, 1995.

[RS90]   M. Rafanelli and A. Shoshani. STROM : a Statistical Object Representation Model. In *Int. Conference on Statistical and Scientific Database Management (SSDBM)*, pages 14–29, Charlotte (USA), 1990. LNCS No. 420, Springer-Verlag.

[RS94]   P. Rigaux and M. Scholl. Multiple Representation Modelling and Querying. In *Int. Workshop on GIS (IGIS'94)*, pages 59–69, Ascona, Switzerland, 1994. LNCS No. 884, Springer-Verlag.

[Sho82]   A. Shoshani. Statistical Databases: Characteristics, Problems, and Some Solutions. In *Int. Conference on Very Large Databases (VLDB)*, Mexico, 1982.

[SM89]   K. S. Shea and R. Macmaster. Cartographic Generalization: When and How to Generalize. In *Auto-Carto 9*, pages 56–67, 1989.

[SS86]   H. J. Schek and M. H. Scholl. The Relational Model with Relation-Valued Attributes. *Information Systems*, 1986.

[vO91]   P. van Oosterom. The Reactive Tree: A Storage Structure for a Seamless, Scaleless geographic Database. In *Auto Carto10*, pages 393–407, 1991.

Specifying Open GIS with Functional Languages[1]

Andrew U. Frank
Werner Kuhn

Department of Geoinformation
Technical University Vienna
Gusshausstrasse 27-29/127
A-1040 Vienna (Austria)

Frank@geoinfo.tuwien.ac.at
Kuhn@geoinfo.tuwien.ac.at

Abstract

The concept of Open GIS depends on precise definitions of data, operations and interfaces. This paper argues for the use of functional programming languages as specification and prototyping tools for Open GIS components. It shows how functional programming languages fulfill the key requirements for formal specification languages and allow for rapid prototyping in addition. So far, it has never been possible to integrate specification and prototyping in a single, easy to use environment. Most existing specification methods lack appropriate tools for checking and prototyping, while existing tools lack either sound semantics or usability or both. The paper discusses the role of specifications in GIS, requirements for specification languages, and presents the basics of algebraic specifications as well as of functional languages. It then describes how functional languages can be used for writing and executing algebraic specifications. A brief example of a GIS data type specification in a functional language is presented, showing how specifications serve to describe differences in the semantics of GIS operations. We conclude that functional languages have the potential to achieve a breakthrough in the problem of specifying interfaces of interoperable components for Open GIS.

1   Specifications and Open GIS

Specifications are essential for software quality and are widely used in industry. For Geographic Information Systems (GIS), they are of special interest in the standardization of data models, transfer methods, Open GIS component interfaces, and database architectures. Practical specification methods are needed for the success of Open GIS architectures in which programs and data collections from different vendors need to cooperate at multiple levels of abstraction [Voisard, and Schweppe, 1994].

1.1   Specifications and Software Development

Specifications allow for a division of labor in software development. They serve as a contract between the software analyst, who understands the application problem, and the programmer, who is concerned with an optimal use of resources. They support producing the software and assessing its correctness.

CASE tools provide informal methods to design, manage, and communicate specifications for software. Positive results from largely informal software design

---

[1] Funding from Intergraph Corporation and from the Austrian Science Foundation is gratefully acknowledged.

methods in general have been reported [Head, 1994], but software practitioners criticize current tools for being too low level. A pointed observation is that CASE tools are nothing but glorified systems to draw diagrams and often do not scale up to large problems, where the amount of documentation becomes overwhelming.

Formal specifications, i.e., specifications written in a formal language with mathematically defined semantics, allow for formal checks and reasoning before programming starts. They can provide support for an automatic program verification [Guttag, Horning, and Wing, 1985]. However, such consistency checks are internal to the formal system and cannot ensure that the specifications capture the intentions of the designer or other real world requirements.

Rapid prototyping has been advocated to achieve programs that correspond not only to specifications but also to the actual user requirements. Prototyping reduces the danger that you get what you ordered, but not what you wanted. In current software design practice, specification and prototyping tools are often separated or only loosely coupled. If a language allowed to write specifications and to execute what has been specified, it could serve as a combined specification and prototyping tool. This paper claims that functional programming languages, extended with recent research results, achieve this goal.

1.2 What is Special about Specifications for Spatial Data?

The need for formal specification languages is common to the whole software industry; problems with interoperability of tools from different vendors plague nearly every user of a computer system. However, the specification problem is more acute for GIS than for most other application areas:

- Economic use of spatial data is only possible if data can be used by many different users from different organizations. The need for a functioning market of spatial base data is larger and this market is growing faster than in most other areas of information technology. Consider as an indicator the offerings for data on CD-ROM: geographic data figure very prominently.
- The structure of geographic data is more complex than that of other data exchanged routinely. It is comparable to, but going beyond, that of CAD data, where similar problems are encountered.
- Sharing data transcends organization boundaries. The consumer usually pays for the data and expects them to be "usable", otherwise legal problems can ensue [Frank, 1992].

1.3 Specifications and the GIS Market

GIS are evolving into multi-vendor software environments, Open GIS, where heterogeneous components cooperate to solve complex spatial problems. Users buy software from different vendors to solve particular parts of their problem: they want to access the database system produced by one company from the mapping tool of another vendor or to assess the spatial dimension of marketing forecasts in a GIS. This movement toward interoperable, open environments will rapidly progress within and outside the GIS industry [O'Callaghan, 1993]. Specifications are the key to achieve this interoperability. They constitute a contract between providers and customers of services in an Open GIS.

Specifications of GIS services provide economical viability for the niche market vendor who can offer tools that are independent of the software environment of a client. If a vendor must provide a special version for any combination of client database system and GIS software, the business cannot operate profitably. GIS tools can only be provided for specific markets if they can be built on top of a general service layer.

Specifications are also essential to access the mass market with GIS software: Selling low cost software can only become profitable if GIS tools provide a standardized service (which can be used and understood independently of a specific vendor) and interact in a standardized way with databases, operating systems and other applications. Specifications are the enabling technique to ensure customer satisfaction with mass products, while also improving special applications that work within open environments.

The problem of data transfers can also be cast into the specification framework [Kuhn, 1994]. This helps to separate the issues of data representation (which are relatively easy to solve) from the critical issues of differences in semantics. The buyers in a "spatial data market" are interested in the information they can obtain from transferred data. They need tools to describe this information or to interpret existing descriptions. Defining this information content or semantics is precisely what a specification does.

The first SSD meeting pointed to the importance of meta data and formalisms to help potential users of spatial data find data in a distributed environment and to transfer them [Smith, and Frank, 1990]. Methods to describe meta data are missing today, current efforts for standardization still struggle with fundamentals of geometric data, and the standards are based on informal semantics. Future standards for Open GIS will need to use formal specifications for defining data semantics and for testing adherence of implementations to standards. Specifications as advocated here can formally define semantics at all levels of a data transfer.

2 Requirements for Specification Languages

Several properties of a specification language are desirable for its use in practice. This section summarizes only the most important ones: expressing semantics, ease of understanding, and rapid prototyping, i.e., a way to check whether the specified semantics are those intended.

2.1 Expressing Semantics

Specification languages must allow for expressing real situations in terms with exactly defined formal semantics. Defining semantics unambiguously and completely is so difficult that it presents one of the main motivations for formal specifications. Most specification methods produce documentation of which only a minimal amount can be checked automatically for well-formedness, completeness, and consistency. While the correctness of a specification with respect to what the designer had in mind can never be formally asserted, clean semantics of the underlying language and formal checking of the syntax make correctness much more likely.

Some data definition languages (e.g., EXPRESS [ISO, 1992]) allow to specify data types, but lack formal semantics. They describe static data types with attributes and relationships, omitting the specification of operations. However, a specification language based on types must have a method to associate data types with operations.

Otherwise the concept of type remains vacuous. Section three describes algebraic specifications which achieve this association.

2.2 Ease of Understanding

Expressive power is a necessary condition for a specification language, but it does not guarantee its success. Specifications must be easy to write and read. Specification languages must help to master the complexity of real world applications and should offer abstractions which are easily understood. Too many specification approaches have stressed the formal aspects of the syntax, disregarding the interpretation of specifications by human readers (as opposed to syntax checkers).

Specifications often produce enormous amounts of documentation, and a common complaint for all specification methods is that they do not scale up. While they work well for the small examples on which they have been developed and tried, they overwhelm the designers when applied to large, real world situations. Despite this complaint, any structured approach to specify a problem before programming is beneficial, nearly independently of the method and tools applied.

2.3 Rapid Prototyping

Organizing a large body of knowledge in a comprehensive fashion must bridge the gap between the cognitive and the formal. Due to the difficulty of writing and reading specifications, many errors are not detected before an implementation is completed. Rapid prototyping has been the industry's answer to this dilemma. It was motivated by the difficulty in the software design process to capture real world semantics. Prototyping is clearly preferable to testing of production code, as it can be done much earlier in the development process, where changes are relatively easy and cheap.

A specification language with a prototyping capability allows for executable specifications. By demonstrating program behavior in such a way, it becomes possible to observe deviations from the intended behavior immediately. Deviant behavior is easy to detect for humans, while the underlying violation of semantics cannot always be easily discovered in a formal description.

3 Algebraic Specifications

There is a growing consensus that formal specification methods are necessary for projects of some complexity; however, it is often unclear what method to choose. Algebraic specifications [Guttag, Horowitz, and Musser, 1978; Liskov and Guttag, 1986] combine the advantages of data abstraction (supporting object-oriented modeling) with an axiomatic method (abstracting from particular execution models) and a functional style (offering clean semantics). In addition, they are easier to learn, read, and write than most other styles.

An algebraic specification defines the behavior of an operation by axioms. These axioms state the operation's effects in terms of other operations on the same data type. One differentiates constructor operations which construct or change an object and observers which report its state. The behavior of the constructor operations is expressed either in terms of other constructors or by observers. The well known example of a stack shows how the effect of a push operations is expressed with the observer top (to check the top element) and the additional constructor pop (to remove the top element):

```
top (push (item, stack)) = item
pop (push (item, stack)) = stack
```

This method of description is formally self-contained and complete. It says all about the behavior of push without relying on the semantics of another domain (e.g., of arrays or lists). Note that the variables used in the axioms are implicitly universally quantified, i.e., the above equations hold for all possible stacks and items. There are informal rules for generating axioms which are easy to follow and achieve sufficient completeness and consistency in the sense of [Liskov and Guttag, 1986].

4 Functional Programming Languages

In functional programming languages, everything is a function returning a value. LISP is the oldest and probably most often used functional language, but APL and ML are other well known examples. One distinguishes pure functional languages, where functions are mathematically pure, produce only one result, and do not have side effects, from others which allow side effects to varying degrees. A comprehensive survey and pointers to the literature can be found in [Hudak, 1989].

4.1 Functions as Fundamental Building Blocks

Functional programs consist of the application of functions to some values. The basic control structure is recursion. For example, a typical implementation of factorials in a language like Gofer [Jones, 1994; Thiemann, 1994] looks like this:

```
fac n = if n==0 then 1 else n * fac (n-1)
```

In pure functional languages, the functions produce only one result value and do not have side effects. The input parameters are not changed, nor are there any other global variables that carry state. This fulfills one of the major desires of programming language designers, to achieve locality of concerns: all effects of a function can be seen in its own code and no other effects must be considered.

4.2 Referential Transparency

By the same token, pure functional programming languages achieve "referential transparency", i.e., an expression always describes the same value. Destructive assignments are not possible, as a value can only be assigned once to a variable. This seems a very strong restriction, but guarantees that mathematical proofs of program behavior are straightforward and can use regular logic, without specific inference rules for each control structure [Dijkstra, 1977]. It allows mathematical reasoning about programs based on substitution. Understanding behavior and reasoning about it becomes much simpler and errors are easier to spot. Referential transparency is also found in (pure) Prolog and is probably one of the reasons why Prolog programming has been so successful.

4.3 Type Inference

Functional programming languages in the tradition of ML [Milner, 1978] are strongly typed. Every object has a particular type and the compiler checks that operations can only be applied to objects of the appropriate type (similar to Pascal and other strongly typed languages). Other functional languages like LISP are untyped or the types are checked at run time. A strong typing discipline is helpful for design as it helps discover problems early in the design.

The work on ML showed that the types need not always be provided by the programmer (as in Pascal or C++), but can be inferred by the compiler. Given the obvious types of constants (3 is an integer, 3.57 is a float) the types of variables and expressions can be logically deduced by a type inference mechanism (e.g., inferring from "a = 3.5 + 2.1" that a is of type float). This achieves the same as a strict type system with programmer-provided types, but eliminates the need to define each variable with its type and reduces program clutter.

4.4 Recent Extensions

Substantial progress has recently been made in the theory of functional programming languages. A new type theory allows for a conceptually clean treatment of inheritance. The application of ideas from category theory, in particular monad transformers, has the potential to overcome limitations of functional languages in dealing with state.

Class-Based Polymorphism

Polymorphism, i.e., the ability of an operation to be applied to arguments of varying types, is very important for modeling spatial data and operations. The intersection of two curves, for example, is the same operation, independent of the type of curves; intersection of two geometric objects has some common behavior for any combination of points, lines, and areas.

Separating the different aspects of polymorphism and combining them with a type hierarchy (inheritance) is conceptually difficult. Current programming languages often mix design issues with implementation concerns. Jones has designed and implemented (in Gofer) a class-based type system with polymorphism, which models multiple-inheritance in a clean way [Jones, 1994].

Dealing with State

The lack of side effects and "updates in place" in functional programming languages have hindered state-based concepts (like databases or I/O) and had to be overcome with loopholes in the past. Some functional languages (e.g., LISP, APL) have included extensions to the strict functional model to make them more usable.

Recently, a coherent extension of the theory has been developed which shows how to integrate database access and I/O into a pure functional framework [Peyton Jones, and Wadler, 1993; Liang, Hudak, and Jones, 1995]. Imperative aspects (e.g., sequences of operations and side effects) are properly expressed without breaking the functional syntax or semantics. This makes functional languages usable and attractive for the specification and prototyping of database interoperability within Open GIS environments.

Implementations exist and have been used to build standard read and write operations for I/O. Efforts to provide graphical user interface tools in a functional language are underway. The tools to connect to database services are available and semantically more suitable methods, better integrated with the type system, are being studied. It is likely that ideas from the functional database studies [Shipman, 1981] can be reused.

5 Using Functional Languages for Specifications

Functional programming languages satisfy some key requirements for specification languages. On the other hand, they do not support some common features of specification environments. This section discusses the pros and cons of using functional languages for writing specifications.

5.1 Advantages

The use of functional programming languages for writing specifications offers three key benefits:

- *formality*: formal specifications allow for automatic checking of well-formedness, completeness, and consistency;
- *executability*: the specifications can be used as executable prototypes and deviations from intended behavior can be detected and corrected immediately;
- *extendibility*: new specifications can be integrated based on a sound type theory with polymorphism [Jones, 1994].

Furthermore, functional programming languages are readily available (often in the public domain) and possess some additional desired properties:

- functions can be combined to form algebras, allowing for an algebraic specification style;
- referential transparency permits mathematical reasoning by substitution;
- a lean syntax that is very close to standard mathematics affords ease of writing and reading.

Thus, functional programming languages satisfy the key requirements for specification languages. They share with specification languages a tendency to mathematical formalism and brevity of expressions (APL provided an extreme example). The functional language Gofer, for example, is about three to five times more compact than equivalent, highly modularized Pascal code (even more for C++, if object-oriented features are being used). One of the major contributions to reduce clutter is the type inference mechanism of languages in the ML tradition.

5.2 Limitations

Functional programming languages do not have all properties of the most advanced formal specification environments: they are not designed for a formal verification of specifications, nor for version management, or for documentation and cooperation in teams.

The major issue is documentation of modular decomposition: how is a complex system subdivided into parts. Here, for both specification languages and functional programming languages, additional tools are necessary such as class browsers of the kind used in Smalltalk environments. CASE tools and visual programming environments are much more advanced in this respect, but there are no reasons why such tools could not be constructed for a functional language.

5.3 Constructive vs. Declarative Axioms

Axioms, when expressed in a functional language, are restricted to a constructive form: the left hand side of the axiom has to be a simple expression or contain only constructor operations. This excludes axioms stating general behavior without supplying a rewrite rule on the right hand side. For instance, it is not possible to say that an operation is transitive or reflexive, or to define a matrix inverse by stating that a matrix multiplied with its inverse produces the unit matrix.

This restriction is necessary to allow for execution and, by the same token, to simplify program proofs. According to our observations, it does not affect the use of functional programming languages for specifying GIS objects. In fact the theory of algebraic specifications [Guttag, Horowitz, and Musser, 1978] is based on the exact same restriction. Many operations are defined as simple expressions which can be copied from text books (e.g., coordinate transformations, geometric constructions). Data types like lists and trees are easily specified by constructive axioms.

The type system can be used to ensure compatibility of definitions according to non-constructive axioms. This resembles the practice in physics to check the dimensions of formulae. Non-constructive axioms can also be used for testing that an implementation conforms to the intended behavior. Boolean functions, testing the intended behavior, are defined and called with appropriate arguments. For example, a function

```
commutative op a b = (a `op` b) == (b `op` a)
```

can be used to test if an operation op is commutative (for a particular pair of arguments). Such tests can be automated by supplying lists of appropriate test cases and applying the test functions to them.

5.4   From Specification to Implementation

Any specification language must be compared with the target implementation language to assure that the specifications can be implemented. There are two issues:

- potential mismatch in concepts
- speed of execution.

The influence that a specification language exerts on the design of the system must be assessed and the effect on the later implementation considered. If the specification and implementation languages differ widely, the implementation requires a substantial redesign. It is then typically very difficult and costly to show that the actual implementation corresponds to the system specified. This may be necessary if different companies are involved and for time- or safety-critical systems.

In contrast to special-purpose specification languages, functional programming languages raise the additional question of execution speed, i.e., whether translation to another language is necessary to achieve efficiency. From the point of view of specifying the behavior of complex spatial objects in GIS, possible efficiency shortcomings of current functional environments are not important. What matters, particularly in an Open GIS environment, is to have an implementation-independent formalism that can be used to describe the semantics of data and operations and to execute these descriptions for test purposes.

Functional languages have been assumed to be inherently slow [Backus, 1978]. New implementation methods based on advanced mathematics seem to overcome this problem to a large extent. Compiled functional code may just be two to five times slower than a C program, i.e., fast enough for many applications. In the long run, functional programming languages may become efficient enough for implementations in most situations. In the short run, many GIS application programming languages are orders of magnitude slower than standard programming languages. Functional languages can therefore already now improve on the performance of application programming languages.

5.5 Our Experience

In Gofer and related languages, we have found a practical tool allowing for a combination of the advantages of formal specifications with those of rapid prototyping. Our experiments have confirmed that such a tool (Gofer or a possible future merger of Gofer with Haskell [Hudak *et al.*, 1992]) provides the expressive power as well as the ease of use necessary for realistic applications in GIS. Gofer is very close to a standard algebraic notation and can be understood with hardly any explanations of the syntax. It is easy to learn and we had students (not from computer science) write non-trivial specifications for geometric data types within weeks.

We have also used Gofer in a "Surveying and Information Systems" course to specify data structures (e.g., a search tree) and to demonstrate their behavior. Gofer is being used in introductory programming courses at some universities [Thiemann, 1994]. We consider to use it as the first programming language for surveying engineering students, replacing an introductory course in Pascal which cannot cover data structures appropriately. In research, we have used Gofer for extensive experiments in specifying hierarchical graph models [Car, and Frank, 1995] and temporal reasoning [Frank, 1994].

6 A Specification Example

A recent discussion in the North-American Open GIS Consortium raised the issue of how to decide on point equality. Obviously, different systems cooperating in a heterogeneous environment can use different semantics in their equality operations. Interoperability is only possible if these semantics can be described independently of the implementations and succinctly presented to the user of an Open GIS service. The following simplified example achieves this using the functional language Gofer to write algebraic specifications for point data models.

Let us assume three different data models for the storage of point data. System A stores simple lists of coordinates and determines point equality based on coordinate values. System B represents points by coordinates and names and compares point names to decide equality. System C uses the same data type as system B, but decides equality like system A, comparing coordinate values.

The specifications focus on equality operations, leaving additional operations on points (such as a distance) unspecified. While Gofer would offer more compact ways to write these specifications (using classes), the code as written here has the advantage of being largely self-explanatory. The Gofer keyword "data" introduces the definition of a (abstract) data type, while the keyword "type" defines just a type synonym. The signatures of functions list the function name, followed by an argument list. Finally, the axioms describe the behavior of the functions by equations. The crucial difference among the three specifications lies in their last axioms, defining the different semantics of equality.

Data Model of System A
```
type Coord = Int
data Point = New (Coord, Coord)
x        ::       Point -> Coord
y        ::       Point -> Coord
equal    ::       (Point, Point) -> Bool
x (New (cx,cy)) = cx
y (New (cx,cy)) = cy
equal (p,q) = (x(p) == x(q)) && (y(p) == y(q))
```

Data Model of System B
```
type Coord = Int
type Name = String
data Point = New (Coord, Coord, Name)
x        ::       Point -> Coord
y        ::       Point -> Coord
name     ::       Point -> Name
equal    ::       (Point, Point) -> Bool
x (New (cx,cy,n)) = cx
y (New (cx,cy,n)) = cy
name (New (cx,cy,n)) = n
equal (p,q) = name (p) == name (q)
```

Data Model of System C
```
type Coord = Int
type Name = String
data Point = New (Coord, Coord, Name)
x        ::       Point -> Coord
y        ::       Point -> Coord
name     ::       Point -> Name
equal    ::       (Point, Point) -> Bool
x (New (cx, cy, n)) = cx
y (New (cx, cy, n)) = cy
name (New (cx, cy, n)) = n
equal (p,q) = (x(p) == x(q)) && (y(p) == y(q)).
```

The specifications show clearly that the decision of equality between two points depends on other operations, i.e., equality of strings or of coordinates. Assuming a transfer of point data between two systems: even if both systems used the same data model (e.g., both have data model of system B), two points may be determined to be the same in the first and different in the second system. This can happen if the full definition of equality is not the same, e.g., if string equality is case sensitive in one of the two systems. The algebraic specifications expressed in the functional language Gofer reveal these semantic differences in their axioms.

7 Conclusions

Specification methods are important for GIS design, because GIS are highly complex software systems. The currently available commercial systems with their limitations and known bugs are demonstrating that GIS is stretching current software design methods to the break point. The evolution toward Open GIS, where software components from different vendors cooperate, will only succeed if the interfaces between components can be formally defined. Open GIS depend crucially on formal, testable specifications. A component needs to be testable for compliance with the intended behavior so that components causing a problem can be identified and rectified. This is a commercial and legal necessity, which may decide on the viability of the whole idea of Open GIS.

This paper has argued that functional programming languages can and should be used to specify GIS software. Functional languages are suitable for specifications because they support the standard methods of mathematical proofs, in particular, substitution of equal terms. This effect of referential transparency is not found in imperative programming languages whose complex proof rules cannot be handled by most practitioners. Furthermore, functional programs are executable, allowing the specifiers to check whether they have specified what they wanted. Since it is impossible to formally prove that a program does what a designer wants, executable specifications are the best possible approximation.

Current practice to help with interoperability is based on two practical tools: test suits and reference implementations. Test suits are sequences of test cases which are processed and compared with the "correct" results. Reference implementations can be used similarly. For any input, the result for the reference implementation and the system under consideration must be the same. Functional programming can be used in both cases to check implementations, with the key advantage that the specification represents the code of the reference implementation. It can be interpreted much easier than traditional programming code and it can be analyzed using standard mathematical logic.

Our experience has convinced us that functional programming languages like Gofer or Haskell offer an appropriate compromise solution to the various requirements for a specification language in practice. They are currently limited in dealing with I/O and databases, but the theory to deal with these shortcomings is developing rapidly. The same theory seems to explain the interaction of modules in a much simpler way than previously possible. Performance of functional programming languages is rapidly improving and they naturally lead to parallel computations.

Acknowledgments

John Eisner (then working on the North-American datum readjustment) introduced the first author to the topic of data abstraction in Copenhagen, 1981. Benoît David (IGN, Paris) pointed us towards CAML, a functional programming language in the ML tradition, in Paris, 1992. John Herring, Kevin Hammond, and Simon P. Jones provided helpful comments on drafts of this paper, as did four anonymous reviewers.

References

Backus, J. "Can Programming Be Liberated from the von Neumann Style? A Functional Style and Its Algebra of Programs." *Communications of the ACM* 21 (1978): 613-641.
Car, A., and Frank, A.U. "Formalization of Conceptual Models for GIS using GOFER." In *GIS/LIS '95 Central Europe in Budapest*, 1995.
Dijkstra, E.W. "Guarded Commands, Nondeterminacy and Formal Derivation of Programs." In *Current Trends in Programming Methodology, Vol. 1: Software Specification and Design*, ed. Yeh, R.T., 1977: 233-242.
Frank, A.U. "Acquiring a digital base map - A theoretical investigation into a form of sharing data." *URISA Journal* 4 (1 1992): 10-23.
Frank, A.U. "Qualitative Temporal Reasoning in GIS - Ordered Time Scales." In *6th International Symposium on Spatial Data Handling in Edinburgh, UK*, IGU, 1994: 410-430.

Guttag, J.V., Horning, J.J., and Wing, J.M. *Larch in Five Easy Pieces*. Digital Equipment Corporation, Systems Research Center, 1985.

Guttag, J.V., Horowitz, E., and Musser, D.R. "The Design of Data Type Specifications." In *Current Trends in Programming Methodology*, ed. Yeh, R.T., Vol. 4: Data Structuring. Prentice Hall, 1978: 60-79.

Head, G.E. "Six-Sigma Software Using Cleanroom Software Engineering Techniques." *Hewlett-Packard Journal* 1994 (June 1994): 40-50.

Hudak, P. "Conception, Evolution, and Application of Functional Programming Languages." *ACM Computing Surveys* 21 (3 1989): 359-411.

Hudak, P. *et al.* "Report on the functional programming language Haskell, Version 1.2." *SIGPLAN Notices* 27 (5 1992).

ISO. *The EXPRESS language reference manual*. ISO TC 184, 1992. Draft International Standard ISO/DIS 10303-11.

Jones, M.P. *Qualified Types: Theory and Practice*. Ph.D. Thesis, Programming Research Group, Oxford University, Cambridge University Press, 1994.

Kuhn, W. "Defining Semantics for Spatial Data Transfers." In *6th International Symposium on Spatial Data Handling in Edinburgh, UK*, IGU, 1994: 973-987.

Liang, S., Hudak, A P., and Jones, A M. "Monad transformers and modular interpreters." In *ACM Symposium on Principles of Programming Languages in* ACM, 1995.

Liskov, B., and Guttag, J. *Abstraction and Specification in Program Development*. The MIT Electrical Engineering and Computer Science Series, Cambridge, MA: The MIT Press, 1986.

Milner, R. "A Theory of Type Polymorphism in Programming." *Journal of Computer and System Sciences* 17 (1978): 348-375.

O'Callaghan, J.F. "The Impact of Applications and Information Technologies on Geographic Information Systems." In *GIS: Technology and Applications, Far East Workshop on GIS in Singapore*, edited by Hongjun, Lu, and Beng, Chin Ooi, World Scientific, 1993: 1-6.

Peyton Jones, S.L., and Wadler, P. "Imperative functional programming." In *ACM Symposium on Principles of Programming Languages (POPL) in Charleston*, ACM, 1993: 71-84.

Shipman, D.W. "The Functional Data Model and the Data Language DAPLEX." *ACM Transactions on Database Systems* 6 (March 1981).

Smith, T.R., and Frank, A.U. "Very Large Spatial Databases - Report from the Specialist Meeting." *Journal of Visual Languages and Computing* 1 (3 1990): 291-309.

Thiemann, P. *Grundlagen der funktionalen Programmierung*. Leitfaden der Informatik, Stuttgart: B. G. Teubner, 1994.

Voisard, A., and Schweppe, H. "A Multilayer Approach to the Open GIS Design Problem." In *2nd ACM GIS Workshop in Gaithersburg, MD*, edited by Pissinou, N., and Makki, K., ACM Press, New York, 1994: 23-29

Load-Balancing in High Performance GIS: Declustering Polygonal Maps*

Shashi Shekhar[1] Sivakumar Ravada[1] Vipin Kumar[1]
Douglas Chubb[2] Greg Turner[3]

[1] Computer Science Dept., University of Minnesota, Minneapolis, MN[†]
[2] Research and Technology Division, U.S. Army CECOM, RDEC, IEWD
[3] Information Processing Branch, Army Research Laboratory

Abstract. A high performance geographic information system (GIS) is a central component of many real-time applications of spatial decision making. The GIS may contain gigabytes of geometric and feature data (e.g. location, elevation, soil type etc.) stored on a hierarchy of memory devices and represented as grids and large sets of polygons. The data is often accessed via range queries (like polygon clipping) and map-overlay queries. For example, a real-time visualization program retrieves the visible subset of GIS data around the current location of simulator via range queries fetching a million points/second. Such performance can be obtained only with major advances in exploiting parallelism and spatial database techniques within the computational geometry algorithms for range and map-overlay queries.

In this paper, we develop and experimentally evaluate data partitioning and load-balancing techniques for range queries in High Performance GIS. We implement static and dynamic load-balancing methods on a distributed memory parallel machine (Cray T3D) for polygon data, and we experimentally evaluate their performance. Preliminary results show that both the static and dynamic load-balancing methods are necessary for improved performance but are not sufficient by themselves. We propose a new quasi-dynamic load-balancing (QDLB) technique which achieves better load-balance and speedups than traditional methods. On 16 processors, we are able to process range queries in under 0.12 seconds for a map with 329,296 edges, where the range query size is 20-25% of the total area of the map. We are also able to achieve average speedups of 14 on 16 processors.

Keywords: High Performance, Geographic Information Systems, Range Query, Declustering Methods, Load-Balancing, Polygon Clipping.

* This work was supported by Army High Performance Computing Research Center under contract the auspices of the Department of Army, Army Research Laboratory cooperative agreement number DAAH04-95-2-0003/contract number DA/DAAH04-95-C-0008.
† Authors email address: [shekhar|siva|kumar]@cs.umn.edu

1 Introduction

A high performance geographic information system (HP-GIS) is a central component of many applications like real-time terrain visualization, situation assessment, and spatial decision making. For example, visualization software retrieves the visible subset of spatial data around the current location of simulator via range queries (fetching a million points/second), and a graphics engine then displays the 3-D image of the data set as shown in Figure 1. As the user moves over the terrain, the part of the map that is visible to the user changes over time, and the graphics engine has to be fed with the visible subset of polygons for a given location and user's viewport. This requires retrieving the visible subset of polygons and computing their geometric intersection with the current viewport of the user. Figure 2 shows a map and a typical range query on a sample map. Polygons in the map are shown with dotted lines. The range query is represented by the rectangle and the result of the range query is shown in solid lines.

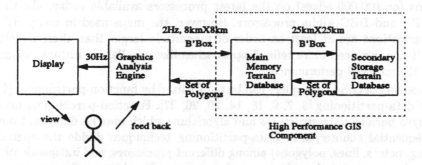

Fig. 1. Components of a Terrain Visualization System.

Problem Formulation: The range query for the GIS can be stated as follows: Given a rectangular bounding box B and a set of polygons S_P, the result of a range query over the set of polygons is given by the set query_retrieve$\{x | x = P_i \cap B$ and $P_i \in S_P\}$, where $\cap$ gives the geometric intersection of two polygons. We call this problem the GIS-range-query problem. Note that the GIS-range-query problem is similar to the polygon-clipping problem [21] in computer graphics. In this paper, we focus on parallelizing the GIS-range-query problem over a set of processors to meet the high performance requirements imposed by a typical HP-GIS.

1.1 Related work and Our Contributions

The existing sequential solutions for the GIS-range-query problem [5, 12, 25] cannot be directly used as a solution to the GIS-range-query problem due to the high performance requirements of the application. For example, the limit

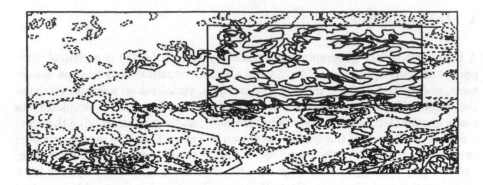

Fig. 2. A sample map used in our experiments.

on response time (i.e. half a second, as shown in Figure 1) for solving a GIS-range-query problem allows the processing of maps with no more than 1500 polygons (or 100,000 edges) on the latest processors available today, like the Power PC and DEC-Alpha processors. However, the maps used in many HP-GIS applications are at least an order of magnitude larger than these simple maps. Hence, we need more refined approaches like parallel algorithms, which deliver the required performance.

Processing of GIS-range-query can be parallelized by function-partitioning [1, 2, 4] or data-partitioning [3, 7, 9, 13, 14, 20, 26, 27]. Function-partitioning uses specialized parallel data-structures and algorithms which may be different from their sequential counterparts. Data-partitioning techniques divide the spatial data (e.g. points, lines, polygons) among different processors, and independently execute the sequential algorithm on each processor. In addition, the processors may exchange partial results during the run time. In this paper, we only focus on data-partitioning techniques.

Spatial data can be partitioned and allocated statically [3, 7, 8, 9, 10, 13, 14, 17, 22, 27] or dynamically [20, 26]. Static partitioning (or declustering) and load-balancing methods divide and allocated the data prior to the computation process. In contrast, dynamic load-balancing techniques divide and/or allocate work at run time. It has been shown that customized declustering techniques based on space partitioning with mapping functions [8, 27], proximity based local load-balance [13, 14, 17, 22], and similarity graph-partitioning [10, 22] are needed to effectively decluster spatial data. It has been shown [3, 7, 27] that static partitioning is adequate for achieving good load-balance where work can be estimated accurately before execution-time (e.g. in case of uniformly distributed point data). The work imposed by a polygon for an arbitrary range-query cannot be estimated accurately before execution-time. Thus, both static and dynamic load-balancing is needed for parallelizing range queries on polygonal maps [26].

In this paper, we develop and experimentally evaluate data-partitioning and load-balancing techniques for range queries on polygonal maps. Specifically, we extend three declustering methods that were developed for point data to polygon data, and then we experimentally measure their performance for the current problem. We implement static and dynamic load-balancing methods for polygon data on a distributed memory parallel machine (Cray T3D) and experimentally evaluate their performance. We show that both the static and dynamic load-balancing methods are necessary but not sufficient by themselves for improved performance. We propose a new quasi-dynamic load-balancing technique which performs better than both static and dynamic methods and achieves better load-balance and speedups. In addition, we theoretically analyze and construct the cost models for our algorithms, implement the algorithms on an existing distributed-memory parallel processor, and experimentally evaluate their performance. Even though we conduct the experiments on Cray T3D, note that, the proposed methods are valid for any distributed memory system due to their low communication overhead.

1.2 Scope and Outline of the Paper

In this paper, we focus on the evaluation of load-balancing schemes for the GIS-range-query problem. At present, the work in this paper is done in the context of main memory terrain databases. We plan to extend our work to secondary and tertiary storage in the near future. Also note that, in this paper we do not consider the hardware based clipping algorithms which are popular in computer graphics.

Several other techniques like preprocessing of the polygon data can be used to reduce the sequential cost of the range query and intersection computation. The cost of the range-query can also be reduced by noting that at any given point in time, the next range-query will spatially overlap with the previous range-query. Even though these are all related to reducing the cost of a GIS-range-query, we do not consider these issues in this paper.

The rest of the paper is organized as follows. In Section 2, we briefly discuss the basic concepts and the sequential algorithm. Section 3 introduces the declustering methods and load-balancing methods. In Section 4, we describe the experiments and evaluate the load-balancing methods with experimental data. Finally, Section 5 gives conclusions and future work.

2 Basic Concepts

In this section, we first discuss a sequential algorithm for the GIS-range-query problem and develop a cost model for this approach. We then introduce basic concepts in parallel computing.

2.1 A Representative Sequential Algorithm

The sequential algorithm uses a filter and brute force approach, and it is divided into three stages: (i) Approximate filtering of the set of all polygons in the map,

(ii) Intersection computation of the bounding box with candidate polygons, and
(iii) Polygonization of the result.

Approximate filtering is carried out by a multi-dimensional search structure
such as the grid file [23], which is used as an indexing method for spatial data. We
simplify the grid file discussed in [23] for the main memory environment and an
example grid file for this environment is given in Figure 3. The space partitioning
for the polygons is shown in Figure 3(a). The Grid file directory and buckets
are shown in 3(b) with the corresponding polygon identifiers (referred to as ids
in the rest of the paper) in each cell. These ids are used as an index into the
structure shown in 3(c) to access the rest of the data for that polygon. For each
range (i.e. bounding box in this case), the grid file performs 2 binary searches
(one search along each axis) and determines the range of cells that overlap the
given bounding box. It then merges the lists of polygon ids from each of the
cells in the computed range and returns the resulting list of polygon ids. Note
that other search structures such as Range-trees [24] and R-trees [12] can also
be used in place of the grid file for this approximate filtering.

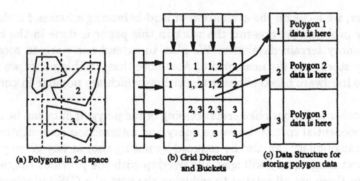

(a) Polygons in 2-d space   (b) Grid Directory and Buckets   (c) Data Structure for storing polygon data

Fig. 3. An example main memory grid file with polygon ids stored in the buckets.

Intersection computation is done using a simple filter and brute force method.
In the case of the GIS-range-query problem, filter and brute force approach is
competitive to plane sweep and triangulation-based approaches. Filtering in this
step is at edge level, in contrast to the polygon-level filtering in the approximate
filtering step. In the filtering step, all the edges of the polygon that have the sum
$X + Y$ of both the vertices less than $X_{min} + Y_{min}$ are filtered out, where $(X_{min},
Y_{min})$ is the lower left corner of the bounding box. Similarly, all the edges with
vertices above the region $X_{max} + Y_{max}$ are filtered out, where (X_{max}, Y_{max})
is the upper right corner of the bounding box. After this filtering step, all the
edges that are not filtered out are checked for possible intersections with the
bounding box. For increasing the efficiency of the filtering step, all the polygon
data is initially pre-processed as follows: (i) The smallest enclosing rectangular
box for each polygon is computed and stored along with the polygon data, and
(ii) the vertices of each polygon are sorted on $X + Y$ value and stored in that

order, along with their original order in the input. With this ordering, all the vertices above/below a given $X+Y$ value can be determined with a single binary search operation. Alternately, plane-sweep [5, 24] can be used for computing the intersection points.

Polygonization of the result from the set of intersection points, clipped vertices, and clipped line segments is performed in linear time, using a simple traversal of the vertices and intersection points in the result. A polygon is constructed by following a clipped vertex (or intersection point) and moving to the next vertex (or intersection point). If each vertex (or intersection-point) is associated with its next and previous nodes, traversing these nodes in counter-clockwise order gives the resulting polygon. Alternative approaches for polygonization are presented in [21, 25].

2.2 Cost model

We characterize the main components of the sequential algorithm which mainly dominate the computation cost, using a simplified cost model. Note that the worst-case asymptotic complexity for the intersection computation between a polygon with n edges and a rectangle is $O(n)$, since there are $4 \times n$ line segment pairs to be checked for intersections. In the case of our intersection computation algorithm, we sort the vertices of each polygon on $X+Y$, resulting in $O(n \log n)$ time complexity. Thus, asymptotically, our algorithm is worse than the simple brute force method. But note that we do the sorting only once for each polygon and it is done in the preprocessing step. Hence the cost per range-query does not include the sorting cost, and we do not include this cost in our analysis. In the following discussion, we present only the dominant portions of per range-query cost. In our cost model, we assume uniform distribution of polygons in the input for simplicity of interpretation.

The cost of the approximate filtering step via the grid file is dominated[1] by the cost of merging and copying the resulting list of polygon ids. Let γ be the number of polygons per unit area of the input. Then, the average number p_u of unique polygons picked up by the grid file for a range query of size $W \times H$ is $\gamma((WH) + \delta^2(W + H))$, where δ^2 is the average area of a grid cell. But note that polygon ids may be duplicated in multiple grid cells, resulting in more than p_u numbers for merging. Let σ be the average number of grid cells spanned by each polygon. Then, on an average, each polygon id is duplicated in σ cells selected by the grid file, resulting in σp_u numbers to be merged. These σp_u numbers are distributed over WH/δ^2 cells. Hence, the merging of WH/δ^2 lists takes time proportional to $\sigma p_u \lg(WH/\delta^2)$. This is approximately equal to $\gamma \sigma W H \lg(WH/\delta^2) t_c^1$, (assuming that the WH factor dominates the $W + H$ factor), where t_c^1 is the cost of merging per polygon id.

The cost of the intersection computation is dominated by the number of actual intersection computations performed in this stage. To compute this cost,

---

[1] If the polygon data is to be copied from the disk to the main memory for each query, this cost is dominated by the cost of copying the polygon data to the main memory.

Table 1. Cross validating the cost model for the sequential algorithm.

Map Size	Cost-type	Bbox Size		
		300	250	200
$2X$	Measured	0.318 ± 0.06	0.294 ± 0.05	0.194 ± 0.06
	Estimated	0.366	0.265	0.180
$4X$	Measured	0.517 ± 0.07	0.468 ± 0.07	0.303 ± 0.06
	Estimated	0.579	0.413	0.275
$8X$	Measured	0.808 ± 0.12	0.717 ± 0.06	0.554 ± 0.07
	Estimated	0.994	0.703	0.462
Parameter Values	$t_c^1 = 16\kappa$	$t_c^2 = 16\kappa$	$t_c^{31} = 256\kappa$	$t_c^{32} = 24\kappa$

let α be the number of edges per unit area of input, and let α' be the filtering efficiency of the binary search, given as a factor of edges selected from the set of candidate edges after grid file filtering. Then, $(WH)\alpha\alpha'$ gives the number of average intersection computations performed per range query. Finally, the cost of polygonization of the result is dominated by the size of the result. This result is comprised of two sets of polygons: (i) the set of polygons which were completely inside the bounding box, and (ii) the set of polygons that actually intersect the bounding box. This cost is then proportional to the number of intersection points $2(W + H)\beta$, plus the number of edges $WH\alpha\alpha'$ in the result which do not intersect the bounding box, where β is the average number of intersection points per unit-length bounding box.

The sequential cost T_{seq} is then given by:
$$T_{seq} = \gamma\sigma WH \lg(WH/\delta^2)t_c^1 + (WH)\alpha\alpha't_c^2 + 2(W + H)\beta t_c^{31} + (WH)\alpha\alpha't_c^{32}$$
$$= WH[\gamma\sigma\lg(WH/\delta^2)t_c^1 + \alpha\alpha'(t_c^2 + t_c^{32})] + 2(W + H)\beta t_c^{31}$$
Here,
t_c^2: the cost of 8 comparisons
t_c^{31}: the cost of updating resulting edges per intersection point
t_c^{32}: the cost of copying a vertex to the result.

We cross-validated the cost-formula with the actual run-time for different map sizes and for different sizes of range-queries. A summary of these observations is given in Table 1. Actual run-time is represented as $Mean \pm SD$ and is averaged over 50 range-queries. The values of the t_c parameters are also given in the table. Here, the constant κ depends on the system and is determined by the clock rate of the system.

2.3 Parallel Architectures and Communication costs

Shared-address-space architecture provides hardware support for read/write access by all processors to a shared memory. In a message-passing (or distributed memory) architecture, processors are connected with an interconnection network, and processors can interact with each other only by passing messages. In this paper, we are concerned only with message-passing architectures, as they are the most widely used architectures in today's parallel processing systems. In our experiments, we used the Cray T3D, which is a distributed-memory machine with a three-dimensional wrap around mesh-interconnection network. This has 512 processors (each processor is a DEC-Alpha running at 150MHz) with 64 MBytes local memory at each processor.

The time taken to communicate a message between two processors in the network is the sum of time t_s, to prepare a message for transmission and time t_w, taken by the message to traverse the network to its destination. A single message with m words can be sent from one processor to a neighboring processor in time $t_s + t_w m$. A message containing m words can be broadcast from a processor to $P - 1$ other processors (one-to-all communication) in time $(t_s + t_w m) \lg P$ [19].

Parallel run-time T_P of an algorithm on P processors includes parallel computation time and communication time. In the ideal case, parallel computation time is given by T_{seq}/P, where T_{seq} is the sequential run-time of the algorithm. Speedup and efficiency are two important parameters by which a parallel algorithm can be evaluated. Speedup S is defined as T_{seq}/T_P, and efficiency is defined as S/P. Speedup for a parallel implementation can be due to (i) reduced page faults and swapping, and to (ii) increased computational power compared to the sequential implementation. Memory swapping and page faults are reduced in a parallel implementation, due to the smaller amount of the data each processor has to hold. This effect often results in superlinear speedups for GIS problems, due to the high memory requirements of GIS problems [3, 7]. Hence, it is desirable to isolate and distinguish the effect of page swapping from the effect of increased computational power for clear interpretation of the results.

The effectiveness of a load-balancing technique is measured by the load imbalance ratio, the increase in work due to the synchronization and communication, and the non-parallelized work in the parallel implementation [19]. The load imbalance factor is defined as $(1 - \frac{Average\ work\ at\ all\ the\ processors}{Maximum\ work\ at\ any\ processor})$ and the total overhead of a parallel implementation is defined as $PT_P - T_{seq}$. Even though the overhead measure is dependent on the load imbalance factor, it is not completely determined by this imbalance factor. Hence, it is desirable that a load-balancing technique exhibit lower values for both these measures.

3 Load-Balancing Techniques

Parallelizing the GIS-range-query on a distributed memory system involves allocating equal amounts of work to each processor so as to effectively use the available processors. These work allocations can be done either statically or dynamically. Static allocations require that the data be initially distributed among different processors so that the processors can work on their local data for each range-query. On the other hand, dynamic methods try to allocate work to idle processors during run time. In this section, we first discuss different ways to divide the work among the processors. We then discuss different factors that can affect the performance of a parallel formulation of the GIS-range-query problem, and we propose a method for parallelizing the sequential algorithm for the GIS-range-query problem.

3.1 Different Levels of Decomposition

A GIS-range-query can be parallelized either by dividing the set of polygons or by the bounding box among different processors. In general, both the bounding box and the set of polygons can be divided into many combinations as shown in Figure 4. These combinations can be grouped into four types: Type I has no division of data. Type II divides the set of polygons into subsets of polygons. However, each polygon is treated as an atomic unit and sub-division at polygon level is not allowed. In contrast, type III divides the areas of individual polygons/bounding-box among different processors. Type IV schemes divide both the areas and the edges of individual polygons and the bounding box. The potential advantage of type III and IV schemes over type II scheme is the possibility of better load-balancing and lower processor idling, resulting in reduced parallel computation time [26]. However, note that types III and IV schemes result either in increased total work or in increased work for polygonization of the result.

| | Options for Dividing the Polygon Data | | | |
	No Division	subsets of polygons	subsets of small polygons	subsets of edges
No Division	I	II	III-a	IV-a
Divide into small boxes	III-b	III-c	III-d	IV-b
divide into Edges	IV-c	IV-d	IV-e	IV-f

(Options for Dividing Bounding Box)

Fig. 4. Alternatives for Polygons/Bounding Box division among processors.

Let T_{comm} be the response-time overhead, due to additional communication cost, or the increased cost for polygonization of the resulting polygons for type III and IV schemes. The gain in parallel-computation time due to improved load-balancing is bounded by the difference between the ideal value (T_{seq}/P) and the actual T_P value achieved by type II scheme. The net gain in response time by any type III or IV scheme over type II scheme is bounded by $[T_P(\text{scheme II}) - \frac{T_{seq}}{P} - T_{comm}]$. This gain is positive only when polygon size distributions are extremely skewed, leading to high load imbalances for type II schemes. At present, the data maps in our application domain do not satisfy these conditions, and the maps and range queries do not cause significant load imbalances, as is evident from our experimental observations documented later.

In the rest of this paper, we focus on type II schemes, which divide the polygon set into subsets of polygons, which are then assigned to different processors, using the static and dynamic load-balancing methods described later in this section. Figure 5 describes the steps in type II scheme. In this scheme, the bounding box is initially broadcast to all processors. Each processor then executes the sequential GIS-range-query algorithm on the local set of polygons. After processing the local data, a processor checks for any load imbalances and seeks more work from another processor which has not yet finished its work. The load-balancing methods discussed later in this section are used for this purpose.

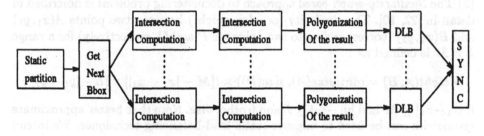

Fig. 5. Different modules of the parallel formulations.

3.2 Declustering Strategies for Polygonal Maps

The Declustering problem for the GIS-range-query problem can be stated as follows: Given a set of polygons, P processors, and a set of queries, divide the set of polygons among P processors, such that the load at each processor is balanced for a given query. Usually, terrain data (which is a set of polygons) has non-uniform distribution and variable size polygons, which makes it difficult to develop a strategy that will be optimal for all queries. It is known that the declustering problem is NP-hard even for point data [22]. Several heuristic methods that have been proposed in the literature for solving the declustering problem for point data are based on the ideas of space partitioning with mapping functions, local load-balance methods, and similarity-based methods [22].

We define a polygon-to-point transformation function and use point-based static-declustering methods for declustering the polygon data. In the following discussion, let $bb(A)$ be the smallest rectangular box enclosing polygon A, where the box is represented by its two corners (x_{min}, y_{min}) and (x_{max}, y_{max}). We define a function *point* from the set of polygons to the set of 2-dimensional points as

$$point(A) = (\frac{x_{min} + y_{min}}{2}, \frac{x_{max} + y_{max}}{2})$$

where $bb(A) = \{(x_{min}, y_{min}), (x_{max}, y_{max})\}$. Further, let $size(point(A))$ denote the number of edges in the polygon A.

In this paper, we examine the following three point-based declustering methods: (1) *Space Partitioning with Mapping-function-based methods* provide a mapping function from the domain of data items to the set of processor ids, assuming that all data items and queries are equiprobable. We use a mapping function based on the Hilbert Space-filling curve [6, 16]. (See [27] for a survey of other mapping functions for declustering.) (2) *Local load-balancing methods* [22, 17] consider a sample window of space (similar to the actual range-query) at a time, and try to equally distribute the load in that window to all the processors. We use a rectangle as the sample window and balance the load in that window by considering the number of edges corresponding to that window at each processor. (3) The *Similarity-graph-based* approach to declustering problems is described in detail in [22, 10]. The similarity (or edge weight) between two points $A(x_1, y_1)$ and $B(x_2, y_2)$ (corresponding to two polygons P and Q, respectively) for a range $L \times M$ is defined as

$$Weight(A, B) = min(size(A), size(B)) \times ([M - |x_1 - x_2|] \times [L - |y_1 - y_2|])$$

if $|x_1 - x_2| \leq M$ and $|y_1 - y_2| \leq L$ and 0 otherwise. Note that better approximate geometries can be used to improve static load-balancing techniques. We intend to examine these techniques in our future work.

3.3 Dynamic Load-Balancing (DLB) Methods

If static declustering methods fail to equally distribute the load among different processors, then the load-balance may be improved by transferring some polygons to idle processors using dynamic load-balancing techniques. A typical dynamic load-balancing technique addresses three issues: (1) Which processor should an idle processor ask for more work, (2) How much more work should an idle processor fetch, and (3) How to contain the communication overhead?

Methods to decide who should an idle processor ask for more work are discussed and analyzed in [19, 20]. These methods can be divided into two categories: (1) In pool-based DLB method, a fixed processor has all the available work and an idle processor asks this fixed processor for more work. (2) In a peer-based DLB method, all the work is initially distributed among different processors and an idle processor selects a peer processor as the donor of work using random polling, nearest neighbor, and global or local round robin. In this paper, we use a pool based DLB method. In future, we intend to complete a comprehensive evaluation of alternative techniques.

Granularity of work division determines how much work is transferred between a donor processor and an idle processor. This granularity may depend on the size of the remaining work, the number of processors, and the accuracy in estimating the remaining work. Several strategies like self-scheduling [11], factoring scheduling [15], and chunk scheduling [18] exist for determining the amount of work to be transferred.

In case of a work transfer, the number of messages and the amount of information exchanged between the processors determines the communication overhead for that work transfer. Since the data needed to represent a polygon can be very large, exchanging the polygon data between processors can be very expensive. By selectively duplicating the polygon data on different processors, load-balancing can be achieved by exchanging only the polygon ids. Since the polygon id is only a word of data, this will result in minimum communication overhead for each data transfer. Note that this replication of polygonal data at different processors results in memory overhead.

3.4   Our Approach: Quasi-Dynamic Load-Balancing (QDLB)

In our approach, we use a two-level pool-based DLB method. We call this method QDLB, since the pool is declustered statically but allocation of work from this pool is done dynamically. This is a two-level scheme, since we use an initial static declustering of the data along with dynamic load-balancing.

In the QDLB method, a processor is designated the *leader* of the group of processors. This leader processor maintains a pool of shared work. Initially, all the data is initially declustered into two sets, S_a and S_b. This declustering is done depending on the desired size of the shared pool of polygons. (In our experiments we got the best performance when S_b was between 40-60% of the total data.) The data in S_a is then statically declustered among all the processors. The data in S_b is also statically declustered into x buckets and is replicated at all the processors. Note that any of the static-declustering methods discussed in Section 3.2 can be used for this static-declustering purpose. The value of x is dependent on the size of S_b and should be tuned, depending on the data (in our experiments, a value between $4P$ and $8P$ resulted in good performance).

When a bounding box for the next range query is received, the *leader* processor broadcasts the bounding-box parameters to all the other processors in the group. After receiving the bounding-box parameters, each processor performs the approximate range query and retrieves the candidate polygons that correspond to its local data for the set S_a. In addition, the *leader* processor performs the approximate filtering for the data in the set S_b and places the resulting polygons in a shared pool of buckets, according to their initial bucket assignment. Each processor then independently works on its local data that corresponds to the polygons from the set S_a. When a processor finishes work on the data from S_a, it fetches polygon ids corresponding to the next available unprocessed bucket. This requires the transfer of b_s numbers, where b_s is the number of polygons retrieved for that bucket. This process repeats as long as there are unprocessed buckets at the *leader* processor.

Pseudocode for the general QDLB method is given in Figure 6. The QDLB method has the drawback of having a single processor as the *leader*. This would affect performance, as the contention at the *leader* process increases for increased P. This contention can be reduced by using the buddy-set method, as described next.

```
TYPE pidSet = 0..P−1;
VAR input_polygon: Set of Polygons map to processor using DECLUSTER();
apprx_strct: record
              local: Array [pidSet] of grid files  map[i] to processor i;
                      /* corresponding to data from S_a */
              global: Array [pidSet] of grid files  map[i] to processor i;
                      /* corresponding to data from S_b */
          endrecord;
PROCEDURE Approx_filter()
  BEGIN
      parallel for(pid in pidSet) do
        filtered_polyids_local[pid] = Aprx_filter(apprx_strct[pid].local, bbox);
        if(pid = 0)
            filtered_polyids_global[pid] = Aprx_filter(apprx_strct[pid].global,bbox);
      endfor;
  END;
PROCEDURE Parallel_Intersect(bbox: BBox)
  VAR result: Array [pidSet] of set of of polygons map[i] to processor i;
      filtered_polyids_local: Array [pidSet] of set of polygon−ids map[i] to processor i;
      filtered_polyids_global: Array [pidSet] of set of polygon−ids map[i] to processor i;
      isect_pts: Array [pidSet] of set of inter_sect points map[i] to processor i;
  BEGIN
      one_to_all_broadcast(0, pidSet, bbox);
      parallel for(pid in pidSet) do
      Approximate_filter();
      isect_pts[pid] = Isect_module(filtered_polyids_local[pid],input_polygon[pid],bbox);
      result[pid] = Reconstruct_module(isect_pts[pid]);
      endfor;
      parallel while (more work) do
      lock_shared_pool(leader); /* lock the shared pool at leader */
      poly_ids = fetch_next(polygon ids from next unprocessed bucket_id);
      unlock();
      isect_pts[pid] = Isect_module(poly_ids, input_polygon[pid], bbox);
      result[pid] = Reconstruct_module(isect_pts[pid]);
      endwhile;
  END
```

Fig. 6. Pseudo-code for the Quasi-Dynamic Load-Balance Parallel Formulations.

Buddy-Set Method: Buddy sets are constructed by dividing the number of processors into k ($k \geq 1$) mutually exclusive sets $(P^1, P^2, \ldots, P^k)$ called buddy sets. A processor in each P^i is designated to be the leader of that buddy set and is denoted by $leader(P^i)$. The initial data set S is declustered into k mutually exclusive sets $(S_1, S_2, \ldots, S_k)$, such that S_i corresponds to the processor set P^i. Each S_i is further declustered into two partitions S_i^1 and S_i^2 (corresponding to S_a and S_b). Now for each i, $1 \leq i \leq k$, the polygons in S_i^1 are declustered among the processors in set P^i. The polygons in S_i^2 are declustered into x buckets and are duplicated at all the processors in P^i. With this data distribution, all the processors construct a grid file for the polygons in their corresponding sets S_i^1 and each $leader(P^i)$ constructs another grid file for the polygons for each S_i^2. Now each buddy-set can independently perform the QDLB method.

3.5 Cost Model for Parallel Formulations

In the static-declustering methods, the computing load coefficient T_c on each processor is not perfectly balanced, which leads to processor idling. In addition, the static load-balancing method has one communication step of broadcasting the bounding box to all the processors. This takes time $(t_s + 16t_w) \lg P$, since we need to transmit four floating-point numbers (x_{min}, y_{min}, x_{max}, y_{max}), each of 4-bytes size. Let ν_s be the load-imbalance factor due to the static load-balancing. Then the total parallel response time T_P for the static load-balancing method can be expressed as:

$$T_P = \frac{T_{seq}}{(1 - \nu_s)P} + (t_s + 16t_w) \lg P$$

We can express T_{seq} as the sum of the cost of filtering plus the cost of the rest of the computation (i.e. intersection computation and polygonization):

$$T_{seq} = T_{fil} + T_{rst}$$

In the case of a purely dynamic load-balancing method ($S_a = 0\%$, $S_b = 100\%$), where a single processor performs the grid file computation for each range-query (and work is distributed to idle processor subsequently), the cost can be expressed as:

$$T_P = T_{fil} + \frac{T_{rst} + T_{comm}}{(1 - \nu_d)P} + (t_s + 16t_w) \lg P$$

where T_{comm} is the communication overhead for work transfers and ν_d is the load-imbalance factor for the dynamic load-balancing method. Note that the filtering cost is not shared among all the processors, and this results in non-parallelizable overhead. Due to this overhead, purely dynamic methods do not perform well for bigger data sets.

QDLB method eliminates the non-parallelizable overhead of the purely dynamic methods. In the QDLB method, some load imbalance is tolerated for reduced communication cost. Let ν_q be the load imbalance factor using the quasi-dynamic technique. The cost of the QDLB method, when n polygon ids are exchanged between processors, is given by:

$$T_P = \frac{T_{seq} + xt_s + 4nt_w}{(1 - \nu_q)P} + (t_s + 16t_w) \lg P$$

The cost of this behavior can be approximated by dividing the sequential cost, plus the communication overhead for work transfers, by the number of processors in the group. The size of the pool size should be small enough so that no processor needs to wait for the *leader* processor to finish the filtering step. In addition, the pool should be large enough to be able to offset the load imbalance caused by static declustering of non-shared data. Also note that load imbalance will still be present in the QDLB method, but this load imbalance will be lower than the load imbalance in static methods. And by choosing a sufficiently large number of buckets, this load imbalance can be reduced.

4 Experimental Analysis

We compare the performance of different declustering methods for a range of map sizes and for a different number of processors. In addition, we compare the proposed QDLB method with the existing methods, and then show how performance improves for the QDLB method when compared to purely static and dynamic load-balancing methods. Our experiments are carried out on the Cray T3D parallel computer at the Pittsburgh Super Computing Center.

We use spatial vector data for Killeen, Texas which is divided into seven themes representing the attributes slope, vegetation, surface material, hydrology, etc. We used the "slope" attribute-data map with 729 polygons and 41162 edges as a base map in our experiments (this is denoted by $1X\_map$). For studying the effect of increased map size, we derived new maps from this base map using the following method: Scaling down the base map along the x-axis by two and combining two such scaled down maps by translating one of the scaled-down maps along the x-axis results in a map of 1458 polygons with 82324 edges ($2X\_map$). A similar technique is used by alternately scaling down along the y-axis and the x-axis to get maps of different sizes as shown in Table 2.

Table 2. Maps and range-queries used in our experiments

Map	#Polygons	#edges	range-query	
			size	number
1X	729	41162	25%	75
2X	1458	82324	25%	75
4X	2916	164648	25%	75
8X	5832	329296	25%	75

We conducted different experiments to measure the effect of both the number of processors and the map size on the performance of the different parallel GIS-range-query algorithms discussed in this paper. For this, a sequence of 75 range queries is constructed such that the sequence of the center points of the range query represents a random walk on the data set. Post-processing is done on this sequence to ensure that all range queries are unique and that the range-query lies completely within the map. The size of each range query is approximately 25% of the total area of the map. In all our measurements, we obtain the run time of the program for each of the 75 queries and report the observed mean of these 75 values. Figure 7 shows our experimental methodology. The number of different options we tried for each parameter is shown in parentheses, and the number of possible combinations after each module is also shown in the figure.

In our experiments, we only measure and analyze the cost per bounding box and exclude any preprocessing cost. This preprocessing cost includes the cost of sorting the polygon data on $X + Y$, the cost of declustering the data among different processors, and the cost of loading the data from the disk to

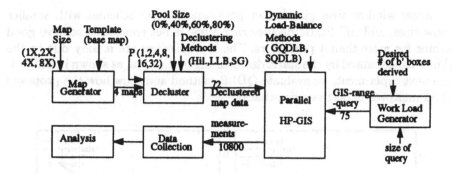

Fig. 7. Experimental Method for Evaluating Load-Balancing Methods for the parallel GIS-range-query.

the main memory. Note that this preprocessing cost is paid only once for each data set that corresponds to the current window of interest. As the query range moves out of the current window, new data is fetched from the disk discarding data for the old window. Since the next location of the window can be pre-determined, preprocessing the new data need not affect the performance of the rest of the system. Moreover, once a new data set is loaded into the main memory, it would be active for several minutes before the window moves out of the current range. Thus, this would leave several minutes for preprocessing the next data set. Hence, in this study, we are only interested in measuring the performance of our algorithm in terms of the variable cost per bounding box (or range query) for the preprocessed data.

4.1 How Do Map Declustering Techniques Compare?

We conduct two experiments to study the effect of declustering achieved by the three static declustering methods: Hilbert, local load-balance (LLB), and similarity-based methods. In this experiment, we study the effect of a different number of processors for the maps $1X\_map$ and $8X\_map$. Here, only static declustering is used, and no run-time load-balancing is performed. The data is initially distributed among different processors, and each processor works on its local data for each range query. The only communication required for each bounding box is a broadcast of the parameters of the bounding box by processor zero to all other processors. Figure 8 shows the results of this experiment. In 8(a), speedups are shown for map = $1X\_map$ and in 8(b) speedups are shown for map = $8X\_map$. In this figure, the x-axis gives the number of processors, and the y-axis gives the speedup value. In the figure, "llb-10" refers to the Local Load-Balancing method with a sample window that is 10% of the total map area. Similar notation is used for sample window of 30% area. Similarity graph method is used with a sample window of area 30% of the total area of the map. The main trends observed from these graphs are that: (i) Bigger maps lead to better load-balancing and better speedups for most schemes, (ii) Schemes with bigger window sizes give better performance than schemes with smaller window sizes, and (iii) Static declustering alone is not enough to achieve good speedups for more than 4 processors. The low speedups are mainly due to the load imbalance caused by the static declustering of the data, as shown in Table 4. In the next experiment, we evaluate QDLB method and show how the proposed method improves upon these drawbacks.

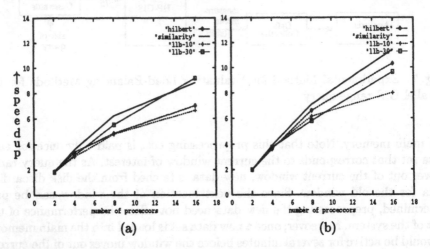

Fig. 8. Speedups for different static-declustering methods. Speedups for maps 2X and 8X are given in (a) and (b) respectively.

4.2 Evaluation of the Quasi-Dynamic Load-Balancing Method

In this experiment, we study the performance of the QDLB method. Table 3 gives the speedups achieved by the QDLB method as the size of the shared pool increases for $P = 16$ and $k = 2$ on the $8X\_map$. We used the similarity-graph method for declustering the data. Note that shared pool size = 0% is the purely static load-balancing method. We observe that the QDLB method outperforms purely static methods (pool size = 0%). Pool size affects performance in a non-linear fashion with a point of diminishing returns. These results show the need for quasi-dynamic schemes with two-level declustering. We do not the report the results for the case with shared pool size = 100%, due to the high memory requirements of this case. (In preliminary experiments, a purely dynamic method performed worse than the QDLB method.) When all the data is put into the shared pool, all this data needs to be replicated at all the processes. In this case, the data does not fit into the main memory of each node of the parallel machine. As noted earlier in Section 2, this results in increased memory faults, leading to increased run-times. To compare the results of different schemes on the same scale, we do not include the results for this purely dynamic scheme. But note that this brings out another drawback of purely dynamic schemes.

Table 3. Speedups for QDLB method and purely static load-balancing methods.

Method	Static	QDLB		
Shared_pool_size	0%	40%	60%	80%
Speedup	10.25	13.18	14.24	12.65

The effectiveness of QDLB method in achieving a good load-balance is shown in Table 4. The data shown in Table 4 is represented as $Mean \pm SD$ for the 75 range queries used in our experiment. The column *Avg. Static* gives the average static execution time over 16 processors and 75 range-queries. The column *Max. Static* gives the maximum static execution time over 16 processors, averaged over 75 range-queries. Similarly, *Avg. Total* time is the average total time over 16 processors for 75 queries, and *Total* is the total parallel run time averaged over 75 range-queries. In this experiment, we observe that the QDLB method has a load imbalance factor of 0.34 for the static part of the computation, and an imbalance factor of 0.10 for total run time. Even though the load-balance resulting from static partitioning of the data is quite uneven, the quasi-dynamic method succeeds in improving the load-balancing.

Table 4. Performance Evaluation of QDLB for P = 16 and k = 2.

Method	Avg. Static	Max. Static	Avg. Total	Total	Speedup
QDLB	0.0379 ± 0.006	0.0582 ± 0.010	0.0846 ± 0.003	0.0941 ± 0.003	14.2 ± 1.85

5 Conclusions and Future Work

Data-partitioning is an effective approach towards achieving high performance in GIS. Partitioning polygonal maps is difficult, due to the varying sizes and extents of the polygons and the difficulty of estimating the work load. Hence, special techniques are needed to parallelize the GIS-range-query problem.

In this paper, we experimentally evaluated different load-balancing schemes for the GIS-range-query problem and proposed a QDLB method which outperforms purely static and dynamic schemes. We showed that static/dynamic load balancing alone may not be enough to achieve good speedups as the number of processors increases beyond 4. In the proposed approach, we use the ideas of declustering in a hierarchical fashion, increasing the load balance over purely static methods and decreasing the communication cost over purely dynamic methods.

We are expanding the experimental work towards a more comprehensive comparison of static, dynamic, and quasi-dynamic load-balancing techniques. We are planning to scale up to larger numbers of processors, larger maps, and queries. We would like to improve the cost models and cross-validate them with the experimental data. We would also like to examine alternative declustering techniques based on better approximate geometries and work-load estimation. We also plan to extend our work to map-overlay problems and other computationally intensive HP-GIS operations. Another major effort would focus on high performance techniques for secondary and tertiary storage terrain mapping and the effect of I/O (e.g. swapping) and indexing methods. Finally, we would like to evaluate these techniques on the workstation clusters which are common in many GIS applications.

Acknowledgments This work is sponsored by the Army High Performance Computing Research Center under the auspices of the Department of the Army, Army Research Laboratory cooperative agreement number DAAH04-95-2-0003/ contract number DAAH04-95-C-0008, the content of which does not necessarily reflect the position or the policy of the government, and no official endorsement should be inferred. This work is also supported by Federal Highway Authority and the Minnesota Department of Transportation. We would like to thank the Pittsburgh Super Computing Center for providing us with access to the Cray T3D. We would also like to thank Christiane McCarthy, Mark Coyle and Andrew Fetterer for improving the readability and technical accuracy of this paper.

References

1. A. Aggarwal, B. Chazelle, L. Guibas, C. O'Dunlaing, and C. Yap. Parallel computational geometry. In *Proceedings of the 25th IEEE Symposium on Foundations of Computer Science*, pages 468–477, 1985.
2. S. G. Akl and K. A. Lyons. *Parallel Computational Geometry*. Prentice Hall, Englewood Cliffs, 1993.
3. M. P. Armstrong, C. E. Pavlik, and R. Marciano. Experiments in the measurement of spatial association using a parallel supercomputer. *Geographical Systems*, 1:267–288, 1994.
4. M. J. Atallah and M. T. Goodrich. Efficient plane sweeping in parallel. In *Proceedings of the 2nd Annual ACM Symposium on Computational Geometry*, pages 216–225, 1986.
5. J. L. Bentley and T. A. Ottmann. Algorithms for reporting and counting geometric intersections. *IEEE Transactions on Computers*, c-28(9):643–647, 1979.
6. T. Bially. Space-filling curves: Their generation and their application to bandwidth reduction. *IEEE Transactions on Information Theory*, IT-15(6):658–664, 1969.
7. G. Brunetti, A. Clematis, B. Falcidieno, A. Sanguineti, and M. Spagnuolo. Parallel processing of spatial data for terrain characterization. In *Proceedings of the ACM workshop in GIS*, 1994.
8. H. C. Du and J. S. Sobolewski. Disk allocation for product files on multiple disk systems. *ACM Transactions on Database Systems*, 7, March 1982.
9. W. R. Franklin et al. Uniform grids: A technique for intersection detection on serial and parallel machines. In *Proceedings of the 9th Conference on Automated Cartography, American Society for Photogeometry and Remote Sensing*, pages 100–109, 1989.

10. M. T. Fang, R. C. T. Lee, and C. C. Chang. The idea of declustering and its applications. In *Proceedings of the International Conference on Very Large Databases*, 1986.

11. Z. Fang, P.-C. Yew, P. Tang, and C.-Q.Zhu. Dynamic processor self-scheduling for general parallel nested loops. In *Proceedings of the International Conference in Parallel Processing*, August 1987.

12. A. Guttman. R-trees: A dynamic index structure for spatial searching. In *Proceedings of the SIGMOD Conference*, pages 47–57, 1984.

13. E. G. Hoel and H. Samet. Data parallel r-tree algorithms. In *Proceedings of the 1993 International Conference on Parallel Processing*, 1993.

14. E. G. Hoel and H. Samet. Performance of data-parallel spatial operations. In *Proceedings of the 20th VLDB Conference*, pages 156–167, 1994.

15. S. F. Hummel, E. Schonberg, and L. E. Flynn. Factoring - a method for scheduling parallel loops. *Communications of the ACM*, pages 35–90, August 1992.

16. H. V. Jagadish. Linear clustering of objects with multiple attributes. In *Proceedings of the 1990 ACM SIGMOD International Conference on Management of Data*, pages 332–342, 1990.

17. I. Kamel and C. Faloutsos. Parallel r-trees. In *Proceedings of the International Conference on Management of Data, ACM SIGMOD*, 1992.

18. C. Kruskal and A. Weiss. Allocating independent subtasks on parallel processors. *IEEE Transactions on Software Engineering*, pages 1001–1016, October 1985.

19. V. Kumar, A. Grama, A. Gupta, and G. Karypis. *Introduction to Parallel Computing: Design and Analysis of Algorithms*. The Benjamin/Cummings Publishing Company, Inc., 1994.

20. V. Kumar, A. Grama, and V. N. Rao. Scalable load balancing techniques for parallel computers. *Journal of Distributed Computing*, 7, March 1994.

21. Y. Liang and B. A. Barsky. An analysis and algorithm for polygon clipping. *Communications of the ACM*, 26, November 1983.

22. D. R. Liu and S. Shekhar. A similarity graph-based approach to declustering problem and its applications. In *Proceedings of the Eleventh International Conference on Data Engineering, IEEE*, 1995.

23. J. Nievergelt, H. Hinterberger, and K. D. Sevcik. The grid file: An adaptable, symmetric multikey file structure. *ACM Transactions on Database Systems*, 9(1):38–71, 1984.

24. F. P. Preparata and M. I. Shamos. *Computational Geometry*. Springer-Verlag, New York, 1985.

25. B. R. Vatti. A generic solution to polygon clipping. *Communications of the ACM*, 35, July 1992.

26. F. Wang. A parallel intersection algorithm for vector polygon overlay. *IEEE Computer Graphics & Applications*, March 1993.

27. Y. Zhou, S. Shekhar, and M. Coyle. Disk allocation methods for parallelizing grid files. In *Proceedings of the Tenth International Conference on Data Engineering, IEEE*, 1994.

Implementation of the ROSE Algebra:
Efficient Algorithms for Realm-Based Spatial Data Types

Ralf Hartmut Güting[1], Thomas de Ridder[2], Markus Schneider[1]
gueting@fernuni-hagen.de, thomas.deridder@fernuni-hagen.de,
markus.schneider@fernuni-hagen.de

[1] Praktische Informatik IV, Fernuniversität Hagen, D-58084 Hagen, GERMANY
[2] Praktische Informatik III, Fernuniversität Hagen, D-58084 Hagen, GERMANY

Abstract: The ROSE algebra, defined earlier, is a system of spatial data types for use in spatial database systems. It offers data types to represent points, lines, and regions in the plane together with a comprehensive set of operations; semantics of types and operations have been formally defined. Values of these data types have a quite general structure, e.g. an object of type *regions* may consist of several polygons with holes. All ROSE objects are *realm-based* which means all points and vertices of objects lie on an integer grid and no two distinct line segments of any two objects intersect in their interior. In this paper we describe the implementation of the ROSE algebra, providing data structures for the types and new *realm-based geometric algorithms* for the operations. The main techniques used are (parallel) traversal of objects, plane-sweep, and graph algorithms. All algorithms are analyzed with respect to their worst case time and space requirements. Due to the realm properties, these algorithms are relatively simple, efficient, and numerically completely robust. All data structures and algorithms have indeed been implemented in the *ROSE system*; the Modula-2 source code is freely available from the authors for study or use.

Keywords: Spatial data types, algebra, realm, finite resolution, numerical robustness, efficient algorithms, plane sweep, ROSE.

1 Introduction

We consider a *spatial database system* to be a full-fledged database system with additional capabilities for representing, querying, and manipulating geometric data (for a survey see [Gü94]). Such a system provides the underlying database technology needed to support applications such as *geographic information systems* and others. Spatial data types like *point*, *line*, and *region* provide a fundamental abstraction for modeling the structure of geometric entities, their relationships, properties, and operations. Their definition and implementation is probably the most fundamental issue in the development of spatial database systems.

There have been quite a few proposals for systems of spatial data types and operations, or *spatial algebras*; they have been embedded into query languages, implemented in prototype systems, and some of them have been defined formally. For a discussion and references see [GüS93b, Gü94]. This paper continues the development of one such proposal, the *ROSE algebra* [GüS93b], which has a number of interesting features: (i) it offers (values of) data types of a very general structure, (ii) has a complete formal definition of the semantics of types and operations, (iii) has a discrete geometric basis (so-called *realms*, see below) which allows for a correct and robust implementation in terms of integer arithmetics, (iv) treats consistency between distinct geometric objects with common parts, and (v) has a general object model interface which allows it to cooperate with different kinds of database systems.

This work was supported by the DFG (Deutsche Forschungsgemeinschaft) under grant Gu 293/1-2.

The development of the ROSE algebra so far consists of three steps: (1) the concept of a *realm* [GüS93a] as a *discrete* geometric basis, (2) the formal definition of the *ROSE algebra* itself offering *realm-based* spatial data types and operations [GüS93b], and (3) the *ROSE system* as an implementation of the ROSE algebra, which realizes its types and operations by providing efficient data structures and algorithms defined over a discrete grid. This third step is the subject of this paper. Let us briefly review the first two steps.

A *realm* conceptually describes the complete underlying geometry of a particular application space in two dimensions. Formally, a realm is a finite set of points and line segments over a discrete grid (see Figure 1(a)) such that (i) each point and each end point of a line segment is a grid point, (ii) each end point of a realm segment is also a point of the realm, (iii) no realm point lies within a realm segment (which means on it without being an end point), and (iv) no two realm segments intersect except at their end points. The idea is now to construct the geometries of spatial objects by composing them from realm primitives (see Figure 1(b)). The realm concept solves numerical robustness and topological correctness problems, enforces geometric consistency of related spatial objects, and enables one to formally define spatial data types or algebras on top of it that enjoy nice closure properties not only in theory but also in an implementation.

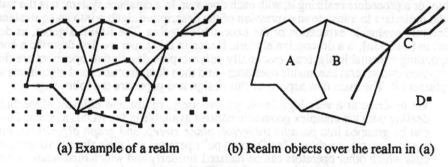

(a) Example of a realm   (b) Realm objects over the realm in (a)

Figure 1

The *ROSE algebra* [GüS93b] offers three data types called *points*, *lines*, and *regions* whose values are *realm-based*, i.e. composed from elements of a realm, together with a comprehensive set of operations. Figure 2 illustrates these data types.

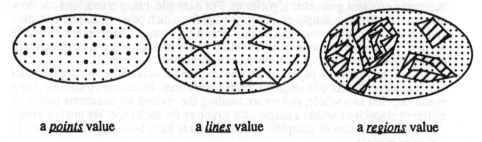

a *points* value   a *lines* value   a *regions* value

Figure 2. Examples of spatial values

The structure of spatial objects is defined in terms of the notions of an *R-point*, an *R-block* and an *R-face*. For a given realm *R*, an *R-point* is a point of *R*. An *R-block* is a connected set of line segments of *R*. An *R-face* is essentially a polygon with holes that can be defined over realm segments. Then a value of type *points* is a set of *R-points*, a value of type *lines* is a set of disjoint *R-blocks*, and a value of type *regions* is a set of edge-disjoint *R-faces* (where edge-disjoint means that two faces may have a common vertex, but no common edge).

There are four classes of spatial operations: (1) spatial predicates expressing topological relationships (e.g. **inside, intersects, meets**), (2) operations returning atomic spatial data type values (e.g. **intersection, plus, minus, contour**), (3) spatial operators returning numbers (e.g. **dist, perimeter, area**), and (4) spatial operations on sets of database objects (e.g. **sum, closest, fusion**). The signature of the first three groups of operations of the ROSE algebra can be found in the Appendix, for the meaning of operations see [GüS93b]. The operations of the fourth group have not yet been implemented because they require the implementation of the object model interface (described in [GüS93b]) which is not yet available.

The topic of this paper is the *implementation of the ROSE algebra*. To be precise, we must distinguish between a *descriptive* and an *executable* algebra [Gü89, BeG92]. A *descriptive algebra* offers types and operations at a conceptual level which can be used to formulate queries; its semantics are given by defining a "carrier" set of objects for each sort of the algebra and a function for each operator. An *executable algebra* describes the actual representations and query processing algorithms present in a system; hence in such an algebra there is a data structure associated with each sort (or type) and an algorithm, or a procedure realizing it, with each operator. In a database system, it is the task of the optimizer to translate an expression of the descriptive algebra into an equivalent, efficiently evaluable expression of the executable algebra. The ROSE algebra, as defined in [GüS93b], is a descriptive algebra. Hence in this paper we first describe a corresponding executable algebra - essentially polymorphic descriptive operators are decomposed into several executable operators - and then data structures and algorithms to implement it. The main new aspects of this design and paper are the following:

- We describe at a very high level, yet precisely, robust and efficient algorithms dealing with the complex geometric entities available in the ROSE algebra. They can be grouped into *parallel traversal, plane sweep,* and *graph algorithms*. For each paradigm, we show a few "prototype" operators and their algorithms and discuss which other operators can be realized similarly and which modifications are necessary. Many algorithms require only linear time, the remaining ones $O(n \log n)$ time where n is a bound on the size of the operand objects.
- All spatial objects processed by the operations are realm-based, i.e., they are defined over a discrete basis and in particular no two segments intersect within their interiors and no point lies within a segment. These properties can be exploited for designing efficient geometric algorithms. For example, many operations can now be realized through a simple parallel traversal for which otherwise more complex and expensive plane sweep algorithms would be needed. When plane sweep is needed, it is simpler because no intersection points of segments can be discovered during the sweep (e.g., a static sweep event structure can be used).
- In contrast to traditional papers on algorithms, the focus is not on finding the most efficient algorithm for one single problem (operation), but rather on considering a spatial algebra as a whole, and on reconciling the various requirements posed by different algorithms within a single data structure for each type. We are not aware that implementations of complete spatial algebras have been described before in a similar manner.
- The implementation is designed for use in a spatial database system. In particular, representations for spatial data types do not use pointer data structures in main memory, but are all embedded into compact storage areas which can be efficiently transferred between a main memory buffer and disk. Data structures are also designed to allow for realm updates.
- The ROSE system has actually been implemented and is running; the complete source code is available from the authors for study or use [Ri95]. The implemen-

tation was done in Modula-2 for UNIX systems. We feel it is important to make such well-designed "modules" for spatial DBMS systems available to the research community.

The importance of a *finite-precision / finite-resolution computational geometry*, as described in this paper, defined on a uniform, discrete grid such that points, end points of line segments, vertices of polygons etc. have integer coordinates instead of arbitrary floating-point coordinates, has been emphasized by Greene and Yao [GrY86] as well as Yao [Ya92]. Finite-precision geometry has so far only been studied by a few researchers (overviews can be found in [KeK81, Ov88b, Ov88c]). Problems considered are, for example, the nearest neighbour searching problem [KaM85], range searching on a grid [Ov88a, Ov88b], the point location problem [Mü85], the computation of rectangle intersections and maximal elements by divide-and-conquer [KaO88b], computing the convex hull of a set of points, reporting all intersections of a set of arbitrarily oriented line segments, and the calculation of rectangle intersections and maximal elements by using the plane-sweep technique [KaO88a, Ov88b]. To our knowledge, geometric algorithms over a discrete domain for more complex structures like those of the ROSE algebra have not been described in the literature.

The paper is structured as follows: In Section 2 an executable algebra is designed for the given descriptive ROSE algebra. In Section 3 we give a high-level specification of data structures for the representation of ROSE objects which provides a basis for the subsequent description of algorithms. Section 4 introduces *realm-based geometric algorithms* for the implementation of ROSE operations. Section 5 shows the actual data structures used and discusses some important implementation concepts.

2 Descriptive and Executable ROSE Algebra

In this section we develop an executable algebra for the given descriptive ROSE algebra. Essentially this means that we have to decompose each polymorphic descriptive operator into corresponding executable operators for the possible combinations of data types. Both algebras use *second-order signature* [Gü93] as the underlying formalism. Second-order signature allows one to define a type system together with an algebra over that type system. In particular, it is possible to describe polymorphic operations by quantification over *kinds*. For the purpose of this paper it suffices to view kinds just as type sets; the two relevant sets are EXT = {*lines, regions*} and GEO = {*points, lines, regions*}. Here are a few examples of spatial predicates of the ROSE algebra:

$\forall$ *geo* in GEO. $\forall$ *ext$_1$*, *ext$_2$* in EXT. $\forall$ *area* in *regions*[area-disjoint].

geo × *geo*	→ *bool*	=, ≠, disjoint
geo × *regions*	→ *bool*	inside
ext$_1$ × *ext$_2$*	→ *bool*	intersects
area × *area*	→ *bool*	adjacent, encloses

Here *geo* is a type variable ranging over the three types in kind GEO so that the first three operations can compare two values of equal type and the inside operation can compare a *points*, a *lines*, or a *regions* value with a *regions* value. The intersects operation can be applied to two values of the same or different type within kind EXT. The notation *regions*[area-disjoint] is an attempt to capture the structure of partitions of the plane (into disjoint regions) in the type system. It ensures that the two operands given to the adjacent or encloses operator are two regions taken from the same partition of the plane, hence they are either disjoint or equal; for details see [GüS93b]. For the executable algebra this is not relevant and we can introduce executable operators with functionality *regions* × *regions* → *bool*.

In the executable algebra, we generally need different algorithms for the different data types. For example, it is obvious that an algorithm which examines the disjointness of two *points* objects will be different from an algorithm which determines whether two *regions* objects overlap. Hence the descriptive operator **disjoint** is mapped to the three executable operators:

points × *points*	→ *bool*	**pp_disjoint**
lines × *lines*	→ *bool*	**ll_disjoint**
regions × *regions*	→ *bool*	**rr_disjoint**

The Appendix lists the signature of the ROSE algebra and shows its translation into executable operators. For example, the first line of the ROSE signature shown above is represented as follows:

Descriptive Operator	Executable Operator	PT	PS	G	TC
geo × *geo* → *bool* =	pp_equal, ll_equal, rr_equal	x			$O(n)$
≠	pp_unequal, ll_unequal, rr_unequal	x			$O(n)$
disjoint	pp_disjoint, ll_disjoint	x			$O(n)$
	rr_disjoint		x		$O(n \log n)$

The last four columns of this table describe the algorithmic technique used to implement this (group of) executable operators (PT = parallel traversal, PS = plane sweep, G = graph algorithm) and the worst case time complexity. The algorithms are discussed below. There is a gap in the table because we have not yet studied efficient algorithms for distance problems (operator **dist** of the third group).

3 Specification of Data Structures for the Types

Algorithms for the executable ROSE operators need to access, and sometimes to build, the data structures representing values of the three types *points*, *lines*, and *regions*. Rather than describing these data structures directly in terms of arrays, records, etc., we first introduce a higher level description which offers suitable access and construction operations to be used in the algorithms. Basically, we define a little abstract data type for each of the three data structures. In a second step, one can then design and implement the data structure itself.

The specification of an abstract data type consists of a many-sorted signature together with a set of laws, or equations, defining the behaviour of operations. To be precise, we use a slightly different specification method sometimes called "denotational specification" (e.g. [Kl83]). It simply means that we assign semantics to the sorts and operations of the many-sorted signature directly by defining carrier sets for the sorts and functions for the operations on these carrier sets, i.e., we define a little algebra for each of the three data structures representing *points*, *lines*, or *regions* values, respectively. In other words, we give a concrete mathematical model for the data type instead of a set of laws. In fact, the whole ROSE algebra itself has been defined by the same method.

For most executable operators it turns out to be sufficient to regard a spatial object as an *ordered sequence of elements* where it is possible to access these elements consecutively and to insert a new element into the sequence. Hence this is our basic strategy for modeling the three data structures.

Before we can introduce the algebra *points*, a few notations are needed. Realms and realm-based spatial objects are defined over a finite discrete space $N \times N$ with $N = \{0, ..., m-1\} \subseteq \mathbf{N}$. $P_N = \{(x, y) \mid x \in N, y \in N\}$ denotes the set of all N-points. Furthermore, an (x, y)-lexicographic order is assumed on P_N which is defined as $p_1 < p_2 \Leftrightarrow x_1 < x_2 \vee (x_1 = x_2 \wedge y_1 < y_2)$.

algebra *points*

sorts *points*, P_N, *bool*

ops

new	:		$\rightarrow$ *points*
select_first	:	*points*	$\rightarrow$ *points*
select_next	:	*points*	$\rightarrow$ *points*
end_of_pt	:	*points*	$\rightarrow$ *bool*
get_pt	:	*points*	$\rightarrow P_N$
insert	:	*points* $\times P_N$	$\rightarrow$ *points*

sets $\underline{points} = \{(pos, < p_1, ..., p_n >) \mid pos \geq 0; n \geq 0; \text{for } 1 \leq i \leq n, p_i \in P_N;$
$\text{for } 1 \leq i < n, p_i < p_{i+1}\}$

functions Let $P = (i, < p_1, ..., p_n >) \in \underline{points}$ and $p \in P_N$.

$new() = (0, \Diamond)$

$$select\_first(P) = \begin{cases} (1, < p_1, ..., p_n >) & \text{if } n \geq 1 \\ (0, \Diamond) & \text{otherwise} \end{cases}$$

$$select\_next(P) = \begin{cases} (i+1, < p_1, ..., p_n >) & \text{if } 1 \leq i < n \\ (0, < p_1, ..., p_n >) & \text{otherwise} \end{cases}$$

$end\_of\_pt(P) = (i = 0)$

$$get\_pt(P) = \begin{cases} p_i & \text{if } 1 \leq i \leq n \\ undefined & \text{otherwise} \end{cases}$$

$$insert(P, p) = \begin{cases} (j, < p_1, ..., p_n >) & \text{if } \exists j \in \{1, ..., n\}: p = p_j \\ (1, < p, p_1, ..., p_n >) & \text{if } p < p_1 \\ (n+1, < p_1, ..., p_n, p >) & \text{if } p > p_n \\ (j+1, < p_1, ..., p_j, p, p_{j+1}, ..., p_n >)2 & \\ \quad \text{if } \exists j \in \{1, ..., n-1\}: p_j < p < p_{j+1} \end{cases}$$

end *points*.

The **sorts** and **ops** parts describe the syntax of the algebra, i.e., the signature. The **sets** and **functions** parts give the semantics in terms of carrier set and function definitions. The algebra *points* contains the sorts *points* (to be defined), P_N, and *bool*. The carrier set of the sort *points* is defined as the set of all ordered sequences $< p_1, ..., p_n >$ of n N-points together with a pointer indicating a position within the sequence. The symbol $\Diamond$ denotes the empty sequence. Functions manipulate such values, for example, *select_first* positions the pointer *pos* on the smallest element of the point sequence, and *get_pt* yields the point at the current position.

A crucial idea for the representation of the relatively complex *lines* and *regions* values, which is the basis for most of our algorithms, is to regard them as *ordered sequences of halfsegments*. Let $S_N = \{(p, q) \mid p \in P_N, q \in P_N\}$ denote the set of N-segments. The equality of two N-segments $s_1 = (p_1, q_1)$ and $s_2 = (p_2, q_2)$ is defined as $s_1 = s_2 \Leftrightarrow (p_1 = p_2 \wedge q_1 = q_2) \vee (p_1 = q_2 \wedge p_2 = q_1)$. W. l. o. g. we normalize S_N by the assumption that $\forall s \in S_N : s = (p, q) \Rightarrow p < q$ which enables us to speak of a *left* and a *right end point* of a segment. Let further $H_N = \{(s, d) \mid s \in S_N, d \in \{left, right\}\}$ be the set of *halfsegments*. A halfsegment $h = (s, d)$ consists of an N-segment s and a flag d emphasizing one of the N-segment's end points which is called the *dominating point* of h. If $d = left$ then the left (smaller) end point of s is the dominating point of h, and h is called *left halfsegment*. Otherwise, the right end point is the dominating point of h, and h is called *right halfsegment*. Hence, each N-segment s is mapped to two halfsegments $(s, left)$ and $(s, right)$. Let dp be the function which yields the dominating point of a halfsegment.

For two distinct halfsegments h_1 and h_2 with a common end point p, let α be the enclosed angle such that $0 < \alpha \leq 180°$ (an overlapping of h_1 and h_2 is excluded by the realm properties). Let a predicate *rot* be defined as follows: $rot(h_1, h_2)$ is true iff h_1 can be rotated around p through α to overlap h_2 in counter-clockwise direction. We can now define a complete order on halfsegments which is basically the (x, y)-lexicographic order by dominating points. For two halfsegments $h_1 = (s_1, d_1)$ and $h_2 = (s_2, d_2)$ it is:

$$h_1 < h_2 \Leftrightarrow dp(h_1) < dp(h_2)$$
$$\vee (dp(h_1) = dp(h_2) \wedge ((d_1 = right \wedge d_2 = left) \vee (d_1 = d_2 \wedge rot(h_1, h_2))))$$

We now define the algebra *regions* (the algebra *lines* is almost the same, see below). The carrier set of the sort *regions* is defined as the set of ordered sequences $< h_1, ..., h_n >$ of halfsegments where each halfsegment h_i has an attached *set of attributes* a_i whose elements are values of some new sort *attr*. Attribute sets are used in algorithms to attach auxiliary information to segments.

algebra   *regions*

sorts   *regions*, H_N, *attr*, *bool*

ops

new	:	$\rightarrow$ *regions*
select_first	: *regions*	$\rightarrow$ *regions*
select_next	: *regions*	$\rightarrow$ *regions*
end_of_hs	: *regions*	$\rightarrow$ *bool*
get_hs	: *regions*	$\rightarrow H_N$
get_attr	: *regions*	$\rightarrow$ *attr*
update_attr	: *regions* $\times$ *attr*	$\rightarrow$ *regions*
insert	: *regions* $\times H_N$	$\rightarrow$ *regions*

sets $\underline{regions} = \{ (pos, < h_1, ..., h_n >, < a_1, ..., a_n >) \mid$
  (1) $pos \geq 0, n \geq 0$
  (2) $\forall i \in \{1, ..., n\} : h_i \in H_N, a_i \subseteq attr$
  (3) $\forall i \in \{1, ..., n-1\} : h_i < h_{i+1}$ $\}$

functions   Let $R_h = < h_1, ..., h_n >$, $R_a = < a_1, ..., a_n >$, $R = (i, R_h, R_a) \in \underline{regions}$, and $h \in H_N$.

$$new() \quad = \quad (0, \Diamond, \Diamond)$$

$$select\_first(R) \quad = \quad \begin{cases} (1, R_h, R_a) & \text{if } n \geq 1 \\ (0, \Diamond, \Diamond) & \text{otherwise} \end{cases}$$

$$select\_next(R) \quad = \quad \begin{cases} (i + 1, R_h, R_a) & \text{if } 1 \leq i < n \\ (0, R_h, R_a) & \text{otherwise} \end{cases}$$

$$end\_of\_hs(R) \quad = \quad (i = 0)$$

$$get\_hs(R) \quad = \quad \begin{cases} h_i & \text{if } 1 \leq i \leq n \\ \text{undefined} & \text{otherwise} \end{cases}$$

$$get\_attr(R) \quad = \quad \begin{cases} a_i & \text{if } 1 \leq i \leq n \\ \text{undefined} & \text{otherwise} \end{cases}$$

$$update\_attr(R, a) = \begin{cases} (i, R_h, < a_1, ..., a_{i-1}, a, a_{i+1}, ..., a_n >) & \text{if } 1 \le i \le n \\ \text{undefined} & \text{otherwise} \end{cases}$$

$$insert(R, h) = \begin{cases} (j, R_h, R_a) & \text{if } \exists\, j \in \{1, ..., n\} : h = h_j \\ (1, < h, h_1, ..., h_n >, < \varnothing, a_1, ..., a_n >) & \text{if } h < h_1 \\ (n + 1, < h_1, ..., h_n, h >, < a_1, ..., a_n, \varnothing >) & \text{if } h > h_n \\ (j + 1, < h_1, ..., h_j, h, h_{j+1}, ..., h_n >, & \\ \quad < a_1, ..., a_j, \varnothing, a_{j+1}, ..., a_n >) & \\ \quad \text{if } \exists\, j \in \{1, ..., n-1\} : h_j < h < h_{j+1} \end{cases}$$

end   *regions.*

Note that the algebra *regions* just offers manipulation of halfsegment sequences; it does not ensure that a sequence indeed represents a correct *regions* value as defined in the ROSE algebra. The algorithms using this structure are responsible for constructing only sequences that indeed represent *regions* values. The algebra *lines* (not presented here) is identical to the algebra *regions* except for all the parts related to attributes which are not needed.

Simple implementations for each of the three data types (algebras) would represent a sequence of n points or halfsegments in a linked list or sequentially in an array; the latter representation would also be compatible with the "compact storage area" requirement needed for efficient database loading/storing. In this case, all operations except for *insert* need $O(1)$ time; *insert* requires $O(n)$ time for arbitrary positions and $O(1)$ time for appending an element at the end of the sequence. Such a representation would in fact be quite good for all "parallel traversal" algorithms of the ROSE algebra, because result objects are always constructed in the lexicographic point or halfsegment order and can therefore be built in linear time.

The actual implementation in the ROSE system uses for all three structures an AVL-tree embedded into an array (the array serving as a storage pool for nodes); the elements, i.e. points or halfsegments, are additionally linked in sequence order. With this representation, all operations except *insert* need $O(1)$ time and *insert* $O(\log n)$ time. The requirement to support insertion in $O(\log n)$ time actually does not come from the ROSE algebra but from the connection with realms; realm updates due to insertion of points or segments into the realm must be propagated to ROSE objects residing in a database [GüS93a]. This means that the data structures should support replacement of a segment in a *lines* or *regions* object by a chain of segments, i.e., the segment must be deleted and the replacement segments be inserted into the structure. Unfortunately, a consequence of this is that the parallel traversal algorithms cannot construct the result objects in linear time any more, but need $O(k \log k)$ for this where k is the size of the result object. This is a case of conflicting requirements, as mentioned in the introduction. On the other hand, deriving the internal structure of a *lines* or *regions* object (e.g. faces and holes) which is needed to complete the construction (see Section 5) requires $O(k \log k)$ time anyway.

4 Algorithms for the Executable Algebra

This section introduces *realm based geometric algorithms* whose characteristic features are numerical robustness, topological correctness, closure properties, and efficiency. Realm-based algorithms are more efficient than their Euclidean counterparts. The design of these algorithms is based on traversal techniques, on the plane-sweep paradigm, and on graph theory. Realm-based geometry deals with spatial objects that are defined over the *same* discrete domain and assumes that no two segments intersect within their interiors and that no point lies within a segment.

Executable operators are grouped by the applied algorithmic technique. For each group we show and explain some example algorithms.

4.1 Algorithms with Simple or Parallel Object Traversal

A number of operators of the executable ROSE algebra can be realized by a simple or parallel traversal (scan) through the point or halfsegment sequence of one or two objects. To simplify the description of algorithms, for each possible combination of two spatial data types two operations are introduced which allow for a parallel traversal through two ordered sequences of elements (halfsegments, points).

As an example, we consider the two operations for two *regions* objects. The operation $rr\_select\_first(R_1, R_2, object, status)$ selects the first halfsegment of each of the *regions* objects R_1 and R_2 (compare to the function *select_first* of algebra *regions*) and positions a logical pointer on both of them. The parameter *object* with possible values {*none, first, second, both*} indicates which of the two object representations contains the smaller halfsegment. If the value of *object* is *none*, no halfsegment is selected, since R_1 and R_2 are empty. If it is *first* (*second*), the smaller halfsegment belongs to R_1 (R_2). If it is *both*, the first halfsegments of R_1 and R_2 are identical. The parameter *status* with possible values {*end_of_none, end_of_first, end_of_second, end_of_both*} describes the state of both halfsegment sequences. If the value of *status* is *end_of_none*, both objects still have halfsegments. If it is *end_of_first* (*end_of_second*), R_1 (R_2) is empty. If it is *end_of_both*, both object representations are empty.

The operation $rr\_select\_next(R_1, R_2, object, status)$ searches for the next smaller halfsegment of R_1 and R_2; parameters have the same meaning as for *rr_select_first*. Obviously, this is realized by *select_next* operations of the two objects.

Both operations together allow one to scan in linear time two object representations like one ordered sequence. Analogous operations can be defined for two *lines* objects (*ll_select_first, ll_select_next*) and a *lines* and a *regions* object (*lr_select_first, lr_select_next*). For the comparison of halfsegments with points, the dominating points of the halfsegments are used so that *points* and *lines* objects (*pl_select_first, pl_select_next*) as well as *points* and *regions* objects (*pr_select_first, pr_select_next*) can be treated in a similar way.

In the sequel we discuss algorithms for the operations (see algorithms below):

points × *regions*	→ *bool*	pr_on_border_of
points × *points*	→ *points*	pp_plus
lines × *lines*	→ *bool*	ll_intersects

Operator **pr_on_border_of** determines whether all points of a *points* object lie on the faces' boundaries of a *regions* object. Hence the algorithm checks whether for each point p of a *points* object P (denoted as $p \in P(P)$) a halfsegment h of a *regions* object R (denoted $h \in H(R)$) exists whose dominating point is equal to p. The while-loop of the algorithm is executed as long as no point is found which is in P but not a dominating point of a halfsegment of R and as long as none of the object sequences is exceeded. For the predicate to be *true*, termination of the while-loop must not have occurred because a point was found which is not on the boundary of R (*object ≠ first*). This implies that termination is due to reaching the end of one or both sequences, and the predicate is *true* if this was not the *regions* sequence alone (*status ≠ end_of_second*).

Operator **pp_plus** forms the union of two *points* objects. The algorithm just scans the point sequences of the two objects and merges them into a new *points* object.

Operator **ll_intersects** examines whether two *lines* objects L_1 and L_2 intersect. According to the definition of the ROSE algebra it yields *true* if both objects have no common (half)segments but at least one common point which is not a *meeting point* but an inter-

```
algorithm pr_on_border_of
input: A points object P and a regions object R
output:    true, if ∀ p ∈ P(P) ∃ h ∈ H(R) : p = dp(h)
           false, otherwise
begin
    pr_select_first(P, R, object, status);
    while (object ≠ first) and (status = end_of_none) do
        pr_select_next(P, R, object, status);
    end-while;
    return (object ≠ first) and (status ≠ end_of_second)
end pr_on_border_of.
```

```
algorithm pp_plus
input: Two points objects P₁ and P₂
output:    A points object P_new containing all points
begin
    P_new := new();
    pp_select_first(P₁, P₂, object, status);
    while status ≠ end_of_both do
        if object = first then p := get_pt(P₁)
        else if object = second then p := get_pt(P₂)
        else if object = both then p := get_pt(P₁)
        end-if;
        P_new := insert(P_new, p);
        pp_select_next(P₁, P₂, object, status);
    end-while;
    return P_new
end pp_plus.
```

```
algorithm ll_intersects
input: Two lines objects L₁ and L₂
output:    true, if no common segment exists, but a common
           point which is not a meeting point
           false, otherwise
begin
    ll_select_first(L₁, L₂, object, status);
    if object = first then act_dp := dp(get_hs(L₁))
    else if object = second then act_dp := dp(get_hs(L₂))
    end-if;
    act_obj := object; found := false; count := 0;
    while (status = end_of_none) and (object ≠ both) do
        ll_select_next(L₁, L₂, object, status);
        if (status ≠ end_of_both) and (object ≠ both) and not
            found then
            if object = first then
                new_dp := dp(get_hs(L₁))
            else if object = second then
                new_dp := dp(get_hs(L₂))
            end-if;
            if new_dp ≠ act_dp then (* new point *)
                act_dp := new_dp; count := 0;
                act_obj := object;
            else if object ≠ act_obj then (* object switch *)
                count := count + 1; act_obj := object;
                found := found or (count > 2);
            end-if;
        end-if;
    end-while;
    return found and (object ≠ both);
end ll_intersects.
```

---

section point. Point p is a *meeting point* if the angularly sorted list of halfsegments of L_1 and L_2 with the same dominating point p can be subdivided into two sublists so that one list contains only halfsegments of L_1 and the other list only halfsegments of L_2. The idea is now to walk around p, scanning the segments, and to count the number of "object changes" in this ordered list of halfsegments of L_1 and L_2. Point p is a meeting point if this number is less than or equal to two; otherwise an intersection point has been found. The while-loop of the algorithm terminates if either the end of one of the objects has been reached or a common halfsegment has been found. In the latter case the result value is *false* (object ≠ both), in the first case the decision is based on whether at least one intersection point has been found or not (*found*). The algorithms for the other operators are similar. The complete list of operators that can be treated by (parallel) traversal is indicated by column PT in the Appendix. For all predicates and for operations returning numbers (e.g. l_length) realized by PT algorithms, the worst case time complexity is $O(n)$, where n is the total number of points or halfsegments in the one or two operands. For operations returning new spatial objects the time bound is $O(n + k \log k)$ where k is the number of points or halfsegments in the result object; $O(n)$ time is needed for scanning the operands and $O(k \log k)$ for constructing the result. Since $k = O(n)$, this is always bounded by $O(n \log n)$.

4.2 Algorithms Using the Plane-Sweep Paradigm

Plane-sweep [PrS85, Me84] is a popular technique of computational geometry for solving geometric set problems which transforms a two-dimensional problem into a sequence of one-dimensional problems which are easier than the original two-dimensional one. A vertical *sweep line* sweeping the plane from left to right stops at special points called *event points*, which are generally stored in a queue called *event point schedule*. The event point schedule must allow one to insert new event points discovered during processing; these are normally the initially unknown intersections of line segments. The state of the intersection of the sweep line with the geometric structure being swept at the current sweep line position is recorded in vertical order in a data structure called *sweep line status*. Whenever the sweep line reaches an event point, the sweep line status is updated. Event points which are passed by the sweep line are removed from the event point schedule. Note that in general an efficient fully dynamic data structure is needed to represent the event point schedule and that in many plane-sweep algorithms an initial sorting step is needed to produce the sequence of event points in x-order (or xy-lexicographic order).

In the special case of realm-based geometry where no two segments intersect within their interiors, the event point schedule is static (because new event points cannot exist) and given by the ordered sequence of points or halfsegments of the operand objects. No further explicit event point structure is needed. Also, no initial sorting is necessary since the plane-sweep order of points and segments is our base representation of objects anyway.

If a left (right) halfsegment of a *regions* object is reached during a plane-sweep, its segment component is stored into (removed from) the segment sequence of the sweep line status sorted by the order relation *above*. A segment s lies *above* a segment t if the intersection of their x-intervals is not empty and if for each x of the intersection interval the y-coordinate of s is greater than the one of t (except possibly for a common end point where the y-coordinates are equal). Points and halfsegments of *lines* objects are used to query the sweep line status.

The sweep line status structure and its operations can also be described as an algebra (a formal description is omitted here) with an ordered sequence of segments as a carrier set where each segment has an attached set of attributes and a pointer indicates the position within the sequence. The operation *new_sweep* produces and initializes the sweep line status. The operation *add_left* (*del_right*) inserts (removes) the segment component of a left (right) halfsegment into (from) the ordered segment set of the sweep line status. The operations *pred_of_s* and *pred_of_p* yield the position of the greatest segment that is smaller than a reference segment and point, respectively. The operations *current_exists* and *pred_exists* allow one to check whether a current segment and the predecessor of the current segment, resp., exists in the sweep line status. The operation *set_attr* sets the attribute set for the current segment, and the operations *get_attr* and *get_pred_attr* yield the attribute set of the current and the preceding segment, respectively. For the sweep line status an efficient internal dynamic structure like the AVL tree can be employed (and is used in the ROSE system) which realizes each of the operations *add_left*, *del_right*, *pred_of_s*, and *pred_of_p* in worst case time $O(\log n)$ and the other operations in constant time.

In the sequel for all algorithms we assume that all those halfsegments of a *regions* object R have an associated attribute *InsideAbove* where the area of R lies above or left of its segment. This *segment classification* can be computed by a plane-sweep algorithm (not shown here) which views all segments intersecting the current sweep line from bottom to top. It is obvious that the lowest segment obtains the attribute *InsideAbove*, the following does not, the third again obtains it, etc. Whether the attribute *InsideAbove* is associated with a segment depends on the assignment of the attribute to the immediate preceding segment in the sweep line status. This segment classification is called at the end of the construction of a *regions* object and the attribute stored with each halfsegment. It requires $O(n \log n)$ time for an object with n halfsegments.

The first class of plane-sweep algorithms considers the relationships between a *points* or *lines* object and a *regions* object. The algorithm scheme is to insert only the segments of the *regions* object into the sweep line status and to use the elements of the *points* and *lines* object, resp., as query elements. The operations of this class have the following signature:

points × *regions*	→	*bool*	pr_inside
lines × *regions*	→	*bool*	lr_inside, lr_intersects, lr_meets
regions × *lines*	→	*bool*	rl_intersects, rl_meets
regions × *lines*	→	*lines*	rl_intersection

As examples, we show the algorithms for pr_inside and rl_intersection (see algorithms on the next page). The algorithms for the other operations are similar. The algorithm pr_inside checks whether all points of a *points* object P lie within the areas of a *regions* object R. A point of P may coincide with an endpoint of a segment of R. Both objects are traversed in parallel during a plane-sweep. The segment components of the left halfsegments of R together with the associated attribute *InsideAbove* are inserted into the sweep line status, the segment components of the right halfsegments are removed. If a point p of P does not coincide with a dominating point of a halfsegment of R, the existence of a segment in the sweep line status immediately below p is checked. If no segment is found, then p definitely lies outside of R. Otherwise, it must be checked if the attribute *InsideAbove* has been assigned to the segment. If this is the case, then p lies inside of R, otherwise outside. The while-loop of the algorithm is executed at most $l+m$ times (l the number of points of P, m the number of halfsegments of R). The loop terminates when all points of P have been examined or when a point has been found which does not lie in R. The insertion of a left halfsegment into and the removal of a right halfsegment from the sweep line status needs $O(\log m)$ time. A point which coincides with the dominating point of a halfsegment can be ignored, since it lies definitely within R. For all other points the preceding segment in the sweep line status has to be searched which also needs $O(\log m)$ time. Altogether, the worst case time complexity of pr_inside is $O((l + m) \log m)$.

The algorithm for rl_intersection produces in a similar way a new *lines* object which contains all segments lying within R. It is crucial for the correctness of this algorithm that we can be sure that a complete (half)segment lies within R, if its dominating point lies within an area of R. This is because the boundary of R cannot intersect the interior of the segment due to the realm properties. This algorithm requires $O((l + m) \log m + k \log k)$ where k is the size of the result object and l and m the size of the *lines* and *regions* operand, respectively.

For all other operations of this class, the time complexity is $O((l + m) \log m)$ if m is the size of the *regions* operand and l the size of the other operand. Of course, for $n = l + m$, $O(n \log n)$ is a simpler upper bound for all operations.

The second class of plane-sweep algorithms considers the relationships between two *regions* objects.

regions × *regions*	→	*bool*	rr_disjoint, rr_inside, rr_area_disjoint, rr_edge_disjoint, rr_edge_inside, rr_vertex_inside, rr_encloses, rr_intersects, rr_meets, rr_adjacent
regions × *regions*	→	*regions*	rr_intersection, rr_plus, rr_minus

Note that here the immediate application of the technique introduced above is impeded by the fact that *regions* objects may have holes. Hence, for the algorithms of this class

```
algorithm pr_inside
Input: A points object P and a regions object R
output:    true, if all points of P lie in the area of R
           false, otherwise
begin
    S := new_sweep();
    inside := true;
    pr_select_first(P, R, object, status);
    while (status ≠ end_of_first) and inside do
        if (object = both) or (object = second) then
            h := get_hs(R); (* Let h = (s, d) . *)
            attr := get_attr(R);
            if d = left then
                S := add_left(S, s);
                if InsideAbove ∈ attr then
                    S := set_attr(S, {InsideAbove});
                end-if
            else
                S := del_right(S, s);
            end-if
        else
            S := pred_of_p(S, get_pt(P));
            if current_exists(S)
                then inside := (InsideAbove ∈ get_attr(S))
                else inside := false
            end-if
        end-if;
        pr_select_next(P, R, object, status);
    end-while;
    return inside;
end pr_inside.
```

```
algorithm rl_intersection
Input: A lines object L and a regions object R
output:    A new lines object L_new containing all halfseg-
           ments of L whose segment components lie in R
begin
    L_new := new(); S := new_sweep();
    lr_select_first(L, R, object, status);
    while status = end_of_none do
        if object = second then
            h := get_hs(R); (* Let h = (s, d) . *)
            attr := get_attr(R);
            if d = left then
                S := add_left(S, s);
                if InsideAbove ∈ attr then
                    S := set_attr(S, {InsideAbove});
                end-if
            else S := del_right(S, s);
            end-if
        else if object = both then
            h := get_hs(L); L_new := insert(L_new, h);
        else
            h := get_hs(L); (* Let h = (s, d) . *)
            S := pred_of_s(S, s);
            if current_exists(S) and
                (InsideAbove ∈ get_attr(S)) then
                L_new := insert(L_new, h);
            end-if;
        end-if;
        lr_select_next(L, R, object, status);
    end-while;
    return L_new;
end rl_intersection.
```

we introduce the concepts of *overlap numbers* and *segment classification*. A point of the realm grid obtains the *overlap number k* if it is covered by (or part of) k *regions* objects. For example, for two intersecting simple polygons the area outside of both polygons gets overlap number 0, the intersecting areas get overlap number 2, and the other areas get overlap number 1. Since a segment of a *regions* object separates space into two parts, an inner and an exterior one, each segment is associated with a pair (m/n) of overlap numbers, a *lower* (or right) one m and an *upper* (or left) one n. The lower (upper) overlap number indicates the number of overlapping *regions* objects below (above) the segment. In this way, we obtain a *segment classification* of a fixed set of *regions* objects and speak of (m/n)-segments. For two *regions* objects (we only consider binary operators here) m, $n \leq 2$ holds; of the nine possible combinations only seven describe valid segment classes. This is because a $(0/0)$-segment contradicts the definition of a *regions* object, since then at least one of both *regions* objects would have two holes or an outer cycle and a hole with a common border. Similarly, $(2/2)$-segments cannot exist, since then at least one of the two *regions* objects would have a segment which is common to two outer cycles of the object. Hence, possible (m/n)-segments are $(0/1)$-, $(0/2)$-, $(1/0)$-, $(1/1)$-, $(1/2)$-, $(2/0)$-, and $(2/1)$-segments. Examples of (m/n)-segments are given in Figure 3.

As an example for the plane-sweep algorithms of the second class we show the algorithm for rr_inside (see algorithm on the next page) which tests whether a *regions* object R_1 is completely contained in a *regions* object R_2. This means that all segments of R_1 must lie within the area of R_2 but no segment (and hence no hole) of R_2 may lie within R_1. If we consider the objects R_1 and R_2 as halfsegment sequences together with the segment classes, the predicate rr_inside is true if (1) all halfsegments that are *only* el-

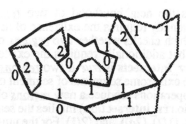

Figure 3. Segment classification

ement of R_1 have segment class (1/2) or (2/1), since only these segments lie within R_2, (2) all halfsegments that are *only* element of R_2 have segment class (0/1) or (1/0), since these definitely do not lie within R_1, and (3) all *common* halfsegments have segment class (0/2) or (2/0), since the areas of both objects lie on the same side of the halfsegment. In the case of a (1/1)-segment the areas would lie side by side so that R_1 could not be contained by R_2. In the algorithm, whenever a segment is inserted into the sweep line status, first the pair (m_p/n_p) of overlap numbers of the predecessor is determined (it is set to (*/0) if no predecessor exists). Then the overlap numbers (m_s/n_s) for this segment are computed. Obviously $m_s = n_p$ must hold; n_s is also initialized to n_p and then corrected. If R_1 has l and R_2 m halfsegments, the while-loop is executed at most $n = l + m$ times, since each time a new halfsegment is visited. The most expensive operations within the loop are the insertion and the removal of a segment into and from the sweep line status. Since at most n elements can be contained in the sweep line status, the worst case time complexity of the algorithm is $O(n \log n)$ which is also valid for all other operations of this class.

The other operations mostly require slight modifications of the algorithm above. The algorithm for **rr_edge_inside** forbids common segments, the algorithm for **rr_vertex_inside** even common points, a problem which to treat is a little bit more complicated. The operation **rr_area_disjoint** yields *true* if both objects have no common areas and only allows (0/1)-, (1/0)-, and (1/1)-segments. The operation **rr_edge_disjoint** additionally forbids common segments (no (1/1)-segments) and **rr_disjoint** even common points which needs a little bit more effort. The operation

```
algorithm rr_inside
input: Two regions objects R₁ and R₂
output:   true, if R₁ lies within R₂
          false, otherwise
begin
    S := new_sweep();
    inside := true;
    rr_select_first(R₁, R₂, object, status);
    while (status ≠ end_of_first) and inside do
        if (object = first) or (object = both)
            then h := get_hs(R₁); (* Let h = (s, d). *)
            else h := get_hs(R₂); (* Let h = (s, d). *)
        end-if;
        if d = right then
            S := del_right(S, s);
        else
            S := add_left(S, s);
            if not pred_exists(S)
                then mₚ/nₚ := */0
                else mₚ/nₚ := get_pred_attr(S)
            end-if;
            mₛ := nₚ;
            nₛ := nₚ;
```

```
            if ((object = first) or (object = both)) and
                (InsideAbove ∈ get_attr(R₁))
                then nₛ := nₛ + 1
                else nₛ := nₛ − 1
            end-if;
            if ((object = second) or (object = both)) and
                (InsideAbove ∈ get_attr(R₂))
                then nₛ := nₛ + 1
                else nₛ := nₛ − 1
            end-if;
            S := set_attr(S, (mₛ/nₛ));
            if object = first then
                inside := ((mₛ/nₛ) ∈ {(1/2), (2/1)})
            else if object = second then
                inside := ((mₛ/nₛ) ∈ {(1/2), (2/1)})
            else
                inside := ((mₛ/nₛ) ∈ {(0/2), (2/0)})
            end-if;
        end-if;
        rr_select_next(R₁, R₂, object, status);
    end-while;
    return inside;
end rr_inside.
```

rr_adjacent which checks the neighbourhood of two _regions_ objects is equal to **rr_area_disjoint** but additionally requires the existence of at least one (1/1)-segment. The operation **rr_meets** which checks whether two _regions_ objects meet in a point is equal to **rr_edge_disjoint** but additionally requires the existence of at least one common point. The operation **rr_intersects** is _true_ if two _regions_ objects have a common area which means that there exist some segments of segment class (0/2), (1/2), (2/0), or (2/1). The following three operations produce a new _regions_ object. The intersection of two _regions_ objects (operation **rr_intersection**) implies the search for all segments with segment classification (0/2), (1/2), (2/0), and (2/1). For the union of two _regions_ objects (operation **rr_union**) all (0/1)-, (1/0)-, (0/2)-, and (2/0)-segments are collected. The computation of the difference of two _regions_ objects R_1 and R_2 (operation **rr_minus**) requires all (0/1)- and (1/0)-segments of R_1, all (1/2)- and (2/1)-segments of R_2, and all common (1/1)-segments. The operation **rr_encloses** yields _true_ for two _regions_ objects R_1 and R_2 if each face and hence each segment of R_2 is contained in a hole of R_1. Note that this condition does not mean that R_1 and R_2 are area-disjoint, since it is possible that another face of R_1 lies within R_2. Here a method is used which gives the overlap numbers a different interpretation: We do not consider the overlapping of object areas but the overlapping of the single cycle areas of an object. In this way, the exterior of R_1 gets the number 0, the area of a face of R_1 the number 1, and a hole the number 2. If a hole of R_1 contains another face of the same object, this face gets the number 3 and a hole of this face the number 4, etc. If we compute such a segment classification for R_1, then R_1 encloses R_2 if all segments of R_2 lie on a level with even overlap number (greater than 0).

4.3 Graph Algorithms

A realm can be interpreted as a spatially embedded planar graph [GüS93a]. Hence, a _lines_ or a _regions_ object defined over such a realm can also be regarded as a planar graph $G = (V, E)$ where the vertex set V is the set of all end points of the segments and the edge set E is the set of all segments of the object. Note that such an _embedded planar graph_ represents not only the usual incidence relationships between nodes and edges, but also the _neighbourhood relationship among segments incident to the same node_. This graph-theoretic view offers two primitive operations, illustrated in Figure 4, that are crucial for the algorithms discussed in this section: For a given halfsegment, (i) find its two neighbours incident to the same node w.r.t. the counter-clockwise order, and (ii) find the "partner halfsegment" representing the same segment (which is equivalent to following an edge of the graph).

Figure 4. Relationships in a graph

Basically, the data structure needed to support these two primitives in $O(1)$ time is an adjacency list for each node containing the outgoing edges in counter-clockwise order. As it happens, the halfsegment sequence representing a _lines_ or _regions_ object is already close to the desired structure because it contains all halfsegments with the same dominating point as a compact subsequence in counter-clockwise order (this fact has already been used in algorithm **ll_intersects**). What is needed additionally is a pointer from each halfsegment to the partner halfsegment. For convenience, we also doubly link the halfsegments around a node. Figure 5 shows a *lines* object and its graph representation in two arrays *Edge* and *Node* (explained below).

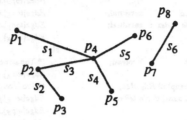

index	h	pred	succ	link	node_index		index	on_stack
1	h_1^l	1	1	5	1		1	false
2	h_2^l	3	3	4	2		2	false
3	h_3^l	2	2	6	2		3	false
4	h_2^r	4	4	2	3		4	false
5	h_1^r	8	6	1	4		5	false
6	h_3^r	5	7	3	4		6	false
7	h_4^l	6	8	9	4		7	false
8	h_5^l	7	5	10	4		8	false
9	h_4^r	9	9	7	5			
10	h_5^r	10	10	8	6			
11	h_6^l	11	11	12	7			
12	h_6^r	12	12	11	8			

Figure 5. Graph Representation of a *lines* object

This is essentially the temporary representation of a *lines* or *regions* object used in the ROSE system as a basis for graph algorithms. In array *Edge*, field *h* contains the half-segment. The fields *pred* and *succ* contain the indexes of the preceding and succeeding halfsegments in the counter-clockwise order; *link* is the index of the partner halfseg-ment. The field *node_index* points into the second array *Node*.

The data structure definition and an algorithm for creating this temporary representation are shown on the next page. In algorithm `init_edge_and_node_array`, the while-loop is executed once for each halfsegment. All operations within the loop need constant time except for linking a right with its corresponding left halfsegment which requires $O(\log n)$ time where n is the number of halfsegments of the *lines* or *regions* object. Hence the whole algorithm has time complexity $O(n \log n)$. After initialization of the arrays, for an index of an element we can find its predecessor, successor, opposite half-segment, and node information in constant time.

```
const      MaxComp = ...;                              (* New or first point reached. *)
type       EdgeRec = record                            topᵥ := topᵥ + 1;
                     h            : Hₙ;                 Node[topᵥ].on_stack := false;
                     pred, succ   : cardinal;          Edge[topₑ].node_index := topᵥ;
                     link, node_index : cardinal;      Edge[topₑ].succ := topₑ;
                     end;                               Edge[topₑ].pred := topₑ;
           NodeRec = record                          else
                     on_stack     : boolean;           (* The same dominating point. *)
                     end;                               Edge[topₑ].node_index := topᵥ;
var        Edge = array [1..MaxComp] of EdgeRec;        (* Produce doubly-linked ring. *)
           Node = array [1..NoOfPoints] of NodeRec;     Edge[topₑ].pred := topₑ - 1;
                                                        Edge[topₑ].succ := Edge[topₑ - 1].succ;
                                                        Edge[topₑ - 1].succ := topₑ;
algorithm init_edge_and_node_array                      Edge[Edge[topₑ].succ].pred := topₑ;
input: A lines object L (or a regions object R)       end-if;
output:    The two arrays Edge and Node              if d = right then
begin                                                   < Compute index i of the corresponding left half-
    topᵥ := 0;                                            segment of the array Edge in the range 1 to topₑ
    topₑ := 0;                                            by using binary search. >
    old_dp := (m, m); (* outside of the realm *)         Edge[topₑ].link := i;
    L := select_first(L);                                Edge[i].link := topₑ;
    while not end_of_hs(L) do                          end-if;
        topₑ := topₑ + 1;                               old_dp := act_dp;
        h := get_hs(L); (* Let h = (s, d). *)           L := select_next(L);
        Edge[topₑ].h := h;                            end-while;
        act_dp := dp(h);                                return Edge, Node;
        if (act_dp ≠ old_dp) or (topᵥ = 0) then      end init_edge_and_node_array.
```

This graph-theoretic view is used to realize the executable operators l_interior, r_contour, l_count, and r_count which have the following signature:

lines	→	regions	l_interior
regions	→	lines	r_contour
lines	→	int	l_count
regions	→	int	r_count

Here l_interior determines a _regions_ object formed from the areas enclosed by segments of a _lines_ object, r_contour returns a _lines_ object formed from the segments of only the outer cycles of the faces of a _regions_ object (holes are omitted). The other two operations return the number of components which is the number of blocks (connected components) for a _lines_ object and the number of faces for a _regions_ object. As an example, we show the algorithm for r_contour.

The main problem is the assignment of the segments to the correct _outer and hole cycles_ which according to the face definition is unique [GüS93a]. According to that definition, the _regions_ object in Figure 6(a) consists of two faces rather than of a single face with a hole.

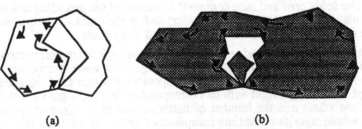

(a)   (b)

Figure 6. Traversal of Cycles

An important observation is that for the *first* halfsegment of any cycle (with respect to the order of halfsegments) we can decide whether it belongs to an outer cycle or a hole. It is a left halfsegment and belongs to an outer cycle iff the attribute *InsideAbove* has been set, otherwise to a hole.

We adopt the following strategy: If for a given left halfsegment it is known that it belongs to an outer cycle, then we traverse the graph forming a *minimal* cycle containing that segment. This works as follows: For the given halfsegment, get the partner halfsegment (i.e. follow the edge). From the partner, go around that node to the *predecessor* in the counter-clockwise order. Follow that edge, etc. As soon as the node of the initial segment is reached again, a complete cycle has been found and its segments can be marked as outer segments.

This strategy works fine for the regions object in Figure 6(a) where it correctly determines the left face. However, in Figure 6(b) the cycle would include the hole segments. Therefore the strategy is refined as follows: If the first segment belongs to an outer cycle, then try to form a minimal cycle traversing the graph as described above. Put each encountered halfsegment on a stack and mark its node as being *on_stack*. As soon as a node is encountered which is on the stack already, two cases are possible:

- Case 1. This is the node of the initial segment. Then a complete outer cycle has been found. Remove all segments from the stack, marking them as outer segments, and also from the graph. Repeat the procedure for the remaining segments.
- Case 2. This is not the initial node. Then a hole cycle has been found. Remove segments from the stack until the current node is found there, marking them as hole segments. Remove these segments also from the graph. Then continue building the outer cycle. - Before removing segments from the stack one must store the next segment of the outer cycle in order to avoid continuing with some other face that may lie in the hole, as shown in Figure 6(b).

If the first segment belongs to a hole, then try to form a *maximal* cycle by going always to the *successor* around a node. Apart from that, proceed in the same way as for outer cycles. However, if here a node is encountered which is not the initial one, then a cycle belonging to another hole has been found sharing a vertex with the hole cycle of the initial segment.

On the next page we present two algorithms. Algorithm **cycle_classification** classifies the segments of a *regions* object as outer or hole segments, following the strategy just discussed. Here the type *EdgeRec* is extended by the fields *visited* and *inside_above*. The first field is initialized by the value *false*; the latter field is true if a halfsegment of the *regions* object has the attribute *InsideAbove*. A variable *top* always contains the index of the top stack element; it is implicitly changed by the stack operations *push* and *pop*. "Remove *Edge[j]* from the graph" means remove the edge from the cycle of segments around its node. This algorithm requires $O(n \log n)$ time for a regions object with n halfsegments due to the included preprocessing step for computing the *Edge* and *Node* arrays; apart from that it needs only $O(n)$ time.

The second algorithm **r_contour** then computes the contour of a *regions* object by using the first algorithm. After cycle_classification has been done, this is trivial and needs only $O(n)$ additional time. The total time for **r_contour**, as presented, is $O(n \log n)$.

The algorithm for **l_interior** first follows a similar strategy as **cycle_classification** to extract only complete cycles from a *lines* object. It then uses plane sweep to remove any cycles enclosed by other cycles. This algorithm needs $O(n \log n)$ time. Computing the components in a *lines* object (**l_count**) can be done by a simple depth-first traversal [AhHU83]. Determining the number of components (faces) in a *regions* object is also a by-product of cycle classification. The last two algorithms require $O(n)$ time once the graph representation has been constructed.

```
algorithm cycle_classification
input: A regions object R
output: A modified regions object R whose halfsegments ob-
        tain the attribute HoleSegment if they belong to a hole
        and OuterSegment otherwise.
begin
    init_edge_and_node_array(R);
    top := 0;
    for i := 1 to < number of segments in Edge > do
        if not Edge[i].visited then
            if Edge[i].inside_above then (* Outer cycle. *)
                Node[Edge[i].node_index].on_stack := true;
                push(i); Edge[i].visited := true;
                first_node_index := Edge[i].node_index;
                l := Edge[i].link;
                push(l); Edge[l].visited := true;
                repeat
                    j := Edge[l].node_index;
                    if not Node[j].on_stack then
                        Node[j].on_stack := true;
                        j := Edge[l].pred;
                        push(j); Edge[j].visited := true;
                        l := Edge[j].link;
                        push(l); Edge[l].visited := true;
                    else if j = first_node_index then
                        while top > 0 do (* Outer cycle. *)
                            j := pop();
                            < Remove Edge[j] from the graph. >;
                            < Set attribute OuterSegment for
                              Edge[j]. >;
                            Node[Edge[j].node_index].on_stack
                              := false;
                        end-while
                    else (* Hole cycle. *)
                        rem := Edge[l].pred; count := 0;
                        repeat
                            k := pop();
                            < Remove Edge[j] from the graph.>;
                            < Set attribute HoleSegment for
```

```
                              Edge[k]. >;
                            Node[Edge[k].node_index].on_st
                              ack := false;
                            if Edge[k].node_index = j then
                                count := count + 1
                        end-if
                        until (j = Edge[k].node_index) and
                              (count = 2);
                        push(rem); Edge[rem].visited := true;
                        l := Edge[rem].link;
                        push(l); Edge[l].visited := true;
                    end-if
                until top = 0;
            else (* Hole cycle. *)
                < Proceed analogously. >
            end-if
        end-if
    end-for;
end cycle_classification.


algorithm r_contour
input: A regions object R
output: A lines object L containing the halfsegments of all
        outer cycles of R.
begin
    L := new();
    cycle_classification(R);
    R := select_first(R);
    while not end_of_hs(R) do
        attr := get_attr(R);
        if OuterSegment ∈ attr then
            h := get_hs(R);
            L := insert(L, h);
        end-if;
        R := select_next(R);
    end-while;
    return L;
end r_contour.
```

4.4 Special Algorithms

The diameter operator of the ROSE algebra determines the maximal extent of an object, that is, the maximal distance between any two vertices. The implementation of the corresponding three executable operators p_diameter, l_diameter, and r_diameter uses special algorithms different from the three techniques mentioned before. The computation of all distances between any two points of an object is too time-consuming. To reduce the number of elements, we determine the convex hull of the object, since the diameter of the convex hull is equal to the diameter of the whole object [PrS85]. An algorithm which calculates the convex hull of the point set of a simple polygon in linear time can be found in [Me84]. An algorithm which computes the diameter of a convex polygon in linear time is shown in [PrS85]. The combination of these two algorithms is used in the ROSE system to realize the three diameter operations in $O(n)$ time for an object with n points or halfsegments.

5 Implementation

In this section we discuss in more detail the actual representation of ROSE objects and some differences between the conceptual view of algorithms, as presented above, and the actual procedures in the system. On the next page, the representation of a *regions* object is shown (for *points* and *lines* objects it is similar). A *regions* object is given as (a pointer to) a record whose last component is an array *elem*; one can dynamically allocate storage to represent *regions* objects of any desired size. The array serves as a storage pool for three different kinds of nodes representing *halfsegments*, *faces*, or *holes*, respectively. Halfsegments are organized in an AVL-tree to allow for updates in $O(\log n)$ time; additional pointers connect all halfsegments within the object, within a face, and within a cycle (outer cycle or hole cycle) into linked lists ordered in halfsegment order. Additionally all faces, and for each face its holes, are linked. Hence the complete structure of a *regions* object is explicitly represented and access operations are offered (in the module hiding this representation) to perform all kinds of scans in linear time. Furthermore, bounding boxes are stored for the object, each face, and each hole. The record contains general information about the object such as the root segment of the AVL-tree, fields for *perimeter*, *diameter* and *area*; the *attr* field tells which of these values have already been computed for this particular object.

In Section 4.3, we have described the graph algorithms from a conceptual point of view. What really happens is that the graph structure is analyzed at the time of *closing* an object, that is, after all segments have been inserted. More precisely, the construction of a *regions* object consists of the following steps:
- Allocate storage, insert *n* halfsegments into the AVL-tree.

To close the object:
- Perform an inorder traversal of the tree to link all halfsegments of the object; compute the bounding box.
- Use plane sweep to compute *InsideAbove* attributes (sketched in Section 4.2).
- Use algorithm cycle_classification (including init_edge_and_node_array) to attach a unique *cycle number* to each segment.
- Use a second plane sweep (a variant of the previous one) to determine for each hole segment the cycle number of the outer cycle of its surrounding face.
- In a final scan of the complete list of segments, link all segments within faces and cycles (this is possible since each segment has now an associated cycle number and face number) and compute the remaining information such as bounding boxes, links of faces and holes, etc.

Clearly the whole construction takes no more than $O(n \log n)$ time and $O(n)$ space. An analogous strategy is used for the more simple *lines* and *points* objects. Because all this information is now explicitly available in the data structures, the algorithms and running times for some operations change: all no_of_components algorithms perform a simple lookup in $O(1)$ time. The algorithm for r̄_contour simply scans the list of faces and for each face the list of segments of its outer cycle which requires only $O(k \log k)$ time (where *k* is the size of the result object). For operators computing **diameter**, **length**, **area** and **perimeter**, only the first call takes $O(n)$ time; the value is then stored with the object so that subsequent calls are lookups in $O(1)$ time. Further differences between the algorithms described above and the actual procedures result from:
- *Use of filter techniques*. Most operations first compare bounding boxes of objects, some in a second step also component bounding boxes, in order to avoid running the more expensive algorithms on the actual halfsegments, whenever possible. Such strategies are well-known (e.g. [OrM88, Gü94]).
- *Estimating the size of the result* is necessary in all operations constructing new objects to allocate the appropriate amount of storage for them.

For further details, we recommend the study of [Ri95].

```
TYPE
  OBJATTRIBS  = (Closed, Perimeter, Diameter, Area);

  ATTRIBSET   = SET OF OBJATTRIBS;

  COMPATTRIBS = (InsideUp, HoleSegment);

  COMPSET     = SET OF COMPATTRIBS;

  FIELDTYPE   = (HalfsegField, FaceField, HoleField);

  SELECTTYPE  = (RegionsSelected, FaceSelected, CycleSelected);

  REGIONSELEM = RECORD
                  CASE kind : FIELDTYPE OF
                    HalfsegField:
                      h               : HALFSEGMENT; (* Key-element. *)
                      attrib          : COMPSET;     (* Element status.*)
                      left            : CARDINAL;    (* AVL-tree. *)
                      right           : CARDINAL;
                      height          : CARDINAL;
                      next_in_regions : CARDINAL;              (* In order lists.*)
                      next_in_face    : CARDINAL;
                      next_in_cycle   : CARDINAL;
                    | FaceField:
                      face_bbox       : BBOX;        (* Face bounding box. *)
                      first_in_face   : CARDINAL;    (* First halfsegment. *)
                      last_In_face    : CARDINAL;    (* (Help pointer.) *)
                      last_in_cycle   : CARDINAL;    (* (Help pointer.) *)
                      first_hole      : CARDINAL;    (* First hole in face. *)
                      last_hole       : CARDINAL;    (* (Help pointer.) *)
                      next_face       : CARDINAL;    (* Face list. *)
                    | ELSE
                      hole_bbox       : BBOX;        (* Hole bounding. *)
                      first_in_hole   : CARDINAL;    (* First Halfsegment. *)
                      last_In_hole    : CARDINAL;    (* (Help pointer.) *)
                      next_hole       : CARDINAL;    (* Hole list. *)
                  END;
                END;

  REGIONS     = POINTER TO RECORD
                  attr      : ATTRIBSET;   (* The object's status. *)
                  perimeter : REAL;        (* Length of Segments. *)
                  diameter  : REAL;        (* Diameter. *)
                  area      : REAL;        (* Area of object. *)
                  bbox      : BBOX;        (* Bounding box. *)
                  count     : CARDINAL;    (* Number of faces. *)
                  holes     : CARDINAL;    (* Number of holes. *)
                  free      : CARDINAL;    (* Number of free fields. *)
                  first_idx : CARDINAL;    (* Idx of smallest halfseg. *)
                  face_Idx  : CARDINAL;    (* Idx of first face. *)
                  root_idx  : CARDINAL;    (* Idx of root of AVL-tree. *)
                  act_Idx   : CARDINAL;    (* Idx of selected halfseg. *)
                  act_face  : CARDINAL;    (* Idx of selected face. *)
                  sel_kind  : SELECTTYPE;  (* Kind of traversal. *)
                  max_idx   : CARDINAL;    (* Idx of largest half-field. *)
                  act_hole  : CARDINAL;    (* Idx of selected hole. *)
                  elem      : ARRAY [1..MaxInRegions] OF REGIONSELEM
                END;
```

6 Conclusions

We have described the implementation of a large part of a spatial algebra for database systems - that is, the almost complete implementation of the first three groups of operators of the ROSE algebra (only the dist operator is missing) which deal with "atomic" objects (whereas the fourth group manipulates set of database objects). Use of high-level primitives has made it possible to describe a relatively large number of algorithms in compact, precise notation. We are not aware of any similar work - treating a whole algebra by giving precise algorithms including analysis of their complexity.

The fact that ROSE objects are realm-based has led to relatively simple, efficient, and numerically robust algorithms. All manipulations of objects are discrete (entirely based on integer arithmetics); real numbers occur only to describe properties such as length or area of objects. A crucial concept is the use of ordered halfsegment sequences as a base representation of objects. Manipulation of such sequences in parallel traversal or plane sweep implements most operations efficiently. On the other hand, we have also shown how the structure of objects (faces, holes, etc.) can be determined by graph algorithms and be represented in the data structures.

The ROSE system is available for study or use, currently in the form of a stand-alone Modula-2 library [Ri95]. It is in principle suitable for use in database systems since all objects have compact representations. However, for a serious integration it is necessary to solve the problem of managing very large ROSE objects in a way that is compatible with the DBMS object and storage management. We are currently working on the definition and implementation of a general "algebra interface" between an external implementation of a system of data types and a database system. The ROSE algebra will be made available under such an interface and integrated into the Gral system [Gü89, BeG92]. In this approach, it is only necessary to replace the array components "at the end" of object representations by identifiers of so-called "database arrays" which behave exactly like ordinary arrays but have their own page sequences and buffer management and interact properly with DBMS transaction management. This is a straightforward, technical modification of the ROSE algebra; algorithms remain unchanged.

Another aspect of integration into a database system is the connection to the underlying realms, in particular the propagation of updates from the realm to ROSE objects in a database [GüS93a]. Our realm implementation is almost completed. All these integration aspects will be described in a forthcoming paper.

Appendix

The structure of this table is explained in Section 2. In column "time complexity" (TC), n denotes the total size of the operand(s), m the size of the *regions* operand (only used if there is just one), and k the size of the result object.

Descriptive Operator		Executable Operator	PT	PS	G	TC
$geo \times geo \rightarrow \underline{bool}$	=	pp_equal, ll_equal, rr_equal	x			$O(n)$
	≠	pp_unequal, ll_unequal, rr_unequal	x			$O(n)$
	disjoint	pp_disjoint, ll_disjoint	x			$O(n)$
		rr_disjoint		x		$O(n \log n)$
$geo \times \underline{regions} \rightarrow \underline{bool}$	inside	pr_inside, lr_inside		x		$O(n \log m)$
		rr_inside		x		$O(n \log n)$
$\underline{regions} \times \underline{regions} \rightarrow \underline{bool}$	area_disjoint	rr_area_disjoint		x		$O(n \log n)$
	edge_disjoint	rr_edge_disjoint		x		$O(n \log n)$
	edge_inside	rr_edge_inside		x		$O(n \log n)$
	vertex_inside	rr_vertex_inside		x		$O(n \log n)$
$ext_1 \times ext_2 \rightarrow \underline{bool}$	intersects	ll_intersects	x			$O(n)$
		lr_intersects, rl_intersects		x		$O(n \log m)$
		rr_intersects		x		$O(n \log n)$

Descriptive Operator	Executable Operator	PT	PS	G	TC
$ext_1 \times ext_2 \to \underline{bool}$ meets	ll_meets	x			$O(n)$
	lr_meets, rl_meets		x		$O(n \log m)$
	rr_meets		x		$O(n \log n)$
border_in_common	ll_border_in_common, lr_border_in_common, rl_border_in_common, rr_border_in_common	x			$O(n)$
$area \times area \to \underline{bool}$ adjacent	rr_adjacent		x		$O(n \log n)$
encloses	rr_encloses		x		$O(n \log n)$
$\underline{points} \times ext \to \underline{bool}$ on_border_of	pl_on_border_of, pr_on_border_of	x			$O(n)$
$\underline{points} \times \underline{points} \to \underline{points}$ intersection	pp_intersection	x			$O(n + k \log k)$
$\underline{lines} \times \underline{lines} \to \underline{points}$ intersection	ll_intersection	x			$O(n + k \log k)$
$\underline{regions} \times \underline{regions} \to \underline{regions}$ intersection	rr_intersection		x		$O(n \log n)$
$\underline{regions} \times \underline{lines} \to \underline{lines}$ intersection	rl_intersection		x		$O(n \log m + k \log k)$
$geo \times geo \to geo$ plus	pp_plus, ll_plus	x			$O(n + k \log k)$
	rr_plus		x		$O(n \log n)$
$geo \times geo \to geo$ minus	pp_minus, ll_minus	x			$O(n + k \log k)$
	rr_minus		x		$O(n \log n)$
$ext_1 \times ext_2 \to \underline{lines}$ common_border	ll_common_border, lr_common_border, rl_common_border, rr_common_border	x			$O(n + k \log k)$
$ext \to \underline{points}$ vertices	l_vertices, r_vertices	x			$O(n + k \log k)$
$\underline{regions} \to \underline{lines}$ contour	r_contour			x	$O(n \log n) / O(k \log k)$
$\underline{lines} \to \underline{regions}$ interior	l_interior			x	$O(n \log n)$
$geo \to \underline{int}$ no_of_components	p_no_of_components	x			$O(n) / O(1)$
	l_no_of_components, r_no_of_components			x	$O(n \log n) / O(1)$
$geo_1 \times geo_2 \to \underline{real}$ dist	pp_dist, pl_dist, pr_dist, lp_dist, ll_dist, lr_dist, rp_dist, rl_dist, rr_dist				
$geo \to \underline{real}$ diameter	p_diameter, l_diameter, r_diameter	*special algorithm*			$O(n) / O(1)$
$\underline{lines} \to \underline{real}$ length	l_length	x			$O(n) / O(1)$

Descriptive Operator		Executable Operator	PT	PS	G	TC
regions → _real_	area	r_area	x			$O(n) / O(1)$
	perimeter	r_perimeter	x			$O(n) / O(1)$

References

[AhHU83]   Aho, A.V., J.E. Hopcroft, and J.D. Ullman, *Data Structures and Algorithms*. Addison-Wesley, Reading, Massachusetts, 1983.

[BeG92]   Becker, L., and R.H. Güting, Rule-Based Optimization and Query Processing in an Extensible Geometric Database System. *ACM Transactions on Database Systems 17 (1992)*, 247-303.

[GrY86]   Greene, D., and F. Yao, Finite-Resolution Computational Geometry. Proc. 27th IEEE Symp. on Foundations of Computer Science, 1986, 143-152.

[Gü89]   Güting, R.H., Gral: An Extensible Relational Database System for Geometric Applications. Proc. of the 15th Intl. Conf. on Very Large Databases (Amsterdam, The Netherlands), 1989, 33-44.

[Gü93]   Güting, R.H., Second-Order Signature: A Tool for Specifying Data Models, Query Processing, and Optimization. Proc. ACM SIGMOD Conf. (Washington, USA), 1993, 277-286.

[Gü94]   Güting, R.H., An Introduction to Spatial Database Systems. *VLDB Journal 3, 4 (1994) (Special Issue on Spatial Database Systems)*, 357-399.

[GüS93a]   Güting, R.H., and M. Schneider, Realms: A Foundation for Spatial Data Types in Database Systems. Proc. of the 3rd Intl. Symposium on Large Spatial Databases (Singapore), 1993, 14-35.

[GüS93b]   Güting, R.H., and M. Schneider, Realm-Based Spatial Data Types : The ROSE Algebra. Fernuniversität Hagen, Informatik-Report 141, 1993. To appear in the *VLDB Journal*.

[KaM85]   Karlsson, R.G., and J.I. Munro, Proximity on a Grid. *Proc. of the 2nd Symp. on Theoretical Aspects of Computer Science*, Springer-Verlag, LNCS 182, 1985, 187-196.

[KaO88a]   Karlsson, R.G., and M.H. Overmars, Scanline Algorithms on a Grid. *BIT 28 (1988)*, 227-241.

[KaO88b]   Karlsson, R.G., and M.H. Overmars, Normalized Divide-and-Conquer: A Scaling Technique for Solving Multi-Dimensional Problems. *Information Processing Letters 26 (1988)*, 307-312.

[KeK81]   Keil, J.M., and D.G. Kirkpatrick, Computational Geometry on Integer Grids. *Proc. of the 19th Annual Allerton Conference on Communication, Control, and Computing*, 1981, 41-50.

[Kl83]   Klaeren, H.A., *Algebraische Spezifikation*. Springer Verlag, Berlin, 1983.

[Me84]   Mehlhorn, K., *Data Structures and Algorithms 3: Multidimensional Searching and Computational Geometry*. Springer Verlag, 1984.

[Mü85]   Müller, H., Rastered Point Location. *Proc. Workshop on Graphtheoretic Concepts in Computer Science*, Trauner Verlag, 1985, 281-293.

[OrM88]   Orenstein, J., and F. Manola, PROBE Spatial Data Modeling and Query Processing in an Image Database Application. *IEEE Trans. on Software Engineering 14 (1988)*, 611-629.

[Ov88a]   Overmars, M.H., Efficient Data Structures for Range Searching on a Grid. *Journal of Algorithms 9 (1988)*, 254-275.

[Ov88b]   Overmars, M.H., New Algorithms for Computer Graphics. *Advances in Computer Graphics*, Eurographics Seminars, Springer Verlag, 1988, 3-19.

[Ov88c]   Overmars, M.H., Computational Geometry on a Grid: An Overview. *Theoretical Foundations for Computer Graphics and CAD*, Springer Verlag, 1988, 167-184.

[PrS85]   Preparata F.P., and M.I. Shamos, *Computational Geometry*. Springer Verlag, 1985.

[Ri95]   de Ridder, T., The ROSE System. Modula-2 Program System (Source Code). Fernuniversität Hagen, Praktische Informatik IV, Software Report 1, 1995. Available as a LaTeX file for printing and/or as a compressed collection of ASCII files.

[Ya92]   Yao F.F., Computational Geometry. Algorithms and Complexity. *Handbook of Theoretical Computer Science*, vol. A, Elsevier Science Publishers B.V., 1992, 343-389.

A 3D Molecular Surface Representation Supporting Neighborhood Queries[1]

Thomas Seidl and Hans-Peter Kriegel

Institute for Computer Science, University of Munich
Leopoldstr. 11 B, D-80802 München, Germany
email: { seidl I kriegel }@dbs.informatik.uni-muenchen.de

Abstract: Applications in molecular biology more and more require geometric data management along with physicochemical data handling. Thus, 3D structures and surfaces of molecules become basic objects in molecular databases. We propose the neighborhood query on graphs such as molecular surfaces as a fundamental query class concerning topological information on patch adjacency. Furthermore, we suggest a patch-based data structure, called the *TriEdge structure,* first, to efficiently support neighborhood query processing, and second, to save space in comparison to common 2D subdivision data structures such as the quad-edge structure or the doubly-connected edge list. In analogy to the quad-edge structure, the TriEdge structure has an algebraic interface and is implemented via complex pointers. However, we achieve a reduction of the space requirement by a factor of four. Finally, we investigate the time performance of our prototype which is based on an object-oriented database management system.

Keywords: 3D molecular modeling, graphs in spatial databases, surface representation, neighborhood query, surface approximation, database systems in molecular biology.

1 Introduction

The fundamental 3D objects in molecular biology and computational biochemistry are large molecules with several hundreds to thousands of atoms. There are various applications that require access to the 3D structure of the molecules, as it is provided for proteins by the Brookhaven Protein Data Bank (PDB) [Ber 77]. Up to now, the PDB contains 3,000 proteins, enzymes, and viruses [PDB 95]. For each entry, along with information on the chemical structure of the protein, the 3D coordinates of its atoms are stored in a text file.

In the last years, a new topic has been emerging in the area of protein engineering: the prediction of molecular interaction, called the *docking problem.* Several methods has been suggested to meet the one-to-one docking problem [Con 86], [BMH 92], [FNNW 93], [HT 94]: which constellation of two given proteins represents a stable complex? A constellation is the relative position of a molecule with respect to its docking partner, and may be described by six parameters: three coordinates for translation in 3D space, and three Euler angles for rotation (cf. figure 1). Since all of these six degrees of freedom to compose two molecules together in 3D space are continuous, the constel-

1. This research was funded by the German Ministry for Research and Technology (BMFT) under grant no. 01 IB 307 B. The authors are responsible for the content of this paper.

lation space is infinite. Common discretizations of protein surfaces result in thousands of points, and each of them can represent a possible docking site.

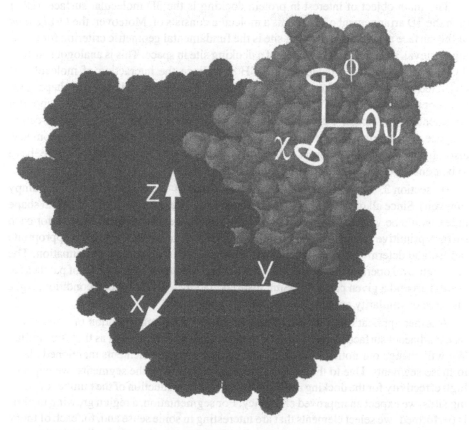

Fig. 1. Example complex: beta trypsin with trypsin inhibitor (PDB code 2PTC)

In our project "BIOWEPRO: a Database System for Protein Docking", we are faced with the one-to-many docking problem: select such proteins from the PDB that are able to form a stable complex in interaction with a given query protein, and determine appropriate constellation parameters. When considering the number of proteins in the database $(3 \cdot 10^3)$ and the number of possible docking sites on a protein in the database $(> 10^3)$ and on the query protein $(> 10^3)$, the search space at least has an overall size of billions of protein-protein-constellations [EKSX 95].

Thus, docking retrieval is a new and challenging application for spatial database systems. Due to the enormous size of the search space, a multi-step query processing architecture is recommended. In spatial database systems, this paradigm efficiently supports the processing of point and region queries as well as spatial joins [BHKS 93], [KSB 93], [BKSS 94]. Additionally, we perform various steps of preprocessing: first, we determine various geometric and physicochemical features of the molecular surface, e.g. local shape index values [Koe 90]. From these, we build up a feature index [Ald 94] to improve the filter step. Second, we apply a segmentation method to diminish the constellation space [EKX 95].

The main object of interest in protein docking is the 3D molecular surface, rather than the 3D arrangement of the atoms a molecule consists of. Moreover, the *local shape* of the surface at a possible docking site is the fundamental geometric criterion for docking retrieval, rather than the location of a docking site in space. This is analogous to similarity retrieval in CAD databases [SKSH 89]. Since the interaction of molecules is restricted to the docking sites, we do not require a description of the global shape (outline, contour) of molecules. An access method for molecular surfaces has to support a representation of possible docking sites that is independent from location and direction in space, i.e. invariant with respect to translation and rotation. Along with the geometry, also physicochemical properties determine molecular interactions and, therefore, have to be considered when representing molecular surfaces.

In section 3, we will see that molecular surfaces are smooth but quite bumpy (uneven). Since all of the bumps have similar atomic size, the selectivity of a local shape index would be very low when based on infinitesimal neighborhoods. Instead, for each surface primitive (patch or point, resp.), we collect its neighbors within an appropriate radius, and determine the local shape via a paraboloid as a simple approximation. The basic retrieval operation is the *neighborhood query:* select a connected set of patches (or points) around a given patch (or point, resp.) bound by a neighborhood condition, e.g. a distance or similarity criterion.

Another application of the neighborhood query is the segmentation of protein surfaces: adjacent surface elements will be grouped to segments as long as they are similar. We will change our notion of docking site from the surface elements mentioned above to these segments. Due to the resulting homogeneity within the segments, we expect a high effectivity for the docking retrieval, and due to the reduction of the number of docking sites, we expect an improved efficiency. For segmentation, a region growing method is performed: we select elements that are interesting in some sense and, for each of them, we perform a neighborhood query controlled by an appropriate similarity criterion.

Neighborhood query processing requires access to adjacency information, as it is provided by common data structures like the quad-edge structure [GS 85], or the DCEL [PS 85]. In this paper, we propose a new basic technique to store molecular surfaces, reducing the storage requirement by a factor of four. Since our method is based on topology, it supports effective and efficient processing of queries on the molecular surface structure. We formally introduce the general neighborhood query, and give an algorithm to process it. Two applications are considered in detail: local surface approximation and surface segmentation. We implemented our method in C++ on top of the object-oriented database management system ObjectStore [OHMS 92].

The paper is organized as follows: in section 2, we refer to related work, and in section 3, we review a common subdivision of molecular surfaces and give a specification to represent their topological structure. In section 4, we formally define the neighborhood query and show its application to surface approximation and segmentation. In section 5, the TriEdge data structure is presented that supports efficient processing of neighborhood queries. Section 6 contains first evaluation results, and section 7 concludes the paper with a summary and an outlook to future work.

2 Related Work

As we will illustrate in section 3, molecular surfaces are 2-manifolds that can be represented by a common subdivision. Therefore, we investigate the literature for any hints how to efficiently store 2D subdivisions in database systems. The articles describing molecular surface calculation as found in molecular biology [Con 83], computer graphics [VBW 94], and computational geometry [HO 94] do not mention their surface representation method. In [HO 94] only, there is a hint that extended van-der-Waals surfaces are stored with the quad-edge structure. More investigations of surface graph structures and retrieval are found in the area of solid modeling, graphs in spatial databases, and graph algorithms for recursive query processing.

In the field of solid modeling, the quad-edge structure is a quite common storage method for 2D subdivisions [GS 85]. As a short review to the concepts behind the quad-edge structure, we cite from [GS 85], page 80, while carefully adapting the notation to the style as required in our implementation environment: "For any oriented and directed edge e we can define unambiguously its vertex of *origin*, $e.Orig()$, its *destination*, $e.Dest()$, its *left face*, $e.Left()$, and its *right face*, $e.Right()$. We define also the *flipped* version $e.Flip()$ of an edge e as being the same unoriented edge taken with *opposite orientation* and same direction, as well as the *symmetric* of e, $e.Sym()$, as being the same undirected edge with the *opposite direction* but the same orientation as e." On page 81, the basic traversal functions are introduced: "We can define the *next edge with same origin*, $e.LEdge()$, as the one immediately following e (counterclockwise) in this ring. Similarly, given an edge e we define the *next counterclockwise edge with same left face*, denoted by $e.Lnext()$, as being the first edge we encounter after e when moving along the boundary of the face $F = e.Left()$ in the counterclockwise sense as determined by the orientation of F. The edge $e.Lnext()$ is oriented and directed so that $e.Lnext().Left() = F$ (including orientation)."

The quad-edge structure is implemented by records representing four views to a single undirected edge, or two directed half-edges, respectively. Each edge record contains four pointers *Data*, two of them to the adjacent vertices, providing the access required for the evaluation of $Orig()$ and $Dest()$, and the remaining two to the adjacent faces $Left()$ and $Right()$. The traversal functions $Sym()$, $LEdge()$, $Lnext()$ etc. are supported by four complex pointers (e,r) from an edge record to the edges following in clockwise and counterclockwise direction around the corresponding vertices $Orig()$ and $Dest()$ (cf. figure 2). This way, a cycle $(e,r).Sym().Sym() = (e,r)$ is stored as a whole in one record: the evaluation of $(e,r).Sym()$ does not require dereferencing the pointer r, but only changing the 'view' component r, whereas the other operations like $LEdge()$ require dereferencing t. In the TriEdge structure, $LEdge()$ cycles are clustered rather than all of the $Sym()$ cycles (cf. section 5).

Since molecular surfaces are 2-manifolds, we do not require generalizations as for the modeling of (non-planar) 3D subdivisions [DL 89] or of subdivided d-manifolds for arbitrary dimensions d [Bri 93]. Molecular surfaces are orientable, therefore we drop the $Flip()$ operation. For reasons of static typing, we want to distinguish explicitly between the surface graph and its dual graph, and thus, do not provide the operation $Rot()$ which serves for changing the view to the dual of the graph, exchanging vertices with faces. Whereas supporting $Flip()$ would cost a few bits per edge record, $Rot()$ would be for free.

244

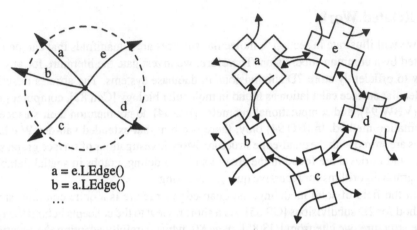

a = e.LEdge()
b = a.LEdge()
...

Fig. 2. An LEdge ring and the corresponding linked quad-edge records (cf. [GS 85])

The quad-edge implementation is similar to the doubly-connected-edge-list (DCEL) from [PS 85], with two differences: first, the quad-edge structure is defined in terms of an edge algebra, leading to a more comfortable interface to edges, their symmetric and dual edges, in comparison to the DCEL. Second, the complex pointers of the quad-edge structure contain a simple pointer to an adjacent edge record, and additionally, unlike a DCEL entry, an offset value representing the view to the referenced edge. Exactly this idea of an algebraic interface together with a complex pointer concept is used for our TriEdge structure as described below. This approach is well supported by the object-oriented data model and leads to an easy integration.

In [DMP 93], a unified topological model called Plane Euclidean Graph (PEG) is proposed to integrate the various domains of information a spatial database system is concerned with. Spatial queries are classified into topological, set-theoretic, and metric queries. Our neighborhood query obviously qualifies for the topological class, but also for the metric or a thematic one, dependent on the neighborhood criterion specified. As a data structure for the PEG, a modification of the DCEL is proposed that additionally can hold isolated points as well as isolated edge components inside faces.

Questions concerning graphs in spatial databases also are investigated in [EG 94]. The graphs consist of nodes, edges, and explicit paths, and are used to represent networks. The examples are taken from the domain of geographical information systems with highways, roads, and rivers, etc. as instances of explicit paths. A type REG is mentioned occurring as parameter for operations inside and intersection, but the concept of faces that are defined inherently by edge cycles is not considered explicitly. In our application domain, we require these faces e.g. for visualizing molecular surfaces. The faces represent the patches of a molecular surface, and provide access to the underlying solid which is an atom sphere, a probe sphere, or a torus. The edge cycles bounding the faces represent the bordering arcs that form the trimming curves when rendering the patches. The dual view of the graph — considering the patches to be vertices instead of faces — helps when traversing the surface graphs.

As an interesting contribution in [EG 94], the selection of a subgraph around a node is provided by the operation circle: $graph_i \times node_i \times num_j \times (edge_i \to num_j) \to graph_i$. The circle function is specified by parameters for the graph, center, and radius along with an edge cost function, and is processed performing Dijkstra's single-source shortest path algorithm. The specification of our conditional neighborhood is very similar to this concept. As an extension, we do not restrict it to the case of a radius bounding the path length, but support general conditions as relations between an arbitrary node and the center of the neighborhood. Additionally, the neighborhood query also supports symbolic similarity criteria and is not restricted to numerical distance comparisons.

Our system is based on an object-oriented data model. In [Jia 92] and [Jia 94], graph structures in relational databases are considered for the purpose of effective expression and efficient processing of recursive queries. For instance, SQL is extended by path expressions for the specification of transitive closures of relations. The graph structure of recursive relations is exploited to perform efficient query processing via graph algorithms. In consideration of a paging environment, algorithms for efficient graph traversal are analyzed. As a result, breadth-first traversal algorithms appear to be preferable.

3 Molecular Surfaces

In molecular biology, the surface of a molecule is defined to be the solvent accessible surface for any solvent probe radius α [Ric 77]. This surface is equivalent to the boundary of the weighted 3D α-hull: for $\alpha > 0$, the α-hull of a set s of spheres is the complement of the union of all open spheres of radius α intersecting no sphere of s [VBW 94]. For $\alpha = 0$, the α-hull is equal to the union of all spheres of s, and for $\alpha \to \infty$, the α-hull of s coincides with the convex hull of s. Various implementations for the calculation of molecular surfaces are published [Con 83], [VBW 94], [Sch 94], [HO 94].

Molecular surfaces have a strong regularity, and there are three types of patches they consist of: convex spherical patches, saddle-shaped rectangles, and concave spherical triangles (cf. figure 3). These types depend on the number of atoms that the probe sphere is in simultaneous contact with when rolling over the molecule. Since the algorithms enforce the atoms to be in general position, ensuring the probe sphere never being in simultaneous contact with more than three atoms, the complexity of the algorithms is reduced drastically. Obviously, this also holds for the representation of molecular surfaces.

At first sight, such patch-based representations of molecular surfaces seem to be difficult to manage: there are different types of patches with a different number of vertices, etc. Thus, triangulated surface representations are quite common to be used for docking purposes, and also for visualization. However, there are strong advantages for the patch-based representation: first, for a particular molecule and a given probe radius α, the solvent accessible surface is well defined in its structure and its shape. Second, for any given point density, the patchwork can be refined to a dotted surface, but not vice versa. Third, every patch is homogeneous with respect to the curvature, and the normal vector of a surface point is determined by the geometric parameters of the patch it lays on, i.e. via the associated atom sphere, torus, or probe sphere, respectively. Overall, we prefer a patch-based surface representation rather than a point-based method or an arbitrary triangulation.

Fig. 3. Surface of a portion of hemoglobin [Con 83].

In the following, we present a patch-based representation for molecular surfaces, providing access to the patches via an edge algebra. Guibas and Stolfi introduced such an algebra for 2D subdivisions as a specification for their quad-edge structure [GS 85]. Since the quad-edge structure is general enough to store 2D subdivisions which are embedded in 3D space, it is an appropriate storage structure for subdivisions of molecular surfaces as described above: let the faces stand for the surface patches, the edges for the arcs bordering each patch, and the vertices for the corner points of the patches. This view is adequate e.g. for visualization purposes, since the patches provide access to the underlying solid being an atom sphere, a probe sphere, or a torus. The edge cycles bounding the faces represent the bordering arcs that form the trimming curves required for rendering the patches. The dual view to this surface graph is intuitive for traversal purposes: consider the patches to be the vertices of the graph, the edges remain being associated to the arcs, and the faces represent the corner points (cf. table 1).

molecular surface	2D subdivision	ditto, dual view
corner point	vertex	face
patch border arc	edge	edge
surface patch	face	vertex

Tab. 1. Components of molecular surfaces, mapped to components of a 2D subdivision

As an interface for our surface representation, we specify required edge functions as follows. An illustration of the operations is given in figure 4. We implement this specification as a C++ module for the object-oriented database system ObjectStore. How-

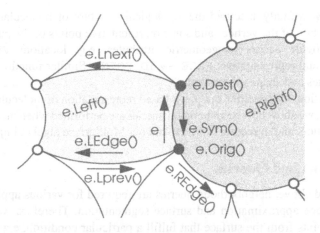

Fig. 4. Illustration of the MolSurface algebra

ever, to demonstrate the relationships between the functions, we give an algebraic specification with axioms. From the EDGE → EDGE functions, Sym and LEdge or Sym and Lnext are primitive, the others are derived with respect to the axioms:

```
SPEC MolSurface;
TYPES EDGE, FACE, VERTEX;
FUNCTIONS
    Sym, LEdge, REdge,
    Lnext, Lprev:        EDGE -> EDGE;
    Left, Right:         EDGE -> FACE;
    Orig, Dest:          EDGE -> VERTEX;
    an_edge:             FACE -> EDGE;
    an_edge:             VERTEX -> EDGE;

AXIOMS (for all EDGE e, FACE f, VERTEX v)
    e.Sym().Sym() == e;
    e.REdge().LEdge() == e;
    e.Lnext() == e.Sym().REdge();
    e.Lprev() == e.LEdge().Sym();
    e.Sym().Orig() == e.Dest();
    e.LEdge().Orig() == e.Orig();
    f.any_edge().Left() == f;
    v.any_edge().Orig() == v;
END MolSurface.
```

In addition to the algebra, we define an iteration statement to assign all the edges e around a face or a vertex counterclockwise to an edge variable e. Thereby, the edge cycle is traversed by the Lnext or LEdge function, resp., until the first edge is reached a second time. Syntactically, we map the iteration clause to a `for` statement via the macro mechanism of C++: `forall_around_face(e,face){...}` and `forall_around_vertex(e,vertex){...}`.

Until now, we only specified the topological structure of molecular surfaces. To yield the location of the vertices and some representative points of the patches, further functions provide access to geometric attributes, e.g. location: VERTEX $\rightarrow$ 3D_POINT, and representative: FACE $\rightarrow$ 3D_POINT. Similar functions deliver thematic attributes and shape information.

In this section, we specified our patch-based representation of molecular surfaces. In the following, we show how neighborhood queries are performed when they are based on this specification, and in section 5, we explain our MolSurface algebra implementation.

4 Neighborhood Queries

As mentioned above, neighborhood queries are required for various applications such as local surface approximation and surface segmentation. Therefore, we select such patches or points from the surface that fulfill a particular condition, e.g. an euclidean distance criterion in case of the approximation, or a criterion of similarity in case of the segmentation.

Formally, we specify the conditional neighborhood of a patch p as follows: for any molecular surface graph g and predicate c over a pair of patches, the *c-neighborhood* of a patch p, $n_c(p)$, is defined to be the maximal connected subgraph of g restricted to the patches v that fulfill the predicate c(v,p). Thus, for each $v \in n_c(p)$, one of the following properties holds: (i) c(v,p) and (v=p), or (ii) c(v,p) and an adjacent patch of v is in $n_c(p)$. In other words we can say: $n_c(p)$ contains only patches p that (1) fulfill the condition c together with p: c(v,p), and (2) are reachable from p via patches that all belong to $n_c(p)$.

The neighborhood query simply consists in the selection of a c-neighborhood: for any patch p of the surface s, and any predicate c(•,•), select all patches from s that belong to $n_c(p)$. In the following, we explain two applications of neighborhood queries.

Various applications of the general concept of neighborhood queries can be thought of. The condition c can be a criterion of surface distance, equivalence, etc. We give three examples taken from the context of docking retrieval.

(1) Segmentation of molecular surfaces. As a condition c, we provide a similarity criterion, e.g. two patches are similar if they both are saddle-shaped, or if they have the same sign for the electrostatic potential. We perform segmentation via a region growing algorithm: therefore, we have to provide a set of patches to be used as sprouts. For each of the patches in the sprout set, we perform a neighborhood query that is controlled by condition c. The resulting segments may have various extensions on the surface and in 3D space, since they are not bound by a spatial distance criterion. Also, they may overlap. When providing a similarity criterion with a very low significance, a single segment can include the whole surface.

(2) Local approximation of the molecular surface. As an early step in the computation of the local shape index [Koe 90] of a patch p, we approximate the neighborhood of p on the surface, e.g. by a paraboloid (cf. figure 5). With a radius parameter r, the locality of the approximation is controlled. For instance, a so called euclidean neighborhood query consists in the selection of all the patches that are reachable from p within the euclidean distance r. In this case, the condition c simply is a comparison: c(v,p) = '$\text{dist}_{\text{euclid}}(v, p) < r$'.

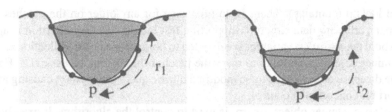

Fig. 5. Local approximation of the molecular surface with different radii r_1 and r_2

(3) Determination of local extrema. In [Con 86], knobs and holes are defined to be surface points that have an extreme solid angle value with respect to their neighbors. As a generalization, our neighborhood query supports specifying arbitrary neighborhood radii leading to different degrees of locality. Thus, various radii can be investigated with respect to their appropriateness for the purpose of docking retrieval.

Neighborhood query processing. After sketching some applications of the neighborhood query, we now present a simple implementation. We perform neighborhood query processing via a graph traversal algorithm:

```
void Neighborhood ( PATCH* p, CONDITION* cond,
                    os_Set <PATCH*>& result)
{
   os_List <PATCH*> open();
   PATCH *h, *v;
   result.clear();

   if (cond->eval(p,p))
     { open.insert(p); result.insert(p); }

   while (h = open.remove_first())
     // expand current patch h:
     forall_around_face( e, h )
     {
        v = e.Right();
        if (not result.contains(v)
            and cond->eval(v,p))
          { result.insert(v); open.insert(v); }
     }
   return;            // result is reference param
}
```

Two container objects are used in our algorithm: result and open. In result, we collect all the patches that belong to the specified neighborhood, and deliver it at the end of our procedure. The only methods applied to result are empty initialization, insertion, and lookup (contains). There is no relevance for any order on the patches, and, therefore, an arbitrary data structure supporting fast lookup and fast insertion is appropriate to hold the result variable. We decided to hold the result collection explicit in a container object, rather than to mark the patches that belong to result. For the latter, the database objects have to be modified during query processing, causing avoidable effort for concurrency control.

The other container object, open, is used to control the algorithm. It exactly contains such patches that are known to qualify for the result, and that have to be expanded later. A patch v that does not fulfill the condition $c(v,p)$ will not be inserted into open, since none of its successors belongs to the specified neighborhood $n_c(p)$, except if it is reachable from p by another path not containing v. Each step of the iteration begins with the extraction of an element from open. We always fetch the first element from open, and since we always insert the new elements at the end, a breadth first search is performed on the surface. This strategy could be changed to other (heuristic) strategies by inserting new patches at appropriate positions into open. For instance, the insertion of patches at the beginning of open would result in a depth first search. The capability of specifying the traversal strategy requires open to be an ordered collection.

5 The TriEdge Data Structure

Up to here, we declared our objects of interest, specified access operations, and presented a basic query class with applications. We presented a specification for a surface representation that supports the expression of neighborhood queries. Since the schema is topology-based, providing connectivity information, neighborhood queries are supported very efficiently. The remaining question is how to implement this specification. In this section, we explain our technique, whereas in section 6, the space reduction factor is shown in detail, and a first runtime evaluation of our prototype is presented.

Obviously, the quad-edge structure qualifies for this purpose. However, it requires 36 bytes per record, when adjusted to a multiple of four. Real molecular surfaces have a size of some thousand patches and edges, for a common probe radius of 1.4 Å which is the size of a water molecule. Therefore, the storage requirement for the surface topology information of a single molecule is hundreds of kilobytes. In table 2, a sample is given for a few molecules from the PDB, which are identified by the PDB entry code. Since the number of proteins in the PDB currently is 3,000 [PDB 95], the size of our 3D protein database for docking retrieval comes into the range of gigabytes. Therefore, an efficient implementation is crucial.

Our data structure for the MolSurface specification reduces the storage requirement for topology information by a factor of four compared to a straightforward implementation by the quad-edge structure. The approach to implement the MolSurface specification consists of two steps: first, we reduce the complexity of the representation by mapping the molecular surface graph to an equivalent but simpler graph structure. Second, we exploit the strong regularity of the new structure as a key property for an efficient data structure. Overall, we save space and, therefore, time for the reduced amount of data transfer within the database system.

The main observation concerns the structure of molecular surfaces and the role of the saddle patches: every saddle patch connects two convex patches and two concave

molecule	PDB code	number of atoms	number of patches	number of edges	size for quad-edge records
Prealbumin, chain a	2PAB-A	872	3,710	7,380	260 kbytes
Prealbumin, chain b	2PAB-B	872	3,776	7,524	265 kbytes
Beta-trypsin	2PTC-E	1,629	5,606	11,160	393 kbytes
Trypsin inhibitor	2PTC-I	454	1,990	3,972	140 kbytes
Subtilisin novo	2SNI-E	1,983	6,220	12,396	436 kbytes
Chymotrypsin inhibitor	2SNI-I	513	2,116	4,224	149 kbytes

Tab. 2. Surfaces of real proteins

triangles. Both types, the convex and the concave patches, are surrounded by cycles of saddle patches. This is analogous to faces and vertices of a 2D subdivision graph that are surrounded each by a cycle of edges. We exploit the analogy to develop a new storage method for molecular surfaces, and call the new structure the *simplified surface graph* (SSG) (figure 6).

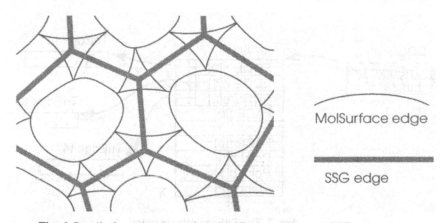

Fig. 6. Detail of a molecular surface: MolSurface edges and SSG edges

Due to this strong relationship to molecular surfaces, an SSG also is a 2D subdivision graph, consisting of vertices, edges, and faces. However, instead of mapping the vertices to corner points, the edges to arcs, and the faces to patches as we did for molecular surfaces, we now associate the vertices to the concave triangles of the molecular surface, the edges to the saddle patches, and the faces to the convex patches (cf. table 3). The number of edges to be stored is reduced drastically: every edge of a molecular surface graph belongs to exactly one saddle, and every saddle is bound by four (molecular) edges. Therefore, a molecular surface graph has four times as many edges as saddle patches, and, equivalently, four times as many edges than the SSG.

A second key observation leads us to a further reduction of the storage space. Since an SSG is a 2D subdivision, we could use the quad-edge structure to store it in the database. However, we can exploit a basic property of an SSG: all of the SSG vertices have a degree of three, since there are only triangles among the concave patches, due to the

molecular surface	molecular surface graph	simplified surface graph
corner point	vertex	—
patch border arc	edge	—
concave triangle	face	vertex
saddle rectangle	face	edge
convex patch	face	face

Tab. 3. Association of molecular surfaces to graph components

general position of the atoms: $e.\text{LEdge}()^3 = e$ for every EDGE_{SSG} e. Therefore, we store the edge cycles around the SSG vertices in arrays with a fixed length of three, rather than using any dynamic structure. This observation leads us to the TriEdge structure which consists of records that contain three SSG half-edges, all of them belonging to the same LEdge_{SSG} cycle. Similar to the quad-edge structure, an edge is represented by a complex pointer (t,v) that consists of a simple pointer t to the TriEdge record, and of a component v ('view') that specifies which SSG half-edge of the LEdge cycle is represented (cf. figure 7).

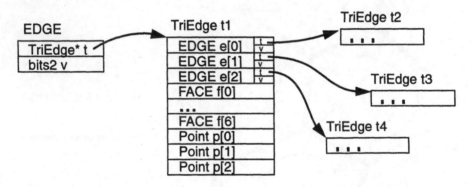

Fig. 7. The TriEdge data structure

A TriEdge record contains three complex edge pointers to store the connectivity information. Due to the mapping from SSG to molecular surface, a TriEdge record has to provide access to seven patches: the concave triangle as an image of the SSG vertex, the three saddle patches as images of the three SSG edges, and the three convex patches as images of the SSG faces that are adjacent to the saddles. Since the corner points are shared between the patches, we associate them to the TriEdge records rather than to the patches. For SSG, the implementation of the basic operations would be as follows:

LEdge_{SSG}: $(t,v) \rightarrow (t,\ v \oplus_3 1)$

Sym_{SSG}: $(t,v) \rightarrow (*t).e[v]$

Since a TriEdge record represents three SSG half-edges, the view v is in the range [0..2]. For molecular surfaces, a TriEdge record represents twelve half-edges (cf.

figure 8a) and, therefore, requires the view v being in the range of [0..11]. Since all of the elements of an LEdge cycle are represented by the same TriEdge record, the LEdge operation requires no dereferencing of the TriEdge pointer of an edge, but only a change of the view v. This function is the same for all edges and, therefore, can be carried out via lookup in a constant table LEDGE: [0..11] → [0..11], implemented simply as an array. For the Sym operation, dereferencing a TriEdge pointer is required in six cases, in the other six cases a change of the view is sufficient. When providing further arrays SYM, LEFT, and ORIG, the basic MolSurf operations are implemented as follows:

LEdge $_{\text{MolSurf}}$:   `(t,v)` → `(t, LEDGE[v])`

Sym $_{\text{MolSurf}}$:   `(t,v)` → `if (v >= 6) then (t, SYM[v])`
                                   `else (*t).e[v/2].correct(v)`

Left $_{\text{MolSurf}}$:   `(t,v)` → `(*t).f[LEFT[v]]`

Orig $_{\text{MolSurf}}$:   `(t,v)` → `(*t).p[ORIG[v]]`

In figure 8b, the arrays mentioned are shown. The asterisk (*) entries in the array SYM indicate that a traversal to the adjacent TriEdge record has to be performed. In these cases, the view component v of the result has to be adjusted to refer to its correct partner half-edge. This issue is delegated to the edge method `correct` which is implemented as follows: (t,w).correct(v) → (t, 2*w + (if odd(v) then 0 else 1)).

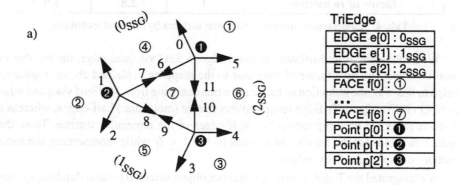

Fig. 8. a) a TriEdge record represents twelve molecular half-edges
        b) four arrays to implement the basic operations

6 Evaluation

First, we investigate the space requirement for the TriEdge structure in comparison to directly storing molecular surfaces using the quad-edge structure, and in comparison to an implementation of the SSG by the quad-edge structure. We assume the vertices and the patches to be referenced by 4-byte pointers, and the records being adjusted to a multiple of four bytes. In a packed representation, the bits for the 'view' component can be held in a single 4-byte word. Let e denote the overall number of edges on the molecular surface. Table 4 shows the reduction of storage space for molecular surfaces by the factor 3.9 when considering topological information as well as references to geometrical information.

storage requirement		MolSurf via quad-edge	SSG via quad-edge	SSG via TriEdge
references per record to ...	adjacent records	4	4	3
	patch corners	2	4	3
	surface patches	2	4	7
bytes per record (bpr)		**36**	**52**	**56**
number of molecular half-edges represented by a single record		2	8	12
number of records (#r)		e	e / 4	e / 6
total bytes (bpr · #r)		36 · e	13 · e	9.33 · e
factor of reduction		**1**	**2.8**	**3.9**

Tab. 4. Storage requirement for molecular surfaces by different techniques

When changing from MolSurf via quad-edge to SSG via quad-edge, the number of records is reduced by a factor of four, due to the mapping explained above. Figure 8a helps to illustrate the reduction of factor six when changing from MolSurf via quad-edge to SSG via TriEdge: a TriEdge record covers twelve (molecular) half-edges, whereas a quad-edge record only represents two half-edges of the molecular surface. Thus, the reduction factor for the number of records is $12/2 = 6$ while representing the same number of molecular (half-)edges.

We integrated the TriEdge structure into our object-oriented protein database system based on the C++ interface of the OODBMS ObjectStore. From our prototype, we obtained the following results of the runtime behavior of the TriEdge structure on an HP-9000/735 workstation under HP-UX 9.01: inserting molecular surfaces takes only a few seconds of elapsed time. The steps performed were reading the surface structure from a text file, creating the TriEdge records as well as the patch objects, and connecting the TriEdge records, all embraced by a transaction begin and commit (table 5).

From further experiments, we obtained the processing time for some selected euclidean neighborhood queries. The elapsed time is shown in table 6 for various radii. We determined the values as an average over 1,000 calls each, performed on a patch on the protein 2pab.a. From the first experiments, we could not recognize any difference in the

molecule	2pab.a	2pab.b	2ptc.e	2ptc.i	2sni.e	2sni.i
number of patches	3,710	3,776	5,606	1,990	6,220	2,116
insertion time (sec)	6.1	6.1	8.8	3.3	9.7	3.6

Tab. 5. Insertion time for molecular surfaces into the database

runtime between a breadth-first and a depth-first evaluation strategy. As expected, the runtime grows nearly linear with respect to the number of neighbors (cf. figure 9).

radius (Å)	number of neighbors	msec per query
1.0	3	0.1
2.0	7	0.6
3.0	16	2.0
4.0	21	4.2
5.0	71	7.4
6.0	130	14.2
7.0	177	19.3
8.0	231	24.0
9.0	280	31.2
10.0	355	36.3
11.0	452	51.1
20.0	1,607	164.0

Tab. 6. Runtime of neighborhood queries for a patch of
the protein 2pab.a (average over 1,000)

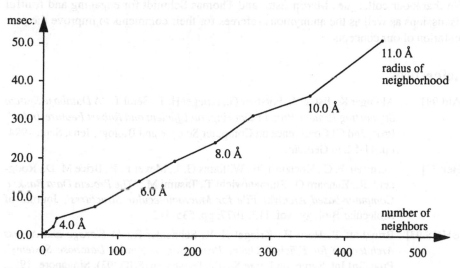

Fig. 9. Dependency of the runtime on the number of neighbors

7 Conclusion

In this paper, we presented the notion of molecular surfaces as fundamental 3D objects in database systems for molecular biology and computational chemistry. Along with the geometric and the physicochemical properties, in particular the topological structure of molecular surfaces has to be represented. As a basic operation, we defined the neighborhood query that is required for applications like local surface approximation and surface segmentation. The technical contribution of the paper is the introduction of the TriEdge data structure as an implementation of molecular surface graphs providing efficient support for neighborhood query processing. It leads to a considerably reduced space requirement compared to the well-known quad-edge structure. First experimental results show the query processing time to be in the range of milliseconds. The insertion time may be improved when integrating the molecular surface calculation program into the database system, thus avoiding text file input.

In our future work, we will integrate (1) circular edges (these are not bound by any corner point) that occur on molecular surfaces in some cases, e.g. when small atom chains stick out from the molecule, and (2) convex patches that are bound by more than one edge cycle which also may occur in some rare cases. After all, we will apply our representation and query processing technique to the docking problem.

A very challenging problem is the clustering of TriEdge records: how can query processing be improved by applying clustering techniques? In our prototype, we still rely on the default clustering of the database management system. A promising approach is managing the records by a spatial access method, since topological proximity implies geometric vicinity but not necessarily vice versa. Also the question about the adequate traversal strategy needs further investigation.

Acknowledgement

We thank our colleagues Martin Ester and Thomas Schmidt for engaging and fruitful discussions as well as the anonymous referees for their comments to improve the presentation of our concepts.

References

[Ald 94]   Aldinger K., Ester M., Förstner G., Kriegel H.-P., Seidl T.: *'A Database System Supporting Protein-Protein-Docking: an Efficient and Robust Feature-Index'*, Proc. 2nd GI Conference on Computer Science and Biology, Jena, Sept. 1994, pp. 41-52, in German.

[Ber 77]   Bernstein F. C., Koetzle T. F., Williams G. J., Meyer E. F., Brice M. D., Rodgers J. R., Kennard O., Shimanovichi T., Tasumi M.: *'The Protein Data Bank: a Computer-based Archival File for Macromolecular Structures'*, Journal of Molecular Biology, Vol. 112, 1977, pp. 535-542.

[BHKS 93] Brinkhoff T., Horn H., Kriegel H.-P., Schneider R.: *'A Storage and Access Architecture for Efficient Query Processing in Spatial Database Systems'*, Proc. 3rd Int. Symp. on Large Spatial Databases (SSD '93), Singapore, 1993, Lecture Notes in Computer Science, Vol. 692, Springer, pp. 357-376.

257

[BKSS 94] Brinkhoff T., Kriegel H.-P., Schneider R., Seeger B.: *'Efficient Multi-Step Processing of Spatial Joins'*, Proc. ACM SIGMOD Int. Conf. on Management of Data, 1994, pp. 197-208.

[BMH 92] Badel A., Mornon J. P., Hazout S.: *'Searching for geometric molecular shape complementarity using bidimensional surface profiles'*, Journal of Molecular Graphics, Vol. 10, 1992, pp. 205-211.

[Bri 93] Brisson E.: *'Representing Geometric Structures in d Dimensions: Topology and Order'*, Discrete & Computational Geometry, Vol. 9, 1993, pp. 387-426.

[Con 83] Connolly M. L.: *'Solvent-Accessible Surfaces of Proteins and Nucleic Acids'*, Science, Vol. 221, 1983, pp. 709-713.

[Con 86] Connolly M. L.: *'Shape Complementarity at the Hemoglobin $\alpha_1\beta_1$ Subunit Interface'*, Biopolymers, Vol. 25, 1986, pp. 1229-1247.

[DL 89] Dobkin D. P., Laszlo M. J.: *'Primitives for the Manipulation of Three-Dimensional Subdivisions'*, Algorithmica, Vol. 4, 1989, pp. 3-32.

[DMP 93] De Floriani L., Marzano P., Puppo E.: *'Spatial queries and data models'*, Proc. European Conference on Spatial Information Theory (COSIT '93), Lecture Notes in Computer Science, Vol. 716, Springer, 1993, pp. 113-138.

[EG 94] Erwig M., Güting R. H.: *'Explicit Graphs in a Functional Model for Spatial Databases'*, IEEE Transactions on Knowledge and Data Engineering, Vol. 6, No. 5, 1994, pp. 787-804.

[EKSX 95] Ester M., Kriegel H.-P., Seidl T., Xu X.: *'Shape-based Retrieval of Complementary 3D Surfaces from a Protein Database'*, Proc. GI Conf. on Database Systems for Office Automation, Engineering, and Scientific Applications (BTW '95), Informatik aktuell, Springer, 1995, pp. 373-382, in German.

[EKX 95] Ester M., Kriegel H.-P., Xu X.: *'Knowledge Discovery in Large Spatial Databases: Focusing Techniques for Efficient Class Identification'*, Proc. 4th Int. Symposium on Large Spatial Databases (SSD '95), Portland, Maine, 1995.

[FNNW 93] Fischer D., Norel R., Nussinov R., Wolfson H. J.: *'3-D Docking of Protein Molecules'*, Proc. 4th Annual Symposium on Combinatorial Pattern Matching (CPM '93), Padova, Italy, in: Lecture Notes in Computer Science, Vol. 684, Springer, 1993, pp. 20-34.

[GS 85] Guibas L., Stolfi J.: *'Primitives for the Manipulation of General Subdivisions and the Computation of Voronoi Diagrams'*, ACM Trans. Graphics, Vol. 4, No. 2, 1985, pp. 74-123.

[HO 94] Halperin D., Overmars M. H.: *'Spheres, Molecules, and Hidden Surface Removal'*, Proc. 10th ACM Symp. Computational Geometry, 1994, pp. 113-122.

[HT 94] Helmer-Citterich M., Tramontano A.: *'PUZZLE: A New Method for Automated Protein Docking Based on Surface Shape Complementarity'*, Journal of Molecular Biology, Vol. 235, 1994, pp. 1021-1031.

[Jia 92] Jiang B.: *'I/O-Efficiency of Shortest Path Alogrithms: An Analysis'*, Proc. IEEE Int. Conf. Data Engineering, 1992, pp. 12-19.

[Jia 94] Jiang B.: *'Processing non-relational database queries—a comparison of various proposals'*, Informatik Spektrum, Springer, Vol. 17, 1994, pp. 373-383, in German.

[Koe 90]   Koenderink J. J.: *'Solid Shape'*, MIT Press, Cambridge, MA, 1990.

[KSB 93]   Kriegel H.-P., Schneider R., Brinkhoff T.: *'Potentials for Improving Query Processing in Spatial Database Systems'*, invited talk, Proc. 9èmes Journées Bases de Données Avancées (9th Conference on Advanced Databases), Toulouse, France, 1993.

[OHMS 92]   Orenstein J., Haradhvala S., Margulies B., Sakahara D.: *'Query Processing in the ObjectStore Database System'*, Proc. ACM SIGMOD 1992, pp. 403-412.

[PDB 95]   Protein Data Bank: *'Quarterly Newsletter No. 71 (Jan 1995)'*, Brookhaven National Laboratory, Upton, NY, 1995.

[PS 85]   Preparata F. P., Shamos M. I.: *'Computational Geometry—An Introduction'*, Springer, 1985.

[Ric 77]   Richards F. M.: *'Areas, Volumes, Packing, and Protein Structure'*, Annual Reviews in Biophysics and Bioengineering, Vol. 6, 1977, pp. 151-176.

[Sch 94]   Schmidt T.: *'Calculation of Protein Surfaces using Spatial Access Methods'*, Master thesis, Institute for Computer Science, Technical University of Munich, 1994, in German.

[SKSH 89]   Schneider R., Kriegel H.-P., Seeger B., Heep S.: *'Geometry-based Similarity Retrieval of Rotational Parts'*, Proc. Int. Conf. on Data and Knowledge Systems for Manufacturing and Engineering, Gaithersburg, ML, 1989, pp. 150-160.

[VBW 94]   Varshney A., Brooks F. P., Wright W. V.: *'Computing Smooth Molecular Surfaces'*, IEEE Computer Graphics & Applications, Vol. 14, No. 5, 1994, pp. 19-25.

An Inferencing Language for Automated Spatial Reasoning About Graphic Entities

Paul Scarponcini
Graphic Data Systems
Englewood, CO
pxs@gdscorp.com

Daniel C. St. Clair
University of Missouri-Rolla
Engineering Education Center
stclair@umrgec.eec.umr.edu

George W. Zobrist
Department of Computer Science
University of Missouri-Rolla

Abstract

A method is proposed for automated reasoning about graphic entities. First, a formal representation scheme is suggested for persistently storing graphic information as fundamental graphic entity types. Next, fundamental relationships between these types are identified. A formal, graphic entity reasoning based inference language (GERBIL) is then presented to implement the relationships. An architecture is proposed, linking a computer graphic system for persistent entity storage with a knowledge based system shell for inferencing. A prototype system, Dafne, demonstrates proof of principle.

1 Background

1.1 Problem Definition

A two-dimensional Computer Graphics System (CGS) is capable of storing points, lines, and polygons (Foley et. al. 1990). If it is a Computer Aided Design (CAD) system, these graphic primitives can be used to depict real world objects on a drawing like walls, doors, and columns on an architectural floor plan. In the case of a Geographic Information System (GIS), they can represent real world features, like cities, roads and counties on a map. But the CGS has no knowledge about what the graphic primitives represent. Consequently, it cannot reason about the relationships between drawing objects or map features.

Without the ability to reason, a CGS can only provide back to the user that information which the user explicitly entered into the system. Consider the GIS map of the United States shown in Figure 1. New York and Boston might be depicted as two points on the map. Each would be labeled with a text string comprised of letters which spell the city's name. A scale bar might be shown to help the reader of the map understand relative distances between cities. From this map, the reader would be able to determine if New York is near Boston. Here, *near* is defined as being less than some predefined straight line distance. The *near* conclusion would have to be reached by the reader; a conventional CGS would not be able to make this inference.

Fig. 1. GIS Map of the USA.

A conventional CGS knows about the two points used to represent the cities; it remembers their x and y coordinates as measured from some origin. It does not know that the points indeed represent cities. In fact, it has no understanding of what a city is. It knows about the letters contained within the text strings but does not know that the letters spell the name of a city nor does it know that the string is associated with the point. With a layer based CGS, all points used to represent cities are stored on a separate city layer. The CGS still cannot understand that each point represents an individual city.

An object based CGS stores sets of graphic primitives together as graphic objects (GDSC 1995). It allows the user to name these objects based upon the real world entities they represent. For example, a map might include an object named CITY:BOSTON which is comprised of a point and the corresponding text string. The CGS now knows that the entire object represents a city. Alternatively, the point primitive could be separated out into a separate object called POINT: SPATIAL:CITY:BOSTON. Now the CGS realizes that the object is a point which spatially locates a city called Boston. If the CGS were provided with a rule that told it how to infer the nearness of two points, it would be able to determine if Boston is near New York.

1.2 Representation Schemes

Numerous representation schemes have been proposed for storing graphic information. These can be grouped into various levels of abstraction based upon semantic content. At the lowest level of abstraction, raster image bitmaps provide a storage mechanism for individual pixel intensities or color, representing a set of values of a particular attribute. There is no explicit data structure for representing inter-pixel relationships.

At the next level, graphic primitives are used to represent graphic images. Van Dam and Sklar (Foley and van Dam 1990) propose a simple raster graphics package including such primitives as lines, polygons, rectangles, circles, ellipses, text strings and areas. Several graphics standards have been created which operate at this graphic primitive level of abstraction (Arnold and Duce 1990), including GKS and PHIGS. Standards which focus on transferring graphic data include CGM, IGES, and SDTS.

At the third level of abstraction, graphic primitives are grouped into more meaningful structures. The GKS enables grouping primitives into segments; PHIGS uses a centralized structure store for hierarchically organizing primitives. Most GIS and CAD systems allow graphic primitives to be grouped together into layers or coverages. Each layer contains graphics relating to a class of real world entities. For example, all graphics relating to doors on an architectural plan may appear on the door layer. The layer mechanism does not segregate each door instance as an identifiable entity. Standards have been proposed by individual clients as well as organizations (Schley 1990) which specify layer content.

Even more complex representation schemes enable graphic objects to assume an identity, representing a real world entity complete with attributes and behavior. Object based systems such as Graphic Data Systems Corporation's Graphic Data System (GDS) require that all graphic primitives be part of a user-definable entity or object (GDSC 1995) For example, all primitives needed to represent an individual door are grouped together into a door object. These objects can then be instantiated at specific locations on a drawing. A viewing mechanism can be used to collect individual objects into dynamic "layers."

In addition to the data structures used to store individual or sets of graphic primitives, a mechanism is required for spatially searching those primitives (Samet and Webber 1988). Sherer et al (1990) offers a good evaluation of various approaches, including linked lists, quad trees, multidimensional (K-D) trees and variations of these three. Numerous other indexing schemes have been proposed.

The highest level of abstraction identified above offers the most promise for supporting automated graphic reasoning. The higher level graphic objects have an identity which enables them to be related to each other and to the real world entities they represent. They are comprised of graphic primitives which define their geometry and spatial location. A reasoning mechanism which functions at the graphic object level is easier to develop.

1.3   Graphic Reasoning

The topic of graphic reasoning can be addressed from four perspectives. These include geometric, spatial, topological and imagistic reasoning. The literature is not clear or consistent with respect to this segmentation. However, this segmentation approach is useful in trying to understand what is meant by graphic reasoning.

Geometric reasoning shall be defined as reasoning about geometric properties of objects. More specifically, it relates to the shape and size of the object. Geometric reasoning is used in robotic and motion planning, machine vision and in solid modeling (Kapur and Mundy 1989). In motion planning, the geometry of obstructing objects is critical to avoidance detection (Woodbury and Oppenheim 1988). In machine vision, the geometric shape of an object is used to distinguish it in a scene

(Hutchinson et al 1989). Walker et al (1988) agree that shape is important to object recognition. They believe that geometric reasoning is key to a knowledge-based vision system.

In solid modeling, geometry is used to define the shape and features of individual components (Marefat and Kashyap 1990). In manufacturing Computer Aided Design (CAD) Systems, solid geometry can be defined by Constructive Solid Geometry (CSG) or by boundary representation (B-rep) (Miller 1989). Computer Aided Manufacturing (CAM) deals with machining features which are based on shape. Geometric reasoning is used to convert from CSG or B-rep structures into shape features used in the machining process.

Spatial reasoning shall be defined as reasoning about the location of an object or its position relative to another object from a particular point of view. In a mapping application, spatial reasoning can address visibility, shortest path and localization queries (Holmes 1989). Visibility queries determine if there is a clear line of sight between two objects. Shortest path determines the minimal distance between the two objects. A localization query determines all points within the locale of a position, that is, within a prescribed radius distance. Holmes is explicit in stating an unobstructed distance. Hence, the locale is not a simple circular area.

Jungert (1989) and Mukerjee and Joe (1989) propose symbolic algebra for spatial reasoning based upon relative locations of objects. Jungert lists objects in row and column strings as they positionally occur left to right and top to bottom. "Less than," "equal to" and "edge to edge with" are the three operators in the algebra. Mukerjee and Joe use thirteen interval logic predicates for single dimensional relations and then extend this orthogonally to handle two dimensional relations.

Topological reasoning shall be defined as reasoning about connectivity, order, adjacency and containment. Kuipers and Levitt (1988) define two levels of topology relevant to their Tour model maps: "(1) a topological network of places and paths and (2) the containment and boundary relations of places and paths with regions." The first level defines the connectivity between a place and path using the on (place, path) relation. A partial ordering results from the order (place 1, place 2, path) relation. Paths have direction, resulting in two boundary regions, left (path) and right (path). This enables their second level of topology which relates to regions.

Egenhofer and Franzosa (1991) define a minimal set of purely topological spatial relations through a formal representation. Areas are defined as a set of points called point-sets. Their boundary and interior are considered separately. Four relations are defined between two point-sets based upon whether or not their boundaries and/or interiors intersect. This results in sixteen possible binary topological relations based upon empty and non-empty intersection sets of the boundaries and interiors. When restricted to polygonal areas in a plane, this reduces to the proposed minimal set of nine relations.

Imagistic reasoning shall be defined as reasoning with visually perceived information or imagery (Narayanan 1992). Research in the representations that underlie imagery, visual processes which support it and the role of imagery in inference has increased with the acceptance of a new discipline called cognitive science. This discipline has resulted from the synthesis of psychology, linguistics, computer science, philosophy and neuroscience (Stillings et al 1987). It attempts to understand human perception, thought, remembrance, language understanding, learning and other mental functions. Understanding how humans store and utilize imagery may provide useful representation and inferencing schemes for computers.

How people store images is perhaps the greatest debate in the area of imagistic reasoning. Kosslyn (1987) proposes that mental images are stored as analogs of visual images, enabling "the conscious experience of 'seeing,' but with the 'mind's eye' rather than with real ones." Pylyshyn (1981) leads the propositional school of thought. Cognition associated with imagery "should be explained in terms of processes which operate upon symbolic encoding of rules and other representations (such as beliefs and goals)." This would be consistent with other modalities.

Chandrasekaran and Narayanan (1992) offer a third approach. They propose a discrete symbolic representation scheme with well defined rules of formation. Latecki and Pribbenow (1992) argue for combining depictorial and propositional inferencing.

An automated reasoning system needs to support geometric, spatial and topological reasoning. Insights into how human beings perform imagistic reasoning suggest potential graphic representation schemes and reasoning processes for an automated reasoning system.

2 Automated Graphic Reasoning System

A formal representation scheme has been proposed for representing real world entities as domain independent classes of graphic objects. Potential relationships between such entities have been identified. Rules have been defined to enable the CGS to determine which relations hold between pairs of graphic objects and therefore between the two real world entities they represent.

2.1 Fundamental Graphic Entity Types

In an object based CGS, graphic entities represent real world objects on paper. To enable the CGS to support graphic reasoning, two domain independent, orthogonal classification schemes have been developed to categorize these graphic entities (Scarponcini et. al. 1993). One scheme considers dimensionality, the other deals with functionality.

Dimensionally, graphic entities can be pointil, lineal, or areal. Pointil entities have zero dimensions and relate to a single location like a point in space or a single point of intersection, like a topological node. Lineal entities have dimension in a single direction at a time. These might be spatially or geometrically attributed lines or merely topological links or edges. Areal entities are two dimensional, but planar. They include polygonal areas and topologically sensitive polygons.

Functionality identifies how the graphic entities are used. These include spatial, topological (nodal and edge), identificational, and representational. Spatial entities provide the function of locating real world objects in space. For multidimensional entities, they also provide geometric description. Topological entities define topological relationships with other entities. These include nodal relationships, such as connectivity, and edge relationships such as adjacency and containment. Representational entities portray the real world object on the map or drawing. These representations can be further identified using identificational graphic entities.

Each graphic entity belongs to one of the three dimensional classes as well as one of the five functional classes. This results in thirteen types of entities, since pointil-edge and areal-nodal combinations are undefined (see Figure 2 below). A real world object can be represented graphically by any combination of graphic entity types, hence the designation of fundamental. On the state roadway map in Figure 3, a symbol of an airplane designates a real world entity of an airport. Using Fundamental Graphic Entity Types (FGET), a pointil-spatial (PS) type graphic entity would define the airport's location. The graphic primitives used to create the airplane symbol would comprise a graphic entity of the pointil-representational (PR) type. The text string label defining the name of the airport would comprise a graphic entity of the pointil-identificational (PI) type. If the map were an airline's route map, as in Figure 4, each airport would be represented by a dot with routes shown as arcs. Here, a pointil-nodal (PTn) type entity could be used to define an airport in order to support automated routing. Route links would be stored as lineal-nodal (LTn) entities.

Functional Supertypes	Dimensional Supertypes		
	Pointil	Lineal	Areal
Spatial	PS	LS	AS
Topological Nodal	PTn	LTn	–
Topological Edge	--	LTe	ATe
Identificational	PI	LI	AI
Representational	PR	LR	AR

Fig. 2 Fundamental Graphic Entity Types
by Functional and Dimensional Supertypes

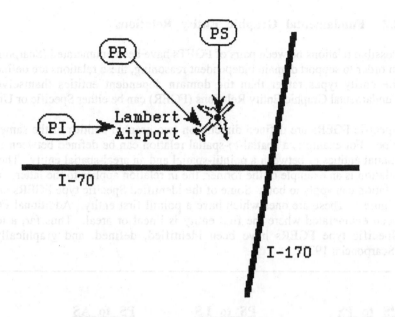

Fig. 3.   State roadway map with FGETs labeled

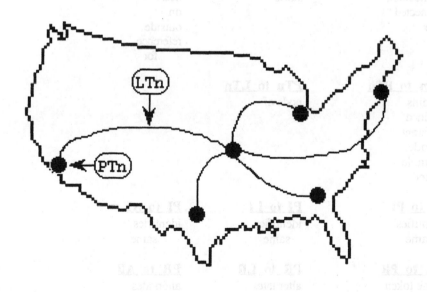

Fig. 4.   Airline route map with FGETs labeled

2.2 Fundamental Graphic Entity Relations

Possible relations between pairs of FGETs have been enumerated (Scarponcini 1992). In order to support domain independent reasoning, these relations are defined between the entity types rather than the domain dependent entities themselves. These Fundamental Graphic Entity Relations (FGER) can be either Specific or Universal.

Specific FGERs are defined directly on two graphic entities of the same functional type. For example, a spatial-to-spatial relation can be defined between two pointil-spatial entities or between a pointil-spatial and an areal-spatial entity. The *connected* relation is an example of the former, the *in* relation applies to the latter, and the *near* relation can apply to both. Some of the identified Specific type FGERs are shown in Figure 5. These are ones which have a pointil first entity. Additional FGERs have been enumerated where the first entity is lineal or areal. Thus far, a total of 128 Specific type FGERs have been identified, defined, and graphically depicted (Scarponcini 1992).

PS to PS	PS to LS	PS to AS
adjacent	at vertex	at vertex
at	ends	center of
close	near	in
collinear	on	margined by
connectable	starts	near
connected		on
near		outside
		reference
		for

PTn to PTn	PTn to LTn
adjoins	node of
chained	
different	
nodes	
linkable	
linked	

PI to PI	PI to LI	PI to AI
identifies	identifies	identifies
same	same	same

PR to PR	PR to LR	PR to AR
same token	alternates	alternates
alternates		

Fig. 5.   Specific Fundamental Graphic Entity Relations
where first entity is pointil

Universal FGERs are either association, transitive or symmetric. Association FGERs derive from inter-entity association links. A pointil-spatial entity may be location-association for (that is, used to locate) a pointil-representational entity, as in the case of the airport symbol in Figure 3 above. This results in the complementary association FGERs *location-for* and *located-by*.

By virtue of the association, the pointil-representational entity can now participate in specific FGERs which were defined for pointil-spatial entities. Hence, if the entity which locates the airport symbol is in a county, then the airport symbol can be construed to be in the county, implying that the airport itself is in the county. These relations are referred to as transitive FGERs: if A is *location-for* B and A is *in* C, then B is *in* C.

Symmetric relations are intuitive. Given two entities, a and b, of the same functional type and a Specific FGER like *near*, then a *near* b implies b *near* a.

2.3 Fundamental Graphic Entity Functions

A set of Fundamental Graphic Entity Functions (FGEF) have also been defined. Following an object oriented paradigm (Booch 1991), these functions are owned by members of the FGET classes. In an object oriented CGS, they would be encapsulated with the graphic entity and its data. In a more conventional object based CGS, they exist as procedures or functions which manipulate graphic entity data but which are external to the entities themselves.

The FGEFs are defined for each FGET. All spatial entity types, for example, have multiple functions called Distance-to, which calculate the distance to a second entity. This second spatial entity is passed as an argument of the function. Based upon the dimensional type of the entity executing the function, and the entity passed as an argument in the function, the CGS knows which Distance-to function to execute. If both are pointil-spatial, the function might use the Pythagorean Theorem to calculate the distance between the two point locations using their respective x and y coordinate data. This is consistent with the concept of polymorphism.

2.4 Knowledge Representation Scheme

A production system (Luger and Stubblefield 1989) is comprised of a set of production rules and an inference engine which applies Modus Ponens. Production rules are of the form:

IF: Conditions
THEN: Conclusion.

Here Conditions is the conjunction of first order logic sentences to be evaluated. Conclusion is the set of first order logic sentences to be asserted if the Conditions are True. Modus Ponens is the rule of inference used to infer the Conclusion (Q) from the Conditions (P) and the production rules (P ===> Q). An inference engine selects the appropriate rule to process. It then matches the rule's Conditions with facts it already knows in order to infer the Conclusion.

First order logic sentences are atomic sentences or the combination of atomic sentences connected by logical operators. These operators specify conjunction ($\wedge$), disjunction (v), implication (===>) and equivalence (<==>). An atomic sentence is a relational expression or the negation of one. Each relational expression is comprised of an n-ary relation constant plus a set of n object terms. These object terms can either be object constants representing a specific object, object variables representing a class of objects with similar properties, or a functional expression which maps one or more objects into another object in the universe of discourse (Genesereth and Nilsson 1987).

A production rule in a knowledge base may be written as:

Rule 1:
IF: R1 (f_1, F (f_1))
THEN: R2 (f_1).

Here, R1 (f_1, F (f_1)) and R2 (f_1) are first order logic sentences, each comprised of a single relational expression. The relation R1 is defined over an object variable, f_1, and a functional expression, F (f_1), which has that same object variable as its only term. The relation R2 is defined over a single object variable. If R1 is true for a particular variable substitution for f_1, then R2 can be inferred for the same variable substitution.

In a production system, a context base is used to store non-persistent facts. It might include the fact that R1(f_1,F(f_1)) is True for the variable substitution of f_1 = A, that is:

R1 (A, F (A)).

An Inference Engine derives knowledge by applying rules in the knowledge base to facts in the context base. In forward chaining, the inference engine begins with known conditions and concludes whatever it can from these conditions. From Rule 1 and the fact R1 (A, F(A)), the system would conclude R2 (A). Here R1 (A, F(A)) matches the IF condition of Rule 1 for f_1 = A. It therefore concludes the THEN side with the same variable substitution.

In backward chaining, the system begins with a hypothesis and works backwards from the hypothesized conclusions to the conditions which support the hypothesis. To test the hypothesis that R2 (A) is true, Rule 1 is selected since its THEN side matches the hypothesis with a variable substitution of f_1 = A. The same substitution is made for all occurrences of f_1 on the IF side. All IF conditions are then tested. If they are all determined to be True, the hypothesis is supported. The IF conditions can either be true by matching facts in the context base or by setting up the condition as a new hypothesis and proving it true by evaluating all of its conditions.

2.5 GERBIL

The Graphic Entity Reasoning-Based Inference Language, GERBIL, is comprised of production rules. The set of valid relations is the predefined set of FGERs. These FGERs are defined over a set of objects and functional expressions. The objects are graphic entities classified by FGET. The functions are the set of predefined FGEFs.

An example of a GERBIL rule is the PS-near-PS rule:

IF: p1.Type = PS
                     p2.Type = PS
                     p1.Distance-to(p2) <= t

THEN: Near (p1,p2,t).

The Condition for this rule consists of the conjunction of three sentences. The first sentence, p1.Type = PS is a relational expression in infix notation. The relational constant is Equals. The first term is a functional expression, or FGEF, called Type. Assuming an object oriented implementation, Type is owned by the graphic entity designated by the object variable p1. Using the notation above, this would be equivalent to Type (p1). The object constant PS is the designation for the pointil-spatial FGET. The second sentence is similar to the first, except that it contains the object variable p2.

Sentence three is also in infix notation, with the relation being Less-than-or-equal-to. The first term is the FGEF Distance-to owned by the graphic entity represented by the object variable p1. Here p2 is an argument passed to the function. The object variable t is used to specify the tolerance or maximum distance allowable between p1 and p2. The Conclusion is a single relational expression utilizing the FGER constant Near followed by three object variable terms.

As an object variable, p1 can represent any object in the universe of discourse. In this context, it can represent any graphic entity in the CGS. Once p1 is bound to a specific graphic entity, this substitution is valid throughout all occurrences of p1 in the entire rule. The same holds true for p2. Nothing precludes p1 and p2 from being bound to the same graphic entity since this is not explicitly precluded in the rule Conditions.

A Graphic Reasoning System (GRS) can employ the PS-near-PS rule to determine if New York and Boston are near each other, i.e., if they are within 100 miles of each other. The hypothesis to be tested is the rule's Conclusion:

Near (New York, Boston, 100).

To test the hypothesis, each Condition sentence must be evaluated. If all are true, then the Conclusion is also true. The variable substitutions made in the Conclusion must be reflected in the Conditions. In other words, the object variables p1, p2, and t are bound to the object constants New York, Boston, and 100, respectively. If there exists a graphic entity called New York, and it is a pointil-spatial entity, then

Condition sentence one is true. If a graphic entity called Boston is also a pointil-spatial entity type, then sentence two is likewise true. The New York object is then sent a message to execute its Distance-to function, taking Boston as its sole argument. The value returned is the point-to-point distance between New York and Boston. If this is less than 100, sentence three and hence the Conclusion are true.

The PS-near-PS rule, like all GERBIL rules, is domain independent. There is no requirement that p1 and p2 be cities on a map. It is possible for p1 to be the location for an airport symbol on a map and for p2 to be a school symbol. The same rule could reason about whether the airport is near the school. Furthermore, the graphic entities do not have to be map features. On an architectural floor plan of a building, it is possible to determine if there are exit signs near all doors for example.

Specific rules.

The FGER *near* is defined between any two spatial FGET entities, including pointil, lineal, and areal types. This results in the following set of GERBIL rules, with classification similar to FGERs themselves. As a Specific FGER, *near* results in the following GERBIL rules:

PS-near-PS	LS-near-PS	AS-near-PS
PS-near-LS	LS-near-LS	AS-near-LS
PS-near AS	LS-near-AS	AS-near-AS

The PS-near-LS rule determines whether a pointil-spatial graphic entity is near a lineal-spatial one. For example, is New York near the Hudson River? The PS-near-LS rule is similar to the PS-near-PS rule:

IF: p1.Type = PS
                l1.Type = LS
                p1.Distance-to(l1) <= t

THEN: Near (p1,l1,t).

The second term in the Conclusion is now a linear-spatial FGET. This is verified by the second Condition sentence. The last Condition sentence sends a message to the graphic entity identified by p1 along with the name of the lineal-spatial entity. Based upon the object oriented concept of polymorphism, pointil-spatial entities can have multiple functions or methods called Distance-to. At execution time, the system knows which to execute based upon the data type of the arguments passed in to the function. In the PS-near-LS rule, a different Distance-to function is executed than was executed in the PS-near-PS rule because the argument is a linear-spatial pointer or identifier. Instead of using the Pythagorean Theorem, this version of the Distance-to function might project the point onto the line and then calculate the distance from the original point to the point of projection. The exact method is encapsulated in the pointil-spatial entity and is of no consequence to the GRS.

The PS-near-AS, LS-near-LS, LS-near-AS, and AS-near-AS rules are similar variations of the PS-near-PS rule. The remaining three Specific rules, LS-near-PS, AS-near-PS, and AS-near-LS can then derive from these. For example, the LS-near-PS rule is:

IF: Near (p1, l1, t)

THEN: Near (l1, p1, t).

The set of nine xS-near-yS rules test the *near* relation between any two graphic entities. The GRS does not need to know what these graphic entities represent nor does it need to know the FGET of each entity. If the hypothesis Near (A, B, 10) is proposed, the GRS will search its GERBIL knowledge base for all rules having Near as a relational constant in their Conclusion followed by three terms. All nine would meet this criteria. They would all be added to the Agenda. The Inference Engine would select one of these rules to fire. It would bind the variables in the Conclusion with the values in the hypothesis. It would then evaluate the Conditions for the specific rule, making whatever variable substitutions are appropriate. If all Conditions are true, the Conclusion is reached. If any Condition fails, the next rule is selected and the process continues. With the *near* rules, the first two Conditions check the FGETs of the hypothesis arguments. In this manner, only the appropriate *near* rule's Distance-to function is actually executed.

There are 141 Specific GERBIL rules which have been developed for testing the 128 identified Specific FGERs (Scarponcini 1992). Some relations can be satisfied with multiple conditions, each expressed as an individual GERBIL rule. For example, a lineal-spatial entity is considered to be *in* an areal-spatial entity if it is totally within it, if one end is in and one is out, or if both ends are out but part of the intervening line is in. Separate rules test each of these three conditions.

Universal rules.

Universal rules are used to test Universal FGERs of the symmetric, association, and transitive types. The symmetric rule applies to symmetric binary FGERs whose arguments are of the same FGET. The x-FGER-y-symmetry rule takes the generalized form of:

IF: x.Type = y.Type
                 symmetric-FGER (y, x)

THEN: symmetric-FGER (x, y).

Near is a symmetric FGER. Rewriting the above rule results in the x-Near y symmetry rule:

IF: x.Type = y.Type
                 Near (y, x)

THEN: Near (x, y).

If New York is near Boston, then Boston is near New York. Both FGETs must be identical, since New York near the Hudson River does not imply that the entire Hudson River is near New York.

The Universal association rules pertinent to spatial FGETs derive from the fact that any FGET which is not spatial can be located by one that is. The two spatial association rules are:

x-located-by-y rule:

IF: Member-of (y.Type, (PS, LS, AS))
              not Member-of (x.Type, (PS, LS, AS))
              x=y.Locates

THEN: Located-by (x, y)

x-location-for-y rule:

IF: Located-by (y, x)

THEN: Location-for (x, y).

Universal transitive GERBIL rules derive from transitive FGERs. Spatial ones result because binary relations on two spatial FGETs, identified as SS:FGERs, also hold for FGETs which are located by spatial FGETs of the same dimensional supertype (pointil, lineal, or areal). Three rules result. The first addresses the case where the first entity is spatial and the second one is not. In the second case, only the second entity in the relation is spatial. In the third case, neither entity is spatial but each is located by a spatial graphic entity. In general form, these three rules are:

xS-xy:SS:FGER-y rule:

IF: x1.Functional_supertype = S
              y1.Functional_supertype /= S
              y2.Dimensional_supertype = y1.Dimensional_supertype
              Location_for (y2, y1)
              xy:SS:FGER (x1, y2)

THEN: xy:SS:FGER (x1, y1)

x-xy:SS:FGER-yS rule:

IF: x1.Functional_supertype /= S
              y1.Functional_supertype = S
              x2.Dimensional_supertype = x1.Dimensional_supertype
              Location_for (x2, x1)
              xy:SS:FGER (x2, y1)

THEN: xy:SS:FGER (x1, y1)

<u>x-xy:SS:FGER-y rule:</u>

IF: x1.Functional_supertype /= S
              y1.Functional_supertype /= S
              x2.Dimensional_supertype = x1.Dimensional_supertype
              y2.Dimensional_supertype = y1.Dimensional_supertype
              Location_for (x2, x1)
              Location_for (y2, y1)
              xy:SS:FGER (x2, y2)

THEN: xy:SS:FGER (x1, y1).

For example, assume x1 is a pointil-spatial graphic entity and y1 is a lineal-topological-nodal one, located by a lineal-spatial entity y2. The first rule can be written with p (as in pointil) substituted in for x and l (lineal) for y. Select the pointil-lineal Spatial Spatial relation (pl:SS:FGER) to be *near*. Then the first rule becomes:

<u>PS-pl:SS:FGER-L rule:</u>

IF: p1.Functional_supertype = S
              l1.Functional_supertype /= S
              l2.Dimensional_supertype = l1.Dimensional_supertype
              Location_for (l2, l1)
              Near (p1, l2)

THEN: Near (p1, l1).

In other words, if p1 is Spatial (it is), l1 is not Spatial (it is not; it is Topological nodal), l2 and l1 have the same dimensionality (they are both linear), l2 is location for l1, and p1 is near l2, then p1 is near l1. It is not necessary for this rule to verify that l2 is Spatial. Recall that this is checked during the subgoal verification of Location-for (l2, l1).

2.6 Dafne

A prototype Graphic Reasoning System called Dafne has been developed. A representative subset of FGERs were implemented to prove of validity of the concept.

The Dafne system architecture is shown in Figure 6. Graphic Data Systems' Graphic Data System (GDS) is the underlying object based Computer Graphics System (GDSC 1995). Graphic entities are stored as objects with classification based upon Fundamental Graphic Entity Types. A GIS roadmap (Figure 7) and an architectural floor plan (Figure 8) were used as representative graphic compositions.

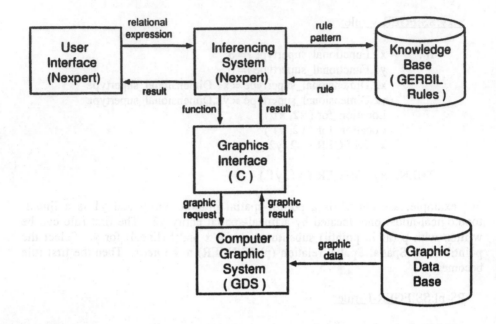

Fig. 6. Dafne system architecture

Representative GERBIL rules have been encoded in a knowledge base using Neuron Data's Nexpert Object software (Neuron Data 1990). Nexpert is linked to GDS via a C language program. FGEFs are encoded in this program. Nexpert also provides the user interface to Dafne.

To determine if two cities are near each other, the user proposes the hypothesis Near (New York, Boston, 100). Nexpert looks for rules with Near as a Conclusion and adds them to its Agenda. One rule is selected and fired. Nexpert's Inference Engine backward chains through the fired rule and any necessary supportive rules in an attempt to find all Conditions to be true. If so, Nexpert concludes the hypothesis that New York is near Boston. If any sentence in the rule requires graphic information, the appropriate C language FGEF is automatically called to retrieve the necessary information from the graphic entities existing in the underlying GDS graphic data base.

Dafne was able to determine relations between graphic entities such as *near* and *in*. Tests were successfully performed on both the roadmap and on the floorplan without necessitating any changes to the GERBIL rules in the knowledge base or to the C encoded FGEFs.

Fig. 7.   GIS roadmap for Dafne reasoning

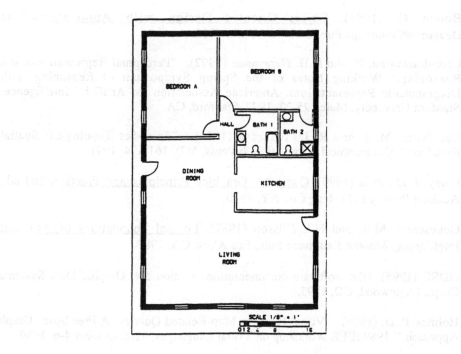

Fig. 8.   Architectural floor plan for Dafne reasoning

3 Conclusions

It was decided that GERBIL would initially focus on binary relations on AEC and GIS graphic entities with at most two dimensions. These simplifying constraints enabled the focus to be on the identification and classification of entities and on the reasoning process itself. The result is a robust, formal language which promises to be extendible to n-ary relations on multi-domain entities including surfaces and solids.

Dafne successfully demonstrates the proposed GERBIL language and GRS architecture. Dafne is able to infer implicit knowledge not explicitly stored in the underlying graphics data base. It can therefore be concluded that Dafne demonstrates GERBIL's ability to support automated geometric, spatial, and topological reasoning.

Future work might include extensions of the GERBIL language into higher order spaces and further development of the Dafne prototype. Implementation issues relating to inter-FGET associations, optimization strategies for reasoning as well as graphic object searching, and other performance and integrity related areas should be explored.

4 References

Arnold, D.B. and D.A. Duce (1990). ISO Standards for Computer Graphics: The First Generation. Butterworths, London, 1990.

Booch, G. (1991). Object Oriented Design with Applications, the Benjamin/Cummings Pub. Co., New York, 1991.

Chandrasekaran, B. and N.H. Narayanan (1992). "Perceptual Representation and Reasoning." Working Notes of the Spring Symposium of Reasoning with Diagrammatic Representations, American Association for Artificial Intelligence, Stanford University, March 25-27, 1992, Stanford, CA.

Egenhofer, M. J. and R. D. Franzosa (1991). "Point-Set Topological Spatial Relations." Geographical Information Systems, 5(2), 161-174, 1991.

Foley, J. D., et al (1990). Computer Graphics Principles and Practice, 2nd ed., Addison-Wesley Publishing Co., NY, 1990.

Genesereth, M.R. and N.J. Nilsson (1987). Logical Foundations of Artificial Intelligence, Morgan Kaufmann Pub., Los Altos, CA, 1987.

GDSC (1995). GDS software documentation, version 5.4, Graphic Data Systems Corp., Englewood, CO, 1995.

Holmes, P. D. (1989). "Visual Reply to Map-Related Queries--A Free Space Graph Approach." 1989 IEEE Workshop on Visual Languages, 92-8, October 4-6, 1989.

277

Hutchinson, S. A., R. L. Cromwell and A. C. Kak (1989). "Applying Uncertainty Reasoning to Model Based Object Recognition." Proceedings CVPR '89 IEEE Computer Society Conference on Computer Vision and Pattern Recognition, 541-8, June 1989.

Jungert, E. (1989). "Symbolic Expressions Within a Spatial Algebra: Unification and Impact Upon Spatial Reasoning." 1989 IEEE Workshop on Visual Languages, 157-162, October 4-6, 1989.

Kapur, D. and J. L. Mundy, ed. (1989). "Geometric Reasoning and Artificial Intelligence: Introduction to the Special Volume." Geometric Reasoning, 1-11, MIT Press, Cambridge MA, 1989.

Kosslyn, S. M. (1987). "Seeing and Imagining in the Cerebral Hemispheres: A Computational Approach." In Readings in Cognitive Science: A Perspective from Psychology and Artificial Intelligence, Morgan Kaufmann Publishers, Inc., San Mateo, CA, 1988.

Kuipers, B. J. and T. S. Levitt (1988). "Navigation and Mapping in Large-Scale Space." AI Magazine, 9(2), 25-43, Summer 1988.

Latecki, L. and S. Pribbenow (1992). "Combining Depictorial and Propositional Inferences for Processing Spatial Expressions." Working Notes of the Spring Symposium on Reasoning with Diagrammatic Representations, American Association for Artificial Intelligence, Stanford University, March 25-27, 1992, Stanford, CA.

Luger, G.F. and W.A. Stubblefield (1989). Artificial Intelligence and the Design of Expert Systems, the Benjamin/Cummings Pub. Co., New York, 1989.

Marefat, M. and R. L. Kashyap (1990). "Geometric Reasoning for Recognition of Three-Dimensional Object Features." IEEE Transactions on Pattern Analysis and Machine Intelligence, 12(10), 949-65, October 1990.

Miller, J. R. (1989). "Architectural Issues in Solid Modelers." IEEE Computer Graphics and Applications, 9(5), 72-87, September 1989.

Mukerjee, A. and G. Joe (1989). "Representing Spatial Relations Between Arbitrarily Oriented Objects." MIV-89 Proceedings of the International Workshop in Industrial Applications of Machine Intelligence and Vision, 288-91, April 10-21, 1989.

Narayanan, N. H. (1992). Preface to Working Notes of the Spring Symposium on Reasoning with Diagrammatic Representations, American Association for Artificial Intelligence, Stanford University, March 25-27, 1992, Stanford, CA.

Neuron Data (1990). Nexpert Object software documentation, version 2.0, Neuron Data Inc., Palo Alto, CA, 1990.

Pylyshyn, Z. W. (1981). "The Imagery Debate: Analogue Media Versus Tacit Knowledge." In Readings in Cognitive Science: A Perspective from Psychology and Artificial Intelligence, Morgan Kaufmann Publishers, Inc., San Mateo, CA, 1988.

Samet, H. and R. E. Webber (1988). "Hierarchical Data Structures and Algorithms for Computer Graphics." IEEE Computer Graphics and Applications, 48-68, May, 1988.

Scarponcini, Paul (1992). An Inferencing Language System for Automated Graphic Reasoning, UMI, Ann Arbor, MI, 1992.

Scarponcini, P., D.C. St Clair and G.W. Zobrist (1993). "Fundamental Graphic Entity Types to Support Graphic Reasoning," presented at InterSymp93, Baden-Baden, Germany, August 1993.

Schley, M. K., ed. (1990). "CAD Layer Guidelines: Recommended Designations for Architecture, Engineering, and Facility Management Computer-Aided Design. American Institute of Architects Press, Washington, D.C.

Sherer, A. D., B. S. Stanojevich, and R. J. Bowman (1990). "SMALS: A Novel Database for Two-Dimensional Object Location." IEEE Transactions on Computer-Aided Design of Integrated Circuits and Systems, 9(1), 57-65, January, 1990.

Stillings, N. A., et. al. (1987). Cognitive Science An Introduction. MIT Press, Cambridge, MA, 1987.

Walker, E. L., M. Herman, and T. Kanade (1988). "A Framework for Representing and Reasoning About Three-Dimensional Objects for Vision." AI Magazine, 9(2), Summer 1988.

Woodbury, R. F. and I. J. Oppenheim (1988). "An Approach to Geometric Reasoning in Robotics." IEEE Transactions on Aerospace and Electronic Systems, 24(5), 630-46, September, 1988.

Inferences from Combined Knowledge about Topology and Directions*

Jayant Sharma and Douglas M. Flewelling

National Center for Geographic Information and Analysis
University of Maine
Orono, ME 04469-5711
{jayant, dougf}@mecan1.maine.edu

Abstract

Separate mechanisms exist for the compositions of binary topological relations and binary direction relations. They are appropriate for homogeneous spatial reasoning, i.e., the inference of new topological relations from a set of topological relations, or the derivation of new direction relations from a set of direction relations; however, these composition mechanisms are insufficient for heterogeneous spatial reasoning, such as the inference of spatial relations from the combination of topological relations and cardinal directions. This paper discusses the shortcomings of current inference methods for heterogeneous spatial reasoning and presents a new method for heterogeneous direction-topology reasoning. The results demonstrate that using a canonical model, in particular Allen's interval relations, leads to a powerful heterogeneous reasoning mechanism. The spatial objects are approximated by their minimum bounding rectangles and the topological and direction relations are mapped onto interval relations. Compositions are performed using the composition table for interval relations. The results of the compositions are then reverse mapped onto directions. This process enables complex three-step inferences over topological and direction relations such as A West of B, B overlap C, and C West of D imply A West of D.

1 . Introduction

The power of spatial reasoning has gained increasing attention within the GIS research community. Over the last few years, a substantial amount of research has focused on new methods to derive higher-level spatial information from more basic spatial information. Particular progress was made in the areas of developing formalizations of direction and topological spatial relations, the composition of qualitative spatial relations, and the design of qualitative spatial inference engines. These findings provide a foundation for spatial information systems that support spatial analysis without the need of transforming any spatial knowledge into the domain of Cartesian coordinates and point-line-area representations. Instead, reasoning with imprecise and incomplete information may be achieved in a purely qualitative matter or, when necessary and available, augmented by quantitative information.

This paper provides a novel contribution to the problem of spatial-relation reasoning by considering inferences from topological *and* direction relations. In most cases, topological relations and cardinal directions have been studied extensively in an

---

* This research was partially supported by the National Science Foundation under grants IRI-9309230 (Principal Investigator: Max J. Egenhofer) and SBR-8810917 for the National Center for Geographic Information and Analysis, and a University of Maine Graduate Research Assistantship (UGRA). This support is gratefully acknowledged.

isolated fashion with great success. Examples are the 4-intersection for binary topological relations (Egenhofer and Franzosa, 1991), the conceptual neighborhood for orientation relations (Freksa, 1992), 2-D strings (Chang *et al.*, 1987), and symbolic arrays (Papadias and Sellis, 1992). At the same time, only little attention has been paid to the interrelationships between topology and directions and how knowledge about topological relations may help in deriving knowledge about cardinal directions. For example, *A* North of *B* and *C inside B* implies *A* North of *C*. In a paper on reasoning about spatial relationships for picture retrieval systems Sistla *et al.* (1994) present some inference rules that use knowledge of topological relations to derive direction relations, without resorting to any general theory that justifies the rules. Their particular example was a three step inference namely, *A* West of *B*, *B overlap C*, and *C* West of *D* imply *A* West of *D*. This paper fills this gap by presenting such a general theory and shows how Sistla's inference rules, and some others, follow from this theory. We base our work on the results of the 4-intersection for binary topological relations, and Allen's interval relations for one dimensional temporal intervals. The results give a sound theoretical basis for inferences such as the one above.

The remainder of this paper is structured as follows: Section 2 describes related work in reasoning about spatial relations. Section 3 outlines models for spatial relations and their composition. Section 4 explains the need for a heterogeneous reasoning mechanism that can combine inferences from knowledge of topological and direction relations. The canonical representation and model that enables heterogeneous reasoning is described in Section 5. The advantages of this canonical model are explained in Section 6, and conclusions and future work are discussed in Section 7.

2. Related Work in Topology-Direction Reasoning

Related work in topology-direction reasoning (Figure 1) has been done on (i) defining the composition of topological and orientation relations taken together (Hernández, 1994) with the result being pairs of topological/orientation relations; (ii) defining direction relations between extended objects in terms of interval relations, thereby facilitating the retrieval of spatial objects from a database using an R-tree based indexing mechanism (Papadias, 1994; Papadias *et al.*, 1995); and (iii) defining direction relations between extended objects using the 4-intersection (Abdelmoty and El-Geresy, 1994; Abdelmoty and Williams, 1994).

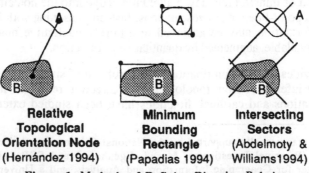

Relative Topological Orientation Node (Hernández 1994)   **Minimum Bounding Rectangle** (Papadias 1994)   **Intersecting Sectors** (Abdelmoty & Williams1994)

Figure 1. Methods of Defining Direction Relations

Hernández (1994) defined a combined topological and orientation relation structure called the relative topological orientation node (rton), which has the same relative neighborhood structure as the combined relations. The orientation relations are defined for point abstractions of the objects, and while methods for defining orientation relations for extended objects are described they are not used in determining the composition tables for topological/orientation relation tuples. The rton is used as an abstract map to represent the combined relationship between two objects such as disjoint/right, i.e., A is disjoint from and to the right of B. Composition is accomplished using the rtons as a store for the intermediate results and allows inferences such as if A disjoint/right B, B disjoint/right-back C then A disjoint/right or disjoint/right-back C. The compositions are defined only for the cases where objects are disjoint or touch and both the orientation and topological relation are known. This work was extended (Clementini *et al.*, 1994) to handle composition of distance/orientation tuples. The distance relations are qualitative distances such as close, far, and very far. Our present work seeks to develop a canonical representation and model that uses information regarding either the topological or direction or both relations.

Papadias (1994) defined cardinal direction relations between extended objects using a form of interval relations. He represents each object by a two-point abstraction, that is the lower-left and upper-right corners of the objects MBR called the first and second point, respectively. Direction relations are defined in terms of these abstractions. For example A is said to be strong_north of B if the Y-coordinate of the first point of A is greater than the Y-coordinate of the second point of B. Similarly, A is said to be weak_north of B if the Y-coordinate of the second point of A is greater than the Y-coordinate of the second point of B and the Y-coordinate of the first point of A is between the Y-coordinates of the two points of B. The directions North-West, North-East, South-West, South-East, South, East, and West are defined similarly. The advantage of using this two-point abstraction is that each direction relation corresponds to a fixed subset set of the 169 possible relations between two MBRs. This facilitates the retrieval of objects satisfying a specified direction relation from a spatial database that uses a spatial index based on rectangles, for example the R-tree.

Abdelmoty and colleagues (Abdelmoty and El-Geresy, 1994; Abdelmoty and Williams, 1994) extended the 4-intersection formalism for topological relations to represent cardinal directions. Each object's bounding rectangle together with four lines extending from the corners of the rectangle are used to divide the space external to the object into four semi-infinite areas. The direction relation between two objects is defined using the intersections of the components of these areas. Their formalism works for point or extended objects. The extended objects may be disjoint, overlapping, or one can contain the other permitting the definition of relations such as A is in the Northeast of B. A further advantage of their work is that it is valid for any frame of reference, that is intrinsic, extrinsic, or deictic. The work presented in this paper assumes an extrinsic frame of reference.

3. Models for the Composition of Spatial Relations

The *composition* of spatial relations is a useful inference mechanism that permits the derivation of a spatial relation between two objects A and C based on their relation with a common object B. The composition of A r_1 B with B r_2 C $\Rightarrow$ A r_3 C is denoted by r_1 ; $r_2 \Rightarrow r_3$. The composition may often result in a set of relations denoted by { }, for example r_1 ; $r_2 \Rightarrow \{r_3, r_4, r_5\}$. Consistency requirements dictate that the inferred set of relations between objects A and C be the set intersection of the compositions over common objects. For example if A r_1 B ; B r_2 $C \Rightarrow \{r_3, r_4, r_5\}$ and A r_1 D ; D r_2 $C \Rightarrow \{r_3, r_5, r_6\}$ then the set of possible relations between A and C is $\{r_3, r_5\}$. Such inferences require a definition of the spatial relations involved and the corresponding composition tables that define the results of each possible composition. The formalization of the relations and their compositions taken together form the model for spatial reasoning used in this paper.

3.1 Allen's Interval Relations

The thirteen possible relations between one dimensional intervals were described by Allen (1983) in his landmark paper on reasoning with temporal intervals. Figure 2 shows the geometric interpretation of these interval relations for one-dimensional objects A and B.

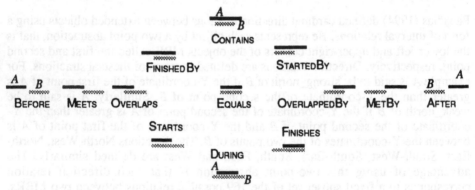

Figure 2. Allen's interval relations.

The composition of interval relations determines the relation, or set of possible relations, between intervals A and C based on the knowledge of the relations between A and B, and B and C. For example, MEETS ; CONTAINS $\Rightarrow$ BEFORE and hence A MEETS B and B CONTAINS C implies A BEFORE C.

The observation that Allen's interval relations are essentially topological relations in 1-dimension enhanced by the distinction of the order of the space leads to the possibility of using them as a canonical model for performing heterogeneous reasoning about direction and topological spatial relations between extended objects.

3.2 Topological Relations

The model used for reasoning about topological relations is based on the 4-intersection (Egenhofer and Franzosa, 1991), a generic model that applies to point sets as well as to any other topological data model such as cells or simplicial complexes (Egenhofer, 1993). The 4-intersection distinguishes eight binary topological relations, which will be referred to by *disjoint, meet, overlap, equal, inside, coveredBy, contain,* and *covers* (Figure 3). These topological relations can be considered as Allen's interval relations less their spatial ordering. Thus *disjoint* maps onto BEFORE or AFTER, *meet* maps onto MEETS or METBY, *overlap* maps onto OVERLAPS or OVERLAPPEDBY and so on. The *composition* of binary topological relations describes the topological constraint between two objects A and C based on the knowledge of the two topological relations between A and B, and between B and C (Egenhofer, 1994) For example, *meet* ; *contain* $\Rightarrow$ *disjoint* and hence A *meet* B and B *contain* C implies A *disjoint* C.

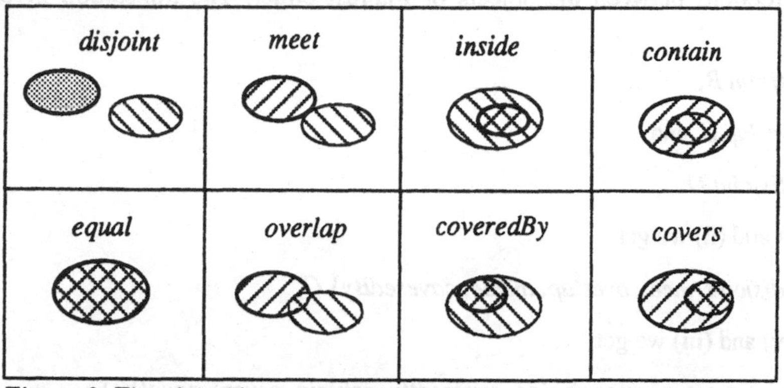

Figure 3. The eight binary topological relations between simple regions.

3.3   Direction Relations

Qualitative directions describe qualitative spatial relations with respect to a reference frame. Most common are cardinal directions (*North, South, East, West*) and their refinements such as *North-East* and *South-West* (Frank, 1992; Peuquet and Ci-Xiang, 1987). Most formalizations of cardinal directions assume that the objects of concern are point-objects. Since we are interested in spatial reasoning about topological relations and cardinal directions, it makes little sense to focus on point objects—all point objects are topologically disjoint or coincide, so any spatial reasoning of this form is of little challenge. Instead, we will employ a notion of cardinal directions that is fairly strict, but can be generalized to objects of higher dimensions.

Let A be a spatial object homeomorphic to a connected point-set embedded in a Cartesian plane such that each point P is specified by a pair of coordinates (P_x, P_y). The cardinal direction *West* between two points P and Q is defined as follows: P is *West* of Q if $P_x < Q_x$. *North, South* and *East* are defined similarly.

Based on the point relations, directions between spatial objects A and B are defined as follows: A is *West* of B if all points of A are *West* of all points of B, that is, for any pair of points p and q, such that $p \in A$ and $q \in B$, p is *West* of q. The composition of cardinal directions as defined above permits only inferences of the kind D_i ; $D_i \Rightarrow D_i$, where $D_i \in \{North, South, East, West\}$ (Frank, 1992).

4.   The Need for Heterogeneous Reasoning

For a situation where a heterogeneous inference is necessary consider that we are given four spatial objects such that A is *West* of B, B *overlap* with C, and C is *West* of D. The question is, "What is the cardinal direction between A and D?" By constructing a graphical rendering of this configuration the conclusion that A must be West of D

becomes evident (Figure 4), however with the given sole inference methods for directions and topology (Section 2), it is impossible to come to the same conclusion through symbolic manipulations. Since no direction relation exists between *B* and *C*, and none is specified between *B* and *D* a composition-based inference is impossible for the direction between *A* and *D*. Mere translation between direction relations and topological relations (*X West Y* $\Rightarrow$ *X disjoint Y*) provides insufficient information to infer directions between the objects of interest either. The translation gives the relations

(i) *A disjoint B*,

(ii) *B overlap C*, and

(iii) *C disjoint D*.

From (i) and (ii) we get

(iv) *A {disjoint, meet, overlap, inside, coveredBy} C*.

From (iv) and (iii) we get

A {disjoint, meet, overlap, inside, coveredBy, contain, covers, equal} D,

which essentially provides no information because it represents the universal relation.

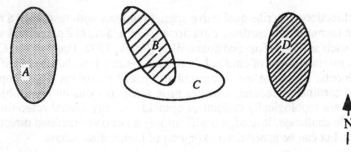

Figure 4. An example demonstrating the utility of topology-direction reasoning:
A West B and *B overlap C* and *C West A* $\Rightarrow$ *A West D*

5. Using the Canonical Method for Heterogeneous Reasoning

The overall goal is a mechanism for determining the composition of topological with direction relations or direction with topological relations resulting in either topological or direction relations (Figure 5). For example, we wish to perform inferences such as *A West of B*, *B overlap C*, and *C West of D* implies *A West of D* and *A disjoint D*.

| Topological Relations | $\odot$ | Cardinal Directions | $\Rightarrow$ | ? Topological Relations
? Cardinal Directions |

Figure 5. The goal: compositions over topological relations and cardinal directions.

Simple translations into either system of inferences is insufficient to solve the problem. With strict definitions for cardinal directions we may translate them to the topological relations *disjoint* or *meet* thereby permitting compositions over topological relations. However the results of such compositions frequently result in multiple possibilities or even no information. For example, translating A *North* of B and B *North* of C gives A *disjoint* B and B *disjoint* C. The composition *disjoint* ; *disjoint* gives the set of all possible relations, that is, {*disjoint, meet, overlap, equal, inside, coveredBy, contain, covers*}. The mapping of topological relations to cardinal directions is not established since *disjoint* maps to any of {*North, South, East, West*}, *equal, inside, coveredBy, contain,* and *covers* map onto the relation, same location, while *overlap* or *meet* do not map onto any cardinal direction.

In order to perform heterogeneous spatial reasoning one could map both topological and directions relations between spatial objects onto a canonical form in which compositions can be performed (Figure 6). The result of the composition is then mapped back onto cardinal directions or topological relations assuming one-to-one mappings between the canonical form and topological relations or cardinal directions are defined.

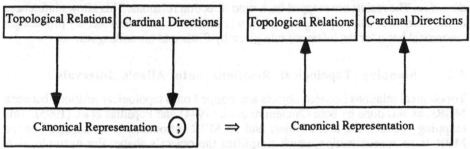

Figure 6. Using a canonical representation.

The mapping onto interval relations gives an approximation of the original spatial relations since there is some loss of information. In particular for topological relations this loss is due to the fact that the mapping is many-to-many. As evident from Figure 8 the interval relation MEETS could result from either topological relation *disjoint* or *meet* and *meet* maps onto one of 11 possibilities among interval relations. For direction relations we would need two interval relations, one each along the X- and Y-axis.

The particular approach used in this paper is (Figure 7):

(i) We use Allen's interval relations and their composition table as the canonical form.

(ii) To facilitate the mappings we use MBRs as an approximation for the spatial objects. Henceforth, mapping onto interval relations along either the X- or Y-axis is straightforward.

(iii) Reverse mappings from interval relations to cardinal directions. This mapping from is a partial one since at present we do not define cardinal directions for extended objects that have a containment relationship. That is, the interval relations EQUAL, DURING, and CONTAINS do not map onto any cardinal direction. The mapping from interval relations to topological relations is less well-defined presently and will be investigated in future.

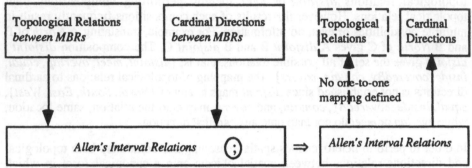

Figure 7. Using interval relations for heterogeneous spatial reasoning.

Compositions of relations are then computed using Allen's composition table for interval relations (Allen, 1983). Given such a heterogeneous reasoning mechanism we can then perform sequences of compositions such as *direction* ; *topological relation* ; *direction*. The results are mapped back onto direction relations. This allows inferences of the form *direction* ; *topological relation* ; *direction* ⇒ *direction* thereby providing a theoretical basis for the inference rule given by Sistla and his colleagues.

5.1   Mapping Topological Relations onto Allen's Intervals

Topological relations between objects are mapped onto topological relations between MBRs, as was done by both Clementini *et al.* (1994) and Papadias *et al.* (1995). This mapping between the actual object and its MBR introduces some ambiguities the MBR is an approximation which simplifies the object's shape. For example, if A *covers* B then the relationship between their MBRs may be *covers*, *contains*, or *equal*.

The benefit of using MBRs is that the reasoning mechanism is applicable for both areal and linear objects and hence there are no exceptions or special cases to be considered. Another advantage of using MBRs is that the MBR topologic relationships can be viewed as a combination of two interval relationships.

Topology of intervals is well understood and Allen's (1983) relationships can be easily integrated into the reasoning model used here. There are 169 possible binary topological relations between MBRs of two objects. Mapping these relations to the corresponding interval relation is accomplished by examining each axis of the MBRs separately. Figure 8 shows possible MBR configurations for each topological relation between two objects and the corresponding X-axis interval relations. Thus if two objects are disjoint then any one of the thirteen interval relations may hold between the X-axis projection of these objects.

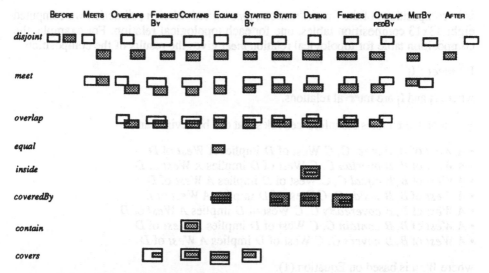

Figure 8. MBR topological mapped onto X-axis interval relations.

5.2 Mapping Direction Relations onto Allen's Intervals

The MBR is also used to create a mapping of direction relations between extended objects. The rules defined earlier are applied to the MBR. Thus *East-West* and *North-South* relations correspond directly to the axial interval relations and vice-versa. As an example, mappings are given for the direction *West* and are defined as follows:

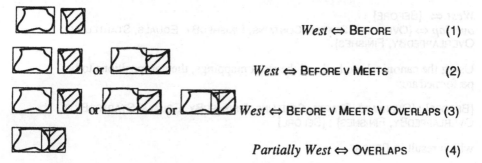

$$West \Leftrightarrow \text{BEFORE} \qquad (1)$$

$$West \Leftrightarrow \text{BEFORE} \vee \text{MEETS} \qquad (2)$$

$$West \Leftrightarrow \text{BEFORE} \vee \text{MEETS} \vee \text{OVERLAPS} \quad (3)$$

$$Partially\ West \Leftrightarrow \text{OVERLAPS} \qquad (4)$$

An example of a situation where *Partially West* occurs is the relationship between New York, Vermont, and Maine. Since New York is *Partially West* of Vermont but not *East* of it, and Vermont is *West* of Maine we can infer that New York is *West* of Maine. This inference can be made by using Allen's interval relations and their composition table. Considering the projections of the MBRs on the X-axis the composition in this case is OVERLAPS ; AFTER which results in BEFORE. Thus we conclude that New York is West of Maine.

6. Results from Using the Canonical Method

Given the mappings onto interval relations any sequence of compositions over cardinal directions or topological relations can be computed. Since our specific interest is in compositions of the form *direction* ; *topological relation* ; *direction* we computed eight 13x13 composition tables, one for each topological relation. For example, the composition table for topological relation *meet* gives the results of the composition

I_i ; *meet* ; I_j

where I_i and I_j are interval relations.

Based on these tables the inferences rules that can be devised are:

- *A West* of *B*, *B meet C*, *C* West of *D* implies *A West* of *D*
- *A West* of *B*, *B overlap C*, *C* West of *D* implies *A West* of *D*
- *A West* of *B*, *B equal C*, *C* West of *D* implies *A West* of *D*
- *A West* of *B*, *B inside C*, *C* West of *D* implies *A West* of *D*
- *A West* of *B*, *B coveredBy C*, *C* West of *D* implies *A West* of *D*
- *A West* of *B*, *B contain C*, *C* West of *D* implies *A West* of *D*
- *A West* of *B*, *B covers C*, *C* West of *D* implies *A West* of *D*

where *West* is based on Equation (1).

The inference given by Sistla *et al.* (1994) is *A dir B*, *B overlap C*, *C dir D* implies *A dir D*, where *dir* is one of {*West, East, North,* or *South*}. We systematically applied the canonical method of Allen's interval relations to derive the complete set of such rules over direction and topological relations which includes the above stated rule.

To illustrate the validity of Sistla's rule we use following mappings from direction and topological relations to interval relations:

West ⇔ {BEFORE}
overlap ⇔ {OVERLAPS, STARTS, CONTAINS, FINISHEDBY, EQUALS, STARTEDBY, OVERLAPPEDBY, FINISHES}.

Using the canonical method and the strict mappings, the compositions to be performed are:

{BEFORE} ; {OVERLAPS, STARTS, CONTAINS, FINISHEDBY, EQUALS, STARTEDBY, OVERLAPPEDBY, FINISHES} ; {BEFORE}

which result in BEFORE.

The above stated rules hold even if we relax the definition of *West* to that in Equation (2), to include the situation where the MBRs meet along one side. The compositions to be performed are:

{BEFORE, MEETS} ; {OVERLAPS, STARTS, CONTAINS, FINISHEDBY, EQUALS, STARTEDBY, OVERLAPPEDBY, FINISHES} ; {BEFORE, MEETS}

which result in BEFORE.

It is not possible to relax the definition further to include OVERLAPS as in Equation (3) because the compositions with OVERLAPS provide a result which includes every relation except AFTER and METBY. The compositions to be performed are:

{BEFORE, MEETS, OVERLAPS} ; {OVERLAPS, STARTS, CONTAINS, FINISHEDBY, EQUALS, STARTEDBY, OVERLAPPEDBY, FINISHES} ; {BEFORE, MEETS, OVERLAPS}

which result in {BEFORE, MEETS, OVERLAPS, STARTS, CONTAINS, FINISHEDBY, EQUALS, STARTEDBY, OVERLAPPEDBY, FINISHES, DURING}.

Using the definition for *Partially West*, Equation (4), gives the same result. The compositions to be performed are:

{OVERLAPS} ; {OVERLAPS, STARTS, CONTAINS, FINISHEDBY, EQUALS, STARTEDBY, OVERLAPPEDBY, FINISHES} ; {OVERLAPS}

which result in {BEFORE, MEETS, OVERLAPS, STARTS, CONTAINS, FINISHEDBY, EQUALS, STARTEDBY, OVERLAPPEDBY, FINISHES, DURING}.

The definition, *Partially West*, is useful though for situations such as the example given in Section 5.2. The composition, over cardinal directions, is New York *Partially West* of Vermont ; Vermont *West* of Maine, where *West* is defined by Equation (2). In terms of interval relations the composition is

{OVERLAPS} ; {BEFORE, MEETS}

which results in {BEFORE}

and hence we can conclude that New York is *West* of Maine.

7. Conclusions and Future Work

This paper has presented a method for inferences using combined knowledge of topological and direction relations. The use of Allen's intervals, as a canonical representation for both topological and direction relations, has permitted a limited but useful amount of reasoning to be performed. Even in situations which produce non-atomic results there may be some useful information derived. In the composition Partially West ; *overlap* ; *Partially West* it is still possible to say Not *East*.

Future work will include:

• Reasoning with interval relations for both axes to generate compositions for *Northeast, Southeast, Southwest,* and *Northwest.*

While this extension is straight forward, the complexity of the problem is increased due to number of ambiguous situations that can result.

• Compositions for other sequences of relations, for example *topological* ; *direction* ; *topological.*

The result of this sequence of compositions being direction and topological relations. This would permit inferences like: *A Inside B* ; *B North C* ; *C covers D* ⇒*A North* of D and *A disjoint D*.

• Testing different definitions for direction relations between extended objects.

The strict definition of *West* (Equation 1) can be relaxed as in Equations 2 and 3. Similarly the definition for *Partially West* could be relaxed to be OVERLAPS or

FINISHEDBY. This relaxation would allow inferences such as determining that Oregon is *West* of Wyoming given that Oregon is *West* of Montana and Montana is *Partially West* of Wyoming.

• Using information about legacy in reverse mappings.

Legacy information will help reduce the ambiguity when mapping back from interval to topological relations since it provides information about the initial mapping of topological relations onto interval relations.

8. References

Abdelmoty, A. I., and El-Geresy, B. A. (1994). An Intersection-Based Formalism for Representing Orientation Relations in a Geographic Database. In *2nd ACM Conference on Advances in GIS Theory*. Gaithersburg, MD: ACM Press.

Abdelmoty, A. I., and Williams, M. H. (1994). Approaches to the Representation of Qualitative Spatial Relationships for Geographic Databases. In M. Molenaar (Ed.), *Advanced Geographic Data Modelling (AGDM 94)*. Delft, Netherlands: Netherlands Geodetic Commission.

Allen, J. F. (1983). Maintaining Knowledge about Temporal Intervals. *Communications of the ACM, 26*(11), 832-843.

Chang, S. K., Shi, Q. Y., and Yan, C. W. (1987). Iconic Indexing by 2-D strings. *IEEE Transactions on Pattern Analysis and Machine Intelligence, PAMI-9*(6), 413-428.

Clementini, E., Sharma, J., Egenhofer, M. J. (1994a). Modelling Topological Spatial Relations: Strategies for Query Processing. *Computers and Graphics, 18*(6), 815-822.

Clementini, E., Di Felice, P., and Hernández, D. (1994b). *Qualitative Representation of Positional Information* (Technical Report), University of L'Aquila.

Egenhofer, M. J. (1993). A Model for Detailed Binary Topological Relationships. *Geomatica, 47*(3 & 4), 261-273.

Egenhofer, M. J. (1994). Deriving the Composition of Binary Topological Relations. *Journal of Visual Languages and Computing, 5*, 133-149.

Egenhofer, M. J., and Franzosa, R. (1991). Point-Set Topological Spatial Relations. *International Journal of Geographic Information Systems, 5*(2), 161-174.

Frank, A. (1992). Qualitative Reasoning about Distances and Directions in Geographic Space. *Journal of Visual Languages and Computing, 3*(4), 343-371.

Hernández, D. (1994). *Qualitative Representation of Spatial Knowledge*. New York: Springer-Verlag.

Papadias, D. (1994) *Relation-Based Representation of Spatial Knowledge*. PhD. Thesis. National Technical University of Athens.

Papadias, D., and Sellis, T. (1992). Spatial Reasoning Using Symbolic Arrays. In A. U. Frank, I. Campari, and U. Formentini (Ed.), *From Space to territory: Theories and Models of Spatio-Temporal Reasoning*, (pp. 153-161). Pisa, Italy: Springer-Verlag.

Papadias, D., Theodoridis, Y., Sellis, T., and Egenhofer, M. J. (1995). Topological Relations in the World of Minimum Bounding Rectangles: a Study with R-trees. In *ACM SIGMOD*. San Jose, CA: ACM Press.

Peuquet, D. J., and Ci-Xiang, Z. (1987). An algorithm to determine the directional relationship between arbitarily shaped polygons in the plane. *Pattern Recognition*, 20(1), 65-74.

Sistla, A. P., Yu, C., and Haddad, R. (1994). Reasoning about Spatial Relationships in Picture Retrieval Systems. In *20th International Conference on Very Large Databases*. Santiago, Chile.

2D Projection Interval Relationships: A Symbolic Representation of Spatial Relationships

Mohammad Nabil*, John Shepherd and Anne H.H. Ngu

School of Computer Science and Engineering
University of New South Wales
Sydney 2052, Australia
{nabil,jas,anne}@cse.unsw.edu.au

Abstract. Spatial relationships are important ingredients for expressing constraints in retrieval systems for spatial databases. In this paper we propose a unified representation of spatial relationships, 2D Projection Interval Relationships (2D-PIR), that integrates both directional and topological relationships. We propose a graph representation for pictures that is based on 2D-PIR. This graph representation can be constructed efficiently and leads to an efficient algorithm for "picture matching".

1 Introduction

Spatial relationships lie at the heart of spatial reasoning and form a vital part of spatial query languages. Two major kinds of spatial relationships have attracted the attention of researchers: directional relationships such as *left_of*, *right_of*, *above*, *below*, etc., (or in terms of *east*, *west*, *north*, *south*, etc.) and topological relationships such as *disjoint*, *touch*, *overlap*, *covers*, etc. Such relationships are used as constraints in spatial query expressions. For example, the following queries explicitly use directional relationships as constraints to retrieve an object: "find a gas station which is located west of a region in a map" or "find a picture containing a computer on the top of a table to the right of a bookcase".

To the best of our knowledge, very few attempts have been made in the literature to reason about directional and topological relationships under a unified representation. However, integration of directional and topological relationships is very useful, since it gives more expressive power than each individual kind of relationship alone. For example, with only directional relationships, we can say that The Netherlands are to the west of Germany, and with only topological relationships, we can say that Germany and The Netherlands have a common border (*meet*), but until we can deal with both kinds of relationship we cannot reason about The Netherlands being a western neighbour of Germany.

This paper describes 2D Projection Interval Relationships (2D-PIR), a simple but powerful representation which provides a unified framework for spatial

---

* On leave of absence from the Department of Agroindustrial Technology, Bogor Agricultural University; currently at School of Computer Science and Engineering–UNSW

(directional and topological) relationships. It is inspired by Allen's and Chang's work in [1] and [2]. This representation not only integrates directional and topological relationships but also describes detailed directional relationships between spatial objects. For example, using traditional directional relationships it is difficult to express directional relationships between The Netherlands and Germany since there exist parts of Germany which are west of, east of, north, as well as south of The Netherlands. By using interval relationships 2D-PIR we can express the spatial relationship between The Netherlands and Germany more completely and more precisely. Note that 2D-PIR is a symbolic representation: each spatial object is represented by a symbol. A symbolic picture is a digraph where nodes of the graph are symbols representing spatial objects and edges of the graph are labelled by 2D-PIR relationships.

This paper only considers 2D spatial objects (regions); however it is easy to extend to higher dimensional spatial objects. The core idea is that regions are projected along the x and y axes and then, using Allen's operators, spatial relationships among objects are encoded. This method has several advantages: (a) it is simple (that is, to derive a 2D-PIR representation is straightforward), (b) it is an efficient representation in terms of storage, (c) it can be as a basis for efficient picture matching (both exact and similarity matching) and spatial reasoning can be developed on top of this representation.

The remainder of this paper is organised as follows. Section 2 presents related work. In Section 3 we discuss Allen's interval relationships and Chang's 2D-strings. We then describe our model for representing spatial relationships. Section 4 discusses how we apply this model for picture retrieval. Section 5 discusses some possible extensions and applications. Finally we present our conclusions and suggestions for future development in Section 6.

2 Related Work

2.1 Directional Relationships

Directional relationships are heavily used in everyday life. We frequently mention an object based on its directional relationship with another object. For example, a mouse is to the right of a keyboard or Munich is north of Rome. According to [15] and [16] directional relationships are fuzzy concepts since they depend on human interpretation. Note also that directional relationships are influenced by the angle of view and orientation of objects.

Peuquet and Ci-Xiang [15] have developed a model for directional relationships between polygons by incorporating size, shape and distance. They also provide an algorithm to determine directional relationships between polygons in 2D space. Some characteristics of their directional relationships are: they are binary, each direction is coupled with a semantic inverse, the area of acceptance for any given direction increases with distance. Some other characteristics are that the area of acceptance for any given direction increases with the dimension in the facing direction of the reference object in relation to the second object, and in the selection between a pair of objects as the reference, the one which is "perceptually prominent" (the larger one) is preferred. In [16], fuzzy concepts were introduced into directional relationships, to account for the fact that such relationships are not necessarily exclusive. For example, if an object is above and to the left of another object, it may be perceived as being *above*, *left_of*, or some degree of both of these.

2.2 Topological Relationships

Topological relationships are relationships which are invariant under topological transformation (that is, they are preserved if the objects are translated, rotated, or scaled) [4].

Egenhofer [5] uses the concepts of *boundary* and *interior* of pointsets to derive topological relationships between two-dimensional regions (pointsets) embedded on a two-dimensional plane (R^2). If A and B are two regions, A^0 and ∂A denote the interior and boundary of A respectively, then all of the possible topological relationships between A and B can be derived from the possible combinations of intersection between their boundaries and interiors; that is $\partial A \cap \partial B, A^0 \cap B^0, \partial A \cap B^0$, and $A^0 \cap \partial B$. Each of these intersections is either empty (0) or non-empty (1). This results in 16 possible combinations as shown in Table 1.

	$\partial A \cap \partial B$	$A^0 \cap B^0$	$\partial A \cap B^0$	$A^0 \cap \partial B$	Relationships' Name
r_0	0	0	0	0	A and B are *disjoint*
r_1	0	0	0	1	*
r_2	0	0	1	0	*
r_3	0	0	1	1	*
r_4	0	1	0	0	*
r_5	0	1	0	1	A *contains* B or B *insides* A
r_6	0	1	1	0	A *insides* B or B *contains* A
r_7	0	1	1	1	A *overlaps* B (disjoint boundary)
r_8	1	0	0	0	A *meets* B
r_9	1	0	0	1	*
r_{10}	1	0	1	0	*
r_{11}	1	0	1	1	*
r_{12}	1	1	0	0	A *equals* B
r_{13}	1	1	0	1	A *covers* B
r_{14}	1	1	1	0	A *covered_by* B
r_{15}	1	1	1	1	A *overlaps* B (intersecting boundary)

*) indicates there is no topological relationship (proved in [5]).

Table 1. Topological relationships created from four intersections

There are nine valid topological relationships between two regions. But r_5 and r_6, r_{13} and r_{14} are inverses of each other. There are two *overlaps* relationships (r_7 and r_{15}) since disconnected boundaries are allowed. If boundaries are assumed to be connected, then r_7 is excluded. Hence, there are eight topological relationships: *disjoint, contains, insides, overlaps, meets, equal, covers* and *covered_by*. Note that these relationships are mutually exclusive.

3 2D Projection Interval Relationships

A 2D Projection Interval Relationship (2D-PIR) is a symbolic representation of directional as well as topological relationships among spatial objects. It adapts two existing representation formalisms (Allen's temporal intervals and 2D-strings) and combines them in a novel way to produce the unified representation. Note that in this paper we only deal with 2-dimensional spatial objects; higher dimensional spatial objects are a subject for future research, but appear to be a straightforward extension of the ideas presented here. The basic idea is that each spatial object is projected along the x and y axes forming an x-interval and y-interval for the object. Using the intervals and Allen's 13 interval relationships, spatial relationships are established. Before we discuss our method, we review Allen's interval relationships and 2D-strings.

Allen [1] proposed an interval-based temporal representation and introduced a method to derive relationships between intervals. Intervals can be represented by their endpoints assuming that every interval consists of a fully ordered set of points of time. Thus an interval is represented as an ordered pair of points with the first point less then the second, and so on. Based on this representation, thirteen relationships (seven relationships have inverses, one relationship has no inverse) are derived as shown in Table 2.

A 2D-string is a symbolic representation of a picture originally suggested by Chang et al. [2]. The representation is constructed from the original picture by stating directional relationships relative to a grid superimposed on the picture. An example is shown in Figure 1, where the upper-case letters represent spatial objects lying in the region of the plane bounded by each grid cell. Note that object A is large enough that it spans two cells.

DE		
	B	C
A	A	

Fig. 1. A symbolic picture

In Figure 1, we can straightforwardly determine directional relationships among objects. For instance, object B is on the *left_of* object C, object D

Relationship	Symbol	Symbol for Inverse	Pictorial Example
X *before* Y	<	>	XXXXX YYYYY
X *equal* Y	=	=	XXXXX YYYYY
X *meet* Y	m	mi	XXXXXYYYYY
X *overlaps* Y	o	oi	XXXXX YYYYY
X *during* Y	d	di	XXXXX YYYYYYYYYY
X *starts* Y	s	si	XXXXX YYYYYYYYYY
X *finishes* Y	f	fi	XXXXX YYYYYYYYYY

Note: X and Y are intervals

Table 2. Allen's interval relationships

is in the same set as (i.e. "near to") object E, and object C is at the *upper_right* of object A.

A 2D-string is a pair made up of the "symbolic projections" of a picture along the x-axis and y-axis. Construction of a 2D-string for a picture commences by laying a grid over the picture; the idea is that objects are partitioned over the cells of the grid (as in Figure 1). To generate a 2D-string from a picture, we scan along the x-axis, looking at the projections of objects on this axis, and describing the relationships between the objects using the operators "=", "<" and ":" ("=" represents the relationship "at the same projected location as", "<" represents the relationship "to the left of" and ":" represents "in the same set as" relation (note that ":" $\Rightarrow$ "=")). For example, in Figure 1, the x-axis relationships are: $A = D : E < A = B < C$. We then repeat this scan along the y-axis, to generate another string of relationships between objects (or, more precisely, their projections on the y-axis). In the example, this corresponds to: $A = A < B = C < D : E$. The 2D-string of the picture is the pair of object relationship strings.

More formally, a 2D-string is defined as follows: Let V be a set of symbols representing spatial objects. Let A be the set {"=", "<", ":"} of spatial relationships where $A \cap V = \emptyset$. A 1D-string over V is any string $x_1x_2...x_n, n \geq 0$, where the x_i are in V. A 2D-string over V, written as (u, v) is defined to be $x_1y_1x_2y_2...y_{n-1}x_n$, $x_{p(1)}z_1x_{p(2)}z_2...z_{n-1}x_{p(n)}$, where $x_1...x_n$ is a 1D-string over V, $p : \{1, ..., n\} \rightarrow \{1, ...n\}$ is a permutation over $\{1, ...n\}$, $y_1, ...y_{n-1}$ is a 1D-string over A and $z_1, ...z_{n-1}$ is a 1D-string over A. For Figure 1, V = {A,B,C,D,E}. The 2D-string representing it is $(A = D : E < A = B < C, A =$

$A < B = C < D : E$) which is called an *absolute* 2D-string. If the symbol "=" is omitted then the 2D representation becomes ($AD : E < AB < C, AA < BC < D : E$) which is called a *normal* 2D-string. If the symbol ":" is also omitted then the 2D-string becomes ($ADE < AB < C, AA < BC < DE$) which is called a *reduced* 2D-string. The *augmented* 2D-string is the *reduced* 2D-string where a permutation function is included in 2D string representation. The *augmented* 2D-string of the above picture is ($ADE < AB < C, AA < BC < DE, 145623$). The integer 145623 is a permutation function which represents positions of symbols in the second string in respect to the first string. For example the first A of the second string occupies the first position in the first string and the second A of second string occupies the fourth position in the first string. The *absolute* 2D-String provides a precise encoding of a picture, but is not a particularly efficient encoding scheme. The *normal* 2D-string provides more efficient encoding and the *reduced* 2D-string provides the most efficient encoding. However, in a *reduced* 2D-string the absolute positioning information is lost. The *augmented* 2D-string preserves positioning information so that picture reconstruction is not ambiguous.

There are several extensions of 2D-strings, but the main idea remains that a picture is partitioned over a grid before the 2D-string is generated. For example, in [11] a picture is partitioned both parallel to the x and y coordinate axes, where the partitions are performed at all the extreme points of all objects in the picture.

2D-PIR also uses the projection concept from the 2D-string representation. It differs from the 2D-string representation in using Allen's interval relationships over the projections of the entire objects along the x and y axes, rather than $\{<, :, =\}$. There is thus no need to partition the image initially. A consequence of this approach, however, is that we must use a *graph*, rather than a *string*, to represent the relationships among the objects in a picture.

Using Allen's operators (interval relationships), directional relationships between intervals, which are the projections of objects in both the x and y axes (interval projection relationships), can be generated. Furthermore they can also be used to capture topological relationships, especially for rectangular objects. The main advantage of this method is that it offers more information about spatial relationships between objects in a picture as compared to traditional method. In other words, it has more expressive power than traditional methods. We will illustrate this power later.

A 2D-PIR between two spatial objects A and B is (χ, ψ). The domain of χ and ψ are $\{<, =, m, o, d, s, f, >, mi, oi, di, si, fi\}$ which are symbols for interval relationships. Note that χ represents the interval relationship between objects A and B projected along the x-axis, and ψ represents the interval relationship between objects A and B projected along the y-axis. Figure 2 illustrates this.

In Figure 2 2D-PIR between A and B is $(<, oi)$, between A and C is $(<, m)$ and between B and C is (fi, si). Let us consider these relationships. What kind of information do we get when the 2D-PIR for A and B is $(<, oi)$? First, it tells us that A and B are *disjoint* and A is *left of* B since $x_A < x_B$. Secondly, it

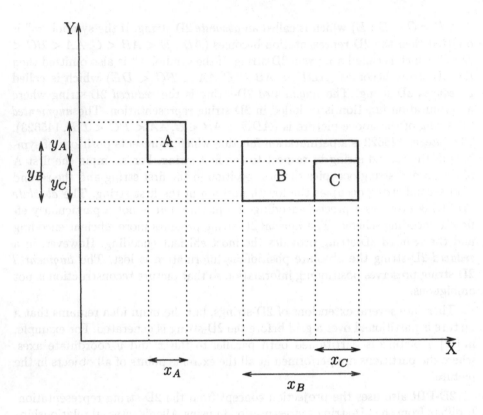

Fig. 2. A 2D-projection picture

informs us that *part of* A is *above* B since y_A *oi* y_B or y_B *o* y_A. Now, we turn to B and C. The 2D-PIR between B and C is (fi, si). The information we can get from this relationship is: 1) B *covers* C (or C *covered by* B), 2) C is located on the bottom-left of B. Thus, we can infer that C is covered by B on the bottom-left.

The above example shows only rectangular objects whose boundaries are parallel to the x and y axes. The shape of real world objects is rarely so simple or regular. To solve this problem, the 2D-string representation uses a minimum bounding rectangle (MBR) on each object, with rectangle boundaries parallel to horizontal (x) and vertical (y) axes. Adopting this approach effectively means ignoring the orientation of objects. In the case of 2D-PIR, this causes problems, as depicted in Figure 3. In this figure, 2D-PIR between A and B is (di, di). The relationship that would be inferred is B *inside* A (A *contains* B) which is incorrect. There are two alternatives to solve this problem.

The first approach introduces topological relationships into 2D-PIRs. A 2D-PIR is now defined as a triple (δ, χ, ψ) where δ is a topological relationship from

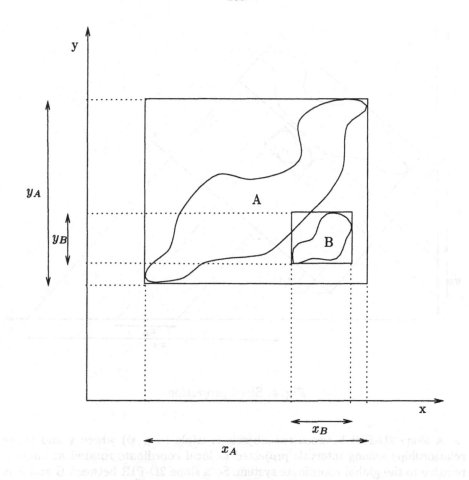

Fig. 3. Another 2D-projection picture

the set $\{dt, to, ct, in, ov, co, eq, cb\}^2$. By introducing these topological relationships, bounding rectangles are not needed. The relationship between A and B will be (dt, di, di) which indicates that A and B are *disjoint* objects and B is *surrounded by* A. The triple (dt, di, di) is interpreted as the "surrounded by" relationship, since $\chi = di$ and $\psi = di$ implies that there exists *parts of* A which are *right, left, above* as well as *below* B.

The second approach uses *true* MBRs (that is, MBRs whose boundaries are governed by an orientation angle φ). Each object is surrounded by an MBR, and then a local coordinate system is created whose axes are parallel to the edges of the MBR for the largest object. Next, projection is performed based on a local coordinate system (slope projection) as explained in [9, 10]. Figure 4 is an example of slope projection of objects in Figure 3.

---

[2] These represent the topological relationships *disjoint, meets, contains, insides, overlaps, covers, equal, covered_by*

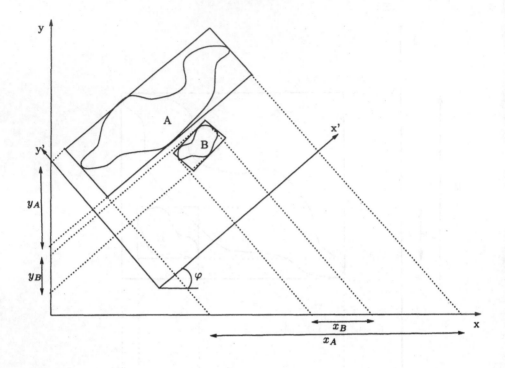

Fig. 4. Slope projection

A slope 2D-PIR between two objects is triple (φ, χ, ψ) where χ and ψ are relationships among intervals projected in local coordinate rotated at angle φ relative to the global coordinate system. So a slope 2D-PIR between B and A is $(\varphi, d, <)$ which tells that A is *above* and *disjoint* with B and part of A is *left of* as well as *right of* B according to the orientation angle φ. Note that the angle φ is available when the MBR of an object is computed.

Both approaches have advantages and disadvantages. The first approach guarantees the correctness of derived spatial relationships. However, it requires extra power to compute the topological relationships. One may refine this approach for objects whose relationship is (dt, di, di) or (dt, d, d) (that is disjoint objects whose MBRs overlap completely). For example, in Figure 3, if B is on the other side of A then the 2D-PIR relationship is still (dt, di, di). To discriminate these situations, the bigger object (in this case A) is divided using vertical strips corresponding to the smaller object's (in this case B) projection on the x-axis (this is also applied on the y-axis). This subdivides A into at most three pieces, where each piece a has 2D-PIR relationship with B. Final relationships between A and B will be a sequence of three 2D-PIR relationships.

The second approach provides a simple solution, since the angle φ is available when the MBR of an object is computed However, it allows incorrect spatial relationships to be derived if the MBR of an object overlaps another object as depicted in Figure 5.

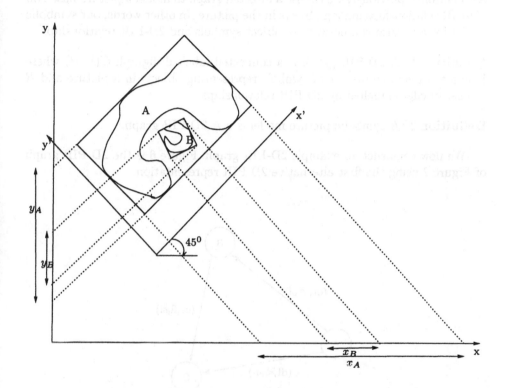

Fig. 5. Picture with MBR objects completely overlap

In Figure 5, the spatial relationships between A and B using the first and second approaches are (dt, di, di) and $(45, di, di)$ respectively. Note that $\varphi = 45^0$ means the orientation angle of the referred object is parallel to the x-axis. Note also that the first approach gives the correct spatial relationship between A and B. A *disjoint* with B and $\chi = di$ and $\psi = di$ can be interpreted as B is *surrounded by* A. The second approach cannot detect that A and B are *disjoint*. The relationship $(45, di, di)$ between A and B is best interpreted as B *inside* A, which is incorrect.

Both approaches are useful for different applications. For example, in multimedia databases, retrieval of images based on *similarity* is a central idea. For this application, both alternatives could be used. The first alternative will guarantee that only correct answers are returned. The second alternative will give more answers and some of them will not be valid answers to the query. In picture similarity retrieval, users generally expect to have to do some post-filtering of query results. However, we prefer to use the first alternative, since it guarantees the correctness of spatial relationships among objects in a picture. Hence, it is possible to develop reasoning mechanisms on it.

The above discussion provides the basis for our symbolic model for pictures. As mentioned previously we choose a directed graph to model a picture based on 2D-PIR relationships among objects in the picture. In other words, our symbolic model for a picture is a network of object symbols and 2D-PIR relationships.

Definition 1. A 2D-PIR graph is a connected labelled digraph $G(V, R)$ where V is a finite non-empty set of symbols representing objects in a picture and R is a set of edges labelled by 2D-PIR relationships.

Definition 2. A symbolic picture model is a A 2D-PIR graph.

We now construct an example 2D-PIR graph. Figure 6 is the 2D-PIR graph of Figure 2 using the first alternative 2D-PIR representation.

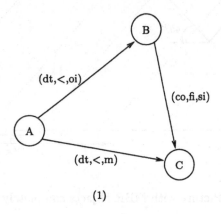

(1)

Fig. 6. A 2D-PIR graph

4 Picture Retrieval Using 2D-PIR

In the previous section, we formally defined 2D-PIR graphs. Since a picture is represented by a graph then to decide whether or not two pictures are equivalent or similar it is necessary to compare the corresponding graph representations. The fundamental equality relationship between graphs is known as *graph isomorphism*. Two graphs G_1 and G_2 are *isomorphic* if there exists a 1-1 and onto function $f : V(G_1) \to V(G_2)$ such that $xy \in E(G_1)$ if, and only if

$f(x)f(y) \in E(G_2)$ [8]. Detecting graph isomorphism in the general case is known to be NP-Hard. However, if we construct our 2D-PIR graphs carefully, we can devise efficient processing algorithms for them. The basic idea is to choose a fixed topology for the graph representing a picture. Using the characteristics of directional relationships that were described in the previous section, the graph construction method is simple and straightforward.

4.1 Graph Construction

The graph that represents a picture can be constructed using the following simple algorithm.

Algorithm: Graph construction
input: A preprocessed picture (all objects are recognised and all necessary
information such as topological and projection relationships
have been computed)
output: A directed graph (adjacency list) representing the picture
begin
(1) Arrange objects from left to right and top to bottom (that is objects
in the picture are sorted based on their position left-right and then
top-bottom priority.
(2) Let P be the ordered set of objects in a picture based on the arrangement
(3) in (1) for each object O_i in P
(4)   create a linked-list of 2D-PIR relationships with the rest of the objects.
(5) endfor
end.

The time complexity of this algorithm is easily analysed. Lines 1 and 2 are $O(1)$ and lines 4 to 5 are $O(e)$ where e is the number of edges in the graph which is always $(n^2 - n)/2$ (n is the number of objects in the picture). Thus, the complexity of the algorithm in term of objects is $O(n^2)$. Figure 7 is an example of a picture and its corresponding graph (adjacency list) constructed by the algorithm.

4.2 Picture Matching

There are two kinds of picture retrieval: picture retrieval based on exact matching and picture retrieval based on similarity matching. Both of these retrieval techniques can be supported by the 2D-PIR representation using a picture matching algorithm that will be presented shortly. The 2D-PIR representation can retrieve pictures based on sub-picture match (exact and similar) using the same algorithm. Note that if symbolic pictures are constructed using the previous graph construction algorithm, then the picture matching algorithm is simple and straightforward.

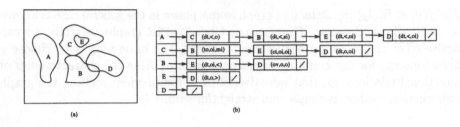

(a)   (b)

Fig. 7. A picture (a) and the corresponding graph (adjacency list) (b)

Algorithm: Picture matching
input: two 2D-PIR graphs (G_1 and G_2) representing pictures P_1 and P_2.
output: integer 0 : no-match
               integer 1: P_1 is a sub-picture of P_2
               integer 2: P_1 is equivalent of P_2
begin
    (1)   if $V(G_1) = V(G_2)$ then
    (2)   for $v_i \in V(G_1)$
    (3)   if linked-list of $v_i \in V(G_1)$ = linked-list $v_i \in V(G_2)$
    (4)   continue
    (5)   else return 0 /*no match*/
    (6)   endif
    (7)   return 2 /* P_1 is equivalent with P_2 */
    (8)   endfor
    (9)   elseif $V(G_1) \subset V(G_2)$ then
    (10)   for $v_i \in V(G_1)$
    (11)   find $v_j \in V(G_2)$ such that $v_i = v_j$
    (12)   if each element of linked-list v_i is also element of linked-list v_j
    (13)   continue
    (14)   else return 0 /*no match*/
    (15)   endif
    (16)   return 1 /*P_1 is sub-picture of P_2*/
    (17)   endfor
    (18)   else return 0 /*no match*/
    (19) endif
end.

A query picture in the above algorithm is a picture or a picture sketch which is used by a user to pose a query. The above algorithm assumes that a query picture contains at most the same number of objects as the number of objects in the intended picture stored in a database. This assumption seems reasonable since users tends to make relatively simple queries containing only a small number of objects. However, the algorithm can be modified easily if a query picture is allowed to be "super-picture" of a database picture. The algorithm can also be extended to deal with a query picture which overlaps a database picture.

This algorithm is dominated by lines 2 to 8 or line 10 to 17, which require $(n^2 - n)/2$ comparisons – that is, $O(n^2)$ in the worst case. Note that n is the number of objects in P_1. It is efficient when compared to the general graph isomorphism algorithm that needs $n^2 n!$ comparisons [8]. It is also better than the 2D-string matching algorithm which is $O(M) + O(N^2 * lp^3)$. Note that both M and N in the 2D-string matching algorithm are the number of entries in matching tables which are greater than the number of objects in a picture (since the 2D-string method uses partition) and lp is the maximum length of matching tables.

Let us look at some examples and demonstrate how the algorithm works. **Example 1.** shown in Figure 8 has two pictures: a query picture (QP) and a database picture (DP).

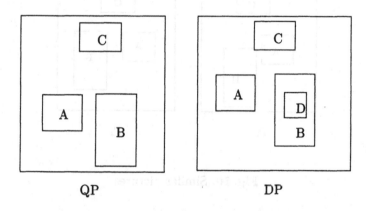

QP   DP

Fig. 8. Example 1: picture matching

Figure 9 contains graphs (symbolic picture models), represented as adjacency-lists, for QP and DP constructed by the graph construction algorithm.

These graphs are inputs for the picture matching algorithm. The execution of the algorithm is as follows: since the nodes of QP are a subset of the nodes of DP ($V(QP) \subset V(DP)$), the algorithm executes lines 10 to 17. The linked-list comparison between the same element (node) of QP and DP (line 16) is always true, so the algorithm will return 1 (QP is a sub-picture of DP).
Example 2. Replace the symbol C in QP of Example 1 with another symbol, e.g. M. The picture matching algorithm will quickly detect that QP does not match with DP (line 18).

The picture matching algorithm described above performs exact matching. This type of matching is probably not very useful for certain applications. For

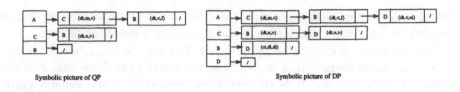

Symbolic picture of QP   Symbolic picture of DP

Fig. 9. Symbolic pictures of Figure 8

example, in multimedia applications similarity retrieval is preferred. Consider picture 10

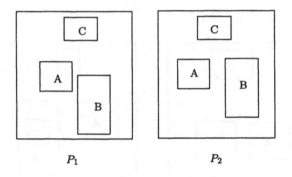

P_1 P_2

Fig. 10. Similar pictures

Using the picture matching algorithm above, pictures P_1 and P_2 are considered "not to match", since the relationships between A and B in P_1 $(dt, <, oi)$ and P_2 $(dt, <, f)$ are different. However, most users would consider P_1 and P_2 to be similar.

It is not our intention to discuss similarity matching in detail, so we simply highlight some important aspects of similarity matching using the 2D-PIR representation. The core idea is how to *measure* that two pictures are considered similar. By quantifying the concept "*degree of similarity*", we can perform useful retrieval operations such as thresholding and ranking.

The degree of similarity between two pictures represented using 2D-PIR picture is dependent on the degree of similarity between their corresponding 2D-PIR relationships. The degree of similarity between 2D-PIR relationships, in turn, is dependent on the degree of similarity between components of 2D-PIRs. For example, the degree of similarity between $(\delta_1, \chi_1, \psi_1)$ and $(\delta_2, \chi_2, \psi_2)$ is dependent on the degree of similarity between δ_1 and δ_2, χ_1 and χ_2, and ψ_1 and ψ_2. As a result, it is necessary to construct similarity metrics both for topological relationships (δ) as well as for interval relationships (χ or ψ).

The notion of *topological distance* as well as closest-topological-relationship-graph developed in [6] can be used to measure the degree of similarity between two topological relationships.

A metric for interval distance can be developed from the notion of *conceptual neighbours* introduced by Freksa [7]. According to Freksa, two intervals are *conceptual neighbours*, if they can be directly transformed into one another by continuously deforming (i.e shortening, lengthening, moving) the intervals (in a topological sense). For example, the relationship *before* ($<$) and *meets* (m) are conceptual neighbours, since they can be transformed into one another directly by lengthening one of the intervals.

The algorithm for similarity matching is almost the same as the algorithm for exact matching, except that, instead of returning 0, 1 or 2, it returns a measure of the degree of similarity. For similarity retrieval, a sequence of pictures governed by the degree of similarity with the query picture will be retrieved. The final decision as to which picture is appropriate is left to a secondary filtering stage.

5 Application and Extension

A potential application of this work is in fast picture retrieval from a multimedia database. Current work in content-based retrieval for images uses colour, texture and shape [14, 3, 12, 13]. The present work can be used to enhance current retrieval methods. Picture retrieval using spatial relations, as presented in this paper, is also useful for Geographical Information System (GIS) and Computer Aided Design (CAD) applications.

Our definition of symbolic picture models using 2D-PIR graphs directly supports graphical query. Using this scheme, the user draws a query in a window using a mouse. This picture query will be translated to a 2D-PIR graph and, using our picture matching algorithm, the intended picture(s) can be retrieved.

2D-PIR can be extended to 3D-PIR to represent spatial relationships in a three dimensional space. An object in three dimensional space can be projected into x, y, and z axes to form 3D-PIR.

2D-PIR can potentially be extended to moving objects by incorporating time intervals into the relationships, forming spatiotemporal relationships. A 2D-PIR model of a picture can be extended to spatiotemporal projection relationships (ST-PIR) to represent relationships among moving objects in a scene. This extension of 2D-PIR looks promising, since ST-PIR will significantly reduce the storage requirement for representing moving objects in a scene, and hence moving object queries can be answered in a reasonable time.

6 Conclusion

This paper proposes a unified representation of spatial relationships using 2D-PIR. A 2D-PIR is a spatial relationship representation that integrates topological and directional relationships in one unified representation. This paper also proposes a method for symbolic modelling of pictures using 2D-PIR graphs. A 2D-PIR graph is a graph where the nodes represent the objects in a picture and the edges are labelled by spatial relationships represented by 2D-PIR.

We have shown that using minimum bounding rectangles (MBR) with boundaries parallel to horizontal and vertical axes will cause problems in 2D-PIR relationship interpretation. We propose two alternative solutions: slope projection and introduction of topological relationships into 2D-PIR representation. Slope projection does not solve the interpretation problem for overlapping MBR; however, it is a simple solution and may be preferred for certain applications where correctness is not very important or applications where there are not many overlapping objects. Introducing topological relationships into 2D-PIR guarantees a correct interpretation of a 2D-PIR relationship, but extra computation is needed to derive topological relationships.

A symbolic picture model using a 2D-PIR graph is a simple, yet powerful representation of a picture. A 2D-PIR graph is constructed from a picture using a simple, efficient method. The construction also leads to a graph structure for which we develop an efficient picture-matching algorithm, which can perform both exact matching and similarity-metric matching.

2D-PIR relationships as well as 2D-PIR graphs have the potential for application to GIS, CAD, multimedia databases and image databases. Using 2D-PIR graphs, picture retrieval can be implemented relatively efficiently. In addition, it supports a direct graphical query facility (e.g. by drawing in a window).

Further possibilities for this work include: spatial reasoning using 2D-PIR, extending 2D-PIR to 3D-PIR, extending 2D-PIR and 2D-PIR graphs for moving objects (incorporating time in 2D-PIR).

References

1. J. F. Allen. Maintaining knowledge about temporal intervals. *Communications of the ACM*, 26(11):832–843, November 1983.
2. S. K. Chang, Q. Y. Shi, and C. W. Yan. Iconic indexing by 2D strings. *IEEE Transactions on Pattern Recognition and Machine Intelligent*, PAMI-9(3):413–428, 1987.
3. T.-S. Chua, S.-K. Lim, and H.-K. Pung. Content-based retrieval of segmented images. In *Proceedings Second Annual ACM Multimedia Conference*, 1994.
4. E. Clementini, P. Felice, and P. van Oostrom. A small set of formal topological relationships suitable for end-user interaction. In *Advances in Spatial Databases*, volume 692 of *Lecture Notes in Computer Science*, pages 277–295. Springer-Verlag, 1993.
5. M. J. Egenhofer. Point-set topological spatial relations. *Int. J. Geographical Information Systems*, 5(2):161–174, 1991.
6. M. J. Egenhofer and K. K. Al-Taha. Reasoning about gradual changes of topological relationships. In A. Frank, I. Campari, and U. Formentini, editors, *Theories and Methods of Spatio-Temporal Reasoning in Geographic Space*, number 639 in Lecture Notes in Computer Science, pages 196–219. Springer-Verlag, 1992.

7. C. Freksa. Temporal reasoning based on semi-intervals. *Artificial Intelligence*, 54(1-2):199–227, 1992.
8. R. Gould. *Graph Theory*. The Benjamin/Cummings Publishing Company, Inc, California, 1988.
9. E. Jungert. Qualitative spatial reasoning from the observer's point of view–toward a generalization of symbolic projection. *Pattern Recognition*, 27(6):801–813, 1994.
10. E. Jungert. Rotation invariance in symbolic slope projection as a means to support spatial reasoning. In *Workshop on Spatial and Temporal Interaction: Representation and Reasoning*, pages 166–170. 1994.
11. E. Jungert and S. K. Chang. An image algebra for pictorial data manipulation. *CVGIP: Image Understanding*, 58(2):147–160, September 1993.
12. H. Lu, B.-C. Ooi, and K.-L. Tan. Efficient image retrieval by color content. Department of Information Systems and Computer Science, National University of Singapore, 1994.
13. R. Mehrota and J. E. Gary. Feature-based retrieval of similar shapes. In *9th International Conference on Data Engineering*, pages 108–115, April 19-23 1993.
14. W. Niblack, R. Barber, W. Equitz, M. Flicker, E. Glasman, D. Petkovic, P. Yanker, C. Falautsos, and G. Taubin. The QBIC project: Querying images by content using color, texture, and shape. Research Report, Report Rj 9203(81511), IBM Almanden Research Center, San Jose, CA., 1993.
15. D. J. Peuquet and Z. Ci-Xiang. An algorithm to determine the directional relationship between arbitrary-shaped polygons in the plane. *Pattern Recognition*, 20(1):65–74, 1987.
16. T. Takahashi, N. Shima, and F. Kishino. An image retrieval method using inqueries on spatial relationships. *Journal of Information Processing*, 15(3):441–449, 1992.

Topological Relations between Discrete Regions

Stephan Winter*

Institute for Photogrammetry, University of Bonn, Germany

Abstract. Topological reasoning is important for speeding up spatial queries, e.g. in GIS or in AI (robotics). While topological relations between spatial objects in the vector model ($\mathbb{R}^2$) are investigated thoroughly, we run into inconsistencies in the raster model ($\mathbb{Z}^2$). But instead of reducing our requirements in case of reasoning in raster images we change from simple raster to a cellular decomposition of $\mathbb{R}^2$ — what we call a hyper-raster — which is also discrete, but preserves the topology of $\mathbb{R}^2$. The discrete representation reduces the computational effort against the vector model.

We will introduce a data structure for the hyper-raster, which represents regions, curves and points. Then we will present algorithms for digitization (vector/hyper-raster conversion). With the hyper-raster the intersection sets, as needed for the determination of a topological relation between two objects, are calculated simply by logical joins of binary images. Without extending our model we can also compute further refinements of the relationships.

1 Introduction

Topological relations have been found useful for speeding up spatial queries, e.g. in GIS or in AI (robotics). The analysis of topological relations may reduce the burden of geometric computations. Sometimes they are solely sufficient, and no further geometric analysis is needed. Therefore, topology should be taken into consideration in spatial data modeling.

While topological relations between spatial objects in the vector model ($\mathbb{R}^2$) can be based on Euclidean topology, which has lead to a symbolic reasoning framework (e.g. Egenhofer and Franzosa 1991, Egenhofer and Herring 1991, Clementini and Di Felice 1994), the *'digital topology'* of the raster model ($\mathbb{Z}^2$, Kong and Rosenfeld 1989, Latecki 1992) is not as powerful and needs conceptual extensions of the cited framework (Egenhofer and Sharma 1993). Instead of reducing our requirements in case of reasoning in raster images we propose to change from simple raster to a cellular decomposition of $\mathbb{R}^2$ (Kovalevski 1989) — what we call a hyper-raster —, which is also discrete, but preserves the topology of $\mathbb{R}^2$.

- We show that the hyper-raster is an intuitive and convenient model to describe topological properties and relations, contrary to the raster. We

* Supported by the *Deutsche Forschungsgemeinschaft*, Sonderforschungsbereich 350.

demonstrate the suitability for topological reasoning by applying Egenhofer's framework of 9-intersections (Egenhofer and Franzosa 1991), without any contradiction or conceptual difference to the vector model.

- The finiteness of the decomposition, in combination with a separate storage of hyper-raster element types, allows to applicate image processing algorithms (Kovalevski 1989, Bieri and Metz 1991). This will speed up the reasoning. We show in a practical example how to apply the reasoning framework to the hyper-raster.

In this paper we concentrate on relations between regions without holes. This is taken as an example, because the hyper-raster is neither limited in representing spatial objects of other dimensions, or holes, nor in topological properties. Both are pointed out in the corresponding sections. Also taking into consideration holes, or lines and points, would only cause additional complexity in reasoning, and would take away the intuitive clarity of this short paper.

This paper has the following structure. After an overview of the relevant notions of topology we summarize the work of others in topological reasoning. Then we introduce the hyper-raster model and a proper data structure for the representation of regions, curves and points. We will also describe the vector-to-hyper-raster conversion. After transferring the 9-intersection to the hyper-raster we specify the calculation of the 9-intersection. The calculation is reduced to logical joins of binary images. Without model extensions we can also compute further refinements of the relationship by image analysis, e.g. the number, the size, the dimension or the shape of intersection components.

An example will demonstrate the operability. The properties of the hyper-raster recommend it as a possible component to integrate vector-based and raster-based spatial data models.

2 Topological Models for GIS

In this chapter we give a short summary of the notions of *algebraic* and *digital* *topology*, pointing out the conceptional difference of vector and raster. Furthermore we introduce the hyper-raster as a regular cellular complex.

2.1 Euclidean Topology

In $\mathbb{R}^2$ we refer to Euclidean topology. Euclidean space is a topological space, that means (Jänich 1994):

Definition 1. A *topological space* is a pair $(X, \mathcal{O})$ of a set X and a set $\mathcal{O}$ of subsets of X, called the open sets, which satisfy

1. the union of open sets is open,
2. the intersection of finitely many open sets is open,
3. $\emptyset$ and X are open.

To become a metric space, a distance measure d has to be introduced additionally. Confining here to Euclidean topology, the Euclidean distance is chosen.

Definition 2. If (X, d) is a metric space, then a subset $V \subset X$ is called *open*, if for all $x \in V$ an $\varepsilon > 0$ exists with the sphere $K_\varepsilon(x) := \{y \in X | d(x, y) \leq \varepsilon\}$ in V. The set $\mathcal{O}(d)$ of all open subsets of X is called the *topology of the metric space* (X, d).

The topology of $\mathbb{R}^2$ is used widely in *data modeling* (e.g. Herring 1987, Bennis *et al.* 1991, Pigot 1991, Molenaar *et al.* 1994, Pilouk *et al.* 1994), and also in *topological reasoning* (Egenhofer and Franzosa 1991, Clementini and Di Felice 1994, and Hernández 1994).

In $\mathbb{R}^2$ Jordan's curve theorem is valid, which is important in the following sections:

Theorem 3. *A simple closed and continuous curve divides the plane into two regions, the interior and the exterior.*

2.2 Digital Topology

This short summary of topological deficiencies of raster images is to contrast with the hyper-raster, which is based on Euclidean topology. The hyper-raster follows in the next section.

A raster is a two-dimensional array of elements with integer coordinates, which can also be interpreted as a lattice $\mathbb{Z} \times \mathbb{Z}$. The raster is only of trivial topology, because the definition of a distance notion is possible, but all sets in a raster are open. Mathematicians speak of *digital topology*, but we have to pay attention to the different meaning of the notion in image processing literature.

Because in a raster we can not distinguish between open and closed sets, the difference between the closure of a pixel set and the open interior is empty, so we have no boundary in a raster. Also Jordan's curve theorem is only applicable with additional definitions of a neighborhood and a boundary curve (Kong and Rosenfeld 1989).

The '*digital topology*', as surveyed by Kong and Rosenfeld (1989) for the use in binary image analysis, differs from the above mentioned topology, because it does not refer to the definition of a topological space. To avoid paradoxa, all topological notions were defined algorithmically, and not by a derivation from the definitions of Sect. 2.1.

However, Kong and Rosenfeld discuss topological properties of binary image arrays. An interior (resp. exterior) boundary curve is introduced as a sequence of interior (resp. exterior) border points. These substitutes for boundary curves have a certain extent. Topologically they are 2D-sets, i.e. regions. Only with different concepts of pixel neighborhood for foreground and background is Jordan's curve theorem valid in the raster model. But these definitions cause contradictions if we permute foreground and background. Latecki *et al.* (1995) limit the

raster model by excluding the pixel compositions which cause paradoxical interpretations, thus foreground-background contradictions will not occur. However,
in this limited model, curves have to be defined as two-dimensional structures.

This *'digital topology'* of Kong and Rosenfeld, further restricted by some
conditions concerning the size and shape of regions, is used by Egenhofer and
Sharma (1993), as referred in Section 3.2. They have to model the results of the
topological deficiencies, while our proposal to use the hyper-raster instead does
not leave Euclidean topology.

2.3 Cellular Decomposition

We are now prepared to introduce the hyper-raster. Using notions from the
Euclidean topology (Sect. 2.1) we define (Jänich 1994):

Definition 4. We call a topological space an *n-cell*, if it is homeomorphic to
$\mathbb{R}^n$.

A *cellular decomposition* $(X, \mathcal{E})$ of a topological space X is a decomposition
of X into parts $\mathcal{E}$, which are cells by themselves.

We distinguish further:

Definition 5. The *interior* of a region $\mathcal{R}$, $\overset{\circ}{\mathcal{R}}$, is a connected and open complex
of dimension 2.

The *closure* of a region $\mathcal{R}$, $\overline{\mathcal{R}}$, is the minimal sub-complex which contains the
interior of $\mathcal{R}$ and all faces of the elements of $\overset{\circ}{\mathcal{R}}$.

The *boundary* of a region $\mathcal{R}$, $\partial\mathcal{R}$, is now $\partial\mathcal{R} = \overline{\mathcal{R}} \setminus \overset{\circ}{\mathcal{R}}$.

The *complement* $\mathcal{R}^c$ of a region $\mathcal{R}$ is $\mathcal{R}^c = X \setminus \overline{\mathcal{R}}$.

It follows that the boundary of a region is at the same time the boundary of
its complement.

For example, the *vector model* of spatial databases is based on an irregular
cellular decomposition of a surface (2.5D) or a plane (2D). In the vector model
boundaries of regions are represented as closed polygons. Polygons are continuous curves by nature, because the line segments are connected by common
vertices. Therefore, Jordan's curve theorem (Theorem 3) is valid for the vector
model.

To overcome the topological problems with $\mathbb{Z}^2$, Kovalevski (1989) proposes
a *regular* cellular decomposition of the plane. This decomposition only limits
the set of considered structures in $\mathbb{R}^2$ to regular shaped cells, but it preserves
the topology of $\mathbb{R}^2$, as the decomposition is embedded in the continuous plane
(homeomorphism). This decomposition is able to substitute the image model[2]
of $\mathbb{Z}^2$ (raster).

---

[2] 1D-edge elements between raster pixels have already been used in image segmentation, there better known as *crack edges* (see e.g. Ballard and Brown 1982, Bässmann
and Besslich 1991.

To decompose the plane, we choose axis-parallel, open quadrangles of the side length 1 as 2-cells. 1-cells are faces of 2-cells, and 0-cells are faces of 1-cells (Fig. 1), the empty cell is admitted also. In this cellular complex a *curve* is a connected chain of 1D- and 0D-cells.

Fig. 1. A cell complex, replacing one pixel.

Kovalevski (1989) picks up the cellular decomposition for the use in image analysis, proposing a cell list data structure and algorithms for image encoding, and Bieri and Metz (1991) apply a tree structure for storing cellular decomposed binary images.

In the remainder of this paper we will call the regular cellular complex a *hyper-raster*, according to Bieri and Metz. Also we will present an own data structure, which is to demonstrate the applicability of topological reasoning more intuitively.

3 Topological Reasoning in GIS

The main use of topological reasoning in spatial databases is to analyze topological relationships before extensive geometric computations. A symbolic reasoning method for the vector model, based on the topology of cell complexes, has been built up by Egenhofer and Franzosa (1991) and Egenhofer and Herring (1991), which we will summarize shortly.

3.1 The 9-Intersection Model in $\mathbb{R}^2$

Egenhofer and Franzosa proposed a method of representing topological relationships by calculating the four intersection sets of the interior and the boundary of two regions without holes, i.e. regions with connected boundaries (*4-intersection model*). They found eight unique and mutually exclusive relations. Egenhofer and Herring expanded the model to a *9-intersection*, also taking into consideration the exterior of regions $\mathcal{R}$, $\mathcal{R}^c$. The 9-intersection can be denoted by a matrix $\mathbf{I}_{33}$:

$$\mathbf{I}_{33} = \begin{pmatrix} \mathring{A} \cap \mathring{B} & \mathring{A} \cap \partial B & \mathring{A} \cap B^c \\ \partial A \cap \mathring{B} & \partial A \cap \partial B & \partial A \cap B^c \\ A^c \cap \mathring{B} & A^c \cap \partial B & A^c \cap B^c \end{pmatrix} \tag{1}$$

The five additional intersection sets of the I_{33} also allow to handle relations between regions with holes and relations between regions, lines and points (cf. Table 1). However, they do not allow to refine the eight relations of regions with more details (cf. Table 2), as it is done by other indicators (Sect. 3.3).

Table 1. Number of real relations between spatial objects (taken from Egenhofer and Herring (1991)). The first item refers to simple objects, the second item (bracketed) to complex objects (complex region: region with holes; complex line: line with more than two boundary points).

Relation between ...	region	line	point
region	8 (18)	19 (20)	3
line		33 (57)	3
point			2

Table 2. The eight topologic relations between two regions without holes, associated with the 9-intersection I_{33}.

$$\begin{pmatrix} \emptyset & \emptyset & \neg\emptyset \\ \emptyset & \emptyset & \neg\emptyset \\ \neg\emptyset & \neg\emptyset & \neg\emptyset \end{pmatrix} \quad \begin{pmatrix} \emptyset & \emptyset & \neg\emptyset \\ \emptyset & \neg\emptyset & \neg\emptyset \\ \neg\emptyset & \neg\emptyset & \neg\emptyset \end{pmatrix} \quad \begin{pmatrix} \neg\emptyset & \neg\emptyset & \neg\emptyset \\ \neg\emptyset & \neg\emptyset & \neg\emptyset \\ \neg\emptyset & \neg\emptyset & \neg\emptyset \end{pmatrix} \quad \begin{pmatrix} \neg\emptyset & \emptyset & \emptyset \\ \emptyset & \neg\emptyset & \emptyset \\ \emptyset & \emptyset & \neg\emptyset \end{pmatrix}$$
$$\text{DISJOINT} \qquad\qquad \text{MEETS} \qquad\qquad \text{OVERLAPS} \qquad\qquad \text{EQUALS}$$

$$\begin{pmatrix} \neg\emptyset & \neg\emptyset & \neg\emptyset \\ \emptyset & \neg\emptyset & \neg\emptyset \\ \emptyset & \emptyset & \neg\emptyset \end{pmatrix} \quad \begin{pmatrix} \neg\emptyset & \emptyset & \emptyset \\ \neg\emptyset & \neg\emptyset & \emptyset \\ \neg\emptyset & \neg\emptyset & \neg\emptyset \end{pmatrix} \quad \begin{pmatrix} \neg\emptyset & \neg\emptyset & \neg\emptyset \\ \emptyset & \neg\emptyset & \neg\emptyset \\ \emptyset & \emptyset & \neg\emptyset \end{pmatrix} \quad \begin{pmatrix} \neg\emptyset & \emptyset & \emptyset \\ \neg\emptyset & \neg\emptyset & \emptyset \\ \neg\emptyset & \neg\emptyset & \neg\emptyset \end{pmatrix}$$
$$\text{COVERS} \qquad \text{COVEREDBY} \qquad \text{CONTAINS} \qquad \text{CONTAINEDBY}$$

Referring to the complex calculation of the additional sets — the exterior of the treated regions is much larger, or goes to infinity, compared to the size of the treated regions themselves — Egenhofer and Herring propose a combination of the 4-intersection and additional criterion to resolve ambiguities in the extended analyses. Egenhofer *et al.* (1994a), who are also interested on regions with holes, solve ambiguities by reasoning about generalized regions, neglecting the holes. But as we will see, the complexity of calculation with the exterior of spatial objects can be eliminated (Sect. 4.4).

In this paper we confine ourselves to regions without holes. The hyper-raster would also work with objects of other dimensions, or with regions with holes, in full accordance to the vector model. However, we prefer a clearly arranged example for topological reasoning, having only eight distinct relations. Another reason is the reference to the work of Egenhofer and Sharma (1993), who adapted the 9-intersection to the raster, for regions without holes. In principle, in the hyper-raster the 4-intersection would be sufficient for representing the expected eight relations. But due to comparability to the raster we will draw up the 9-intersection in the following. Should we ever want to extend the reasoning in hyper-raster we would have to use the 9-intersection in any case.

3.2 The 9-Intersection Model in $\mathbb{Z}^2$

Egenhofer and Sharma (1993) applied the 9-intersection to raster regions, using a 4-adjacency and the interior boundary (which has a diameter of one pixel), in concordance with the '*digital topology*' (Sect. 2.2). Constraints about consistent combinations in the 9-intersection reduce the number of possible relations from $2^9 = 512$ to 16, all with a geometric interpretation. These relations can be ordered in a conceptual-neighborhood-graph, which has clusters comparable to the relations of $\mathbb{R}^2$.

The number of relations differs from those which occur in $\mathbb{R}^2$. The first reason is the two-dimensional boundary, which allows intersection sets that would be inconsistent in $\mathbb{R}^2$. The second reason is the conceptual deficiency in the limitation to interior boundaries, which leads Egenhofer and Sharma to the interpretation that topology in the discrete space is based not only on coincidence of boundaries but also on neighbored boundaries. This is a problematic point of view, because it is more the deficiency of '*digital topology*' than of discretisation, as we will show for the hyper-raster.

3.3 Refinements of Topological Reasoning

The literature presented some ideas which described topological relations more detailed as by a binary I_{33}. We will pick up them for reasoning in the hyper-raster.

One refinement of modeling topological relationships was the idea of replacing the binary intersection matrix by a matrix indicating the dimension of an intersection set: -1D (for $\emptyset$), 0D, 1D, or 2D, cf. Table 3 (Clementini *et al.* 1993).

Egenhofer (1993) also specifies topological relations in a more detailed way, by additional numerical topological invariants: the dimension of intersections, and the number of components of an intersection set. Other topological invariants are added in a multiple representation framework in Egenhofer *et al.* (1994b).

4 The Hyper-Raster Model

Now we propose to applicate the cellular decomposition of $\mathbb{R}^2$ (cf. Sect. 2.3) as a data model for digital images. We develop here a data structure for the hyper-raster, which we will use later for topological reasoning (Sect. 4.4).

Table 3. The possible dimension of intersection sets.

	$\overset{\circ}{B}$	∂B	B^c
$\overset{\circ}{A}$	$\{-1D \vee 2D\}$	$\{-1D \vee 1D\}$	$\{-1D \vee 2D\}$
∂A	$\{-1D \vee 1D\}$	$\{-1D \vee 0D \vee 1D\}$	$\{-1D \vee 1D\}$
A^c	$\{-1D \vee 2D\}$	$\{-1D \vee 1D\}$	$\{-1D \vee 2D\}$

A sketch of the hyper-raster shows 2D picture elements, enriched by edge and node elements (Fig. 2). While the hyper-raster consists of elements with different dimensions, behavior and meaning, a data structure for the hyper-raster should be able to distinguish between the element types, too. The data structure should also be able to handle all spatial entities of the plane: points, curves and regions. Furthermore we want to preserve the two-dimensional array structure to apply image processing algorithms later.

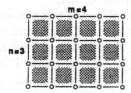

Fig. 2. The hyper-raster with separable element types: picture elements, edges and vertices.

Therefore, we now introduce a class *hyperimage*, which consists of separate matrices for the element types, and of methods to handle the interrelation of the matrices and to adopt image processing algorithms.

4.1   Hyperimage: a Hyper-Raster Data Structure

Data elements of the class *hyperimage* are a matrix C for the 2D-cells, a matrix E for the horizontal and vertical edge elements, and a matrix N for the vertices. A cell decomposition of an area of size $n * m$ will lead to $n * m$ 2D-cells, $(n + 1) * m$ horizontal edges, $n * (m + 1)$ vertical edges, and $(n + 1) * (m + 1)$ vertices[3] (cf. Fig. 2).

---

[3] On the other hand Bieri and Metz (1991) propose to normalize the hyper-raster, which yields other numbers.

Storing vertical edges and horizontal edges separately, e.g. in matrices **V** and **H**, has some disadvantages[4]. But the unique matrix **E** we introduced instead of **V** and **H** maintains the connectedness of the boundary, by 8-adjacency. **E** is built by resampling the hyper-raster into a matrix rotated by 45° and scaled by $\sqrt{2}$. Then each edge element is associated with one rotated pixel (Fig. 3, cf. also Fig. 6) (Kropatsch 1985, Kropatsch 1986).

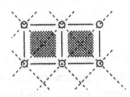

Fig. 3. A rotated matrix can store all edge elements.

While the size of **H** and **V** is together $2nm+n+m$, the size of **E** is $(n+m)^2 = 2nm+n^2+m^2$. So, if memory becomes a problem, the implemented data model should be changed, e.g. to a list structure.

Separating the hyper-raster elements requires access methods (rules) to identify the faces of a single element of C, $c_{i,j}$, and vice versa. The four vertices of a picture element $c_{i,j}$ are found at $n_{i,j}$ (north-west), $n_{i+1,j}$ (south-west), $n_{i+1,j+1}$ (south-east), and $n_{i,j+1}$ (north-east). The upper edge of $c_{i,j}$ is found at $e_{i+j,\text{rows}-i+j}$, the left edge is found at $e_{i+j,\text{rows}-i+j-1}$, and so on. The access rules are part of the data encapsulation.

With this set of three separate matrices we have to model two different tasks:

- to represent the spatial entities (point, curve, region), we introduce a set of *labeling* matrices C_l, E_l, and N_l. C_l contains region labels, with the condition that one pixel may only belong to one label class, E_l contains curve labels, and N_l point labels, both with the same condition.
  Because in this paper we concentrate on regions (without holes), in the remainder we only refer to C_l.

- to represent the boundaries of spatial entities, we introduce *boundary* matrices C_b, E_b, and N_b. Because 2-cells are boundaries of volumes — which we exclude —, we can remove C_b from this set. Then E_b contains the arcs of the boundaries of regions, and N_b contains both, the vertices of the boundaries of regions, and the bounding vertices of curves. Storing a point's boundary is not necessary because it coincides with the point.
  Also here the context of this paper allows us to confine ourselves to *region boundaries* in E_b and N_b.

---

[4] For example, a boundary of a rectangle splits in **H** into two components, the upper and the lower boundary, and in **V** into the left and the right boundary. This is undesired in some applications, like contour detection.

The elementary data type of the labeling matrices depends on the maximum number of spatial objects (# labels), while the type of the boundary matrices depends on the amount of information we wish to store. In the simplest case binary matrices — (*boundary element, not boundary element*) — are sufficient.

4.2 Digitization

To convert a vector data set into a hyper-raster, the digitization rules are slightly different from those for the raster, with regard to curves and points. Digitizing a point means labeling the nearest 0-cell in N_l. Digitizing a curve requires to label a closed chain of 1-cells (in E_l) between start and end vertex (in N_b). A region will be digitized by converting the boundary, a closed polygon, into E_b and N_b, and afterwards labeling the interior in C_l. Some attention has to be paid to avoid degenerated regions. A degeneration consists of 1-cells in the boundary (and, because of redundancy, also of 0-cells) which have no 2-cell labeled as interior. This can occur, if the resolution of the discretisation is not sufficient (cf. Fig. 4).

The digitization rules are implemented as a part of the constructor of a hyperimage. If a vector data set of regions is digitized, the result is a fully segmented and classified matrix C_l, and binary matrices E_b and N_b. With regard to topological reasoning, the matrices E_b and N_b, although redundant to a large degree, are both are necessary (cf. Table 4).

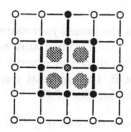

Fig. 4. Degenerated region: a 1-cell of the boundary with no interior neighbor cells.

A topological relation is a binary relation, i.e. a relation between two spatial objects. Therefore, it is sufficient to digitize the two regions in question (if we start with vector data sets), or to extract single regions (if we start with hyper-raster maps). Such a set of (binary) *extract matrices* C_e, E_e, and N_e, build for each of both regions, can be limited in size to a bounding rectangle of the region. In C_e the interior of the region is foreground, and the exterior of the region is background, and in E_e and N_e the boundary of the region is foreground.

Our presented data structure is now complete for topological reasoning. The next step is to transfer the 9-intersection to the hyper-raster and then to apply it in the *hyperimage*.

4.3 The 9-Intersection in the Hyper-Raster

In the hyper-raster, we find exactly the eight relationships between regions which exist in $\mathbb{R}^2$. Egenhofer and Sharma (1993) cite five conditions to select the relations which really occur in $\mathbb{R}^2$ from the 512 possible states of the 9-intersection. In raster they may apply the first three conditions (which leads to remaining 16 relations), but here also the latter two conditions can be applied (leaving the known eight relations):

Condition 4 *If the interior of A intersects with the boundary of B then it must also intersect with the exterior of B, and vice versa.*

Condition 5 *If both interiors are disjoint then the boundary of A cannot intersect with the interior of B, and vice versa.*

Proof. Condition 4 follows from the hyper-raster property that intersections with boundary elements can only exist of 1D- or 0D-cells. But if an 1D-cell (and the more a 0D-cell) belongs to the interior of A, then both neighbored 2D-cells belong to A, too. Compared to it an 1D-cell of the boundary of B inevitably neighbors with one 2D-cell of the interior of B and one 2D-cell of the exterior of B. Therefore, an intersection of the interior of A with the boundary of B implies that at least one neighbored 2D-cell of the boundary must fall on the exterior of B, and one on the interior of B. $\qquad\square$

Proof. Condition 5 rests upon the same hyper-raster property. An 1D-cell of the boundary of A, and more an 0D-cell, inevitably neighbors with one 2D-cell of the interior of A, and one 2D-cell of the exterior of A. If the boundary of A intersects with the interior of B, then at least one 2D-cell of the interior of A intersects with a 2D-cell of the interior of B. $\qquad\square$

In principle, conditions from the vector model to exclude inconsistent combinations of the 9-intersection hold true for the hyper-raster analogously. That is because of the common spatial model of cellular decomposition. A confinement to regular cells is invariant to topological modeling. With that we may expect, that topological relations between spatial objects of other dimensions, or between regions with holes, will coincide to the vector model, too.

4.4 The 9-Intersection in the *Hyperimage*

With the *hyperimage* the 9-intersection is very fast to compute, contrary to the situation in the vector model. We have only to overlay the extracted object matrices (taking care of their different origin). The overlay is done by joining them with a logical '∧' pixel by pixel (this is equivalent to ∩ in set denotation).

Then the foreground of the overlay represents an intersection set, or a part of it. As one property of the '$\wedge$'-operator the overlay can be limited to the overlap of the bounding rectangles of the considered regions.

Now we show how to enlarge the binary extracted matrices into three-valued matrices[5], specifying the *interior*, *boundary*, and *exterior* of a region $\mathcal{R}$. For simplicity we omit the index e of the extraction matrices in the following, and the foreground pixels of a matrix we denote by '$\mathcal{F}$'.

$$
\begin{aligned}
C(\overset{\circ}{\mathcal{R}}) &= \bigcup c_{i,j} \mid c_{i,j} \in \mathcal{F} \\
C(\partial\mathcal{R}) &= \emptyset \\
C(\mathcal{R}^c) &= \bigcup c_{i,j} \mid c_{i,j} \notin \mathcal{F} = \bigcup c_{i,j} \setminus \{C(\overset{\circ}{\mathcal{R}})\}
\end{aligned}
\tag{2}
$$

C_e contains no boundary information and is really binary, therefore.

$$
\begin{aligned}
E(\overset{\circ}{\mathcal{R}}) &= \bigcup e_{i,j} \mid (e_{i,j} \notin \mathcal{F}) \wedge (\sum(e_{k,j} \in \mathcal{F}) = \text{odd}), \text{ with } k = 0\ldots i-1 \\
E(\partial\mathcal{R}) &= \bigcup e_{i,j} \mid e_{i,j} \in \mathcal{F} \\
E(\mathcal{R}^c) &= \bigcup e_{i,j} \mid (e_{i,j} \notin \mathcal{F}) \wedge (\sum(e_{k,j} \in \mathcal{F}) = \text{even}), \text{ with } k = 0\ldots i-1 \\
&= \bigcup(e_{i,j} \setminus \{E(\overset{\circ}{\mathcal{R}}), E(\partial\mathcal{R})\}
\end{aligned}
\tag{3}
$$

Since E_e contains no degenerated elements (cf. Sect. 4.2), an element $e_{i,j}$ belongs to the interior of a region, if it is not boundary and if an odd number of boundary elements precede in the row i.

Also, $e_{i,j}$ is interior if it is not boundary, and if at least one neighbored 2-cell belongs to the foreground (interior).

To determine $N(\overset{\circ}{\mathcal{R}})$, we have to check for each $n_{i,j}$ if it is not boundary, and if at least one neighbored 2-cell belongs to the foreground (interior).

$$
\begin{aligned}
N(\partial\mathcal{R}) &= \bigcup n_{i,j} \mid n_{i,j} \in \mathcal{F} \\
N(\mathcal{R}^c) &= \bigcup n_{i,j} \setminus \{N(\overset{\circ}{\mathcal{R}}), N(\partial\mathcal{R})\}
\end{aligned}
\tag{4}
$$

With that we can denote the three topological sets of a region $\mathcal{R}$ which occur in I_{33} as:

$$
\begin{aligned}
\overset{\circ}{\mathcal{R}} &= C(\overset{\circ}{\mathcal{R}}) \cup E(\overset{\circ}{\mathcal{R}}) \cup N(\overset{\circ}{\mathcal{R}}) \\
\partial\mathcal{R} &= C(\partial\mathcal{R}) \cup E(\partial\mathcal{R}) \cup N(\partial\mathcal{R}) \\
\mathcal{R}^c &= C(\mathcal{R}^c) \cup E(\mathcal{R}^c) \cup N(\mathcal{R}^c)
\end{aligned}
\tag{5}
$$

These sets can be used to evaluate the intersection sets in I_{33}. Intersections between matrices of different types are empty *per definitionem*, so we may reduce for example the interior-interior intersection set between two regions $\mathcal{A}$ and $\mathcal{B}$ to the following equation:

$$
\overset{\circ}{\mathcal{A}} \cap \overset{\circ}{\mathcal{B}} = (C(\overset{\circ}{\mathcal{A}}) \cap C(\overset{\circ}{\mathcal{B}})) \cup (E(\overset{\circ}{\mathcal{A}}) \cap E(\overset{\circ}{\mathcal{B}})) \cup (N(\overset{\circ}{\mathcal{A}}) \cap N(\overset{\circ}{\mathcal{B}}))
\tag{6}
$$

---

[5] An alternative way is directly to extract ternary matrices (*interior, boundary, exterior*), but we are interested in the binary matrices for further processing.

However, we are mainly interested in intersection sets being empty or not, and only less interested in the completeness of an intersection set. Therefore, we now refer to the possible dimensions of the nine intersection sets[6] (Table 3).

Proposition 6. *If an intersection set is either of dimension 2 or empty, and if the intersection set is not empty, there must exist a (non-empty) set $C(\mathcal{A}) \cap C(\mathcal{B})$.*

Proposition 7. *If an intersection set is either of dimension 1 or empty, and if the intersection set is not empty, there must exist a (non-empty) set $E(\mathcal{A}) \cap E(\mathcal{B})$.*

Proposition 8. *If an intersection set is either of dimension 0 or empty, and if the intersection set is not empty, there must exist a (non-empty) set $N(\mathcal{A}) \cap N(\mathcal{B})$.*

All three propositions are self-evident and do not need further proof. Now, following Table 3, Proposition 6 is used for deciding about the intersection sets i_{11}, i_{31}, i_{13}, and i_{33}. With Proposition 7 we decide for the intersection sets i_{12}, i_{21}, i_{23}, and i_{32}. Only the boundary-boundary intersection is not fixed in the dimension. It may be both, 1D or 0D. That means that Propositions 7 and 8 are not applicable. Therefore, we need the

Proposition 9. *If a non-empty boundary-boundary intersection set exists, there must also exist a non-empty set $N(\partial\mathcal{A}) \cap N(\partial\mathcal{B})$.*

Proof. The boundary is foreground in E and N (see (3,4)). Then it follows from hyper-raster consistency that each foreground pixel $e_{i,j}$ is bounded by two foreground pixels $n_{k,l}$ and $n_{m,n}$ (minimum condition for 1D-intersection). On the other hand, if the intersection is 0D, it is evident that $E(\partial\mathcal{A}) \cap E(\partial\mathcal{B})$ is empty, so there must exist a non-empty $N(\partial\mathcal{A}) \cap N(\partial\mathcal{B})$. □

With these considerations we can now reduce the calculations for the intersection sets of I_{33} to the overlays given in Table 4. As one consequence we directly gather from that table that there is no further need to build $N(\overset{\circ}{\mathcal{R}})$ or $N(\mathcal{R}^c)$.

4.5   Refinements in the Hyper-Raster

For transferring the refinements to the hyper-raster we will use the overlay of extraction matrices more extensively. Several additional measures can be calculated:

- the *dimension* of an intersection set. As in the vector model, this concerns only the boundary-boundary intersection, which can be 1D or 0D (or -1D, in case of ∅). The dimension is determined by the type of the matrix which contains the intersection set: if $E(\partial\mathcal{A}) \cap E(\partial\mathcal{B})$ is not empty, then this set is 1D, and if only $N(\partial\mathcal{A}) \cap N(\partial\mathcal{B})$ is not empty, then the set is 0D. The dimensions of the other intersection sets are fixed.

---

[6] In Sect. 4.3 we have shown that these dimensions will hold in hyper-raster, too.

Table 4. Operations to calculate the intersection sets of I_{33} from hyperimage matrices.

	$\overset{\circ}{B}$	∂B	B^c
$\overset{\circ}{A}$	$C(\overset{\circ}{A}) \cap C(\overset{\circ}{B})$	$E(\overset{\circ}{A}) \cap E(\partial B)$	$C(\overset{\circ}{A}) \cap C(B^c)$
∂A	$E(\partial A) \cap E(\overset{\circ}{B})$	$N(\partial A) \cap N(\partial B)$	$E(\partial A) \cap E(B^c)$
A^c	$C(A^c) \cap C(\overset{\circ}{B})$	$E(A^c) \cap E(\partial B)$	$C(A^c) \cap C(B^c)$

- the *number of separations*. This is done by counting the connected components (Lumia *et al.* 1983, Bässmann and Besslich 1991) in the intersection matrices. The intersection matrices of **C**'s and **E**'s are sufficient for this task, because a junction is at least 1D.
- *component features*. Performing feature extraction yields a list of further parameters, characterizing the single intersection component: the size, the perimeter, the main axes, compactness, the center of gravity, the orientation, and other features. These parameters are no topological invariants (e.g. Bässmann and Besslich 1991).
- the *type* of boundary-boundary intersections (*crossing / touching*). This type follows from contour tracking through both considered **E** matrices.

5   Example

We may be interested in the topological relation between the following regions A and B (Fig. 5). Assume, that the two vector sets refer to the same real world object, but it is associated in one GIS map with three boundary points, and in another with four boundary points.

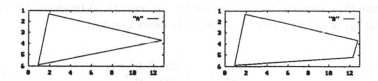

Fig. 5. A region in two different vector maps.

The digitization into discrete *hyperimages* (one per vector region) follows Sect. 4.2. The result are three matrices C_e, E_e, and N_e for each region (Fig. 6).

With these matrices we create intersection matrices (Fig. 7) and determine the topological relation between $\mathcal{A}$ ('the region from map A') and $\mathcal{B}$ ('the region from map B').

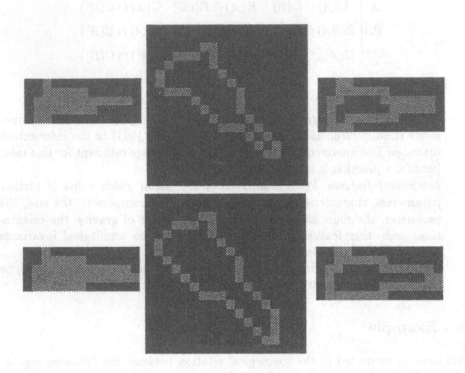

Fig. 6. The hyperimage matrices $\mathbf{C}_e(\mathcal{A})$, $\mathbf{E}_e(\mathcal{A})$, and $\mathbf{N}_e(\mathcal{A})$ (top line), $\mathbf{C}_e(\mathcal{B})$, $\mathbf{E}_e(\mathcal{B})$, and $\mathbf{N}_e(\mathcal{B})$ (bottom line). Foreground is bright. We can also see the rotation and scale of $\mathbf{E}$.

From the intersection matrices we can derivate the 9-intersection matrix (the element i_{33} is not evaluated because it is never empty):

$$|\mathbf{I}_{33}| = \begin{pmatrix} 26 & 0 & 0 \\ 10 & 24 & 0 \\ 9 & 12 & - \end{pmatrix} \tag{7}$$

This matrix is equivalent to the topological relation COVEREDBY $(\mathcal{A}, \mathcal{B})$ (cf. Table 2). A refined description of the relation will contain:

- Dimension of boundary-boundary intersection: 1D.

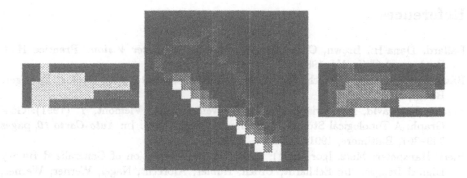

Fig. 7. The intersection sets of the C-, E- and N-matrices. The sets are differentiated by gray intensities.

- Number of components:

$$\text{no\_components}\,(\mathbf{I}_{33}) = \begin{pmatrix} 1 & 0 & 0 \\ 2 & 2 & 0 \\ 1 & 2 & (1) \end{pmatrix} \tag{8}$$

Further attributes of the components are not evaluated here.

6 Conclusions

We have presented a model and a data structure to realize a topological reasoning between two regions without holes in images within the topology of $\mathbb{R}^2$. Our model overcomes the topological defect of the simple raster model, and is able to compute easily and quickly a detailed description of topological relations. The model is capable of reasoning with objects of other dimensions, and with holes, which has to be demonstrated later.

The proposed data structure is intuitively clear, and the adapted size of the reasoning area to the overlap of bounding rectangles speeds up the reasoning enormously. Compared to the complex calculations in $\mathbb{R}^2$, we are in advantage because binary images are discrete and the applied image processing needs no higher computations than comparison and counting. The proposed *hyperimage* structure is well suited for demonstrating intersection sets, but up to now is not optimized for memory and access. Changing the structure is possible in the object-oriented paradigm.

Therefore, we propose to choose the hyper-raster as a general model for topological reasoning in spatial databases and GIS. Some work is required to complete the model for curves and points, and to open the model to the whole world of image processing tasks, e.g. for image segmentation, contour tracking *et cetera*. But the advantages which compensate for this work, are, in particular, explicit elements for edges and vertices, and a discrete computation space.

References

Ballard, Dana H.; Brown, Christopher M. (1982): *Computer Vision*. Prentice Hall, Englewood Cliffs, NJ, 1982.

Bässmann, Henning; Besslich, Philipp (1991): *Bildverarbeitung Ad Oculos*. Springer, Berlin, 1991.

Bennis, K.; David, B.; Morize-Quilio, I.; Thevenin, J. M.; Viemont, Y. (1991): Geo-Graph: A Topological Storage Model for Extensible GIS. In: *Auto-Carto 10*, pages 349–367, Baltimore, 1991. ACSM — ASPRS.

Bieri, Hanspeter; Metz, Igor (1991): A Bintree Representation of Generalized Binary Digital Images. In: Eckhardt, Ulrich; Hübler, Albrecht; Nagel, Werner; Werner, Günther (Eds.), *Geometrical Problems of Image Processing*, pages 72–77, Berlin, 1991. Akademie Verlag.

Clementini, Eliseo; Di Felice, Paolino (1994): A Comparison of Methods for Representing Topological Relationships. *Information Sciences 80*, pages 1–30, 1994.

Clementini, Eliseo; Di Felice, Paolino; van Oosterom, Peter (1993): A Small Set of Formal Topological Relationships Suitable for End-User Interaction. In: Abel, D.; Ooi, B. (Eds.), *Advances in Spatial Databases*, pages 277–295, New York, 1993. 3rd Symposium on Large Spatial Databases SSD '93, Springer LNCS 692.

Egenhofer, Max J.; Franzosa, Robert D. (1991): Point-set topological spatial relations. *Int. Journal of Geographical Information Systems*, 5(2):161–174, 1991.

Egenhofer, Max J.; Herring, John R. (1991): Categorizing Binary Topological Relationships Between Regions, Lines, and Points in Geographic Databases. Technical report, Department of Surveying Engineering, University of Maine, Orono, ME, 1991.

Egenhofer, Max; Sharma, Jayant (1993): Topological Relations Between Regions in R^2 and Z^2. In: Abel, D.; Ooi, B. (Eds.), *Advances in Spatial Databases*, pages 316–336, New York, 1993. 3rd Symposium on Large Spatial Databases SSD '93, Springer LNCS 692.

Egenhofer, Max J.; Clementini, Eliseo; di Felice, Paolino (1994): Topological relations between regions with holes. *International Journal of Geographical Information Systems*, 8(2):129–142, 1994.

Egenhofer, Max J.; Clementini, Eliseo; Di Felice, Paolino (1994): Evaluating Inconsistencies among Multiple Representations. In: Waugh, Thomas C.; Healey, Richard G. (Eds.), *Advances in GIS Research*, pages 901–919, Edinburgh, 1994. Proc. 6th Int. Symp. on Spatial Data Handling.

Egenhofer, Max J. (1993): A Model for Detailed Binary Topological Relationships. *Geomatica*, 47(3 & 4):261–273, 1993.

Hernández, Daniel (1994): *Qualitative Representation of Spatial Knowledge*. LNAI 804. Springer, Berlin, 1994.

Herring, J.R. (1987): TIGRIS: Topologically Integrated Geographic Information System. In: *Auto-Carto 8*, pages 282–291, Baltimore, 1987. ACSM — ASPRS.

Jänich, Klaus (1994): *Topologie*. Springer, Berlin, 4. edition, 1994.

Kong, T. Y.; Rosenfeld, A. (1989): Digital Topology: Introduction and Survey. *CVGIP 48*, pages 357–393, 1989.

Kovalevski, V. A. (1989): Finite topology as applied to image analysis. *CVGIP 46*, pages 141–161, 1989.

Kropatsch, Walter G. (1985): A pyramid that grows by powers of 2. *Pattern Recognition Letters*, 3:315–322, 1985.

Kropatsch, Walter (1986): Grauwert- und Kurvenpyramide, das ideale Paar. In: Hartmann, G. (Ed.), *Mustererkennung 1986*, pages 79–83, Berlin, 1986. 8. DAGM-Symposium, Springer.

Latecki, Longin; Eckhardt, Ulrich; Rosenfeld, Azriel (1995): Well-Composed Sets. *Computer Vision and Image Understanding*, 61(1):70–83, 1995.

Latecki, Longin (1992): *Digitale und Allgemeine Topologie in der bildhaften Wissensrepräsentation*, Band 9 der Reihe DISKI. infix, St. Augustin, 1992.

Lumia, Ronald; Shapiro, Linda; Zuniga, Oscar (1983): A New Connected Components Algorithm for Virtual Memory Computers. *Computer Vision, Graphics, and Image Processing*, pages 287–300, 1983.

Molenaar, Martien; Kufoniyi, O.; Bouloucos, T. (1994): Modelling Topologic Relationships in Vector Maps. In: Waugh, Thomas C.; Healey, Richard G. (Eds.), *Advances in GIS Research*, pages 112–126, Edinburgh, 1994. Proc. 6th Int. Symp. on Spatial Data Handling.

Pigot, Simon (1991): Topological Models for 3D Spatial Information Systems. In: Mark, David M.; White, Denis (Eds.), *Auto-Carto 10*, pages 368–392, Baltimore, 1991. ACSM-ASPRS.

Pilouk, Morakot; Tempfli, Klaus; Molenaar, Martien (1994): A Tetrahedron-based 3D Vector Data Model for Geoinformation. In: Molenaar, Martien; de Hoop, Sylvia (Eds.), *Advanced Geographic Data Modelling*, pages 129–140, Delft, 1994. Netherlands Geodetic Commission.

Generating Seeded Trees from Data Sets*

Ming-Ling Lo and Chinya V. Ravishankar

Electrical Engineering and Computer Science Department
University of Michigan–Ann Arbor
1301 Beal Avenue, Ann Arbor, MI 48109
mingling, ravi@eecs.umich.edu

Abstract. In this paper we study the problem of how to perform spatial joins between two data sets with no pre-computed spatial indices. No techniques appear to exist to date that specifically target this problem. Our solution is also useful in the context of query optimization for complex spatial queries. In addition, we demonstrate that simple sampling techniques can be effective in reducing spatial join costs.

We extend the work in [LR94, LR95] and introduce the bootstrap-seeding technique, which allows seeded trees to be constructed directly from input data sets. We can thus dynamically construct two seeded trees for two data sets and perform a spatial join between them. The task of bootstrap-seeding comprises the subtasks of determining the number and the contents of the slots, and constructing the tree. Simple sampling techniques are used to determine the slot contents efficiently.

Our experiments show that spatial joins using our methods are very comparable in performance to that of joins between the same data sets with pre-computed R-trees, and confirm the viability of our method. When joining two data sets with different sizes, our studies suggest that it would be beneficial to bootstrap an initial seeded tree for the smaller data set, and then to construct a seeded tree for the larger data set using copy-seeding and the seed level filtering technique.

1 Introduction

Spatial join operations are important and expensive operations in spatial databases. However, relatively little work has been done on them. The large sizes of the data sets involved is only one reason for the high cost of spatial joins. In addition, since the values of spatial attributes can not be totally ordered, join methods developed for traditional databases cannot be used directly in spatial joins. Existing spatial join algorithms can generally be divided into those based on tree-like indices [LR94, LR95, BKS93, Gut84, BKSS90, FSR87, SRF87] and those based on other methods such as spatial join indices [Rot91, LH92, Val87] and z-ordering [Ore89, Ore90, Ore91].

Most of these methods assume that some spatial indices have been constructed for both operand data sets of the spatial join [BKS93, Gut84, BKSS90,

---
* This work was supported in part by the Consortium for International Earth Science Information Networking.

FSR87, SRF87], or that some pre-computation has been done before a spatial join is invoked [Rot91, LH92, Val87]. If an operand data set does not have a pre-computed spatial index, the cost of constructing one at join time can be prohibitive. Such requirements place a operational burden on the spatial database system, since it may not be cost-effective to maintain index structures for all data sets regardless of their patterns and frequencies of usage. Furthermore, such requirements can be impossible to satisfy in many situations. For example, the inputs to a spatial join may be the results dynamically generated by other database operations, in which case no spatial indices would exist for such input data sets. Since most spatial indices are designed for incremental updates rather than all-at-once construction, building spatial indices dynamically at join time can be very expensive.

Our work in [LR95] first demonstrated the feasibility of dynamically constructing spatial index structures, called *seeded trees*, to perform spatial joins. In that work, one operand data set was assumed to have a pre-computed tree-like spatial index. A *seeded tree* index was then constructed for the the data set without a spatial index, using information extracted from the index existing for the other operand data set. We have also shown that the cost of this approach is much lower than that of building an R-tree index for the second data set [LR94, LR95]. There are two reasons for the low costs of the seeded tree join method. First, constructing a seeded tree dynamically is much cheaper than constructing R-tree dynamically. Second, joining a R-tree and a seeded tree constructed with information from it is cheaper than joining two independently constructed R-trees.

However, that work represents only a partial solution to the problem. The approach to seeded tree construction in [LR94, LR95] required copying and then possibly transforming the upper levels of an existing R-tree index. If neither operand data set had a pre-computed spatial index, we would be forced to construct at least one R-tree dynamically, the cost of which could be exorbitant. The relative magnitudes of the costs of constructing R trees and seeded trees are illustrated in Fig. 1.

In this paper, we study methods to construct seeded trees directly from their associated data sets, with no pre-existing index structures, while retaining construction and join cost advantages. We show how to generate seeding information directly from the data sets, and without relying on existing index structures.

1.1 Bootstrapping Seeded Trees

This approach to seeded tree construction involves three steps: determining the structure of the seed levels, sampling the input data set to extract information, and building the seed levels of the index using this information. We call the method of generating seeding information directly from the data set *bootstrap seeding* to distinguish it from that of [LR94, LR95]. That earlier method, based on copying information from an existing index, will be called *copy seeding*.

To join two spatial data sets without existing spatial indices, we first build a seeded tree by bootstrapping from one operand data set. Then we build a

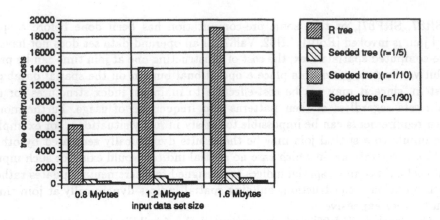

Fig. 1. Costs of constructing R trees and seeded trees. r is the ratio of the cost of accessing a disk page sequentially to that of accessing it randomly.

copy-seeded index tree for the other data set by copying the upper levels of the bootstrap-seeded tree. Thus, the bootstrap-seeded index plays the role of the pre-computed R-tree when one exists. After both seeded trees are built, they are joined to produce the final result. The tree matching algorithm is the same as that between two R-trees, or between a seeded tree and an R-tree [LR94, LR95, BKS93].

This paper makes three significant contributions by demonstrating the feasibility of bootstrap seeding. First, it solves a problem that was hitherto prohibitively expensive, namely the problem of spatial joins when no spatial indices exist. Second, it makes a significant contribution to spatial query optimization by giving the spatial query optimizer new alternatives while planning for the execution of queries. For example, consider a complex spatial join between three spatial data sets of equal size A, B and C (see Fig. 2). Assume A has a pre-computed R-tree, while B and C do not. Furthermore, assume the selectivity between B and C is much lower than that between A and B, or that between A and C. Without bootstrap seeding, we would be forced to join A–B and A–C first. However, with bootstrap seeding, we can perform the B–C join first and exploit its low selectivity by constructing seeded trees for B and C. Third, it demonstrates the viability of using sampling techniques in helping with spatial joins.

This paper is organized as follows. Section 2 first describes the structure and the basic algorithm for constructing seeded trees. Section 3 discusses how to build a seeded tree directly from an input data set. This task involves the subtasks of determining the topology of seed levels, extracting information from the data set, and constructing the seed levels using this information. The tasks are elaborated in sections 4, 5, and 6, respectively. Section 7 discusses issues in joining two seeded trees. Section 8 presents experimental results, and section 9 concludes this paper.

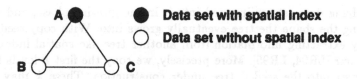

Fig. 2. Join graph for a complex spatial join. Data set A has a pre-computed R-tree, data sets B and C have not.

2 Seeded Tree Basics

This section outlines the basic algorithms of constructing seeded trees and using them in spatial joins. For details please refer to [LR94, LR95]. Structurally, a seeded tree consists of the *seed levels* and *grown levels* (see Fig. 3). The tree nodes at the seed levels are called *seed nodes*, and those at the grown levels are called *grown nodes*. The seed levels start from the root and continue consecutively for a small number of levels. The grown levels span from the children of the last seed level to the leaf level. As with R-tree nodes, a non-leaf node in the seeded tree contains entries of the form (mbr, cp), where cp points to a child node, and mbr is the minimum bounding rectangle of all objects contained in the child node. A leaf node contains entries of the form (mbr, oid), where oid refers to a spatial object in the database, and mbr is the bounding box of that object.

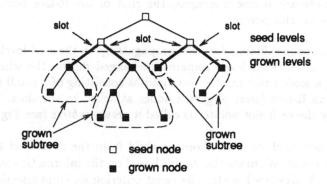

Fig. 3. Example of a seeded tree.

The construction of a seeded tree consists of a *seeding phase*, a *growing phase* and a simple *clean-up phase*. The seed levels are numbered from 0 (the root level) through $k-1$, and the grown levels span from level k to level l (the leaf level).

2.1 Seeding and Growing Phases

In the seeding phase the seed levels of a seeded tree is determined. These upper levels will be used to guide the growth of the tree when the data object of the underlying data set are inserted into it in the growing phase, and will help determining the shape the tree eventually grows into. With copy seeding, this is done by extracting information from another tree-like spatial index, calling a *seeding tree* [LR94, LR95]. More precisely, we copy the first k levels from the seeding trees into the seeded tree under construction. These k may undergo some transformation before they are used in subsequent tree construction. With bootstrap seeding, this is done by extracting information from the underlying data set, the details of which will be discussed in the following sections. We call each (mbr, cp) pair at level $k-1$ a *slot*, and level $k-1$ of the seeded tree, the *slot level*.

During the growing phase, data objects of the underlying data set are inserted into the seeded tree, and the tree grows accordingly. To insert a data object, we traverse the tree from the root to the slot level, at each level choosing a suitable node to traverse from the next level. Eventually the slot level is reached and a slot chosen for inserting the data. If this is the first insertion through this slot, the child pointer of the slot will be NULL. In this case, a new grown node is allocated, the child pointer is set to point to the new node, and the data object inserted into it. Otherwise the data are inserted into the grown node found through the slot pointer. This grown node behaves like the root of an ordinary R-tree. When it overflows due to insertions, it will be split into two grown nodes, and a third grown node allocated to become the parent of the two nodes. The slot pointer is modified to point to the new root. Subsequent insertions through this slot behave like ordinary R-tree insertions, the root of the R-tree being the node pointed to by the slot pointer.

Recall that node splitting does not propagate up to the seed levels, and that the structure of the seed levels remains unchanged during the whole growing phase. Thus, a seeded tree can be visualized as consisting of a small tree of seed nodes, with an R-tree forest of grown nodes attached to the slots. The R-tree pointed to by the each slot pointer is called a *grown subtree* (see Fig. 3).

At each seed level we must choose a child from the next level to traverse, until a slot is found. We make this choice based on the information stored in the bounding box fields of each node. The exact criterion for child selection depends on whether the value stored is a central point or an area. If central points are stored, we choose a child whose central point is close to the central point of the data being inserted. If areas are stored, we choose a child that yields the smallest bounding box area after insertion, subtracting from it the sum of the areas of the old bounding box and the input rectangle. This criterion is the same as that used in R-tree construction.

The *clean-up phase* begins after all data object in D_S are inserted into the seeded tree. The bounding box fields of seed node are adjusted to be the true minimum bounding boxes of their children. Slots containing no data objects are deleted and relevant data structures made consistent.

2.2 Using Linked Lists in Growing Phase

To avoid random disk accesses due to buffer overflow at the growing phase, we use intermediate linked lists to assist in tree construction. During the growing phase, if we estimate that the tree size will be larger than the buffer size, the data inserted through a slot will not be built into a grown subtree immediately, but first organized into a linked list of data pages, attached to the slot. The linked lists grow as data objects are inserted. Eventually all data pages in the buffer will be allocated. If we now want to insert an additional data object into a linked list in which all data pages are full, we write all linked lists longer than a small pre-defined constant to disks, freeing up most of the buffer space. The insertion process then proceeds as before. When all data objects in D_S are inserted, we can start constructing grown subtrees from the linked lists. For each slot, an R-tree is built using the data objects stored in the linked lists grown under that slot. The slot pointer is modified to point to the root of this R-tree.

Using such intermediate linked lists, we can construct the grown subtrees one by one instead of all together. Since there are many slots in the seeded tree, and hence many grown subtrees, the average size of a grown subtree is much smaller than the size an R-tree built with the same input data. The chances of a grown subtree overflowing the buffer are therefore much smaller, and the number of random disk access is significantly reduced. The price this method must pay is an increase in the number of sequential accesses for writing and reading the linked lists. However, since sequential access is much faster than random access in disk I/O, this results in much faster construction times.

3 Bootstrapping Seeding

Now we consider how a seeded tree may be built directly from an input data set. Our objective is to generate a seeded tree which can be constructed efficiently and result in efficient join with other seeded trees.

From [LR94, LR95], we know how to construct a seeded tree given its seed levels. Thus, our first task is to determine the seed levels for bootstrap seeding. That is, we must determine the topology of the seed levels and the contents of the various seed nodes. We have found that the structure and contents of the slots are most important to the success of the method. The contents of the slots decide in large measure how the lower levels of the index (the grown levels) develop. The number of slots used in the seed levels also affects tree construction costs and join performance. The key to bootstrap seeding thus lies in determining the number and contents of the slots.

Finding the optimal set of slots for bootstrap seeding requires involved analysis of the characteristics of the data sets participating in the join, and of the system resources available for join processing. Since we intend to construct seeded trees on the fly, we prefer an efficient but sub-optimal method. We divide the task of determining the slots into the two subtasks of determining their number and of determining their contents. The system resources and data set sizes determine the number of slots. The data set contents determine the contents of the slots.

Spatial data sets being generally quite large, it is infeasible to examine them in entirety in making such determinations. Instead, we sample the data sets and determine the slot contents based on the samples. Our experiments have shown that an appropriately-chosen sample preserves enough information about the data set to serve our purposes.

The task of finding a set of slots for bootstrap seeding thus consists of the following steps:

1. Determining the number of slots S.
2. Taking a sample of size k efficiently from the input data set.
3. Placing the S slots on the map area using information in the sample.

Once the set of slots is determined, we can build the seed levels by simply constructing an R-tree using this set of slots as input. In section 4, we show that the number of slots is so determined that the size of seed levels is always smaller than the available buffer size. Therefore, the cost of constructing this R-tree requires limited CPU costs and *no* I/O cost whatsoever. Once the seed levels are built, the tree growing process for both bootstrap- and copy-seeding is exactly as described in [LR94, LR95].

4 Determining the Number of Slots

For copy seeding, determining the number of slots is not an issue, since the seed levels are copied from another tree, thereby determining the number slots. However, it is clearly an issue for bootstrap seeding.

parameter	definition	parameter	definition
D	input dataset size (# blocks)	d	number of data item
B	buffer size (# blocks)	S	number of slots
l	number of seed levels	h	tree height
N_s	number of nodes in seed levels	n_i	number of nodes at level i
n_l	number of nodes at slot level	f_{max}	maximum fanout
f_{min}	minimum fanout	f_{ave}	average fanout of whole tree
f_i	average fanout at level i		

Table 1. Parameters in seeded tree construction

This section discusses the relationship between the desirable number of slots, the system buffer size, and input data set sizes. We will show that for given buffer and data set sizes, there is a preferred range of choices for the number of slots. Table 1 lists the parameters used in our discussion. Without loss of generality, we assume that a tree node, a buffer page, and a disk page are of the same size. There can be many ways of organizing spatial data. We assume that a data set contains, for each spatial object, a 16-byte minimum bounding box and a 4-byte pointer to the detailed description of the object. We also assume that the seeded tree has large node fanout, so that the size of a tree is approximately the size of its leaf level.

4.1 Algorithm Requirements

For feasibility and efficiency of the seeded tree algorithm, we require the following constraints on the structure of seeded trees:

R1 The size of the seed levels should
    R1.1 be smaller than the buffer size.
    R1.2 occupy a small fraction of the buffer so as to obtain good tree construction performance.
R2 The average grown subtree size should
    R2.1 be smaller than the the available buffer space to avoid random disk access during grown subtree construction.
    R2.2 occupy a small fraction of the available buffer for good performance during actual join.

Requirement R1 Requirement R1.1 is expressed as $N_s < B$. For large fanout, we have $n_i \ll n_{i+1}$, for $1 \le i < h$, and $N_s = \sum_{i=1}^{l} n_i \approx n_l$. Therefore, we require $n_l < B$.

To obtain better performance, we use R1.2 and require seed level nodes to occupy only a fraction of the buffer, which translates into formula $n_l < B/E$, or

$$S < \frac{B \cdot f_l}{E}, \tag{1}$$

where $E > 1$ is a tunable constant.

Requirement R2 Requirement R2.2 states the average grown subtree size should be smaller than a fraction of the available buffer space. Since the input data set has D blocks, each grown subtree must hold D/S blocks of input data on average. A leaf node of a grown subtree is f_{ave}/f_{max} full on average, hence a grown subtree needs $(\frac{D}{S})/(\frac{f_{ave}}{f_{max}})$ leaf nodes to hold D/S blocks of input data. With large fanout, the number of leaf nodes is approximately the number of nodes of the tree, and the average size of a grown subtree is thus $(\frac{D}{S})/(\frac{f_{ave}}{f_{max}})$ nodes.

Let B' be the buffer space available after holding the seed levels in the buffer. Since the size of the seed levels is approximately n_l, $B' = B - n_l$. Requirement R2.2 is expressed as

$$\frac{D \cdot f_{max}}{S \cdot f_{ave}} < \frac{B'}{C}$$

for some tunable constant $C > 1$. Using $s = n_l \cdot f_l$ and $B' = B - n_l$, this formula can be rearranged into $n_l > \frac{CDf_{max}}{(f_{ave}f_l)} \cdot \frac{1}{B-n_l}$. Using K to denote the factor $CDf_{max}/(f_{ave}f_l)$ and solving for n_l, we get a lower bound for n_l:

$$\frac{B - \sqrt{B^2 - 4K}}{2} < n_l. \tag{2}$$

Bounds on Number of Seed Levels and Number of Slots Using (1) and (2) and $S = n_l \cdot f_l$, we can derive bounds for the number of slots as follows:

$$\frac{(B - \sqrt{B^2 - 4K})f_l}{2} < S < \frac{Bf_l}{E}. \tag{3}$$

4.2 Requirements Imposed by Intermediate Linked Lists

The previous requirements guarantee the feasibility of the algorithm and good performance during the join phase. For the intermediate linked list mechanism to provide substantial benefit during the tree construction phase, we further require

R3 The total number of slot should be

R3.1 smaller than the number of buffer pages to avoid buffer thrashing, and thus random disk accesses, during linked list construction.

R3.2 smaller than a fraction of buffer pages to obtain good performance during grown subtree construction.

There are two reasons for R3.2. When we write a batch of linked lists to disk, the pages at the end of the linked lists are, on average, half-full. When the number of slots is large and the linked lists are short on average, the fragmentation problem becomes serious. For example, if the number of slots is equals the number of buffer pages, the average linked list length will be be 1 when a batch write occurs. In this case, 50% of of the information moved by I/O effort is useless. There is also a second and more serious problem. The total number of random reads incurred when reading linked lists back from disk to build grown subtrees is proportional to the number of slots. Let N_{ba} be the average number of batches a slot participated in the batch writes[2] The number of random reads required to read the linked lists back to memory is $S \cdot N_{ba}$. Therefore, it is beneficial to make the number of slots as small as possible.

Requirement 3 can be formally expressed as $S < \frac{B'}{Q}$, where $Q > 1$ is a tunable parameter. The above formula can be solve for S:

$$S < \frac{B}{Q + \frac{1}{f_l}}.$$

---

[2] When a linked list is shorter than a tunable threshold, it does not participate in the batch write.

Since $Qf_l + 1 > E$, and hence $\frac{B}{Q+\frac{1}{f_l}} < \frac{B \cdot f_l}{E}$, for reasonable choices for parameters, when considering all three requirements, the bounds on n_l becomes

$$\frac{(B - \sqrt{B^2 - 4K}) \cdot f_l}{2} < S < \frac{B}{Q + \frac{1}{f_l}}. \tag{4}$$

Note that the upper bound depends on buffer size and average leaf node fanout only. The lower bound is a monotonically increasing function of the data size set. When we plan to construct two seeded trees with the same set of slots, we must ensure that the number of slots satisfies the bounds imposed by both data sets simultaneously. This means we need only to apply inequality 4 to the larger data set size to derive the bounds for the number of slots.

5 Taking Samples

After determining k, the number of slots, we must sample from the input data set. The number of samples n would be a function of k. If the seeded tree is being constructed for data that is the output of some other operations in the same query, we can sample as the output is produced. Sampling would incur no additional I/O costs.

In many cases, we expect the data set to reside in a data file. If the data in the data file are known to be randomly distributed, that is, the placement of data in the file has no relation to the closeness in space of the objects they represent, the sampling task would be easy. We can simply read the first n items sequentially from disk and use them as sample. The sampling cost is very small in this case. In practice, we cannot rely on the data set having this property. Often spatial closeness of data does effect in the closeness of data in the file. In these cases, we have to sample randomly from the file.

If the number of samples is small in comparison to the size of the file, we can read the necessary disk blocks through random access. If the number of samples is large relative to the size of the file, it would be cheaper to sequentially access all disk blocks and perform the sampling. Algorithms such as those in [Vit85, Vit84, Ahr85] can be used to sample this sequential data stream.

The expected number of disk blocked accessed as a function of the size of the random sample has been presented in [Yao77]. Let m be the total number of disk blocks in the data file, n be the total number of data items and k be the size of the random sample. The expected number of accessed disk block X_D is

$$X_D = m \cdot \left[\prod_{i=1}^{h} \frac{nd - i + 1}{n - i + 1} \right] \quad \text{where } d = 1 - 1/m. \tag{5}$$

A simpler expression for a tight lower bound of this formula is [Yao77, Car75]

$$X_D = m(1 - (1 - 1/m)^k). \tag{6}$$

Let ρ be the ratio of the cost of a sequential disk block access to that of a random block access. If $X_D > m \cdot \rho$, it will be cheaper to perform random sampling through sequential reads. Approximating X_D with 6, this condition can be expressed as

$$k > \frac{\ln(1-\rho)}{\ln(1-1/m)}. \tag{7}$$

Whether it is cheaper to sample by sequentially accessing the data file depends on the ratio ρ and the number of blocks in the file. As an example, assume there are $100,000$ data items in a data file, each occupying 20 bytes. The file will have 2000 blocks. If the ratio ρ is $1/5$, it would be cheaper to sample by sequentially reading all blocks for sample sizes over 447 items. If the ratio is $1/30$, the threshold becomes 68 items.

There are other ways to reduce sampling costs. For instance, when a sample of size k is needed, we can first read in a some small number b of blocks from the data file and then obtain our k data samples from these b blocks. However, the feasibility of this approach depends on how the data are clustered in the file. As our purpose is to demonstrate the viability of building seeded trees from data sets, and the sampling cost does not dominate the overall cost of join, we do not pursue this approach further.

6 Slot Placement

In this section, we discuss how to generate a set of S slots from a sample set of size k. We have the following guidelines for choosing slots for a bootstrap-seeded tree.

- Place slots at or near the centers of clusters of data. This strategy inserts data objects that are close to each other into the same grown sub-tree, reduces dead area in bounding boxes of sub-trees, and improves performance.
- Avoid letting one slot cover too many data objects. Otherwise, we may have a grown sub-tree that overflows the buffer. Thus, we might want to place more than one slot in large clusters.
- Use point slots, i.e., slots whose bounding box value is a point. In [LR94], we have observed that setting the contents of slots to their center points at the beginning of the growing phase results in seeded trees that are more efficient during tree matching. Using point slots also simplifies the task of determining slots for bootstrap-seeded trees, as we need to worry about setting fewer parameters.

The study of cluster analysis in statistics [Eve93, KR90] addresses problem similar to ours. However, techniques developed there do not apply directly to our context for several reasons. First, most cluster analysis is assumed to be performed off-line. Therefore, expensive, multiple-pass algorithms can be used to analyze the clustering structure of data sets. For bootstrap seeding, we cannot afford expensive off-line computation. Second, our purpose is not to determine the precise clustering structure of data sets, but rather, to choose slots that support efficient spatial operations. Therefore, we are interested in identifying fast but formally less rigorous methods.

6.1 Direct Sample Placement

The simplest method is to directly use the data objects in sample set as the slots. In the method, the number of sampled objects is set to be the number of slots, that is, $k = S$. After taking a size S sample from the data file, we calculate the center point of the sample data objects, which are then used as slots. The method is simple and straightforward, and is used as basis of comparison in our study.

6.2 Nearest Group Center Placement

As noted above, it would be advantageous to place the slots inside data clusters. Moreover, it is useful to place more slots inside clusters that have more data objects. We adopt the following somewhat stricter criterion:

Given a spatial data set and the number of slots S, place the S slots in the map area so that the sum of distances from the center of each data object to its nearest slot is minimized.

In this section, we discuss a heuristic to approach this goal. This method forms S groups of data, each representing a slot. Data objects from the sample set are placed one by one into the group whose center of gravity is nearest to the center of the object. The slot contents are set to the centers of gravity of the groups at the end of this processing.

The method is described in detail as follows. For each slot, we form a *data group*. Each group has a center of gravity and a weight. That is, each group is represented by triple (u, v, w), where (u, v) is a vector describing the position of the center of gravity, and w is the weight of the group.

At first, we randomly choose S data objects from the sample set, each to initialize one data group. For each such object with center at (x, y), its associated group is initialized to $(x, y, 1)$.

For each remaining data object with center at (u, v), we then identify the group (x, y, w) whose center of gravity is nearest to (u, v). The object is added into this group and the group triple is updated to

$$\left(\frac{wx + u}{w + 1}, \frac{wy + v}{w + 1}, w + 1 \right) \tag{8}$$

When all objects in the sample set are processed, the centers of gravity can be output as slots.

This method is sensitive to how we initialize the group centers. To avoid instability, we can go through the sample data set more than once. At the end of each pass, we reset the group weights to smaller values, and re-insert all sample objects into their nearest group.

The parameters of this method are the number of passes and the value to which we reset the group weights at the beginning of a new pass. The ratio of the sample set size and slot number is another parameter of this method. This method requires the sample size k to be several times greater than the slot number S. Again, we are interested in an efficient but suboptimal method, not in fine-tuning these parameters. We set the number of passes to two and reset the weights to one third its original value at the beginning of the second pass. The ratio of sample set size and slot number is set to 20. Note that when the ratio and the number of passes are one, the method degenerates into the direct sample placement method.

7   Joining Two Seeded Trees

Consider a spatial join between two data set D_R and D_S, neither of which has any spatial index. Suppose we choose data set D_R and bootstrap a seeded tree T_R directly from it. Next we need to build a seeded tree T_S for D_S. There are three ways to obtain the seed levels for T_S:

1. Copy the seed levels of T_R as when it is built.
2. Use the same seed levels originally constructed for T_R.
3. Construct the seed levels of T_S by bootstrapping from D_S.

The first two alternatives fall into the category of copying seeding. The third is bootstrap seeding. Our experiments show the first alternative outperforms the second alternative slightly. The third alternative incurs additional sampling and slot placement costs in tree construction without providing better performance in tree matching. In the following discussion, all seeded tree joins use the first alternative unless indicated otherwise.

After both seeded trees are built, we join these trees using the same tree matching algorithm used to join two R-trees, or one R-tree and one seeded tree [BKS93, LR94, LR95]. Since the tree matching algorithm does not restrict the types of the participating trees, it proceed exactly as before.

7.1   Seed-Level Filtering

Seed level filtering [LR94] is a technique that we can use to enhance join performance when one participant is a seeded tree. It works as follows. Say we are building a seeded tree by copy-seeding from an existing R-tree. When data objects are inserted into the new seeded tree, we can check to see if the object overlaps at least one bounding box in the nodes at the slot level. If not, the object will not overlap any object in the R-tree and need not be inserted at all. Using this technique in the construction of seeded trees results in smaller seeded trees, saving costs in subsequent processing. Seed level filtering is useful if the data set used to construct the seeded tree is large and only a portion of the data objects in the data set overlap data objects in the R-tree.

This technique is particularly useful with joins between two seeded trees. In this context, we can first bootstrap a seeded tree from the smaller of the two data sets, and then construct a seeded tree for the larger data set by copy-seeding. Seed level filtering can be applied to the larger data set in the during construction of the second tree.

One argument against bootstrapping from the smaller data set could be that the common seed levels are built using less information, and may hence result in inferior tree join performance. However, our experiments show that even without seed level filtering, the penalty for using the smaller data set for bootstrapping (and thus to determine the common seed levels) is marginal. Using seed level filtering, bootstrapping from the smaller data set allows us to filter objects from the larger data set, potentially screening more data objects from participating in the subsequent processing. The benefits of filtering objects from the larger data set far outweigh any penalties for bootstrapping with the more limited information in the smaller data set.

8 Experiments

Assume we need to perform a spatial join between data sets D_R and D_S, both without pre-computed spatial indices. We will call the seeded tree constructed for D_R, T_R, and that constructed for D_S, T_S.

For simplicity, we assume that the disk page size and the memory page size are both 1K bytes, as are the node sizes for both seeded trees. The data files are assumed to contain entries consisting of a 16-byte bounding box and a 4-byte object identifier. We also assume a dedicated buffer of 512 pages.

We studied data of different degrees of spatial clustering. The degree of clustering was controlled by a simple scheme, similar to the one in [LR94]. When generating a data set of $x \times y$ objects, we first generated x *cluster rectangles*, whose centers were randomly distributed in the map area. We then randomly distributed the centers of y data rectangles within each clustering rectangle. By controlling the total area of the clustering rectangles, we could control the degree of clustering of the data set. The smaller the total area of the clustering rectangles, the more clustered the data set. The length and the width of each clustering rectangle was chosen randomly and independently to lie between 0 and a predefined upper bound. This upper bound controlled the total area of the clustering rectangles. The size and shape of data rectangles were similarly chosen using a smaller upper bound. When clustering rectangles or data rectangles extended over the boundary of the map area, they were clipped to fit into the map area. When a data rectangle extended over the boundary of its clustering rectangle, it was not clipped. In the experiments, the number of data objects per cluster was set to be 200, and the number of clustering rectangles was set according to the total number of data objects. Without loss of generality, the map area under study was assumed to range from 0 to 1 along both X and Y axes.

The degree of clustering of the data sets used in our experiments were categorized as high, medium, or low, meaning that the side lengths of the clustering rectangles were no larger than 0.03, 0.04, and 0.09, respectively. We used four join dataset pairs A, B, C, and D, respectively. A, B, C contained data sets of cardinalities 100k and 40k, respectively. The data sets in D had cardinalities 100k and 80k. The degree of clustering in A, B, and C was low, medium, and high, respectively. The degree of clustering in D was medium.

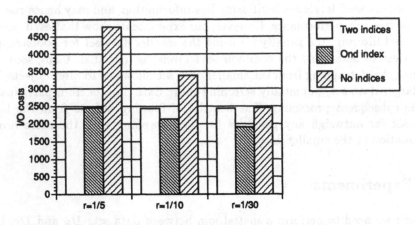

Fig. 4. Costs of spatial joins under various conditions.

A preview of the performance of our method may be appropriate at this point. Although we assume no pre-existing indices, and are addressing an inherently more difficult problem, the performance of our method compares very favorably with the easier cases where indices pre-exist. Figure 4 illustrates the total join costs of for three scenarios, with different numbers of pre-existing indices. Data set pair B was used as input data set. Column "Two indices" is the cost of joining two pre-existing R-trees. No construction costs are incurred in this case. Column "Once index" is the combined cost of constructing a seeded tree for the smaller data set and that of joining the seeded tree with a pre-existing R-tree for the larger data set. Column "No indices" is cost of constructing two seeded trees plus that of joining them[3]. The costs are shown under different assumptions for ρ, the ratio of the costs of sequential and random I/O. In the first group of columns, labeled "$r = 1/5$", the value of $\rho = 1/5$. In the second and the third groups, $\rho = 1/10$, and $\rho = 1/30$, respectively. As Fig. 4 shows, even in the case in which there is not any pre-computed spatial indices, the costs of dynamically constructing two seeded trees and then joining them is quite comparable to the cost of joining two R-trees pre-computed from the same input data sets.

Figure 5 shows the break up of the total cost of spatial joins on data set pair B, with the number of slots set to 100. The columns labeled "input" show the cost

---

[3] The number of slots used is 100.

of Initially reading in the input data sets during tree construction. The columns labeled "sampling bound" are the maximum possible costs of sampling from the larger of the two data sets. This value is the upper bound on sampling cost in all cases. The columns labeled "processing" shows all other costs, including the costs incurred during the growing phases of the two seeded trees and those during tree matching. As seen in the figure, the upper bound on the sampling cost is very small under all assumptions, which makes it less rewarding to optimize on the sampling costs. The input costs are fixed and are also small portions of the total costs. Our experiments on other data set showed similar cost break-downs. The numbers lists in the following discussion are the processing costs only only. Also, different ρ ratios in general demonstrated the same trends in various experiments. For clarity of presentation, we will show only the performance numbers obtained under the assumption of $\rho = 1/30$.

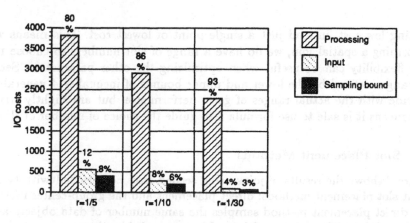

Fig. 5. Break-ups of seeded tree join costs.

8.1 Choice of Number of Slots

We studied the effect of using different numbers of slots on the performance of seeded-tree joins. We were particularly interested in studying whether the lower and upper bounds derived in Sect. 4 were useful guides to choosing slot numbers. The group-center sampling method was used to determine the values of slots after their number was decided.

We chose the values of parameters C and Q to be 3 in inequality 4, which means that the average grown subtree size and the number of slots will both be about 1/3 of the number of pages in the buffer. For the buffer and data set sizes used, this formula yields 16 and 165 as the lower and upper bounds respectively, for the number of slots.

Figure 6 shows the effects of slot numbers, using data sets A, B and D. Two observations are of interest. First, there is in general a range of slot numbers

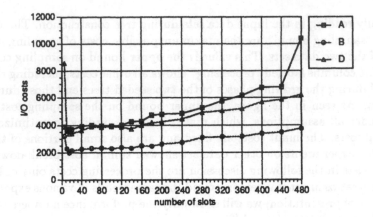

Fig. 6. Effect of slot number on seeded tree join performance.

yielding low cost, instead just a single point of lowest cost. This means when performing a spatial join, we do have a range of slot numbers to choose from. This flexibility can be useful when optimizing the other parameters. Second, the ranges defined by the lower and upper bounds of inequality 4 generally do coincide with the actual ranges of good performance, but are slightly stricter. This means it is safe to use formula 4 to guide the choice of number of slots.

8.2 Slot Placement Methods

Figure 7 shows the results of joins using seeded trees constructed with two different slot placement methods: direct placement and the group-center methods. The direct placement method samples the same number of data objects as the number of slots. The number of data objects sampled by the group center methods is a parameter of the method. Here we set that number to be 20 times the number of slots. The group center method used here makes two passes, resetting the group weights at the start of the second pass to 1/3 of their values at the end of the first pass.

As Fig. 7 shows, the performance of the direct placement method is surprisingly close to that of the group center method. This demonstrates the adaptability of the seeded tree construction algorithm and robustness of the performance of seeded trees. Even if the slots are not placed in the best positions, the performance of the seeded tree join shows very little degradation. The closeness of the two methods precludes the need for testing group center method with smaller sample size-slot number ratios.

8.3 Seed Level Filtering and Data Set Sizes

As discussed earlier, given two data sets with no indices, we can bootstrap the initial seeded tree for either the larger or the smaller data set, and use that index to copy-seed the second. Figure 8 shows the performance differences between

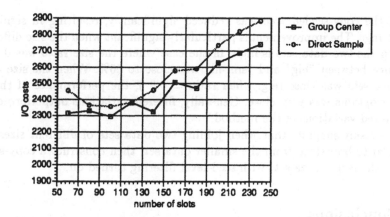

Fig. 7. Performance of boot-strap seeded trees constructed with different slot placement methods.

such choices. Consider first the lines labeled "big" and "small", which show join performance using the larger and smaller data set as the basis for bootstrapping, respectively. The data sets used here were of medium clustering and the larger of the two data sets was always of cardinality 100,000. The X-axis is the ratio of the size of the smaller data set to that of the larger data set. The performance of the two alternatives is quite close, with the "big" variation being slightly better.

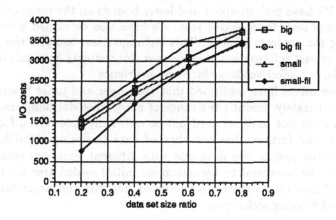

Fig. 8. Effect of seed level filtering.

When we turned on the seed level filtering technique [LR94], the situation reversed. When the larger data set was used for bootstrapping and filtering was applied the smaller data set ("big-fil"), the improvements were marginal. On the other hand, when the roles were reversed and the larger data set was filtered, many more data objects became exempt from insertion into the tree. Thus the size of the copy-seeded tree was reduced significantly, resulting in significant cost savings. The improvement is particularly significant when the size difference between the two data sets is high. In the case where the size ratio was 0.2, the difference between "big" and "sml-fil" was close to 50%. When the size of the two data sets was close (e.g. when ratio = 0.8), the performance of the two filtering options was very close. Generally, filtered variations outperformed the non-filtered variations of the method.

This result suggests that when joining two data sets of different sizes, it is beneficial to bootstrap from the smaller data set, then construct a copy-seeded tree for the larger data set, with seed-level filtering turned on.

9 Conclusions

In this paper we studied the problem of how to perform spatial joins between two data sets with no pre-computed spatial indices. To the best of our knowledge, no solution has hitherto existed for this problem in the context of spatial joins. Solving this problem also contributes to query optimization for complex spatial queries. In addition, we have demonstrated the feasibility of using sampling techniques to advantage in spatial joins.

We have extended the work in [LR94, LR95] and introduced the bootstrap-seeding technique, which allows seeded trees to be constructed directly from underlying data sets. The task of bootstrap-seeding is divided into that of determining the number of slots, assigning values to slots, and constructing the index tree. We have derived upper and lower bounds on the range of the acceptable number of slots for a seeded tree. We have also developed a technique for determining the contents of slots. This technique first samples the underlying data set to extract information, then derives slot contents from this information using simple, but effective data clustering heuristics.

Our experiments have confirmed that the upper and lower bounds we have derived do accurately describe the range of acceptable slot numbers. They also indicate that the slot contents need not be optimally determined for good join performance, and further, that complicated data clustering algorithms are unnecessary. When joining two data sets with different sizes, our results suggest that it would be beneficial to bootstrap an initial seeded tree for the smaller data set, and then to construct a copy-seeded tree with the larger data set using the seed level filtering technique.

References

[Ahr85]   J. H. Ahrens. Sequential random sampling. *ACM Transactions on Mathematical Software*, 11(2):157–169, June 1985.

[BKS93]   Thomas Brinkhoff, Hans-Peter Kriegel, and Bernhard Seeger. Efficient processing of spatial joins using R-trees. *Proceedings of ACM SIGMOD International Conference on Management of Data*, pages 237–246, May 1993.

347

[BKSS90] Norbert Beckmann, Hans-Peter Kriegel, Ralf Schneider, and Bernhard Seeger. The R*-tree: An efficient and robust access method for points and rectangles. *Proceedings of ACM SIGMOD International Conference on Management of Data*, pages 322–332, May 1990.

[Car75] A. F. Cardenas. Analysis and performance of inverted data base structures. *Communications of ACM*, 18(5):253–263, May 1975.

[Eve93] Brian Everitt. *Cluster Analysis*. Edward Arnold, London, third edition edition, 1993.

[FSR87] Christos Faloutsos, Timos Sellis, and Nick Roussopoulos. Analysis of object oriented spatial access methods. *Proceedings of ACM SIGMOD International Conference on Management of Data*, pages 427–439, 1987.

[Gut84] Antonin Guttman. R-trees: A dynamic index structure for spatial searching. *Proceedings of ACM SIGMOD International Conference on Management of Data*, pages 47–57, Aug. 1984.

[KR90] Leonard Kaufman and Peter J. Rousseeuw. *Finding Groups in Data, An Introduction to Cluster Analysis*. John Wiley & Sons, Inc., New York, 1990.

[LH92] Wei Lu and Jiawei Han. Distance-associated join indices for spatial range search. In *Proceedings of International Conference on Data Engineering*, pages 284–292, 1992.

[LR94] Ming-Ling Lo and C. V. Ravishankar. Spatial joins using seeded trees. In *Proceedings of ACM SIGMOD International Conference on Management of Data*, pages 209–220, Minneapolis, MN, May 1994.

[LR95] Ming-Ling Lo and C. V. Ravishankar. Seeded trees for spatial joins: Structure and implementation. Technical report, Department of EECS, University of Michigan, Ann Arbor, Michigan, 1995.

[Ore89] J. A. Orenstein. Redundancy in spatial databases. In *Proceedings of ACM SIGMOD International Conference on Management of Data*, Portland, OR, 1989.

[Ore90] Jack Orenstein. A comparison of spatial query processing techniques for native and parameter spaces. In *Proceedings of ACM SIGMOD International Conference on Management of Data*, pages 343–352, 1990.

[Ore91] Jack Orenstein. An algorithm for computing the overlay of k-dimensional spaces. In O. Gunther and H.-J Schek, editors, *Advances in Spatial Databases (SSD '91)*, pages 381–400, Zurich, Switzerland, August 28-30 1991. Springer-Verlag.

[Rot91] D Rotem. Spatial join indices. In *Proceedings of International Conference on Data Engineering*, pages 500–509, Kobe, Japan 1991.

[SRF87] T. Sellis, N. Roussopoulos, and C. Faloutsos. The R$^+$-tree: A dynamic index for multi-dimensional objects. In *Proceedings of Very Large Data Bases*, pages 3–11, Brighton, England, 1987.

[Val87] P. Valduriez. Join indices. *ACM Transactions on Database Systems*, 12(2), 1987.

[Vit84] Jeffery Scott Vitter. Faster methods for random sampling. *Communications of the ACM*, 27(7):703–718, July 1984.

[Vit85] J. S. Vitter. Random sampling with reservoir. *ACM Transactions on Mathematical Software*, 11:37–57, March 1985.

[Yao77] S. B. Yao. Approximating block access in database organizations. *Comm. of ACM*, 20:260–261, Apr. 1977.

Spatial Join Strategies in Distributed Spatial DBMS

David. J. Abel[1], Beng Chin Ooi[2], Kian-Lee Tan[1,2], Robert Power[1],
Jeffrey X. Yu[3]

[1] CSIRO Division of Information Technology
Computing Science and Information Technology Building
GPO Box 664, Canberra, ACT 2601, Australia

[2] Department of Information Systems & Computer Science
National University of Singapore
Lower Kent Ridge, Singapore

[3] Department of Computer Science, Australian National University
Canberra, ACT 0200, Australia

Abstract. In a distributed spatial database system, a user may issue a query that relates two spatial relations that are stored at different sites. Because of the sheer volume and complexity of spatial data, spatial joins between two spatial relations at different sites are expensive in terms of computation and transmission cost. In this paper, we examine the problems of spatial joins between sites, and present spatial join processing strategies used in a heterogeneous spatial database system. Preliminary experimental results are reported.

1 Introduction

Queries in spatial databases frequently involve relationships between two spatial entities. These relationships include *containment, intersection, adjacency* and *proximity*. For example, the query "which schools are adjacent to areas zoned for industrial purposes?" requires an adjacency relationship, while the query "which police stations are more than 1 kilometre from a major road?" involves a proximity relationship. To answer these queries, spatial joins are used to materialise the relationships between the two spatial entities. Like the relational join operation, spatial joins are expensive, and have received much research attention recently [Gun93, BKS93, BKSS94, GaG94, LoR94].

While spatial database research to date has largely focused on single-site environment, some prospective applications now call for distributed spatial databases. A representative example is in government agencies where the sharing of core data sets across agencies has been shown to provide high savings [Tom93]. Legislative and organisational requirements make it very difficult to establish a single unified database; rather data sharing must be approached as a problem in distributed access to many autonomous databases.

To realise the full potential of a distributed spatial database system, many issues have to be addressed. Most of these issues are similar to those that arise in designing heterogeneous database systems [RIDE93]. These include the integration of existing schemas and data, the processing and optimisation of distributed queries, and transaction processing issues. However, the issue of processing a distributed spatial query has been largely ignored.

In a distributed spatial database system, a user may issue a query that joins two spatial relations that are stored at different sites. Unlike conventional distributed databases where the transmission cost is dominant [OzV91], both the transmission cost and the processing cost may be comparable for distributed spatial databases because of the sheer volume and complexity of spatial data. In this paper, we focus on the design of distributed spatial join algorithms. We propose a new spatial join algorithm that is based on the concept of *spatial semijoins*. Like its relational counterpart, a spatial semijoin eliminates objects before transmission to reduce both transmission and local processing costs. This elimination is performed as a spatial selection on one database using an *approximation* to the spatial descriptions of the other. All the algorithms studied are based on single-dimensional approximations obtained from object mapping. In particular, locational keys are used to linearise spatial objects. To study the effectiveness of semijoin-based approaches, we conducted extensive experiments on real data sets. The results show that the methods are effective in reducing total processing cost in distributed join processing. To our knowledge, there is no reported work on distributed spatial join processing. This is the first of its kind to address the issue.

The remainder of this paper is organised as follows. In the next section, we describe the distributed architecture in which this work is targeted. We also look at the issues involved in processing distributed spatial queries. In Section 3, we examine distributed join processing, introduce the spatial semijoin and describe how it can be used for join processing. Section 4 describes the join strategies that are based on semijoins. Results from experiments with a representative database are described and analysed in Section 5. We summarise our findings and discuss on-going work in Section 6.

2 The Virtual DataBase

The work done in this paper is one of our on-going research activities in designing the Virtual DataBase system (VDB) [AOP+94]. The Virtual Database is a specialist server in a distributed environment which clients view as a single database containing all the information to be sourced from other agencies through distributed databases.

The architecture, as shown in Figure 1, follows the widely-used reference model for architectures for federated database of Sheth and Larson [ShL90]. Note that only one local database is shown in the schematic. The VDB itself is the part of the total system enclosed in the large oval. Dashed lines represent information transfers made when a local database is registered with the VDB.

Solid lines between components represent transfers of commands and data made during the processing of a request by a client system.

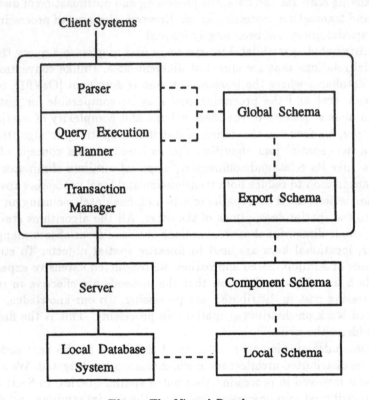

Fig. 1. The Virtual Database.

Four types of schema are present:

- the global schema defines the classes accessible to clients. It also includes, only for reference within the VDB, the procedures to materialise the classes from the local databases and some information on the costs of performing operations within the local databases. The schema is defined in terms of the VDB data model;
- the local schema of a local database defines its complete schema, using the local database management system DDL;
- the component schema reexpresses the local schema of a local database in terms of the VDB data model;
- the export schema of a local database defines the data which the local database is prepared to make accessible through the VDB. It can also include information which is implicit in the design of the local database schema.

Client systems express operations by the VDB. The execution of an operation is:

- commands are parsed, with checks against the Global Schema. The output is passed to the Query Execution Planner (QEP);
- The QEP assembles the query plan, essentially a sequence of operations to be performed by the VDB local processor and the local databases. This phase also includes query optimisation in which the QEP selects between possible sets of commands and their sequencing to minimise the total cost of the operation. The query plan is passed to the Global Transaction Manager (GTM);
- The GTM is responsible for retrieving data that are available at its site, and issuing commands, in a generic form, to the database drivers of the local databases. The drivers reexpress those commands in their database system's native command language, execute the command, and pass data back to the GTM. The GTM is also responsible for monitoring successful completion of operations, for error recovery and for operations by the VDB local processor.

Various techniques for generating and processing query plans proposed for non-spatial heterogeneous database systems are being adopted by the VDB. However, unlike many other systems, we have to be concerned about the large volume of large data items. It has traditionally been assumed that transmission of data dominates distributed query processing performance, and as a result, many algorithms have been designed to minimise transmission cost [OzV91]. This assumption is probably due to the days when network speeds were slow and wide area networks were assumed. While the transmission costs of exporting a spatial data set from one site to another can be high, this assumption may not be valid in distributed spatial databases where local area networks are used. This is because of the high speed local area network and the high local processing cost for spatial operations. The local processing cost cannot be ignored since

- many spatial databases of real-world interest are very large, with sizes ranging from tens of thousands to millions of objects;
- spatial descriptions of objects are typically extensive, ranging from a few hundred bytes in Land Information System applications to megabytes in natural resource applications [Abe93]; and
- many basic spatial operations such as testing the intersection of two polygons are expensive.

As a broad indication of relative costs of operations, transmission of a land parcel spatial description (with an average size of 48 bytes) over an Ethernet Local Area Network requires 0.5 milliseconds. On the other hand, retrieving a polygon from a database of 50000 polygons using an intersection qualification costs in the region of 2 milliseconds on a SUN SPARC-10 machine. The challenge then is to develop more efficient distributed spatial join strategies that take into account both the transmission cost and local processing cost.

In this paper, unless otherwise stated, R and S represents two spatial relations. R resides at site R_{site} and S at site S_{site}. A spatial join between R and S

is on the spatial attributes $R.A$ and $S.B$. The result of the spatial join is to be produced at site S_{site}.

3 A Framework for Semijoin-Based Spatial Join

A straightforward approach to perform a spatial join between R and S is to transmit the whole of R from R_{site} to S_{site}.[4] The spatial join can then be performed at S_{site} using an existing uniprocessor join algorithm. This method, though simple, incurs high transmission cost and high local processing cost.

In this section, we present an alternative approach that is based on the concept of semijoin. We will first look at the semijoin operator for spatial databases called *spatial semijoin*, and then present a framework for designing semijoin-based algorithms.

3.1 The Spatial Semijoin

In conventional distributed databases, the semijoin operation [BeC81] has been proposed to reduce transmission costs. The θ-semijoin of a relation R with another relation S on the join condition $R.A \theta S.B$ is the relation $R' \subseteq R$ such that all the records in R' satisfy the join condition, where θ is a scalar comparison operator (i.e. $<, >, <=, >=, =$).[5] The join of R and S, that are located at sites R_{site} and S_{site} respectively, can be performed using a semijoin in three steps. First, S is projected on the joining attribute at S_{site}, and the distinct values of the result, say S', is transmitted to R_{site} . Next, the semijoin of R and S' is performed at R_{site} to give R', which is sent to S_{site}. Finally, the join of R' and S is performed at S_{site} to produce the join result. Since R' has fewer records than R, transmitting R' is cheaper. Additionally, there is some saving in local processing costs for evaluation of the final join at site S_{site}. Clearly, there are additional local processing and transmission operations to be performed and a design objective is to ensure that there is a net saving in cost.

The semijoin concept can be readily adapted to perform joins in distributed spatial databases. However, the conventional semijoin has to be extended for additional considerations that are peculiar to spatial databases. These considerations are:

- The conventional semijoin uses the distinct values of the joining attribute in S to minimise the transmission cost from S_{site} to R_{site} and the cost to evaluate the semijoin. However, as most spatial descriptions are intrinsically complex data types and represent irregular, non-overlapping partitions of

---

[4] An alternative solution is to transmit the index of R also. This can take advantage of join algorithms that are based on indices [BKS93, LoR94] provided the indices at both sites are similar. However, since joins are usually performed on subsets of relations (as a result of selections), it is no longer clear how much could be gained by transmitting the index of R.

[5] In [BeC81], θ is set to "$=$".

space, there is no direct equivalent to a projection on a single-value attribute where the joining attribute is a spatial description. Consider, for example, a relation representing soil types in a region. Each record then describes a polygonal area occupied by a certain soil type. These polygons are represented as arrays of the coordinates of their vertices. In natural resource databases, spatial descriptions are typically hundreds to thousands of bytes long [BKS93]. For cadastral databases, descriptions are much smaller, but still in the region of 100 bytes [Abe93]. Therefore, transmitting the spatial descriptions remains costly.

- Evaluation of relationships such as containment, intersection and adjacency between two polygons is complex and expensive compared to testing equality of two single-value attributes. For example, our study shows that testing intersection of two polygons each with an average of six vertices costs 250 microseconds on a SUN SPARC-10 workstation, while the equality test of two single-value attributes is of the order of 0.1 microseconds.

To cut down on the transmission cost and local processing cost to evaluate the semijoin on the spatial attributes of R and S, we propose that approximations to the objects in R and S and a computationally less expensive, but weaker, spatial relationship be used. The approximations and the weaker spatial relationship must satisfy the *property of conservation*, i.e. for two objects that are spatially related, their approximations must also be related by the weaker relationship. For example, as shown in Figure 2, an object e_2 is possibly contained in object e_1 only if its approximation E_2 intersects with e_1's approximation E_1.

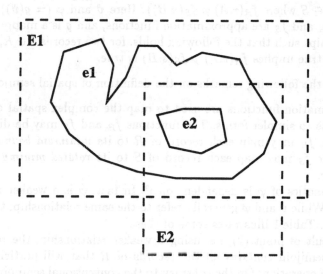

Fig. 2. E_1 overlaps E_2, and e_1 includes e_2.

To some extent, the idea of spatial semijoins using weaker relationships is similar to joins on approximations in [Gun93]. Table 1 lists some examples of **relationships and their approximations.**

$e_1 \theta e_2$	$E_1 \Theta E_2$
e_1 within distance d from e_2 (measured between centerpoints)	E_1 within distance d from E_2 (measured between closest points)
e_1 overlaps e_2	E_1 overlaps E_2
e_1 includes e_2	E_1 overlaps E_2
e_1 contained in e_2	E_1 overlaps E_2

Table 1. Some examples of operations and their approximations.

Using approximations and a weaker relationship are motivated by two observations. First, the approximation is shorter than the full descriptions of the spatial entity and hence will incur lower transmission costs. Second, geometrically-simple approximations such as the minimum bounding rectangles allow simple evaluation of spatial relationships and so reduce the computation cost when evaluating the semijoin. For example, referring to Figure 2 again, transmitting rectangles with 2 vertices is definitely cheaper than transmitting the irregularly shaped objects. Moreover, checking for rectangle intersection is also cheaper than checking for polygon containment.

The resulting semijoin operation, called *spatial semijoin*, is defined as follows.

Definition 1. Let R and S be two spatial relations, and A and B be attributes of R and S on spatial domains, respectively. The ϑ spatial semijoin between R and S on attributes A and B, denoted $R' = R \overset{s}{\underset{A\vartheta B}{\ltimes}} S$, is defined by $R' = \{r \in R \mid \exists s \in S$ where $f_R(r.A) \; \varphi \; f_S(s.B)\}$. Here ϑ and φ $(= g(\vartheta))$ are *spatial* operators, f_R and f_S are approximation functions, and g is a mapping function on relationships such that the following holds: for two records $r \in R$, and $s \in S$, $r.A \; \vartheta \; s.B$ is true implies $f_R(r.A) \; \varphi \; f_S(s.B)$ is true.

We have the following remarks on the definition of spatial semijoin.

1.) Approximation functions are used to map the complex spatial descriptions of objects to simpler forms. The functions f_R and f_S may be different. For example, f_R may map each record of R to its *minimum bounding rectangle*, while f_S may map each record of S to its *rotated minimum bounding rectangle*.
2.) The semantics of φ is dependent on ϑ. In fact, φ is a weaker relationship than ϑ. While ϑ and φ generally refer to the same relationship, they may be different. Table 1 illustrates some of these.
3.) As a result of point (2), i.e. using a weaker relationship, the result of the spatial semijoin *contains* all the records of R that will participate in the final join operation. On the contrary to the conventional semijoin, where the result of the semijoin is the set of records of R that will participate in the final join operation, the spatial semijoin using a weaker relationship does not

eliminate totally all records that do not contribute to the final answer. In other words, the spatial semijoin result contains both *hits* and *false drops*. Hits are records of R that will satisfy the join operation, ϑ, while *false drops* are those that satisfy the join operation φ but not ϑ.

3.2 The Framework

A distributed spatial join can be pre-processed using a spatial semijoin. The basic framework of a spatial join, $R \underset{A\vartheta B}{\overset{s}{\bowtie}} S$ at site S_{site}, using a semijoin can be expressed as follows.

Framework 1. Distributed Spatial Join Processing Using Semijoin
Input: Two relations R and S with spatial attributes A and B, respectively.
Output: $R \underset{A\vartheta B}{\overset{s}{\bowtie}} S$.

1. $B' = \{s.B \mid s \in S\}$;
2. $B^f = \{f_S(b) \mid b \in B'\}$;
3. **Send** distinct values of B^f from S_{site} to R_{site};
4. **Reduce** R to $R' = \{r \in R \mid \exists b \in B^f$ such that $f_R(r.A) \; \varphi \; b$ where $\varphi = g(\vartheta)\}$;
5. **Send** R' to S_{site};
6. **Perform** $R' \underset{A\vartheta B}{\overset{s}{\bowtie}} S$

The performance of the framework hinges on the approximations to the spatial descriptions of S, i.e. step 2. We restrict our discussion here to three possible approximation functions, illustrated in Figure 3:

- f_S is an identity function $\mathcal{I}$ such that $\forall t \in B', \mathcal{I}(t) = t$. In other words, the spatial descriptions of the records of S are sent to the R_{site}.
- f_S is a 1-1 mapping such that each record of B' is mapped to a record in B^f. However, instead of the complex spatial description, a simpler approximation that bounds the spatial object is used. For example, the the minimum bounding rectangles (MBR) of the records may be used and transmitted.
- f_S is a m-1 mapping such that several records of B' are mapped to the same B^f record. For example, a smaller set of MBRs can be used such that each MBR bounds several spatial objects.

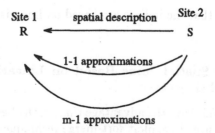

Fig. 3. Different approximations functions for f_S.

The first two approaches lead to B^f having as many records as B. The last approach, on the other hand, has the potential for varying the size of B^f to optimise the total cost of the operation. The first approach has no false drops in R' if $\varphi = \vartheta$, while the last approach has the highest number of false drops in R'. However, the first approach incurs the highest cost in transmitting B^f to the R_{site}, while the last approach requires minimum transmission cost. Since the number of objects being reduced by S using the third approach might not be significant, transmitting R' could still be very expensive. Such an effect will defeat the purpose of a spatial semijoin.

The second and third approaches follow closely the usual practice in spatial database systems of structuring operations as a filter operation using simplified descriptions (or approximations) followed by full evaluation using the full descriptions of objects [Ore86, BKS93, BKSS94, GaG94]. Typically a polygonal object is represented for the filter operation by its MBR, because MBRs are inexpensive to store (16 bytes for single-precision) and spatial relationships between them are inexpensive to evaluate. The filter test is formulated not to reject cases that satisfy the full evaluation. However, it typically will not reject all cases that do not satisfy the full test. Design then seeks a good compromise between the false drops, the costs of the filter operation and the costs of storing and (if necessary) deriving the approximations.

From the definition of the spatial semijoin and the description of the framework, we note that adopting different approximation functions will lead to different families of semijoin-based algorithms. The framework is also independent of the relationship on the joining attributes of R and S. Without loss of generality, we adopt intersection as the relationship in this paper.

4 Semijoins Based on Linearised Single-Dimensional Objects

In this section, we design a basic intersection-join algorithm that uses spatial semijoins. We assume both R and S have existing spatial indices. This is not unreasonable since large spatial relations in practice usually have an existing spatial index. The algorithm exploits the spatial indices in two ways:

- to provide the approximations for spatial objects;
- to perform the semijoin and final join using the indices at the respective site.

Moreover, we assume that the indices are based on linearised single-dimensional objects.

4.1 Uniprocessor Spatial Joins Based on Linearised Single-Dimensional Objects

Sort-merge join methods have the advantage that, in the best case, both data sets are scanned at most once. To exploit sort-merge techniques in spatial databases, the spatial objects must be ordered. Techniques on ordering multi-dimensional objects using single-dimensional values have been proposed [AbS84, Ore86] and one of the most popular ordering techniques is that based on bit interleaving proposed by Morton [Mor66]. In [AbS84], a space is recursively divided into four equal-sized quadrants as in the quad-tree [Sam90], forming a hierarchy of quadrants. For each quadrant, a unique key of base 5 is attached. Figure 4 illustrates an example of key assignment. When these keys are traced, it is the z-order enumeration of grid cells as in [Ore86]. An object that is fully contained by a subspace is assigned its key. To improve the approximation of objects by quadrants, an object is assigned up to k locational keys (In [AbS84], $k = 4$). For example, using $k = 4$, the rectangular object in Figure 4 will be assigned the keys: 1100, 1233, 1300, 1410. The spatial objects are held sorted in ascending sequence by the locational key values, with each member of the sorted list consisting of the object identifier, its MBR and the assigned locational key. A B+-tree is used to provide direct access to the spatial objects based on the locational keys [Abe83].

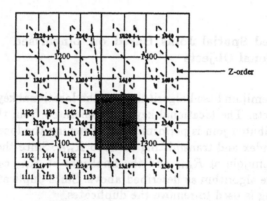

Fig. 4. Assignment of locational keys.

Consider two spatial relations R and S that are to be joined. Figure 5(a) shows the objects in R and S, and Figure 5(b) shows the locational key values of the objects. In this example, we have allowed each object to have a maximum of 4 keys. Joining the two relations can be performed by a merge-like operation along the two sorted lists of locational keys. We note the following. First, the join is a non-equijoin. For example, the locational key value 1240 of S4 matches two locational key values of R1 (namely 1241 and 1242). Second, the result may contain duplicates. This is because each object has multiple keys, and different pairs of keys of the same objects may intersect. For example, there are two resulting pairs between R1 and S4. Finally, the results may contain false drops. Looking at Figure 5(a), we notice that there are only two intersections, but we obtain four. The pair (R1, S2) and (R2, S2) are false drops. This arises because the locational keys are but approximations of the actual objects.

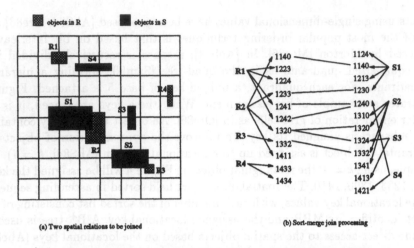

(a) Two spatial relations to be joined   (b) Sort-merge join processing

Fig. 5. Example of two spatial relations and its join processing.

4.2 Distributed Spatial Joins Based on Linearised Single-Dimensional Objects

Our distributed semijoin based algorithm uses the locational keys as approximations to the objects. The locational keys are generated from the MBR of each object. The distributed join is performed by retrieving the locational keys of S from its spatial index and transmitting them to R_{site}. Since the locational keys are sorted, the semijoin at R_{site} and the final join at S_{site} can be performed using a merge-like algorithm as described above. Since duplicates may occur in the result, hashing is used to remove the duplicates.

We note that the semijoin is less complex than the final join. Since the join is a non-equijoin, the scanning of the sorted lists for the final join requires "backing up". On the other hand, the semijoin requires a full scan of R, and at most a full scan of S. This is because it suffices to check that a record of R matches at least one record of S', rather than multiple records of S'.

For the final join, to cut down the cost of I/O when records are backed-up, we cached those records of R' (and S) that join with multiple records of S (and R').

5 A Performance Study

A performance study on the distributed join algorithms was performed to study the effectiveness of the semijoin-based algorithms in evaluating a distributed spatial join. In this section, we present the experiments conducted and their results.

5.1 The Experimental Setup

A data set of the land parcels for the whole State of South Australia was used for the experiments. This database has 762000 records with polygonal spatial descriptions of an average of 6 vertices. Three pairs of test sets were extracted: sets 10R and 10S with 10000 parcels each, 50R and 50S with 50000 parcels, and 100R and 100S with 100000 parcels each. The generation of pairs of sets sought to ensure a controlled number of intersecting parcels. The database was initially divided into three parts corresponding to three geographic regions of South Australia, so that the upper part contained 280000 parcels, the middle 245000 parcels and the lower 237000 parcels. The set 10R was generated by randomly selecting two thirds of the records (i.e. 6666 parcels) from the upper part and one third (i.e. 3334 parcels) from the middle. The set 10S was generated by selecting one third of the records from the middle part and two thirds from the lower. The objects of S are translated by 100m northward and eastward. In this way, the objects in the database that appear in both R and S become "different". The other pairs of test sets were similarly generated. Tests showed that there were 135 intersections between objects in the pair 10R and 10S, 3253 in the pair 50R and 50S and 13096 in the pair 100R and 100S.

The performance of the various algorithms was compared on the total time for the distributed spatial join processing. We omit the cost of producing the final result since it is the same for all strategies. The total cost to perform a distributed spatial join is given as:

$$C_{total} = C_{transmit} + C_{cpu} + C_{io}$$

where $C_{transmit}$, C_{cpu} and C_{io} respectively represent the transmission, CPU and I/O cost required for the join.

The transmission cost incurred includes the cost of transmitting the approximations of S, S', from S_{site} to R_{site}, and to transmit records of R that will participate in the final join, R', from R_{site} to S_{site}.

The CPU cost comprises several components. These include the cost to initiate I/Os, to extract the approximations, to perform the semijoin at R_{site} and to perform the final join at S_{site}.

The I/O cost comes from fetching records for generating S' at S_{site}, storing S' at R_{site}, fetching S' for and performing the semijoin, fetching R', storing R' at S_{site}, refetching R' for and performing the final join.

The various algorithms were implemented on a SUN SPARC-10 machine. The evaluation of the algorithms was conducted by performing the semijoin and the final join using the data sets. These provided information on the size of the approximations used to evaluate the semijoin and the size of the semijoin result. We also monitored the CPU usage and the number of page accesses. While the value of the CPU cost monitored reflects the CPU usage, the transmission and I/O cost are computed respectively as follows:

$$C_{transmit} = \text{number of bytes transmitted} \cdot \frac{1}{\omega_{bandwidth}}$$

$$C_{io} = \text{number of page accesses} \cdot io$$

where $w_{bandwidth}$ represents the bandwidth of the communication network and io represents the cost per page access. In our study, the default value for $w_{bandwidth}$ is 100KBytes/sec and the default I/O cost to retrieve a 8 KBytes I/O block is 0.025 sec. The system is also assumed to have a buffer size of 10 MBytes.

With the data sets that we have, each object has an average of 2.3 locational keys, so the 10K relations have about 23K locational keys. Table 2 summarises the data for the various relations used.

	Relation R			Relation S		
Cardinality	10K	50K	100K	10K	50K	100K
Total number of keys	23189	115484	231426	23175	115904	232169

Table 2. Total number of locational keys.

5.2 The Algorithms Studied

We evaluated three strategies based on locational keys. They are:

- **Algorithm QT-N.** This is the naive algorithm which transmits R and the associated locational keys to S_{site}, and evaluates the join directly.
- **Algorithm QT-4.** This algorithm uses a semijoin. The locational keys of all objects in S are used as the approximations. These locational keys are readily available from the leaf nodes of the B$^+$-tree for S. In our study, each object has at most four locational keys.[6] Duplicate locational keys are removed before transmission.
- **Algorithm QT-C.** In algorithm QT-4, there may be redundancy in the approximations of S. First, a region represented by a locational key may be contained in a region represented by another locational key. Second, 4 regions represented by 4 distinct locational keys may be merged into a bigger region represented by a single locational key. To remove such redundancy, the approximations of S are *compacted* before transmitting to R_{site}. We denote the new algorithm QT-C. Note that compaction does not result in any loss of information. While compaction minimises the size of the approximations to be transmitted and the cost of the semijoin, it also incurs additional CPU cost to compact the approximations.

We have also conducted preliminary tests on a nested-loops algorithm that transmits R to S_{site}, and performs the join as a series of spatial selections of R records on S. The results turned out to be bad. It is always worse than algorithm QT-N, and performed as much as 4 times worse than algorithm QT-N. As such, we omitted the nested-loops algorithm in our experiments.

---

[6] We can derive a family of algorithms with different numbers of locational keys. Our preliminary study, however, shows that 4 locational keys perform well.

Cardinality	QT-4			QT-C		
	S'	R''	R'	S'	R''	R'
10K/10K	22045	4113	2011	11571	4113	2011
50K/50K	92385	36892	16977	14188	36892	16977
100K/100K	158470	86532	38005	8128	86532	38005

Table 3. Number of objects transmitted for locational key based algorithms.

5.3 Experiment 1: Effect of Relation Sizes

In this experiment, we study the effect of relation sizes on the performance of the algorithms. Figure 6 shows the result of the experiment when both relations R and S are of the same size. In the figure, the lower, middle and upper bars represent the CPU, transmission and I/O cost respectively. The corresponding information on the number of objects transmitted for the semijoin-based algorithms are tabulated in Table 3. In the table, S' corresponds to the number of locational keys of S transmitted to R_{site}, R' is the cardinality of the semijoin result (i.e. number of objects of R in the semijoin result), and R'' is the corresponding number of locational keys for the semijoin result.

A number of observations can be made, bearing in mind they are valid only within the context of the characteristics of the data sets used (particularly the short spatial descriptions of the Land Information Systems data) and of the relatively high transmission rate assumed. First, for all the algorithms, the local processing cost $(C_{cpu} + C_{io})$ is comparable to the communication cost. In fact, for the semijoin based algorithms, the processing cost is larger than the communication cost. This confirms that local processing cost cannot be ignored during query processing for distributed spatial joins.

Second, we note that the algorithms based on semijoins outperform the naive approach. For algorithm QT-N, the communication cost dominates performance. Algorithm QT-4 performs better since it is able to cut down the size of the data to be transmitted.

Third, we see the benefits of compaction. Though compaction incurs some additional processing cost, it also cuts down on the processing cost of the semijoin and the number of approximations to be transmitted. The savings as a result of compaction are more than its overhead. This result is reflected as we see algorithm QT-C outperforming QT-4. We also observe that QT-C is more effective for large S. This is because for large S, more approximations can be compacted.

These results demonstrate that semijoin-based algorithms are effective. Moreover, it shows that approximations to objects, which are usually readily available in existing indices, can be reused in performing the semijoin.

To study the effect that the sizes of joining relations have on the algorithms, we also conducted experiments using relations of different sizes. Figure 7 shows the results of the experiments. We see that both algorithms QT-4 and QT-C are inferior to QT-N when S is larger than R. This is expected because for large

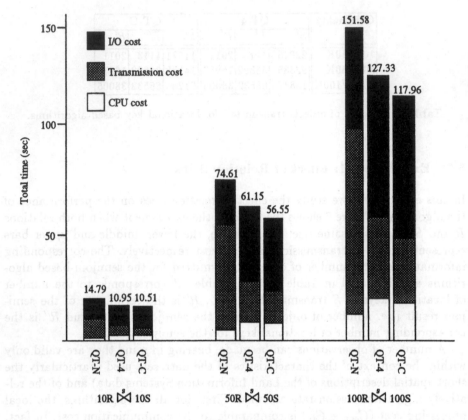

Fig. 6. Comparisons of locational key based algorithms.

S, transmitting the large number of approximations of S to R_{site} is not less expensive than transmitting the entirety of the smaller R to S_{site} Thus, the savings gained in reducing R cannot outweigh the overhead. This is true in our experiments because the length of a spatial description is relatively small – an average of 48 bytes.

For the remaining cases, we observe that the semijoin-based algorithms outperform QT-N. This further demonstrates that semijoin algorithms are effective for distributed spatial databases.

5.4 Experiment 2: Effect of Communication Bandwidth

To understand more fully the effects of transmission rates on the algorithms, we also performed sensitivity studies that vary the transmission rates. Figure 8 shows the result of these tests as the communication bandwidth varies from 20KBytes/sec to 100KBytes/sec, and Figure 9 shows the results when the communication bandwidth varies from 100KBytes/sec to 1MBytes/sec. This effectively models the range of network speeds from WAN to LAN. For each scenario, two sets of tests were conducted, one for small spatial descriptions (50 bytes)

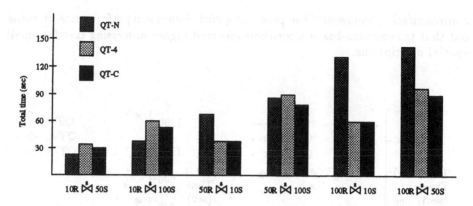

Fig. 7. Locational keys based joins of different relation sizes.

and the other for large spatial descriptions (1000 bytes). Both relations used contain 100 K records.

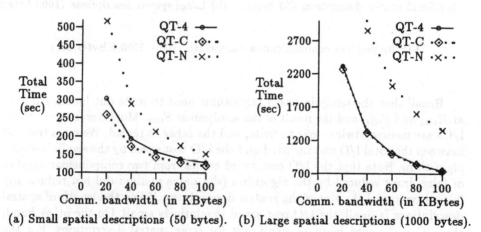

(a) Small spatial descriptions (50 bytes). (b) Large spatial descriptions (1000 bytes).

Fig. 8. Vary the communication bandwidth (20 – 100 KBytes/sec).

From Figure 8, we see that the semijoin-based algorithms are superior in all cases. Moreover, we observe that they are more effective at lower communication bandwidth and/or large spatial descriptions. This is because at low communication bandwidth and/or large spatial descriptions, the cost to transmit the entirety of R from R_{site} to S_{site} increases drastically. The ability of the semijoin-based algorithms to prune away objects that do not satisfy the join condition makes them attractive.

The results shown in Figure 9 give a slightly different picture. When the bandwidth gets larger (> 300 KBytes/sec), we see that the naive join algorithm is superior for data with small spatial descriptions. This is because at such high communication bandwidth, the processing cost dominates performance. It turns out that the semijoin-based algorithms incurred higher processing cost for small spatial descriptions.

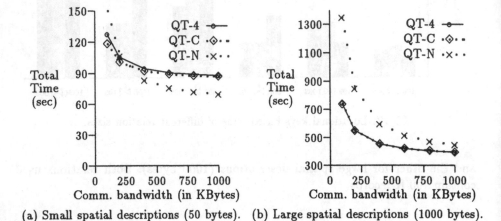

(a) Small spatial descriptions (50 bytes). (b) Large spatial descriptions (1000 bytes).

Fig. 9. Vary the communication bandwidth (100 – 1000 KBytes/sec).

Recall that the semijoin-based algorithms need to write out locational keys at R_{site} and S_{site}, and the result of the semijoin at S_{site}. Moreover, most of these I/Os are incurred twice – one to write, and the other to reread. We see a tradeoff between the total I/O cost incurred and the I/O cost saved by the semijoin-based algorithms. Note that the I/O cost saved comes from two components: number of false drops reduced by the algorithm (the naive method did not reduce any false drops), and the size of the spatial descriptions. When the length of spatial descriptions is small, the I/O cost saved is relatively small. On the other hand, the I/O cost saved becomes significant for large spatial descriptions. For the naive method, the I/O cost incurred increases much faster with the size of spatial descriptions.

5.5 Experiment 3: Effect of Record Length of Spatial Descriptions

Since record length of spatial descriptions of spatial applications varies widely, we also study the effect of varying record length. Figures 10(a) and 10(b) show the results when the communication bandwidths are at the extremes – very low of 20 KBytes/sec and very high of 1MBytes/sec. We vary the length of spatial descriptions from 50 bytes to 1 KBytes for joins of 100R and 100S. The lower end of the range (towards 50 bytes) models LIS applications with their small spatial descriptions while the higher end (towards 1 KBytes) represents GIS applications with long spatial descriptions. Note that varying the length of spatial descriptions affects both the I/O and communication costs. We note that the semijoin-based algorithms always outperform the naive approach regardless of the length of spatial descriptions. The longer the spatial descriptions, the higher the communication cost and I/O cost. The results confirm the observations made earlier. At low communication bandwidth, the naive approach is always inferior to the semijoin-based techniques. But the naive approach still has its place for small spatial descriptions and high communication bandwidth. This implies that the semijoin-based algorithms are more effective for applications with large spatial descriptions such as GIS applications.

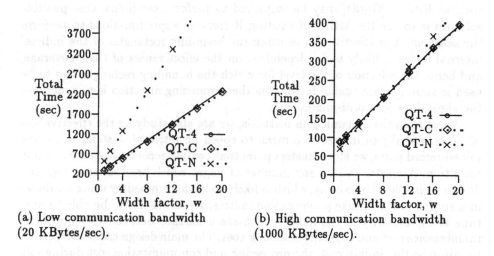

(a) Low communication bandwidth (20 KBytes/sec).

(b) High communication bandwidth (1000 KBytes/sec).

Fig. 10. Vary the record width (record width = 50w bytes)

Note that the difference between the two semijoin algorithms is not significant. In fact, the difference decreases as the length increases. This is so since compaction only benefits the transmission of the approximations which do not change with the length of the spatial descriptions, i.e. the total cost is increasing while the saving due to compaction stays constant.

6 Discussion

The spatial semijoin has been presented as a basis for improved algorithms for evaluation of joins on distributed spatial databases. Its formulation and application drew on the concepts of the semijoin of conventional databases and of the filter test of spatial query processing. We described and presented a novel semijoin-based algorithm that employs single-dimensional locational keys as approximations. The overhead of transmitting approximations may be reduced by compacting the keys. Our experimental study showed that semijoin algorithms provide useful reductions in the cost of evaluating a join in most cases.

Our results showed that a naive join method still has its place. We plan to look at how the optimiser can determine when a semi-join or naive techniques should be applied. Moreover, besides compaction which is non-loss, we plan to look at how approximations may impact the performance of the algorithm. For example, if the region represented by a set of locational keys forms 75% of a larger quadrant, then it may be beneficial to replace these locational keys by a single locational key that represent the larger quadrant. This will cut down on the number of approximations to be transmitted but will increase the number of false drops. We have also already begun exploring how multi-dimensional indices such as R-trees [Gut84] may be employed to perform semijoins. One possible solution is to use the MBRs of existing R-trees as approximations to perform the semijoin. The effectiveness of using the bounding rectangles of the indices' internal nodes is likely to be dependent on the effectiveness of their coverage, and hence the selection of the level for which the bounding rectangles are to be used is an important tuning factor. Another promising direction is to generalise the algorithms for multi-join queries.

Apart from the dynamic join methods, we are also studying the effectiveness of using spatial join indices as a mean to speed up retrieval. Instead of storing joined record pairs, we store clusters pairs that contain records that satisfy a join condition. A cluster can be any number of pages which are clustered together due to their spatial proximity, which is likely to be determined by using a subtree in a spatial index. Unlike previous join indices, we would like to be able to fine-tune the granularity of the index to achieve a balance between the join index maintenance cost and the join processing cost. The main design criteria are hence to minimise the update cost, the processing and communication cost during join processing. If such an index is used to maintain join results from two different sites, updates will pose a problem for non-tightly coupled systems. Incremental updates, or only using the join index for approximate answers are the solutions being considered. We shall report such a study in a future paper.

References

[Abe83] D.J. Abel: A B$^+$-tree Structure for Large Quadtrees. *Computer Vision, Graphics and Image Processing*, 27, 19-31, 1983.

[AbS84] D.J. Abel and J.L. Smith: A data structure and retrieval algorithm for a database of areal entities. *Australian Computer Journal*, 16, 147-154, 1984.

[Abe93] D.J. Abel: Some Evolutionary Paths for Spatial Database. *International Symposium on Next Generation Database Systems and Then Applications, NDA '93*, 1-10, 1993.

[AOP+94] D.J. Abel, B.C. Ooi, R. Power, K.L. Tan, G. Williams, X. Zhou: The Virtual Database: A Tool for Migration from Legacy LIS. *Proceedings of AURISA 94*, 117-126, Nov. 1994

[BeC81] P. Bernstein, D. M. Chiu: Using semi-joins to solve relational queries. *Journal of ACM 28*, 25-40, 1981.

[BKS93] T. Brinkhoff, H. Kriegel, and B. Seeger. Efficient processing of spatial joins using r-trees. *Proc. ACM SIGMOD International Conference on Management of Data*, 237–246, 1993.

[BKSS94] T. Brinkhoff, H. Kriegel, R. Schneider and B. Seeger. Multi-step processing of spatial joins. *Proc. ACM SIGMOD International Conference on Management of Data*, 197–208, 1994.

[GaG94] Volker Gaede and Oliver Gunther: Processing Joins with User-Defined Functions, *Institut fur Wirtschaftsinformatik, Humboldt-Universitat zu Berlin*, TR-94-103, 1994.

[Gun93] Oliver Gunther: Efficient computation of spatial joins. *IEEE Proc. Int. Conference on Data Engineering*, 50-59, 1993.

[Gut84] A. Guttman: R-trees: A dynamic index structure for spatial searching. In *Proc. ACM SIGMOD Int. Conf. on Management of Data*, 47–57, 1984.

[LoR94] M. Lo and C. V. Ravishankar. Spatial joins using seeded trees. *Proc. ACM SIGMOD International Conference on Management of Data*, 209–220, 1994.

[Mor66] G. M. Morton. A computer oriented geodetic data base and a new technique in file sequencing. IBM, Ottawa, Canada, 1966.

[Ore86] J.A. Orenstein: Spatial query processing in an object-oriented database system. *Proc. ACM SIGMOD Int. Conf. on Management of Data*, 326-333, 1986.

[OzV91] M.T. Ozsu, P. Valduriez: *Principles of distributed database systems.* Prentice-Hall, 1991.

[RIDE93] Proceedings of the 3rd Workshop on Research Issues in Data Engineering: Interoperability in Multidatabase Systems, (ed) H.J. Schek, A.P. Sheth, B.D. Czejdo, IEEE CS Press, 1993.

[Sam90] H. Samat: The Design and Analysis of Spatial Data Structures, *Addison-Wesley*, 1990.

[ShL90] A. P. Sheth and J. L. Larson: Federated database systems for managing distributed, heterogeneous, and autonomous databases. *ACM Computer Surveys*, Vol.22, No.3, 183-235, 1990.

[Tom93] Tomlinson Associates Ltd, GIS Planning - Land Status and Assets Management, Office of Geographic Data Coordination, Melbourne, Victoria, 1993.

Comparison and benchmarks for import of VPF geographic data from object-oriented and relational database files*

David Arctur, Eman Anwar, John Alexander and Sharma Chakravarthy

GeoPlan Center, 431 Arch Building
University of Florida, Gainesville, FL 32611, USA
E-mail: arctur@ufl.edu

Miyi Chung, Maria Cobb and Kevin Shaw

Mapping, Charting and Geodesy Branch, Code 7441
U.S. Naval Research Laboratory
Stennis Space Center, MS 39529, USA
E-mail: {chung,cobb,shaw}@dmap.nrlssc.navy.mil

Abstract. This paper presents some of the advantages accrued from adopting an object-oriented (OO) data model versus the relational data model when representing and managing a Vector Product Format (VPF) database, specifically the Digital Nautical Chart (DNC) for Norfolk Harbor, Virginia. An OO-DNC prototype viewer capable of importing, displaying and editing DNC feature data both from relational-format and from object-format files was developed using the Smalltalk language. The differences in performance between the relational import and the object import were then compared across several DNC coverages. The results indicate a significant increase in performance when adopting the OO paradigm; specifically the OO-DNC viewer imported feature data from object-format files from 6 to 15 times faster than from the relational-format files. It should be noted that these figures are NOT the result of comparing a commercial object-oriented database managment system (ODBMS) against a commercial relational database management system (RDBMS), but rather the result of reading both relational-oriented and object-oriented data file formats using an object-oriented program written in Smalltalk. Nevertheless, we feel these results indicate a significant functionality and performance improvement can be obtained by using an OO framework for the data and software.

1 Introduction

The Vector Product Format (VPF), developed by the U.S. Defense Mapping Agency (DMA) and defined in [7], has become part of the DIGEST international standard formats for representing geographical data. VPF is a *georelational* specification which uses a relational data framework [6] for storing both attribute and geo-spatial information about the geographic features represented. A number of database products based on the VPF standard have been developed, such as the Digital Chart of the World

---

*This work has been sponsored by the U.S. Defense Mapping Agency and the U.S. Naval Research Laboratory.

(DCW), the Digital Nautical Chart (DNC), the World Vector Shoreline (WVS) and others. Each of these VPF derivatives has different sets of geographic features and attributes. As the DNC specification [8] is one of the most complex it was chosen for this study at the request of the Naval Research Laboratory (NRL).

Of late there has been a great increase in the utilization of the object-oriented paradigm in various areas such as software engineering, database design and implementation, and computer integrated manufacturing (CIM). This warrants examination of the possible adavantages, if any, that may accrue as a result of the adoption of the object-oriented paradigm in geographic information systems (GIS) applications.

Before presenting the approach and results for comparing object-oriented and relational data organization, it is useful to first give a brief description of the current VPF georelational structure, using for illustration the Norfolk Harbor DNC database (see Fig. 1).

2 Summary of DNC Data Structures

The DNC is a general purpose database format designed to support GIS applications such as marine navigation. The design of the DNC is an extension of the VPF base specification. In this section we provide a description of the content, data format, and design of a DNC database.

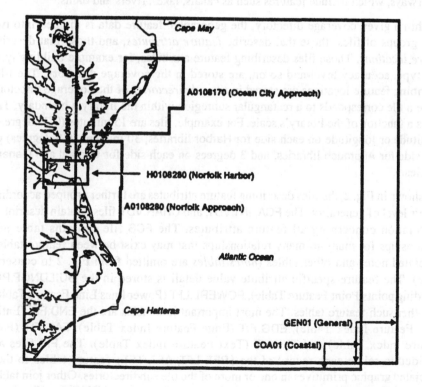

Fig. 1. DNC01 Libraries for the Chesapeake Bay Area Database

The DNC organizes geographic data for distribution on CD-ROM discs where each disc or disc set contains the database of geographic information for a particular region. For example (see Fig. 1), the Chesapeake Bay area surrounding Norfolk, Virginia has been coded as database DNC01. This database is organized using the hierarchical directory structure shown in Fig. 2. The name of the topmost directory represents the name of the database. The DNC01 directory contains two files: the Database Header Table (DHT) which provides general information about the database (source, date of creation, revision level, etc.) and the Library Attribute Table (LAT), which provides the boundaries of each library in terms of decimal degrees of latitude and longitude. As defined in the VPF specification and illustrated in Fig. 1, a *library* defines a geographic boundary and scale, where a larger scale implies a closer-in view and a smaller scale implies a further-out view. Thus, the A0108280 library has a smaller scale and presumably lesser accuracy and precision of data than in the H0108280 library. The different libraries are chosen to handle the different scaling factors utilized during data collection. A database-level directory can have an arbitrary number of libraries; in Fig. 2 we show for example two of the library directories, A0108280 and H0108280.

A library subdirectory is further divided into *coverages*, each of which contains the data for logically- and spatially-organized groups of geographic *features*. For example, the CUL coverage represents Cultural Landmarks, which include buildings, power lines, streets, railroads and other feature classes. The IWY coverage represents Inland Waterways, which include features such as canals, lakes, rivers and dams.

Within a given coverage directory, the geographic feature data is divided into two main groups of files: those that describe *feature attributes*, and those that describe *feature locations*. Those files describing feature attributes, for example building type, road type, accuracy level and so on, are stored in the coverage directory. The files describing feature locations are stored in *tile subdirectories* of the coverage directory, where a tile corresponds to a rectangular subregion within the library's boundary. Tile size is a function of the library's scale. For example, tiles are 15 minutes (0.25 degrees) of latitude or longitude on each side for Harbor libraries, 30 minutes (0.5 degrees) on each side for Approach libraries, and 3 degrees on each side for Coastal and General libraries.

As shown in Fig. 2, the files describing feature attributes are further grouped according to their level of generality. The FCA, INT.VDT, and CHAR.VDT files contain descriptive information concerning all feature attributes. The FCS file contains table-join relationships for many-to-many relationships that may exist between feature tables, associated notes and other tables (*notes tables* are omitted from Fig. 2 to conserve space). The feature-specific attribute value detail is stored in the BUILDNGP.PFT (Building points Point Feature Table), POWERL.LFT (Power lines Line Feature Table), and other such feature tables. The most important join tables are the END.FIT (Entity Node Feature Index Table), EDG.FIT (Edge Feature Index Table), FAC.FIT (Face Feature Index Table) and TXT.FIT (Text Feature Index Table). The FIT files are provided to relate each record of the {PFT, LFT, AFT, TFT} feature tables to their associated graphic primitives in one or more of the tile subdirectories. Other join tables and index files may also be employed, as defined in the VPF and DNC specifications.

Finally, within the tile subdirectories, the geographic coordinate data is organized into END (Entity Node), CND (Connected Node), EDG (Edge or Polyline), FAC (Face or Polygon), and TXT (Text) files. Full spatial topology is supported, such that: Entity Node records have a foreign key to their "containing face" primitive record; Connected Node records have a foreign key to their "starting edge" primitive record; and Edge records have foreign keys to their start node, end node, left face, right face, left edge and right edge primitive records. Face primitives consist of a foreign key to the RNG (ring) table, which indicates the starting edge primitive for each face. The VPF specification defines a "winged-edge topology" rule, by which a face primitive is assembled from tracing the comprised edge primitives. Text primitives consist of a textual label and a

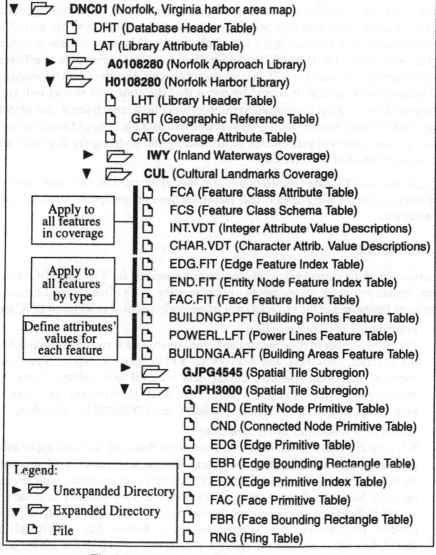

Fig. 2. DNC01 Database Directory Structure (partial)

"shape line" that describes the location and path along which the text label is to be displayed. Text features are not topological structures, but simple cartographic elements for identifying certain features at an arbitrary location, such as the name "Chesapeake Bay."

Edge and Text primitives have variable-length records. To facilitate faster access to these primitives DNC specifies an additional index file, named EDX and TXX respectively, to be stored in each tile subdirectory. The direct byte offset for each record of the EDG or TXT files is stored in the associated EDX and TXX file, sorted by the primary key in the tile-level EDG or TXT primitive file.

There is still another layer of data required to represent DNC features, which is the *spatial index*. VPF specifies an *adaptive binary tree* framework for managing spatial indexes of point, edge and face primitives. Spatial tree cells' keys are stored in additional index files for association with their contained features for use in spatial queries and display. The OO-DNC prototype viewer currently uses a more efficient *quadtree spatial data manager* [17], thus we do not concern ourselves with the standard VPF spatial index system. It should be noted that the choice of spatial indexing framework does not affect the comparative import times between relational- and object-format files. The real issues regarding these alternative data file formats have to do with the comparative ease and performance of associating and updating the attributes and location coordinates of DNC features.

A final note on VPF data organization is that the relational files have their schema description within the file's header. This facilitates dynamic interpretation and import of feature data.

3 Motivation

Examination of the current relational organization specified for VPF and DNC shows several limitations which we attempt to overcome using an OO framework. Currently, the primary limitations of the geo-relational framework specified in VPF and DNC are:

- *Intensive use of system resources*
  The large number of files, indexes and cross-references involved in representing the libraries, coverages and features in VPF databases impose significant overhead in system resources during data retrieval and updates. There are approximately 3500 (mostly small) files used to represent just sixteen megabytes of data in the combined A0108280 and H0108280 libraries alone.

- *Record keys maintained by the application*
  It is a characteristic of the relational framework that each database application program must maintain the primary and foreign key values used to relate records in the various tables. Given VPF's complex organization, with several layers of hierarchical composition of features, the many-to-many associations among features and primitives, and the number of index tables used to improve retrieval performance, even simple changes in feature data are difficult to accomplish while maintaining referential integrity among all the tables. It is also a significant challenge to publish such changes to other customers of a

database product, who may have made additional modifications themselves. Due to these difficulties no tools are provided on the database CDROM to make changes of any kind to the DNC feature data.

- *Structural constraints of the VPF database design*
  In order to make the data more manageable, the VPF-specified directory structure divides a product database into libraries, coverages and tiles. This produces a severe limitation with respect to spatial topology as arbitrary restrictions on the scope of feature adjacency information are made. For example, spatial topology is only maintained among features within a single tile of a single coverage and library.

Due to these and other issues, loading of feature data from the VPF database files is very time-consuming using VPFVIEW, the public-domain viewer application provided with the database on each CDROM. And while commercial GIS tools can be used for some of the operations in which VPFVIEW is inadequate, such tools require costly equipment, software, training and experience. These drawbacks clearly are not the result of inadequate understanding or skill in designing and implementing relational databases, but an indication that the relational model may be inappropriate for this type of data. Furthermore, given DMA's goal of providing VPF products for use by customers having limited computing resources or experience, professional GIS tools will not be a practical workaround for many users.

Thus, the main goal of this project was to develop a non-commercial GIS framework with better performance than VPFVIEW, that would additionally permit editing and updating of VPF feature data. To meet this goal, we chose to implement an object-oriented prototype application.

4 Emergence of Object-Oriented Systems

While OO language compilers and tools have been in development since the late 1960's [10], commercial availability did not occur until the early 1980's. It was not until the latter part of the 1980's that commercial object-oriented database management systems (ODBMSs) became generally available and reliable. Since that time, there has been a virtual explosion of development in this field, including applications of ODBMSs for handling geographic data (see [1] and [5] for more extensive bibliographies of this literature). However, within the GIS user community there has been slow acceptance of this technology (surprisingly, slower in the U.S. than in Europe), as none of the current OO GIS products yet approach the breadth of functionality offered by conventional GIS software. This situation is rapidly changing. Regardless of any perceived immaturity in the marketplace, properly-developed OO frameworks offer significant, fundamental advantages over the relational model, as described below.

- *Improved Use of System Resources*
  In Smalltalk, applications typically appear to the operating system as a small number of large, monolithic processes and data spaces, rather than many small ones. Within a single operating system process, a Smalltalk application is

typically managing many lightweight threads of activity and control. In addition, within a single large data space in memory or on disk, a Smalltalk application dynamically allocates and reorganizes the space needed for objects in a very efficient manner. This achieves much more effective utilization of the operating system resources, and greatly reduces data I/O. These facilities, e.g. effective memory utilization, can also be achieved in other OO programming languages such as C++, however, it is the responsibility of the application programmer to program such facilities.

- *Encapsulation of Structure and Behavior*
  In non-OO programming systems (including relational database applications), data structures are passive: they have no control over which procedures may act on them, or on what those procedures may do with them. Thus, they cannot be "responsible" for their own state. For instance, different procedures can unknowingly interfere with each other by making changes to the same data structure or database record. Such problems can be very difficult to identify and debug in large, complex applications.

  In the OO paradigm, each object has its own state as well as a set of methods/procedures that are allowed to access and change that state. Thus, objects are in charge and capable of protecting their own state, i.e., changes to their state can take place only by invoking the appropriate procedures within the object's definition. (This varies somewhat among OO languages; Smalltalk is strictest about enforcing an object's encapsulation of state.) This architecture results in inherently more manageable applications, as programmers can be concerned with greatly reduced scope of possible side-effects from the changes they make in an object's behavior.

  Another advantage of having a set of procedures which access and change an object's state is the ability to associate customized "triggers" which fire when these methods/procedures are invoked. To elaborate, triggers can fire in response to any granularity of change in an object's state as required by the application. This is in contrast to the relational model where triggers can be associated when 'entire' tuples are inserted, deleted and updated, i.e. it is not possible to associate a trigger with the update of a specific attribute of a relation.

- *Unique Object Identifiers*
  Most commercial RDBMSs provide very limited support for maintaining the referential integrity of associations between tables. Typically, this support is limited to enforcement during schema evolution. It is assumed that the database application programmers will manage runtime referential integrity among associated data records within the various programs that access the database (this also relates to the encapsulation issue just mentioned). This is an error-prone assumption that becomes increasingly problematic as applications grow and change. The data dictionary for a typical relational database does not store the relationships *between* tables, only for the components *within* tables. This is true as well in the VPF and derivative products' specifications. It is the responsibility of the application programmer developing a VPF viewer, for

example, to carefully study the product specification documents in order to understand how the various database and feature tables are linked, and to ensure proper use of the primary and foreign keys among all tables.

In Smalltalk and commercial ODBMSs, each object is guaranteed a unique identifier, with which the application developer should never need to be concerned. Unlike the situation with relational tables that requires application programmers to maintain primary and foreign key values linking records among different tables, an OO system automatically manages all object identifiers and linkages for the programmer. The OO programmer's task is simply to *point* one object to another object whenever needed to establish an association, without needing to know the value or address of the pointer. As far as the programmer needs to be concerned, *objects simply hold onto pointer references to other objects*. This has significant ramifications. Instead of needing to join tables to assemble a complex object's complete state as one would in a relational database, a query need only specify an element of a given object's state and the rest of the object is found quickly and directly by following its constituent pointer references. This allows complex "object webs" to be created, retrieved and updated far more quickly and with less system resource overhead than much simpler relational objects that involve table joins. This is why OO data structures can be used for arbitrarily-deep hierarchical composition applications such as CAD and GIS.

The foregoing discussion barely touches on the issues and potentials of OO systems. The reader is referred to [2], [16] for discussion of analysis and design issues with OO applications; and to [9], [11], [12], [14], [15], [18] for guidance in OO concepts and the Smalltalk language. This is by no means an exhaustive list of references, but will provide a good starting point for learning about this technology. The remainder of the paper will discuss the tools chosen for addressing these requirements, and the results achieved.

5   Method

This section consists of two parts, the first dealing with a rationale and description of the development tools used, and the second dealing with the OO-DNC model and the benchmark design.

5.1   Development Platform And Tools

The Smalltalk language and tools, as implemented in the VisualWorks product from ParcPlace Systems, Inc. [14], [15], together with the ENVY/Manager source code revision management system from Object Technology International [13], were chosen as the development system for this project. There were many reasons for this choice, both esoteric and practical:

- Smalltalk, generally considered the most uniformly object-oriented programming system, has very simple syntax and semantics that are easily learned, and which are followed consistently throughout the implementation of the language and its development tools, most of which are written in Smalltalk. Its power lies in this simplicity, reflectiveness, and the self-extensible library of object classes. This leads to sharply increasing gains in productivity of development as one builds experience with the language and tools. Rather than focussing on mastery of complex rules of syntax and semantics as in C, C++ and many other languages, one focuses on learning how to use the development tools most effectively and on understanding the extensive class library of reusable objects. The ParcPlace version of Smalltalk includes the largest class library (over 800 object classes and 8000 methods), as well as the most extensive and robust tools for development.

- OTI ENVY/Manager, developed for and with Smalltalk, provides one of the richest and most seamlessly integrated source code configuration management tools available today for any programming language. This kind of facility is almost essential to support development of large applications by multiple programmers, and was an invaluable part of the project.

- ParcPlace Smalltalk and OTI ENVY run on several versions of UNIX, as well as MS-Windows and Macintosh platforms. These development tools produce platform-portable source code and binary object data files.

- While no commercial ODBMS was used in this phase of the project, it was recognized that this would become an important component of the system at a later date. Many leading ODBMS vendors have, or are developing, Smalltalk language interfaces, generally for the ParcPlace version of Smalltalk as this is the predominant commercial version available on UNIX systems. With an ODBMS that supports both Smalltalk and C++ interfaces, a database developed in Smalltalk should be accessible to software written in C++. At the time of this writing, very recent efforts at ODBMS standards development [3] specifically address both C++ and Smalltalk language bindings and other issues.

5.2 OO-DNC Model

By the time of this project, the GeoPlan Center at the University of Florida (UF) already had been developing and refining a framework of OO tools and techniques on which the OO-DNC could readily be built, using two popular versions of Smalltalk (ParcPlace Systems' VisualWorks, and Digitalk's Smalltalk/VPM for OS/2 [9]). The tools developed at UF included a spatial data management facility based on the quadtree structure; a generalized approach for representing interdependent GIS feature data with extensive attributes and flexible symbology; and a windowed, graphical user interface for working with spatial data that supports zoom and pan over the map region. A derivative of this system has now been developed for the OO-DNC model. The base framework for OO-DNC comprises 66 classes and nearly 400KBytes of compiled code. To this the DNC01 database feature set adds another 108 classes and 50KBytes of code.

Summary Of BOSS. A significant component of the OO-DNC data model for purposes of this benchmark is the Binary Object Streaming Service (BOSS), an optimized import/export facility developed by ParcPlace Systems for storing complex object webs on disk [4], [14]. Objects are stored in an internal, platform-portable, binary format that allows for more compact storage and faster retrieval. This alone will account for a significant performance improvement. In addition, BOSS correctly deals with the difficult problem of managing "circular references" (back-pointers between objects), as well as providing a means of processing object definitions at runtime without the need for the Smalltalk compiler. There is no practical limit to the depth and complexity of object hierarchies and webs which can be stored on disk in BOSS format. However, it is not intended to replace a database manager since it lacks transaction management semantics. Below we describe the means by which BOSS makes objects persistent.

The mechanism for writing an object to the archive can be best characterized as a depth-first recursive procedure. To understand this process it helps to visualize the object to be stored as a tree of objects. BOSS begins a depth-first traversal of this structure and represents and stores each object reached (or alternatively each node in the tree) provided this object has not been encountered beforehand. Reaching an object X that has been previously encountered implies that X's representation exists in the archive, i.e., it has been previously stored. When this situation is encountered, the depth-first traversal from object X downwards is halted and a reference to its stored representation is placed at that point. In this way multiple copies of the same object on the archive are avoided. Another situation that can cause a depth-first traversal to halt is when immediate values such as integer, string, etc. are encountered.

In order for BOSS to ensure that objects are only stored once, two dictionaries of associations are maintained, specifically, the writerMap and the readerMap. The writerMap maintains the association of an object with its index, i.e. object->index. This table is used while the archive is being constructed in determining if a newly referenced object has already been written into the archive. If it has, then the traversal stops at that point downwards and the object's object index is written in its place. On the other hand, if the object is not present in the writerMap, an index is created and added. Similarly, the readerMap maintains the association of an index with is respective object, i.e., index->object. The readerMap is stored on the archive itself and when the archive is opened, the readerMap is used to help build each object's contents.

As with a commercial ODBMS, BOSS also deals with the issue of allowing "cut points" in object webs. For example, it is unwise to store a reference to the host window system, such as a pointer from the feature objects to the map display window, in the BOSS file. This will "pull" a very large and undesireable portion of the Smalltalk memory space into the disk file. All that should be stored in the BOSS disk file is the actual feature data. In place of a potentially undesireable object reference, the programmer can cause a symbolic representation to be stored, from which the appropriate links can be reestablished upon later import.

BOSS-format file storage of OO-DNC feature objects was utilized in this study because it offered the most comparable file format for persistent object-oriented feature data storage, in comparison with the VPF geo-relational file format. A reasonable extension of this benchmark study would be to compare optimized Relational-DBMS management of the geo-relational database against optimized Object-DBMS management of the OO-DNC database.

6 Benchmark Design

Fig. 3 illustrates the main steps in getting feature data from the disk to the screen. At the stage of feature processing depicted here, it is assumed that the database has already

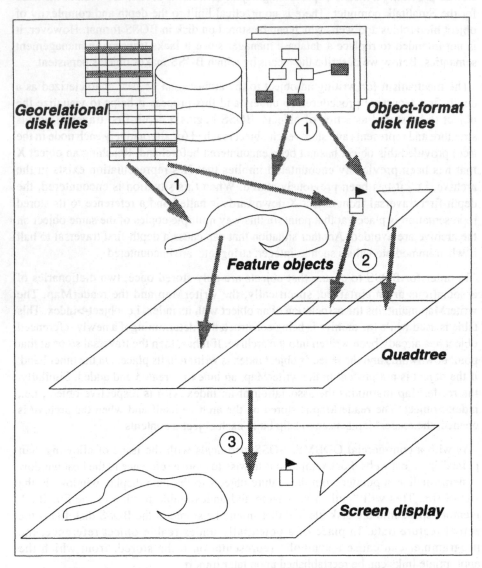

Fig. 3. Spatial features are (1) imported either from relational VPF files
or from object-format files, then (2) placed in quadtree, and (3) rendered on screen.
Note that each *object-format file* contains whole features, while 4 or more *georelational
files* are required to define each individual feature.

been "installed," meaning that:

- the database, library and coverage header files have already been read, and necessary definitional information stored in memory;
- all necessary associations (primary-to-foreign key links) between the geo-relational tables have been determined and are stored in memory, including complex joins where applicable;
- a runtime web of database definitional objects has been generated and is held in memory, which will be used to initialize the DNC features as they are imported into the object model; and
- Smalltalk classes corresponding to all the features which occur in the current DNC database have already been created.

These conditions assure that the benchmark testing of the system's performance for reading DNC data is minimally influenced by definitional tasks, and that both the geo-relational import and the object-format file import are on as equivalent a basis as possible. Table 1 below describes the respective import procedures in more detail. It is quickly apparent why there might be little contest between object-file and relational-file import in this study. Besides the huge difference in file I/O, there is also a huge difference in processing work to make OO-DNC feature objects from the relational files as opposed to the BOSS-format files. Furthermore, it was not possible to compare object vs. relational import on an even playing field in this study for the simple reason that a maximally-optimized means of processing the relational data files was not available, as it was for processing object-format data files. Given all these factors, it is expected that the object-file import would outperform the relational import.

The benchmark test runs were organized around whole groupings of point features and line features, by coverage, for the two libraries A0108280 (Norfolk Approach) and H0108280 (Norfolk Harbor). These were chosen for the sake of convenience, as these groupings are easily specified for importing from either data format, and offer a broad range of feature loads. As seen in Figs. 4-5, the number of point features per import batch varied from 2 to nearly 12,000. The range was between 5 and 6500 for line features. While we did not make repeated measurements of each import test for statistical averaging purposes, we felt this variation in feature load would provide adequate sampling for our purposes. The tests were limited to point and line features, as import of area and text features had not yet been completed in the OO-DNC prototype.

These tests were conducted on an IBM RS/6000 model 350 (20MHz) Unix workstation, with 32MB RAM, 3GB local disk capacity (which contained all the data used for the tests), Motif window manager, and no other application software or user processes at the time of the benchmarks. The amount of RAM required by the Smalltalk system at runtime varied from 9MB with no DNC features imported, to 22MB with CUL (Cultural), ECR (Earth Cover), and LIM (Boundary Limits) for both the Norfolk Approach and Harbor libraries imported (the maximum amount of simultaneous feature loading that was attempted). For the benchmarks however, each coverage was imported to a fresh workspace with no other coverages loaded, for consistency of comparison. This would not necessarily reflect actual usage patterns, of course.

Table 1: Relational and Object Import Procedures

Relational Import	Object Import
1. Open one of END.FIT, EDG.FIT files.	1. Open BOSS-format feature class file.
2. Sequentially parse fixed-length *.FIT records, identifying the feature class for each record.	2. Invoke optimized routine for parsing BOSS-format files, which performs steps 3 - 5.
3. Create a new instance of correct feature class object.	3. Read BOSS header for object index table.
4. Open and read feature attributes from *.PFT, *.LFT file into new feature object's local storage.	4. Scan through file, creating new instance of each object stored.
5a. For variable-length primitive data (EDG): open and reposition primitive index file (EDX); read offset and byte length for primitive data record.	5. Sequentially rebuild instance variables' values by creating new instances of linked objects, including feature attributes, location coordinates, and bounding rectangle.
5b. Open and reposition primitive data file (END, EDG); read coordinate data into OrderedCollection object, and convert from text strings to efficient byte-integer array form.	6. Place new feature instance in quadtree based on its bounding rectangle.
6. Edge features: open, reposition and read bounding rectangle from EBR primitive data file. Point features: create a small bounding rectangle around the location point.	7. Repeat steps 1 - 6 for each feature class in the selected coverage to import, or for next BOSS-file segment of current feature class if more than 1000 features (file I/O - memory efficiency threshold).
7. Place new feature object in quadtree based on its bounding rectangle.	
8. Repeat steps 2 - 7 for all feature classes of *.FIT file; repeat steps 1 - 7 for each of END.FIT and EDG.FIT of the selected coverage to import.	
Total files processed: approx. 3500. *Total file space: approx. 16 MBytes.*	*Total files processed: approx. 200.* *Total file space: approx. 15.5 MBytes.*

7 Findings

The two graphs below show 5.7- to 14.8-times factor improvements in import performance with the object format data file over the geo-relational format data file. These were plotted on log-log scales because of (a) the very large range along the X-axis, and (b) the magnitude of difference between the two curves in each figure. These results appear reasonable from a number of perspectives:

- Far fewer files need to be opened and processed to import object-format data, than to import relational VPF data. This is primarily due to the utilization of BOSS for the object file storage.

- The reduced margins of improvement found when importing a very small number of features could be due to some initial overhead to process an object-format data file, which is still less than that needed to begin to process the relational files. The OO approach showed much greater economies of scale than the relational approach, as the number of features increased. This is probably due to the simpler, direct-pointer nature of relationships to decode within the object-format data file, in comparison with the key-matching joins needed to decode the relational data files.

- The similarities in dips and peaks between the object and relational curves in the line-feature plot (at least for large numbers of features to import) most likely reflect peculiarities in the feature data. For instance, some line-features have many more coordinate points per feature than others. The point-feature imports, having only a single coordinate location per feature, resulted in much smoother curves with increased feature loads, as would be expected.

The amount of time to load the imported features into the quadtree (step 2 in Fig. 3) was almost negligible, in comparison with the import from disk. This time averaged about 1.5 seconds per thousand features, regardless of the feature size. It was found that, as the quadtree became very densely populated with point features (such as those in the hydrography coverages), the quadtree loading time began to slow down slightly. The time required to perform queries for features in the quadtree was also dependent on the total number of features present.

8 Conclusions

The OO-DNC model developed so far achieves an order-of-magnitude improvement in the time to load features from disk; supports spatial queries that cross tiles, coverages and even libraries; and allows direct examination *and modification* of all feature attributes and coordinates. Standard colors, symbols, line types, and area-fill patterns may be specified and stored for each feature class, yet be overridden if needed for individual features. Standard map display capabilities such as zoom and pan over the map region are supported.

While these results and potentials are very positive, some cautions and questions remain to be addressed. Although considerable efforts were made to ensure that the relational import methodology took maximum advantage of index tables to improve

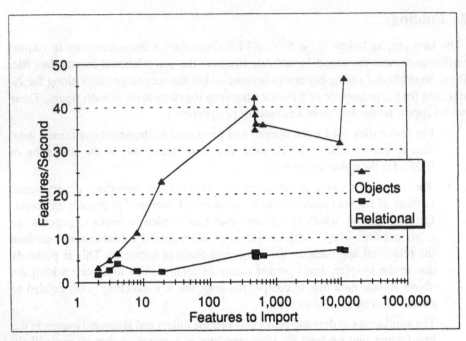

Fig. 4. Import Performance with Point Features

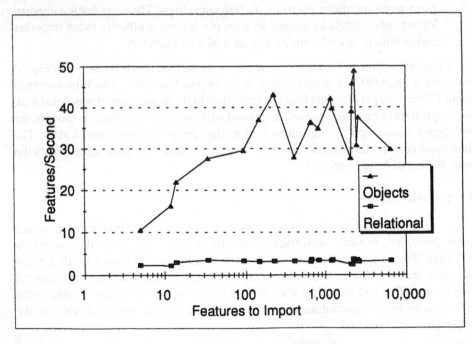

Fig. 5. Import Performance with Line Features

performance, the join technique followed was essentially the "indexed loop" approach. More efficient join techniques are likely, such as the "hash join" approach, but the degree of fragmentation in the DNC feature data files has made them difficult to implement so far. Also, the benchmark tests did not include area or textual features, though it is expected that these will behave similarly to the line features. And while the OO-DNC model here retains the spatial topology information imported from the original relational data files, there is no mechanism yet in place for maintaining this information within the OO framework. Investigation of the best means of handling this is a task for the FY95 phase of the project.

This project has shown very promising preliminary results that can be realized with object-oriented technology. GIS data complexity will only increase as computing resources continue to improve, and it does not appear that pure-relational database frameworks are as well suited to serve in this application field as OO systems.

References

1. F. Bancilhon, C. Delobel and P. Kanellakis: *Building an Object-Oriented Database System: The Story of O₂*, Morgan-Kaufmann, 1992.

2. G. Booch: *Object-Oriented Analysis and Design, with Applications*, Benjamin/Cummings, 1994.

3. R. Cattell: *The Object Database Standard: ODMG-93, Release 1.1*, Morgan-Kaufmann, 1994.

4. M. Christiansen: "Persistent Object Management Using the ParcPlace Binary Object Streaming Service," In: Smalltalk Report, pp. 4-10, SIGS Publishing, October 1994.

5. B. David, L. Raynal and G. Schorter: "GeO₂: Why objects in a geographical DBMS?" In: Proceedings to the Third International Symposium on Large Spatial Databases, SSD-93, pp. 264-276, Springer-Verlag, 1993.

6. C. J. Date: *An Introduction to Database Systems*, Addison-Wesley, 1983.

7. Defense Mapping Agency: *Product Specifications for Digital Nautical Chart*, Draft Document No. MIL-D-89023, DMA, Fairfax, VA, 1993.

8. Defense Mapping Agency: *Military Standard: Vector Product Format*, Draft Document No. MIL-STD-2407, DMA, Fairfax, VA, 1993.

9. Digitalk, Inc: *Smalltalk/VPM Object-Oriented Programming System: Tutorial and Programming Handbook*, Digitalk, Los Angeles, CA, 1989.

10. A. Goldberg: *A History of Personal Workstations*, ACM Press, 1988.

11. A. Goldberg and D. Robson: *Smalltalk-80: The Language*, Addison-Wesley, 1989.

12. W. LaLonde: *Discovering Smalltalk*, Benjamin/Cummings, 1994.

13. Object Technology International, Inc.: *ENVY/Manager: A Team Programming Environment for Objectworks/Smalltalk, User Manual, Release 1.43*, OTI, Ottawa, Ontario, 1994.

14. ParcPlace Systems, Inc.: *VisualWorks Reference Guide, Release 2.0*, PPS, Sunnyvale, CA, 1994.

15. ParcPlace Systems, Inc.: *VisualWorks User's Guide, Release 2.0*, PPS, Sunnyvale, CA, 1994.

16. J. Rumbaugh, et. al.: *Object-Oriented Modeling and Design*, Prentice-Hall, 1991.

17. H. Samet: *The Design and Analysis of Spatial Data Structures*, Addison-Wesley, 1990.

18. D. Smith: *Concepts of Object-Oriented Programming*, McGraw-Hill, 1991.

Compressing Elevation Data*

Wm Randolph Franklin

Electrical, Computer, and Systems Engineering Dept., 6026 JEC,
Rensselaer Polytechnic Institute, Troy, New York 12180–3590
(518) 276–6077, Fax: (518) 276–6261
wrf@ecse.rpi.edu

Abstract. This paper compares several, text and image, lossless and lossy, compression techniques for regular gridded elevation data, such as DEMs. Sp_compress and progcode, the best lossless methods average 2.0 bits per point on USGS DEMs, about half the size of gzipped files, and 6.2 bits per point on ETOPO5 samples. Lossy compression produces even smaller files at moderate error rates. Finally, some technques for compressing TINs will be introduced.

1 Introduction

Since Digital Elevation Model (DEM), or, similarly, Digital Terrain Elevation Data (DTED), files are so large, minimizing storage space is important. Altho storage space becomes ever cheaper, the data has higher and higher resolution. Besides the cost of the space, the data file size also affects transmission time and cost. Even within one computer, since processors are getting faster faster than busses and memories are getting faster, smaller data can lead to faster computation. Therefore, altho the question has been studied by many people since computers were first used in cartography, it is still appropriate to ask: How should we compress elevation data?

The first decision is whether to use a general- or a special-purpose compression algorithm; this is not at all clear. The special-purpose method, such as a Triangulated Irregular Network (TIN), can take advantage of the peculiar nature of elevation data, and of the desired error behavior. However, a general-purpose algorithm might have so much effort devoted to its development that it might perform quite well on elevation data, even though not designed specifically for that. In fact, in computer engineering, special purpose machines have generally been failures for that reason. Such failures include most of the machines developed in all the following categories: Lisp machines, floating point processors, database engines, special graphics engines, and parallel machines.

In this paper, we test compress a regular gridded sample digital elevation file with some older, generally available, compression algorithms, such as compress, gzip

*Partial support was provided by NSF grant CCR-9102553.

and JPEG, then with some new, lesser-known algorithms, such as lossless JPEG, ha, codetree, progcode, and sp_compress, and then with some semi-custom algorithms where we compress the hi-order bytes of the data separately from the lo-order bytes. We measure the efficiency of the methods in terms of the number of *bits per point* (bpp) in the compressed file, as well as the compression ratio relative to an uncompressed binary file (which is already smaller than an uncompressed ASCII file). We consider both lossless and lossy algorithms, and in the latter case measure the error compared to the bpp. We study the size penalty associated with partitioning the file into many small pieces before compression, which facilitates accessing only a small part of the file later without needing to uncompress all of it. We then try the best methods on 1024×1024 extracts from 24 randomly-selected $3''$ USGS DEMs and on 4 extracts from the ETOPO5 files.

Finally, we will consider some ways that a specifically topographic format, the TIN, might be compressed.

2 Review

This review will first consider data compression and entropy, then effects of errors in DEMS on interesting properties, and finally other operations on DEMs, which might be affected by errors.

For an excellent introduction to data compression in general, see the Usenet comp.compression Frequently Asked Questions file (FAQ)[12]. It discusses Huffman, Lempel-Ziv-Welch (LZW), JPEG, and others, and gives references. Nelson[23] is a good introduction to the standard compression algorithms, and includes floppies with code. Whitten[39] describes a suite of programs for text and image compression. One non-technical issue inhibiting optimal compression is the large number of patents on the most popular methods.

Burrough[1] and Peuquet[25] consider data compression issues in GIS. Fractals, as presented in Clarke and Schweizer[6], might also be used to compress terrain. Neumann[24] introduces information issues, such as entropy, in representing the topological relations in a map.

Carter[2] describes the errors in the $3''$ DEMs, produced by interpolating contours on 1:250K maps, which we use in this study. Walsh et al[36] also discuss this problem.

Weibel[38] filters gridded DEMs in various ways. He uses global filtering doing smoothing as in image processing by convolving with a 3×3 or 5×4 filter. He compares this with a selective filtering to eliminate points that do not add anything to our characterization of the surface. He tests a 220×390 elevation grid to see whether generalization changes essentials of the terrain, such as hill sharing and RMS error. Shea and McMaster[32] also discuss generalization.

Chang and Tsai[4] found that lowering DEM resolution hurt the accuracy of the calculated slope and aspect of the terrain. Carter[3] shows that the 1 meter resolution particularly affects the aspect, causing a bias towards the four cardinal directions, and suggests smoothing the data. Lee et al[19] analyze the effect of elevation errors on feature extraction. Fisher[10] considers the effect on visibility.

One operation often performed on terrain data is visibility determination, De Floriani and Magillo[7]. Puppo et al[26] use a parallel machine to convert a DEM to a TIN. They scale the elevation to 8 bits and perform experiments on grids of up to 512 × 512, reporting results for a 128 × 128 grid. For example, for a 30 meter accuracy 497 of the 16,384 points are selected. This TIN is then used to calculate line-of-sight-communication in De Floriani et al[8].

Drainage pattern determination is another frequent DEM operation, as described by McCormack et al[22]. Skidmore[33] extracts properties of a location, such as being on a ridge line, from a DEM. Franklin and Ray[11, 27] do visibility calculations on large amounts of data.

The use of a linear quadtree with 2-D run-length encoding and Mortin sequences is discussed in Mark and Lauzon[21]. The storage can be about 7 bits per leaf. Waugh[37] critically evaluates when quadtrees are useful, while Chen and Tobler[5] find that quadtrees always require more space for a given accuracy than a ruled surface. Dutton[9] presents a region quadtree based on triangles, not squares. This quaternary triangular mesh defines coordinates on a quasi-spherical world better than a planar, Cartesian, system does. Leifer and Mark[20] use orthogonal polynomials of order up to 6 and quadtrees for a lossy compression of three 256 × 256 DEMs. Their work anticipates ideas used in wavelets and in the best methods that we will see later in this paper.

3 Compression Review

Here is a quick summary of some of the major themes in compression. *Huffman* coding measures the number of times each symbol in a file occurs, and uses fewer bits to represent the more common symbols. In English text, instead of using 7 bits for each character, E might be stored as *00*, which Q might be *10110010*. The limitation is that adjacencies, such as that Q is almost always followed by U, are not used. Huffman is optimal if there are no such relations, except for a roundoff error since each symbol must be coded with an integral number of bits even if its probability is not exactly an inverse power of two.

Arithmetic coding improves on Huffman in that case by coding symbols with real fractional numbers. Only enough bits to uniquely identify the symbol are stored. Arithmetic coding usually uses floating point math, and can be subject to roundoff errors, which will cause errors in the uncompressed file, unless care is taken in the implementation. Huffman and arithmetic coding are often used inside other schemes to compress calculated coefficients.

Run-length encoding represents strings of the same repeated symbol as a count. The *GIF* (Graphics Interchange Format) image format common on PCs uses this (and other techniques). This method is excellent for line drawings. A step more sophisticated than this is *delta* encoding, which calculates the difference of each pixel of an image from the previous pixel, and then uses some other method, such as run-length encoding, to compress the differences. Facsimile transmission does this in 2-D, calculating the difference of one row from the previous row, then within that row of differences, calculating second order differences across it. The 2-D differencing is about 10% better than 1-D.

The above two methods are *lossless*; the original file is completely reconstructible. For images, *lossy* methods are often used since they may allow much greater compression without much visibly hurting the image.

Wavelets[13] offer a new technique that appears quite powerful; some of the best compression systems described below are based on this.

JPEG, from its designers, the Joint Photographic Experts Group, is a standard image compression method that splits the image into blocks, does a discrete cosine transform frequency analysis of each block (similar to a Fourier transform), deletes components that should not be very visible, and Huffman codes some things. JPEG is usually lossy. It has a parameter to control how lossy, with a lossier file being smaller. JPEG was designed to compress hi-quality photographic images, with 24 bpp (3 colors at 8 bits). This contrasts to GIF, which assumes only 8 bpp. JPEG does not do so well compressing line drawings and text, with sharp jumps in intensity between adjacent pixels. There is also *LJPEG*, lossless JPEG. LJPEG may use various techniques, such as 2-D differencing, as well as a lossy JPEG followed by a compressed correction table. Huang and Smith[15] have an implementation that compresses binary (raw) PBM files. 2-D differencing also appears in other methods.

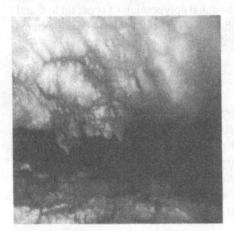 

Fig. 1. Sample Adir512: Lake Cham- **Fig. 2.** 1024 × 1024 Section of ETOPO5 plain West DEM at 512 × 512

4 Lossless Compression Experiments

We started by experimenting with several lossless compression techniques on adir512, a 512 × 512 reduction of the USGS Lake Champlain West DEM, shown in Figure 1[1], obtained from the 1201 × 1201 DEM with the program pnmscale. This is not one corner of the DEM, but is the whole DEM at a lower resolution. We used this conservative choice since a 512 × 512 corner of the DEM, with the points still spaced at 3″, would have compressed either better or worse depending on which corner we used, as shown later in Table 6 . The file contains a mix of a mountainous region in the southwest, with a plane in the center west and a lake in the center east. The 262, 144 points range in elevation from 22 to 1,568 meters.

---

[1] The printed greyscale image was histogram-equalized with xv to improve legibility.

The purpose of these experiments was to determine the relative performance of the various methods, so that we could select a few methods to apply to files of various sizes. The next test case was `adir1024`, a 1024 × 1024 corner of the Lake Champlain West DEM, first whole, then partitioned into smaller and smaller blocks. This demonstrated that altho a particular method might compress different files of the same size by amounts ranging over a factor of three, the relative performance of different methods applied to the same file did not vary much. This is why these experiments might have some general validity on other data sets.

Finally we tested a few methods on a 1024 × 1024 block of 24 other randomly selected DEMs. We saw the same behavior again. Altho compression ratios varied over a factor of 10, the ratio of the size achieved by the `progcode` method to the size achieved by `gzip`, varied by only a factor of 2. That is,

$$\frac{\max_{i=1,24}\left(\frac{\text{size}(\text{progcode}(\text{file}_i))}{\text{size}(\text{gzip}(\text{file}_i))}\right)}{\min_{i=1,24}\left(\frac{\text{size}(\text{progcode}(\text{file}_i))}{\text{size}(\text{gzip}(\text{file}_i))}\right)} = 2.$$

In the following numbers, we will generally ignore header information in the files since the headers are a small fraction of the file size, which fraction gets smaller as the data gets larger.

The raw ASCII file, with each point stored as three to five characters, depending on the number of digits in the elevation (plus a separator), as takes 964,532 bytes. Using a binary file with two bytes per number reduces the space to 524,288 bytes. This is a smaller reduction than expected since 33.6% of the elevations are only 2 digits. Nevertheless, the binary file is useful since it is much faster to read since formatted I/O is rather compute-bound.

The Unix `compress` command, applied to the ASCII file, produces a 289,408 byte file, altho in only 3 CPU seconds on a Sun Sparc 10/30 workstation. A better compression program is `gzip`, part of the Free Software Foundation suite of free GNU software. `gzip` has an option for the amount of time spent to compress. At the default setting, applied to the original ASCII file, the compressed file is 263,270 bytes, produced in 21 seconds. `gzip -9`, the slowest smallest setting, produces a file of 258,016 bytes in 37 seconds. Since the latter took almost twice as long to compute, the default setting is probably appropriate.

`Gzip`, in 7 seconds, compresses the above binary file to 230,889 bytes. `Gzip -9` creates a slightly smaller 230,179 byte file in 14 seconds. This shows that treating the file as numbers, rather than as simple text is somewhat better. How good might we potentially do?

Among the 262,144 points, there are only 1,436 different elevations. Thus, a table of the existing elevations plus 10 bpp are almost sufficient. What is the information theoretic Huffman lower bound, ignoring relations between adjacent points? Let n_i be the number of points with the i-th elevation, counting from lo to hi, and let the total number of points be $N = \sum n_i$. Then lower bound, also called the entropy of the data, is, in bits,

$$N \log_2 N - \sum_i n_i \log_2(n_i)$$

For this data, the frequencies range from 71 elevations occurring once, to one elevation occuring 28,674 times. The entropy is 280,753 bytes, or 8.6 bpp. Clearly, ignoring correlations in the elevations is expensive.

The above entropy calculation ignores autocorrelations in the data. Therefore consider a 1-D differencing, along a linear array of the points. There were 501 different differences ranging from −158 to +750, with 156 deltas occurring once, $\Delta = 0$ occurring 80,125 times, and the next most frequent delta occurring 15,577 times. The resulting file's entropy is 163,125 bytes, or 5.0 bpp, so using deltas gave us a factor of 1.7.

4.1 Ha

Ha0.999[14] is a recent (1995) compression program by Harri Hirvola designed for general files, either text or images. It has two methods, which are described in the documentation thus:

> *1-ASC:* Default method using sliding window dictionary followed by arithmetic coder. Offers quite good compression on wide variety of file types.

> *2-HSC:* Compression method based on finite context model and arithmetic coder. Quite slow for binary data, but offers very good compression especially for longer text files.

We tried both methods on both the ASCII and the binary heights. Compressing the binary data was, as usual, about 10% better. Ha-2 was somewhat smaller than ha-1, and sometimes faster, sometimes slower. Ha-2 on the binary data gave 3.2 bpp. However, ha is about twice as slow as gzip.

4.2 Splitting the Data Into Planes

Since the GIF format and many image processing implementations require 8-bit data, we might split our 16-bit data into two separate 8-bit planes, containing the hi-order and lo-order bytes, respectively, of each elevation, and encode each plane separately. Of three different compression algorithms applied to the hi file, GIF was the best, somewhat better than gzip on the binary file. Gzip was slightly the best on the low file, but all the method were close enough that the difference is probably not significant.

Combining GIF on the hi with gzip on the binary lo gave 191,670 bytes, or 5.9 bpp, or less efficient than some following methods.

Splitting also illustrates a weakness in gzip. It compressed the 1-byte-per-point lo file down to 182,038 bytes. However, we tried expanding the lo file to 2 bytes per point, with the hi byte always zero. Gzip compressed this only to 217,335 bytes, 20% worse. This also occurred when the hi file was expanded to 2 bytes per point. Gzip's compressed size grew from 9.711 to 11,433 bytes. Also gzip on the two halves of the file was more efficient than gzip on the whole file. This was true for the file in either ASCII or binary. In the latter case, the difference was 17%.

4.3 Said and Pearlman

Said and Pearlman[28–31] have several new lossless and lossy image compression algorithms and programs. The uncompression programs are separate in order to facilitate validating the results. Sp_compress is a lossless progressive transmission method using arithmetic coding. Progressive transmission means that lo-resolution data is transmitted first in the file, then it is refined. This is useful since an uncompresser could be written for previewing a file via a lo-speed communication medium before deciding whether to get the whole file. Sp_compress compressed adir512 to 96,413 bytes, or 2.94 bpp, in 5 seconds.

Progcode is another lossless compression program, which produces a slightly larger file. Its decoder, progdecd, altho not written to uncompress a truncated file, calculates what the mean-squared error (MSE) would be if a lower bit rate were used. The MSE shows that progcode is quite conservative with the compressed file size, presumably to prevent possible roundoff errors similar to what can occur with arithmetic coding. For example, progcode compressed adir512 to 98,993 bytes, or 3 bpp, in 6 seconds. However when this compressed file is decoded at a rate of only 1.2 bpp, progcode reported that the result was identical to the original file. This means that progcode could presumably be modified losslessly to compress this file to only 32,322 bytes, which is a very high compression ratio. In our compression experiments, after running progcode on a file, we often ran progdecd at various bit rates to find the smallest rate at which it reported no differences in the uncompressed file. We name this number the progcode *extrapolated* rate to indicate that we expect that this rate might be possible with a modified progcode, but that we don't yet have a program that does it.

The obvious question is whether the low progcode extrapolations might be due to some error. However the Said and Pearlman program codetree, described later in the lossy compression section, suggests that the progcode extrapolations are correct. When using codetree, we give it a bit rate, and it writes a file of the corresponding size. Then the separate uncompression program decdtree uncompresses that file, compares it to the original, and reports the mean-squared error.

In this example, codetree at 1.2 bpp compressed the file to 39,322 bytes. Decdtree at that bit rate reported a mean-squared error of 1.45, where the maximum elevation was 1,568. We also converted the uncompressed file to PGM format, differenced it with the original, and calculated the histogram of the absolute differences between the original file and the 1.2 bit per point compression, as shown in Table 1 on the following page.

Said and Pearlman's sp_compress and progcode are by far the best. Ha-2 on the binary file is second, far behind, with gzip well behind it. Splitting the file into hi and lo bytes and compressing them with GIF and gzip respectively was better than only gzip. Two conclusions are evident.

1. Generic compression algorithms, usually in the image processing domain, are so good that there may be no need to design special algorithms for Digital Elevation Models.

2. The two best algorithms are less than two years old, which shows that compression research is still progressing.

Table 1. Histogram of Errors Caused by Compressing `Adir512` With `Codetree` at 1.2 Bpp

Absolute Difference	Number of Points
0	111,725
1	102,975
2	34,851
3	9,794
4	2,301
5	425
6	61
7	11
8	1

Progcode has one restriction: the size of the data array must be a power of two. This poses a problem with DEMs, which have 20% more than a power of two rows. The easy solution, for the programmer, is to let the user repartition his data to suit the program, but a better solution might be to pad the DEM to the next power of two, 2048 × 2048, which increases the total size by a factor of 2.9.

How efficiently does progcode compress a file with large blocks of zeros? We made two tests of compressing a file, then padding it with zeros to double its size, and compressing that. The first file was adir512; the second adir1024. The latter was statistically a little different in that it was a subsquare of the DEM, and not a subsample of the whole, as was the former. As Table 2 on the next page shows, the compressed padded files were each 16% larger than the corresponding compressed unpadded file. There are some internal parameters in progcode, which are now set for medical images. If they were fine-tuned for the statistical properties of elevation data with large blocks of zeros, then this 16% padding penalty might be reduced. Alternatively, instead of padding the file up, it might be partitioned, quadtree-style, into smaller blocks each of an acceptable size. At some minimum size, such as 8 × 8 perhaps, we might stop splitting and start zero-padding. Then, since there is little overhead in compressing small blocks, each block could be feasibly separately compressed.

Since the actual size of the compressed file actually needed by progcode for error-free compression seems to be much smaller than the whole file, we considered that for the first test case. However, the results were comparable. The 512 file needed 1.2 bpp for error-free reconstruction, while the padded 1024 file need 0.35 bits per padded point, or 1.4 bits per original point, or about 16% more.

Sp_compress requires only that the number of rows and columns each be a multiple of four so the padding problem does not arise here. We reported above how well it handles padded files since this is one measure of its optimality.

Table 2. Compression Efficiency on Zero-Padded DEMs

	Adir512		Adir1024	
	Original	Padded	Original	Padded
Number of rows	512	1024	1024	2048
Progcode:				
Compressed file size	98,993	113,641	254,952	295,857
Ratio	1.16		1.16	
Bits per original point	3.0	3.5	1.95	2.26
CPU Time	5	15	25	82
Sp_compress:				
Compressed file size	96,413	103,884	246,923	275,327
Ratio	1.08		1.11	
Bits per original point	2.9	3.2	1.9	2.1
CPU Time	5	15	21	62

4.4 Summary

Table 3 on the following page summarizes the compression algorithms that don't split the data into planes. We conservatively calculated the compression ratio relative to the binary file size, not to the original ASCII file. Table 4 shows the results when the elevations were first split into hi and lo order bytes, and the two files compressed separately. Showing the compression ratios for the separate bytes didn't seem meaningful.

Finally, in these tests, we used Sun Sparc IPC and 10/30 Unix workstations, and programmed in C++ with the Apogee compiler. Tomas Rokicki's dvips, Jef Poskanzer's Portable Bit Map (PBM) package, Netpbm version, and John Bradley's xv were also very useful.

5 Lossy Compression Experiments

Since elevation data can have many errors[2], and in any case is represented only to the nearest meter, it is a waste to store the data at a higher accuracy than is justified. Therefore *lossy* compression methods might be appropriate sometimes. Indeed, sometimes we gather data faster than we can easily store or transmit it. Altho the our first suggestion here might be simply to lower the spatial resolution or to truncate the number of bits used to store each point, a more sophisticated approach, such as one of the algorithms described below, might allow us to keep more information in fewer bpp.

5.1 Scaling the Elevations

There are a large number of image processing compression methods. Altho their underlying theory is general, many implementations are for only 8-bit data. There is also some precedent in the literature for scaling elevations to 8 bits for research purposes. In adir512, scaling destroys $\log_2 \left(\frac{1568}{256} \right)$, or slightly more than 2 bpp, or 65K bytes. The

Table 3. Comparison of Various Compression Methods on `Adir512`

Method	File Size (A)	Time	Ratio $\left(\dfrac{524{,}288}{A}\right)$	Bpp $\left(\dfrac{A}{32{,}768}\right)$
Lossless:				
Original ASCII file	964,532		0.54	29.4
Binary file	524,288		**1.0**	16.0
Compress	289,408	3	1.8	8.8
Entropy of the elevations	280,753		1.9	8.6
Gzip on the ASCII file	263,270	21	2.0	8.0
Gzip-9 on ASCII	258,016	37	2.0	7.9
Ha-1 on ASCII	256,396	40	2.1	7.8
Gzip on binary	230,899	7	2.3	7.0
Gzip-9 on binary	230,179	14	2.3	7.0
Ha-1 on binary	224,904	18	2.3	6.9
GIF on hi and gzip-bin on lo	191,670		2.7	5.9
Ha-2 on ASCII	179,146	30	2.9	5.5
Entropy of the deltas	163,125		3.2	5.0
Ha-2 on binary	163,115	38	3.2	5.0
Progcode	98,993	6	5.3	3.0
Sp_compress	96,413	5	5.5	2.9
Extrapolated Progcode	32,322		16.4	1.0
Scaled down; otherwise lossless:				
Binary file	262,144		2.0	8
GIF	123,986		4.2	3.8
Gzip	103,413		2.0	3.2
Lossless JPEG	64,935		8.1	2.0
Scaled down and lossy:				
JPEG 75	14,798		35	0.45
JPEG 50	10,408		50	0.32
JPEG 25	7,275		72	0.22

resulting file is now quantized in 6 meter intervals, so the maximum error introduced by this is 3 meters, and the average error is 1.5. Datasets with a greater maximum elevation will have larger errors.

After scaling the elevations, the binary file is one byte per element, or 262,144 bytes. Gzip compresses this file to 103,413 bytes. Note that this size, plus the destroyed bits, is still less than the gzipped original file, showing in yet another way that altho gzip is an excellent compression program, it can be suboptimal.

Converting the scaled file to a GIF file (which is exact, but requires 8-bit data) gives a 123,986 byte result, somewhat worse than gzip. LJPEG gives 64,935 bytes, showing

Table 4. Comparison of Compression Methods on the `Adir512` Split into Hi and Lo Bytes

Method	File Size	Ratio	Bpp
	(A)	$\left(\dfrac{262,144}{A}\right)$	$\left(\dfrac{A}{32,768}\right)$
Hi bytes:			
Original	262,144	1	8
`Gzip` on ASCII	11,393	24	0.35
`Gzip` on binary	9,711	27	0.30
GIF	9,632	27	0.29
Lo bytes:			
Original	262,144	1	8
`Gzip` on ASCII	226,246	1.15	6.9
`Gzip` on binary	182,038	1.4	5.6
GIF	227,833	1.15	7.0
Combined:	(A)	$\left(\dfrac{524,288}{A}\right)$	$\left(\dfrac{A}{32,768}\right)$
Original	524,288	1	16
`Gzip` on each ASCII file	237,639	2.2	7.3
GIF on each file	237,465	2.2	7.3
GIF on hi and `gzip`-binary on lo	191,670	2.7	5.9

that elevation data has similar statistical characteristics to photographic images. This may be partly due to smoothing during the data generation, in which cliffs in the real world can be smoothed into gradual slopes.

5.2 Lossy Compression of the Scaled Data

JPEG compression, by the xv program, at the default parameter setting of 75%, gives a 14,798 byte file. (The JPEG parameter scale is arbitrary, and does not mean, say, 75% accuracy.) Parameters of 50 and 25 give files of 10,408 and 7,275 bytes respectively. The compression is quite impressive, if you can tolerate the errors. Table 5 on the following page shows a histogram of the errors for three JPEG parameter setting. For the 75 parameter, 1/2 of the elevations were not changed by JPEG compression, the average elevation was changed by 0.626 scaled units, which is 4 original units (meters), and the worst change was 8 scaled units. The RMS error is 1.015 scaled units, 6.2 original units.

xv also has a smoothing parameter for JPEG compression. However it doesn't have much effect; setting it to the high value of 50% reduced the compressed files by about 2%.

Table 5. Histogram of Errors Caused by Various JPEG Parameter Settings on the Scaled
`Adir512`

Absolute		Frequency	
Error	JPEG 75	JPEG 50	JPEG 25
0	138,263	68,016	38,916
1	93,265	132,363	112,120
2	23,265	38,104	53,840
3	5,597	14,512	27,545
4	1,321	5,616	14,294
5	337	2,196	7,157
6	79	860	3,864
7	14	314	2,120
8	3	102	1,139
9		42	561
10		15	265
11		4	159
12			76
13			41
14			28
15			10
16			6
17			2
18			0
19			1
File Size	14,798	10.408	7,275
Bpp	0.45	0.32	0.22

5.3   Said and Pearlman

Said and Pearlman also have two lossy compression programs, `Codetree` and
`fastcode`, using wavelet compression. `codetree` adds arithmetic entropy-coding,
which improves the compression a little, but increases the time a lot. With these programs, you specify the desired number of bits per pixel, and whether the input data is
smooth (used for optimizing the compression). However, since `progcode` also gives
almost as good lossy compression, by decoding only part of the compressed file, we used
that. Figure 3 on the next page shows the RMS (Root-Mean-Square) error of the compressed file for sizes ranging from 0.025 to 1.2 bpp, at which bit rate the reconstructed
file is identical to the original.

We can now compare `prograte` to JPEG on the scaled data. For example, JPEG-
75 has 0.45 bpp, and an RMS error of 6.2. However, `prograte`'s RMS error at this
reconstruction rate is 3.9. `Codetree`'s RMS error at 0.45 bpp is 3.5. Alternatively,
these programs can achieve an RMS error of 6.2 with a coding rate of only 0.25 bpp.
Therefore they are almost twice as efficient as JPEG on the scaled file.

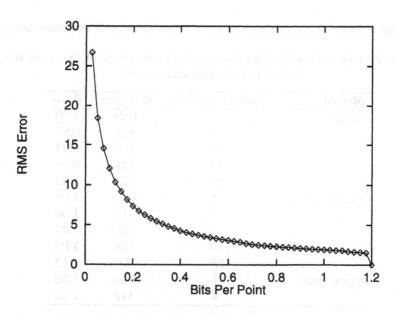

Fig. 3. Lossy Compression `Adir512`

Table 6. Effect of Quartering `Adir1024` Before Compressing

Method	Compressed File Size	Compressed Quarters Sizes	Ratio
Gzip	757,013	307137+208268+144059+75078=734,542	97.0%
Sp_compress	246,923	98463+63387+53490+32239=247,579	100.3%
Progcode	254,952	100400+64831+55301+33477=254,009	99.6%

6 Compressing the DEM in Pieces

One objection to compressing data is that using any part of the file requires uncompressing the whole file. We could partition the file into pieces and compress them separately, but then the total size of all the compressed pieces might be larger than the compressed single file. To test this, we split `adir1024` into four 512 × 512 pieces. Table 6 shows that quartering the file has little effect, but sometimes slightly improves the compression. While this might not always obtain, it suggests that splitting the file before compressing should not be disastrous.

This table also suggests how variable compression can be. With either method the largest compressed quarter was triple the size of the smallest. This could cause a problem in practice since a program handling compressed files would either have to dynamically allocate storage according to each file's size, or else always have enough storage reserved for the rare worst case.

What if we split `adir1024` into 16 pieces of 256 × 256 and compress them sep-

Table 7. Effect of Partitioning `Adir1024` Into Blocks Before Compressing

Ratio is the ratio of the total of the sizes of all the compressed blocks to the size of `Adir1204` compressed as one file.

Method	Number of Blocks	Block Size	Ratio
Gzip	1	1024	1.00
	4	512	0.97
	16	256	0.97
	64	128	0.99
	256	64	1.02
Sp_compress	1	1024	1.00
	4	512	1.00
	16	256	1.02
	64	128	1.05
	256	64	1.13
Progcode	1	1024	1.00
	4	512	1.00

arately? `Gzip` gives files ranging from 12,684 to 81,199, for a total size of 731,067 bytes, still smaller than the compressed complete file. The `sp_compressed` files range from 6,386 to 27,098 bytes, for a total of 251,042 bytes, or only 1.7% larger than the original compressed file. What about partitioning `adir1024` into 64 blocks of 128 × 128? The `gzipped` files range from 357 to 21,739 bytes, totaling 747,438 bytes. With `sp_compress`, the files range from 279 to 7,455 bytes, totaling 258,489 bytes. What about 256 blocks of 64 × 64? `Gzip` produced files from 45 to 5,827 bytes, totaling 771,455 bytes. `sp_compress` crashed while compressing three of the files, which were almost all zeros, so we used `progcode` for them. The 256 files ranged from 27 to 2,217 bytes, totaling 279,060 bytes. Table 7 summarizes these results, which may be stated briefly thus: Compression is useful even when we wish to use only a portion of the file.

7 Large Scale Test of 24 DEM Samples

In the above section, it seems that `progcode` is the best lossless compression of elevation data. Does this extend to other data? The full test was to take a random sample of all the USGS DEMs[35] (except Alaska because of its different size). For each letter of the alphabet (except X and Z), we took the alphabetically first available DEM starting with that letter. They are shown in Figure 4 on the following page. We losslessly compressed a 1024 × 1024 extract from each file thrice, with `gzip` (for comparison since it is so popular), `progcode`, and `sp_compress`.

Table 8 shows the resulting number of bpp, and the compression ratio, measured relative to the binary file size. We report the arithmetic average, not the, lower, geo-

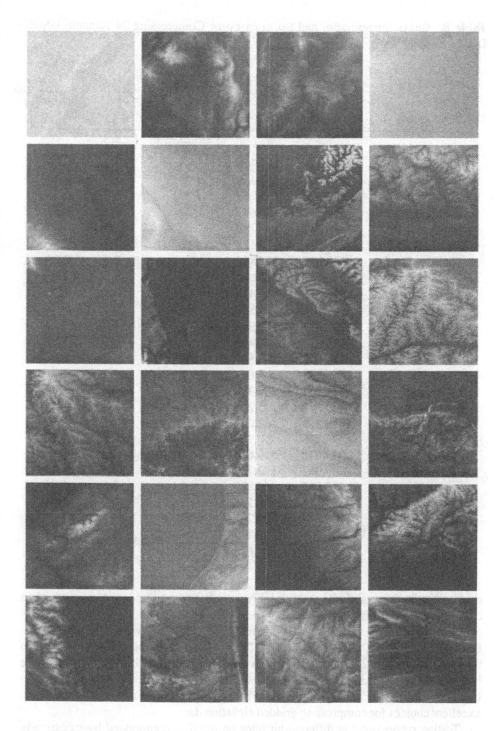

Fig. 4. The 24 Sample USGS DEMs

Table 8. `Gzip`, `Progcode`, and `Sp_compress` Compressing 24 Random USGS DEMs

File	Gzipped Binary File Size (A)	Progcode File Size	Progcode Compression Ratio $\left(\dfrac{2097152}{A}\right)$	Progcode Bpp $\left(\dfrac{8A}{1024^2}\right)$	Sp_compress Bpp
Aberdeen E	159,605	119,465	17	0.9	0.88
Baker E	1,003,125	448,446	4	3.4	3.32
Caliente E	935,762	395,299	5	3.0	2.93
Dalhart E	274,551	170,611	12	1.3	1.27
Eagle Pass E	360,627	193,790	10	1.5	1.46
Fairmont E	260,759	170,128	12	1.3	1.27
Gadsden E	620,059	312,823	6	2.4	2.29
Hailey E	1,082,799	425,666	4	3.3	3.15
Idaho Falls E	286,591	174,438	12	1.3	1.31
Jacksonville W	103,181	79,852	26	0.6	0.58
Kalispell E	993,627	472,969	4	3.6	3.52
La Crosse E	795,570	472,465	4	3.6	3.51
Macon E	374,493	219,867	9	1.7	1.62
Nashville E	566,738	285,661	7	2.2	2.11
O'Neill E	379,707	208,384	10	1.6	1.55
Paducah E	440,521	235,205	8	1.8	1.74
Quebec E	660,238	282,027	7	2.2	2.09
Racine E	73,776	50,908	41	0.4	0.36
Sacramento E	1,014,075	516,623	4	3.9	3.85
Tallahassee E	309,067	192,788	10	1.5	1.42
Ukiah E	927,052	460,870	4	3.5	3.45
Valdosta E	157,818	118,538	17	0.9	0.88
Waco E	346,640	203,288	10	1.5	1.52
Yakima E	898,159	353,717	5	2.7	2.61
Total	13,024,540	6,563,828	7.7	2.1	2.0

metric mean at that bottom since this is more conservative and also more relevant when compressing and storing many files at once.

Note that both the `gzipped` and our compressed sizes vary wildly from file to file. Each original file was $2 \cdot 1024^2 = 2,097,152$ bytes. All the compression times were in the range from 12 to 26 seconds. In every case, `sp_compress` and `progcode` were better than `gzip`, compressing the whole set of 24 files down to 2.0 and 2.1 bpp, respectively, or half the size of `gzip`. Therefore, both `sp_compress` and `progcode` seem excellent choices for compressing gridded elevation data.

Testing `progdecd` at different bit rates on the files compressed by `progcode` showed that on the average there were no differences at an uncompression rate of 0.7 bpp. This shows us a goal for lossless compression.

8   Compressing ETOPO5

The *ETOPO5* file for the northern hemisphere is an array of 1080×4320 elevations or depths, spaced at $5'$ of arc. We extracted 4 1024×1024 subsets, starting 56 rows down from the North Pole, and starting at the first column, and at multiples of 1024 columns later. Fig. 2 shows the fourth section. Then we tried `gzip`, `progcode`, and `sp_compress` on them, with the results shown in Table 9. `sp_compress` looped on section 2, so we used `progcode` for that one. This data does not compress so much since the elevation range is much greater (about 19,000). `Sp_compress` or `progcode` are still better than `gzip`.

Table 9. Comparison of Various Compression Methods on ETOPO5 Sections

Method	Section	Size (A)	Time	Ratio $\left(\dfrac{2097152}{A}\right)$	Bpp $\left(\dfrac{8A}{1024^2}\right)$
Original file	1-4	2,097,152		**1.0**	16
Gzip	1	1,011,838	14	2.1	7.7
	2	1,188,712	19	1.8	9.1
	3	1,413,901	20	1.5	10.7
	4	1,367,549	19	1.5	10.4
	Average	1,245,500		1.7	9.5
Sp_compress	1	726,955	27	2.9	5.5
	2	failed			
	3	829,678	29	2.5	6.3
	4	882,405	19	2.4	6.7
Progcode	2	819,326	33	2.6	6.3
	Average	814,591		2.6	6.2

9   Compressing a TIN

Altho regularly gridded data compresses quite well, how might we compress a TIN file? There are the (x, y, z) coordinates of the points, and the six neighbors (on average) of each point.

Let the number of points in the original DEM be N, typically, $1201^2 = 1,442,401$. Let K be the number of points selected to be in the TIN. If the TIN is to be worth using, then $K \ll N$. The easiest way to store the points is to list their coordinates in the original DEM, at a cost for each (x, y) of $2 \log_2 N$ bits/point. However, the smaller information-theoretical space comes from the number of subsets of K points selected from N, and is

$$\frac{1}{K} \log_2 \text{binom}(N, K) \approx \lg N - \lg K$$

bits per point, where binom(N, K) counts binomial combinations, e.g., binom($5, 2$) = $5!/2!/(5-2)! = 10$. If, say, $K = 65,535$, then this is a significant reduction from 20.5 to 4.5 bits per point.

Compressing heights is hard since the irregular topology makes run-length encoding difficult, tho not necessarily impossible. Compressing the topology is harder. If there is nothing stored inside each triangle, then they might be constructed as needed from the point adjacencies.

The average point has six neighbors, and the simplest implementation is an array of the ID numbers of the neighbors. 16 bits per ID, plus a count, gives about 100 bits per point. This is by far the dominant storage cost. Note that the storage cost for a hierarchical structure will be even larger. There are more compact methods of storing a planar graph, so that each edge requires only a few bits. The compact format has to be expanded before the graph can be traversed, but that's already the case with the points. To understand the compact planar graph structure, consider how to store a binary tree compactly.

With the simple binary tree format, each node contains two pointers, for its two sons. We can traverse and update this structure, but it costs 32 bits per node (if there are under 2^{16} nodes). We might instead store only the information about whether or not each node has a left son, and whether it has a right son, in 2 bits total per node. We traverse the tree in some well-defined recursive order, such as the node, then its left subtree, and finally its right subtree, listing the 2 bits for each node in sequence. Following that, we can list in sequence any internal information about each node.

We can extend this to a planar graph, though the structure is more complicated; see Jacobson[16, 17], Kannan et al[18], and Turan[34]. An unlabeled triangulation can be stored in $3 + \lg 3 \approx 4.6$ bits per node; the K labels require another $K \lg K$. The graph would probably need to be expanded before being used.

Altho the TIN initially does not seem competitive with the regular grid compression methods described earlier, with these succinct codings, it might be. Which is actually better remains an open question.

10 Summary

We have studied many compression algorithms for regularly gridded terrain elevation files, including both generic image processing methods, and some semicustom ones. The generic image processing compression algorithms perform so well that there appears no need to design algorithms specifically for elevation data. This also allows us to take advantage of the continuing progress in image processing algorithms. For example, the best algorithms that we studied are all quite new. With sp_compress, for example, USGS DEMs compress down to an average of 2 bpp. There is a wide variation in the compressability of different data; however the relative performance of various methods on any particular file does not vary widely.

Compression should not hinder interactive use of the data; partitioning one test file into 256 blocks before compressing increased thae total size by only 13%.

Several open questions remain. Can these methods be improved by fine-tuning internal parameters for the statistical properties of elevation data, if those properties are, in fact, different than the scenes that the algorithms were designed for? Can the very low bit-rates at which `progdecd` reports an exact reconstruction be extended into a new compression program at those rates? Since lossy compression is much more compact, often far below 1 bpp at moderate mean squared errors, how much lossiness can we tolerate before essential properties of the data such as drainage patterns and visibility are damaged?

References

[1] P. A. Burrough. *Principles of Geographical Information Systems for Land Resources Assessment.* Clarendon Press, Oxford, 1986.

[2] J. R. Carter. Relative errors identified in USGS gridded DEMs. In *Autocarto*, volume 9, pages 255–265, 1989.

[3] J. R. Carter. The effect of data precision on the calculation of slope and aspect using gridded DEMs. *Cartographica*, 29(1):22–34, Spring 1992.

[4] K.-T. Chang and B.-W. Tsai. The effect of DEM resolution on slope and aspect mapping. *Cartography and Geographic Information Systems*, 18(1):69–77, 1991.

[5] Z.-T. Chen and W. Tobler. Quadtree representations of digital terrain. In *Proceedings, Auto-Carto London*, volume 1, 1986.

[6] K. C. Clarke and D. M. Schweizer. Measuring the fractal dimension of natural surfaces using a robust fractal estimator. *Cartography and Geographic Information Systems*, 18(1):37–47, 1991.

[7] L. De Floriani and P. Magillo. Visibility algorithms on DTMs. *Int. J. Geographic Information Systems*, 8(1):13–41, 1994.

[8] L. De Floriani, P. Magillo, and E. Puppo. Line of sight communication on terrain models. *Int. J. Geographic Information Systems*, 8(4):329–342, 1994.

[9] G. Dutton. Locational properties of quaternary triangular meshes. In K. Brassel and H. Kishimoto, editors, *4th International Symposium on Spatial Data Handling*, volume 2, pages 901–910, Zürich, 23-27 July 1990.

[10] P. F. Fisher. Algorithm and implementation uncertainty in viewshed analysis. *International Journal Of Geographical Information Systems*, 7:331–347, Jul–Aug 1993.

[11] W. R. Franklin and C. Ray. Higher isn't necessarily better: Visibility algorithms and experiments. In T. C. Waugh and R. G. Healey, editors, *Advances in GIS Research: Sixth International Symposium on Spatial Data Handling*, pages 751–770, Edinburgh, 5–9 Sept 1994. Taylor & Francis.

[12] J.-L. Gailly. Comp.compression Frequently Asked Questions. Usenet, posted to comp.compression, ftpable from rtfm.mit.edu:/pub/usenet/news.answers/compression-faq/part[1-3], webbable from http://www.cis.ohio-state.edu/hypertext/faq/usenet/compression-faq/top.html, 25 Feb 1995.

[13] J.-L. Gailly. What is wavelet theory? http://www.cis.ohio-state.edu/hypertext/faq/usenet/compression-faq/part2/faq-doc-3.html, 25 Feb 1995.

[14] H. Hirvola. (HA, a small file archiver utility). ftp://ftp.nl.net/gopher/NLnet-connected/aipnl/ha_src/, Jan. 1995. Mentioned in the comp.compression FAQ.

[15] K. Huang and B. Smith. Lossless JPEG codec. ftp://ftp.cs.cornell.edu:/pub/multimed/ljpg.tar.Z, June 1994.

[16] G. Jacobson. *Foundations of Computer Science*, volume 30, chapter Space-efficient static trees and graphs. 1989.

[17] G. Jacobson. *Succinct Static Data Structures*. PhD thesis, Carnegie-Mellon, Jan. 1989. Tech Rep CMU-CS-89-112.

[18] S. Kannan, M. Naor, and S. Rudich. Implicit representation of graphs. *SIAM Journal On Discrete Mathematics*, 5:596–603, Nov. 1992.

[19] J. Lee, P. K. Snyder, and P. F. Fisher. Modeling the effect of data errors on feature extraction from digital elevation models. *Photogrammetric Engineering And Remote Sensing*, 58:1461–1467, Oct. 1993.

[20] L. A. Leifer and D. M. Mark. Recursive approximation of topographic data using quadtrees and orthogonal polynomials. In N. R. Chrisman, editor, *Autocarto 8: Proceedings Eighth International Symposium on Computer-Assisted Cartography*, pages 650–659, Baltimore, 29 March – 3 April 1987. ASPRS and ACSM.

[21] D. M. Mark and J. P. Lauzon. Linear quadtrees for geographic information systems. In *Proceedings of the International Symposium on Spatial Data Handling*, volume 2, pages 412–430, Zurich, 20–24 August 1984.

[22] J. E. McCormack, M. N. Gahegan, S. A. Roberts, J. Hogy, and B. S. Hoyle. Feature-based derivation of drainage networks. *Int. J. Geographic Information Systems*, 7(3):263–279, 1993.

[23] M. Nelson. *The Data Compression Handbook*. M&T Books, Redwood City, Calif. USA, 1991.

[24] J. Neumann. The topological information context of a map/ an attempt at a rehabilitation of information theory in cartography. *Cartographica*, 31(1):26–34, Spring 1994.

[25] D. J. Peuquet. A hybrid structure for the storage and manipulation of Very Large Spatial Data Structures. *Computer Vision, Graphics, and Image Processing*, 24(14), 1983.

[26] E. Puppo, L. Davis, D. de Menthon, and Y. A. Teng. Parallel terrain triangulation. *Int. J. Geographic Information Systems*, 8(2):105–128, 1994.

[27] C. K. Ray. *Representing Visibility for Siting Problems*. PhD thesis, Electrical, Computer, and Systems Engineering Dept., Rensselaer Polytechnic Institute, May 1994.

[28] A. Said. An image multiresolution representation for lossless and lossy compression. (submitted), July 1994.

[29] A. Said and W. A. Pearlman. A new fast and efficient image codec based on set partitioning in hierarchical trees. (submitted), presented in part at the IEEE Symp on Circuits and Systems, Chicago, May 1993.

[30] A. Said and W. A. Pearlman. Reversible image compression via multiresolution representation and predictive coding. In *Proceedings SPIE*, volume 2094: Visual Commun. and Image Processing, pages 664–674, Nov. 1993. email: amir@densis.fee.unicamp.br, pearlman@ecse.rpi.edu.

[31] A. Said and W. A. Pearlman. (new image coding and decoding programs). ftp://ftp.ipl.rpi.edu/pub/-EW_Code/, Apr. 1995.

[32] K. S. Shea and R. B. McMaster. Cartographic generalization in a digital environment: When and how to generalize. In *Autocarto*, volume 9, pages 56–67, 1989.

[33] A. K. Skidmore. Terrain position as mapped from a gridded digital elevation model. *Int. J. Geographic Information Systems*, 4(1):33–49, 1990.

[34] G. Turan. Succinct representations of graphs. *Discrete Applied Math*, 8:289–294, 1984.

[35] USGS. 1:250K DEMs. ftp://edcftp.cr.usgs.gov/pub/data/DEM/250.

[36] S. J. Walsh, D. R. Lightfoot, and D. R. Butler. Recognition and assessment of error in geographic information systems. *Photogrammetry Engineering and Remote Sensing*, 53:1423–1430, 1987.

[37] T. Waugh. A response to recent papers and articles on the use of quadtrees for geographic information systems. In *Proceedings of the Second International Symposium on Geographic Information Systems*, pages 33–37, Seattle, Wash. USA, 5–10 July 1986.

[38] R. Weibel. Models and experiments for adaptive computer-assisted terrain generalization. *Cartography and Geographic Information Systems*, 19(3):133–153, 1992.

[39] I. H. Witten, A. Moffat, and T. C. Bell. *Managing Gigabytes: Compressing and Indexing Documents and Images*. Van Nostrand Reinhold, 1994.

Author Index

Abel, David 348
Alexander, John 368
Anwar, Eman 368
Arctur, David 368

Blott, Stephen 117

Chakravarthy, Sharma 368
Chubb, Douglas 196
Chung, Miyi 368
Cobb, Maria 368

de Ridder, Thomas 216
Dettori, Giuliana 152

Ester, Martin 67

Finke, Ulrich 29
Flewelling, Douglas 279
Frank, Andrew 184
Franklin, Wm. Randolph 385

Gaede, Volker 96
Güting, Ralf Hartmut 216
Gyssens, Marc 14

Han, Jiawei 47
Henrich, Andreas 132
Hinrichs, Klaus 29
Hjaltason, Gísli 83

Koperski, Krzysztof 47
Kriegel, Hans-Peter 67, 240
Kuhn, Werner 184
Kuijpers, Bart 1
Kumar, Vipin 196

Lo, Ming-Ling 328

Möller, Jens 132

Nabil, Mohammad 292
Ngu, Anne 292

Ooi, Beng Chin 348

Paredaens, Jan 1
Power, Robert 348
Puppo, Enrico 152

Ravada, Sivakumar 196
Ravishankar, Chinya 328
Rigaux, Philippe 170

St. Clair, Daniel 259
Samet, Hanan 83
Scarponcini, Paul 259
Schneider, Markus 216
Scholl, Michel 170
Seidl, Thomas 240
Sharma, Jayant 279
Shaw, Kevin 368
Shekhar, Shashi 196
Shepherd, John 292

Tan, Kian-Lee 348
Turner, Greg 196

Van den Bussche, Jan 1
Van Gucht, Dirk 14
Vandeurzen, Luc 14
Vckovski, Andrej 117

Winter, Stephan 310

Xu, Xiaowei 67

Yu, Jeffrey 348

Zobrist, George 259

Lecture Notes in Computer Science

For information about Vols. 1–879
please contact your bookseller or Springer-Verlag

Vol. 880: P. S. Thiagarajan (Ed.), Foundations of Software Technology and Theoretical Computer Science. Proceedings, 1994. XI, 451 pages. 1994.

Vol. 881: P. Loucopoulos (Ed.), Entity-Relationship Approach – ER'94. Proceedings, 1994. XIII, 579 pages. 1994.

Vol. 882: D. Hutchison, A. Danthine, H. Leopold, G. Coulson (Eds.), Multimedia Transport and Teleservices. Proceedings, 1994. XI, 380 pages. 1994.

Vol. 883: L. Fribourg, F. Turini (Eds.), Logic Program Synthesis and Transformation – Meta-Programming in Logic. Proceedings, 1994. IX, 451 pages. 1994.

Vol. 884: J. Nievergelt, T. Roos, H.-J. Schek, P. Widmayer (Eds.), IGIS '94: Geographic Information Systems. Proceedings, 1994. VIII, 292 pages. 19944.

Vol. 885: R. C. Veltkamp, Closed Objects Boundaries from Scattered Points. VIII, 144 pages. 1994.

Vol. 886: M. M. Veloso, Planning and Learning by Analogical Reasoning. XIII, 181 pages. 1994. (Subseries LNAI).

Vol. 887: M. Toussaint (Ed.), Ada in Europe. Proceedings, 1994. XII, 521 pages. 1994.

Vol. 888: S. A. Andersson (Ed.), Analysis of Dynamical and Cognitive Systems. Proceedings, 1993. VII, 260 pages. 1995.

Vol. 889: H. P. Lubich, Towards a CSCW Framework for Scientific Cooperation in Europe. X, 268 pages. 1995.

Vol. 890: M. J. Wooldridge, N. R. Jennings (Eds.), Intelligent Agents. Proceedings, 1994. VIII, 407 pages. 1995. (Subseries LNAI).

Vol. 891: C. Lewerentz, T. Lindner (Eds.), Formal Development of Reactive Systems. XI, 394 pages. 1995.

Vol. 892: K. Pingali, U. Banerjee, D. Gelernter, A. Nicolau, D. Padua (Eds.), Languages and Compilers for Parallel Computing. Proceedings, 1994. XI, 496 pages. 1995.

Vol. 893: G. Gottlob, M. Y. Vardi (Eds.), Database Theory – ICDT '95. Proceedings, 1995. XI, 454 pages. 1995.

Vol. 894: R. Tamassia, I. G. Tollis (Eds.), Graph Drawing. Proceedings, 1994. X, 471 pages. 1995.

Vol. 895: R. L. Ibrahim (Ed.), Software Engineering Education. Proceedings, 1995. XII, 449 pages. 1995.

Vol. 896: R. N. Taylor, J. Coutaz (Eds.), Software Engineering and Human-Computer Interaction. Proceedings, 1994. X, 281 pages. 1995.

Vol. 897: M. Fisher, R. Owens (Eds.), Executable Modal and Temporal Logics. Proceedings, 1993. VII, 180 pages. 1995. (Subseries LNAI).

Vol. 898: P. Steffens (Ed.), Machine Translation and the Lexicon. Proceedings, 1993. X, 251 pages. 1995. (Subseries LNAI).

Vol. 899: W. Banzhaf, F. H. Eeckman (Eds.), Evolution and Biocomputation. VII, 277 pages. 1995.

Vol. 900: E. W. Mayr, C. Puech (Eds.), STACS 95. Proceedings, 1995. XIII, 654 pages. 1995.

Vol. 901: R. Kumar, T. Kropf (Eds.), Theorem Provers in Circuit Design. Proceedings, 1994. VIII, 303 pages. 1995.

Vol. 902: M. Dezani-Ciancaglini, G. Plotkin (Eds.), Typed Lambda Calculi and Applications. Proceedings, 1995. VIII, 443 pages. 1995.

Vol. 903: E. W. Mayr, G. Schmidt, G. Tinhofer (Eds.), Graph-Theoretic Concepts in Computer Science. Proceedings, 1994. IX, 414 pages. 1995.

Vol. 904: P. Vitányi (Ed.), Computational Learning Theory. EuroCOLT'95. Proceedings, 1995. XVII, 415 pages. 1995. (Subseries LNAI).

Vol. 905: N. Ayache (Ed.), Computer Vision, Virtual Reality and Robotics in Medicine. Proceedings, 1995. XIV,

Vol. 906: E. Astesiano, G. Reggio, A. Tarlecki (Eds.), Recent Trends in Data Type Specification. Proceedings, 1995. VIII, 523 pages. 1995.

Vol. 907: T. Ito, A. Yonezawa (Eds.), Theory and Practice of Parallel Programming. Proceedings, 1995. VIII, 485 pages. 1995.

Vol. 908: J. R. Rao Extensions of the UNITY Methodology: Compositionality, Fairness and Probability in Parallelism. XI, 178 pages. 1995.

Vol. 909: H. Comon, J.-P. Jouannaud (Eds.), Term Rewriting. Proceedings, 1993. VIII, 221 pages. 1995.

Vol. 910: A. Podelski (Ed.), Constraint Programming: Basics and Trends. Proceedings, 1995. XI, 315 pages. 1995.

Vol. 911: R. Baeza-Yates, E. Goles, P. V. Poblete (Eds.), LATIN '95: Theoretical Informatics. Proceedings, 1995. IX, 525 pages. 1995.

Vol. 912: N. Lavrac, S. Wrobel (Eds.), Machine Learning: ECML – 95. Proceedings, 1995. XI, 370 pages. 1995. (Subseries LNAI).

Vol. 913: W. Schäfer (Ed.), Software Process Technology. Proceedings, 1995. IX, 261 pages. 1995.

Vol. 914: J. Hsiang (Ed.), Rewriting Techniques and Applications. Proceedings, 1995. XII, 473 pages. 1995.

Vol. 915: P. D. Mosses, M. Nielsen, M. I. Schwartzbach (Eds.), TAPSOFT '95: Theory and Practice of Software Development. Proceedings, 1995. XV, 810 pages. 1995.

Vol. 916: N. R. Adam, B. K. Bhargava, Y. Yesha (Eds.), Digital Libraries. Proceedings, 1994. XIII, 321 pages. 1995.

Vol. 917: J. Pieprzyk, R. Safavi-Naini (Eds.), Advances in Cryptology - ASIACRYPT '94. Proceedings, 1994. XII, 431 pages. 1995.

Vol. 918: P. Baumgartner, R. Hähnle, J. Posegga (Eds.), Theorem Proving with Analytic Tableaux and Related Methods. Proceedings, 1995. X, 352 pages. 1995. (Subseries LNAI).

Vol. 919: B. Hertzberger, G. Serazzi (Eds.), High-Performance Computing and Networking. Proceedings, 1995. XXIV, 957 pages. 1995.

Vol. 920: E. Balas, J. Clausen (Eds.), Integer Programming and Combinatorial Optimization. Proceedings, 1995. IX, 436 pages. 1995.

Vol. 921: L. C. Guillou, J.-J. Quisquater (Eds.), Advances in Cryptology – EUROCRYPT '95. Proceedings, 1995. XIV, 417 pages. 1995.

Vol. 922: H. Dörr, Efficient Graph Rewriting and Its Implementation. IX, 266 pages. 1995.

Vol. 923: M. Meyer (Ed.), Constraint Processing. IV, 289 pages. 1995.

Vol. 924: P. Ciancarini, O. Nierstrasz, A. Yonezawa (Eds.), Object-Based Models and Languages for Concurrent Systems. Proceedings, 1994. VII, 193 pages. 1995.

Vol. 925: J. Jeuring, E. Meijer (Eds.), Advanced Functional Programming. Proceedings, 1995. VII, 331 pages. 1995.

Vol. 926: P. Nesi (Ed.), Objective Software Quality. Proceedings, 1995. VIII, 249 pages. 1995.

Vol. 927: J. Dix, L. Moniz Pereira, T. C. Przymusinski (Eds.), Non-Monotonic Extensions of Logic Programming. Proceedings, 1994. IX, 229 pages. 1995. (Subseries LNAI).

Vol. 928: V.W. Marek, A. Nerode, M. Truszczynski (Eds.), Logic Programming and Nonmonotonic Reasoning. Proceedings, 1995. VIII, 417 pages. 1995. (Subseries LNAI).

Vol. 929: F. Morán, A. Moreno, J.J. Merelo, P. Chacón (Eds.), Advances in Artificial Life. Proceedings, 1995. XIII, 960 pages. 1995 (Subseries LNAI).

Vol. 930: J. Mira, F. Sandoval (Eds.), From Natural to Artificial Neural Computation. Proceedings, 1995. XVIII, 1150 pages. 1995.

Vol. 931: P.J. Braspenning, F. Thuijsman, A.J.M.M. Weijters (Eds.), Artificial Neural Networks. IX, 295 pages. 1995.

Vol. 932: J. Iivari, K. Lyytinen, M. Rossi (Eds.), Advanced Information Systems Engineering. Proceedings, 1995. XI, 388 pages. 1995.

Vol. 933: L. Pacholski, J. Tiuryn (Eds.), Computer Science Logic. Proceedings, 1994. IX, 543 pages. 1995.

Vol. 934: P. Barahona, M. Stefanelli, J. Wyatt (Eds.), Artificial Intelligence in Medicine. Proceedings, 1995. XI, 449 pages. 1995. (Subseries LNAI).

Vol. 935: G. De Michelis, M. Diaz (Eds.), Application and Theory of Petri Nets 1995. Proceedings, 1995. VIII, 511 pages. 1995.

Vol. 936: V.S. Alagar, M. Nivat (Eds.), Algebraic Methodology and Software Technology. Proceedings, 1995. XIV, 591 pages. 1995.

Vol. 937: Z. Galil, E. Ukkonen (Eds.), Combinatorial Pattern Matching. Proceedings, 1995. VIII, 409 pages. 1995.

Vol. 938: K.P. Birman, F. Mattern, A. Schiper (Eds.), Theory and Practice in Distributed Systems. Proceedings,1994. X, 263 pages. 1995.

Vol. 939: P. Wolper (Ed.), Computer Aided Verification. Proceedings, 1995. X, 451 pages. 1995.

Vol. 940: C. Goble, J. Keane (Eds.), Advances in Databases. Proceedings, 1995. X, 277 pages. 1995.

Vol. 941: M. Cadoli, Tractable Reasoning in Artificial Intelligence. XVII, 247 pages. 1995. (Subseries LNAI).

Vol. 942: G. Böckle, Exploitation of Fine-Grain Parallelism. IX, 188 pages. 1995.

Vol. 943: W. Klas, M. Schrefl, Metaclasses and Their Application. IX, 201 pages. 1995.

Vol. 944: Z. Fülöp, F. Gécseg (Eds.), Automata, Languages and Programming. Proceedings, 1995. XIII, 686 pages. 1995.

Vol. 945: B. Bouchon-Meunier, R.R. Yager, L.A. Zadeh (Eds.), Advances in Intelligent Computing - IPMU '94. Proceedings, 1994. XII, 628 pages.1995.

Vol. 946: C. Froidevaux, J. Kohlas (Eds.), Symbolic and Quantitative Approaches to Reasoning and Uncertainty. Proceedings, 1995. X, 420 pages. 1995. (Subseries LNAI).

Vol. 947: B. Möller (Ed.), Mathematics of Program Construction. Proceedings, 1995. VIII, 472 pages. 1995.

Vol. 948: G. Cohen, M. Giusti, T. Mora (Eds.), Applied Algebra, Algebraic Algorithms and Error-Correcting Codes. Proceedings, 1995. XI, 485 pages. 1995.

Vol. 949: D.G. Feitelson, L. Rudolph (Eds.), Job Scheduling Strategies for Parallel Processing. Proceedings, 1995. VIII, 361 pages. 1995.

Vol. 951: M.J. Egenhofer, J.R. Herring (Eds.), Advances in Spatial Databases. Proceedings, 1995. XI, 405 pages. 1995.

Vol. 952: W. Olthoff (Ed.), Object-Oriented Programming. Proceedings, 1995. XI, 471 pages. 1995.

Vol. 953: D. Pitt, D.E. Rydeheard, P. Johnstone (Eds.), Category Theory and Computer Science. Proceedings, 1995. VII, 252 pages. 1995.

Vol. 954: G. Ellis, R. Levinson, W. Rich. J.F. Sowa (Eds.), Conceptual Structures: Applications, Implementation and Theory. Proceedings, 1995. IX, 353 pages. 1995. (Subseries LNAI).

Vol. 956: X. Yao (Ed.), Progress in Evolutionary Computation. Proceedings, 1993, 1994. VIII, 314 pages. 1995. (Subseries LNAI).

Vol. 957: C. Castelfranchi, J.-P. Müller (Eds.), From Reaction to Cognition. Proceedings, 1993. VI, 252 pages. 1995. (Subseries LNAI).

Vol. 958: J. Calmet, J.A. Campbell (Eds.), Integrating Symbolic Mathematical Computation and Artificial Intelligence. Proceedings, 1994. X, 275 pages. 1995.